Rupert Hugh Morris

The History of the Church and Parish of St. Mary-on-the-Hill, Chester

Together with an account of the new church of St. Mary-without-the-Walls

Rupert Hugh Morris

The History of the Church and Parish of St. Mary-on-the-Hill, Chester
Together with an account of the new church of St. Mary-without-the-Walls

ISBN/EAN: 9783337037758

Printed in Europe, USA, Canada, Australia, Japan

Cover: Foto ©Lupo / pixelio.de

More available books at **www.hansebooks.com**

THE HISTORY

OF THE

CHURCH AND PARISH

OF

St. Mary-on-the-Hill

CHESTER

TOGETHER WITH AN ACCOUNT OF THE NEW CHURCH

St. Mary-without-the-Walls

BY THE LATE

J. P. EARWAKER, M.A., F.S.A.

AUTHOR OF "EAST CHESHIRE," AND EDITOR OF "SOME MAN CHESTER WILLS," ETC., ETC.,
HONORARY SECRETARY OF THE RECORD SOCIETY OF LANCASHIRE AND CHESHIRE

EDITED BY

RUPERT H. MORRIS, D.D., F.S.A.

TO

The Most Noble

HUGH LUPUS,
DUKE OF WESTMINSTER, K.G.,

Lord Lieutenant of Cheshire,

WHO HAS MOST UNGRUDGINGLY AND CONSTANTLY
FOR MANY YEARS PAST
DEVOTED TIME AND INFLUENCE
TO THE FURTHERANCE OF ALL UNDERTAKINGS
THAT COULD TEND TO THE HAPPINESS AND WELL-BEING

OF

CHESTER AND ITS INHABITANTS,

This Work

IS

MOST RESPECTFULLY AND GRATEFULLY

DEDICATED.

List of the Founders of this Work.

His Grace THE DUKE OF WESTMINSTER, K.G.
The late Rev. CANON THOMAS EATON, M.A. (*Past Rector*).
ADMIRAL T. L. MASSIE.
CAPTAIN EDWARD R. MASSIE, J.P.
The late ALDERMAN ROBERT FROST, J.P.
ALDERMAN CHARLES BROWN, J.P.
The late ALDERMAN WILLIAM JOHNSON, J.P. (*Past Churchwarden*).
The late DR. DAVIES-COLLEY, J.P.
The late Mr. J. R. BAKER (*Past Churchwarden*).
Mr. FRED. BULLIN, J.P.
Mr. HENRY FINCHETT-MADDOCK (*Past Churchwarden*).
Mr. JOHN GAMON (*Past Churchwarden*).
Mr. J. G. HOLMES (*Past Churchwarden*).
Mr. GEORGE PARKER (*Past Churchwarden*).
Mr. REGINALD POTTS.
The late Mr. JAMES SALMON, J.P. (*Past Churchwarden*).
Mr. HENRY TAYLOR, F.S.A. (*Past Churchwarden*).

PREFACE.

The late Mr. J. P. Earwaker had been engaged for several years in collecting materials for the History of St. Mary's, and he had seen through the press some 170 pages of the present Work, when the hand of death was suddenly laid upon him, and it was left to others to take up the pen which he had dropped, and carry the Work through to completion. Sad and pathetic as were the circumstances under which I was called upon to undertake this task, and difficult, of necessity, as it is to take up the threads of a history which have been arranged by another, it was less difficult than it might well have proved to be, owing to the excellent method and order which obtained with Mr. Earwaker.

The mass of materials collected by him for this purpose is very great, but so carefully was it grouped in sections that my chief task lay in selecting and compressing within reasonable compass the copious and valuable information gathered together, and in studying to preserve a due proportion in the matter to be included.

The Pedigrees I have printed without any alteration or correction, exactly as they were left. Mr. Earwaker was so remarkable for accuracy and patience in investigation that, failing his revision, they could not well receive any other.

Our readers will, I hope, be interested in the valuable particulars contained in the somewhat lengthy extracts from the Churchwardens' books. No apology is needed for printing in full such important records. The limit of space prescribed prevented any further extension of this reproduction, but a sufficient number of extracts has been exhibited to show how closely the history of St. Mary's Church followed the political and ecclesiastical history of the country at large. They illustrate in a remarkable manner the important changes in ritual, and in a less degree in doctrine, during the years of Henry VIII., Edward VI., Queen Mary, and Queen Elizabeth. They also contain many curious references and old dialect words. Some extracts, too, have been given from the later accounts to the year 1800, with special reference to any entries which are interesting, or which throw light on the manners and customs of bygone years, or which refer to public events in Chester or in the kingdom generally.

A very full series of extracts has been given from the Parish Registers, including those for the years 1547-1553 and 1570-1574, from the Harleian MSS. in the British Museum, and from the official transcripts in the Bishop's Registry at Chester, for various years between 1601 and 1627, the original Registers being lost.

An account is printed of the Old Monuments in the Church to the Troutbeck family and others, with copies of important monumental inscriptions, all now destroyed. These are taken from manuscripts in the British Museum, not generally known, one of which has only recently been acquired.

A list of "Founders of the Work" is appended, without whose co-operation and pecuniary support the Work could not have been undertaken. From these it is proper to select for special mention the name of His Grace the Duke of Westminster, patron of the two Rectories of St. Mary's-within-the-Walls and St. Mary's-without-the-Walls, who, in addition to his munificent gifts to both Churches, old and new, has been a liberal subscriber to the fund raised for the publication of this History. To this honoured name must be added that of Mr. Henry Taylor, who has been most indefatigable in promoting the Work, grappling with almost insuperable difficulties, and keeping the project in view, when others had almost despaired of its ever arriving at completion.

Thanks are due and are most gladly given for the valuable assistance rendered by Admiral Massie and Captain Edward Massie, who placed at our disposal their valuable collection of Cheshire pedigrees; to Venerable Archdeacon Barber, Rector of St. Mary's-within-the-Walls; to Rev. Henry Grantham, Rector of St. Mary's-without-the-Walls; to Mr. John Gamon, the learned and courteous Registrar of the Diocese, whose stores of Diocesan documents were always readily accessible; and to Mrs. Earwaker, whose facile pen has done much to embellish this volume. There will, doubtless, be many others who assisted the late Mr. Earwaker in preparing for this History, and who, it is hoped, will accept this thankful recognition of their kindly service.

RUPERT H. MORRIS.

St. Gabriel's Vicarage,
Warwick Square, S.W.

TABLE OF CONTENTS.

	PAGE
DEDICATION	iii
LIST OF FOUNDERS OF THE WORK	iv
PREFACE	v-vi
ST. MARY-ON-THE-HILL—THE CHURCH—CURIOUS ENTRIES IN CHURCHWARDENS' ACCOUNTS—LIST OF VESTMENTS AND ORNAMENTS—ALTERATIONS IN THE FABRIC	1–11
RE-ARRANGEMENT OF THE ECCLESIASTICAL PARISH OF ST. MARY'S, &c.	11–13
THE CHURCH OF ST. MARY-WITHOUT-THE-WALLS—ROMAN REMAINS FOUND—LIST OF GIFTS	13–18
THE PRESENT CHURCH OF ST. MARY-ON-THE-HILL—THE MODERN STAINED GLASS—COMMUNION PLATE—BELLS	19–26
SPECIAL INCIDENTS IN THE PAST HISTORY OF ST. MARY'S—TRIAL OF WITCHES	26–30, 182
THE CHANTRIES AND ALTARS FORMERLY IN ST. MARY'S CHURCH	30–33
THE OLD HERALDIC STAINED GLASS AND OLD MONUMENTS	33–44
MONUMENTAL INSCRIPTIONS NOW IN THE CHURCH	45–58
INSCRIPTIONS IN THE CHURCHYARD	58–59
MONUMENTAL INSCRIPTIONS AND TABLETS FORMERLY IN THE CHURCH	60–76
LIST OF THE RECTORS OF ST. MARY'S	77–104
THE REGISTERS OF ST. MARY'S	105–177
EXTRACTS FROM OTHER REGISTERS RELATING TO PERSONS AND PLACES CONNECTED WITH ST. MARY'S PARISH	177
OLD CHESHIRE FAMILIES CONNECTED WITH ST. MARY'S	183–196
PEDIGREE OF WORSLEY OF CHESTER AND BIRKENHEAD ...	192
THE CHARITIES OF ST. MARY'S	197–200
THE SUNDAY EVENING LECTURE AT ST. MARY'S ...	200–201
LIST OF CHURCHWARDENS, 1536–1897	202–210
CHURCHWARDENS' ACCOUNTS, 1536–1565	211–255
PEDIGREES: BRERREWOOD OF CHESTER—GAMULL—WESTON—ACTON—PRESCOTT—FOULKES—CURRIE—MANLEY OF THE LACHE, OF PULTON—ELLIS—BROWNE OF NETHERLEIGH—MORGELL—BROCK—BROWNE OF UPTON—HUNT—HOLME	256–288
INDEX NOMINUM	289–300
INDEX RERUM	301–303

LIST OF ILLUSTRATIONS.

St. Mary's-without-the-Walls ...	... *Frontispiece*
Arms of Sir Robert Brerewood—Sir Francis Gamul—Randle Holme	1
St. Mary-on-the-Hill—Exterior	To face page 1
,, —Interior	,, 12
,, —Ground Plan ...	,, 14
,, —Portion of Oak Roof	,, 20
Old Communion Plate	,, 22
Randle Holme's House ...	,, 25
Masonic Window in Memory of Randle Holme	,, 33
Monument to Thomas Gamul, Recorder of Chester	,, 41
Monument to Philip Oldfield ...	,, 43
Mural Monument to Randle Holme ...	,, 46
Arms and Crest of Oldfield ...	44, 193
Coat of Arms of Ralph Worsley, Esq., 1573	59, 188
Coat of Arms on the Brass to Rowland Waring, 1695 ...	76
Arms and Crest of Troutbeck ...	186
Boss, Oak Roof, St. Mary's-on-the-Hill.	201, 210

ST. MARY-ON-THE-HILL, CHESTER.

SIR ROBERT BRERLWOOD	SIR FRANCIS GAMUL	RANDLE HOLME
Knt., Recorder of Chester, Judge of the King's Bench, &c.	Knt. and Bart., who entertained King Charles I. at Chester in 1645.	(Father, son, grandson, and great-grandson), the four well-known Chester Antiquaries.

ARMS OF THREE OF THE OLD FAMILIES CONNECTED WITH ST. MARY'S.

St. Mary-on-the-Hill, Chester.

HE PARISH OF ST. MARY-ON-THE-HILL, CHESTER, extends beyond the city boundaries, and includes the township of Gloverstone, which is wholly within the city, and those of Upton, Moston, Claverton, and Marleston-cum-Lache in Broxton Hundred, and Little Mollington in Wirral Hundred. Of these townships, Gloverstone is a very small one, closely adjacent to St. Mary's Church, and although entirely within the city of Chester, is yet a distinct township, and not subject to the city jurisdiction. Upton, Moston, Claverton, Marleston-cum-Lache, and Little Mollington, are all in the near neighbourhood of Chester. Exactly opposite to St. Mary's Church, but on the further side of the river Dee, is Handbridge, a hamlet in Claverton township, in which the new church of St. Mary-without-the-Walls has recently been erected. Saltney, a growing hamlet on that side of the Dee, is partly in St. Mary's parish (Claverton township), but chiefly in Hawarden parish, in the county of Flint.

B

The Church.

THE CHURCH of St. Mary, or, as it was more generally called, "St. Mary-on-the-Hill," ranked next to the abbey church of St. Werburgh and the collegiate church of St. John, as one of the most important of the many churches in Chester. Built on high ground above the river Dee, and in close proximity to the Castle of Chester, from which it is only separated by a broad and deep fosse, it was almost certainly erected by one of the early Norman Earls of Chester, whose chief stronghold the Castle of Chester was. It was most probably built early in the twelfth century, and it was certainly in existence in the middle of that century, when the advowson was given by Randle Gernons, the fourth Earl of Chester, who held that important position from the year 1128 to 1153, to the Abbey and Convent of St. Werburgh at Chester.[1]

St. Mary's remained in the possession of this rich and famous abbey till its dissolution in the year 1540, so that for quite four hundred years the clergy who officiated there were all presented by that abbey. After the dissolution of St. Werburgh's, the advowson of this church was granted to the then newly-created Dean and Chapter of Chester, but in consequence of certain disputes, they lost it, and it became the property of John Brereton, of Wettenhall, Esquire, who is found presenting to it in 1554. It was subsequently sold, together with a moiety of the Wettenhall estate, to the Wilbrahams of Dorfold, near Nantwich, and by the marriage of the Rev. Robert Hill, of the Hough, in Wybunbury, county Chester, with the daughter of the Rev. John Wilbraham, it passed to that family, and in 1819 was sold to the Earl Grosvenor, whose grandson, the Duke of Westminster, is the present owner.

In common with most of our parish churches, we know little or nothing of the early history of St. Mary's or how it gradually grew in size and importance during mediaeval times. Although it is clear that it was several times rebuilt or enlarged, yet it is impossible to give any definite dates when these alterations took place. In 1433, as will subsequently be shown, William Troutbeck, Esq., and Joan his wife built a chapel at the east end of the south aisle, and in 1444 they founded a chantry there, dedicated to the Holy Trinity. This chapel unfortunately fell down in 1661, and its fall utterly destroyed the handsome effigies of its founders, and others which had been placed there. It remained in ruins till 1693, when it was rebuilt by the parishioners, to whom it had been conveyed in 1691 by the Earl of Shrewsbury, who, as the direct descendant of the Troutbecks, was its then owner.

In 1536 there is a very interesting entry on the fly-leaf of the earliest volume of the Churchwardens' Accounts to the effect that on the dissolution of Basingwerk Abbey, near Holywell, in Flintshire, in 1535, the parishioners of St. Mary's had purchased the "choir"—most probably the choir or chancel roof,—and had put it up in their own church. The exact words of this entry are as follows :—

"Also in ther tyme *i.e.*, the two churchwardens mentioned as holding office when the book was begun, 27th Henry VIII., 1536] the quere [choir] was boght at basewerke and sett uppe with all costs and

[1] Chartulary of St. Werburgh, Chester. *Harl. MS.* 1965. f. 23. In this grant the church is described as "St. Mary of the Castle" *(vel. Marie de Castro).*

chargis belongynge to the same, more ouer the churche flowre, the chauncell and Seynt Katherine chappell the[y] did tyle in ther tyme."

But if the mediæval history of the church is defective, St. Mary's is exceptionally fortunate in possessing a remarkably fine series of Churchwardens' Accounts, from which the later history may be deduced with great clearness. These Accounts, which begin in 1536, are not only the earliest and the most perfect of any that I know of in the whole of Cheshire, but they go back to the early part of the sixteenth century, and so afford a very striking picture of the ecclesiastical history of a parish church from just prior to the Reformation down to modern times. They are wonderfully perfect, the receipts and disbursements of the churchwardens from that early date having been preserved almost without a break. Great interest, too, attaches to these records, for, as will be noticed, they commence in the middle of the reign of Henry VIII., at a time when he and his Privy Council were engaged in suppressing all the larger abbeys and monasteries throughout the kingdom, and so paving the way for the establishment of the reformed religion, which Edward VI. and his advisers carried out. Very many people seem to think that the dissolution of the abbeys and monasteries was synonymous with the suppression of the Roman Catholic ritual throughout the realm, but such records as these early Churchwardens' Accounts show how fallacious such a theory is. It is clear from them that until the end of Henry VIII.'s reign, that is down to 1547, the ritual in vogue at St. Mary's, and no doubt also in all other parish churches, was that of Roman Catholicism, and the various entries are most quaint and suggestive.[1]

St. Mary's was abundantly supplied with vestments of all kinds ; copes, albs, tunicles are mentioned, as a matter of course, as are also the quire books and procession books, and the "organs" which supplied the music for the services. There are constant references to the "clock" and to "the bells," of which there seem to have been six, including a "great bell" and a small "anthem bell," which would be rung at the elevation of the host. A large amount was expended each year in the purchase of wax to supply the church with candles, and the making of the large wax candles, which are called "surges" or "sergesses," and weighed about twenty pounds each, seems to have been an important event in the parish, and to have necessitated the giving of "beyrich" or "barrage," or what we should now term "an allowance," to the workmen employed at this labour.[2] Entries relating to this occur regularly year by year, together with others referring to "St. Stephen's lights," that is, to the candles burning before an image of St. Stephen placed somewhere in the church. There are regular entries for supplying the lamp in the church with oil, for "scouring" or cleaning the lamp, and the "chaldeners" as well as "the brasen censer" and "the cross." The "frankincense" and the charcoal used in the church form constant items in the wardens' accounts, and there are many interesting references to the great church festivals and the way the clergy educated the people by exhibiting to them some of the great mysteries of religion symbolically. Thus at Easter there are entries referring to the Easter sepulchre, such as "pay'd for nayles, pynes, and thred to heng the sepulcre," paid for "the sepulcre lights," and also for "cordys [cords] to the pascall," that is the large "paschal" or candlestick used at Easter. At Christmas there seems to have been a special decoration made

---

[1] I have here made use of the summary of these Accounts, which I drew up for a paper read before the Chester Archæological and Historic Society, in October 1887, and printed in the second volume of the *Journal* of that Society issued in 1889. Some few corrections and additions have been made where opportunity occurred.

[2] It is my intention, if space permits, to print at the end of this book a large number of extracts from these most interesting accounts, and, if possible, to print some of the earlier years in full. All the references in the text here given can then easily be verified, and explanations of the meanings of the rare or uncommon words will be given.

B 2

Dame Margerie Saillion Prioresse of the house and Priory of our Blessed Lady within the Cit Chestre, and the Convent of the same place on 20 February 1533 lets to Richard Sneyde, of Chester land &c in Northgate street, by a deed sealed with dark green wax circumn "SCOIE PRIORISSE & COVENTUS MONTABULI) STE MARIE CESTRE."
Ches. Archl Socy. Vol I

For Thurllow see this of Stores see Chesh. Historic Soc.? vol 5 p 93

ST. MARY-ON-THE-HILL, CHESTER.

of holly, which is regularly referred to as "the holyn," and there are entries for "the condullys [or candles] for the same," and occasional references to a sort of scenic arrangement in which the moon and stars figured prominently. Thus, in 1540, "paide for nayles and tymber to make the mone under the holyn," and " paide for hanging the roppe in the pulle [pulley] for the holyn." and " for making a skaffolde to take down the mone." Again, in 1544, " paid for candles to ye sterr and to ye hollyn."

In 1539 there is a curious entry " for settying up and schestyng [chesting] the holy goste," and in 1540 "paide for wyre to sett uppe the holy goste," by which is meant a figure of a dove symbolising the Holy Ghost. There are also entries " paid for a purse to carry ye sacrament " and for " a cord to the vayle." And, curiously enough, in the same year, 1544, in which these last two entries occur, there is the first reference to the Bible, when " a cheyne to the Byble " was paid for. There are also entries paid for rushes at Easter and Pentecost, and also for taking the old rushes out of the church. Rushes were used to strew on the floor of the church to keep it warm.

In 1537 there is an entry " for makynge and gyldynge 4 buttons to the best cope and the velvet cope," and another for " 3 gyrdyllis to the best shute [suit]." The clerk, too, was yearly provided with a "rochet," which is a white linen vestment like a surplice. In 1539 there are several entries about the raising up of the high altar, and when it was done the wardens entertained their neighbours at the cost to the parish of 4d. The "holy water stock" was set up this year, and a small sum was paid " for a cord to the curtyn before the high altar."

In 1542 a porch was built on the north side of the church, the stones for which came from the ruins of St. Mary's Nunnery; and another porch was also built on the south side, and in the following year a chamber was erected over one of these porches, and fitted up as a living room for one of the priests serving in the church ; and in this year, 1543, the pulpit was also made. There are occasional references to the rood loft, and in 1547, the first year of King Edward VI., the holy "rood," or figure of our Lord on the Cross, was taken down, and in this year we have the first record of "white-liming " or whitewashing the church, in order to get rid of any paintings or other ornamentation there might be on the walls.

These entries continue much the same till about the year 1550, when, with the introduction of the reformed religion, by command of Edward VI., great changes took place. In 1549 a book for the Communion and two psalters, and a book called " The Paraphrases," were purchased by the wardens, and in 1550 the lead from " the holy water stocke " was sold for five shillings. In this latter year a large sum was paid " for takyng downe the alters and tyling the churche flore," and another sum was paid for mending the glass windows, in which the old stained glass, with inscriptions beseeching prayers for the souls of those who had given them, had probably been broken.[1]

In 1553 Chester was visited by the commissioners appointed by the Privy Council—John [Bird] Bishop of Chester, Thomas Smith, mayor of the city, Sir Laurence Smith, knight, and Roger Hurleston, gentleman—to inquire as to "all and singular the copes, vestments, chalices, ornaments, and goodes," of all and every the churches, chapels, &c., within the city ; and an inventory, now in the Record Office, London, was made of all such as they had sold for the king's use, and also "of the chalices, copes, and vestments of cloth of gold " by them received and retained for the king's use, as well as " such goods, crosses, plate, or bells " as had been sold or stolen by

---

[1] A full account of the old heraldic stained glass formerly in the church windows, with the inscriptions placed there, will be subsequently given.

the parishioners and others. As regards St. Mary's, the copes, vestments, &c., belonging to the church were sold for £10 13s. 6d.—a larger sum than was paid for the vestments of any other church in the city, not excepting the cathedral. The goods, &c., delivered to the churchwardens on the 28th May, 1553, to be kept in the church till the king's pleasure was further known, are set out as follows :—

A chalice with a paten of silver, weighing 10 ounces.
Two copes, three table clothes [or, as we should call them, altar cloths].
A payre of organs. A hanging for the table of linen. A pillow of silk.
Five great bells in the steeple, and an anthem bell and a clock.
Four towels, a surplice, and all the bookes in the church now used.

In the volume of Churchwardens' Accounts there is a list of the vestments, &c., in 1553, which had been either delivered up to the king's commissioners, or retained by the churchwardens for the use of the parish. This list, which is most interesting, is as follows (the spelling being modernised) :—

Delivered to Mr. Branshank our best suit there to be kept in safety to the use of the parish, one cope of gold, one vestment of gold, and two tunicles of gold, and one albe belonging to the same suit which they were lapped in.

 Item delivered there to be kept in safety to the use of the parish one cope of red satin.
 Item one red satin vestment.
 Item two tunicles of satin.
 Item two vestments of black chamlet.
 Item two albes belonging to the best suit.
Memorandum that these be the goods delivered to the King's Commissioners :
 Item a cope of red velvet.
 Item a cope of red scarlet.
 Item a vestment of green silk.
 Item a vestment of scarlet.
 Item a vestment of green satin of Bruges.
 Item a vestment of white silk.
 Item two tunicles with all things belonging to them.
 Item a hanging to an altar with squirrels (?) of gold.
 Item two corporas cases of gold and corporas clothes within them and one of silk and a cloth within the same.
Item at the same time we sold certain of the church goods, and these are our receipts :
 Received for banners and a veil cloth and certain hangings that belong to the altar, 10s.
 Received for certain pixes, and for certain "parers" belonging to the best suit, 8s. 8d.
 Received for two coffers and four spears, 8s.
 Received for certain hangings that belonged to the altars in the church, 3s. 4d.

This was in May, 1553. In July of that year the king, Edward VI., died, and Queen Mary succeeded him, and being a Roman Catholic, that religion at once revived. Many of the vestments, &c., formerly belonging to the church were, no doubt, restored to it, and in the Accounts for that year and for 1554 such entries as the following speak for themselves :—

Paid for "makyng of the altres," 17d.
Paid to "the carver for a frame to the table of the high altar," 16d.

Paid for "settinge vp of the angell," 6d.[1]
Paid for "gilding of an image of our Lady," 20d.
Paid for "painting the table to the high altar," 4s.
Gathered in the parish "for the makying of the Rode," 8s. 4d.
Paid "for the holy watter bockytt," 3s. 3d.
Paid "for sayinge of masse to a prest in the wytson weke," 12d.
Paid "for the making the Rode," 12s., for "gilding the Rode," 13s., &c., &c.

In the following year, 1555, there are payments for "frankincense and charcoal," for "mending the cloth before the high altar," and once more "for candles for the holyn," "for the holyn to the star and mone," and "for makying the mone and all such thyngs belongen to ytt." There are other entries in 1557 for making a star and for painting and gilding it, &c.

Queen Mary died in November, 1558, and was succeeded by Queen Elizabeth, and the reformed Protestant religion was once more in the ascendant. This shows itself in these Accounts. The rood was taken down in 1559, a communion table was provided and a communion book, and in 1562 the rood loft itself came down, as well as the altars, the church was painted throughout, and the Ten Commandments put up. There is no mention of the "organs" after 1553, when it is probable they had been taken down; but in 1565 there is an entry to the effect that "the organ pipes lying in the cofer were weighed and found to be just five score pounds."[2] Once more, nine years later, in 1574, a joiner was paid for taking down "the organ case," and there was received "of y⁶ virginall maker for y⁶ organ wyndowes," 18d. In 1573, the sum of 3s. 2d. was received for eleven pounds of brass, "beinge y⁶ bucket and y⁶ owld cense [censer]," showing that all the articles formerly used in the church were gradually got rid of.

In 1581 the church was whitewashed, and the pillars and the arches appear to have been painted red. In 1583 the Ten Commandments "with other texts of Scripture" were painted on the walls, and in 1602 we have a further payment "for paintinge, writinge sentences and layinge the pillars and windowes of the church in redde, and writing the X Commandments at large." This had to be done again in 1616. In 1622 the church was ornamented by "the King's Armes wrought on a table [or board] with gould and oyle cullers" by Randle Holme, and costing £3. In 1630, the church was beautified (?) in the manner set out in the following entry:—

P⁴ vnto M⁶ Holme for layinge the puilpitt, readinge place, pooremans box and fontt in oyle greene, for gildinge the hobbs of the puilpitt cover and the starrs vpon itt and the fontt stone. And to Robert Thorneley for layinge the church windowes and arches and Saint Katerins Ile in redd, for writeinge of all the sentences in compartements vpon the walls, for layinge the doores, dyall, clockehouse and starr in color, for layinge of all the carved worke in greene and yellowe, for marblinge the greatt pillers and workeinge the Comandements.

li s. d.
v. xiii. iiii.
[£5 13s. 4d.]

The following list of the "church goods" drawn up in 1631 seems of sufficient interest to print in its entirety, as showing what constituted the possessions of a large parish church in the time of Charles I.:—

An Inventory of Church goods delivered by me, M⁶ Randle Holme, jun., one of the late Church

---

[1] In 1556 this entry occurs: "Payd for the Angell that the sacrament ys in, xlijd."

[2] They were sold, and there was received in the next year for 82 pounds of "orgayne pypes" at 5d. the pound, 34s. 2d., and it is recorded in 1567 that "ther remayneth of orgayne pipes in the churche cofer in weight, xxj."

wardens of this p'ish of St. Maryes, vnto Thomas Johnson and Thomas Welshman, now Church wardens, the 20th day of May, 1631, as wittnesse their hands vnder written.

Imp^r a new parchment booke for a Regester.	a new booke of homileys in folio.
bushop Juells workes in tow bookes.	a large Church bible in folio.
an other bible in folio the Clark redeth in.	a Comon praier booke in folio for the p'son.
an other Seruice booke for the Clarke.	an other ould Comon prayer booke.
16 bonds of them whos names may be seene which have mony of the p'ish or [are] bound to the p'ish as apereth in folio ante in the yeare 1630 of the Accounts.	
a pulpit cloth of red velvett.	a blew Cushion for pulpit and [a] Casse to put it in.
a lynnen Table Cloth & one course one.	3 Surplesses.
a Comunion Table, a Carpet for the Comunion Table.	a payre of Iron Snuffers, 5 chime hommars of Iron, a Crow of Iron.
3 stocks for wheles in the bellfree.	a square piece of tymber a yard long.
a beare [bier] to Carry Corpes to the Church.	a booke in 4to to be sayd the 5th of November.
a booke of Cannons.	a booke of Comon prayer to be red in tyme of plage [plague].
3 books of Articles.	a book of Comon prayer to be red in tyme of warr.
a statute booke of xxixth of Q. Eliz [1587].	a statute book of first of K. James [1603].
a booke of Instructions from the king.	an order for pennance.
a breefe for bowes & Arrows from the king.	10 roales of papers in the chest.
8 hanging plates for Candles.	ould banners in the Chest.
a Comunion Cupp of Silver & Couer of the same.	a gilt leder [leather] Cusshion.
2 Chestes to keepe the Church goods in.	one roule contayning 3 church mapps of the seates.

also xi^s iiij^d [11s. 4d.] of mony wch I had in my hand.

(*Signed*) THOMAS JOHNSONNE
THOMAS WELLSHMAN."

From an entry in 1639 referring to the "mens seates on the south side the church" it is evident that at St. Mary's, as in so many other churches, the men sat on one side of the church and the women on the other.

In February, 1646, Chester capitulated to the Parliamentary forces after having undergone a long and close siege, and in that year the following memorandum referring to St. Mary's, and written by one of the Randle Holmes, occurs in *Harl. MS.* 1994 :—

"1646. This yeare all the curious windowes and figures [therein] were by the Roundheads caused to be taken downe & defaced and cutt in quarrells confusedly, and [the repairs] cost the parish in the workmanship x" [£10]."[1]

During the Civil War, St. Mary's seems to have suffered much, so that Randle Holme, jun. (the third of that name), who was one of the two churchwardens in 1657, collected a large sum of money "towards the repair of the steeple and the bells," and a list of those who contributed towards this object is given in the volume of the Churchwardens' Accounts.[2] In this same year

---

[1] I do not find any reference to this in the Churchwardens' Accounts for that year or subsequently, but they are rather badly kept at this period. Randle Holme, living in the parish, and taking an active interest in the church, would be likely to know of this destruction.

[2] If space permits, this list, giving the names of all the chief inhabitants of the parish, will be printed in the Appendix.

the old font was done away with in accordance with the spirit of the times, and 5s. was paid " for a faire Bason to hold water in when Infants are baptized," and a further sum of 2s. to the smith " for makeing a round iron to sett it on in yᵉ church " !

In 1659, on the outbreak of the " Cheshire Rising," which was only the prelude to the restoration of Charles II. in the following year, Chester Castle was held against the insurgents, and this entry occurs in *Harl. MS.* 1929, in an account of affairs in Chester :—

"1659. Aug. 1. Sᵗ Marys steeple [was] demolished by souldiers from the Castle by command from Col. Croxton, the governor, because the castle should be kept against the gentlemen that came to the city for the defence . . . of the King and Parliament."

And again when Sir George Booth and his party had been defeated, and Hawarden Castle had been surrendered to the forces of the Parliament, the following entry occurs in the same MS. :—

"1659. Aug. 21. Harden Castle delivered up this morning. Many gentry brought in prisoners, some surrendering themselves, many citizens put in the Castle and Sᵗ Maries church."

In *Harl. MS.* 2125, f. 335, it is stated under date 5th November, 1659, that the governor of the Castle, Colonel Croxton, " ordered St. Mary's steeple to be pulled down " ; but whether this really refers to the lowering of the tower in August of that year, or to a still further pulling down in November, is not very clear. The entries in the Churchwardens' Accounts for that year are as follows :—

Paid to the Masons for takeing down part of the steeple 4 05 0
Paid more to a workman for takeing down the battlements of the steeple 0 01 0

In the following year the restoration of the monarchy was received at St. Mary's with the usual rejoicings, and the King's arms were once more set up in the church. But, curiously enough, the communion table had gone astray, and sixpence was paid for a warrant to search for it, and fourpence was " spent on the constables in goinge about to search for the table " ! In 1661, Troutbeck's Chapel, as already stated, fell down, and there are several entries about viewing " the ruines of the church," and obtaining a " Brief " for its repair. In 1666 this " Brief money " had only realised £45.

In 1676, and again in 1706, there are entries for " building the church porch," and in 1678 and 1680 more money was spent on the repair of the church and " St. Catherine's chancel." In 1693 is this notice : " Memorandum that in the year 1693 the south part of the church formerly called Troutebeckes Chapple was repaired." In 1728 a small gallery was erected at the west end of the church, and " on Sunday, November 24th, 1745, the churchyard walls of St Mary's-on-the-Hill were taken down, and the materials taken into the Castle,"[1] which was done to protect the castle in case the rebels in the " young Pretender's " insurrection of that year should gain possession of the city.

From that date to comparatively modern times, little was done to the church beyond the erection of galleries and keeping the building in repair, and there is nothing in the Churchwardens' Accounts calling for special comment. In August, 1793, an organ was put up in the west gallery given by Mr. Challiner at a cost of £173.[2] The appearance of the building early in this century is shown in the accompanying illustration taken from a now very scarce volume of

---

[1] Cowper's MSS. quoted by Ormerod, vol. i. p. 248. There is an entry in the Churchwardens' Accounts for this year : " Paid for securing Ch. books and plate at yᵉ time of the Rebellion, 3s."

[2] Hemingway's *History of Chester*, 1831, vol. ii. p. 106.

THE CHURCH.

etchings of churches, &c., in Chester, published about 1816.[1] It shows the north side of the church, the north porch, the high clerestory windows, and the low squat tower, which had never been raised[2] since it was lowered in 1659 (see *ante*). In front of the railings are the figures of three soldiers from the adjacent castle.

The following description of the church at this time was written by the late Dr. Ormerod for his *History of Cheshire*, published in 1819 :—

"It is built of red stone and consists of a tower, containing six bells, a nave and chancel, with side aisles, and subordinate chancels at the end of these aisles. The nave is divided from the side aisles by three pointed arches on each side, and by another pointed arch from the chancel; and each subordinate chancel is also divided from its aisle by a pointed arch and by an obtuse one from the principal chancel. Of these last, the arch on the north side has been modernised. The windows on this side are more obtusely pointed than the others, and contain fragments of stained glass: among others, the arms of Brereton and Ipstones, and a golden tun, probably intended as a rebus. In the south chancel is a very handsome octagonal font, now disused, which has been anciently ornamented with gilding and painting."

It may be added that a portion of the chapel at the east end of the south aisle was used as a small vestry, with a door leading into it from the churchyard, and in another portion of this chapel the font was placed. Prior to 1830, the octagonal font above mentioned had been replaced by a modern one.[4] A rather flattering view of the church, taken about 1830, is shown in an excellent lithograph by Miss Georgina Jackson, of which the opposite plate is a careful reproduction.

Sir Stephen Glynne, Bart., of Hawarden Castle, visited St. Mary's on three occasions, and has left the following descriptions of the church, which will now be read with interest.[5] His first visit was in 1830.

"This church is entirely of late Rectilinear, but superior in style to most of the churches in Chester, though built of friable stone, with some bad modern alterations of windows. It consists of a nave with side aisles and a chancel with side chapels, with a low western tower, the upper part of which is modern, but having a panelled west door much worn. The parapets of the church are embattled, and within the north porch is a doorway with quatrefoil panelling in its continuous mouldings. The nave has on each side three Tudor arches with octagonal piers, and the chancel opens to each chapel by one very wide arch of like form. There is a clerestory with numerous windows; those of the aisle and chancel are large, with contracted arches, but some have been despoiled of their tracery, particularly on the south. The east window is good, and lately filled with tolerable stained glass, and the east wall lately repaired, and its gable crowned by a new cross. There is in the nave a very handsome panelled ceiling with stars, and in the north chapel

---

[1] This is entitled "Twelve Etchings of Public Buildings in Chester," by G. Batenham, and I consider myself very fortunate in possessing a copy of this rare little book. It also contains etchings of the two tombs in St. Mary's, those of Philip Oldfield and Thomas Gamull, neither of which is very accurately drawn.

[2] In Pigot's *History of Chester*, 1815, p. 81, it is stated that "the steeple of this church is only seventeen yards [51 feet] high; it was repaired and the upper part renewed in 1715, when its further elevation was objected to by the governor of the castle lest it should command a view of the castle-yard." I am rather sceptical as to the truth of this statement, as there is no reference to these repairs in 1715 in the Churchwardens' Accounts.

[3] To the new edition of Ormerod's *History*, the editor has added a note that "the fine panelled ceiling of the nave is in oak, and is traditionally said to have once belonged to the Abbey of Bazingwarke (*sic*) in Flint." This is most probably the case, as pointed out in the description of the present church (*see* p. 20), where this roof is described. *See* also page 2, where the removal of the choir roof from Basingwerk Abbey is mentioned.

[4] Hemingway's *History of Chester*, vol. ii., p. 106.

[5] These descriptions are taken from Sir Stephen Glynne's account of the churches in Cheshire, now being edited for the Chetham Society by Canon Atkinson.

of the chancel is a monumental effigy of a late Rectilinear tomb. The interior is tolerably neat, though the pews are ugly. A west gallery extending across the whole church contains an organ."

Subsequent visits were paid in 1849, 1852, and 1861, the descriptions being as follows:—

"The church has been improved in many respects lately. The south aisle has been externally much restored, and new windows of three lights inserted. The exterior much cleansed." [1849.]

"In the south chapel of the chancel is a piscina at the south-east.

"The stained glass of the east window is partly modern, partly of ancient fragments.

"The font has an octagonal bowl on a stem of similar form. The chancel arch is rather straight sided, dying into the wall, and appears to be older than the rest of the chancel, which is probably *temp.* Henry VIII. A fine obituary window of stained glass is in the north chapel, and another in the south chapel. Great improvements have lately taken place; the pews in the chancel and its chapels are removed, and replaced by open seats enclosed by new open screens of wood, erected by the daughters of the late Dr. Currie. The gallery at the west end is removed, and the organ, which has been rebuilt and arranged in a very appropriate manner, placed on the ground under the tower arch. A neat low screen divides the north aisle from the north chapel. The windows south of the nave have curious foliated brackets in their interior jambs, level with the sills, and in the south wall appear curious ancient paintings in fresco recently brought to light." [1852.]

"Further improvement—new open seats replace the pews, organ moved to south aisle of chancel, and tower arch opened. Tower in course of being raised." [1861.]

Shortly after the Rev. Thomas Eaton became rector of St. Mary's, he effected a few repairs in the church, but much more was done by his successor, the Rev. W. H. Massie, who would have completely restored it had not his unexpected death in January, 1856, prevented him.[1] During some restorations made by him in 1843 in the south aisle, a small but interesting mural painting was uncovered on the east wall at the end of that aisle. This shows the figure of our Lord on the Cross, with St. Mary on the one side, and St. John on the other, and further along the figure of an archbishop in full eucharistic vestments, wearing a mitre and holding a crozier in the left hand. Above the crucified Saviour is the figure of a king,[2] crowned and robed, holding a sceptre in the right hand. It has been conjectured that this represents Henry VI., in whose reign the Troutbeck Chapel at the end of this aisle was built. The floriated background of this painting and the other details are shown in the annexed illustration, taken from the *Journal of the Chester Archaeological Society*, vol. i., p. 400. The remains of this mural painting are still to be seen in the church.

The Rev. Charles Bowen, who succeeded Mr. Massie, issued an appeal for funds to restore the church on the 8th March, 1861, and meeting with a very liberal response, was ultimately enabled to expend £2,200 on that object. He greatly improved the tower by adding 30 feet to its height, and by removing the organ from under the tower, enabled the fine pointed tower arch and west window to be seen. The whitewash was scraped from the walls, and the old pews were replaced by open benches. The chancel was laid with encaustic tiles, and the general appearance of the church was very greatly improved in every way.

---

[1] It is recorded of him that "he restored the chancel, repaired and adorned the richly-toned organ, brought out from beyond their accumulated plaster the original oaken roofs," and also filled many of the windows with stained glass. Owing to his exertions, the large east window was filled with stained glass to the memory of those of the 23rd Royal Welsh Fusiliers who had perished in the Crimea.

[2] This figure has also been described as "a regally attired figure, not improbably representing the Virgin as Queen of Heaven".

On a brass plate fixed in the tower is this inscription:—

This church was repewed and restored and the tower elevated to the present height in the year of our Lord 1861.

CHARLES BOWEN, Rector.
JOHN JONES, } Churchwardens.
HUGH ROBERTS, }

JAMES HARRISON
[Architect].

During the time that the Rev. W. H. Massie, the Rev. Charles Bowen, and the Rev. Henry Grantham, held the rectory of St. Mary's, various important changes were effected in the parish. In the first place, by the erection of new churches in the outlying districts of Lache and Upton; secondly, by a rearrangement of the parish boundaries of some of the churches within the city; and thirdly, by the erection of the fine church of St. Mary-without-the-Walls, and the transference to it of the old church plate, and all the old registers, &c., belonging to St. Mary-on-the-Hill, whilst that church was constituted the parish church for the united parishes of St. Bridget's and St. Martin's. As these changes are very important historically, and at the same time by no means easy to describe with clearness, I gladly avail myself of the following summary of them, kindly drawn up by John Gamon, Esq., the Bishop's secretary and Registrar of the diocese of Chester, for the purpose of this work.

REARRANGEMENT OF THE ECCLESIASTICAL PARISH OF ST. MARY'S, ETC.

In 1855 a section of St. Mary's parish was assigned, as part of a consolidated chapelry, formed out of the parishes of St. Mary, and of Hawarden, in the county of Flint, to the Church of the Holy Epiphany, Lache, now better known as the Church of the Holy Epiphany, Saltney; this assignment being confirmed by an Order of the Queen in Council, dated the 24th September, 1855.

Afterwards, on account of the migration of population from the centre to the suburbs of the city and the intermixture of the city parishes—an intermixture in many cases quite bewildering in the administration of a parish, and perhaps only to be accounted for by reference to the several territories and possessions of religious houses in the city before the dissolution of the monasteries—it had long been considered desirable to effect exchanges of territory by way of consolidating the ecclesiastical divisions allotted to the various churches and their clergy. This was commenced in the year 1880, with the approval of the then Bishop of Chester (Bishop Jacobson), by the present Dean of Chester (the Very Rev. John L. Darby), who, in his capacity of Archdeacon of Chester, drew up a scheme for this consolidation, a task of no little intricacy and requiring much patient adjustment with regard to the many interests affected by it.

This scheme, elaborated in all its details, received the approval of the Bishop, the Ecclesiastical Commissioners for England, and the Archbishop of York, and was partly carried into effect in 1881 by the allotment to St. Peter's Church and its rector of all that portion of the parish of St. Oswald's within the walls of the city, and parts of other parishes adjoining, an arrangement sanctioned and confirmed by an Order of the Queen in Council of the 26th August, 1881.

Again, in 1882, the township of Upton, an outlying part of St. Mary's parish, was assigned to the Church of the Holy Ascension, Upton, a chapel-of-ease of St. Mary's, and created a separate benefice in the patronage of the Duke of Westminster, who made a considerable augmentation to its endowment by the transfer to Upton church of tithe rent-charge of St. Mary's, in compensation for which transfer his Grace paid to the Ecclesiastical Commissioners for England, by way of benefaction to St. Mary's, the sum of £3,000. This assignment was confirmed by Order of the Queen in Council, dated the 30th day of November, 1882.

But the most intricate and, perhaps, the most important part of the scheme remained to be accomplished, involving the building of a new church, south of the river Dee, in the parish of St. Mary's, which should serve as the parish church for the larger portion of St. Mary's parish, lying on the south of that river and an adjoining part of the parish of St. Bridget, which was wholly separated from its parish church and the rest of its own parish by intervening territory of St. Mary's. These two sections of the city parishes constituted a district of considerable importance from the large and increasing population contained within their bounds, and a proposal for their consolidation, together with sundry adjustments of boundaries, by which all that portion of St. Mary's within the city walls was allotted to the parish churches of St. Bridget and St. Michael, and better defined limits were set to the parish of St. Bridget on its eastern side, and to the parish of Holy Trinity on its northern boundary, was in 1883 submitted by Archdeacon Darby to the Duke of Westminster, the patron of St. Mary's. His Grace not only highly approved of the proposal, but, with his characteristic munificence, at once declared his intention of facilitating its accomplishment by building a new parish church in St. Mary's parish, on the south side of the river, at his own expense.

With this promise by the Duke of Westminster all difficulties disappeared, and the noble generosity with which the new church was built and surrounded with its handsome rectory and enlarged elementary schools will ever be dwelt upon with affectionate remembrance by all who admire the grace and symmetry of the church and the excellency of its structure or who are privileged to worship within it.

The new church was completed in 1887, and was consecrated by the Right Reverend William, Lord Bishop of Chester (now Bishop of Oxford), the successor to Bishop Jacobson, on the 18th day of June in that year, by the name of "The Church of St Mary-without-the-Walls, Chester," and was, by an Order of the Ecclesiastical Commissioners for England, dated the 14th day of July, 1887, substituted for the ancient church of St Mary's-on-the-Hill, Chester, as the parish church of the parish of St Mary.

By two Orders of the Queen in Council, both dated the 15th day of September, 1887, ratifying and confirming schemes proposed by the Bishop of Chester with the consent of the several patrons and incumbents of the city parishes affected, and recommended by the Archbishop of York, a large portion of St Mary's parish lying within the walls of the city was transferred, with several minor adjustments, to the parish of St Bridget; another portion of St Mary's parish was allotted to the parish of St Michael, and the whole of the ancient parish of St Bridget on the south side of the river Dee consolidated with the rest of St Mary's parish on that side of the river as the ecclesiastical parish of the rectory and new parish church of St Mary-without-the-Walls.

The names of the patrons and incumbents consenting to the schemes referred to were,

his Grace the Most Noble Hugh Lupus, Duke of Westminster, the Rev⁴ Henry Grantham, Rector of S⁺ Mary's, the Right Honourable Edward Henry Earl of Derby, the Rev⁴ Edward Marston, Rector of Holy Trinity, Chester, the Bishop of Chester, patron of S⁺ Bridget's with S⁺ Martin's, and the Venerable Edward Barber, Archdeacon of Chester and rector of S⁺ Bridget's with S⁺ Martin's.

The ancient church of S⁺ Mary-on-the-Hill having, upon the Order for substitution of the new church of S⁺ Mary in place of this ancient parish church, become a chapel-of-ease of S⁺ Mary's parish, was transferred to the parish of S⁺ Bridget with that portion of S⁺ Mary's parish annexed to the parish of S⁺ Bridget, and having been recently repaired and restored it is now constituted the parish church for the parish of S⁺ Bridget with S⁺ Martin, and so will resume its interesting and useful position among the churches of the city as a memorial of the religious life and energy of days gone by and of the vigour with which this life and energy still flourish amongst us.

It remains only to congratulate the Dean of Chester on the success with which his well considered proposals have been carried into effect, and the high appreciation the changes have met with from the clergy and people interested in them.

THE CHURCH OF ST. MARY-WITHOUT-THE-WALLS.
(NOW THE PARISH CHURCH OF ST. MARY'S.)

When the Duke of Westminster decided to build a new church in the southern part of St. Mary's parish, on the other side of the river Dee, he selected an elevated plot of land in Handbridge, adjacent to the main road there. This road is not far from the line of the old Roman street leading from Chester (Deva) to Uriconium, and as it was known, from the Roman remains previously found there, that there had been a Roman cemetery along the line of this street, the excavations for the foundations of the new church were watched with much interest. Mr. G. W. Shrubsole has kindly sent me the following particulars of the various remains found there :—

Roman Remains found on the site of St. Mary-without-the-Walls, &c.

In excavating the foundations for the nave and tower, beyond a few coins of the Constantine family and a Roman bronze fibula, nothing of importance was discovered. But when the excavations for the chancel were reached, it was evident that the line of the Roman cemetery had been found. The surface soil there was crowded with fragments of Roman pottery, representing every variety of fictile ware. Below this came the clay, in which, at depths of four or five feet, interments were met with. These were well shown in the making of a drain from the chancel to the high road in a south-easterly direction. The section then exposed disclosed interments at intervals of two or three yards, which were of two kinds: firstly, the ordinary black cinerary urn, and secondly, a circular pit, two or three feet in diameter, containing burnt bones, charcoal, &c., but no pottery. The amount of burnt *débris* suggested that several cremated bodies had been placed in these pits. The absence of lamps, and indeed of any memorial beyond the urn, suggested that this might be the common burying-place of the Roman legionaries. The urns were so friable that not one was recovered entire. A large case filled with the more interesting of the fragments of pottery may be seen in the Grosvenor Museum.[1]

The site and surroundings of the church are also interesting.

[1] See also Thompson Watkin's *Roman Cheshire*, p. 219. It is there stated that about seven interments were found, and some fine fragments of Samian ware, one nearly an entire vessel.

1. The Roman cemetery bordered, for a mile or more, the Roman street from Deva, across a ford over the river opposite old St. Mary's, and thence across the fords at Eaton or Aldford (Oldford) to Uriconium. The site of the church, as already noticed, is on part of the Roman cemetery, and the east end of the building is on the margin of the Roman street.

2. The field on the north-east side of the church, well seen from the city walls opposite, as rising with a gentle slope from the ford across the river (the rock at this point being cut down to the water's edge) has several points of interest. It possesses a figure of Minerva carved on a scarped rock face, which is almost unique in England as a relic of Roman work *in situ*. The Roman street passed through the centre of this field to the east of the church and on the higher part of it and on the east side of the Roman street is the site of the so-called " King Edgar's Palace." This is marked in Braun's plan of Chester, made about 1570, " Ruinosa domus Comitis Cestriensis," " Edgar's Palace;" and this building, I believe with Stukeley, to have been a Roman villa.[1] This field and the one on the west side extending to the new churchyard are the quarries which supplied the material for paving the Roman street to Eaton. Slabs of sandstone six and eight inches thick have been found along the present Eccleston road at a depth of three feet. Ten and fifteen feet of rock have here been cut away over two acres of ground, and the Roman figure on one of the rock surfaces supplies the clue to identify the workers.

A fuller account of this field, which has recently been presented by the Duke of Westminster to the Corporation as a recreation ground, will be found later on in the account of Handbridge, and the various other Roman remains from there will also be described, and if possible, illustrated.

To return to the new church. The foundation stone was laid in the presence of a large and fashionable gathering on Monday, the 20th July, 1885. There was a brief service, at which the rector, the Rev. H. Grantham, officiated. In an interval the respond pier-stone of the church was laid as a foundation stone by the Duke of Westminster, a beautifully-wrought trowel and mallet of polished mahogany, with dark walnut handle and silver mounted, being used on the occasion. The trowel bore the inscription : " Presented by the Rector and Committee to his Grace the Duke of Westminster, K.G., on his laying the foundation stone of the Church of St. Mary's-without-the-Walls, Chester, 20th July, 1885." In a cavity of the stone was deposited a hermetically sealed bottle containing photographs of the Duke and Duchess of Westminster and Lady Grosvenor, a plan of the church, and a record of the circumstances which led to its erection, together with the names of the donor, rector, churchwardens, architect and contractors, copies of the local newspapers, and specimens of 1885 silver coinage.

When the ceremony was over, the company adjourned to the site of the Rectory, where, after a brief service, her Grace the Duchess laid the foundation stone of that building.

The work of erecting the church and the rectory was proceeded with without delay, and within two years they were practically completed, and that too without any accident. The church, of which Mr. F. B. Wade, of London, was the architect, is built of the local red sandstone, with dressings of Runcorn stone, in the Early English style. It consists of a nave, with north and south aisles, a south transept, and a vestry and robing-room on the north side. At the west end is a lofty tower and spire, 168 feet in height, and an octagonal baptistry, a somewhat unusual and noteworthy arrangement. The total length of the interior of the church is 141 feet, the nave, including the aisles, being 75 feet by 50 feet ; the chancel measures 43 feet by 21 feet, and the south transept 25 feet by 24 feet. The whole of the interior is faced with stone ashlar, and the body of the church is oak panelled to the height of five or six feet. The floor is composed

---

[1] *See* Pennant's *Tour in Wales*, and Thompson Watkin's *Roman Cheshire*, p. 200.

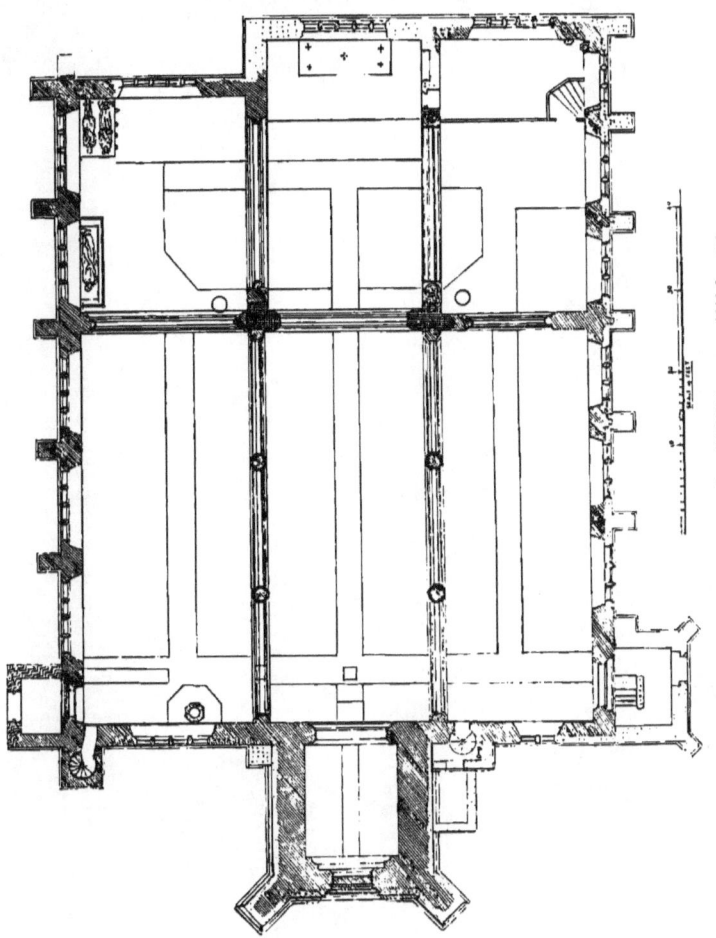

of pine blocks, except the chancel and baptistry, which are laid with Worcester mosaics. The open roofs of the nave, chancel, and aisles, &c., are all of oak.[1] The church will seat seven hundred people, and it has been estimated that the cost of its erection, together with the peal of eight bells, the rectory, and the enlarged schools, cannot have been much less than £40,000. The contractor for the building was Mr. John Thompson, of Peterborough, who was engaged on the restoration of Chester Cathedral.[2] The architect of the Rectory was Mr. E. A. Ould, of Chester, and the builder Mr. Thomas Espley, of Ecclesham.

The church was consecrated by the Bishop of Chester on the 18th June, 1887, and as the occasion was recognised as one of no ordinary importance, there was a very large congregation. It is not often that so large and handsome a building, with a fine peal of bells, an excellent organ, stained-glass windows, a churchyard, rectory house, and schools all complete, is built by one generous donor, and then presented to the public, so that every effort was made to prove to the Duke of Westminster how much his kindness and liberality were appreciated. The parishioners of St. Mary's, as well as many of the inhabitants of Chester, requested permission to furnish the beautiful structure erected for their benefit, and the list of donations and special gifts (printed on page 17), amounting in all to £1,274, shows how willingly they carried out this labour of love. The Bishop of Chester (Dr. Stubbs) was accompanied by the Dean of Chester, the two Archdeacons, the Canons of the Cathedral, the Precentor, and a very large number of the neighbouring clergy. His lordship took for his texts Isaiah lii. 1, and 1 Chronicles xxix. 14, "Awake, awake; put on thy strength, O Zion; put on thy beautiful garments, O Jerusalem"; "Who am I, and what is my people, that we should be able to offer so willingly after this sort? for all things come of thee"; on which he preached a very earnest sermon. In the course of his remarks he said:

"We are met this morning to dedicate with thanks and prayers a very complete and most beautiful new church. It is very beautiful, everything in it and about it is full of voices of love, and of the careful desire to make it as beautiful as it can be made, a fit offering of deep and dutiful and intelligent devotion. This is not, indeed, a fitting time for personal congratulation or compliment. What a gift the munificent heart of the founder has given as the offering of a king to the service of the King of Kings, and what an encouragement and new spring of hope and blessing such a foundation is to those who have at heart the welfare of Church and people, there cannot be a single person here who does not recognise with admiration and gratitude. God loves the cheerful giver, and there is an abundant blessing in the gracious heart, the heart that has grace so to give. In such a feeling we accept and dedicate the church. The words of our founder are the words of David: 'All things come of thee, and of thine own have we given thee.'"

After the dedicatory service was concluded, the following address was presented to the Duke of Westminster:

TO THE MOST NOBLE HUGH LUPUS, DUKE OF WESTMINSTER, K.G.

MAY IT PLEASE YOUR GRACE,

We, the rector and parishioners of St. Mary's, Chester, desire to offer to your Grace our congratulations on the happy occasion of the consecration of the new parish church of St. Mary-without-the-Walls, for which, together with the new rectory and schools, we are indebted to your munificent liberality. The

---

[1] It should also be noted that all the wrought-iron work of the church was designed by the architect himself, and is marked by much beauty and artistic feeling.
[2] Mr. R. M. Searle was clerk of the works, and Mr. B. Darling the contractor's manager.

parishioners of St. Mary's will ever regard with gratitude this magnificent memorial of your Grace's zeal and interest in the welfare of the parish, and of the city and neighbourhood of Chester. We pray that God's blessing may ever rest upon your Grace's labours for the good of those around you, and that you may be long spared to see the fruit of your work in the increase of godliness, piety, and charity amongst us. May many years of happiness be in store for you and her Grace the Duchess, whom we desire most respectfully to include in these our congratulations, good wishes, and prayers.

Signed on behalf of the parishioners, June 18th, 1887.

H. GRANTHAM, *Rector*.

HENRY TAYLOR }
JAMES SALMON } *Sidesmen*.

ALEX McGREGOR }
JOHN GAMON } *Churchwardens*.

The Duke, who spoke with deep emotion, sincerely thanked the rector and churchwardens, and those whom they represented, for their very handsome address, so feelingly written, which, he said, he received with a thankful heart. He must be excused saying anything more then, further than that he hoped and prayed that the work they had begun that day might long continue, and that the church would ever open its gates to a devout congregation. He thanked them sincerely for all they had said and done, and the lord Bishop for the kind words he had used in his sermon.

The peal of eight bells cast by Messrs. Mears & Stainbank, of Whitechapel, London, were rung at intervals during the morning, and at the conclusion of the service, and they attracted much favourable comment for their remarkable sweetness of tone. The clergy were entertained at luncheon in the Parish Room; a supper was given to the workmen and others in the evening. In the following week the children and poor of the parish had a dinner and a tea provided for them. An octave of services was also held in the church during that week.

The whole of the glass in the church, as well as the stained glass in the east and other windows, was designed and manufactured by Mr. Edward Frampton, of Buckingham Palace Road, London. The lofty east window of five lights depicts the Crucifixion, with full-length figures of the Virgin Mary, St. Alban, and St. George. In the three upper central lights are smaller subjects, the Annunciation, the Nativity, and the Salutation. The chancel window on the south side has a figure of St. Luke, whilst the large rose window at the west end depicts our Lord in Majesty, with the emblems of the four Evangelists, and surrounded by angels.[1] The three narrow windows in the baptistry show the baptism of our Lord, St. Philip baptizing the Eunuch, and Cardinal Beaufort baptizing the infant son of Henry the Fifth in the Tower.[2] The south-transept windows have the following subjects: The Pool of Bethesda, and seated figures of Moses and Elijah.[3]

The following is the complete list of the various offerings, both of money and special gifts made to the church, which was presented to the Duke of Westminster, together with the congratulatory address given above. The various money gifts were all employed in procuring the necessary articles of furniture, books, &c., for the use of the church, other than those provided by the special gifts.

---

[1] These windows were the gift of the Duke of Westminster.
[2] Presented by the children of the parish, together with the font.
[3] Presented by Mrs. Robert Roberts and Mr. and Miss Baker.

THE CHURCH OF ST. MARY-WITHOUT-THE-WALLS.

Presented, together with an Address, to His Grace the Duke of Westminster, K.G., on the occasion of the Consecration of St. Mary's-without-the-Walls, Chester, June 18th, 1887.

LIST OF GIFTS.

	VALUE			VALUE	
Mr. Robt. Frost (clock, three dials) £230	0	0	Mrs. Johnson (brass and onyx altar candlesticks)	£6	0	0
Mr. C. W. Potts (the late) (carved oak pulpit)	150	0	0	Mr. E. M. Sneyd Kynnersley	10	0	0
Sir Thos. G. Frost	50	0	0	Mrs. W. A. Gardner (litany desk, in memoriam)	8	0	0
Mr. John Gamon	50	0	0	Mr. John F. Lowe (old silver mounts for service books)	10	10	0
Mr. C. M. and Miss Machell	60	0	0	Mrs. & Mrs J. G. Holmes (altar cloth, red)	42	0	0
Miss Bryars	20	0	0				
Mr. and Mrs. Giles R. Griffith (carved oak lectern, in memoriam)[1]	50	0	0	Mrs. & Miss Taylor (altar cloth, white)	10	0	0
Mr. and Miss Baker (stained glass window, in memoriam)[2]	37	10	0	Mrs. Llewelyn Roberts (do., green)	12	0	0
				Mrs. J. L. Bedford (do., purple)	15	0	0
Mr. Robt. Roberts and family (stained glass window, in memoriam)[3]	15	0	0	Mrs. W. Welsby (bookmarker) } red	2	10	0
				Mrs. T. R. Dimond Hogg (do.) }			
Children of the Parish (font, £40: baptistry windows, £45)	85	0	0	Mrs. & Misses Porter (do., white)	3	0	0
A Friend	2	2	0	Miss Shirley (do., green)	2	10	0
Mrs. Freeman L. Bagnall	6	0	0	Mr. T. Vernon Royle	10	0	0
Mr. Joseph Oakes (the late)	5	0	0	Mrs. Grantham (bible)	5	7	0
The Rector, Rev. H. Grantham (the altar)	10	0	0	Mr. A. W. Dutt (old silver alms dish)	7	10	0
				Mr. & Mrs. A. MacGregor (brass alms dish)	5	0	0
Miss Stillwell (shields for altar candles)	1	0	0				
Mr. S. Golder (brass altar desk)	4	0	0	Mr. & Mrs. Brocklebank (brass & enamel font ewer, in memoriam)	8	0	0
Mrs. Golder (litany book)	1	10	0				
Miss C. F. Smith (book markers, purple)	0	10	0	Mr. T. Appleyard (alms boxes)	4	0	0
				Mrs. Kirkpatrick (altar cruet)	2	15	0
Mr. Jas. Gregg (brass and onyx altar vases)	2	10	0	Mrs. Clegg (the late)	5	0	0
				Mr. & Mrs. E. Grantham	5	0	0
Mrs. and the Misses Revis (alms bag, purple)	4	0	0	Mrs. W. C. Deeley (alms bags, green)	4	0	0
				Mr. & Mrs. H. Moss	25	0	0
General Ingall, C.B. (the late)	5	0	0	Mr. R. Gregg (hymn board)	1	0	0
Mr. T. Miller	1	1	0	Mr. Henry Taylor	5	0	0
The Misses Frost (kneelers for the sanctuary)	5	0	0	Mr. James Salmon	5	0	0
				Miss Sharpe (hymn books)	1	0	0
Mr. Freeman L. Bagnall	4	0	0	Rev. T. R. Dimond Hogg (hymn books)	2	0	0
The Misses Green (pulpit hangings)	3	3	0				
The Sheriff, Mr. T. W. Griffiths, and Miss Griffiths (set of clergy stalls)	15	0	0	Mr. & Mrs. R. P. Royle (font cover)	25	0	0
				A Friend (per the rector)	2	10	0
Mrs. Norton (the late) (set of clergy stalls)	15	0	0	Messrs. T. Wood & Son (umbrella stand for tower entrance)	15	0	0
				Mr. W. Bolland (for church furniture)	2	10	0
Mr. R. Longueville Barker (altar cross, in memoriam)	8	0	0	Miss Bolland (do.)	2	10	0
Mr. S. H. Sleigh (service books)	10	0	0	Mr. T. Smith (cassocks & surplices for organist and verger)	3	3	0
Mrs. & Miss Morris (alms bags, red)	4	0	0				
Mr. E. Kendrick	1	1	0	Mrs. MacGregor	1	0	0
Miss Higgins (altar linen)	4	0	0	Miss Royle (vases)	1	10	0

[1] This lectern bears this inscription, "To the glory of God and in memory of Thomas Griffith, 40 years Alderman of this city, given by his son, Giles R. Griffith, June 18th, 1887."

[2] This window, the most easterly on the south side, has this inscription, "To the glory of God the above window was erected in memory of a beloved brother, who fell asleep April 23rd, 1885."

[3] The inscription beneath the three small cinquefoil windows in the south transept is as follows: "To the glory of God, in memory of Robert Roberts, surgeon, of Hallaton, Leicestershire, first-born child and only surviving one of Robert and Mary Roberts, Chester, who died January 20th, 1883, in the 24th year of his age, this window is erected by those who loved him best. 'Trouble not yourselves, for his life is in him.'"

[4] Inscribed, "Finis coronat opus, in memoriam Cordelia A.M.G."

	VALUE.				VALUE.		
Mr. P. H. Fletcher........................	£5	0	0	Messrs. Lamont & Son (cupboard for altar cloths, &c.)........................	£12	0	0
Mr. Ernest Jones (extinguisher)	1	0	0	Mr. T. Garner (for furniture)............	1	0	0
Sir Philip Grey Egerton (the late)......	15	0	0	A Friend (per the rector, do.)	1	0	0
Mr. J. E. Ewen (the late) (holland covers for altar, lectern, and prayer desks)	5	0	0	Miss Eggers (rector's robes)	6	0	0
Mr. J. Dennis (door mats)...............	4	10	0	Mr. Salusbury K. Mainwaring	10	0	0
Collected by—				Mrs. Bate (the late) (hymn books for congregation)	5	0	0
Mrs. J. Gamon (for surplices and cassocks for choir)	10	5	0	Mrs. Luxmore (for furniture)............	2	0	0
Mrs. Ingall (do.)	3	3	0	Mr. Chas. Dutton (the late) (do)	5	0	0
Mrs. W. T. Giles (do.)	10	2	6	Mr. A. Priestner (do.)	2	0	0
Mrs. W. D. Jolliffe (do.)...............	3	3	0	Mr. W. D. Jolliffe	2	2	0
Mrs. H. Moss (do.)........................	5	0	0	Mr. A. Banks	3	3	0
Mrs. T. Hignett (do.)...................	8	0	0	Mr. Clayton	2	0	0
Mrs. W. C. Deeley (do.)	5	0	0	Mrs. Tarver (sacramental spoon)	0	10	0
Alderman Littler (notice board)	3	0	0	Mr. Green (church board)...............	10	0	0
Mr. W. Bolland (texts on zinc for placing over alms boxes)	5	0	0	Total ...	£1,274	10	6

In 1889, a reredos was presented to the church by the Duke of Westminster, and was dedicated by the Bishop of Chester (Dr. Jayne), on Sunday, 26th May, in that year. It represents the Resurrection, and was designed by Mr. Frederic Shields, and executed by Messrs. Heaton & Co., Cloisonné-Mosaic Co., Limited, London. The west window at the end of the south aisle is filled with stained glass representing the call of St. Matthew (Luke v. 27, 28) with the following inscription underneath :—

To the glory of god, and in memory of Charles Albert, the beloved son of Sir Thomas Gibbons and Lady Frost, born May 29, 1872, died October 26, 1891.

A white marble tablet has been let into the wall of the south aisle bearing this pathetic inscription :

"Faithful unto death."

To the Sacred and ever Cherished Memory

of earth's most valued treasures,

ALEXANDER FEREDAY MURRAY, Aged 18.

ROBERT MURRAY, Aged 17,

Sons of LIEUT.-COL. and MRS. MURRAY, grandsons of MR. and MRS. FEREDAY,

who, with six men, true to duty's call,

faced death and lost their lives to save a drowning comrade

in the South Atlantic, July 16, 1886.

[Ps. cvii. 30.] [Matt. xi. 26.]

THE PRESENT CHURCH OF ST. MARY-ON-THE-HILL.

When, as already explained in the above account, the new church of St. Mary-without-the-Walls was erected by the Duke of Westminster in 1887, it then became the parish church of St. Mary's parish, and the old church of St. Mary-on-the-Hill was constituted the parish church of the united parishes of St. Bridget's and St. Martin's, of which the Ven. Edward Barker, Archdeacon of Chester, was the Rector. In spite of the restorations carried out by Canon Bowen in 1861, already referred to, the church was known to be badly in want of repair, and an examination by Mr. J. P. Seddon, the architect who was called in, showed that any further delay in commencing the work would be highly dangerous.[1] The rector and churchwardens were fortunate in obtaining the services of a strong committee, and in 1888 they issued an urgent appeal for subscriptions, and estimated that an expenditure of £2,500 to £3,000 (afterwards raised to £3,000 to £4,000) was absolutely necessary. Helped by the handsome donation of £1,000 by the Duke of Westminster, the patron of the living, and several other sums of £100 and £50 each, the amount of £2,000 was gradually raised, and the work of restoration was started in 1890. As time went on it was found that more was required than had been originally contemplated, and by the end of 1891 the sum of over £4,500 had been spent on the church, towards which the Duke of Westminster had contributed £2,050.

It was re-opened for divine service on the 11th June, 1891, when an appropriate sermon was preached by the Bishop of Chester (Dr. Jayne). The chief features of the restoration have been the removal of all the galleries in the church, the opening out of the tower arch, the erection of new windows in the north aisle, the rebuilding of the south clerestory and its windows, and the careful repair of the old and beautiful timber roof of the nave. The level of the floor of the nave and aisles has been considerably lowered, giving much greater height to the church generally, and showing the columns to much advantage. The floor has been laid with oak wood blocks on the top of concrete, which effectually closed the old vaults and burial-places inside the building. The chapel at the end of the south aisle, which was formerly used as a vestry and for the organ, has been restored to its original use, and is now available as a chapel for daily services, &c. The old and dilapidated stone font has been removed, and the one formerly in use at St. Bridget's has been transferred to St. Mary's and is placed at the junction of the tower and nave. The organ from St. Bridget's has been erected in the north chapel, and will be used till a larger one can be put up. The architect was Mr. J. P. Seddon, F.R.I.B.A., of London, assisted by Mr. T. M. Lockwood, F.R.I.B.A., of Chester, as local architect, and the contractors were Messrs. S. & W. Pattinson, of Rushington, near Sleaford.

When the church was re-opened the north porch, which it had been found necessary to take down, had not then been re-erected. An appeal, however, was made to the Freemasons of the Province of Cheshire to defray the cost of its erection, in honour of the family of the Randle Holmes of Chester, one of whom, Randle Holme (III.) was not only a prominent Freemason, but was also most closely identified with St. Mary's Church, of which he was churchwarden for two years, and in which he and his ancestors are buried. This appeal, thanks to the energy of Mr. W. H. Finchett, of Chester, was very successful and the foundation stone of the "Randle

---

[1] A report on the church by Mr. Ewan Christian, the architect to the Ecclesiastical Commission, dated 8 Feb. 1888, also pointed out the various repairs which were essential.

Holme Porch," as it is called, was laid with all Masonic ceremony by Lord Egerton of Tatton on Easter Monday, April 18, 1892. The sum of £200 was raised, and on the 10th Nov. 1892, the porch was formally dedicated to the service of God. The following inscription has been placed in the quatrefoil window on the west side.

This porch was rebuilt in the year of our Lord 1892 by the Freemasons of Cheshire, to the Glory of God, and in memory of Randle Holme, of the city of Chester, arms-painter, herald and genealogist, born 1627, died 1700. He was one of the earliest known Cheshire Freemasons, and was baptized and buried in this church, of which he was churchwarden from Easter, 1657, to Easter, 1659. As the author of the Academy of Armory, 1688 (the first book ever printed in Chester), and as one of the collectors of the Randle Holme MSS., now preserved in the British Museum, he (bearing with his grandfather, his father, and his son, the distinctive name of Randle Holme) is thus worthily commemorated in his and their native city, with whose history they were so closely identified, and whose antiquities they did so much to preserve.[1] The corner-stone was laid with Masonic rites by the Right Worshipful the Provincial Grand Master (Lord Egerton of Tatton) on Easter Monday. Completed and dedicated by the Very Worshipful the Provincial Grand Chaplain, in the presence of the Very Worshipful the Deputy Provincial Grand Master (Sir Horatio Lloyd, Knt.), on St. Martin's Eve.

Above this inscription are the old Masons' arms, and below it the arms of Lord Egerton of Tatton. In the other quatrefoil window on the east side are the arms granted to the first Randle Holme by Richard St. George, Norroy King of Arms, on his visitation of Cheshire in 1613.[2]

The present church consists of a nave and chancel, with side aisles and side chapels, and a tower at the west end. The nave is separated from the aisles by three pointed arches, and from the chancel by a high-pointed chancel arch. Each of the side chapels is separated from the chancel and from the aisle by a wide obtusely pointed arch. There is a lofty clerestory containing ten windows on each side above the nave. The tower arch is very lofty and pointed, and at the junction of the nave and tower is placed the font. There is a door at the west end leading through the tower into the church, and one in each of the two aisles, the door on the north side having "the Randle Holme porch" already described.

The nave has a very handsome timber roof beautifully carved. It is divided up into square panels and on the bosses, about the middle, are the letters 𝔐.𝔑.𝔄.𝔇.𝔑. in Old English black letter. On another boss are the initials I.H.C. It is most probable that this handsome carved roof is the old choir roof of Basingwerk Abbey, near Holywell, in Flintshire, which, as already explained, was brought here on the dissolution of that Abbey in 1536 (*see* p. 2). The side aisles have heavy open timber roofs, but are devoid of all ornament. There is a plaster roof in the chancel.

The chapel at the end of the north aisle (as will subsequently be shown) was formerly dedicated to St. Katherine, whilst that at the end of the south aisle was dedicated to the Holy Trinity. This latter chapel was built by the Troutbeck family, of Dunham-on-the-Hill and Chester, in the year 1433. The following inscription has recently been placed in this chapel:—

To the memory of
WILLIAM TROUTBECK, OF DUNHAM, ESQUIRE,
Chamberlain of Chester,

---

[1] A full account of the Holme family, with special reference to the four Randle Holmes will be given later on.

[2] This glass was made by Messrs. Shrigley and Hunt, of Lancaster, and the money for its purchase was collected by Henry Taylor, Esq., F.S.A., the Worshipful Master of the Cestrian Lodge. These arms are given on page 1.

Portion of Oak Roof of St. Mary on the Hill, Chester, showing the Name **Maria** on the Bosses.

(By whom this chantry was founded A.D. 1433.)[1]
SIR WILLIAM TROUTBECK, HIS GRANDSON,
Sergeant of the Bridge Gate,
and other members of the family
who here lie buried,
this tablet is placed by
THE REVEREND JOHN TROUTBECK, D.D.,
Chaplain-in-ordinary to the Queen
and Minor Canon of Westminster.

Above is the coat of arms of Troutbeck,—azure, a wreath of trouts interlaced, proper, and the date, 1892.

THE MODERN STAINED GLASS.

Many of the windows are filled with stained glass. The east window of the chancel, of five lights, depicting Christ commanding his disciples to go forth and teach all nations, was erected to the memory of the Rev. William Henry Massie, who was Rector of St. Mary's from 1848 to 1856. Underneath is the following inscription:

In memory of William Henry Massie, Rector of this Parish, who died January 5, 1856.

The east window of the north aisle, of five lights, depicts the Israelites fighting against the Amalekites, with large figures of Aaron and Hur holding up the arms of Moses. Underneath is this inscription:

In memory of the officers and men of the 23 Reg. R.W. Fusiliers, who fell in the Crimea, from the Victory of Alma to the Storming of Sebastopol, Sep. 1854 to Sep. 1855.

In the north aisle, the two most easterly windows on the north side, of four lights each, are filled with stained glass in memory of the Oldfield family. The one over the Oldfield tomb has the figures of the four Evangelists, and this inscription underneath:

To the glory of God, and in memory of Thomas Brame Oldfield, of Champion Hill, Surrey, who died November xx, MDCCCXLVIII., Aged LX.[2]

The other window, the most easterly of the two, over the Gamul tomb, has the figures of St. James, St. John, St. Peter, and St. Paul, and those of Isaiah, Jeremiah, Ezekiel, and Daniel, and this inscription underneath:

Thomas, son of Leftwich, and great-grandson of Philip Oldfield, died 1731, Thomas, son of the preceding Thomas Oldfield, died 1758, Thomas, son of the last preceding Thomas Oldfield, died 1808, Thomas, grandson of the last preceding, and son of Thomas Brame Oldfield, died 1858.

Underneath this inscription is the following one:

In gloriam Dei, In honorem S. Thomæ Apostoli, In memoriam Thomæ carissimi Familiä Oldfield, Hoc. Mon. Pos. MDCCCLXI.

The east window of the south chapel, of four lights, is filled with stained glass, with this inscription underneath:

---

[1] There is a slight error here. As will subsequently be shown, this chantry chapel was built in the year 1433, but the chantry itself was not endowed or founded till 1444 (see pp. 31-2).

[2] Near this are two modern inscribed brasses to the Oldfield family, the inscriptions on which will be given in the account of the monumental inscriptions in the church.

Erected by a bereaved Mother in loving remembrance of Mary Lewis Barton, who died at Hadley Parsonage, Salop, Feb^r 2nd, 1860, aged 24, and of William Clegg, Lieutenant XI. Reg^t who died at Pieter Maritzburg, Natal, Febr^y 4th, 1865, aged 27.

In the upper part of this window, and in two of the south windows in this aisle, all the fragments of old stained glass which were found in the church are placed, and they are of special interest as being the only examples of old stained glass now to be found in any of the Chester churches. Each of these two south windows, of three lights each, has in the upper part four small narrow lights, each filled with the mediaeval figure of a saint in old glass. In the upper part of the east window are the arms of Brereton quartering Ipstones, and the briar and the tun, a rebus on the name Brereton. There are also the emblems of the Passion, two hands, two feet, and a pierced heart, a chalice, and some fragments of inscriptions.

The most easterly window on the south side of this chapel, of three lights, has stained glass representing the descent of Moses from Mount Sinai with the tables of the law, and is inscribed—

To the honor of God, and in mem. of John Hill, Esq., Attorney General of the Chester Circuit, died April IV., MDCCCXLIX., and his eldest son, Thomas Wilkinson Hill, Esq., Barrister at Law, died Jan. XXV., MDCCCLII. This window was erected by Henrietta Amelia, daughter and sister of the above.

The next window of three lights is filled with stained glass, with this inscription underneath :

Sacred to the memory of Thomas Mawdesley, M.A., Rector of this Parish, who died 2^d Sept^r., 1833, aged 75, and of Mary Anne, his wife, who died 26th April, 1848, aged 89. Thomas, their son, M.A., Incumbent of Chelford in this County, died 21st Jan^y, 1839, aged 50. Othuel, their son, Lieut. R.N., killed on service in the Adriatic. 9th Nov^r, 1812, aged 22. The old and the young are gone to their rest, and they who remain are waiting for a joyful Reunion in and through the merits of our Lord Jesus Christ.

THE COMMUNION PLATE.

As already stated (*see* p. 5, on the 28th May, 1553, the churchwardens of St. Mary's retained, amongst other things, for the services of the church, "a chalice with a paten of silver, weighing ten ounces." In the inventory of the church goods made 20 May, 1631 (*see* p. 7, there is no mention of any paten, but there was "a Comunion cupp of silver and [a] couer of the same." It was this want of a paten which prompted the following gift, which is duly entered in the Churchwardens' Accounts for 1637.

Memorandum thatt sume [some] takeinge notice of the wantt of a siluer plate to serue the bread att Comunions: the 29th of September, 1638, Mrs. Elinor Anderton, wife to Mr. Matthew Anderton, Esqr., did bringe to Mr. Seddon, our then Curate, a little broade siluer Dish with two eares, to be bestowed on the p'ish and [to] remaine in the church for the same vse for euer.

And again in 1639 there is this note :

Memorand : that Mrs. Ales Whittby, widdow, after the death of her late husband, Edward Whittby, Esq., late Recorder of this Citty, did giue and bestowe vpon the Church a longe silver plate, with a foote vnder itt to serue the Comunion bread, and a square quishion with fringe & tassells of cloath att issue

COMMUNION PLATE.
ST. MARY-ON-THE-HILL, CHESTER.

branched [i.e., cloth of issue, embroidered] for the deske for the Comunion table, to remain for the church vse for euer, and were given in Anno Dni, 1639.[1]

The next entry occurs in 1712, when it is recorded that £25 16s. was "paid Mr. Robisson, goldsmith, for the siluer Flagon for the Sacram' as apeeres by his note." In the same year, the same goldsmith was paid 3s. 6d. "for boylinge y° church plate," by which is probably meant cleaning it. Once more, in 1758 it appears that the sum of £7 2s. 3d. was paid "for a silver Challice and cover."

The present Communion plate belonging to St. Mary's Church, and now in use at St. Mary's-without-the-Walls, consists of a silver flagon, two silver Communion cups with covers, and two silver patens. The flagon is eighteen inches high, and the stand at the bottom is five inches across. It has the names "Stephen Sone and William Witter, churchwardens, 1712." This is the flagon purchased in that year for £25 16s. The oldest Communion cup is of Elizabethan character, but its exact date has not been determined. It bears no inscription. A copy of it, made to match it, is probably the one bought in 1758, above referred to.

The oldest of the two patens is the one given to the church in 1639 by Mrs. Alice Whitby, and bears the inscription, "The gift of Mrs. Ales Whitbe to the Parish Church of St. Maries, 1639." The other paten bears the inscription, "The gift of Thomas Barlow,[2] of Upton, to St. Mary's Church in Chester, 1683." There is nothing in the Churchwardens' Accounts relating to this gift except an entry to the effect that Randle Holme was paid "for puttinge Thomas Barlow's Leagisie downe vpon y° Table of Guifts."

As already stated, the above Communion plate is now at St. Mary's-without-the-Walls. The plate now in use at St. Mary's (with the exception of a modern donation) came from the now destroyed church of St. Bridget, and consists of a silver-gilt flagon, two silver chalices, and four silver patens. The flagon has the following inscription on the bottom, "St. Bridget's, Chester. Cha' Price, Sam¹. Nickson, Churchwardens, 1810"; probably showing when it was re-gilt, as it is of much older date. The oldest chalice has these names, "Thomas Bolland, James Johnson, Churchwardens, 1720"; and the other has "Benjᵐ Scott, J. Williams, Churchwardens, 1784." The two oldest patens are thus inscribed, "This and such an other with a guilt Flaggon cup and cover are the gift of Mrs. Hannah Swan to St. Bridget's parish."[3] The other two patens are modern and bear this inscription:—

Two Patens Presented in deep gratitude by Mr. & Mrs. Fereday to the Church of St. Mary-on-the-Hill, Chester, on its becoming the Parish Church of St. Bridget with St. Martin, 1891.

THE BELLS.

From the earliest inventory of the church goods, taken 28th May, 1553 (p. 5), it appears that there were at that time "five great bells in the steeple, and an anthem bell." There are frequent references to these bells in the Churchwardens' Accounts, and to the provision of new bell-ropes,

---

[1] It may here be noted that Mrs. Whitby had made a very handsome gift to the church in 1618, as thus entered in that year's Accounts:—
"Mrs. Alice Whitby, wife to Edward Whitby, Esquire, and Recorder of the Cittie of Chester, gaue to the churche of St. Maryes a pulpit clothe of crymson velvet of foure breades [breadths], the middle breades are embrawdered with goulde and silke, and for it she had the ould pulpit clothe and bestoed it on the churche of Saynte Olaue's [Olive's] in the Citty of Chester."

[2] Mr. Thomas Barlow, of Upton, was buried at St. Mary's, on the 7th September, 1683.

[3] Mrs. Hannah Swan, who was the widow of the Rev. Thomas Swan, for some years Rector of St. Bridget's, was buried in that church on the 12th February, 1696[-7].

&c., and the carrying out of sundry repairs. But in 1597 it would appear that some of the bells were newly cast, as shown by the following entry:—

Rec. about the charges of the bells, of particular persons assessed vpon them, as appeareth by the particulars of their names	xxvij^{li} xvij^s iij^d [£27 17s. 3d.]
It. for old timber	xij^s vj^d
It. for old iron	ix^s j^d
Somme totall receaved about this matter	xxviij^{li} xviij^s x^d [£28 18s. 10d.]
Paid by me about the same charge and allowed by the auditors of the same parishe	xxix^{li} xiiij^s xj^d [£29 14s. 11d.]
So that the parishe rests to me vpon this entry	xvj^s j^d

In 1617 the "anthem bell" was recast at Congleton. I have been a good deal puzzled to explain the meaning of the name of this bell, and to define its use, as I have not met with it elsewhere, and cannot find it described anywhere. I can only conjecture that it is the same as the "sacring bell," which was formerly rung at the elevation of the host, and was in some churches suspended in a small bell-cot placed on the roof directly over the chancel arch.[1] At the Reformation these bells, if retained, were used for other purposes, as seems to have been the case at St. Mary's, where the "anthem bell" had become so worn as to render it necessary to recast it in 1617.

P^d for castinge the Antom bell and the brasse wayinge fourscore and ix^{li} and a halfe, and a brass for the fourth bell beinge caste with it, all vnder one, after ij^d a pound for castinge	xv^s. [15s.]
Spent vppon our selues goeinge to Congerton [Congleton] with the Tanton bell and cominge whome [home] and beinge there[2]	iiij^s vj^d [4s. 6d.]

In 1623 the two largest bells had to be recast, and for that purpose were sent to Holt, not far from Chester, to a bell-founder there named William Clivery or Clibbery.[3]

P^d at the hovlte in castinge the towe biggest great bells	xvj^s
P^d to Mr Langeforde for henginge the belles and makeinge v newe wheles	iij^{li} xiij^s viij^d [£3 13s. 8d.]
P^d to William Cliufrie [Clivery] bellfounder for castinge the belles all newe[1]	xij^{li} [£12]

A few years later, in 1632, the great bell of all was recast, and it was sent to the same bell-founder.

P^d for takeinge downe the greate bell & spentt at borroweinge the windles att the Minster, and for sendinge to Holt for the belfounder	iiij^s xj^d [4s. 11d.]

---

[1] This is the case at Prestbury in Cheshire (see *East Cheshire*, ij., p. 187).

[2] In this same year's accounts is an entry of a payment to Robert Ford, of Wigan, for "casting of towe brasses for the greate bell."

[3] There are not many references to this bell-founder to be met with. See my paper on the subject of Lancashire and Cheshire Bell-founders, &c., *Transactions of the Historic Society, Lancashire and Cheshire*, 1890.

[4] The Congleton bell-founders would appear to have been consulted, but they did not come to terms with the churchwardens who, however, treated them well, and "bestowed vppon Congleton Bellfounders ijs." Another 2s. was also paid "when we agreed with the Bellfounder" from Holt.

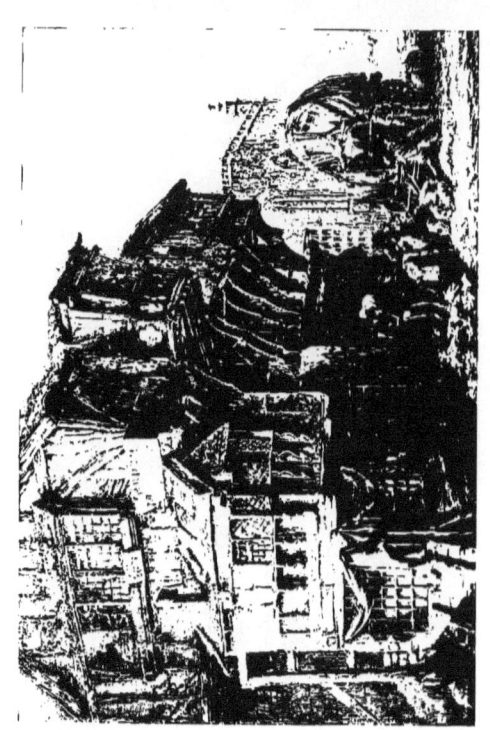

P^d for carriage of the bell to the hoult and back againe.........	xxij^s	[22s.]
P^d to William Cliuery [Clivery] for castinge of the greate bell	vj^{li}	[£6]
P^d for a hundred & odd waight of newe mettall that was added to the bell more than the weight was before[1]	v^{li}	[£5]

In the year 1657 Mr. Randle Holme, Junior (the third of that name), who was then one of the churchwardens, set about the restoration of the tower of St. Mary's, which had been damaged during the Civil War, and was also successful in obtaining a new peal of four bells for it which were cast by the bell-founders at Wigan in Lancashire. He thus records his receipts and expenditure in the Churchwardens' Accounts for that year.

	li	s	d
Receiued in Contribution Money from seuerall cittyzens towards the repaire of the steeple & bells, as appeares by their names, the sume of	17	19	8
Received by an assesm^t leuyed on the parrishners for the same use as appeareth by the names, the sume of..................	61	0	7
Payd to John Mecher for seting a roofe vpon ye Steeple, he being at all charges of flaggeing it to carry away the water, slateing it, to find all the tymber that will goe to it & workmanship. And likewise he to be at the cost of hanging the foure new bells, finding all the iron worke for them, & to make good the brused clappers for wch he had from vs ...	26	10	0
Payd to Mr. Mathew Ellis & Henry Grey for carrying of the broken bell metal to Wigan, staying there till the bells were new cast & bringing them to the church againe	3	0	0
Spent when we went to Wigan to see the bells cast, being foure dayes out, horses & men..	1	0	0
Payd to Geffrey Scot,[2] the bell-founder, for casting of four bells, with their brasses	25	0	0
Spent in drinke amongst his workemen & giuen them in Barrages[3]..	0	15	8
Spent on the Belfounder & his sone in Chester, they being here six dayes to see the bells hanged, and to chipp them to make them tuneable	0	9	4

In the following year, 1658, the great bell was also re-cast at Wigan, Mr. Randle Holme Junior, being still one of the churchwardens, and there are the following entries relating to it in the Churchwardens' Accounts :—

	li	s	d
Imprimis.—Spent when we agreed with the Bell-founder for casting of the great bell	0	2	0
Payd to the bell-founder for casting of the great bell, he being at all charges of takeing it downe out of the steeple, carrying of it to Wigan & backe againe, to hange it up & fitting the irons and head-stock to it........................	12	0	0

[1] There is an entry in this year's Accounts "for hanging up the Anthem bell, being fallen down."

[2] Mr. Geoffrey Scott succeeded Mr. John Scott as a bell-founder at Wigan, but the exact relationship between them is not very clear. (See my paper on Lancashire and Cheshire Bell-founders in the *Transactions of the Historic Society of Lancashire and Cheshire*, 1890.)

[3] "Barrages" were what we should now term "allowances" or drinks to the workmen. It is an obsolete word, which frequently occurs in these Accounts.

Spent on the Belfounder & seuerall of the gentlemen of the parrish when they were about the consultation of the tuneablenesse of the Bells & in drinke to the ringers	0	3 4

Some years prior to this, the anthem bell had been broken, probably during the siege of Chester, for in 1646 the following entry occurs :—

1st for two dayes worke, takeinge downe the breaken Antham Bell and alteringe the frame, and changeinge the head & makeinge itt fitt for the bell that is now vpp, and for placeinge & puttinge itt up & fastening it......................	iij'	iiij^d
1st for carriage of the bell from the Pentice wth Mr. Alderman Holme gott for the p'ish, beinge one of Boughton chapel bells		iiij^d .

In 1657, however, this bell had to be taken down and presumably restored to its original use, as shown by the following entry in the Churchwardens' Accounts :—

Payd for takeing down the little bell which Mr. Harper demanded as belonging to the chapell & hospitall of Boughton	0 0	4

On the 9th May, 1659, a public meeting of the parishioners of St. Mary's was held to prevent abuses by the ringers, and to draw up regulations about the bells. It was decided that the bell-ropes should be kept locked up, except that of the great bell, which the sexton was to use for "tollinge of a passinge bell," and for ringing at five o'clock in the morning and at eight o'clock in the evening. If any of the parishioners wished the other bells to be rung, they had to make arrangements with the ringers, and the churchwardens were to make their own arrangements for ringing the bells on the fifth of November and other special occasions.

The bells at present existing in the tower of St. Mary's are, in the main, those which were placed there in 1657, as above described. They are now six in number, and bear the following inscriptions :—

1. JESUS BE OUR SPEDE.
2. GLORIA IN EXCELSIS DEO.
3. DULCEDINE LOCIS CANTABO TUO NOMINE.
4. JUCUNDITATE SONI SONABO TIBI DOMINE.
5. CHA^s & J^{no} RUDHALL, FEC^t, WILL^m ORFORD & J^{no} GRINDLEY, WARDENS, 1768.
6. This bell has the date only, 1783.

And on each Bell these letters :—
C. W., G. C., R. H.,[1] 1657.   W^2 | S

SPECIAL INCIDENTS IN THE PAST HISTORY OF ST. MARY'S.

Before proceeding with the details of the history of the old church of St. Mary's, its chantries and altars, its monumental effigies and monuments, &c., &c., attention may very fittingly be directed to one or two special incidents which appear noteworthy. For some reason or other, during mediæval times, the church was frequently used for such purely secular

---

[1] The churchwardens for that year were George Chamberlain and Randle Holme, Junior, whose initials are on the bells.
[2] This is the mark of John Scott, of Wigan, bell-founder, the predecessor of Geoffrey Scott, by whom these bells were cast.

purposes as the holding of inquisitions *post mortem*, and inquisitions as to proof of age, &c. Many instances of this may be given, of which the following are examples[1] :—

7. Henry VI. [1429]. Proof of age of Katherine, wife of William Walsh, daughter of Richard de Hatton of Chester, taken in the Church of the Blessed Mary-on-the-Hill, Chester, before the escheator.
19. Henry VI. [1441]. Proof of age of Robert de Lee taken in the Church of the Blessed Mary-on-the-Hill, in the City of Chester, before the escheator.
20. Henry VI. [1442]. Proof of age of Hugh de Calveley.
29. Henry VI. [1451]. ,, ,, of John Starkey.
30. Henry VI. [1452]. ,, ,, of Thomas, son and heir of Sir Peter Gerard, Knt.
33. Henry VI. [1455]. ,, ,, of John, son and heir of Hugh Starkey.
18. Edward IV. [1478]. ,, ,, of Hugh, son and heir of John Starkey of Oulton.
17. Henry VII. [1502]. ,, ,, of Richard, son of Thomas Gerard of Cruewood.

All taken in "the Church of St. Mary-on-the-Hill in the City of Chester."

Other churches were occasionally used for these and similar purposes, an enquiry as to proof of age of John, son of John Bruyn, being taken in the 5th Edward IV. [1465] in Wistaston Church, and so late as the 9th Nov. 32 Henry VIII. [1540], an inquisition was taken in Holy Trinity Church, Chester, relating to certain tanned hides belonging to a Chester shoemaker.[2] But St. Mary's seems to have been more frequently used for such purposes than other parish churches, possibly on account of its proximity to the Castle of Chester, and to the Exchequer and other Courts, which were held there.

Also, owing to its nearness to the Castle, the churchyard of St. Mary's was used for the burial of those persons who were condemned to death at the Assizes held in the Castle, and there are many entries in the Registers showing how common these executions were.[3]

1628—9. James Thornet, a p'soner, buried 17th day of March.
1629. William Harding, a p'soner, buried 7th day of May.
1629. John Hill, p'soner, buried 7th day of July.
1631. John Johnson, Joan Broome, and Katherine Crosse, three p'soners that were executed, buried att the west end of the steeple[4] in churchyard 25th day of Aprill.
1633. Richard Lathom } being 4 [sic] p'soners that were executed, buried in church-
      Katherine Williams } yard on ye south side the 4th day of May.
      James Johnson }
1637. Thomas Briscoe }
      Ralph Wilkinson } 4 p'soners executed, buried at the west end, betwixt the
      Ellen Weld } north porch and the steeple, the 14th day of Aprill.
      Ellen Woodward }

Some of these entries are of special interest, as for instance :—

⁵1616. Tymothie Tatton, a p'soner, buried viij^o die Julij. [In the margin, "p'ssed to death."]
⁵1627. Prisoner pressed, William Wilson, sepultus fuit v^o die Aprilis.
1631. Thomas Laceby, a p'soner, prest to death, bur. in churchyard on the north side the steeple the 23th day of Aprill.

---
[1] The originals of these inquisitions are in the Record Office, London, amongst the Cheshire Records.
[2] *Lancashire and Cheshire Records*, Record Society, vol. vij., p. 216.
[3] The existing Register only begins in 1628.
[4] The "steeple" was the common name for the tower at this time.
[5] These two entries are from the transcripts of the now missing Register, which transcripts are preserved in the Bishop's Registry, Chester.

These instances (and more might be given) of prisoners being "pressed to death" are examples of a terrible penalty now happily long since abolished. If a prisoner refused to plead at all he saved whatever property he had from being forfeited to the Crown, but he had to undergo a special form of punishment. He was stripped naked and laid on his back in a cellar, with his arms and legs stretched out. A board was placed across his body, and on this was piled up weights and stones "as much as he can bear and more," and these remained on him until he either volunteered to plead or till death released him from his sufferings. On the first day he was allowed " three morsels of barley without any drink," and on the second day, " two drinks of stagnant (not running) water, without any bread "; and as the judge said, when he decreed this penalty, " this shall be his diet until he is dead." The duration of this punishment depended on the strength of the prisoner, and in some cases it is known to have lasted from a Saturday till the following Monday night, or more than forty-eight hours, during which the wretched man's suffering must have been intense.

But the most interesting of all these entries is the following, which occurs in the year 1656:—

> 1656. Three witches hanged at Mich'as Assizes, buried in the corner by the Castle Ditch in Church yrd, 8$^{th\,1}$ of October.

As it was probable that the official report of the trial and conviction of these three unfortunate persons might be preserved amongst the Chester Records now in the Record Office, London, a search made there was fortunately successful. The three "witches" were Anne Thornton, of Eaton, near Chester ; Ellen, the wife of John Beech, of Rainow, near Macclesfield ; and Anne, the wife of James Osboston, of the same place, and the following is the account of the respective pleadings and trials[2] :—

TRIAL OF THE THREE WITCHES AT CHESTER, 1656.

At the Session of Chester held in the Commonhall of Pleas in Chester, on Monday the last day of March, 1656, before John Bradshawe, Serjeant att Lawe, Justice of Oliver, Lord Protector of the Commonwealth of England, Scotland, and Ireland, and the Dominions thereunto belonging, of Chester, and Thomas Fell, Esq., the other Justice of the said Lord Protector, of the said County.

The Jurors present that *Ellen, the wife of John Beech, late of Ranowe*, in Cheshire, collier, on the 12th September, 1651, and on divers other days as well before as after, at Ranowe, did exercise and practise the " Invocacon and conjuracon " of evil and wicked spirits, " and consulted and covenanted with, entertayned, imployed, ffedd and rewarded certayn evill and wicked spirits."

On the said 12th day of September the said Ellen Beech did exercise certain "Witchcrafts" upon Elizabeth Cowper, late of Ranowe, spinster, whereby she, from the 12th till the 20th of September, aforesaid, did languish, and upon the said 20th day died.

Anne, the wife of James Osboston, late of Ranowe, in Cheshire, husbandman, on the 12th day of September, 1651, practised certain wicked and divellish acts upon John Steenson, late of Ranowe, husbandman, which caused his death on the 20th of September.

The said Anne Osboston on the 20th November, 1653, at Ranowe exercised "certayn artes and Incantacons " on Barbara Pott, late wife of John Pott, of Ranowe, from the effects whereof she died on the 20th of January then next following.

---

[1] There is apparently a clerical error in this date, which is clearly enough written in the Register. The accounts of the trials of these witches all agree that they were executed on the *15th*, and it is most probable that they would be buried very shortly afterwards, so that the date should be the 15th, or possibly the 18th.

[2] Cheshire Plea Roll, Michaelmas, 1656, Public Record Office, London.

And again on the 17th day of July, 1655, the said Anne Osboston practised sorceries on one John Pott, late of Ranowe, yeoman, from which time he languished until the 5th of August, when he died.

On the 30th of November, 1651, the said Anne Osboston used "enchantments" upon Anthony Booth, late of Macclesfield, in the county of Chester, gent., thereby causing his death on the 1st of April then next following.

And now at the Sessions held at Chester on Monday, 6th October, 1656, came the aforesaid Ellen Beech and Anne Osboston in their proper persons by Richard Golborne, gent., Constable of the Castle of Chester, brought to the bar, and the indictment being seen by the Justices, they instantly demand how the said Ellen Beech and Anne Osboston will acquit themselves of the premises above charged severally against them. Whereupon they doe say severally for themselves that they are not guilty of the trespass or murthers aforesaid and hereupon for their good or evil doe put themselves upon the country. And John Bradshaw, Esq.,[1] who for the Lord Protector doth here on that behalf follow for the said Lord Protector doth the like. The Jurors say that they were guilty of the aforesaid murders, and they were sentenced to be hanged severally by their necks.

John Bradshaw, Esq.,[1] demands execution against them, and he had it at Boughton, in the county aforesaid, upon Wednesday the 15th day of this instant October, about three of the clocke in the afternoone of the same day.

The Jurors of divers hundreds of the said county at the Sessions held as Chester on Monday, Oct. 6th, 1656, present upon their oath that *Anne Thornton, late of Eyton in Cheshire, widow*, on the 9th day of February, 1655[-6], and on divers other days and times, as well before as since, at Eccleston, "not having God before her eyes, but by the instigacon of the Divell beinge moved and seduced [did] with force and arms wickedly, divellishly, and feloniously diverse [*sic* for devise] exercise and practise certayne divellish and wicked actes and Incantacons called Witchcrafts, Inchauntments, Charmes, and Sorceries in and upon one Daniell ffinchett, sonne of Raphe ffynchett, of Eccleston, yoman, beinge an infant of the age of three dayes," whereby he, the said Daniel from the 9th day of February in the year aforesaid until the 11th day of the same month, "did languish, upon which said 11th day he the aforesaid Daniel by the said wicked and devillish Actes soe by her the aforesaid Anne Thornton used, exercised and practised, as aforesaid, upon him the said Daniel, dyed." "And soe the Jurors aforesaid upon their oath aforesaid, doe saye that the aforesaid Anne Thornton, upon the aforesaid 11th day of February, at Eccleston, aforesaid, the aforesaid Daniel ffinchett by the aforesaid wicked and divillish Acts in manner and forme aforesaid, feloniously, voluntarily, and of her malice forethought, did kill and murder contrary to the forme of the statute in that case made and provided, and against the public peace."

And now at the Sessions held at Chester as aforesaid came the said Anne Thornton in her proper person by Richard Golborne, gent., Constable of the Castle of Chester, brought to the bar, and the indictment being seen by the Justices, they instantly demand how the said Anne Thornton will acquit herself of the premises, whereunto the said Anne says that she is not guilty of the murder aforesaid, and hereupon for her good or evil doth put herself upon the country. And John Bradshaw, Esq.,[1] who for the Lord Protector doth here on that behalf follow for the said Lord Protector doth the like. The Jurors say that Anne Thornton is guilty of the aforesaid murder, and that she hath no goods or chattels, lands or tenements in the said county of Chester to the knowledge of the said jurors. Therefore it is considered by the Court that the aforesaid Anne Thornton be hanged by her neck, which was done at Boughton upon Wednesday, the 15th of this instant October, about three of the clock in the afternoon of the same day, according to the custome of the countie aforesaid.

---

[1] This was John Bradshaw, of Congleton, Esq., the Attorney-General for the County Palatine of Chester, who, although bearing the same names as the celebrated John Bradshaw, Esq. (the regicide), the Chief Justice of Chester, before whom these trials were held, was no relation to him. Much confusion has arisen between these two persons.

[Handwritten note at top:] The former notice of a chantry in this Church (extracted from the general Ecclesiastical Survey, 26 Hen VIII [ ]) most probably reg relates to the Troutbeck Chapel — 'Cantaria infra ecclesiam Beate Marie Cestrie. Johannes Button capellanus valet in redd' provenien' de certis terris et tenementis in Civitate Cestrie annexatim per cantaristam ibm recept' ad annuum Cvj' viij'. xma. inde x' viij' Hemingway Vol II p 104

One other entry deserves to be noted here, and that is the burial of the man who had no doubt helped most of these unfortunate persons out of the world.

1643. John Edwards, the Hangman, buried in north church yard 17th of November.

THE CHANTRIES AND ALTARS FORMERLY IN ST. MARY'S CHURCH.

The chantries and altars in the church do not appear to have been very numerous. The chantry chapel at the end of the north aisle was dedicated to *St. Katherine;* whilst that at the end of the south aisle, as will subsequently be shown, was dedicated to *The Holy Trinity;* and at the altars in each of these chapels services were regularly held. In addition to these there was an altar dedicated to *St. Mary,* and generally known as "the St. Mary's service"; and another dedicated to *St. Stephen;* whilst in the St. Katherine's chapel there was placed an image of that saint.

These altars and services are occasionally referred to in old wills and other documents, which are of much interest. Thus, in the will of Matthew Ellis, made 5th February, 1546-7,[1] he desired to be "buryed in Seynt Maries church, within the ile [aisle] wheare I walke," "I also geaue and bequethe vnto the meynteninge of *Seynt Maryes s'vice* and *Seynt Katherines s'vice* one steer worth xxs., or els xxs. of money equally to be devyded betweene theym." He leaves small legacies to each of the following priests: to Sir Edmund Burton, who was the curate, 3s. 4d.; to Sir Richard Stancliffe, 2s.; and to Sir Henry Brown, a silver-gilt ring; whilst 12d. was left "to every preoste of Seynt Maryes."

A still earlier and more important will is that of Thomas Dedwood, of Chester, gentleman, made on the 31st March, 1497.[2] This will, which is in Latin, directs that his body was to be buried in St. Mary's Church, and that a fit priest be found and endowed to celebrate at *the altar of St. Stephen,* in the church of St. Mary aforesaid, for the space of seven years for the benefit of his soul, and the souls of his father and others. "Item to the works of the church of St. Mary,[3] 40s." "Item for three trentals of masses, to be celebrated in the aforesaid church, for my soul, 30s." "Item to the three houses of Friars within the city of Chester, to each, 6s. 8d." "Item to John Badde, chaplain, 10s. to pray for me." He mentions Cicely, his mother, and Joan, his wife. The arms of "Dedwood, who lived in Castle Lane," were formerly in the old glass in the east window of St. Mary's Church (*see* p. 34).

In 1520, in the will of William Milnes, made in that year, he refers to "the image of the Lady Katherine, the Virgin," and to Sir William Bavand, priest and chaplain.

In the general Ecclesiastical Survey, taken 26 Henry 8 [1536], there is mention of a chantry chapel within the church of the Blessed Mary of Chester, of which John Dutton was then chaplain, and which was worth per annum 106s. 8d. arising from certain lands and tenements in the city of Chester. This was most probably the Troutbeck chantry described later on.

At the date of the Bishop's visitation in 1553-4, Sir Nicholas Sedgwick was the curate, paid by the rector, and Sir Thomas Stretbarell was a priest paid by John Robinson, but who

---

[1] Copied in the *Enrolment Books* at the Bishop's Registry, Chester, vol. i., p. 143.
[2] *Harl. MS.* 2131, f. 205.
[3] This would show that some repairs or rebuilding was going on at St. Mary's at this time.

Compare Contract with that of Catterick Church Yorkshire of 1412. Rev James Raine. 1834
Fotheringhay Church in Dugdale's Monasticon Anglicanum.
Monument of Richd Beauchamp, Earl of Warwick, Monos Remains 45. 1826
Will of Henry VI. Building of Eton College
William of Worcester's Itinerary. Nasmith. 8vo 1778.
July 21 1492. Appointment of John Trofford, Chorister, as chaplain for life of Chester Castle. § of Sir John the person named late

THE CHANTRIES AND ALTARS FORMERLY IN ST. MARY'S CHURCH. 31

the latter benefactor was there is at present no evidence. In 1561, in an account of the Chantry lands in Cheshire, there is mention of "the chantry of the St. Mary hills[1] in Chester [in the possession] of Sir John Talbot, Knt.," and worth £5 6s. 8d. per annum.

Two of the old chantry priests at St. Mary's are referred to as follows[2]:—

Sr John Trafford was buryed at St. Maryes in Chester aboute the laste yeare of Kynge Henrye the eyghts Reyne [1546], and had a pencon of tenne pounds per annum.

Sr Richard Stonclyffe was buryed at St. Maryes aforesayd in the seconde or thyrde yere of the regne of Kynge Edward the syxte [1548-9], and had a pencon of . . . per annum.

The burial of the latter priest we know from other sources took place at St. Mary's on the 5th April, 1548.[3]

The Chantry chapel at the end of the south aisle was built by William Troutbeck, Esq., and Joan his wife in the year 1433, and some little information is on record concerning it. The original contract for its erection by Thomas Betes, mason, is a document of much interest, and one of a class of which very few are now extant. It is as follows[4]:—   *Thomas Betes, Mason*

AGREEMENT BETWEEN WILLIAM TROUTBECK ESQ., AND THOMAS BETES, MASON, for building a Chapel at St. Mary's Chester, 1433.

This endenture made bytwene William Troutebek, esquier, on that on[e] p'tie, and Thomas Betes, mason, on that other p'tie, beres wittenesse that the forsaid Thomas has made covenant and granted to the said William that he shall make a Chapel in the chirche yord of Seynte Marie on the Hill, on the south side of the chauncell of the chirche there, that is to wete [to wit] the est ende, the south side and the west ende, conteynynge the length of the chauncell there and xviij fote wide withinne the walles, and as high as hit nedes resonably to be ; with v faire and clenely wroght wyndowes full of light. that is to say on[e] gable wyndow in the est ende with iiij lightes, and iij wyndowes on the south side, ichone [each one] of iij lightes, and on[u] in the weste ende, in the best wise to be devised[5] : and iiij botras [buttresses] on the south side, with a grete arche in the weste ende ; and the chapelle to be battellet above, like to the little closet withinne the castell of Chester, with a corbyl table longynge [i.e., belonging] thereto : and at ayther end iij honest fynyals.

And the forsaid William shall pay to the forsaid Thomas xx^{li} [£20] like as the worke goes forwarde, and also give him a gowne, and alsoe the forsayd William shall fynde fre[e] stone, lyme, sonde, wat' [water] wyndelasse and stuf for to scaffolde with, and such manere necessaries as the forsaid Thomas nedes, and all manere of cariages that longen [i.e., belong] therto ; and the forsaid Thomas shall, by the ov'sight [oversight] of Maester John Asser,[6] make the chappell and all thynges that longen thereto (masoncraft).[7] honestly. In wytnesse of the whech thynge to these p'sentes endentures the p'ties forsaid, aither anendes other haven set to their sealx.

Gyven at Chester the Monday next before the feste of the natyvyte of Seint John the Baptist [June 24] in the yere of Kyng Henry the Sixt after the conquest xj [1433]. *(The Seal gone - Hemingway Vol II f.104)*

[1] This chantry is also referred to in the Minister's Accounts of the Cheshire Chantries. Exchequer Records, 3 and 4 Edward 6, No, 8, membrane 2

[2] Special Commissions 16th Elizabeth. Public Record Office, No. 3258, Diocese of Chester. Stipends and Pensions.

[3] Harl. MS. 2177. Extracts from the earliest Register of St. Mary's, now lost.

[4] Printed in Ormerod's History of Cheshire, new edition, vol. ij., p. 41, from the original in the possession of the Earl of Shrewsbury in 1807. I have added the words in square brackets and the notes, in order to make it more intelligible.

[5] This was probably a small window to be placed above " the grete arche in the west ende," subsequently mentioned, which was to separate this new chapel from the south aisle. The roof of this chapel was probably higher than that of the south aisle, very likely as high as the chancel roof.

[6] This John Asser was appointed master mason for the county of Chester and for North Wales on the 1st March, 11th Henry 6, 1433, on the resignation of John Asser, his father. A Roger Asser was Rector of St. Mary's from 1464 to 1471.

[7] This word is interlined in the original

Finial - the ornament which crowns a pinnacle, canopy, pediment or gable. used by old writers for the whole pinnacle.
And every botrasse fynyssh with a fynyall - Contract for Fotheringhay Church.

A few years later, by a deed dated 23 Henry VI. [1444][1] William Troutbeck and Joan his wife conveyed certain lands in Chester, Woodchurch, Little Christleton, and Ledsham to trustees, and by a deed dated 23 September, 1444, Roger Holme, rector of Astbury, and John Masey, chaplain, reconveyed the same to them " to have and to hold to the said William and Joan for their lives, with remainder to John Troutbeck, their son and the heirs of his body " to provide " one fit and proper chaplain to celebrate divine service for the soul of the said William in the church of St. Mary on the hill, in a chapel called '*La Trinite Chappell*,' built by the said William and Joan, and to pay to the said chaplain yearly £5 6s. 8d."[2]

This is, curiously enough, the only reference to the dedication of this chantry chapel, which I have met with, and unlike St. Katherine's Chapel at the east end of the north aisle, the name of the Trinity Chapel does not seem to have been preserved after the Reformation. It was simply called " Troutbeck's Chapel " from the name of its founders.

Within this chapel a raised altar tomb was erected to the memory of William Troutbeck and Joan his wife, with their effigies at full length, and various coats of arms around it, as fully described in the account of the old monuments in the church (*see* p. 38). There was also in this chapel another very handsome monument to their grandson, Sir William Troutbeck, Knt. In one of the windows was an inscription desiring prayers for the souls of William Troutbeck and Joan his wife, who built this chapel (*see* p. 36).

In the year 1661 this chapel fell down, and the monuments above referred to were all unfortunately destroyed. It remained in ruins for over thirty years, but in 1691 it was conveyed by the then Earl of Shrewsbury, the direct descendant of the Troutbecks, to the parishioners of St. Mary's for ever, and in 1693 they rebuilt it.

The deed conveying this chapel is as follows[3]:—

"To all Xtian People to whome these presents shall come, the Right Hon'ble Charles Earle of Shrewsbury, &c., sendeth Greeting—Whereas the south chancell (commonly called Troutbeck's chappell) parcell of the parish church of St. Maryes upon the Hill, in the city of Chester is, and for divers yeares last past hath byn decayed and out of repayre, and for that the same hath bynn reputed to belong unto the sayd Earle, and his ancestors, the inhabitants of the sayd parish have neglected to repayre the same. Now knowe yee that the sayd Earle, upon the earnest suite and request of the present minister[4] and churchwardens, and the parishioners of the sayd parish of St. Mary on the Hill, in the city of Chester, and for divers other good causes and considerations him the sayd Earle thereunto moveing, and especially that the sayd chancell may be forthwith repayred, and for ever hereafter kept in good repayre by the churchwardens and inhabitants of the sayd parish of St. Maryes upon the Hill and their successors, and the sayd Earle and his heires and assignes for ever fully and clearley acquitted and discharged of, and from the repayre thereof, hath given, graunted, released, and confirmed, and by these presents dothe freely and clearely give, graunt, release and confirm unto John Wrench and John Cotgreave, churchwardens of the sayd parish and parish church, the sayd chappell, or parte of the sayd parish church (commonly called Troutbeck's chappell), and every parte and parcell thereof, with th'appertenances and all the right, title, interest, clayme, and demaund whatsoever of him the sayd Earle, of in and to the same and every part thereof.

[1] This deed was amongst the Shrewsbury charters in 1807 (*see* Ormerod, vol. ij., p. 41, note).

[2] Enrolled on the *Cheshire Recognisance Rolls* for that year.

[3] This is printed in Hemingway's *History of Chester*, vol. ij., p. 105, 1831, and it is there stated to be " an authenticated copy " which had not previously been published, and that " the original is carefully preserved in an iron chest in the church." I regret to say it is not now amongst the St. Mary's Church papers, and I cannot learn what has become of it. Hemingway states that Sir Joseph Jekyll, chief justice of Chester, was instrumental in getting the Earl of Shrewsbury to give this chapel to the parishioners.

[4] This was the Rev. Richard Wright, B.D., rector from 1674 to 1711.

CHESHIRE.

PROGRAMME OF CEREMONY

OF

Laying of the N. E. Corner Stone

OF THE

Randle Holme Porch of St. Mary's Church, Chester,

BY THE

Right Honble. Lord Egerton of Tatton,

Right Worshipful Provincial Grand Master.

AND THE PROVINCIAL GRAND OFFICERS,

On *MONDAY, APRIL the 18th, 1892,*

Province of Cheshire.

Bowdon, April 2nd, 1892.

Worshipful Sir and Brother,

I am commanded by the Right Honourable Lord Egerton of Tatton, Right Worshipful Provincial Grand Master, &c. &c. &c., to summon you to attend an especial

Provincial Grand Lodge

Which will be held at Chester Castle, on Monday, the 18th April, 1892, at One o'clock, for the purpose of laying the Foundation Stone of the Kindle Holme Porch.

— Morning Costume, White Ties and White Gloves. —

Yours faithfully and fraternally,

RICHARD NEWHOUSE, P.M.
Provincial Grand Secretary.

AGENDA.

1.—The Grand and Provincial Grand Officers...

2.—The R.W. Provincial Master and P... ...and Pr. Grand Lodge to be opened at Two o'...

3.—The R.W. Prov. Grand Master... ...Brethren on the Order of Proceedings.

4.—The Brethren will form in Procession to the M... ...where a service will be held, and a collection will be made on behalf of the Building Fund.

5.—The Foundation Stone will be laid by the Right Honourable Lord Egerton, R.W. P.G.M., with full Masonic Honours.

6.—The ceremony being concluded, the Brethren will re-assemble... ...Castle in reverse order, when the especial P.G. Lodge will be closed.

7.—The Vintage Luncheon, Dinner of Address... ...John Lewis, D.P.G., and Bro. Mrs. V.D.

Hemingways says Before which Signature [of Shrewsbury] the arms of the said Earl appendant thereto — Indorsement of the deed. Seled and delivered in the presence of Jo. Howen Griff. Phillips.

THE OLD HERALDIC STAINED GLASS AND OLD MONUMENTS. 33

To have and to hould the sayd chappell or parte of the sayd parish church and every parte thereof, with the appurtenances unto the sayd John Wrench and John Cotgreave and their successors (churchwardens of the sayd parish and parish church for the tyme being) for ever, to the use, benefitt, and behoofe of the inhabitants and parishioners of the sayd parish of St. Maryes upon the Hill for ever, as a free gift of him the sayd Earle, and that freely, clearly, and absolutely, without any manner of lett, suite, trouble, disturbance, or molestation of him the sayd Earle, or of his heires or assignes, or any of them, or of any other p'son or p'sons whatsoever clayming or to clayme by from or under him them or any of them in any wise, att and under the yearly rent of one peppercorne to be payd yearly to the sayd Earle, his heires and assignes on the feast day of St. Michaell Th'arch-Angell (if lawfully demanded), in token only as an acknowledgment for the above-mentioned guifte and graunt.

In witness whereof he the sayd Earle hath hereunto sett his hand and sealle, the fowerteenth day of March, in the third yeare of the raigne of our Sovereign Lord and Lady William and Mary, by the Grace of God over England, &c., King and Queene, Defenders of the ffayth, &c., Anno Dñi. 1690-91. (Signed) Shrewsbury ××

Hemingway in his *History of Chester*, writing of this chapel in 1831, states that " one part of the site of this chapel is a small neat vestry ; and on another, an enclosed angle, in which is a modern font, which latterly replaced an ancient octagonal one formerly ornamented with gilding and painting, but now thrown aside as useless[1] ; here also is an excellent pannelled seat for the convenience of women who come to be churched."

The foregoing is a true copy of the original grant of Charles Earl of Shrewsbury [now the property of the Parishioners of Saint Mary's Church in Chester, usually kept in the parish chest] taken on the fifth day of April, in the year one thousand seven hundred eighty two, by T. Craul. Hemingway p. 106.

THE OLD HERALDIC STAINED GLASS AND OLD MONUMENTS.

Prior to the Reformation the windows of St. Mary's contained a quantity of mediæval stained glass, mostly consisting of shields of arms, and figures either singly or in groups, with inscriptions underneath. The shields of arms were those of well-known families, directly or indirectly connected with the church and parish, members of which had in various ways benefited the church either by donations of lands or money, or by founding chantries, &c. The figures were either single figures placed to commemorate the clergy, or else consisted of groups of figures, father and mother, sons and daughters, mostly depicted kneeling in prayer, and put in by surviving relatives to the memory of the deceased. The inscriptions underneath the figures were usually in Latin, desiring prayers for the souls of those whom they commemorated. In some cases these figures were put in by those who wished to beautify the church by the insertion of stained glass windows, and then the inscriptions, still usually in Latin, desired prayers " for the good estate," or life, of the donor who had caused the stained glass to be made.

At the Reformation the inscriptions desiring prayers for the souls of the dead and all figures of saints were deemed to be inconsistent with the Protestant religion, and orders were given for their destruction all over the country. But local associations and family ties and connections were too strong to be ignored, and in a great many churches this old stained glass was allowed to remain well on to the middle of the reign of Queen Elizabeth, and even down to the time of the Civil War, when religious fanaticism destroyed most of what had so long been permitted to remain.

The fullest account of the old stained glass in St. Mary's is contained in one of the

---

[1] The old oak cover of this octagonal font was discovered some years since buried under one of the pews near the font. The Rev. W. H. Massie in 1854 brought to light some rude painting on it, and a careful drawing of it appears in the *Journal of the Chester Archaeological and Historic Society*, vol. j., p. 402. It represents the baptism of an infant, and dates back to the end of the 17th or the beginning of the 18th century.

F

Trafford. Arg. a cross engrailed Sable.
Trafford. Arg. on a cross engrailed Sa. 5 mullets or } B4.4.

ST. MARY-ON-THE-HILL, CHESTER.

manuscripts belonging to the collection of the Randle Holmes, now fortunately preserved in the British Museum. In this manuscript (*Harleian MS.* 2151, f. 15), one of the Randle Holmes appears to have collected all the notices of this stained glass, which he could find, illustrated with rough sketches of the various shields of arms and of the figures formerly in the windows. This is headed " St. Mary's in Chester, 1578," and no doubt starts with the notes of the glass in the church at that date, probably made by Thomas Chaloner[1] and others. This account is as follows[2] :—

" In the Chancell [window] over the communion table these coates."
[1.] *England* [France and England quarterly.]
[2.] [Prince of Wales.] [The same with a label of three points Argent.]
[3.] *Troutbeck.* [Argent, a fleur-de-lys between three Moors' heads couped Sable.]
[4.] *Venables.* [Azure, two bars Argent, in the fesse point a crescent of the last.]
[5.] [Hugh] *Lupus* [Earl of Chester] [Azure, a wolf's head erased Argent.]
[6.] *Dedwood*[3] *who lived in Castle Lane.* [Sable, two bars Argent ; on a canton of the first a garb between four nails (?) Or.][4]

" In the same great window eastward these three coates with the writting under."
[7.] *Davenport* [Argent, a chevron between three cross-crosslets fitché Sable.]
[8.] [Devias?] [Sable, a chevron between three cross-crosslets, Argent.]
[9.] [Bostock.] [Argent, a fesse couped Ermines.]

Orate pro anima Johannis Dauenport hujus ecclesiæ rectoris qui hanc fenestram fieri fecit MDrrrib.[5]

(*Translated.*) Pray for the soul of John Davenport, rector of this church, who caused this window to be made, 1534.

[10.] [Haydock?] .. [Argent, a cross Sable in dexter chief a fleur-de-lys of the last.]
" In the same window at the bottom is this writting."

Orate pro anima Johannis Willaston[6] **quondam rectoris hujus ecclesiæ et pro animabus . . . . parentum ejus . . . . MCCCC . . . .**

(*Translated.*) Pray for the soul of John Willaston, formerly rector of this church and for the souls of . his parents . 14 . . .

" In another light in the same windowe this coate and writting under it."
[11.] [Argent, a cross engrailed Sable and in dexter chief a fleur-de-lys of the last.]

Orate pro animabus Johannis Leche et Johannæ uroris ejus. . . .

(*Translated.*) Pray for the souls of John Leche and Joan his wife . . .

" In a window at north side of the comunion table by the vestry doore these coates."

---

[1] At this date, 1578, the eldest of the four Randle Holmes was only a child, having been born about 1571.
[2] For the identification and blazon of these coats I am much indebted to my friend J. Paul Rylands, Esq., F.S.A.
[3] Thomas Dedwood was a benefactor to the church and by his will dated 31st March, 1497, left money for a priest to celebrate at the altar of St. Stephen in the church for seven years, &c. (*see* p. 30).
[4] The tinctures of this coat are not given in *Harl. MS.* 2151, but have been taken from the arms given in King's *Vale Royall*, 1656. In the *Harl. MS.* the charges in the canton resemble acorns rather than nails.
  The contracted Latin of the original has in all cases been extended.
[5] John de Wylaston or Willaston was rector of St. Mary's from 1403 to 1430, so that the date of the glass is probably 1430, the date of his death.

[12] *Hulse* [Argent, three piles in point Sable.]
[13] *Warberton* [Argent, a chevron between three cormorants Sable.]
[14] *Troutbeck* [As No. 3, impaling Hulse as No. 12.]
[15] [Troutbeck as No. 3 impaling Argent on a bend Sable three covered cups of the field.] *Rixton.*

"At the bottome of the s^d window this writting."

Orate pro [anima] Ricardi Pencell[1] quondam Rectoris hujus ecclesiæ . . .

(*Translated.*) Pray for the soul of Richard Pencell,[1] formerly rector of this church

' " In one of the high windowes in the chancell this coate."

[16]. [Brereton] [Quarterly 1st and 4th, Argent, two bars, Sable; 2nd and 3rd, Argent a chevron between three crescents Gules. Ipstones.]

"This figure in one of the higher windowes."

A man kneeling on a cushion to the left, with his hands clasped in prayer and a sword on his side; underneath this figure is the following inscription :—

Orate pro bono statu Morgan Broughton. . . .

(*Translated.*) Pray for the good estate of Morgan Broughton . . .

"On the window over against it on the other side the chancell this writting with figures over it "

Orate pro [bono statu] Ricardi Ball qui hanc fenestram fieri fecit . . .

(*Translated.*) Pray for [the good estate] of Richard Ball, who caused this window to be made

"St Katherines Chappell in St Marys Church in Chester

" In the east window on the top of it these coates & at the bottome of the said windowe is the writting vnder them vnder a man & woman with 4 sones & 2 daughters "

[17.] *Brereton* [Argent, two bars Sable, on the upper one a crescent of the field.]
[18.] [Brereton as No. 17 quartering Ipstones as in No. 16.]

Orate pro bono statu Ranulphi Brereton et Ciceliæ et Johanne uxorum suis [*sic*] **ac pro animabus patrum et matrum qui quidam Ranulphus hoc opus vitreum fieri fecit anno domini MDxxiii.**

(*Translated.*) Pray for the good estate of Randal Brereton and Cecily and Joan his wives and for the souls of his father and mother which said Randal caused this glass work to be made in the year of our Lord 1523.

" Above this writting is the figure of a man & his wives with 4 sones and 2 daughters."

[19.] . . . . [Quarterly 1st, Argent, a cross patée Sable, on a chief Or a lion passant holding a cross-crosslet fitchéGules, ? Vawdrey. 2nd, Or a chief indented Gules . 3rd, Quarterly Gules and Argent, four crescents counterchanged, Tatton. 4th, Argent, on a chevron, between three birds (cormorants?) Sable, a mullet Or, Warburton? Crest: on a wreath a moor-cock Or, wattled Gules.]

" Edward Vaudrey of Ridding, Esq., died 17 Marc, 1622."[2]

[20.] [Thelwall, Argent, a fesse Gules between three boars' heads couped Sable.]

---

[1] Richard Pencell, or Pensell, was rector from 1430 to 1458.
[2] I think this coat of arms and inscription refer to some monument, and not to any old heraldic stained glass.

[Handwritten note at top:] My friend, the Author, does not appear to have studied Randle Holme's description of this Tomb in conjunction with Harl. MS. 2129. fol. 184. where occur the notes of Randle Holme taken at Warrington in 1640. He says:—"In Butler's chapel on the north side is a very Auncient monument of a man in armore cutt in Stone in an arch in the wall."
"In the middle (middle) of the Chapel is a faire tombe of Butler with his wife lyinge as the Tombe of Troutbeck in St Maryes in Chester with shields all about, but all the cotes be aworne off." JHS

"In the highest window on the north side in St. Kath. Chapell is this writting" [without any drawing of any arms or figure].

Orate pro animabus [Ricardi] Wyrrall,[1] quondam maioris Cestrie et Agnetis uxoris ejus ac liberorum suorum qui hanc fenestram fieri fecit anno MDxxi.

(*Translated.*) Pray for the souls of [Richard] Wyrrall, formerly Mayor of Chester, and Agnes his wife, and of their children, who caused this window to be made in the year 1521.

"Troutbeck's Chapell in St. Marys in Chester, 1578.

"This chapell now belongs to the Earle of Shrosbury. In the window at the east end are these armes.

[21.] . . . . . . [France and England quarterly with a label of three points Ermine.]
[22.] [Royal Arms.—France and England quarterly.]
[23.] [Prince of Wales—as No. 2.]
[24.] [Earls of Chester. Azure three garbs Or.]
[25.] [. . . . . . Or, three water-bougets Sable.] *? [illegible]*
[26.] *Troutbeck* [As No. 3.]
[27.] [Rixton—Argent, on a bend Sable three covered cups of the field.] *See several times in Warrington Church.*
[28.] [Molyneux—Azure, a cross-moline quarter pierced Or.]

"In the higher south windowe Troutbeeks conte with this writting vnder it."

Orate pro animabus Gulielmi Troutbeck armigeri[2] Cestrie et Johanne uxoris ejus qui hanc capellam fecerunt anno domini MCCCCxxiiij.

(*Translated.*) Pray for the souls of William Troutbeck, Esquire,[3] of Chester, and Joan his wife, who built this chapel in the year of our Lord 1424.

"In the two lower windowes on the said south side are these coates, viz., *Troutbeck* and *Rixton*."

Then follows the description of the two fine old tombs, with marble or alabaster effigies, put up to the memory of the Troutbecks, the founders of this chapel, and their descendants. Randle Holme describes them in these words, writing probably in the middle of the seventeenth century."[3]

"At the side of the south wall of the said Chapell under the high-most window is this monument cut in alabaster, with these coates on the side of it. A man, all in armour save the head, with his sword by his side and a collar of SSS about his neck. He is holding of his wife by the hand, she being in a red gown being furred with ermine, her head tyre richly attyred (as those days were) 2 Angells supporting her cushions under her head, and at her feet a lamb. At his feet is a lion couchant; under his head an helmet mantled with the crest, being a Moors head, the wreath composed of Trout fishes, the head of one over the taile of the other before it.

"At the head end of the tombe are these arms."

The arms sketched are the coat of *Troutbeck* and a curious shield which is not heraldically correct, but which is meant for *Stanley, Earl of Derby*. It may be described as follows:

---

[1] He was Mayor in 1506.

[2] I think there is a word or two missing here, and that it should read *Camerarii Cestrie* (Chamberlain of Chester), an office which was held by the Troutbecks for several generations.

[3] There is a line drawn across the page in the original MS., marking off the latter portion as distinct from the former, which is dated 1578.

per pale, dexter, Or on a chief indented Azure three plates for *Lathom*; sinister Argent on a bend Azure three bucks' heads cabossed Or for *Stanley*; on a chief over all Gules, three legs in armour conjoined at the thighs and flexed in triangle Argent, garnished Or, for the lordship of the *Isle of Man*.

" On the side of the tomb these [four] coats [of arms]."[1]

" 1. Argent a fleur-de-lys between three morions or moor's heads [couped] Sable [*Troutbeck*] impaled with Azure a bend between six covered cups Or [*Boteler*] of Bewsey co. Lanc.].

" 2. Azure a bend between six covered cups Or [*Boteler*] impaled with Argent a fleur-de-lys between three black moor's heads couped Sable [*Troutbeck*].

" 3. Argent two bars Sable [*Brereton*].

" 4. Argent a fleur-de-lys between three moor's heads couped Sable [*Troutbeck*] impaled with Argent three piles in point Sable [*Hulse*]."

" Between every escochion is a saint carved, very curiously wrought."

A rude sketch of the tomb is affixed to this MS. (*Harl. MS.* 2151, f. 16), but beyond showing that it was a raised altar tomb with the two full length effigies lying side by side, the right hand of the man grasping the left hand of the woman, the drawing does not add anything to the above description. Most unfortunately not a single word of the inscription, which would be cut or painted round the four edges of the tomb, is given, so that it is not easy to identify which of the Troutbecks it is meant to commemorate.

" In the middle of this said Chappell is an other faire tombe, which is very curiously wrought, that for the finenesse of the worke it did exceed any tombe or monument of that nature, as any that our English churches can produce. Thus by one described before it was ruinated by the fall of the Roofes and Arch of the church chancell and this chappell.

" It was a faire Tomb of one of ye Troutbecks, the man all in rich armour with a rich border of pearle and stones about his head, on the helmett and on the front of his helmett; over his forehead is engraved JESV NAZERENVS REX; all the plate and edges of his armour curiously wrought as it were inbrothery [embroidery], with a collar of SSS about his neck holding one gauntlett in his . . . . hand and the wife's hand in the other. Under his feet a lion couchant, under his head an helmett mantled, haveing on it a wreath of trouts and a moor's head proper. She hath her head richly attired with a vale over her head, white with a blew gown and a short cercote [surcoat] of black; with rings on her fingers; at her feet a lamb and 2 angells supporting the cushions under her head."

[2] " At the head [these arms]" *Troutbeck* and *Rixton* as before. " At the feet" *Troutbeck* impaling *Rixton* and *Rixton* quartering Argent a fesse Gules, in chief three mullets Sable (? for *Lancelyn* of Poulton-Lancelyn) impaling Argent a fesse . . . for . . . . On the north side (1) Argent two chevrons Gules, on a canton of the last a mullet Or *Warburton ancient*; (2) Argent two bars Azure *Venables* quartering Or three water bougets Sable . . . . ; (3) Argent two bars Gules, on a canton of the last a cross-crosslet fitché Or . . . . ., . impaling Azure a lion rampant Argent . . . . ; (4) Azure cruisily fitché a cinquefoil Or . . . . " On the south side the Tombe " (1) *Troutbeck* impaling *Hulse*, (2) *Troutbeck* with a label of three points impaling quarterly 1 and 4 *Lathom*, 2 and 3 *Stanley*, on a chief over all the arms of the *Isle of Man*. (3) *Venables* impaling *Troutbeck*. (4) *Rixton* impaling *Troutbeck*.

---

[1] In the original manuscript these arms are set down in an abbreviated way much used by the third Randle Holme.
[2] These arms in the original manuscript are set down in the same abbreviated way as those on the monument already described. It is only necessary to give the names of the well-known coats, which are the same as those on the first tomb.

"There was writtings about the top edges of both these monuments, but they were wholly decayed and worn away."

In King's *Vale Royall of England*, printed in 1656, in "The Description of the City and County Palatine of Chester, compiled by Mr. Webb, M^r of Arts," and, as shown by internal evidence, drawn up about the year 1621, the following description of these two tombs is given in the account of St. Mary's Church (p. 43):—

"Upon the South side of the Chancel of this Church standeth a fair Chapel, which is reported to be there erected by the Ancestors of a great and worshipful race of the *Troutbecks*, of great reputation in this County of *Chester*, and of whose Lands many of the Gentlemen of the Shire have now no small portion, though the chiefest of the same are now in the possession of the Right Honourable the Earl of *Shrewsbury*.

"In which Chappel the bodies of some of them, and by all likelihood the Founders of the Chappel, lye in a fair Vault in the middest of the *Chappell*, and for two of them two very fair Tombs of *Alabaster*, the one over the said Vault, the other by the wall on the South side, at the upper end of the *Chappell*, with the Statues of them both, and their Wives, upon the said severall Tombs artificially pourtrayed, whereof one of them is for Sr *Henry Troutbeck*,[1] himself in his compleat armour, and his Lady lying on his left hand, his head upon the hulk of a *Moor's* head : and body [*sic* for the helmet] neatly wrought with a Wreath of Trouts round about it ; and the other is for Sir *Adam Troutbeck*[2] and his Lady, which sheweth that she was a Countesse, her Statue lying upon his right hand and her collar of SS. finely adorning her bare neck, his head supported like the others, and many Escuchions of their Arms, were fairly engraven about both of their said Tombs, which might shew all their marriages and descents but that the same by length of time are grown so dimme, as they cannot be well discerned."

It is almost certain that the tomb in the middle of this chapel was erected to the memory of William Troutbeck, Esq., who died in 1436, and Joan his wife, who built the chapel and endowed the chantry,[3] whilst the other on the south side commemorated his grandson, Sir William Troutbeck, Knt., who died in 1459, and Dame Margaret (Stanley) his wife.

The windows on the north and south sides, or as Randle Holme describes them, "in the body of the church," also contained heraldic stained glass. "In the window next St. Katherine's Chancell or Chappell on the north side are these arms with figures of [a kneeling man and woman and of] sons and daughters behind them." There is a sketch of the shield of arms, quarterly Argent and Sable a cross patonce counterchanged for EATON and sketches of a man kneeling with a sword on his right side, and a woman kneeling habited in furred gown. The following inscription appears to belong to these figures :—

Orate pro bono statu Ricardi Grosvenor et Sibilla uxoris ejus qui hoc opus fecit [*sic*] [anno domini] MDrrib.

(*Translated*.) Pray for the good estate of Richard Grosvenor and Sybil his wife, who made this work [in the year of our Lord] 1524.

"In the second window on the north side this writting but no arms."

Orate pro animabus Ranulphi Hunt et Elizabethæ uxoris ejus et pro

---
[1] This is a pure guess, no such person as Sir *Henry* Troutbeck being known to have existed at all.

[2] The identification of this tomb as that of Sir *Adam* Troutbeck, if such a person ever existed at the date of the tomb, is only a guess like that of Sir Henry Troutbeck already alluded to.

[3] As the shield of Troutbeck impaling Stanley was on this tomb, it is probable that the marriage of Sir William Troutbeck and Margaret Stanley had taken place before it was erected in 1436. This is confirmed by the label of three points being on the arms of Troutbeck, shewing that he was at that time an eldest son.

It does not appear from anything I have been able to collect, whether these reliques of antiquity and superstition were destroyed, but it is probable their demolition may be ascribed to puritanical zeal, when the parliamentary forces had possession of the city about 1647.
Hemingway, Vol II. p 112

THE OLD HERALDIC STAINED GLASS AND OLD MONUMENTS. 39

𝔞𝔫𝔦𝔪𝔞 𝔈𝔩𝔢𝔰𝔦 𝔇𝔞𝔳𝔦𝔡. 𝔒𝔯𝔞𝔱𝔢 𝔢𝔱𝔦𝔞𝔪 𝔭𝔯𝔬 𝔟𝔬𝔫𝔬 𝔰𝔱𝔞𝔱𝔲 𝔡𝔬𝔪𝔦𝔫𝔦 𝔍𝔬𝔥𝔞𝔫𝔫𝔦𝔰 ℌ𝔲𝔫𝔱 𝔠𝔞𝔭𝔢𝔩𝔩𝔞𝔫𝔦, 𝔐𝔞𝔱𝔱𝔥𝔢𝔦 𝔈𝔩𝔩𝔦𝔰 𝔢𝔱 𝔄𝔩𝔦𝔠𝔦𝔢 𝔲𝔵𝔬𝔯𝔦𝔰 𝔢𝔧𝔲𝔰, 𝔮𝔲𝔦 𝔮𝔲𝔦𝔡𝔞𝔪 𝔐𝔞𝔱𝔱𝔥𝔢𝔲𝔰 𝔥𝔞𝔫𝔠 𝔣𝔢𝔫𝔢𝔰𝔱𝔯𝔞𝔪 𝔣𝔦𝔢𝔯𝔦 𝔣𝔢𝔠𝔦𝔱 𝔞𝔫𝔫𝔬 [𝔡𝔬𝔪𝔦𝔫𝔦] 𝔐𝔇𝔛𝔳.

(*Translated.*) Pray for the souls of Randle Hunt and Elizabeth his wife and for the soul of Ellis David. Pray also for the good estate of Sir John Hunt, chaplain, [and] of Matthew Ellis and Alice his wife, the which Matthew caused this window to be made in the year of our Lord, 1515.

"In another window these figures of men and women with their children." A rough sketch shows the kneeling figure of a man with three sons behind him, the eldest having apparently a kind of helmet on his head as if a soldier, and the kneeling figure of a woman with five daughters behind her. The inscription underneath is only fragmentary.

. . . . R. Hunt et uxor' ejus fil' . . . . Ellis et eorum filiorum et filiarum . . . .

(*Translated.*) [Pray for the souls of] R. Hunt and his wife, the daughter of . . . . Ellis, and of their sons and daughters . . . .

"In another north window is Mathew Ellis in a gown and an head piece or helmet on his head and 4 sonnes after him, and his wife in a vaile and 5 daughters after her, but noe arms or writting."

"And in an high window [*i.e.*, in the clerestory] in the middle Ile is written :

𝔒𝔣 𝔶𝔬𝔲𝔯 𝔠𝔥𝔞𝔯𝔦𝔱𝔶 𝔭𝔯𝔞𝔶 𝔣𝔬𝔯 𝔶𝔢 𝔰𝔬𝔲𝔩𝔢 𝔬𝔣 𝔐𝔞𝔱𝔱𝔥𝔢𝔴 𝔈𝔩𝔩𝔦𝔰 𝔞𝔫𝔡 𝔈𝔩𝔦𝔷𝔞𝔟𝔢𝔱𝔥 𝔥𝔦𝔰 𝔴𝔦𝔣𝔢. . . .

"In the west window by the north door are these arms," Argent a pale fusilly Sable [*Savage*] and Argent a griffin segreant Sable [*? Bold*]."

With these the account of the old stained glass formerly in St. Mary's ends, the rest of the pages of this MS. (*Harl.* 2151) devoted to that church, consisting of copies of old monumental inscriptions, &c., which have been incorporated with others, obtained from various sources, in the subsequent pages devoted to the description of the monumental inscriptions formerly existing in the church, but now lost or destroyed.

In the chapel on the north side, formerly dedicated to St. Katherine, there still remain two handsome monuments, which are of much interest. One was erected to the memory of Thomas Gamul, Esq., Recorder of Chester, a member of a very old Chester family, who died in 1613; and the other to the memory of Philip Oldfield, Esq., a distinguished Chester lawyer, who died in 1616. Considering the proximity of the church to the castle and the many vicissitudes it must have passed through, it is extraordinary that both these monuments should be in such an excellent state of preservation as they are now. It is, however, stated on a modern inscription placed near the Oldfield tomb, that on the surrender of the city of Chester to the Parliamentary forces in February 1646, Leftwich Oldfield, Esq., and Sir Francis Gamul "procured an assurance that their respective family tombs in St. Mary's Church should be preserved from injury, as the property they most valued. The result proved the advantage of their forethought, as these two tombs are the only monuments of a like character in Chester, which escaped demolition by the Puritans."

The GAMUL tomb has full-length effigies of Thomas Gamul, Esq., Recorder of Chester, who died on the 10th August, 1613, and of his wife Alice (Bavand), who died in August, 1640.

He is habited in a long gown over his coat and trunk hose, his hands are joined together in prayer and his head is uncovered resting on cushions. He wears a small ruff round his neck and has a pointed beard and moustache. His wife wears a large ruff and a very full pleated dress, having a long cloak, without sleeves, hanging from her shoulders. She has her hair turned back from the forehead under a jewelled head dress; her head rests on two cushions, and her hands are clasped in prayer. Their only surviving son, Francis Gamul, afterwards Sir Francis Gamul, Knt. and Bart., is shown kneeling on one knee at his mother's feet, his head leaning on his right hand and an open prayer book on the other knee. He wears a broad collar, a close-fitting jacket, and trunk hose. On the front of the monument, as shown in the accompanying plate, are two shields of arms and the kneeling figures of three children, two sons and one daughter, each of whom holds a skull, showing that they died in their infancy.[1]

The arms on the front of the monument are as follow :—

The shield towards the head of the monument has six coats: (1) Or, three mallets Sable, *Gamul*. (2) Sable, three leopards' heads Argent jessant a fleur-de-lys of the second, *Ockley*. (3) Argent, a fesse dancette, in chief three escallops Argent, *Euedon*. (4) Gules, three boars' heads couped Argent, *Stapeley*. (5) Azure, a star of six points within the horns of a crescent Sable, *Minshull*. (6) as (1). Over all is a label of three points, and the crest is a trefoil slipped Or, winged Sable, issuing from a ducal coronet Or. This is the coat of arms of Edmund Gamul, Esq., the father, differenced by the label of three points, to show that it is used for the son, Thomas Gamul, Esq., the Recorder, who died in his father's lifetime.

The shield towards the foot of the monument is the same coat of six quarterings, with the label of three points, for Thomas Gamul, impaling the arms of his wife, Alice, daughter of Richard Bavand, of Chester, as follows: (1) Ermine, two bars Gules, in chief two boars' heads couped Sable, *Bavand*. (2) Gules on a bend Or three lioncels passant Sable. . . . . (3) Or, on a chief Gules three trefoils slipped Argent, a crescent Gules for difference, *Banville of Chester*. (4) as (1). The crest of Gamul as before and that of Bavand, on a wreath a boar's head Or pierced in the mouth with an arrow Argent.

The following inscription is on the lower end of the tomb, now much worn and impossible to read in places. The contracted Latin has been extended and corrected from the copy given in King's *Vale Royall* and elsewhere.

OSSIBUS ET MEMORIÆ.

Thomæ Gamuelis, ornatissimi armigeri et juris consulti clarissimi, in quo eximia quædam ingenii suavitas cum summâ morum gravitate ancipiti palmâ contendebat : quique (proh dolor!) in ipso ætatis dignitatisque suæ flore, ardentissimâ febre correptus, et præreptus ; immaturo funere tristissimum toti Cestriæ (cui per aliquot annos præfuerat) a memoriâ multiplicis suæ scientiæ, admirabilis prudentiæ, singularis fidei, spectatissimæ probitatis et pietatis minime vulgaris, desiderium reliquit.

Alicia, uxor quondam beatissima, nunc mœstissima vidua, parvum hoc non-parvi amoris monumentum, multis cum lacrimis precibusque profusis, ponit simul consecratque. In quo ipsa posthac sua quoque ossa recondi et permisceri cineribus tam chari capitis nimis misere cupit : ut ab eo jam mortuo nunquam sejungatur quicum vivo olim conjunctissime et jucundissime vixerat : Vixit autem ille annos

---

[1] These were Thomas and Richard Gamul, who were living in 1603 but died young; and Alice Gamul, who died in 1606, and was buried at St. Oswald's. These figures have been incorrectly described as being three daughters, instead of two sons and one daughter as clearly shown by the costumes. Webb in the *Vale Royall*, by an obvious clerical error, speaks of their holding "skeletons" in their hands instead of skulls and he states that in his time, 1620, the tomb was "compassed with a strong piked grate of iron."

XLII. obiit decimo die Augusti Anno a partu Virginis MDCXIII. Ubi nunc quatuor liberorum lætus parens factus fuerat; quoram tamen hodie unus tantum superstes est, isque minimus natu, nomine Franciscus, puerulus optimæ spei; cui ego quidem omnia bona in hoc uno voto exopto: sit Patri simillimus.

> Hunc tumulum tibi composui, charissime conjux:
> Quo mea mista tuis molliter ossa cubent.
> Dilexi vivum, volo defunctum comitari:
> Nam, quos junxit amor, dissosciare nefas.

The following is a literal translation of the above inscription, with an attempt to represent the Latin verses at the end in rhyme :—

FOR THE BONES AND TO THE MEMORY OF

THOMAS GAMUL, Esquire, a most distinguished man and a very illustrious lawyer, in whom a remarkable sweetness of temperament was worthily matched by a consummate dignity of manner, and who (ah, woe!) in the very flower of his age and high position was attacked, and too early snatched away by a most violent fever. By his premature death he left to all Chester (over which he had for some years ruled) a most sad feeling of loss from the recollection of his manifold knowledge, his remarkable foresight, his conspicuous faithfulness, his tried goodness, and his most rare piety.

ALICE, formerly his most happy wife, now his most sorrowful widow, with many a tear and prayer poured forth, at once erects and dedicates this small memorial of her great love; where too she, out of the depths of her sorrow, wishes her own bones to be hereafter buried and mingled with the ashes of one so dear to her, in order that she may never be separated from him now dead, with whom when once alive she had lived in perfect union and happiness. He lived but 42 years. He died on the 10th day of August, in the year 1613, from the Virgin's maternity.[1] While here on earth he was the joyful parent of four children, of whom, however, one only this day survives, and he the youngest, by name Francis, a little boy of the highest promise; for whom I indeed ardently desire all blessings in this one wish: "May he be in everything most like his Sire."

> [2]"This tomb, dear husband, have I raised for thee,
> Where mixed with thine my bones may gently rest;
> My love in life, with thee in death I'd be,
> 'Tis wrong to break the union love has blessed."

Alice Gamul, the widow of Thomas Gamul, Esq., who erected this monument to his memory, married for her second husband her first husband's successor in the Recordership, Edward Whitby, Esq. He was buried in this tomb on the 25th April, 1639, and she was buried there on the 18th August, 1640.[4]

On the east wall of this north chapel, above this monument is the following inscrip-

---

[1] This expression "a partu Virginis" is a most unusual one, and difficult to translate.

[2] The literal translation is as follows :—
> This tomb I have raised for thee, my dearest husband,
> That here my bones mingled with thine may gently lie asleep.
> I loved thee living, I wish to accompany thee dead,
> For it is wrong to separate those whom love hath joined.

[3] For this translation, and much assistance with others, I am much indebted to an old friend, H. S. B. Price, Esq., M.A., Lincoln's Inn, London.

[4] A fuller account of her and her two husbands, with abstracts of their wills, &c., will be given later on in the account of the Gamul family.

G

tion to the memory of Edmund Gamul, the father of the Recorder, who died in September, 1616, three years after the untimely death of his son :—

> The bodies of the jvst are bvried in peace,
> bvt their name liveth for ever.—Ecclvs 44.
>
> Here lieth the body of EDMVND
> GAMVL, sometime maior of this Ci-
> tie, whoe had 2 wives Elizabeth,
> the davghter of Thomas Case by
> whome hee had issve 3 sonnes and 3
> davghters & Elizabeth, the widdow
> of Will: Goodman sometime maior of
> this City, whoe died withovt issve.
> whoe departed this life in the ye-
> are of his age [79.
> Anno Dom. 1616. Sept. 7].[1]

Webb in the *Vale Royall*, writing of this monument about 1621, says :

"In another Chapell on the North side of the Chancell there is the remembrance of another of like Fame and Work [*i.e.* to Robert Brerewood, Alderman and thrice mayor of Chester previously referred to] and a late Alderman of great and good account, of this City, and of the same time, for whom were to be wished some monument answerable to his worth, there being no more than his Arms, Crest, and this Inscription." And he continues : "But what needs a Monument, when as this Inscription above recited, was but an addition to as fair and beautiful a Tomb, (erected in that very place for his eldest Son *Tho. Gamull*, Esquire, late Recorder of this City and a learned Lawyer, deceased before his said Father) as can be desired ? Or if that son had not yet been intombed, which were to be wished, when as his vertues and reputations live still in a second son of his yet living, [William Gamul of Chester and Crabwall, alderman and mayor of Chester], who both in his own time and since hath born[e] the chief Magistracie in this City with such general applause, as is not expedient for me to publish. And I well knowing his modest disposition, dare not give liberty to my pen to do him all his rights, but thus I return to his Brothers Tomb again."

Over the above inscription to Edmund Gamul, Esq., is his coat of arms, quarterly of six, and his crest, identical with those described on the tomb of his son, the Recorder (but without the label), and on either side of this, two shields of arms, the one bearing Gamul impaling Argent on a bend Gules coticed Sable, three buckles of the first for Case[2] and the other Gamul impaling Argent two bars Gules, for Mainwaring.

The OLDFIELD monument also in this north chapel was erected to the memory of Philip Oldfield, Esq.,[3] a well-known Chester barrister (educated at Gray's Inn, London), who died at Chester on the 15th December, 1616. It is a handsome monument and in a very excellent state of preservation as shown in the accompanying illustration. His life-size effigy is placed on a marble slab, habited in a long gown and wearing a ruff. He is leaning on his right side, the right hand supporting the head, the elbow resting on a cushion, and he holds a roll in the left

---

[1] The inscription finishes at "age," but the age and date of death are filled in from the *Vale Royall*, p. 44.

[2] As stated on the inscription the first wife of Edmund Gamul was Elizabeth, daughter of Thomas Case, of Chester, and the second was Elizabeth, widow of William Goodman, of Chester, and, as I have ascertained from other sources, the daughter of John Thorpe, or Thrope, of Chester (*see* the Gamul pedigree *postea*).

[3] He was the eldest son of Philip Oldfield, of Middlewich, by his wife Elizabeth Swinton, and was born about the year 1541.

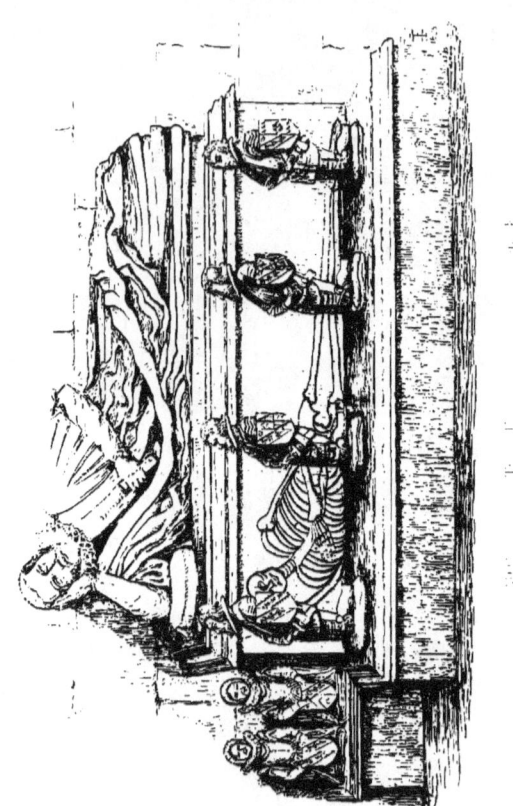

[Handwritten note at top: The tomb of Bishop John Carpenter in Westbury Church obiit 1476. Here he is still remained a cadaver of or alabaster figure of a corpse, lying in a shroud which was represented as withdrawn, so as to expose the skeleton beneath. This design is not very common, and is intended to remind the spectator what he himself will become. These figures were generally laid under the slab, supporting an image of the same person as he appeared in life. In Farnworth Church one of the Attones is misplaced, his head cut off. At St Marys Chester the old pillar sculptured in robes above the tomb is incised below as a skeleton, in the very same attitude in which he lies upon the top. The meaning is simply in all these cases an obvious 'memento mori' ES FUI SUM ERIS 'You are what once I was. I am what you will be.']

THE OLD HERALDIC STAINED GLASS AND OLD MONUMENTS. 43

hand, whilst below him, on the side of the tomb, a skeleton is painted in the same attitude as the figure immediately above it. The marble slab is represented as supported on the shoulders of the kneeling figures of his four sons, their right hands resting on the hilts of their swords, and bearing on their left arms shields on which were painted the arms of Oldfield, impaling those of Wettenhall, Somerford, Mainwaring of Croxton, and Leftwich, respectively. At the head of the tomb are the kneeling figures of his two daughters, holding in front of them shields with the arms of Wettenhall and Shakerly, respectively, impaling Oldfield.

This monument is thus described by Webb in writing about 1621 (King's *Vale Royall*, 1656, p. 46):—

"Neer to the same and close to the same wall [the north wall of the north chapel] was of late erected a very fine Tombe of alabaster curiously adorned, a well-formed statue, lying upon the Table of it, turning itself as it were side-wayes, his right hand supporting his head and his elbow leaning upon a fine Pillow, his three [*sic* for four] sons in their order, placed on the utter [outer] side of the Chest of the Tombe and his two Daughters in the arched end thereof, the same fenced with an Iron grate; and the Inscription over the same, thus."

The inscription to his memory is as follows, the contracted words being extended :—

PHILIPPO OLDFELD, Armigero ob navatam in construendis viis pontibusque operam in eruendis antiquissimis Familiarum stematibus, bene de Comitatu hoc merito. Qui in primum matrimonium Helenæ Gulielmi Berington de Bradwell heredi copulavit ex quâ Thomam & Elizabetham Johanni Wetenhall enuptam genuit: Ad secunda vota convolans Helenam Griffith viduam, filiam Gulielmi Hanmer armigeri duxit, per quam tres filios [et] unam filiam procreavit quorum primogenitum Philippum Mariæ unicæ filiæ et heredi Joannis Somerford de Somerford, armigeri: Michaelem Elenoræ heredi Jacobi Manwaringe de Croxton armigeri, Gulielmum Elizabethæ heredi Roberti Leftwich de Leftwich armigeri, Margeriam filiam Petro Shakerley, primogenito nepoti ex heredibus Galfridi Shakerley de Holme armigeri in matrimonium felicissime elocavit. Jure consulto municipali clarissimo marito suo charissima Helena uxor relicta sepulchrum hoc monumentum consecravit. Obiit 15 Dec., 1616, ætatis suæ 75.

Of this inscription the following translation may be given :—

To PHILIP OLDFELD, Esquire, who deserved well of his county by reason of the work done by him in constructing roads and bridges, as well as in investigating the most ancient pedigrees of its families. He for his first marriage wedded Helen, heiress of William Berington of Bradwell, by whom he begat Thomas and Elizabeth, married to John Wetenhall. Betaking himself to a second choice, he married Helen Griffith, widow, the daughter of William Hanmer, esquire, by whom he was the father of three sons and one daughter. Philip, the eldest of these, he caused to be married to Mary, only daughter and heiress of John Somerford, of Somerford, esquire ; Michael to Eleanor, heiress of James Mainwaring, of Croxton, esquire ; William to Elizabeth, heiress of Robert Leftwich, of Leftwich, esquire : and his daughter Margery to Peter Shakerley, eldest grandson of Geoffrey Shakerley, of Holme, esquire : all most happily. To him her husband, most distinguished as a lawyer and citizen, his dearest wife Helen, who survives him, has dedicated this tomb as a memorial. He died 15th December, 1616, in the 75th year of his age.

The above Latin inscription is the same as that now on the monument, but the contracted Latin has been carefully extended. Underneath it was added, "Peter Shakerley, Esq., eldest son of Sir Geffr. Shakerley, Knt., by Margaret, his first wife, refreshed this inscription in memory" of the said Margaret, his great grandmother, 1724, and on another tablet below was added,

> In June 1788 this tombe & monument was repaired & cleaned by order of the rev. Doctor Richard Jackson

prebendary of Chester, whose mother was wife of
Richard Jackson, Esq., of Betchton House near Sandbach,
in this county, and who was the only daughter of
William Oldfield, Esq., and Lætitia his wife,
and great great grandson of Philip Oldfield Esq and
Ellen his wife of Bradwall in this county.

Strangely enough, both of these latter inscriptions, which Dr. Ormerod describes as existing in 1819, are no longer attached to the monument, having disappeared since that date in some of the many restorations to which the church has been subjected. But in their place the following has been carved on the base of the tomb,

This tomb and monument were repaired and restored
in 1724, by Peter Shakerley, gent, grandson of the above Margaret Shakerley,
in 1788, by Richard Jackson, D.D., 5th in descent from the above Thomas Oldfield,
in 1846 by Thomas Brame Oldfield, 5th in descent from the above William Oldfield.

There are iron railings in front of this monument, and on the standards in the middle and at each corner are three small escutcheons, on which coats of arms are painted.

ARMS AND CREST OF OLDFIELD.

Over this inscription are the arms of *Oldfield*, Or on a bend Gules three crosses patée fitchée, Argent, quartering *Grosvenor*, *Pulford*, *Pheasant*, *Eaton*, and *Stockton*, and the crest, a demi-wivern with wings expanded Argent, crined Or, issuant from a ducal coronet of the second.

The two windows near this tomb are filled with modern stained glass, put up in 1848 and 1861, with inscriptions to recent members of the Oldfield family, which have already been printed on page 21. Two modern brasses bearing the following inscriptions are also affixed to the wall near the Oldfield monument.

In memory of Leftwich Oldfield of Leftwich Hall in this county. He was a zealous Royalist during ye Civil Wars and incurred imprisonm^t and ye sequestr^n of his estate by his faithful adherence to ye Stuarts. On ye surrender of this City to ye parliamentary forces in Feb^r 1646, Sir Francis Gamul and Leftwich Oldfield procured an assurance that their respective family tombs in St. Mary's Church, sh^d be preserved from injury, as ye property they most valued, ye result proved ye advantage of their forethought, as ye two tombs beneath are ye only monuments of a like character in Chester wch escaped demolition by ye Puritans. He married Mary dau^r of Colonel Thos. Croxton of Ravenscroft, in this county & died Augt 6, 1669, aged 50 y^{rs} leaving a large family.[1]

The inscription on the other brass is—

In Memory of William Langston Oldfield, third son of Thomas Brame Oldfield, Esq., of Champion Hill, Surrey, born 24th April 1818, died 4th October, 1849.

---

[1] This inscription is evidently designed to read like the copy of an old one, but I can not find any trace of any such inscription having ever existed in this church prior to the erection of this modern brass.

MONUMENTAL INSCRIPTIONS NOW IN THE CHURCH.

The following is a complete transcript of all the monumental inscriptions now remaining in St. Mary's Church, with the exception of those on the monuments of Thomas Gamul, Esq., and Philip Oldfield, Esq., already described. The church formerly contained a great many other monumental inscriptions, many of much interest, which have been lost or destroyed. An account of as many of these as I have been able to recover from various sources will be given later on.

On the east wall of the north aisle is a marble slab bearing a long Latin inscription to the memory of RALPH WORSLEY, Esquire, who died in the year 1573. The inscription, the contracted Latin being extended where necessary, is as follows[1]:—

Hic subtus humatur Corpus Radulphi Worseley Armigeri | Qui fuit Filius tertius Gulielmi Worseley de | Worseley Meyne in Comitatu Lancastriæ Armigeri Ac | quondam Serviens, scilicet Pagettus Garderobæ | Roharum ac unus Dapiferorum Cameræ invictissimi Principis Henrici octavi, Dei gratiâ Angliæ Franciæ & Hiberniæ | nuper Regis : Cui idem Rex ob bonum & fidele servicium | circum Regiam suam personam impensum, ex Regia sua | magnificentiâ ad terminum vitæ donaverat Officia | Satellitis Coronæ Custodiæ leonum, leonarum & leopardorum | infra Turrim Londonensem ; Portatoris Magnæ Garderobæ | Contrarotulatoris in Comitatibus Cestriæ & Flint | Clerici Coronæ Lancastriæ et Escæator Comitatus | Palatini Lancastriæ aliasque Remunerationes. Hiis | accesserunt | Præstantes animi dotes cœlitus ei Tributæ | Quibus insigniter. erat indutus, nempe Singularis | in Deum Pietas, Multifaria in Pauperes Beneficientia | & mira in cunctos Charitas. Annos octoginta Natus & | ultra xxvij° die Decembris, Anno Domini 1573. expiravit : | Relicta Sobole Alicia conjuge Thomæ Powell | Armigeri (qui hos sumptos fecit) Katherinâ nupta Thomæ | Tutchet, Armigero et Avisia Thomæ Vawdrey Generoso de Joanna , filia Johannis Pike, Armigeri uxore sua progenitis | ———Nullâ Cœlum reparabile Gazâ.

Of this inscription the following translation may be offered :—

Beneath this spot is buried the body of RALPH WORSLEY, Esquire, who was the third son of William Worsley of Worsley Meyne, in the county of Lancaster, Esquire, and was formerly in the service as Page of the Wardrobe,[2] and one of the Stewards of the Chamber of the most mighty Prince, Henry the Eighth, lately by God's grace, King of England, France and Ireland : to whom the same King on account of the good and faithful service spent about his own Royal person, had out of his Royal bounty given, for the term of his natural life, the offices of Sergeant of the Crown, of Warden[2] of the lions, lionesses and leopards within the Tower of London, of Porter of the Great Wardrobe, of Controller[2] in the counties of Chester and Flint, of Clerk of the Crown of Lancaster and of Escheator[3] in the County Palatine of Lancaster, while rewards from other sources were added to these.

Pre-eminent mental gifts were bestowed upon him by Heaven, with which he was remarkably endowed, as for example, rare piety towards God, widely-ranging beneficence towards the poor, and wonderful charity towards all men. Having lived more than eighty years, he died on the 27th day of December, in the year of our Lord, 1573, leaving issue, Alice, wife of Thomas Powell,[4] Esquire (who has defrayed the cost hereof),

---

[1] The original is in small capitals throughout, and the letter "u" is represented by "v." It is much faded.
[2] I am not quite certain if these various offices are correctly translated, as it is not always easy to identify them.
[3] The Escheator was the official before whom the various inquisitions *post mortem*, &c., were taken.
[4] This was Thomas Powell, of Horsley, near Holt, co. Denbigh, Esq.

, Katherine, married to Thomas Tuchet,[1] Esquire, and Avice, married to Thomas Vawdrey,[2] gentleman, his children by his wife Joan, daughter of John Pike, Esquire.

"By no worldly treasure can heaven be won."

On the wall near this monument is a large shield of arms with helmet, crest and mantling. The arms are Argent a chevron, between three hawks[3] Sable, beaked and belled Or and jessed Gules, on the chevron a mullet Or for difference. Crest on a wreath, a hawk Sable, beaked and belled Or and jessed Gules. This, which must be considered as the coat of Worsley of Chester, differs entirely from the arms of the Worsleys of Lancashire.

There is a memorandum in the earliest volume of the Churchwardens' Accounts, under the year 1603, that with regard to the monument of Ralph Worsley, Esq., in as much as "the said Rauffe in his life tyme had been a good Benefactor to this Parish; that the gravestone in St. Katherine's chappell of this Church, now lyinge uppon the corps of the snyde Rauffe with his Armes thereupon and under his inscription in the wall shall not hereafter be taken up or removed, unlesse yt be for some of the yssues or offspringe of the said Rauffe." This was entered in the book at the request of William Powell, gent., 6th April, 1603. The shield of arms above referred to is now fixed in the wall near the mural inscription, and is shown on the cut on page 59.

A large and handsome mural monument, on the north wall of the north aisle to the memory of the second RANDLE HOLME.[4] This monument, which has been elaborately painted and gilded, is shown in the accompanying illustration. On either side of the inscriptions are skulls and cross-bones, &c., believed to be intended for emblems of Freemasonry. The contracted Latin of the original has been carefully extended.

[5] Hoc monumentum in memoriam ponitur Ranulphi Holme aliquando aldermani et justiciarii pacis hujus civitatis Cestriæ majoris ejusdem anno MDCXLIII. Qui quidem Ranulphus filius et heres fuit Ranulphi Holme, aldermani et justiciarii pacis et majoris anno MDCXXXII ejusdem civitatis Cestriæ prædictæ (qui etiam fuit servus domini nostri Henrici principis filii primogeniti Jacobi Regis piæ memoriæ, ac etiam deputatus fuit pro officio armorum in comitatibus palatinis Cestriæ et Lancastriæ et vi comitatuum Nord Walliæ) per Elizabetham uxorem ejus, filiam Thomæ Alcock de civitate Cestriæ et relictam Thomæ Chaloner, de eadem civitate, quandoque Ulster regis armorum pro Hiberniæ regno. Ille fuit filius et heres Thomæ Holme de Cestriæ civitate prædictæ per Elizabetham uxorem ejus, filiam Johannis Devenett de Kinderton, in comitatu Flynt, generosi. Filius fuit ille Gulielmi Holme, domini medietatis villæ de Tranmore per Margarettam uxorem ejus filiam Ricardi Caldy de civitate Cestriæ prædictæ, [ille fuit][6] filius et heres Gulielmi Holme, qui obiit anno I Henrici VIII.; filius et heres Roberti Holme, qui obiit 14 Edwardi IV.; filius et heres Thomæ Holme qui vixit 24 Henrici VI.; filius et heres Johannis Holme domini mediatatis villæ de Tranmoll, qui obiit 4 Henrici V.; filius et heres Roberti Holme, domini mediatatis villæ de Tranmoll, jure uxoris ejus Matildæ filiæ et unius coheredum Richardi de Tranmoll, domini [de] Tranmoll, filii et heredis Gulielmi de Tranmoll per Matildam filiam et unam coheredum Petri de Lymme, filii Gilberti, domini de Lymme qui vixit tempore Edwardi I.

[1] Thomas Tuchett, of Nether Whitley, co. Chester, Esq.
[2] Thomas Vawdrey, of the Riddings, in Bowdon parish, co. Chester, gentleman.
[3] These birds have been described as choughs, but they are clearly meant for hawks as shown by the drawing of the bells and jesses put on the birds when they were used for hawking.
[4] The inscription to the memory of the first Randle Holme, who died in 1654, painted on a board which was in the church in 1817 is now missing. A copy of it will be found in the account of the inscriptions formerly in the church postea. A full account of the Holme family will be given later on.
[5] The Latinity of this inscription is very bad, being apparently a trans'ation of an English epitaph into most wretched "dog Latin."
[6] Rather than put a number of genitive cases, I have taken the words "ille fuit" or "qui fuit" before each "filius," &c., as understood.

Ipse Ranulphus superdictus tempore vitæ ejus duxit in uxorem Catherinam filiam Matthei Ellis de Overlegh in comitatu civitatis Cestriæ generosi, per quam habuit 3 filios et 5 filias, post cujus mortem duxit in uxorem Elizabetham, filiam et heredem Thomæ Dodd, de civitate Cestriæ, relictam Samuelis Martyn, mercatoris; ille in anno 63 ætatis suæ obiit, die dominica 4 Sept. xi Caroli 2^{di}, annoque Domini cɪɔɪoclix.[1]

Neere to this place lyeth interred the bodyes of Sarai, eldest dau^r of Henry Soley, minister of ye Gospell at Forton in ye county of Salop and late wife to Randle Holme, Sworne Servt & Gentleman of his Maties Chamber in Extraordinary to Kinge Charles ye Second, one of [the coun]cill of ye citty of Chester, and deputy to Garter principall Kinge of arms; she had yssue by him Randle, Elizabeth, Kath. Rachell and Sarai y^t died an infant; she died ye 5th of April, anno 1665, aged 36 yeares; and Katherine, sister of ye s^d Randle and late wife to Benj. Harpur, of London, gent., she died the vii of July an'o 1664, aged 34 yeares; and alsoe William Holme, brother of the said Randle and 2nd son of Randle Holme, alderman, died the xxvi day of Aprill anno D'ni 1666 and ye 35 yeare of his age; and Rafe ye yongest sonne of Randle Holme, alderman, died ye day of   anno 1641, aged 4 yeares.[2]

At the top of this monument is a large shield of arms, as shown in the illustration, 1st and 4th *Holme*, 2 *Tranmoll*, 3 *Lymme*, with the *Holme* crest.[3] On either side are two crests, *Holme* and (?) *Tranmoll*. Lower down, just above the inscription, are two other coats, *Holme* impaling Ermine a lion rampant Azure for *Ellis*, and *Holme* impaling Argent on a fess Gules, between two barrulets wavy Sable, three crescents Or for *Dodd*, referring to the two marriages of Randle Holme the second of those names.

On a mural monument placed on the pier of the arch at the east end of the north aisle is this inscription to the memory of the third and fourth RANDLE HOLME.

> Here lyes the Body of Randle
> Holme, gen^t Sewer in extraordinary
> to K: Charles ye 2^d and deputy to ye Kings
> at arms, who died 12th March 1699:
> And Randle Holme his son, deputy to Norroy
> K: att arms, who died 30th day of aug. 1707
> He married Marg^t, daughter of Griffith Lloyd,
> of Llanarmon in the County of Denbigh, gen^t by
> w^m he had issue Sara, Eliz. Kat. Randle, and Kat. who
> died before their Father, and lye
> here Interred

---

[1] The following is a translation of this inscription:—
This monument is placed to the memory of Randle Holme, formerly alderman and justice of the peace of this city of Chester, mayor of the same in the year 1643. The which Randle was son and heir of Randle Holme, alderman and justice of the peace, and mayor in the year 1633, of this city of Chester aforesaid (who was also servant to our lord Prince Henry, eldest son of King James, of pious memory, and was also a deputy for the office of arms in the counties palatine of Chester and Lancaster and the six counties of North Wales), by Elizabeth, his wife, daughter of Thomas Alcock, of the city of Chester, and the relict of Thomas Chaloner, of the same city, and formerly Ulster king of arms for the kingdom of Ireland. He was the son and heir of Thomas Holme, of the city of Chester aforesaid, by Elizabeth, his wife, daughter of John Devenell, of Kinderton, in the county of Flint, gentleman. He was the son of William Holme, lord of the half of the township of Tranmore, by Margaret, his wife, daughter of Richard Caldy, of the city of Chester aforesaid. [He was] son and heir of Robert Holme, of Tranmore, a?ar Tranmoll, aforesaid, by Jane, the daughter of Thomas Poole, of Poole, esquire, [who was] son and heir of William Holme, who died in the first year of Henry VIII. [1509]: son and heir of Robert Holme, who died 14 Edward IV. [1474]: son and heir of Thomas Holme, who lived 24 Henry VI. [1446]: son and heir of John Holme, lord of the half of the township of Tranmoll, who died 4 Henry V. [1416]: son and heir of Robert Holme, lord of the half of the township of Tranmoll, in right of his wife, Matilda, daughter, and one of the coheirs of Richard de Tranmoll, lord of Tranmoll: son and heir of William de Tranmoll, by Matilda, the daughter and one of the coheirs of Peter de Lymme: son of Gilbert, lord of Lymme, who lived in the time of Edward I. [1272-1307].

This Randle, aforesaid, in his lifetime married Catherine, daughter of Matthew Ellis, of Overlegh, in the county of the city of Chester, gentleman, by whom he had three sons and five daughters, after whose death he married Elizabeth, daughter and heir of Thomas Dodd, of the city of Chester, the relict of Samuel Martyn, merchant: he died in the sixty-third of his age, on Sunday, 4th September, 11 Charles II., in the year of our Lord 1659.

[2] The latter part of this inscription is now very much worn and nearly illegible. The dates have never been filled in.

[3] The coat of Tranmoll or Tranmere is Argent a cross engrailed Gules, over all a bend Azure and that of Lymme is Gules a pale fusilly Argent. The ancestors of Randle Holme married the heiresses of each of these families.

Mr. J. P. Rylands on "arms taken from an Old Booke of Arms A.D. 1568" gives for Lancashire famly of Ellis (9?) [Elliot] Or, on a cross sable five crescents argent. Historic Socty Lanc y thed. new Series Vol. I. p. 105 Cowper or Cowplor of Nottinghamshire Mr Cowper says High Sheriff of that County 10 Eliz( ) bore Azure, a fortice erected gules. Guillim p. 476.

ST. MARY-ON-THE-HILL, CHESTER.

At the top is a shield of arms, *Holme* quartering *Tranmoll* and *Lymme*, with an escutcheon of pretence Tenny (or brown) a chevron Or between three fishes naiant Argent [? *Soley*] and underneath the inscription the same coat with another escutcheon of pretence Sable a chevron Or between three antelopes' heads of the second [*Lloyd* of Llanarmon].

On a wooden tablet, formerly in the Overlegh pew, but now fixed on the north wall of the north aisle.

Here lie Interr'd *Mathew Ellis* of Over-leigh in ye County
of ye City of Chester; one of ye Gentlemen of ye Body Guard to King
Henry 8; Son of Ellis ap Dio ap Griffith Successor to Kenrick Sais A
British Nobleman & lineally Descended from Tudor Trevor Earl of
Hereford. He died 20 Apr. 1574; Alice his Wife, died 1547. His Son
Mathew Ellis, of Over-Leigh, Gent. Died 1575, whose Wife, Eliz.
Daughter of Thomas Browne of Nether-Legh, Gent. died 1570, Having
issue Julian, who was Married to Thomas Cowper of Chester, Esqr
Margery, & Mathew Ellis of Over-Legh, Gent. he died 31 July 1613;
his Wife Alice Daughter to Richd Birkenhead, of Manley, Esqr died
6 July 1640 having issue Katherine, wife to Randle Holme of Chester
Gent: And Mathew Ellis of Over-Legh, Gent. who died 3 Nov. 1663
his Wife Elizabeth Daughter to William Hulton of Baddiley, Gent.
died 4 Nov. 1671, their Son Mathew Ellis, Gent., married Anne Daughter
to John Birkenhead of Backford, Esqr, he died 17 Feb. 1685, She died
4 August 1689.
Beati sunt Mortui Qui in Domino Moriuntur.

For Cowper, see Burke's Landed Gentry Vol. Ip 591. under Hincks

Above this inscription is the coat of arms of *Ellis*, Ermine a lion rampant Azure, between the following crests for *Ellis* and *Cowper*, a female affrontée proper, couped at the waist, habited Gules, crined Or, and a demi-wolf Argent, issuant from a mural crown Gules, and holding in its paws a garb Or.

Underneath the inscription are the arms of *Cowper* with three quarterings and these words:—

William Cowper, of Over-Legh, Esqr, in Respect to these, His
Ancestors and Relations, Caused this Decayed Memorial
to be Restored, Anno Dni, 1739.
He died 12th of October, 1767. Aged 66.

On a small brass plate fixed on the north side of the Chancel arch, this inscription, all in capitals:—
At the top a nicely engraved coat of arms, with shield, helmet, crest, and mantling. The arms are on a fess engrailed between three stags' heads, three hunting horns, a crescent for difference. The crest is an arm erect holding in the hand a tassel.

Here Lyeth the Body
of Rowland Waring gen.
Hee dyed May xiii 1695.

On a flat stone at the east end of the north aisle:—
Underneath
are interred the remains of
SUSANNA
wife of JOHN HILL of this city
She departed this life 30 August 1837
Aged 39 years.

On a small white marble stone formerly on the floor
of the north chapel:—
JOHN HILL Esqr
died April 4th 1849
Aged 75.

Christian monuments by John Hicklin, lecture April 1 1850. Chester Arch¹ Soc. Vol I p 38.
About the middle of the 17ᵗʰ century we come to mural slabs, which dropping the effigy altogether, give only an Eulogium on the person represented; and at the same date we have the introduction of those singularly ugly monuments which re-present the deceased as leaning on his elbow, "as if," says Ford, "they died o' the toothache." One of this description of rather an ambitious character stands in the north aisle of St Marys in Chester.

MONUMENTAL INSCRIPTIONS NOW IN THE CHURCH.   49

On an old brass formerly in the north aisle, all in capitals :—

Here lyeth the body of William Brock[1] of Vpton in the county of Chester esq', who by Anne his wife, daughter and co-heyre to Robert Mohune of Baynton in the county of Dorcet esq' had yssue 4 sonnes and 7 daughters Hee dyed on the 4ᵗʰ day of April 1640 ; & Here also liethe the body of Edward Brock his vnkell who died on the 3ᵈ day of October 1639.

A shield of arms (Gules), on a chief [Argent] a lion passant [of the first and ducally crowned Or] for *Brock*, impaling [Gules] a maunch [Ermine] the hand grasping a fleur-de-lis [Or] within a bordure [Argent] for *Mohun*—the colours not indicated.

On a large slab at the east end of the nave, on the north pillar of the chancel arch :—

Above is the coat of arms of Brock within a lozenge.

To the Memory of
Mʳˢ. SUSANNAH BROCK
who died March yᵉ 20ᵗʰ 1766
She was daughter to WILLIAM BROCK Esq'
of Upton in this County,¹
And the last of that Ancient Family.
This Monument was erected by her Nephew & Nieces
the Son and Daughters of JOHN EGERTON Esq'
of Broxton in this County.

On the edge of a pew now in the south chapel :— ᵃ·

✝In the vault beneath lie the remains of Robert ffoulkes of Boughton-Hall, buried Octʳ 1787 and *(Pedigree p.)* his ancestors; also Susanna his wife 1797 ✝ Susanna his daughter 1825, and Mary the wife of Wᵐ Currie M:Dʳ 1813—whose daughters Elizabeth and Jane erected this seat for the use of the parish A:D: 1850.

On a large mural tablet on the north side of the chancel, within the communion rails, all in capitals :—[2]

To the memory of
WILLIAM CURRIE M.D,
Late of Boughton Hall in this county
third son of William Currie Carlyle Esq'
of Cleughheads and Bridekirk in the county of Dumfries.
Eminently skilled in the theory of medicine
quick in discernment, sound in judgment and kind in manner,
he enjoyed during more than fifty years practice
the confidence of all classes of society.
To those qualities which gave dignity to the man
the Holy Spirit added
the higher graces which become the Christian.
He was humane, benevolent and charitable
Revered by all who were acquainted with him,
and inexpressibly dear to those of his own family.
From the study of the Holy Scriptures
he drew the principles which regulated his life
and the peace which marked its decline.
He was born July 17ᵗʰ 1749 and died Aug. 19ᵗʰ 1834
Aged 85."

The three whose names are here recorded
lived in love and died in faith
Looking to no other ground of hope
but the merits of Christ made theirs through faith.

Below this inscription are three shields of arms as follows :—Three lions passant in pale, crest a demi-lion rampant, grasping in both paws a mullet. A saltire, on an escutcheon of pretence three lions passant in pale. A saltire, a mullet in chief for difference. The crest is broken off, the claws of a bird (? a hawk) only being left.

On a tablet in the north chapel :—
Sacred to the memory of
the Revᵈ WILLIAM CURRIE, M.A.
second son of the late Wᵐ. Currie Esqʳ
of Boughton Hall in this County
who died Febʸ. 12ᵗʰ 1844
Aged 53 years.
Underneath are the arms and crest of Currie.

---

[1] For other inscriptions to the Brock family see the account of the inscriptions formerly in the church, but now lost. See also the account of the Brock family *postea*.
[2] For the remainder of this inscription see next page.

a. *Illustrated in Ches Arch¹ Soc¹ Vol I p. 40. Called the Churchwardens Seat. One bench end has a shield with 3 lions passant in pale and a shield with a saltire, a mullet in chief for difference. The arm of the bench end has an excellently carved lion couchant holding in both paws a mullet(?).*

On a mural tablet on the south side of the south chapel :—

In the Vault beneath lie the Remains of
ANNA MARIA CURRIE,
who died Aug. 30th, 1845, aged 57,
Relict of Lieut-Colonel Edward Currie,
who served with much distinction on the personal Staff
of the late General Lord Hill, G.C.B. throughout the
Peninsula Campaigns and fell on the field of Waterloo

where he was employed as an assistant Adjutant General
in the army under the command of Field Marshal
His Grace the Duke of Wellington, K.G., &c.
This humble tribute to the Memory of their lamented
Parents is inscribed by their surviving Children.
John Robert Currie late Capt[n] 95th Regt., Son of the above
died December the seventh, 1845, aged 38.
Arms, in a lozenge, a chevron Ermine between three lozenges, impaling a saltire, in chief a rose.

On either side of the tablet to William Currie, M.D. (*see* previous page), and forming part of it :

To the memory of
Mary
daughter of
ROB[T] FOULKES, ESQ[R]
of Houghton
and wife of
WILL[M] CURRIE, M.D.
a true Christian
a devoted wife
an exemplary
mother
Born Nov. 5th, 1745
Died Dec. 30th, 1812
aged 67.

To the memory of
Susan
daughter of
WILL[M] CURRIE, M.D.
& MARY his wife
in the midst of
bodily weakness
she lived
the life of faith
and died in peace
Born April 25th, 1775
Died Oct. 9th, 1828
aged 53.

On a tablet at the east end of the north aisle, above the Randle Holme stone monument :—

Near this place lieth the Body of
Ann Evers, who died Jan[y] 21st 1782 Aged 67
Also the Body of James Evers
died May 26th 1790 Aged 85 Years
Also the Body of James Evers Grandson
to the above James and Ann Evers
who died Dec[br] 13th 1795 Aged 3 Years
Also the Body of Ann Evers Grandaughter
to the above died Jan[y] 20th 1802 Aged 11 Years
Also the Body of Tho[s] Baxter Evers Grandson
to the above died Feb[ry] 10th 1802 Aged 5 Years
Also in hope of a Joyful Resurrection the Body
of Ann Evers wife of Peter Evers and Mother
of the above Children who departed this Life
August 29th 1825 Aged 70
Also the Body of Peter Evers, died
March 13th 1831 Aged 73.

On a stone tablet on the north wall of the north aisle :—

In Memory of
THOMAS SHUTTLEWORTH
who died March 10th 1838
Aged 62 years
Also of Ellen Chapman
the beloved wife of Edwin Weigh
and only daughter of the above
who died Feb[y] 18th 1841
Aged 20 years.
Our days on earth are as a shadow.

Also of Sarah
wife of the above
Thomas Shuttleworth
who died Jan[y] 12th 1854
Aged 66 years.

I have a grandfather's clock in oak case, with Peter Evers, Chester, painted on the dial.
JH.

[Handwritten note at top:] The Gloggs of Grange, from whom the Gleggs of Irby and Backford descend, became so poor that the last representative was taken out of Dodds Castle, where he was in the Debtor prison, that he might die out of prison, at the end of the 18th Century. The property passing by purchase into the hands of John Leigh Esq of Liverpool whose descendants held the same in 1888.

MONUMENTAL INSCRIPTIONS NOW IN THE CHURCH. 51

In the north aisle, on the north wall, below a tablet to the Shuttleworth family, on a white marble tablet, in capitals :—

In memoriam
viri reverendi
STEPHANI HENRICI FAWCETT LL.D.
hujusce ecclesiæ olim prælectoris,
qui die Januarii xxvi A.D. MDCCXL.
ætatis suæ xxxiii
vitam efflavit
item CATHERINÆ uxoris ejus
quæ obiit MDCCCXLV
ætat. LXI.

On a stone tablet at the west end of the north aisle :—

Mary Egan
widow died the 25th
of December 1785.

On a small white mural monument in the south chapel, near the window containing stained glass to the memory of the Mawdesley family (*see* p. 22).

In loving remembrance of
Robert Mawdesley
late Captain 51st Regiment
died July 4th 1859.
Mary Ann Mawdesley,
died January 30th 1873.
Frances Elizabeth Mawdesley[1]
died May 22d 1891.

On a small black slab, now loose, in the north chapel, but formerly placed on the outside of the church, near the north porch :—

Sacred
to the Memory of
THOMAS BOOTE
who died in Jamaica
in the West Indies
on the 16th Nov. 1821
aged 27.

On a white marble slab, formerly on the floor of the south aisle, much worn :—

JOHN GLEGG of Irbie Hall in this
County Esq died 6 Feb. 1804 :[2]
Aged 72.
BETTY BASKERVYLE GLEGG
his Wife died 9 July 1810
Aged 77.

On an oval mural tablet high up on the wall of the south aisle :—

In this Chancel lieth
the Body of
ROGER WILBRAHAM
late of Dorfold in the County
of Chester Esqr who Departed
this Life on the 24th day of January
1768 in the 52d Year of his Age.

In the south aisle on the south wall, at the west end, near the south door :—

Near this Place
Lieth the Body
of Lieut JAMES THOMSON
who departed this life
the 13th of May 1786
Aged 73.

On a small white marble tablet on the north side of the chancel arch :—

Sacred to the Memory of
EDWARD NASH Esqr
second Son
of the late RICHARD NASH Esqr
of Walberton in Sussex,
who died at Chester Castle,
on the 28th of November 1808 :
Aged 61 Years.
His Remains are deposited
in the Middle Aisle of this Church

[Handwritten marginal note at right:] John Glegg married in 1762 Betty Baskerville Glegg of Withington and Gayton — Baskers Londergeatry † 1572.

---

[1] I am informed this should be more correctly Frances Elizabeth *Martha* Mawdesley.
[2] In the register his burial is entered on the 11th Feb. 1804, and his age is given as 74. His wife's burial was on the 14th July, 1810, her age 77.

H 2

On the mural tablet fixed on the south pillar of the chancel arch facing the nave at the east end. At the top is a coat of arms and crest.

> To the pious Memory
> of MR. JOHN SNOW
> Alderman of Chester,
> Whose Faith and Piety to God,
> Candour to Men,
> Temperance Patience & Honesty
> Deserve a long Commemoration.
> A generous Benevolence
> And Sweetness of Temper
> Appeared in all his Actions;
> But chiefly in his tender care
> And Affection for his Orphan Sisters.
> They
> Sarah, Isabella & Elizabeth
> Erected this Monument,
> the smallest Expression
> of their Grief and Gratitude.
> He Dy'd Oct 2 1749, Ag'd 43

On a mural tablet fixed on the south pillar of the arch separating the south chapel from the south aisle:

> Quiescunt hic reliquiæ
> IOHAN^S COTGREAVE Civit
> Cestr' Cervisiarij qui
> post vitam pietate
> justitia et caritate
> peractam in pace Obijt
> 1mo die Martij 1724
> Ætatis 80.
> Simul conduntur Cineres Elizabeth
> Conjugis charissimæ, quæ placidam
> Expiravit Animan 27e Nov. 1735.
> Ætat 87.[1]

Above is a shield of arms, Sable a fesse dancetté Ermine, between three hunting-horns stringed Or for *Cotgreave*. Crest, a bird Azure rising out of a ducal crown Or, but now broken off.

On the south wall of the south aisle, a mural tablet:—

> A memorial
> of Gratitude and Affection
> to a Revered Father
> whose remains are interred in a Vault near this
> PETER SNOW Esqr of Lache Hall in this County
> died April 27th 1807 Aged 63.
> Also to a Beloved Husband
> EDWARD SHAKFIELD SIMON SNOW Esqr
> who departed this life at Lache Hall June 27th
> 1843 Aged 54.
> His Christian Patience & Resignation during a
> protracted Illness
> of 14 years gained him the Love of all who knew
> him, particularly that
> of his Wife who erects this in commemoration of
> his kind and benevolent
> Disposition
> Also of MARY wife of the above E. S. S.
> SNOW Esqr
> who died at Bath February 23rd 1866 in her 72nd
> year.
> " If we suffer with Christ we shall also reign
> with Him."

On a tablet on the south side of the chancel, high up on the wall, rather worn:—

> Underneath lie the Remains
> of the Rev^d
> MIDDLETON JONES, LL.B.
> late of Crilharth
> in the County of Brecon,
> formerly Rector of this Parish
> who died
> the 9th November, 1775
> Aged 47.

Above is a shield of arms, of which a chevron Sable can now only be made out.

---

[1] (*Translated.*) Here lie the remains of John Cotgreave, of the city of Chester, brewer, who, after a life of piety, justice, and charity, died in peace 1st March. 1724(-5). aged 80. In the same place are deposited the ashes of Elizabeth, his most beloved wife, who died [literally, breathed out her placid soul] on the 27th November, 1735, aged 87.

SNOW granted to Robert Snow Esq. of Savile Row. Arg. a fesse nebulée erm. betw. three antelopes' heads erased arg. Crest - A mount vert thereon an antelope's head erased per pale nebulée erm and az. Burke

SNOW. Cucksand, Co Bedford, and Surrey, a patent by Thomas Hawley, Clarencieux. Per fesse nebulée az & arg three antelopes' heads erased counterchanged, armed or. Crest - An antelope's head erased, per pale, nebulée arg & az. Burke

SNOW. Hertfordshire, London, Westminster, and Wiltshire. Argent. on a fesse betw two bars nebulée sable a lion passant of the field. Burke.

1814. St Marys Churchyard inclosed with iron railings, November.

[1422] THE SPENCE-COTGREAVE FRAUDS.

About 1848 one William Sidney Spence, writing from Priory Place, Birkenhead—which, however, was not his residence—sent a number of letters of the same general tenour to persons who might, he thought, like to have their pedigrees enlarged. One of these is printed in "Notes and Queries" of 11 March, 1854 (1st Series, ix., 221), by which time the writer was dead. It began:—

"Having been engaged by Miss Cotgreave of Netherlegh House, near Chester, to inspect and arrange the title deeds and other documents which belonged to her father the late Sir John Cotgreave, I find a very ancient pedigree of the Cotgreaves de Hargrave in that county, which family became extinct in the direct male line in the year 1724, but which was represented through females by the above Sir J. C. It is the work of the great Camden, anno. 1598, from documents in the possession of the Cotgreave family, and contains the descents of five generations of"—the family of the person to whom the letter was addressed.

The letter then went on to offer extracts, on condition of remuneration, adding: "Miss Cotgreave will allow me to make the extracts and has kindly consented to attest the same."

A specimen of the pedigrees he returned to clients, attested by Miss Cotgreave, has been published in the present series of the "Sheaf."

Other writers in "Notes and Queries" (ix., 275; x., 255) added their experiences; the formulas varied a little from time to time, but several descents and quarterings were always offered.

The matter came up again in the same periodical in 1860 (2nd Series, ix. 61, &c., x. 106), when some further particulars were given; also in 1862 (3rd Ser. i. 8, &c.).

The following statement was made by S. T.:—
"The late Sir John Cotgreave (formerly a Mr. Johnson, who assumed his more aristocratic surname by virtue of being descended from the family) was knighted as Mayor of Chester in 1816, 'on the marriage of the Princess Charlotte.' He married twice: by his first wife (Miss Cross) he had no issue, but by his second, a dressmaker, Miss Harriett Spence, he had children both before and after marriage. Sir John died 1836; his widow survived till 1848. William Sidney Spence was her brother. I have not discovered, nor is it material, whether Lady Cotgreave connived at or derived benefit by the forgeries of her brother, or attested them as he asserted; it is clear, however, that his pedigrees before 1848 (when she died) are verified by the signature of 'Harriet' Cotgreave, and those subsequently by 'Ellen' Cotgreave, the Miss C. whose attestation be offered in all cases after his sister's death."

Spence seems to have died about 1852.

J. B.

MONUMENTAL INSCRIPTIONS NOW IN THE CHURCH. 53

At the west end of the north aisle, on a tablet let into the wall, near the font, in capitals :—
Sacred to the memory of
WILLIAM NEWELL Alderman of this city
died 2nd April 1831 aged 64
Sarah wife of the above
died 17th June 1833 aged 64
And of their children.
John, died 25th April 1797 aged 2
Mira, died 27 June 1807 aged 9
Mary, died 24th March 1823 aged 22
Harriett, died 10th April 1824 aged 21
Frances, died 19th June 1833 aged 25
Sarah, died 21st Feb. 1840 aged 44
William, died 25th April 1848 aged 43
Ann, died 26th August 1866 aged 71
Margaret, widow of John Hassall
died 31st December 1870 aged 71
and of
Emma, died 30th Dec'r 1886 aged 76.

On a mural tablet at the west end of the south aisle :—
Underneath
lie the remains of Sarah wife of
Edward Moss (of this City Miller)
who died Aug'st 29th 1823 aged 40 years
also Thomas, son of the above
Edward Moss, who died June 19th 1825
aged 2 weeks
Also Thomas, son of the above
Edward Moss who died Dec'br 9th 1834
aged 3 weeks
Also Sarah, daughter of the above
Edward Moss who died Dec'br 23rd 1835
aged 9 weeks
Also William son of the above
Edward Moss, who died March 24th 1837
aged 29 years
Also Sarah 2nd wife of the above
Edward Moss, who died March 13th 1838
aged 37 years
Also in this church yard lie the
Remains of the above Edward Moss
who died April 5th 1848 aged 67 years.

On a mural monument of white marble at the west end of the south aisle, the inscription in old English black letter :—
In Loving Memory of
HARRY RANDLE KNOWLES FORD
2nd Lieut. 16th foot, Bedfordshire Reg't
who died of fever
at Rawal Pindi, India,
June 3rd 1891. Aged 21 years.
Eldest son of
Lieut. Col. John Ford, R.A.
and grandson of the late
Rev. F. Ford, Rector of St. Peter's.
[Phil. 1c. 3v.]
Erected by his sorrowing relations.

Arms and Crest of Ford, party per fesse Argent and Ermine a lion rampant. Crest, a lion's head erased.

In the Troutbeck or south chapel, high up on the wall, on a mural tablet :—
Sacred to the Memory of
WATKIN THELWALL Esq'r late Major
in the Bengal Artillery in the East Indies
and second Son of the late
DAVID THELWALL Esq'r of Blanc Vale
in the County of Denbigh who departed
this Life 6th October 1814
in his 76th Year.
He was a truly just Man Sincere in his Friendship Kind and Benevolent to the Poor much Esteemed while Living and in Death ever to be Lamented by his Surviving Widow who Caused this Monument to be Erected.
In the same Vault are deposited the Remains of
ELIZABETH wife of the above named
WATKIN THELWALL. She died 26th August
1816 in the 71st Year of her Age.

On a flat tombstone formerly near the altar steps :—
Hugh Whishaw died 24th of January
1749.
Hugh Whishaw¹ died 4th of January
1780.

¹ For an earlier inscription relating to this family see account of the inscriptions formerly in this church, but now lost.

In the Troutbeck Chapel, painted on a board:
Above is a shield of arms, paly of nine Sable and Or on a bend Azure, three garbs Or; crest a lion statant, for *Duke* and the motto *Christo Duce et Auspice Christo.*

Near to this Pillar, are deposited
the Remains of THOMAS DUKE Esq :
the Senior Alderman and Justice
of the Peace of this City. and
Mayor thereof A.D. 1740.
Just and Upright,
Meek and Charitable,
He lived esteemed
And died lamented,
on the 27th day of November 1764
Aged 76.

On a mural tablet in the south chapel, placed very high :

Sacred to the Memory of MARY EYTON Youngest
Daughter
of CHARLES EYTON of PENTRE MADDOCK in the
County
of Salop Esq' by Mary his Wife who died the 16th
of May 1764
Also MARY his Wife who died the 16th of January
1766
Also MARY THOMAS only Daughter of Capt.
WILLIAM THOMAS
of this City by JANE his Wife Eldest Daughter of
Charles Eyton
who died the 21st December 1766, aged 3 Years and
Eleven Months
Also Capt. WILLIAM THOMAS who died the 28th
October 1769.
This Monument is placed here as a small
Testimony of the
Affection of Mrs JANE THOMAS the only Surviving
Daughter
of CHARLES EYTON Esq' being the last of that
Ancient Family.
Also the above nam'd Mrs JANE THOMAS who died
the 15th of April 1795 Aged 72 Years.
HESTER PULFORD Cousin of the above JANE
THOMAS
Died March 23rd 1803 Aged 82 Years.

Below this inscription is a shield of arms.

A mural tablet on the south wall of the south aisle :—

Sacred
to the Memory of
ROBERT TOPHAM
of this City
whose valuable life was closed
on the 9th December 1834
in the 32nd year of his age.

On a mural tablet on the south wall of the south aisle :—

Underneath
is deposited all that was mortal of
ELIZABETH
the exemplary wife of JOHN WALKER
of this city ASSAY MASTER
She died VI of June MDCCCXXIV
aged XXXVII years
She excelled in all the relative duties of life and
never pained her friends until she died.
Two of her infant children sleep in the same vault.

On a white slab now in the Tower. Above the inscription was the coat of arms of *Cotton*, now gone.
To the Memory of
PETER COTTON late of this City, Gent[1]
Descended from the ancient Family
of Cotton of Cotton in Cheshire
Who happily completed a single sober
& Religious Life,
with eminent Charity
Giving by his Will

	£
For buying of Medicines for the Poor of this City	100
For buying of pious Books for their use	50
To the Blue-coat School in this City	200
To ye School of Witton £50 & to ye Minister there £50	100
To the Poor of Northwich & Witton	50
To the Poor of the Parish of St. Mary £20 & to the Poor of each of the other eight Parishes in this City £10	100

He died Febr. 16 Anno Dom 1715-6 Æt 42.

---

[1] His burial is thus entered in the Register: "Peter Cotton, an Attorney, Gent., Dyed att Mr. Tho. Kirkes house in Castell Lane & Buryed ye 19th Day of Febry. 1715-16."

On a small mural tablet, now placed in the Tower :—
Near
this Place lies Interred
in the hopes of a Glorious Immortality
the mortal part of
Mʀ WILLIAM DAWSON
late of the City of Chester Silk Mercer
who departed this Life
January 16ᵗʰ 1807
Aged 54 Years.

On a small stone, now in the Tower :—
Vnderneath Lyeth yᵉ Bo-
dy of Sarah Davghter
to Ralph Pickmore of
yᵉ City Buchʳ was Bur
Aprill yᵉ 3ʳᵈ 1712.

On a mural monument now in the Tower :—
Near this rest
(in faithfull expectation of the Triumphant call)
the Remains of
RICHARD son of PETER DEWSBURY,
Alderman
who died 18ᵗʰ of August 1756
Aged 19
of LETICIA his Daughter Wife of JOHN DENNIS
who died 13ᵗʰ of January 1768
Aged 37
of the said PETER DEWSBURY
who died 19ᵗʰ of February 1773
Aged 72
of LETICIA his Widow
who died 29ᵗʰ of December 1783
Aged 80.
and of JOHN DEWSBURY DENNIS their grandson
who died 9ᵗʰ of July 1786
Aged 21
RUTH the last of the Family
died 7ᵗʰ of Octʳ 1787 Aged 59.
The memory of the Just is blessed.

On a small oval monument now in the Tower :
Underneath
lie the remains of
Colin Robinson
who died March 16ᵗʰ 1809.

On another oval monument in the Tower :
Near
this place lie the remains
of ISAAC HUNTINGTON
who died April 7ᵗʰ 1793
Aged 80 Years
Also ANN LEACH Daughter
of the above died January
9ᵗʰ 1822. Aged 69.

On a white stone monument also in the Tower :—
Underneath
lie the remains of
THOMAS JONES
Broker, late of this City,
who departed this life
July 11ᵗʰ 1798 Aged 51
Also the remains of
MARY wife of the above
THOMAS JONES
who departed this life
Octʳ 2ⁿᵈ 1808 Aged 62.

On a small white tablet in the Tower, in capitals :—
In Memory of
CHARLES FARQUHAR
Died April 16ᵗʰ, 1875, Aged 34 years
JAMES HARGREAVES
Died March 20ᵗʰ 1875
Aged 16 years and 3 months
of the Band 1ˢᵗ Battⁿ 19ᵗʰ Regiment
Erected as a token of Respect
by the men of the Band
1875.

He is called a "Sergeant of Invalids" at his wife's burial in 1777.

MONUMENTS RECENTLY MOVED TO ST. MARY'S FROM ST. BRIDGET'S.

When St. Mary's became the parish church of the united parishes of St. Bridget's and St. Martin's, as already described, St. Bridget's church was pulled down, and all the mural monuments which it contained were transferred to St. Mary's. These have all been placed in the south chapel, and the letters S.B. have been cut on each of them, so as to show whence they came. A small white marble tablet bearing the following notice has also been placed near them :—

The Monuments marked S.B. were brought here from S. Bridgets church. A faculty to pull down that church and make this the parish church, was decreed June 11th 1891.

On a white marble mural monument :—
Sacred
to the memory of
ELIZA MARIA
the beloved wife of
the REV^D. WILLIAM GIBSON
rector of this parish,[1]
and daughter of
the right reverend J. B. Sumner, D.D.
Lord Bishop of this diocese.
She died in the island of Madeira
on the 29th May 1836
in the 29th year of her age.

. . . .

A white mural monument having an alabaster urn set in a black recess. This inscription underneath :

MARY NELSON
died Jany xxiv. MDCCXCV.
Her husband the Revd Wm Nelson
erected this monument
as a tribute of respect
to her memory.

Underneath this another inscription, but on the same monument :

This tablet is placed
as a tribute of respect to the memory
of
the REV^D WILLIAM NELSON
(late rector of this parish¹) who died
xxi^d September MDCCCX
by his nephew & niece Nelson & Jane Batty.

On a white mural monument :
Near this Monument
lie entombed the Remains of
RICHARD BARKER of Llindir
in the County of Denbigh Esqr
(formerly of this Parish¹)
who died 21st October 1818
Aged 72.
Also of MARY his Wife
who died 20th March 1839
Aged 87.

On a white mural tablet :—
In memory of
PHILIP HUMBERSTON of this City Esquire
who died the 20th of July 1844
Aged 73 Years.
And of his Children CATHERINE MARIA
and MARY who died Infants.
HESTER. who died the 26th of December 1826
Aged 20 Years.
SOPHIA, wife of W. ECCLES of Davenham
Esquire, who died the 28th of May 1839
Aged 30 Years.
FRANCES, widow of the Revd ROBERT YARKER
Vicar of Neston, who died the 4th of January 1855,
Aged 54 Years.
CATHERINE, wife of the REV^D GEORGE PEARSON,
Rector of Castle Camps, who died the 15th of June 1859,
Aged 56 Years.
Also CATHERINA MARIA, widow of
PHILIP HUMBERSTON Esquire
who died the 23rd of August 1859
Aged 82 Years.
Above is a shield of arms— *Humberston* impaling *Cotton*, and the crest of *Humberston*.

---

[1] That is of course the parish of St. Bridget.

On a large white mural monument:—
Near this place
lie interred the remains of
FRANCIS EDGE BARKER of this city Esqr
who departed this life
June 10th 1827
aged 48.
and of HARRIETTE his wife
who departed this life
Feb^r 17th 1846
aged 65.
Also of RICHARD BARKER Esqr of this city,
eldest son of the above,
who died on the 20th of Decr 1877
aged 69.
And of SARAH his wife
who died on the 12th of Novr 1881 aged 69.
Also of
MARIA GLYNNE BARKER,
youngest daughter of the above
Francis Edge and Harriette Barker,
who died on the 9th of July 1887
aged 67.

On a white mural tablet:—
Near this rest the Remains of
PRISCILLA LAWRENSON,
who died the 29th of March 1784
aged 82 Years.
Also the Remains of
LAWRENCE LAWRENSON;
Son of the said Priscilla Lawrenson
who died the 30th of August 1788
aged 46 Years.
He was an Affectionate Husband, a tender Parent,
A sincere Friend, and an Honest Man.
Also MARY Relict of the above
LAWRENCE LAWRENSON;
who departed this Life February 13th 1837
aged 70 Years.
MARTHA LAWRENSON, Daughter of the
above Lawrence, died 6 Jany 1848.

On a white mural monument:—
Sacred to the memory of
THOMAS SHAW, of this city, who died June 20th
1789, aged 50 years,

Also ELIZABETH, wife of the above THOMAS SHAW,
died August 1st 1808,
aged 56 years.
Also of THOMAS, son of the above THOMAS &
ELIZABETH SHAW
died February 22^d 1802, aged 28 years.
and JOHN MELLOR, of this city, died October 27th
1821, aged 52 years.
and of JOHN, son of the above JOHN MELLOR,
died February 28th 1827
aged 31 years.
Also of THOMAS SHAW MELLOR, son of the first
named JOHN MELLOR
died July 26th 1829, aged 34 years.
Likewise of JUSTINA wife of the
first named JOHN MELLOR
died Novr 22nd 1834, aged 65 years.

On a large white mural monument:—
In the church yard near this place
lie the remains of
Owen Foulkes of this city esquire
who departed this life the xix July MDCCCXLV
aged LXXVI years.
Also of Betty his wife
who departed this life the xiv May MDCCCLII
aged LXVII years.
Above the inscription is a small coat of arms—
Gules three boars' heads in pale, couped Argent,
langued Azure, impaling party per chevron Argent
and Or three pheons Sable. Crest, a two-headed
eagle displayed Or.

A white mural monument with a black border:—
ELIZ. JORDAN
died Octr 28th 1782.
JAMES JORDAN
Father of the above
died Decr 31st 1817
Aged 78
Also ABIGAIL JORDAN
wife of the above
JAMES JORDAN
who died April 19th 1823
Aged 79 Years.

On a white mural monument :—

To the memory
of their lamented mother
Mary, during 1. years the wife of
GEORGE HASTINGS
who, after severe and protracted suffering
was taken peacefully and gently to her
heavenly home on the iii December MDCCCXLI
in the LXXVII year of her age.
This tablet
is erected by her grateful and afflicted
son and daughter
who, while they mourn their irreparable loss
find comfort in the thought of her unspeakable gain.
Also the above GEORGE HASTINGS, who died
Decr xxi MDCCCXLVII in the xc year of his age.

On a modern brass plate. —

Erected
by their parents in Memory of
Elizabeth Annie :
daughter of Peter Thomas and Barbara Kelly
who died 22nd Oct : 1868 : aged 3 years :
on board H.M. Ship Malabar :
entering the straits between Aboo Eyle and Jibbel
Zoogur
and of
Catherine Sarah :
who died 8th May : 1864 : aged 5 days
at Jubbulpore.

The following inscription on the modern stone FONT, with marble columns, removed from St. Bridget's and placed under the tower arch may here be given :—

In memory of W. P. HUTTON late rector
of this Parish,[1] who died Aug. 1, 1855, and of Ellen
his wife, who died Feb. 8, 1864.

INSCRIPTIONS IN THE CHURCHYARD.

The old churchyard at St. Mary's is full of graves, and it is difficult to make any selection of inscriptions of sufficient public interest to warrant their being printed here.[2] The following, however, may be given[3] :—

At the west end of the churchyard, on a flat tombstone :—

Sacred
to the Memory of
WILLIAM THREADGOLD
of Bullsbury Mill Essex
Aged 75 Years (of the Foster
Family Margaret Rooding
Hall) & one of the oldest free
Burgesses of Maldon, who
departed this Life Septr 1st
1826.

On a flat tombstone at the south-west corner near the Tower :—

Sacred
to the Memory of
ALICIA O'BRIEN
widow of Christopher James
O'Brien late Lieu^t-Colonel
of the Clare Militia
who departed this life
October 13th 1842 Aged 71.

---

[1] That is St. Bridget's parish.

[2] As might be expected a great many of the tombstones relate to the non-commissioned officers and men of the various regiments who died whilst stationed at the adjacent Castle.

[3] Many of the tombstones now placed in the churchyard, near the church, are plain as if they had been turned over and the inscriptions put face downwards. These may possibly have been turned out of the church at the various restorations.

INSCRIPTIONS IN THE CHURCHYARD.

On a flat tombstone on the north side:

Underneath
lieth the Remains of
WILLIAM OWENS who served
his King and Country Faithfully
as a Non-commissioned Officer
16 Years in the Royal Welch
Fusiliers who departed this
life Nov'r the 11th 1834
Aged 47 Years.

Here lies a true Soldier whom all must applaud,
Many hardships he suffered at home & abroad,
But the hardest Engagement he ever was in
Was the Battle of self in Conquest of Sin.

On the south side of the churchyard is a SUN-DIAL, put on the top of a pillar, which has the appearance of being the cut-down shaft of an old stone cross, the base of which is well preserved. It does not bear any motto but has the names of Samuel Price, Randle Sorton Churchwardens, and the date 1739 with the maker's name S. Davies (?) Fecit.

COAT OF ARMS OF RALPH WORSLEY, ESQ., 1573.
See page 46.)

QUERIES.
[119] THE SUNDIAL IN ST. MARY'S CHURCH-
YARD, CHESTER.
I have been looking at the sundial on the south side of old St. Mary's Church. I read on the dial plate :—
SAMUEL PRICE,
RANDLE SORTON,
CHURCH WARDENS.
1739.
P. DANIEL, FECIT.

The shaft is of white sandstone, square at the base, tapering, the angles chamfered, forming an octagon in section. It has been at one time painted. The base is red sandstone, and octagonal; the upper surface much worn, so much so as to expose an inch or more of the lead in which the shaft is bedded. Now the shaft and base are evidently older than the 18th century work of the dial plate; in fact they are Perpendicular in character, and in harmony with much of the stone work of the church, so much so that I have come to the conclusion that it is the decapitated churchyard cross, subsequently utilised for a sundial. Of this we have many examples. In Owen's "Stone Crosses of the Vale of Clwyd," two instances are given of the cut-down church-yard cross doing duty as a stand for a sundial. They occur at Llanarmon-in-Yale and Llaune-fydd churchyards.

Was the engraver, P. DANIEL, a local man?
Chester.   GEORGE W. SHRUBSOLE.
In the Churchwardens' Accounts for St. Mary's parish, from the 31st May, 1739, to the 7th May, 1740, the only entry about the above sundial is as follows:—
March ye 27th, 1740' Pd Samll
Davis for wrighting 'sic' ye Altar
Peice and Dial in Ch:yard 10 0 8
P. Daniel's name is not mentioned in the accounts. ED.

ST. MARY-ON-THE-HILL, CHESTER.

MONUMENTAL INSCRIPTIONS AND TABLETS FORMERLY IN THE CHURCH.

The importance of St. Mary's Church in days gone by is shown by the number of persons occupying good positions in the city who either lived in the parish or selected that church as their place of burial. As will appear from the following pages, St. Mary's formerly possessed a large number of monumental and other inscriptions, put up to those who were there interred, *not one of which is now in existence!* Thanks, however, to the painstaking care of many Chester antiquaries, I am enabled to give copies of the inscriptions here, and so to hand down to posterity much information relating to family and personal history, derived from these now lost inscriptions, few of which have been printed before. It is not difficult to account for the loss of these memorials, for as the stones became worn and more or less damaged and illegible they would be removed from the church to make room for newer ones, whilst at the same time many of the inscriptions would appear to have been painted on wooden tablets,[1] which would decay more easily even than those of stone.

The chief sources whence the following inscriptions have been derived will be found in the notes attached to each, but it may here be mentioned that I have arranged them as far as possible chronologically; those relating to any one family however being kept together, whilst the contracted Latin, generally very badly copied, has been extended and careful translations appended.

The earliest tombstone of which we have any record is the one placed to the memory of ADAM BIRKENHEAD, who held various important offices in Chester, &c., in the early part of the 16th century. He died in 1516. Randle Holme describes it as "a gravestone inlayed with brasse" in the south aisle, "and having these armes and writting,"[2] the Latin having been extended:—

Hic jacet Adam Birkenhead generosus et Alicia uxor ejus, qui quidem Adam dum vixit fuit Protonotarius et Clericus Coronæ domini Regis in comitatus Cestriæ et Flint et Clericus Coronæ domini Regis apud Lancaster et Receptor Thomæ comitis Derby dominiorum suorum de Hawarden et Mould in Marchias Walliæ,[3] qui obiit nono die mensis Augusti anno domini MDXVI. Quorum animabus propicietur deus.

(*Translated*) Here lies Adam Birkenhead, gentleman, and Alice his wife,[4] the which Adam in his life time was Prothonotary and Clerk of the Crown of the lord the King in the counties of Chester and Flint and Clerk of the Crown of the lord the King at Lancaster, and receiver of Thomas, Earl of Derby, for his lordships of Hawarden and Mold in the Marches of Wales, who died the 19th day of August, in the year of our Lord 1516. On whose souls may God be merciful.

In the margin of this MS. (*Harl. MSS.* 2151) is a sketch of this "gravestone," showing a large tombstone with shields of arms at the four corners, and a space in the lower portion of the stone for the above inscription arranged in four or five lines. It is strange, however, that there is no indication in this sketch of the inlaid figures in brass of Adam Birkenhead and his wife which would undoubtedly be placed there, and which are described in the *Vale Royall* as " his and his

---

[1] One or two of these painted wooden tablets are still preserved at St. Mary's, the inscriptions on which have already been given in the account of the monumental inscriptions, &c., now preserved in the church. More painted wooden tablets, mostly the work of the Randle Holmes, are preserved in St. John's Church, Chester.

[2] *Harleian MSS.* 2151. The inscription is also printed in King's *Vale Royall*, p. 47, in the account of Chester written by Webb about 1621.

[3] In the *Vale Royall* this appears as " domorum suarum de Hawraldyn et in Vmmersh." It is difficult to account for this discrepancy.

[4] This Adam Birkenhead married Alice, the daughter and coheir of John Huxley, of Huxley, co. Chester, gentleman.

MONUMENTAL INSCRIPTIONS FORMERLY IN THE CHURCH. 61

wife's Pictures well cut in brass." The shields at the four corners appear to be (1) *Birkenhead*, three garbs within a bordure; (2) three hunting horns impaling six fleurs-de-lis, 3, 2, and 1 ; (3) a quarterly coat not filled in ; and (4) *Birkenhead*. No colours are given. This large tombstone is most probably the one referred to later on as "the stone," or "the marble stone," in the south aisle. Nothing is now known of it.

A few years since I met with, in private hands, the original grant of a burial-place in the chancel of St. Mary's, granted by the Abbot and Convent of St. Werburgh to a certain John Birkenhead, gentleman, which is interesting enough to print here, in a translated form, as follows[1] :—

GRANT OF A BURIAL-PLACE IN THE CHANCEL OF ST. MARY'S IN 1525.

To all the faithful in Christ, who shall see this our present writing, THOMAS, by divine permission, ABBOT OF THE MONASTERY OF ST. WERBURGH AT CHESTER, and the Convent of the same place, patrons of the parish church of the Blessed Mary the Virgin upon the Hill in the city of Chester, (sends) greeting in our Lord everlasting. Know ye that we, the said Abbot and Convent, with unanimous consent, have granted and conceded to our beloved *John Birkenhead*, gentleman, three yards of land in length and two yards of land in breadth, lying in the Chancel *(in cancellaro)* of the said parish church, where Joan, late the wife of the said John Birkenhead, is interred and now lies. To have and to hold the said land to the said John, his heirs and assigns, for ever. And we, the said Abbot and Convent, appoint our beloved Hugh Peck, our lawful attorney, to deliver seisin of the said land to the said John, in our name, to hold to him and his heirs. In testimony of which we have placed our common seal to this our present writing.

Given in our Chapter House, the 11th day of May, in the 17th year of King Henry the Eighth [1525].

A large portion of the large and beautiful seal of the Abbey of St. Werburgh is still attached to this deed.

There was also "on an old escutcheon [or painted wooden tablet] in the south aisle" this inscription :—

[2] Under the stone in the South Isle lyeth burryed the bodyes of Adam Birkenhead gent and Alice his wife, daughter and co-heire of John Huxley of Huxley, the said Adam dyed the nineteenth of August 1516.

A shield of arms : Sable three garbs Or [? Argent] within a bordure* Argent [*Birkenhead*] impaling Ermine on a bend cotised Gules, three crescents Or [*Huxley*].

"On the wall by Troutbecks Chapell" was this inscription painted on a board :[3]

Under the marble stone in the South Ile lyeth buried the Body of Tho : Birkenhead of Chester gen., 2d son to Henry Birkenhead of Backford Esq'r, who died 12 of November 1644.[4] And Alice his wife, daughter and heire to Tho: Roberts of Chester gen., who died 1 January 1691.[5] They had issue Thomas Birkenhead, who died 5 January 1685, and Elizabeth, who died 21 December 1694,[6] and Henry, died young.

Above the inscription a shield of arms of four quarterings for *Birkenhead*. 1 & 4. Sable three garbs

---

[1] I have also printed this translation in the *Chester Archæological and Historic Society's Journal*, vol. iii., 1890, p. 221.

[2] *Additional MSS.* No. 29781 (British Museum) and *Stowe MS.* 648, a very valuable manuscript recently purchased by the British Museum. This latter manuscript was apparently written by Francis Bassano, a well-known Chester herald, who succeeded the last Randle Holme and died at Chester in 1747. It has his name and that of Mr. Orme, another herald who succeeded him at Chester, on the fly-leaf. On page 4 begins the series of "Monumental Inscriptions in the Parish Church of St. Mary's Chester," which it is clear from internal evidence was collected after 1721 and before 1735, as a Brock inscription put up in that year is not noticed.

[3] This inscription is taken from *Harl. MS.* 2151, *Stowe MS.* 648, and *Add. MS.* 29781 ; the slight variations which occur being corrected from the Registers, &c.

[4] "Thomas Birkenhead gent buried in the south Ile vndr the marble stone 14th day of Novembr 1644. (Register of St. Mary's).

[5] "Mrs Alice Birkinhead widow was bur'd the 4th day of January" 1691-2. (*Ibid.*)

[6] "Mrs Elizabeth Birkinhead was buryed ye 22 day of Decembr" 1694. (*Ibid.*)

William Brereton of Brereton Inv. 1601.
Sir Randal Manwaring of Over Peover, knight Will proved 1612
Cecelia Manwaring of Chester, widow Will proved 1617
Henry Manwaring of Chester Will proved 1610

ST. MARY-ON-THE-HILL, CHESTER.

Or [? Argent] within a bordure Argent [*Birkenhead*]. 2. Ermine on a bend cotised Gules, three crescents Or [*Huxley*]. 3. Or a cinquefoil [? a rose] Gules within an orle of six trefoils Vert [*Thorncliffe*?]. On an escutcheon of pretence Azure a chevron between three dolphins nowed Argent [*Roberts*]. *see page 67.*

In the *Vale Royall* two inscriptions of early date are given as existing in 1621, one of which does not occur elsewhere. The earliest of these was in the Troutbeck Chapel : " near unto the same Tomb that stands over the Vault, lyeth the body of a late Gentlewoman of that progenie [*i.e.*, of the Troutbecks] with this remembrance in a brasse plate upon her stone :

Here lyeth Eglanbie, Daughter to William Troutbeck, and late wife to Rich. Leigh of Chester, who dyed the 11th of March, Anno Dom. 1596."

The other was in the north chapel ; " on the corner of the same Chappel, opposite to the former [*i.e.*, the Oldfield tomb] is fastened the Arms and Crest of a late godly disposed Lady, having been Wife to an Esquire, and a Knight, both of great place and Revenue ; as by the memorial in a fair Table of her Arms, appeares, thus :

K. Domina Mainwaring filia R. Hurle[s]ton de Civitate Cestr. Arm. nupta Will. Brereton de Hanford Ar, et postea Ro. [*sic* for Ra.] Mainwaring de Peever. Equiti Obiit ii April 1518 [*sic* for 1618]."[1]

" This Lady in her life-time was a good benefactor to the City, and repaired some part of the Wall where it was ruinous, and at her decease, gave many charitable gifts, which I willingly would for example have mentioned in this place ; but having no perfect Instructions let this [notice] suffice."

The following may also be quoted here.[2] " At the upper end of this Chappell [*i.e.*, Troutbeck's chapel] lyeth the body of a late famous Citizen *Robert Brerewood*, Alderman, and thrice Maior of this *City*, of whom I find no other *Monument* there, save onely his coat, Crest and streamer advanced over him ; the words whereof are *Labore, prudentia, equitate*, which were well fitted to him, in whom those vertues were all eminent."[3] A rough sketch of the coat of arms, &c., of this Robert Brerewood, who died on the 29th May and was buried in St. Mary's on the 2 June 1601[4] is given by Randle Holme in *Harleian MS.* 2151, where he writes "at the higher end of the Chappell in the wall next to the chancell hangs the penon, coat and crest of Robt. Brerewood 3 tymes maior of Chester."[5] *See page 1 for Coat of arms and Crest*

These inscriptions follow next in chronological order :—

M. Young obiit 13 die Octobris 1620.[6]

A shield of arms : Ermine a goat's head Sable, armed Or for *Young*.

E. Leigh obiit 14 die Martii 1620 [1620-1].[9]

A quartered shield of arms : (1) and (4) Or a lion rampant Gules [*Leigh*, of the West Hall, High Leigh] (2) Gules a pale lozengé Argent [*Lymm*]. (3) Gules a chevron between three lozenges Argent [*Sale*].

---

[1] (*Translated.*) K[atherine] lady Mainwaring daughter of R[oger] Hurleston of the city of Chester Esq. married William Brereton of Hanford (Handforth) Esq. and afterwards Randle Mainwaring of Peover, Knight. She died on the 2nd April 1618. Her Funeral Certificate has been printed by the Record Society, vol. vj., *Cheshire Funeral Certificates*, p. 140. It begins as follows:—" Dame Kathren Lady Manwaring dyed on the seacond daye of Aprill an° 1618 and lyeth interred in St Mareys Church within the City of Chester." This inscription is also given in the *Stowe MS.* 648, where the arms are given thus, *Hurlton* [or *Hurleston*]. (1) Argent a cross of four Ermine spots Sable, (2) Argent, two bends engrailed Sable, (3) Argent a chevron between three stonebows Sable, (4) as (1).   [2] King's *Vale Royall*, p. 43.   (2) *Wogstaff*   (3) *Mualeton*

[3] He then goes on to state that the best monument he has is the reputation of his learned son Edward Brerewood of Oxford and Gresham College in London, then recently deceased. A further account of the Brerewood family will be given later on in this book.   [4] Funeral Certificate (Record Society, vol. vj., *Cheshire Funeral Certificates*, p. 39).

[5] The drawing given by Randle Holme may be thus described. On a tabard and on the sleeves thereof, Ermine, two pallets vairy Or and Azure; on a chief of the last a bezant between two garbs gold for *Brerewood*. Above the tabard and resting upon it is an esquire's helm with a short plain tasselled mantling, thereon the crest, viz., On a wreath two swords in saltire Gules, pomels Or, entiled with a ducal coronet of the last.   These two inscriptions are from the *Stowe MS.* 648

William Brereton of Honford, Esq.

For Sir W.m Brereton and Handforth family see Cheshire Biographies by T. W. Barlow, published 1850.

Handforth Hall. Inscription. Sir Thomas Brereton Bart Inscription on Tomb in Handforth Chapel.

The following Certificate of William Brereton Esq.r 1601, who was grandfather of the Parliamentary General of that name, is signed by the deceased's wife.

William Brereton of Honforde, Esquier, died the fifte daye of June a: d'ni 1601. He maried Katheryne daughter of Roger Hurleston of Chester, gent., and had yssue 3 sons and two daughters, viz: Brian, first sonne, died younge; Rich.d 3 sonne, died yonge; Jane, eldest daughter, died younge.

Will'm Brereton sonne and heir maried Margaret, daughter of Richard Holland of Denton in the county of Lancaster Esquier.

Dorothie Brereton onely daughter now lyvinge.

He bore Argent 2 barres sable; a crescent difference (Brereton) quartered with Argent, a chevron wit' three crescents gules (Ipstones); upon the quarteringe a cross fleurete gu. bezante [or rather charged with five bezants]. (_____). The three (2) coates sa., a starre ar. (Honford of Handforth).

The fourth (3) Gules. a sythe and sheath Or.
(Praers). The last quartered coat as the first.
His creast on a Chapeau az: turned
up Ermyne a Dragon gu: breast creast,
and inside the winges Or.

Sr Wm Brereton (signature)

"This Crest being the ancient Crest of Wm Hanford, whose sole heire
was married to Sr William Brereton, is allowed to Randoll Brereton of
Hanford to Beare and use by me R. Glow: Somerset in May 1584".

See Cheshire Visitation 1580. p. 45 for Crest and Arms as then recorded
by Robert Glover, Somerset. Arms quarterly of eight. 1. Brereton. 2. Malpas. 3 Malpas.
4 Egerton. 5 Ipstones. 6 Hanforth. 7 Praers. 8. Ashton. Crest, a bear's head &c

MONUMENTAL INSCRIPTIONS FORMERLY IN THE CHURCH. 63

John Cooke, glover, Sheriff of this Citty 1616, dyed the 14 day of December, 1625.[1]
A shield of arms for *Cooke*: Argent three stags, two and one Gules.

Lawrence Reading. gent., dyed the 8 day of July, Anno 1630.[2]
A shield of arms: Argent a chevron between three boars' heads erect and erased Sable, tusked Or, for *Reading*.

[3] Thomas Swinton, of the Citty of Chester, gent., dyed upon the 18th day of November, 1637.[4]
A shield of arms : Argent a fess Gules between three boars' heads couped Sable, for *Swinton*.

[5] Eleanor late wife unto Mathew Anderton, Esq. Dyed upon the 22nd day of August Anno Dñi 1639.[5]
A shield of arms of seven quarterings for *Anderton*: (1) Sable three shackbolts Argent, a crescent for difference. (2) Vert three bugle horns Argent, stringed Or. (3) Azure a lion rampant Argent. (4) Azure a chevron between three covered cups Or. (5) Argent a cross ragulé Gules. (6) Per fess Argent and Sable a pale counterchanged three bears' heads Gules. muzzled Or. (7) Argent two bars Gules and on a canton of the second a maunch Argent. Impaling *Gamul*. Or three mallets Sable, and the usual quarterings.

[6] Anne daughter of Sr Randle Mainwaring, of Peever. Knight, and late wife unto Robert Brerewood, Esq., dyed the 23 day of December, Anno Dñi, 1630.[6]
Arms : *Brerewood*—Ermine two pallets vairy Or and Azure, on a chief Azure a bezant between two garbs Or, impaling *Mainwaring* (1) Argent two bars Gules, (2) Azure three garbs Or, (3) as (2). (4) as (1).

"On an old escutcheon formerly on the south side of the pulpit ":—

[7] Katherine eldest Daughter to Mathew Ellis of Overlegh gentleman married Randle Holme y[e] younger Sheriff of this Citty 1633. by whom she had issue three sonnes and five daughters, vidlzt Randle, William. Raphe, Katherine, Elizabeth, who died yonge, Elizabeth againe, Amy, Alice, Helen. She dyed upon the 15th Day of March Anno 1640 [1640-1].

These inscriptions also occur:—

Mrs. Grissell Smith, Daughter to S[r] Samuel Smith, of Dublin, in the Realme of Ireland, Knt., dyed upon the 21 day of December, Anno 1640.[8]
A shield of arms : Per chevron Azure and Gules, three leopards' heads erased Argent, spotted Sable.

---

[1] *Additional* MS. 29781 (Brit. Mus.). His will was proved at Chester in 1626, and is in the Probate Court there.
[2] *Stowe* MS. 648. The earliest Register of St. Mary's, which begins in 1628, thus records his burial : " Lawrence Readinge, gent., buried 11th day of July," 1630. His will, if he made any, is not now preserved at Chester.
[3] *Stowe* MS. 648.
[4] The entry in the Register is as follows :—" Thomas Swinton gent., buried in St. Katherine's Ile before the doore at the feete of Mr. Readings stone the 21st day of N vemb[r]," 1637. He was the son and heir of Richard Swinton, of Knutsford, gent., by his wife Eleanor, daughter of Edmund Gamul, Esq. His Funeral Certificate has been printed by the Record Society, *Cheshire Funeral Certificates*, p. 175.
[5] The entry in the Register is as follows :—" Mrs. Ellinor Anderton, wife of Mathew Anderton, Esq., buried in S[t]. Katherine's Ile under her sone Mr. Thomas Swinton's stone 26th day of August," 1639.
She was the daughter of Edmund Gamul, Esq., who was buried at Chester in 1616 (see the Gamul pedigree *postea*).
[6] Her Funeral Certificate has been printed by the Record Society, vol. vj., *Cheshire Funeral Certificates*, p. 38. It begins as follows :—" Mrs. Anne Brerewood departed this mortalle life in Chester upon the 23 day of December, 1630, and was buried in St. Maryes Church in Troutbecks Chappell there."
[7] *Additional* MS. 29781. This inscription was existing in 1819, and is given by Ormerod in his *History of Cheshire*.
[8] In the Register the entry is " Mrs. Grissell Smith, buried vnder old Mr. Boothes' stone. in St. Katherine's Ile, the 22th day of December," 1640. In the next year, 1641, the following entry throws some light upon this lady's family :—" Elizabeth. an infant and daugh[r]. of Thomas Salisburie, of Leadliookes, Esq., buried in St. Katherine's Ile. xp[e]n it[s]. Aunt, Mrs. Grissell Smith, 8th day of Aprill."

ST. MARY-ON-THE-HILL, CHESTER.

[1] Mrs. Jane, Daughter of John Conway, of Bodrithin, Esq., late wife of Thomas Salisbury, of flint, Esq., dyed the 11 day of September, 1640.[2]

A shield of arms: Gules a lion rampant, Argent crowned Or, between three crescents of the last [*Salisbury*] impaling Sable on a bend Argent between two bendlets, Ermine a rose Gules, between two annulets Sable [*Conway*].

[3] Here in the middle He lyeth buried the Bodyes of Hugh Whickstead sometime Sheriffe and one of the Coroners of this Citty of Chester and alsoe of Alice his wife which said Hugh dyed on the 8 day of November 1646[4] and the said Alice dyed on the 20 day of January 1653. Alsoe of Hugh 2^d son of the said Hugh and Alice who dyed on the 27 day of March 1655.[5]

A shield of arms: Argent, on a bend Azure, between two Cornish choughs proper, three garbs Or, a crescent in chief [*Whicksted*] impaling per bend sinister Ermine and Ermines a lion rampant Or, within a bordure Gules [*Trevor*].

The four following inscriptions relate to the family of BROCK, of Upton, in St. Mary's parish:—

[7] William Brock, of Upton, in the County of Chester, Esq[r], dyed on the 3rd day of Aprill, 1640[8] and Edward Brock, his uncle, dyed on the 3rd day of October, 1639.[9]

Here lyeth Interred the body of Anne, Daugh. and Co-heir to Robert Mohun, of Banton, Esq., and late wife to Wm. Brocke, of Upton, in the County of Chester, Esq., by whom he had issue 11 children. She dyed the 17 day of June, Anno 1660.[10]

A quartered shield of arms: (1) Gules on a chief Argent a lion passant guardant of the first, *Brock*. (2) Gules a fess dancetté Ermine between three bugle horns stringed Or, a crescent for difference, *Colgreave*. (3) Azure a spread eagle Argent [*Ridware*]. (4) Or a fess wavy Sable, in chief three martlets of the last [*Rosingrave*]. (5) Gules two lions passant Argent, a label of three points Or . . . . . . (6) A griffin segreant per fess Gules and Azure [*Hargreve*]. (7) [Sable] a fess humetté Argent a martlet for difference [*Rostock*]. (8) Or a fess Azure [*Vernon*]. (9) Quarterly, Or and Gules a bend Sable [*Malbank*]. (10) Azure three garbs Or, *Earl of Chester*. (11) Azure a wolf's head erased Argent, *Hugh Lupus*. (12) Gules a chevron Argent fretté Sable between three mullets Argent [*Moulston*]. (13) Vert a bend engrailed Ermine [*Wettenhall*?]. (14) Argent on a chief Gules three bezants, a crescent for difference . . . . . (15) Lozengé Or and Azure a chevron Gules . . . . (16) Gules a lion rampant Argent

Impaling (1) Gules within a bordure Argent a hand proper holding a fleur-de-lis Or, issuing out of a maunch Ermine, *Mohun*. (2) Or a chevron between three lozenges Azure, on a chief Gules a spread eagle Or . . . . (3) Sable a lion rampant Argent over all a bend Gules . . . . . (4) as (1).

---

[1] *Stowe MS.* 648.
[2] Thus entered in the Register:—"Mrs. Salisbury widdow buried vnder Readings stone att the entrance of St. Katherines Ile the 13th day of September," 1640.
[3] This inscription occurs in *Harl. MS.* 2151 and in the *Stowe MS.* 648.
[4] There are no entries of burials in this year between the 17th May, 1646, and the 16th January, 1646-7, the Register being defective.
[5] " Mrs. Alice Whicksted widd. buried in the middle He over ag[t] her owne pue doore 22th day of January," 1656-7.
[6] " Hugh Whicksted buriall in Troutbecks Chappell, the 29th day of March," 1655.
[7] *Stowe MS.* 648.
[8] "William Brocke, Esq[r], buried in St. Katherine's Ile, under Mr. Vaudreys stone, 8th day of Aprill," 1640. (St. Mary's Register.)
[9] " Edward Brocke gent. buried in St. Katherines Ile vnder Mr. Vaudreys stone 4th day of October," 1639. (Do., do.)
[10] " Mrs. Brocke of Vpton was Buried in St. Katherines yle vnder her owne ston on the 21th Day of June," 1660. (Do., do.)

[1820] BROOK MONUMENT AT GRAPPENHALL.
Flat stone in Grappenhall churchyard.
VNDER THIS | STONE | LIETH IN | TERED | THE BODY | OF WILLIAM | BROCK ⁖ OF | BRAD= | LEY WITHIN ⁖ | APPLETON | ESQ. | VIRE WHO ⁖ DE= | PARTED THIS | LIFE THE TENTH | DAY OF MAY AND | WAS BVRIED THE | THIRTINTH DAY | OF THE SAME | MONTH ÆTATE | SVE 54
ANNO | DOMINI   1674
[skull and crossbones]   ANON.

[Ormerod (Helsby's) ii. 820 calls the year 1674, and states that William Brook was born in 1622; but the entry of the burial in the parish register reads:—"1674, April 13. Wm. Brook of Upton and Bradley, Esq., in the Chancel of Grappenhall Church."]

*[handwritten at top: ** William Brock, of Upton, Esq. his eldest son, died Aug. 10. 1734, aged 58 years.   Hemingway vol II f. 109]*

MONUMENTAL INSCRIPTIONS FORMERLY IN THE CHURCH. 65

¹ 'Here lyeth the body of William Brock, of Upton, in the County of Chester, Esqr., who by Anne, his wife, Daughter and Co-heir to Robert Mohune, of Baynton, in the County of Dorsett, Esqr., had issue 4 sons and 7 daughters, he dyed the 4 day of Aprill, 1640.² And here alsoe lies the body of Edw⁴ Brock, his uncle, who dyed on the 3 day of October, 1639.³ Alsoe the body of Susanna, Daughter to Joseph Hockenhull, of Shotwick, Esqr., wife to William Brocke, of Upton, Esqr., who was buried 2ᵈ February, 1699.⁴ She had issue 4 sons and two daughters. Alsoe the body of Edward the 4ᵗʰ son to the above mentioned William Brock, Esq., who was buryed May the 23ᵈ, 1713.⁵ John Wilson, grandson to William Brock, Esqr., was buryed September 6, 1714.⁶ Here lyeth the Body of William Brock, Esqr., aged 73 years, who dyed the 10ᵗʰ of Janʳʸ, 1715.⁷ **

'William Brock, of Upton, Esq. married Elizabeth daughter to Sʳ Robert Brerewood, of Chester, Knt., by whom he had issue William, Randle, Anne, and Margaret. She dyed the 17th day of May, 1662.⁹ Katherine, daughter & heir to Edward Gregge, of Bradley, in Appleton in Cheshire, gent, his 2ᵈ wife survived him.¹⁰ He dyed April, 1674, aged 55 years & was buried at Grapenhall.'¹¹

A shield of arms: Gules on a chief Argent, a lion passant guardant of the first for *Brock*, impaling *Brerewood*.

[margin notes: Hist Registers. Church / 1642. Sept 8ᵗʰ William Brocke and Elizabeth Brerewood, Civitat: entries? Taylor's Hist. q Hist. p. ng. §ij.]

¹² Here Lyeth the Body of
WILLIAM BROCK
the Eldest son of William Brock,
of Upton Gent
who was interred the 26 day
of March Aⁿ Dñi 1715¹³
Aged 19 years
Here also lyeth the Body of
THOMAS BROCK
second son of yᵉ aforesaid
William Brock of Upton Gent
who was interred the 20ᵗʰ Day
of May Aⁿ Dñi 1707¹⁴
Aged 7 Years
Also yᵉ Body of ELIZABETH BROCK
Mother of yᵉ above named Children
who died Nov. yᵉ 5 1735¹⁵

---

¹ This important inscription occurs both in the *Stowe MS.* 648 and in *Additional MS.* 29781. Another inscription with a the shield of arms embodying the first portion of this, but differently worded is recorded in the *Stowe MS.* as having been in the church, and is printed on p. 64.

² "William Brocke Esqr. buried in St. Katherines lle vnder Mr.Vaudreys stone 8th day of Aprill," 1640. (St. Mary's Register.)

³ "Edward Brocke gent buried in St. Katherine lle vnder Mr. Vaudreys stone 4th day of October," 1639. (Do., do.)

⁴ " Shusannah yᵉ wife to William Brock Esqr. of St. Oswels Prish was buryed yᵉ 2ᵈ day of Feb." 1699-1700. (Do., do.)

⁵ "Mr. Edward Brock sonn to William Brock of Vpton, Esqr., was Buryed the 23 Day of May, 1713." (Do., do.)

⁶ " John son to Mr. John Wilson of yᵉ Parish of Trinity was Buryed the 6th Day of Septembr, 1714." (Do., do.)

⁷ "William Brock of Upton, seniʳ, Esqʳ, Buryed the 14th Day of January, 1715[-16]."

⁸ *Stowe MS.* 648.

⁹ "Elizabeth Brocke, wife of Mr. William Brocke, of Vpton, buried in St. Katherin yle vnder his owne Ston on the xxiᵗʰ ty of May," 1662. (St. Mary's Register.)

¹⁰ This statement serves to correct the pedigree of Brock, of Upton, hitherto accepted. *See* under the account of the Local umilies *postea*.

¹¹ His burial is thus recorded in the Grappenhall Register :—
1674. May 13. William Brock, of Upton and Bradley, Esqʳ, buried in the chancel of Grappenhall church.
His tombstone bearing the following Inscription, all in capitals, is still to be seen in Grappenhall churchyard :—Under this | one dieth in | terred the body | of William | Brock of Brad- | ley within Appleton Esq | uire who dece | parted this | Life the | 4th | day of May and | was buried the | thirteenth day | of the same | month Ætate | swe 54 anno | Domini | 1674.
The statement on the inscription at St. Mary's that he died . . . . *Aprill* is clearly a clerical error for May

¹² The inscription occurs in *Add. MS.* 29781.

¹³ "William sonne to William Brock juniʳ Esqʳ of Vpton was Buryed the 26ᵗʰ Day of March, 1715."

¹⁴ "Thomas son to William Brock juniʳ Esqʳ of Vpton was Buryed the 20ᵗʰ Day of May 1707."

¹⁵ "Elizabeth Relict to the late Wᵐ Brock Esqʳ of further Northgate Street Bur⁴ yᵉ 8ᵗʰ day of November," 1735.

K

The following long Latin inscription to the memory of SIR ROBERT BRERFWOOD, KNT., a distinguished barrister and one of the Judges of the Court of King's Bench, who died in 1654, is stated by Randle Holme to have been placed " on the screene next to the pulpit on a large table " or tablet, probably of wood, and having at the top two shields of arms, Brerewood impaling Mainwaring, and Brerewood impaling Lee. The transcript of this inscription is full of contractions, so that more than usual difficulty has been experienced in giving it in an extended form.

Hic jacet corpus ROBERTI BRERFWOOD militis, unius Justiciariorum Placitorum coram ipso Rege tenendorum assignatorum, filii et heredis Johannis Brerewood de civitate Cestriæ generosi, qui quidam Robertus Brerewood ad ætatem fere septem decem annorum, anno domini nostri 1605 admissus fuit in Collegium Æneascenum[1] in Academiâ Oxoniensi et post duorum annorum moracionem ibidem ab Academiâ prædictâ decedit et in mense Octobris anno domini 1607 admissus fuit in Hospitium Medii Templi Londoni et postea circa sive [spatium?] septem annorum proximum sequentium ibidem ad Barram vocatus fuit et præterea in initio mensis Decembris anno domini 1637 constitutus fuit unus Justiciariorum domini Regis [in] comitatus Anglesey, Carnarvon et Merioneth et in Quadragesimâ tunc proximum sequente vice suâ fuit Lector infra Hospitium Medii Templi prædicti et præterea in hebdomadâ post festum Paschæ anno domini nostri 1639 electus fuit in officium Recordatoris civitatis Cestriæ prædictæ et præterea [in] termino Trinitatis anno domini nostri 1640 ad generalem vocationem servientium ad legem tunc habitam factus fuit serviens ad legem et postea [in] termino Hillarii anno domini nostri 1641 constitutus fuit per litteras patentes dominæ Reginæ nostræ serviens dictæ dominæ Reginæ ad legem et præterea 5to die Decembris anno domini nostri 1643 factus fuit eques auratus et deinde per litteras patentes domini Regis nostri Caroli gerentes datum 31um die Januarii anno 19° regni regis et in anno domini 1643 factus fuit unus Justiciariorum Placitorum coram ipso Rege tenendorum assignatorum et juratus [fuit] in plenâ curiâ termino Hillarii 6° die ffebruarii apud Oxoniam in officium prædictum et obiit 8° die Septembris anno 1654 ætatis suæ 67.

Ipse tempore suo duas uxores habuit viz., Annam Mainwaring filiam Ranulphi Mainwaring de Peever in comitatu Cestriæ militis, primam ejus uxorem, et Katherinam Lee filiam Ricardi Lee de Lee in comitatu Cestriæ militis, secundam ejus uxorem per quas uxores habuit et reliquit separales exitus filios et filias.[2]

(*Translated.*) Here lies the body of Sir ROBERT BRERFWOOD, Knight, one of the Justices of the Court of King's Bench,[1] son and heir of John Brerewood of the city of Chester, gentleman, who—the same Robert Brerewood—at about the age of 17 years, in the year of our Lord 1605, entered at Brasenose College in the University of Oxford, and after a stay there of two years left the said University, and in the month of October in the year of the Lord 1607, was admitted to the Middle Temple Inn, London, and after being there for just about the space of the next following seven years was called to the Bar, and further in the beginning of the month of December in the year of the Lord 1637 was appointed one of our Lord the King's Justices for the Counties of Anglesey, Carnarvon, and Merioneth, and in the Lent following was in his turn Reader at the Middle Temple Inn, aforesaid, and further in the week after the festival of Easter in the year of our Lord 1639, was chosen to the office of Recorder of the said city of Chester, and further in Trinity Term in the year of our Lord 1640, at the meeting then held of Sergeants-at-Law was made a Sergeant-at-Law, and afterwards in Hilary Term in the year of our Lord 1641 was, by Letters Patent of our Lady the Queen, appointed Sergeant-at-Law to our said Lady the Queen, and further on the 5th day of December in the year of our Lord 1643 was Knighted, and then by Letters Patent of our Lord King Charles, bearing date the 31st day of January in the 19th year of the King's reign, and in the year of the Lord 1643 [*i.e.*, 1643-4], was appointed one of the Justices of the Court of King's Bench and was sworn in to his office

---

[1] This is a very unusual word as "Collegium .Enei nasi " is the proper expression.
[2] If *sive* is right then some such word as *spatium* has to be supplied.
[3] From the curious Latinity of this inscription it is not improbable that it was composed by one of the Randle Holmes.
[4] That is of the Pleas assigned to be taken before the King himself, as distinct from " communia placita," or Common Pleas.

Sir Robert Brerewood compounded for his Estate at £387·10·0

MONUMENTAL INSCRIPTIONS FORMERLY IN THE CHURCH. 67

aforesaid in full Court in Hilary Term on the 6th day of February at Oxford, and died on the 8th day of September in the year 1654, in the 67th year of his age.

In his time he had two wives; namely, Anne Mainwaring, daughter of Sir Randle Mainwaring, of Peever, in the county of Chester, knight, as his first wife, and Katherine Lee, daughter of Sir Richard Lee, of Lee, in the county of Chester, knight, as his second wife; by which wives he had and left separate issue both sons and daughters.

At the foot of the inscription was a shield of arms, Brerewood impaling Mainwaring.

The following very interesting inscription to the memory of a distinguished divine, CHRISTOPHER PASLEY, D.D., is described as being "on an old board fixed to a pillar":—

'In hopes of a glorious resurrection, neere unto this place, lyeth interred the body of CHRISTOPHER PASLEY, Doctor in Divinity, who was first Chaplain in the house to the Lord Keeper of the great Seal of England, afterwards household Chaplain to the Honble House of Derby, sometime Tutor to the Earle of Derby that now is, and late Rector of Hawarden in the County of Flint, dyed upon the [1]7th day of September, Anno Dñi 1658, being aged 63 years.² Resurgam.

Neere whom lyeth the body of John son to William Coventry of Newhouse, in the county of Chester, gent., grandchild to the said Doctor.³

A shield of arms: Argent a fesse between three mullets pierced Sable on the fesse a crescent Or for difference, for *Pasley*. Crest a mullet pierced Argent charged with a crescent Gules. Impaling Argent a bugle horn strung Sable, in chief a mullet Gules, in base a crescent of the last, for . . . . . Crest a bugle horn Argent strung Gules.

This inscription commemorates some members of the well-known family of RAVENSCROFT, of Bretton, co. Flint, but not far from Chester.

'Here within Troutbecks Chappell lyeth Buryed the Bodyes of George Ravenscroft second son to Robert Ravenscroft of Bretton Esqr, who dyed the 28 of October 1657⁴ .Ætatis suæ 35. Robert Ravenscroft 4th son to the said Robert Ravenscroft Esq. who dyed the tenth of ffeb. 1645⁵ .Ætatis suæ 19. Phillip Ravenscroft 6th son to the said Robert Ravenscroft Esq. who dyed the 29 of April 1645⁶ .Ætatis suæ 12.

A shield of six quarterings for *Ravenscroft*: (1) Argent, a chevron Sable between three ravens' heads erased proper [*Ravenscroft*]. (2) Azure a lion rampant guardant amongst fleurs-de-lis Argent [*Holland*]. (3) Argent, three bulls' heads couped Sable [*Stevington*]. (4) Sable three garbs within a bordure Or [*Brickhill*]. (5) Argent on a bend Vert three spades of the first [*Swettenham*]. (6) Azure a chevron between three dolphins nowed [ ].⁷ Presumably Roberts, see page 62 l—3.

---

¹ This inscription occurs in Harl. MS. 2151, Add. MS. 29781, and Stowe MS. 648. The first of these MSS. describes it as hanging upon "the screene which divides the body of the church from St. Katherines Ile, the chancell and Troutbecks chappell."

² The entry of his burial in the Register is as follows:—
"Doekter Parsley was Buried in St. Katherines yle on the xvij^{th} Day of September," 1658.
It would have been most difficult to have identified Christopher Pasley, D.D., under the title of "Doekter Parsley," had this epitaph not been preserved.

³ The entry of this child's burial is as follows:—
"John sonne to Mr. William Coventrey was buried in St. Katherines yle on the first Day of November," 1658.

⁴ *Stowe MS.* 648.

⁵ The entry in the Register is as follows:—"Captaine George Ravenscrofte buried in Troutbecks Chappell the 30th day of October," 1657.

⁶ "Mr. Robert Ravenscroft buried in Troutbecks Chappell the 12th day of February," 1645-6.

⁷ "Mr. Phillip Ravenscroft buried in Troutbecks Chappell upon his Aunt Brerewood first day of May," 1645. Robert Ravenscroft, of Bretton, Esq., married Elizabeth, eldest daughter of Sir Randle Mainwaring, of Peover, Knt., who died Jan. 1633-4. She was sister to Anne wife of Robert Brerewood, Esq. (afterwards knighted), who had been buried at St. Mary's, 23 Dec., 1630, hence the above allusion to "Aunt Brerewood."

⁸ The names of these quarterings have been filled in from the *Visitation of Cheshire*, 1580 (Harleian Society, vol. xviii., p. 194).

K 2

The five inscriptions following relate to the family of BROWNE, of Netherlegh, near Chester.

"On an old board formerly on the south wall."

¹ Phillippa uxor Thomæ Browne de Nether Legh gen' filia Thomæ Berrington de Civitate Cestriæ gen' per quam ipse prædictus Thoma habuit decem filios et quinque filias. In quadragesimo secundo anno ætatis suæ sexto die Maij Anno Domini 1664² obijt in pace erga Deum et Homines.

A shield of arms: Argent two bendlets between as many mullets Sable [*Browne*]. Crest a lion sejant Sable, the dexter paw resting on an escutcheon Argent charged with a mullet Sable. Impaling Sable three greyhounds courant Argent, collared Gules, edged and ringed Or within a bordure of the second [*Berrington*]. Crest out of a ducal coronet a greyhound's head Argent, collared Gules, studded and ringed Or.

³ Hic jacet Corpus Thomæ Browne de Nether Legh in Com' Civit' Cestriæ gen' qui obiit [2]4 die August Anno 1669, Ætatis suæ 49.⁴ In tempore suo duas uxores habuit viz' Phillippam filiam Thomæ Berrington de Civit' Cestriæ gen' per quam uxorem habuit et reliquit separal' exitus filios et filias et secundam ejus uxorem Hannam filiam Rici Leicester de Held in Budworth Magna, relict' Caroli Levesley de Civit' Cestriæ gen', quæ cum supervixit.

A shield of arms: *Browne*, as before, impaling Azure, a fess Gules between three fleurs-de-lis Or, a mullet for difference [*Leicester*]. Crest a wolf's head erased Azure, a mullet for difference.

"On an old escutcheon," a shield of arms for *Parker*: Argent a chevron Sable between three stags' heads caboshed Gules, a label of three points Sable for difference. Crest a stag's head caboshed Gules.

⁵ Here lyeth ye Body of Richard Parker,
Eldest son of Richard Parker of Audley
in the County of Stafford Gent by Phillippa his wife Eldest Dau. to Thomas
Browne of Nether Legh in Cheshire Gent
who died 22 Novemb. 1681 Aged 6 Yeares.

⁶ Hic jacet Georgius Browne tempore pacis studiosus et in Artibus Magister, in Bello Dux, qui post multa pericula tam per marem quam terram, in pace obiit 3 Maii 1653.⁷ Hic etiam jacent Thoma et Thoma, Geo., Sam', Richard, Martha, Elizabetha et Hannah, filii et filiæ Thomæ Browne de Nether Legh gen' fratris prædicti Georgii.

¹ This inscription occurs in *Harl. MS.* 2151, *Stowe MS.* 648, and *Add. MS.* 29781, and is given by Ormerod as existing in 1819. The following is a translation:—Phillippa, wife of Thomas Browne of Nether Legh, gentleman, daughter of Thomas Berrington of the city of Chester, gentleman, by whom he the said Thomas had ten sons and five daughters, she died in the forty-second year of her age, on the 6th day of May, in the year of our Lord 1664, in peace towards God and all mankind.

² "Mrs. Phillippa Brown wife of Mr. Thomas Browne buried on the 9th day of May," 1664.

³ This inscription occurs in *Harl. MS.* 2151, *Add. MS.* 29781, and in the *Stowe MS.* 648, and is given by Ormerod as existing in 1819. The following is a translation:—Here lies the body of Thomas Browne of Nether Legh in the county of the city of Chester, gentleman, who died [2]4th August 1669 in the 49th year of his age. In his day he had two wives, namely, Phillippa, daughter of Thomas Berrington of the city of Chester, gentleman, by which wife he had and left separate issue, both sons and daughters, and for his second wife he had Hannah, daughter of Richard Leicester of He[a]ld in Great Budworth, the relict of Charles Levesley of the city of Chester, gentleman, who survived him.

⁴ "Mr. Thomas Browne was buried the 28^t day of August," 1669.

Add. MS. 29781 and *Stowe MS.* 648. In both these the Christian name is clearly Richard, whilst the entry in the Register is "Thomas son of Mr. Richard Parker was bur. ye 25 of November, 1681. This is, however, a mistake of the copyist, as his baptism is rightly entered at St. Mary's in 1675, "Richard son of Mr. Richard Parker bapt. on the 3rd of November."

⁶ This inscription occurs in *Add. MS.* 29781 and *Stowe MS.* 648, and the latter part only is given by Ormerod. The translation is as follows:—Here lies George Browne, in peaceful times a student and a Master of Arts, in time of war a commander, who after many dangers as well by sea as by land, died peacefully 3rd May, 1653. Here also lie Thomas and Thomas, George, Samuel, Richard, Martha, Elizabeth and Hannah, sons and daughters of Thomas Browne of Nether Legh, gentleman, brother of the said George.

⁷ The following is the entry of his burial in the Register:—"Mr. George Browne buried in Mr. Thomas Browne his brothers seate 6th of May 1653."

MONUMENTAL INSCRIPTIONS FORMERLY IN THE CHURCH. 69

Mathew Browne Gentleman dyed on the 24 day of Novemb' Anno Dñi 1634.
A shield of arms: *Browne*, as before, impaling *Allen*.

"Alice Daughter of Mathew Browne [2] Gentleman late Wife to Thomas Parnell of the City of Chester Ironmonger, dyed on the 5 day of September, 1639.
A shield of arms: *Browne*, as before, a crescent for difference.

The following long inscription relates to the family of BROWNE, of Upton, near Chester. It was "on an old board formerly placed against the North wall."

A shield of arms: *Browne of Upton*, Argent two bendlets Sable between as many pellets. Crest, a demi-lion rampant Ermine, crowned Or, holding in the dexter paw a rose Gules.

[3] "This was set up in the memory of Richard Browne, of Upton, in ye County of Chester, gent, sone and heire to Thomas Browne, by Elizabeth his Wife, daughter to Henry Birkenhead, Esq., Clerk of ye Green Cloth to Queen Elizabeth, sone and heir of Rich. Browne, sone and heir of Thomas Browne, of Upton, aforesaid. The abovesaid Richd Browne died the 4 of January 1624,[1] having had 2 Wives, first Frances, daughter to Sr George Beverley, of Huntington, Knt, who died without Issue, secondly to Mary, daughter to Sr Tho. Aston, of Aston, Knt, by whom he had Issue Thomas Browne of Upton and Richd of London. She after[wards] married Jacques Arnodio, gent, and dyed ye 17 Feb, 1668 [5] Aged 87 Years. Thomas Browne sone and heire died at Munster in Ireland 1643;[6] he married Grissell daughter to . . . . . Dobb of Ireland, by whom he had Issue Thomas, Robt, Francis, Richard, Mary, Judith, Grissell and Dorothy. She died in Childbed ye 19 of June 1641.[6] Thomas Browne sone and heire married Cicely daughter to William Glegge of Gayton Esq, who died in Childbed of her Daughter Cicely the 16 of March Año Dñi 1661.[7]

The following is one of the very few inscriptions relating to the RECTORS of St. Mary's:—

" Here Lyeth the Body of THOMAS KIRKES,[8] Rector of St Maryes, who Departed this Life the 23 Day of November, Anno Dni 1673.

The annexed inscription commemorates PETER GERARD, Esq., of Chester, a physician of repute and skill:—

---

[1] *Stowe MS.* 648. She was buried at St. Mary's on the 8th Sept. 1639, "at the upper end of the South Ile at Troutbecks Chappell doore."
[2] This is mentioned in Ormerod's *History of Cheshire*, where Matthew Browne is described as "of Netherlegh."
[3] *Add. MS.* 29781 and *Stowe MS.* 648. This inscription is also given in Ormerod's *History of Cheshire* in a condensed form.
[4] Buried at St. Werburgh's Church, Chester. See his Funeral Certificate printed by the Record Society, vol. vi. *Cheshire Funeral Certificates*, p. 49.
[5] "Mrs. Marie Arnodio buried on the 20th day of Febrau:" 1667-8. (St. Mary's Register.)
[6] "Mrs. Grissell wife of Mr. Thomas Browne, of Upton, buried at the north side of Readings stone in St. Katherines Ile 20th of June," 1641. (Do., do.)
[7] She was not buried at St. Mary's, but at Heswall in Wirral Hundred.
[8] *Add. MS.* 29781.
[9] For a fuller account of Mr. Kirkes see the account of the Rectors *polea*. His burial is thus entered in the Register:—
" Mr. Kiarkes [*sic*] minister buried upon the xxvth Day of November," 1673.

¹ Hic situs est Vir æque ac Medicus optimus
PETRUS GERARDUS, Armiger,
Ex Antiquâ admodum sui nominis pariter et Illustri
Olim Kingsleiorum familijs Oriundus,
Prioris originem clara hæc propago proxime attigit.
Medicinæ non solum Doctor sed et apud Suos,
Instaurator summus.
Erga Deum Pius, Erga Regem Fidelis, Erga Amicos Perpetuus
Qui dum sanandi Artem maluit Ægrotantibus
quam sibi profuisse;
Studio et itinere frequenti attritus
Lentâ dein tabe confectus
Mebilis obijt Año { Ætatis XXXVIII"
                   { Domini MDCLXXVIII" ²

Uxorem duxit, quæ hoc in piam memoriam posuit Illi Monumentum, Susannam filiam natu maximam Stephani Jackson Londinensis Armigeri: ex quâ liberos suscepit quatuor Stephanum, Petrum Annam, Petrum dein alterum priorem enim idem quod patrem clausit sepulchrum.
Iram et meditare mortem, quum morborum stator hic succubuit.

(*Translation.*) Here lies buried one equally pre-eminent as a Man and a Physician, PETER GERARD, Esquire, descended as well from the very ancient family whose name he bore, as from the formerly illustrious family of the King[s]leys, this distinguished scion was most nearly related to the house of the former. He was not only a Doctor of Medicine, but quite the most eminent man in his profession as a healer. He was characterised by piety towards God, fidelity towards his King, and constancy towards his friends. And in his desire that his skill in healing should profit the sick rather than himself, weakened by zealous work and frequent journeying, and then worn out altogether by a lingering decline, he died a man to be lamented, in the 38th year of his age and in the year of the Lord 1678.

He took as his wife—who has erected this monument to him for an affectionate remembrance—Susan, the eldest daughter of Stephen Jackson, of London, Esquire, by whom he had 4 children: Stephen, Peter, Anne, and then a second Peter, for the same tomb has closed upon the former of that name as upon his Father.

Think on [God's]³ wrath and death, when the Stayer of Diseases has here succumbed.

A shield of six quarterings for *Gerard:* (1) and (6) Argent a saltire Gules [*Gerard*, ancient]. (2) Azure a lion rampant Ermine, crowned Or [*Gerard*]. (3) Azure a lion rampant Argent [*Gerard*]. (4) Vert a cross engrailed Ermine [ ]. (5) Argent an oak tree eradicated and fructed proper [ ]. A crescent over all for difference. Crest a lion's jamb holding . . . . Impaling Argent on a chevron Sable, 3 cinquefoils Argent between as many falcons' heads erased Azure, for *Jackson.* Crest a horse in full course Argent, gouttée

¹ *Harl. MS.* 2151 and *Stowe MS.* 648.

² "Doctor Peter Gerard buried (with a certificate), on y⁰ 9th day of December, 1678." He was the sixth and ultimately the eldest surviving son of Gilbert Gerard, of Crewood, co. Chester, and the Green Hall, in Castle Lane, Chester, Esq., a colonel in the Parliamentary army, by his wife Anne, daughter of William Brettargh, of Brettargh Holt, co. Lane., Esq. He was baptised at Frodsham, 10 Feb., 1640-1, and was educated at Brasenose College, Oxford, where he matriculated 31 July, 1658, B.A. 1662, M.A. 18 Jan. 1664-5, B. and D. Med. 1669, and Fellow of his College. He married (as stated in the inscription) Susanna, daughter of Stephen Jackson, of London, merchant (marriage settlement dated 20 Feb., 1671-2, and the marriage licence 6 April, 1672), by whom he had three sons, Stephen, Peter and Peter, who all died young, and one daughter and heiress, Anne Gerard, who was married at St. Michael's, Chester, on the 12 July, 1705, to Edward Norris, of Chester and Speke, co. Lanc., Esq., M.D., of Brasenose College, Oxford. She died 3 Jan., 1729, aged 53, and was buried at Garston, near Liverpool. Peter Gerard's widow, Susanna, was buried at St. Mary's in 1706, the entry in the Register being as follows: "M⁽ᵗˢ⁾ Susannah Gerrard, widow, of St. Michell Parish, was buryed the 21 day of Aprill, 1706."

³ The word *iram* is very puzzling. It has been suggested that it is a mis-reading of *I* (go) *jam* (now), and that the meaning is "Go now and think on death," &c.

MONUMENTAL INSCRIPTIONS FORMERLY IN THE CHURCH. 71

Gules. About the arms are these four crests: on the right hand, a lion rampant Ermine crowned Or, and an oak tree as in the arms; on the left hand a falcon's head erased Azure, and a pheon point downwards Or.

Other inscriptions are—

"On an old stone, all in capitals."

[1] JOHN WRIGHT of Brewers Hall Esqr.
Departed this Life the 5 Day
of December 1689.[2]
Allso the Body of Catherine
Daughter to John Wright Esq.
Sonn to the above mentioned
John Wright, who Departed this
Life the 1 Day of Decem' 1706.

[3] Near this place lyes the body of Alexander Wynne and Edward Wynne, sons of Edward Wynne of Brithli[4] in the county of Flint Esq' and Elizabeth his wife, daughter of Walter Horton of Catton, in com. Derby, Esq', the said Edward the youngest son dyed the 22[1] of September 1681 and Alexander the eldest son dyed the 2^d of October following and were buried in the same grave.

A shield of arms of six quarterings for *Wynne*: (1) and (6) Gules a lion rampant Argent. (2) Argent a red rose proper. (3) Sable a chevron between three goats' heads erased Or. (4) Or a griffin segreant Gules. (5) Gules a chevron between three pansies (?) Argent.

"On an old escutcheon."

[6] Here lyeth interred ye Body of Iohn
Houseman who was Borne in Kidder
minster in Woostershire gentle
man to ye Honor^{ble} Coll. Rog. Whitley
of Peel Esq'. He departed this Life
in ye 36th Year of his Age & on the
17th day of Nov. Año Dñi 1697.[7]

[8] Here lyeth Interred the Body of Phillip Bateman late of Upton who dyed the 25[9] Day of February and in the Sixtye Eight Yeare of his age Annoque Domini 1697.

And Also the Body of Elizabeth Bateman Wife to Phillip Bateman who dyed the sixth day of September and in the sixty fift Yeare of her Age Annoque Domini 1698.

This inscription commemorating a daughter of one of the rectors of the church, the Rev. RICHARD WRIGHT, B.D., was "on a brass plate" on the north side of the altar rails:

---

[1] *Add. MS.* 29781 and *Stowe MS.* 648.
[2] "John Wright Esqr of Brewers hall was bur' ye 9th day of Decemb^r." 1689.
[3] *Stowe MS.* 648.
[4] ? Brithic, co. Flint.
[5] Should be 27th, he was buried on the 29th, and his brother on the 4th October.
[6] *Add. MS.* 29781.
[7] "Mr. John Houseman was Buryed ye 18th day of Novemb^r," 1697.
[8] *Add. MS.* 29781.
[9] Query the 15th day of February, the entry in the Register being "Phillip Bateman of Vpton was buryed ye 17th day of February," 1697. His wife was buried on the 8th Sept. 1698.

> [1] Hic sita est
> Elizabetha Filiarum ex duabus primogenita
> Richardi Wright S.T.B. hujus ecclesiæ Rectoris
> Et Vxoris Mariæ Fil.' nat.' maximæ
> Joannis Wainwright LL.D. Diœc. Cestr' Cancell'
> obdormivit in pace Virgo pientissima
> Intaminatis moribus et omnigenæ Virtutis Xtianæ
>   Præssidiis munita
>   Secutores relinquens parentes
> Et Mariam sororem etiam Virginem
>   Dolore obrutos
> XII Kal Jun. Año. { Dom. MDCCII.[2]
>   { Ætat XXIII.
> Credentes fore ut resurgant singulorum Cineres
> simulque anhelantes ut una pariter transferantur
> in sedes Beatorum cum cecinerit Tuba ad illustrem
> adventum Domini.

(*Translation.*) Here lies buried Elizabeth, the elder of the two daughters of Richard Wright, B.D., Rector of this church, and Mary his wife, eldest daughter of John Wainwright, LL.D., Chancellor of the diocese of Chester. This most pious maiden, fortified by her unsullied character and the safeguards of Christian worth in every form, fell asleep in peace on the 21st day of May, in the year of our Lord 1702, in the 23rd year of her age, leaving her parents and her sister, also still a maiden, overwhelmed with grief, to follow her.

Believing (as they do) it shall surely come to pass that the ashes of each one rise again, and ardently desiring too that they may be at the same moment carried to the Abodes of the Blessed, when the Trumpet shall have sounded for the glorious Advent of the Lord.

The following inscription relates to the family of WHISHAW,[3] long resident in St. Mary's parish:—

> [4] Here Lyeth the Body of Charles Whishaw who was buried the 25 day of July 1702. Alsoe the Body of Mary late Wife of William Done of the Citty of Chester Gent.[5] who Departed this life the 2ᵈ day of July Anno Dñi 1708. Alsoe the Body of Sarah Lacy Widdow and Relict of Thomas Lacy of Winkley in the County of Lancaster Esqʳ, who Departed this life the 24 of January 1708 in the 73 year of her age. Alsoe the Body of Rebecca Whishaw Daughter to Mr. Hugh Whishaw who dyed the 6 day of August 1710. Alsoe Jane Daughter to Hugh Whishaw Gent was buried the 27 of February 1714. Alsoe Frances[6] the

---

[1] *Add. MS.* 29781 and *Stowe MS.* 648. It is also referred to by Ormerod in 1819 as "on a brass at the north side of the altar rails," but no dates are given !

[2] "Elizabeth Daughtʳ to Mr. Richᵈ Wright Minnister of St. Marys was Buryed the 24ᵗʰ day of May," 1702.

[3] The manor of Hockenhull in Cheshire was bought in 1713 by Mr. Hugh Whishaw, of Chester, and was sold by his son and successor in 1761 to John Walsh, Esq., M.P. (Lyson's *Cheshire,* p. 797). The *Gentleman's Magazine* for 1841 has this obituary notice:—"Dec. 21st, Died in Wilton Crescent, John Whishaw, Esq., M.A., F.R.S., Senior Bencher of Grays Inn. He was the elder son of the late Hugh Whishaw, Esq., of Chester, where he was born about 1764. He was educated at Macclesfield Grammar School and Trinity College, Cambridge. He edited Mungo Park's Travels, and was the friend and executor of Sir Samuel Romilly."

[4] *Stowe MS.* 648, the dates corrected by the Registers. A flat tombstone relating to this family is still in the church (see p. 53).

[5] His marriage is thus recorded in the St. Michael's Register:—
"1704 May 18 Mʳ Willᵐ Done Attorney & Mʳˢ Mary Whishaw Spinstʳ both of Sᵗ Marys parish, were marryd by a licence of yᵉ 16ᵗʰ instant."

[6] Her marriage is thus entered in the St. Mary's Register:—
"1705 Hugh Whishaw Gent of Castell Lane and Mʳˢ Frances Branton were married with a licence yᵉ 23ᵈ day of December."

MONUMENTAL INSCRIPTIONS FORMERLY IN THE CHURCH. 73

wife to Hugh Whishaw Gent was buried the 10th day of October 1717. Alsoe the Body of William Done of this Citty Gent, who was buried the 24 day of Aprill 1719.[1]

This inscription commemorates the Rev. JAMES PEAKE, one of the non-jurying clergy of Cheshire who refused to take the oath of allegiance to William III. in 1688.

> [2] Quiescunt his reliquæ
> Reverendi JACOBI PEAKE
> Ecclesiæ Anglicanæ
> Aliquando Presbyteri,
> Qui Fidem
> Principi suo semel juratam
> Constanti animo vindicavit
> Supremum adusque diem
> Propositi Tenax.
> Obiit Primo die Aprilis
> Anno Salutis MDCCXIX
> Ætatis LXVII.

Another inscription related to the ACTON family.

[3] Thomas Acton sepultus 9 of November 1678. Hannah Acton sepulta 19 of February 1672. Benjamin Acton sepultus 22 of October 1686. Sarah Acton sepulta 31 of March 1697. Thomas & Hannah son and daughter to Mr. John Acton sepulti 20 of December 1688 and the 21 of March 1696.

Elizabeth daughter to Johnson Mainwaring gen' was buried June the 3 day 1717. John son to Johnson Mainwaring Esq' was buried July the 29 1719. Alsoe the Body of Elizabeth the wife of Johnson Mainwaring Esq and daughter to John Acton gen', who was buryed the 2d day of December 1719.

The entries in the Registers of St. Mary's of the various persons mentioned in the above inscription differ somewhat materially as to dates, &c. They are as follows :—

1678. Mr Thomas Acton buried (with a Cert.) on the 26th day of November.
1672. Hannah Wife of Mr Thomas Acton buried on the 18 day of February.
1686. Mr Benjamine Acton was bur. the 13th day of October.
1697. Shusanna the wife to John Acton Gen' was bur. ye 31st day of March.
1689. Thomas, son of Mr John Acton was bur. ye 17th day of December.
1697. Hanna daughtr to John Acton Gen' was Buryed ye 22 day of February.
1717. Elizabeth Daughtr to Mr Johnson Manwaringe of Castell Lane Buryed ye third Day of June.

[1] The burials of the persons named on this tablet are thus entered in the Registers of St. Mary's :—
1702 Charles Whishaw of Castell Lane was bur. ye 25th of July.
1708 Mary ye wife to William Done Gent. of Castell lane an Attorney was Buryed the 5th day of July.
1708 Madam Sarah Lacy of Castell lane Widow was Buryed the 26th day of January.
1710 Rabakah Daughtr to Mr Hugh Whishaw of Castell lane was Buryed the 8th Day of August.
1714 Jane ye Daughtr to Mr Hugh Whishaw an Attorney was Buryed the 27th Day of February.
1717 Mrs Frances Whishaw Wife to Hugh Whi-haw Gen' of St Bridgets Parish Buryed ye 10th Day of October.
1719 William Done Gen' of ye Parish of St Peters an Attorney and Store Keeper was Buryed ye 25th Day of April.

[2] Add. MS. 29781. The following is a translation :—
"Here lie at rest the remains of the Reverend James Peake, sometime a priest of the Church of England: who, resolute in his purpose to his very last day, kept with determination that allegiance to his Prince, which he had once for all sworn to keep. He died on the 1st day of April, in the year of Salvation 1719, and in the 67th year of his age."
The Rev. James Peake was clearly a non-juror, one of the comparatively few clergy who vacated their livings rather than take the oath of allegiance to William III., after having already taken it to James II. He was Vicar of Bowdon, in Cheshire, from 1684 to 1692. By his wife Frances, daughter of Thomas Weston, of Chester, clerk, rector of Christleton, he had two daughters, coheirs, one of whom married Thomas Patten, of Warrington. His widow was buried at St. Mary's, 17 May, 1743.
The entry of his burial in the Register of St. Mary's is as follows :—
"Mr. James Peake Minnist' Dyed in the Parish of St Michaels and Buryed the third Day of April 1719."

[3] Stowe MS. 648. There are several discrepancies between the dates on this monument and those given in the St. Mary's Registers. See the pedigree of this family postea.

L.

1719. John son to John Manwaringe Esqr in Trinity Parish, Buryed the 29th Day of July.
1719. Elizabeth ye wife to Johnson Manwaringe Esqr of Trinity Parish Buryed the second Day of December.

Other inscriptions are :—

[1] Near this place lyeth the body of Mary daughter to Samuell Meadowes buryed ffeb. 19. 1705 [1705-6].

[2] Charles Wilbraham Seaventh Son of Ralph Wilbraham of Dorfold in the County of Chester Esqr and Patron of this Church who dyed the 20 of Aprill 1721 aged 32 Yeares.[3]

[4] Here lie
the Remains of the Rev
RALPH VERNON
Chaplain
to the Right Honourable
the Earl of Cholmondeley
He died the 28th of July 1760
In the 42nd Year of his Age.[5]

The following inscriptions, printed in Ormerod's *History of Cheshire*, published in 1819, as then existing in the church, are no longer to be found there, having disappeared during the various restorations to which it has been subjected. The first relates to the first RANDLE HOLME, the senior antiquary and genealogist of those names.

Attached to a pillar is a board on which are painted the arms of *Holme* quartering *Trammoll* [or *Trammere*] and *Lymme* and impaling *Alcock* (Argent between three scythes Sable on a fesse Gules, an escallop Or). Crests of *Holme* and *Alcock* (on a wreath, an escallop Or between two scythes Sable). Inscription[6] :—

Here beneath lyeth the bodyes of Randle Holme of
ye Citie of Chester,
Ald^r, and Justice of Peace and was Maior thereof 1633,
died ye 16 of Jany 1655, æt 84 ;
Also of Elizabeth his wife,
daughter to Tho. Alcock, and widow to Tho. Chaloner,
gent., she dyed the 24 of May 1635 and [had] yssue two sones
William Holme y^t died 1623,[7] without yssue li-
vinge, and Randle Holme, now living, who
was also maior of this citty 1643.

[1] *Stowe MS.* 648, corrected by the Register of St. Mary's.
[2] *Stowe MS.* 648.
[3] The entry in the Register is as follows :—
"Mr. Charles Wilbraham Brother to Mr. Hugh Wilbraham Rector of this Parish was Buried the 23d Day of Aprill 1721."
[4] *Add. MS.* 29781.
[5] He is described in the Register of St. Mary's as " the Rev. Mr Ralph Vernon, of Bridge Street," and he was buried there on the 31st July, 1760. A " Mrs. Hannah Vernon, widow, of Watergate Street," was buried there on the 2nd February. 1762. She may have been his widow.
[6] This is also copied in the *Stowe MS.* 648, but the arms there noted are not the same as those given by Ormerod.
[7] There seems to have been a separate little monument to this son thus given in the *Stowe MS.* 648, *Add. MS.* 29781, and also by Ormerod, as follows :—
William Holme eldest son of Randle Holme dyed the 10th day of July, 1623.
I am inclined to think that the shields of arms referred to in note 6 were attached to this monument and not to the former one.

[illegible handwritten page]

MONUMENTAL INSCRIPTIONS FORMERLY IN THE CHURCH. 75

Another relates to the BROCK family of Upton.

    Susanna, daughter to Joseph Hockenhull of Shotwick Esq., wife to
        William Brock. [No dates given.[1]]
    William Brock, Esq., died 10 Jan., 1715, aged 73.
    William Brock, of Upton, Esq., his eldest son, died Aug. 10, 1734, aged 58.[2]

Another relates to the family of PRESCOT of Chester.[3]

    Susanna, daughter of George and Anne Prescot, died 3 Feb., 1722.
    Gregory, son of the same, died Oct. 4, 1725.
    Anne, wife of the said George, died 22 Sept., 1740, aged 59 years.
    George Prescot, merchant, died March 10, 1747, aged 67.
    Thomas Prescot, of Eardshaw, co. Cest., Esq., died 29 Oct., 1768, aged 63.

Another relates to the WILBRAHAM family.

    Capt. Peter Wilbraham died Feb. 27, 1765, aged 40.[4]
    Mary, his wife, died Jan. 10 [? 30] 1766, aged 37.[5]

On gravestones in the chancel were the following inscriptions to the children of John and Elizabeth Hill[6]:—

    Emma Jane Barbarah, 3rd daughter, died May 8th, 1810 (15 months); Emma Jane Barbarah, Nov. 8, 1810 (3 months); Elizabeth Anne, 2d daughter, born Aug. 3, 1805, died Jan. 27, 1812; Robert Wilbraham Hill, 4th son, born April 9, 1815, died July 4, 1815.

The following inscription to a distinguished ecclesiastic, GEORGE SNELL, D.D., Archdeacon of Chester and Rector of Wallasey, who died on the 5th February, 1655-6, was accidentally omitted in its proper place.

    [7] Hic situs est GEORGIUS SNELL, S.T.P.
        Archidiaconus Cestriensis, qui per injuriam
        Temporis in Communionem Laicam redactus,
        privatus obiit Feb. 5, 1655.[8]

His burial is thus entered in the Register of St. Mary's:—

    "1655. Docter Snell buried in the Quire neere Mr Pearetrees tombe the 7th day of ffebruary" [*i.e.*, 1655-6].

---

[1] She was buried in February, 1699-1700, the entry in the Register being,
    "Shusannah ye wife to William Brock, Esq., of St. Oswel's Parish, was buryed ye 3d day of Feb. 1699" [1699-1700].

[2] For other Brock inscriptions *see* pp. 49 and 64-5. *See* also the full pedigree of the Brocks in the account of the old families connected with St. Mary's, *postea*.

[3] This large tombstone still exists in the Church (1893), but the inscription is all but illegible. At the top is a brass plate with the arms of Prescot, Argent (?) a chevron between three owls Sable (?) and the inscription begins thus (all in capitals):—
    "Here lieth the body of Susanna" . . . . . rest worn off . . . . till near the end these words are legible . . . . . . "Prescot . . . and a Deputy Lieutenant . . . who departed this life the . . . of October, 1768, aged 63."
For a notice of this family *see* the account of the old families connected with St. Mary's, *postea*.

[4] "Mr Peter Wilbraham Gentleman of St Johns parish was Buried the Second day of March," 1765.

[5] "Mrs Mary Wilbraham of St Johns parish widow was buried the 3d day of Feb." 1766. In the Churchwardens' Accounts her burial is said to have taken place "in ye Rector's chancell."

[6] Other Hill inscriptions will be found in the account of the inscriptions now in the Church (*see* p. 48). John Hill, Esq., was the Attorney-General of the old Chester Circuit (*see* p. 22).

[7] This inscription is not given in any of the three authorities so often before referred to, *Harl. MS.* 2151, *Add. MS.* 29781, and *Stowe MS.* 648, but is printed in the *History of the Cathedral Church at Chester*, 1793, p. 66.

[8] (*Translate l.*) Here lies George Snell, D.D., Archdeacon of Chester, who by the lawlessness of the times, reduced to Lay Communion, died a private man, on the 5th February, 1655[-6].

L 2

He was the son of William Snell, of Charley and Nethercot, co. Devon, by Margaret, his wife, daughter of . . . . . Stranbery, of Stranbery and Eastdown in that county.[1] He appears to have completed his education at St. John's College, Cambridge, of which college he was elected Fellow, but on the 8th July, 1620, he received the degree of Doctor of Divinity " after public performance of exercise " from the University of St. Andrew's.[2] He married Lydia, sister of Dr. John Bridgeman, Bishop of Chester (himself a Devonshire man), by whom he had a family of one son, George,[3] and six daughters.[4] On the 16th January, 1618-19, he was collated by the Bishop (Morton) to the Archdeaconry of Chester. In the same year, 1619, he was appointed to the Rectory of Wallasey, co. Chester,[5] which he held, together with the Rectory of Waverton (to which he was appointed about 1633[6]), till the time of the Civil War, when he would appear to have been turned out by the Parliamentary party.[7] He retired to Chester, and was buried at St. Mary's on the 7th Feb. 1655-6.

[1] Harl. MS. 2040, f. 68ᵇ.

[2] See Harl. MS. 2131, f. 200, where his diploma is given, and where he is described as Fellow of St. John's College, Cambridge.

[3] " 1620(-1) Jan. 8. Thomas, son of Dr. Snell, Archdeacon of Chester, baptized." (Register of Wigan, co. Lanc.)

[4] The eldest of these daughters, Elizabeth, married Thomas Bennett, of Barnston, co. Chester; the second, Margaret, married Thomas Jepson (?), of Maner (?), near Hawarden; the third, Katherine, was unmarried; the fourth, Lydia, married John Parker, of Watford, co. Hertford; the fifth, Dove (?), married Robert Dicas, of Burton, in Gresford parish; and the sixth, Eleanor, was unmarried. (Harl. MS. 2040, f. 68ᵇ.)

[5] He paid his composition for First Fruits for the Rectory of Wallasey 9 Feb. 17 James [1619-20], and again, on a re-presentation to the same rectory, on the 19 May 21 James [1623].

[6] He paid his composition for First Fruits for Waverton on the 30 March, 9 Charles, 1633.

[7] The exact dates of his leaving Wallasey and Waverton are at present uncertain.

COAT OF ARMS ON THE BRASS TO ROWLAND WARING, GENT., 1605
(See page 48.)

List of the Rectors of St. Mary's.

c. 1200 to 1893.

(From the Episcopal Registers at Lichfield and Chester, the Record Office, London, the Parish Registers and Churchwardens' Accounts, &c., &c.)

Temp. King John. [1199-1216.] RICHARD DE COTON.
Presented by Hugh, Abbot of St. Werburgh and the Convent of the same.

The name of this, the earliest known rector of St. Mary's, I fortunately met with in one of the *Harleian MSS.* in the British Museum (*MS.* 1994, f. 262). That MS. is one of the Randle Holme collection, and is mostly in the handwriting of the third Randle Holme, who describes this particular record as "an old roll lent me by Dr. Bridgeman, Deane of Chester in Feb. 1661[-2]." That roll contained an account of certain " Pleas at Chester. 13 Richard II. [22 June 1389 to 21 June 1390] relating to St. Werburghs Abbey and recent presentations to the churches of the Abbey &c." The then Abbot states that "Hugh late Abbot, *temp.* King John, presented to the said church of S¹ Mary-on-the-Hill a certain clerk Richard de Coton, who was admitted on that presentation and instituted and inducted in the time of King John."

The name of no other rector is at present known till the beginning of the 14th century, when the Episcopal Registers at Lichfield supply the following presentations :—

    1314. 3rd Kalends of May [29 April]. ROBERT DE CLIPSTON.
Presented by the Abbot and Convent of St. Werburgh at Chester.

    1324. 18th Kalends of February [15 January]. RICHARD DE ST. EDMUND.
Presented by Edward the King [as Earl of Chester] by reason of the temporalities of the Abbey of St. Werburgh at Chester being vacant and in his hands. [Cause of vacancy not given.]

He occurs on the *Cheshire Recognizance Rolls* on Jan. 20, 1326-7, as "the lord (*dominus*) Richard de S¹ Edmund, parson of the church of S¹ Mary-on-the-Hill, near the Castle of Chester."

This rector was the celebrated RICHARD DE BURY (*i.e.*, Bury St. Edmunds), who was an active statesman and churchman in the reign of Edward III., being created Bishop of Durham in 1333, and Lord Treasurer and Lord Chancellor of England in 1334. At the time of his presentation to St. Mary's he was already Dean of Wells, to which office he was appointed on the 20th Feb. 1322, being described in the Episcopal Register as "Richard de Bury *alias* de Sancto Edmundo." He was also at this time Chamberlain of Chester, appointed in 1321. In 1435, the year of his death, he completed his *Philobiblon*, "a pious memorial of himself before God," a book which has made his memory so dear to Bibliophiles.¹

    1327. 7th Kalends of January [26 December]. ALAN DE RETFORD.
Presented by the Abbot and Convent of St. Werburgh at Chester, on the resignation of the lord (*domini*) Richard de St. Edmund, the last rector.

His name occurs on the *Cheshire Recognizance Rolls* on the 13th Oct. 1328, and 19th July, 1331, in both of which entries he is described as parson or rector of St. Mary's.

---

¹ An interesting account of Richard de Bury was contributed to the *Cheshire Sheaf* in 1880 (vol. ij., pp. 68, 74, and 96) by the late Mr. J. E. Bailey, F.S.A. A much fuller memoir of him by Mr. E. C. Thomas, with a translation of the *Philobiblon*, has since been published.

*Hemingway Vol II p. 106. gives 1342. Thomas de Bexynton (not Byvynton)
and from St Peter's Church (p. 87) in 1349 Robertus de Bexington.
Henry de Belynton ?removing armour-beam to forward the Abbot of Chester died 1345.*

ST. MARY-ON-THE-HILL, CHESTER.

1335. 10th Kalends of August [23 July]. THOMAS DE CAPONHURST.
Presented by the Abbot and Convent of St. Werburgh at Chester, on the resignation of Alan de Retford, the last rector.

1338. 2nd Nones September [4 Sept.]. GUY DE NEWTON.
Presented by the Abbot and Convent of St. Werburgh at Chester, on the resignation of Thomas de Caponhurst, the last rector.

In 1337 this rector was beneficed at Coddington (*Cheshire Recognizance Rolls*). On the same rolls he occurs as parson of St. Mary's on the 19th Jan. 1338-9.

1342. 6th Kalends October [26 Sept.]. THOMAS DE BYVYNTON.
Presented by the Abbot and Convent of St. Werburgh at Chester, on the death of Guy de Newton, the last rector.

He was afterwards rector of Astbury, from 1343 to 1368. It has been conjectured that his name may be the same as Bebington, from the place of that name in Wirral Hundred. He was also for some time rector of Thurstanton in that Hundred.

1343. 7th Kalends November [26 Oct.]. RICHARD DE OCLEGH.
Presented by the Abbot and Convent of St. Werburgh at Chester, on the resignation of Thomas de Byvynton, by reason of an exchange with the church of Astbury.

This rector was presented to Astbury by the Abbot and Convent of St. Werburgh on 9th Kalends Oct. [23 Sept.], 1336, and is mentioned as such on the *Cheshire Recognizance Rolls* in 1342. In 1343, and again on Sept. 11, 1347, he occurs on the same rolls as rector of St. Mary's. His name is sometimes spelt Okley or Okeleye.

[c. 1362]. JOHN DE SHEYNTON.
[Probably presented by the Abbot and Convent of St. Werburgh at Chester, but his presentation has not occurred.]

On the 3rd Ides of March, 1362, John de Sheynton [? Shevington] had a dispensation to leave his church for the purposes of study, and is then spoken of as "Rector of St Mary on the Hill, Chester."

*See Repert h. 36.
f. 440.1*

1363. 18th Kalends December [14 Nov.]. JOHN SQUIER.
Presented by the Abbot and Convent of St. Werburgh at Chester. [Cause of vacancy not stated, but the rectory is said to have become vacant on the Wednesday next following the feast of St. Michael.]

This rector retired in 1403[1] on a pension of 40 marks per annum, of which 20 marks is recorded to have been paid to him on Oct. 17, 1404, by the Abbot of St. Werburgh (*Cheshire Recognizance Rolls*). He is then described as "John Squier of Sainsbury." This pension continued to be paid him up to Jan. 27, 1412-13.

1403. 1st May. JOHN DE WYLASTON.
Presented by the Abbot and Convent of St. Werburgh at Chester. [Although the cause of vacancy is not stated, it was on the resignation of John Squier, the last rector.]

In *Harl. MS.* 2007, f. 83^b, is a copy of a deed dated 1419 to which "John de Willaston parson of the church of the Blessed Mary on the Hill at Chester" was a party. His name frequently occurs on the *Cheshire Recognizance Rolls* from 1405 to 1423, so that he appears to have been a well-known man in Chester.

---

[1] It has been stated that *Richard de Madley* and *John de Altcar* were rectors of St. Mary's c. 1380, but no confirmation of this has occurred, and it is almost certain that John Squier was there from 1363 to 1403.

1395
August 5.

William de Hoton and William de Kirkeby, glover of Chester, give to Hugh Holes, Roger Erneys, William de Wybunbury, Randal de Apelton, John de Weverham, Roger de Draycote, parishioners of the parish of St Mary on the Hill, on behalf of their fellow parishioners, recognizance in 100 marks that William Stake, clerk and "aque bagillarius" of the church of the said parish, should faithfully serve the said parishioners in the said office. Recognizance Rolls of Chester. [18 & 19 Ric. 2. m. 6 d. (7).] 36 Report p. 98.

William de Hoton died in 1396. There was a William de Kirkeby of Chester, barker who in 1393 purchased the bark of oaks in the forest of Mara at 2s. 8d. the oak. (p. 275).

Hugh de Holes was justice of Chester and appears to have been knighted about 1400.

William Stake, clerk does not appear in the list of the Clergy of St Mary on the Hill, and this appears only in the above instance.

William de Wybunbury was a webster or weaver, of the City of Chester and became tenant jointly with other persons of the fulling mills of the Dee for seven years in 1402 at £10.13.4 yearly

LIST OF THE RECTORS OF ST. MARY'S.

He died on the 7th April, 1430, and was commemorated by stained glass placed to his memory in the church (*see* p. 34).

1430. .... April. RICHARD PENSELL.[1]

Presented by William Troutbeck, Esq., on the death of John de Wylaston, the last rector, on the 7th April last.

In *Harl. MS.* 2022, f. 18, is a copy of a deed dated 24 Henry 6 [1446] in which the name of "Richard Pensell, parson of the church of the Blessed Mary" occurs. His name is frequently to be met with on the *Cheshire Recognizance* and *Plea Rolls* in 1433, 1439, &c.

During his incumbency the Chantry Chapel at the end of the south aisle was built by William Troutbeck, Esq., and Joan his wife in 1433 (*see* p. 31), and on the 23rd Sept. 1444, they founded a chantry there and dedicated it to the Holy Trinity (*see* p. 32).

He died in 1458 and, like his predecessor, was commemorated by stained glass placed to his memory in the church (*see* p. 35).

1458. 17th May. JAMES STANLEY.

Presented by the Abbot and Convent of St. Werburgh at Chester, on the death of Richard Pensell, the last rector.

On the 16th Sept. 1464, this rector was presented to St. Peter's, Chester, by the Abbot and Convent of St. Werburgh, having effected an exchange with Roger Asser, the then rector there. He resigned St. Peter's in 1466 and went to Hawarden.

1464. 16th September. ROGER ASSER.

Presented by the Abbot and Convent of St. Werburgh at Chester, on the resignation of James Stanley, the last rector, by reason of an exchange with the church of St. Peter at Chester.

In a chronological account of the city of Chester[2] it is stated that on the 15th January, 1470[-1] "Roger Asser, dean of S' Johns and parson of S' Marys" died.

1471. 10th July. HENRY SMYTH.

Presented by the Abbot and Convent of St. Werburgh at Chester, on the death of Roger Asser, the last rector.

He occurs on the *Cheshire Recognizance Rolls* in 1480.

1498[-9]. 2nd January. JOHN VEYSY, LL.D.

Presented by the Abbot and Convent of St. Werburgh at Chester, on the death of Henry Smyth, the last rector.

1506. 4th August. JAMES STRAITBARELL.

Presented by the Abbot and Convent of St. Werburgh at Chester, by reason of an exchange with the prebend of Alton Boriall in the Cathedral Church of Salisbury.

In the earliest Act Book now preserved at Chester it is stated that this rector was presented on the resignation of Mr. John Veysy, Doctor of Laws, and that "he was admitted instituted and inducted by Magister Robert Cliffe, the Bishop's official at Chester."

[? 1523. 2 May.] MAURICE BIRCHINSHAW, LL.B.

[No particulars as to the presentation of this rector or the cause of vacancy appear to be on record.]

---

[1] The name of *Humphrey Rolley*, presented by Sir William de Atherston, Knt., on the 9th April, 1430, has been given as having been a rector of St. Mary's, but no confirmation of this has occurred, and there is no doubt that Richard Pensell was the rector from 1430 to 1458.

[2] Ormerod's *History of Cheshire*, vol. i, p. 233.

1527[-8]. 9th March. JOHN DAVENPORT, M.A.

Presented by the Abbot and Convent of St. Werburgh at Chester, on the resignation of Maurice Birchinshaw, the last rector.

This rector was commemorated in the old stained glass formerly placed in the east window of the chancel (*see* p. 34).

1534. 11th May. JOHN BRERETON.

Presented by the Abbot and Convent of St. Werburgh at Chester, on the death of John Davenport, the last rector.

This rector was the third son of Sir Randle Brereton, of Shocklach, co. Chester, knight, and brother of Sir William Brereton, Knt., who was beheaded in 1536. He was instituted to the rectory of Bebington, co. Chester, on the 14th March, 1511, and subsequently held the living of Astbury from 1535 to 1542. He also held *both* moieties of the church of Malpas from 1533 to 1542, being the only rector of that church who ever did so. His death occurred in 1542. In some of his presentations he is styled "decretorum doctor," doctor of decrees (?).

1542. 22 November. RICHARD WHITEHEAD.

Presented by Ottiwell Worseley, gentleman, by reason of a grant of the next presentation made by the Abbot and Convent of St. Werburgh at Chester, on the death of John Brereton, the last rector.

The grant of the next presentation above referred to is enrolled in the earliest Institution Book at Chester (1502 to 1576), fol. 14. It bears date 5th Oct. 1536, and is a grant by John, Abbot of the Monastery of St. Werburgh in the city of Chester, of the order of St. Benedict and the Convent of the same, the true and undoubted patrons of the parish church of the blessed St. Mary-on-the-Hill in the said city, to John Byrkenhead, Esq., and Ottiwell Worseley, gentlemen, of the next presentation to the said rectory.

Mr. Richard Whitehead was admitted and instituted on the 25th November, 1542. The original presentation dated 22 Nov. 1542, addressed to John [Bird] Bishop of Chester, and signed " per me Otuelum Worseley," is still preserved in the Bishop's Registry at Chester. It is the earliest original presentation to St. Mary's now preserved there.

On the 14th March, 34th Henry VIII. (1542-3), the advowson of St. Mary's having in the meantime been granted to the Dean and Chapter of the newly created Cathedral of Chester, Henry Man, D.D. (*sacrœ theologiœ professor*) and Dean of the Cathedral of Chester and "the canons or prebendaries of the said Cathedral in chapter assembled," as patrons "of the parish church of the blessed Mary, the Virgin, commonly called the church of the blessed Mary on the hill in the city of Chester," granted to Edmund Gee, Thomas Langley, and William Rogers, *alias* Rogerson, of Chester, the next presentation to the said rectory. To this grant, the original of which is now in the Bishop's Registry at Chester, there is a fragment of the Dean and Chapter seal still remaining.

On the 28th March, 1543, the above grantees made the next presentation to the rectory as follows :—

1543. 28th March. HENRY MAN, D.D.

Presented by Edmund Gee, Thomas Langley, and William Rogers, *alias* Rogerson, of the city of Chester, by virtue of a grant to them of the next presentation by the Dean and Chapter of Chester dated 14th March last past, on the death of Richard Whitehead, the late rector.

This rector was admitted and instituted on the 30th March, 1543, but there would appear to have been some disputes about this presentation, for on the 19th April, the King, Henry VIII., presented another rector as shown by the following entry, duly enrolled, like the previous one, in the first volume of the Institution Books now preserved at Chester.

Dr. Henry Man is stated to have been a Carthusian monk at the Charterhouse, London, and also one of the brethren of Sion College, London. He was the second Dean of Chester, to which office he was

LIST OF THE RECTORS OF ST. MARY'S.   81

appointed on the 8th October, 1541. On the 22nd January, 1546, he was elected Bishop of Sodor and Man, which he held for a time *in commendam* with the Deanery of Chester. He died 17th October, 1556.

1543. 19th April. JAMES COURTHORPE, M.A.

Presented by the King [Henry VIII.] as the true patron of the church of St. Mary in the city of Chester, vacant by the death of the last incumbent [Richard Whitehead].

This rector appears to have been duly admitted and instituted, but the date of institution is not given.

It is not quite clear which of these two rectors succeeded in establishing his claim, but it is probable that HENRY MAN, D.D., who was at that time Dean of Chester, retained St. Mary's. In 1544 the Churchwardens' Accounts record the burial of "Sir *John Acre*," who was no doubt one of the priests serving at St. Mary's.

1546. 23rd April. THOMAS TAYLOR.

Presented by Henry [Man] by divine permission Bishop of Sodor [and Man] and Dean of Chester and the Chapter of the same, on the resignation of the last rector [? Henry Man].

The following entry occurs in the extracts from the old Register of St. Mary's (*Harl. MS.* 2177, f. 113), "S' Thomas Taylor p̃son there was married 16 of November 1550," but the name of his wife is not given. There is also the entry of "Clement son of Tho. Taylor baptized 18 Aug. 1553."

By a deed dated 28th June, 38 Henry VIII. [1546], the Dean and Chapter of the Cathedral church of Christ and the Blessed Mary of Chester, the true patrons of the parish church of the Blessed Mary-upon-the-Hill in the city of Chester, grant to Sir Thomas Caurden, or Cawerden, Knt., his executors and assigns, the next presentation to the said church.[1] By another deed dated on the 11th February, 3rd Edward VI. [1548-9], he transferred this next presentation to Richard Colly, gentleman,[2] who in turn granted it to Randle Brereton of the city of Chester, gentleman, by deed dated 28th May in the same year.

In 1546 *Edmond Burton* is described as Curate at St. Mary's.[3] In 1548 the Churchwardens' Accounts mention "Sir *Henry Browne*,"[4] "Sir George,"[4] and "Sir Oliver,"[4] three priests probably connected with St. Mary's, and in 1550 "Sir *Hugh Ley*" is mentioned, and in 1551 "Sir *Richard Faulkner*." The copy of the earliest Register of St. Mary's, which is now missing, (contained in *Harl. MS.* 2177), records the burial of "Sir *Richard Stancliffe* priest" on the 5th April, 1548, and that of "Sir *Henry Browne*, priest, son of Thomas Browne," on the 13th June, 1553.

1554. 10th September. CHARLES DUCKWORTH.

Presented by John Brereton, of Eccleston, co. Chester, gentleman, by reason of the assignment to him by Margaret Goodman and Ursula Goodman, the assigns of [Sir] Thomas Carden [Knt.], the patron, by reason of the grant of the advowson made to him by the Dean and Chapter of the Cathedral church of Chester dated 28th June, 38th Henry VIII. [1546] [on the deprivation of Thomas Taylor, the last incumbent].

He was admitted and instituted on the 25th Sept. 1554. In the original presentation, preserved in the Bishop's Registry at Chester, the living is said to have been vacant "owing to the deprivation of Sir Thomas Talior the last incumbent."

There would also seem to have been a dispute about this presentation, for on the 15th Sept. 1554, WILLIAM BROGDEN, M.A., was presented by Edward . . . . of Chester, gentleman, and Ellen his wife, administrators of Thomas Bennett of Chester, deceased, by reason of a grant of the next presentation to the said Thomas Bennett by Sir Thomas Cawrden, Knt., the true patron, on the deprivation of Thomas

---

[1] Original deed in the Bishop's Registry at Chester, with a portion of the seal remaining.
[2] *Ibid.—ibid.*
[3] Will in the Enrollment Books at Chester, vol. i., f. 143.
[4] "Sir" was at this time a common designation for a priest or clergyman, and originally signified one who had taken a degree at a university. It was used till the middle of the 17th century, and is to be found in Shakespeare.

Taylor, the last incumbent.[1] Nothing more is known of Mr. Brogden, but Charles Duckworth succeeded to the living and gave a bond to the Bishop dated 6 Oct. 1554.[2] He paid his composition for First Fruits on the 2 March, 1554[-5] and retained possession of the living for over forty years. In 1533-4 Charles Duckworth had been returned at the Bishop's Visitation as a stipendary priest at Aldford paid by the rector, and in 1547 he is described as curate there.

Unfortunately nothing is at present known of the family history of this rector, who was here for such an unusually long period. He died in 1596, but his will, if he made any, is not now preserved at Chester. In the Churchwardens' Accounts there are several references to a *George Duckworth*, who appears to have helped the rector, and who was not improbably his son. Later on another Charles Duckworth was beneficed in the diocese of Chester, and was presented to Dodleston in 1634.

The deprivation of Thomas Taylor was probably due to his being a married man when, on the accession of Queen Mary in July, 1553, the Roman Catholic religion was again revived and many of the married clergy were turned out of their livings.

In 1570 *James Milner* was "Curate of S[t] Marys on the hill in Chester" (*Harl. MS.* 2177. f. 113. Notes from the old Registers of St. Mary's, now lost). In the year 1580 the Churchwardens' Accounts contain an entry to the effect that on the 12 July in that year *Robert Collier*, clerk, came there as Curate. The Churchwardens' Accounts also note the burial in 1587 of "*Sir Hugh Ley*, priest, some time curate." He was here in 1550 (*see* before). see 226.

1596. 4th June. ROBERT COLLIER.

Presented by Richard Brereton, Esq. [of Eccleston], on the death of Charles Duckworth, the last rector.

As recorded in the Institution Book in the Bishop's Registry at Chester (vol. ii., p. 25) he was duly inducted to the rectory of St. Mary-on-the-Hill, by James Milner, clerk [who had been previously the curate there], in the presence of Robert Brerewood, Alderman, Thomas Wierden, Robert Sandford, Randle Whitbie, William Cross, John Houghton (?), clerk of the said church, John Gregory, Thomas Rogerson, Robert Cadie, Richard Crosse, and Thomas Powell. He paid his composition for First Fruits on the 8th July, 1596.[3]

Mr. Collier must have been well known to the parishioners of St. Mary's before he became rector, for it is recorded in the first volume of the Churchwardens' Accounts, "Robert Colliere clarke came to be Curate in this yeare 1580 Julij xij"."

In February 1621-2 Mr. Collier, as Rector of St. Mary's, and Mr. Gill, as "Lecturer" there, contributed the sums of 10 shillings and 5 shillings respectively to the fund raised amongst the clergy of the diocese of Chester towards " the recovery of the Palatinate."[4]

This rector died in the summer of 1623, after having held this living for 27 years. His will, dated 4th July, was proved at Chester on the 6th Aug. 1623. He describes himself as "Robert Collier clarke, Rector of S[t] Maries," and begins by dividing his six "best spoons" equally amongst his three daughters Katherine, Elizabeth, and Jane, "and the other three spoons I leave to my wife, together with my little silver cup, my two kine, my best bed, well furnished, both with linen and woollen, my great press, my great new chest together with tables, chairs," &c., conditionally upon her giving to his daughter Jane as much linen as his other daughters, who were then married, had received. He left the remainder of his goods equally between his daughters, and appointed his son-in-law, Thomas Wright, his sole executor. The will is signed "By me Robert Collier, Rector of S[t] Maries." In a codicil he bequeathed to his other son-in-law, Wm. Smith, "all my Latin Books, according to my promise formerly made," and he left to "Mr. Brereton," prob-

[1] Mr. G. J. Piccope's Notes from presentations and proceedings at Chester.
[2] *Ibid.—ibid.*
[3] Record Society (Lancashire and Cheshire) publications, vol. viij., p. 401.
[4] *Ibid.—ibid.*, vol. xij., p. 60.

LIST OF THE RECTORS OF ST. MARY'S.

ably the patron of the living, "a piece of gold to the value of 22 shillings," and to Mr. John Gill, his curate, "Stultetus (?) on Esaiah" for a remembrance. The only witness to the will is "John Gill, clericus."

The inventory of his effects was taken on the 31st July, 1623, and amongst the items "18 coats of armes or scuchins" are valued at 3s., and "his books of all sorts" at £18 12s. 6d. In his "Study" there were, amongst other things, "3 little desks, a sword, a head piece, 2 daggers and other implements" valued at 7s. 6d. He had in money owing to him £16 12s. *Inventory 1625.*

His daughter, Jane Collier, only survived her father a few weeks. Her will, dated the 20th Sept. 1623, and proved at Chester on the 8th October in that year, contains many items of interest. She desired her body "to be buried upon my father's corpse in the church of St. Marys." "To the poor of St. Marys parish" she bequeathed £5 for a stock "and the poor to have every Good Friday 10s worth of bread." "To the poor of St. Toolors [i.e., St. Olaves] 10s, to St. Michaels 10s. to St. Bridgets 10s, to St. Martins 10s, to Trinity 10s, to St. Peters 10s, to Little St. Johns 10s, to St. Oswalds 15s, and to St. Johns parish 15s." She also bequeathed the following legacies: "to my son John Crosse" £30, "to my brother Smith 22s, to my brother Wright 22s, to Mr. Brereton 20s, to my sister Wright 20s, to her son Timothy 20s and 2 spoons, to my sister Smith and her three sons 20s each, to my mother 20s, to widow Grenwall 20s, to my father in law Crosse 5s, to Joseph Teggen [the parish clerk] 5s," and several other small sums to different persons. She desired her brother [in law], Thomas Wright, to be her executor.

The will is endorsed on the back as that of "Jane Collier *alias* Crosse late of the city of Chester deceased." The executor's accounts are preserved with the will, and some extracts may here be given. *Inventory 1625.*
They are described as "the accounts of Thomas Wright executor of the last will of Jane Collyer, late of *Wills. p.n.*
the parish of St Mary in the city of Chester deceased, made the 13 February 1625[6]."

Item paid for the coffin 7s. 6d.
„ for blacking the coffin 12d.
„ for the loan of blacks for the bier and pulpit 6d.
„ to the ringers for ringing 4s.
„ for beer for the ringers 18d.
„ to Mr. Asbrooke[1] for funeral sermon 20s.
„ to Joseph Tegen, the clerk, for his duties and grave making 18d.
„ to Mr. Gill for redeeming books the decedent had pawned to him 15s.

Mr. *John Gill*, M.A., above referred to was for many years curate at St. Mary's. He is called "Lecturer" in 1622.

1623. 16th December. FRANCIS EDWARDS,[2] M.A.

Presented by Richard Brereton, Esq. [of Eccleston], on the death of Robert Collier, the last incumbent.

He was admitted and inducted on the 23rd December "by John Gyll, Master of Arts, Curate of St. Marys," when he gave the usual bond to the Bishop of Chester. As these bonds are of uncommon occurrence, and are very interesting from the stipulations they contain, I have copied that given by him in full.

Bond to the Rev. father in Christ, John, by Divine permission, Bishop of Chester, in the sum of £100, given by Francis Edwards, clerk, rector of the parish church of St. Mary on the Hill in the city of Chester. Dated 23rd Dec. 1623.

"The Condičon of the within written obligačon is such That yf the within bounden FFRANCIS

---

[1] Mr. Asbrook was "curate of St Johns" in 1622 (Record Society, vol. xij., p. 60), and probably was still there in 1623.
[2] In the Institution Books at Chester (vol. ij., p. 102) there is an entry under date of the 11th August, 1623, that at Bangor on that date the Rev. Father, John, Bishop of Chester (would have) instituted Master THOMAS BRIDGES, clerk, to the rectory of St. Mary-on-the-Hill, in the city of Chester, on the presentation of Mr. . . . . . Brereton, vacant by the death of the last incumbent, but he declined to be instituted. In the margin there is this entry : "Md he would not accept it & therefore could not be inducted."

M 2

EDWARDS clerke instituted unto the Rectory of St Maries within menconed Doe not only preach and expound the word reuently to his best power in the said Church of St Maries at tymes Convenient to the Congregaton there Comitted to his Charge as befitteth his place and Callinge but alsoe Doe every Sabaoth and festiuall Daie, vnlesse hee Can shew iust Cause of his absence or otherwise be licensed by the within named Reuend father or other iudge Competent in that behalfe, instruct the youth of the sayd pishe in the Catachisme and Doe painfully vse Cure and Diligence therein. And further doe att all tymes hereafter against all manner of persons whatsoeuer saue Defend and keepe harmeles the said reuend father of and from all and all manner of Charges, suits troubles and Incumbrances whatsoeuer which may at any tyme hereafter happen to arrise accrue and growe for or by reason of the grauntinge of the sayd Institucon and induccon to the said ffrancis Edwards. And yf it fortune the tytle or presentacon whereby hee was presented to be lawfully Disproved and any other lawfully approved then yf the sayd ffrancis Edwards Doe within one moneth next after warninge giuen vnto him by the sayd reuend father resigne the sayd Rectory and all his right title and interest in and to the same into the hands of the sayd reuend father accordinge to lawe in that behalfe provided then this obligacon to be voyd and of none effect or ells the same to stand and remaine in full power and vertue."

He paid his composition for First Fruits for St. Mary's, and also for Heswall (in Wirral Hundred), of which parish he was also Rector,[1] on the 14th April, 1624.[2]

This rector was the second son of John Edwards, of Cheveley, co. Chester, gentleman, (who died at Cheveley on the 26th Nov. 1637, and was buried at Eccleston church), by his wife Elizabeth, daughter of John Welch, of Bignall Hill, co. Stafford.[3] He was 42 years of age at his father's death and so must have been born about the year 1595. He married Elizabeth, daughter of John Cooke, sometime Sheriff of Chester, by whom he had a large family. Only one of his children was baptized at St. Mary's. The dates of their respective births are as follows: –Francis, born December, 1630; Elizabeth, June 19. 1631; Francis, Oct. 5, 1632; John, Feb. 6, 1633-4; William, June 10, 1635; Ann, June 26, 1636; Thomas, Sept. 25, 1637; Andrew and Peter, Nov. 30, 1638; Theodor, May 24, 1640; Francis, July 13, 1641, and John, Feb. 17, 1642-3.[4] The only children baptized and buried at St. Mary's are thus noticed in the Register :–

1629 ffrancis sonne to Mr ffrancis Edwards Parson yr 10th day of December, baptized.
1630 ffrancis sonne of Mr Parson Edwards bur. 24th day of Aprill.
1641[-2] John sonne of ffrancis Edwards Clerke Rector of this Church buried in the Chancell in the middle of yr crosse walke below the stepps neere the end of the communion table 21th day of Januarie.
1654 A sonne of Parson Edwards buried vnder Mrs Cookes stone 13th day of November.
1659 Anne Edwards Daughter to Parson Edwards was buried in the north yle vnder Mrs Cookes ston on the 18th Day of June.[5]

His name occurs in 1624, 1634, 1635, 1636, and 1639, as paying various sums of money as his contributions from the rectories of St. Marys and Heswall for clerical subsidies, ship-money, the repair of St. Paul's Cathedral, London, &c."

[1] He was presented to Heswall by John Edwards, probably his father, patron for this turn from the Bishop of Chester, and was instituted 12th April, 1624.
[2] Record Society (Lancashire and Cheshire), vol. viij., p. 404.
[3] *Cheshire and Lancashire Funeral Certificates*, Record Society, vol. vj., p. 79.
[4] These particulars are taken from a series of extracts relating to the Edwards family, copied from an old family Bible and printed in the *Genealogist*, N.S., 1886. vol. ij., p. 116. The writer of the earliest entries appears to have been the Thomas Edwards born 1637, who married in 1663 and died 1687 leaving issue. He heads the above list of children thus: "the time of the bearth of my fathers children Borne at heswall in werrall in Cheshire," but he nowhere mentions his father's name and it was only by a comparison of names and dates that I was enabled to identify him.
[5] The burial of this daughter is thus entered in the Register of Holy Trinity, Chester, the month and date being different :— "Ann Edwards Daughter to parson Edwards died at Mrs Hands the 20 of October 1659 and was buried the 22 day of the same month at St Maryes."

Record Society, vol. vij., pp. 78-9, 91, 100-1, 115-6, 119.

LIST OF THE RECTORS OF ST. MARY'S.

It is clear from these entries that Mr. Edwards was still rector in the beginning of the year 1642, but some time in that year he probably resigned, as I find that he was still at Heswall for several years longer. His wife Elizabeth was buried there in 1647, and his own burial is thus entered : " 1653. Francis Edwards, Pastor of Heswall, buried Nov. 20th."[1]

As already stated *Mr. John Gill*, M.A., was "Curate of St. Marys" at the time of Mr. Edwards' appointment as rector in 1623, and in the previous year we find him described as "Lecturer" there (*see* p. 82). His name has not occurred subsequent to 1626, but in the Register under date the 17th July, 1630, there is an entry of the baptism of "Philip sonne to *Thomas Walmesley* Clerke," but it is not probable that he was Curate here, as the transcript of the Register for that year, 1630, is signed "*Richd Kyrke* Curate." In 1636 there is this entry, "Elinor Seddon daughter of William Seddon Clerke baptized 6th day of November," and in 1638 "William Seddon sonne of William Seddon Clerke and now Curate of this Church baptized the 5th day of July."[1]

Of this curate of St. Mary's, *William Seddon*, M.A., we have fortunately some very interesting particulars preserved to us in a letter sent by his son the Rev. Edward Seddon, of Throwley, co. Devon, dated 10th July, 1704, and addressed to the Rev. John Walker, the author of "Sufferings of the Clergy," 1715. This letter supplies such a graphic picture of the times during the Civil War and Commonwealth periods that I have copied almost the whole of it although it is a somewhat lengthy one.[2]

"The Reverend Mr. WILLIAM SEDDON (my most honoured Father) M.A. of Magdalen Coll, in Camb, being about the year of our Lord 1636, settl'd a preacher in one of ye parish Churches, I think St. Maries, in ye city of Chester, was then also possess'd of a Vicarage at Eastham (about six miles distant from y^t City, value 68^{li} per annum), where he liv'd with his wife and family in a very happy condition, till ye Civil war's breaking out, and ye Parliament's forces drawing on to besiege Chester, he was compel'd to withdraw his family and effects into ye City for succour, where his great and good Friend and Pastor, ye Lord Bishop Bridgman, then Lord Bishop of Chester, accommodated him with several rooms and lodgings in his own Palace ; and yet the aged Bishop dreading the hardships of a siege, voided the place, leaving my Father in his Palace, who continued diligent in his ministry, and frequent Preaching to ye Garrison there. And the City being closely besieg'd, and frequently storm'd, my Mother was on ye 12th day of Octob., 1645, delivered of me her 9th child, (all the 9 then living) and said to be ye last y^t was publickly baptiz'd in ye Font of y^t Cathedral there before ye restoracon in 1660. The city being surrendered upon Articles, my Father was shortly apprehended and made Prisoner, and after some short durance was demanded by ye prevailing Powers, why he had not, according to ye Articles of surrender, march'd off with ye Garrison to ye Kings Quarters, to which he reply'd, y^t he thought his Cassock had vnconcern'd him in those Articles, being a Minister in ye City, but above all he had a wife, and many small children there, which if he could see tolerably dispos'd of he would, not vnwillingly, accept the Articles.

"But many complaints being made against him, y^t he had in his preaching reflected upon the proceedings of the prevailing party, and had animated ye Garrison to resist even unto blood, &c., he was remanded to Prison again, and his house permitted to be plunder'd by ye souldiers, who despoil'd him not of his goods only, but of his books and papers, which they exposed to sale at a

---

[1] In the Churchwardens' Accounts for 1636 there is this entry,
"Given Mr Seddon by the Gentlemens appointment in parte of requital of his paines att the fasts xx^s."

[2] This letter first appeared in *Local Gleanings relating to Lancashire and Cheshire*, (an antiquarian periodical edited by me), March 9th, 1877 (vol. ij., No. 517). It was subsequently reprinted in the *Correspondence of Nathan Walworth*, printed by the Chetham Society (vol. cix.), with notes by the late Mr. J. E. Bailey, F.S.A., and in January 1881, it was reprinted in the *Cheshire Sheaf*, Nos. 1450 and 1459. The original is among the collections for Walker's "Sufferings of the Clergy," in the Bodleian Library, Oxford.

[3] An entry in the Eastham Register states that William Seddon, M.A. was inducted into the Vicarage there in February, 1637-8. He was presented "by the King by lapse" and was instituted on the 2nd February, 1637-8.

very low rate ; and so by private directions to some of his friends, he repurchas'd some of the most necessary for his own use. But then an order was drawn up to export his wife and children out of y⁰ City to Eastham (which accordingly was done, several of y⁰ younger sort being put into a wagon with other goods which had escap'd the pillage) where though they had only y⁰ bare walls of a Vicarage house to resort to, yet they found a hearty welcome from y⁰ loial part of the parishioners there, amongst whom they dispers'd themselves, and in a short time after, my Father's confinement was somewhat enlarg'd, and his escape conniv'd at, which gave him y⁰ liberty of going in quest of his wife and children, whom he found in pretty good circumstances amongst his loial friends.

"But another minister (whose name and character I have utterly forgot),[1] being dispatch'd with orders from y⁰ ruling powers at Chester to supply the vicarage at Eastham, and a rumour dispers'd y⁴ my father must be apprehended again, and reduc'd as prisoner to Chester, he scamper'd about privately to the houses of y⁰ loyal Gentry, to whom his character and condition were well known, and then despatched a letter to his elder Brother Mr. Peter Seddon at Outwood in Lancashire (y⁰ place of my Father's nativity) who was then, at y⁰ rate of y⁰ times, turn'd zealous Presbyterian too, and had a son a Captain in y⁰ Parliament's army, acquainting him with y⁰ storm he was under, and requesting him to cover either all or part of his ffamily, till he could weather y⁰ storm ; *to which letter y⁰ main of y⁰ answer he had was y⁴ would he conform himself to y⁰ Godly party, his own merits would protect and prefer him,*[2] which so insens'd my Father y⁴ he never more held any correspondence with him. But in his perambulacons amongst y⁰ loialists, conducted by y⁰ good hand of Providence, he met with one Mr. Bratherton, a Lancashire gentleman and a hearty Cavalier, with whom he had former acquaintance, and who by virtue of a deed of trust from one Mr. Byrom, a gentleman, y⁴ was slain in the King's service, had the donacon of a Parsonage call'd Grapenall [Grappenhall] (which was then vacant by y⁰ death of one Mr. Richardson its incumbent) and the presentacon to this Rectory he freely tendered to my Father, perswading him, with all possible secrecy and expedicon, to post up to y⁰ Commissioners or Tryers of Ministers which accordingly my Father did, and upon examinacon was by them approv'd, and recommended to y⁰ Rectory of Grap'nal, a Parsonage worth about 130ˡⁱ per annum, at 16 or 18 miles distance from Chester, and bordering upon Lancashire.

"Here he settled and fix'd himself, well accepted, and beloved by his Parishioners so y⁴ he had time to re-collect his dispersed Family, and enjoy'd a calm ; but this could not be durable, he was soon haunted with the old rumours of a dangerous delinquent, a malignant &c. and this grew up into menaces of articles and complaints and at last into a moral assurance y⁴ one Major Brooks a Parliamenteer officer, (whose malice he had formerly experienced) intended to seize and apprehend him, which caused him for a time to abscond, and afterwards, upon overt attempts made upon him, to flee into Lancashire, where he was by some friends recommended to one Mr. Fleetwood, of Penwortham (a parish situate near to a great market town called Preston, and about 22 miles distant from Grap'nall in Cheshire) who being a very loial gentleman and impropriator of y⁰ tyths of y⁴ parish, entertained him in y⁰ quality of a chaplain, or curate, to preach at y⁴ little church near adjoining to Penwortham Hall.

"Here my father fixed again in this gentleman's house, entirely beloved of his patron (who allowed him 40ˡⁱ per annum), and of all his parishioners, and having intelligence out of Cheshire, y⁴ my mother, whom he had left at Grap'nall with a strict charge to gett y⁰ place supplyed, and keep possession as long as she could, was with her family ejected y⁰ Parsonage house there, and a new Rector, one Mr. Bradshaw, a rigid Presbyterian (whether by appointment of

---

[1] This was John Murcot, a well-known Nonconformist, a B.A. of Oxford, who had studied under John Ley, the celebrated Vicar of Great Budworth. He "was called to Eastham in Wyrrall in Cheshire" from Astbury, before June 1648, but shortly afterwards became minister at West Kirby in Cheshire.

[2] The words in italics are underlined by Mr. Walker, who has written opposite to them, as if in astonishment. "owne Bro' !"

commoners or usurpacon, I know not), put in, he acquainted his Patron, Mr. Fleetwood with it, who thereupon order'd a poor cottage house, at a little distance from his own Hall, to be fitted up, and added 3 or 4 acres of ground to't, to keep a couple of cows, and here, as in a little ark of rest, my Father seated himself with his wife and 9 children, supported and maintain'd by y⁰ good hand of Providence, which order'd him still y⁰ 40ˡˡ pension from his Patron, and large gratuities from y⁰ Loyalists in those parts, whose children he privately baptiz'd, and performed other ministerial offices, at their requests, according to the antient forms of y⁰ church ; which tho' it gave him sometimes y⁰ trouble of musquetiers to guard him into Preston as a Prisoner, yet upon y⁰ mediacon of the neighb'ring Gentlemen he was soon dismiss'd, and return'd to his family to recount his hazard, with his *olim meminisse juvabit*: and tho' in all this time he had not any allowance of a 5th, or any y⁰ least part from either his Parsonage or vicaridg in Cheshire, nor any temporal state whatever, yet he liv'd cheerfully and contentedly, and saw many of his children comfortably dispos'd of and presently upon y⁰ Restoracon in 1660,¹ he ejected Bradshaw again, who though a rigid Presbyterian yet he then trim'd up, and gott another benefice call'd Lym [Lymm] in Cheshire, where I think he dy'd. And my Father being restored to his Rectory at Grp'nall, resetl'd himself and his family in the parsonage house there, where he, and my mother (y⁰ constant partner of his sufferings) aged each of them about 70 years, departed this life, both in one month and lye buried both in one grave in the chancel there, A.D. 1671."²

c. 1642. RICHARD HUNT, B.D.

His presentation has not occurred, but he was probably appointed on the resignation or death of Francis Edwards. He paid his composition for First Fruits on the 30th April, 18 Charles [1642],³ so that he must have been appointed early in that year.

According to a pedigree in *Harl. MSS.* 2161, f. 158ᵇ, he was the son of William Hunt, of Manchester, by his wife Anne, daughter of William Boulton, of Abram, in the parish of Wigan, co. Lanc. He was born on the 2nd March, 1593-4, and was baptized at the Collegiate Church, Manchester, on the 8th of that month. He was not improbably educated at the Manchester Grammar School, and subsequently at Emmanuel College, Cambridge, where he was admitted on the 7th May, 1610, being described as born in Lancashire. He was a scholar of his college and afterwards Fellow. He took his B.A. degree in 1613, that of M.A. in 1617, and B.D. in 1624.⁴ He married Martha, daughter of Humphrey Cole, of Tillingham, near Bradwell-juxta-Mare, co. Essex, by whom he had an only surviving daughter and heiress, Grace, who married John Joyce, son and heir of Mr. Alderman Joyce, of Salisbury, by whom she had issue.

On the 14th May, 1628, he was presented to the vicarage of Acton, near Nantwich, by Sir Richard Wilbraham, of Dorfold, Bart., and he was also for a time vicar of Walsall,⁵ co. Stafford. In the year 1639 he was elected to the prebendal stall of Tarvin in the cathedral at Lichfield.

---

¹ It appears from the Institution Books at the Public Record Office (*Exchequer Records*) that he was instituted to Grappenhall on the 2 March, 1660[-1], on the presentation of John Bretherton, of Hay, co. Lanc., gent., and subsequently was re-instituted to the same benefice on the 18 Sept. 1661, on the presentation of the King. He signs the Registers there in 1661 as rector.

² Katherine, wife of Mr. Seddon, died on August 22nd, and was buried at Grappenhall on the 24th August, 1671. Her husband survived her a few days only, being buried in the church there on the 8th September, 1671. He left no will, but the inventory of his goods is still preserved at Chester, letters of administration being granted to Robert Proudlove, the husband of his daughter Elizabeth. This Robert Proudlove of Grappenhall was married to *Elizabeth Seddon* by licence at Winwick, co. Lanc., on the 9th Oct. 1662. A few days later, in the same church, *Katherine Seddon* was married to Thomas Birkenhead of Warrington, 20th Oct. 1662 ; and again at Winwick on the 22nd August, 1663, *Eleanor Seddon* married Mr. George Becket, of Middlewich. On the 7th April, 1670, *Frances Seddon* was married at Grappenhall to John Brock, Esq., of Reddish Hall, in Grappenhall (see the Grappenhall Registers).

³ Record Society (Lancashire and Cheshire), vol. viij., p. 406.

⁴ *Palatine Note Book*, vol. iv., p. 79.

⁵ His name, however, is not to be found in Willmore's *History of Walsall*, a topographical work of value, recently published.

He was still at St. Mary's on the 9th May, 1644,[1] as appears from an entry in the Churchwardens' Accounts, but shortly after that he was ejected by the Parliamentary forces, possibly on the surrender of the city to them in the spring of 1646. As will subsequently appear he returned to St. Mary's about 1655, and died there in 1662.

[*c.* Feb. 1647-8.] WILLIAM PEARTREE.

[Probably put in by the Parliamentary authorities on the ejection of Richard Hunt, but he is also stated to have been presented by " the patron."]

Mr. Peartree signed "the Cheshire Ministers' Attestation" on the 6th July, 1648, as "pastor of Marys in Chester," but it is probable he had not been there long, for in the Churchwardens' Accounts under Feb. 13, 1647-8, he is referred to as " Mr. Paretree who is presented unto us by the patron to be our minister."

"Master William Peartree" was "minister" (? Vicar) of Wrenbury from about the year 1630 to 1639. and in September, 1642, amongst the names of the Puritan ministers imprisoned by the Royalists, the name of " William Peartree, late of Nantwich " occurs. On the 12th August, 1646, £30 a year from the tithes of Wybunbury were ordered to be paid for the maintenance of " William Peartree, minister of the church of Wybunbury," so that it must be subsequent to that date that he came to St. Mary's. His name occurs in the Registers of St. Mary's in 1648 as " Mr. Peartree Parson."

He died in March, 1654-5, and his burial is thus recorded in the Register :—

1654[-5] Mr. Pearetree Parson of this Church buried in the Quire against the window the 16th day of March.

His will, if he made one, should now be preserved at Somerset House, London (as no wills were proved at Chester 1650-1659), but a search there has not been successful. Nothing is at present known of his family.

[*c.* 1655.] RICHARD HUNT, B.D.

[Re-instated on the death of William Peartree.]

On Mr. Peartree's death, the previous rector, Richard Hunt, B.D., would appear to have been re-instated in his old living. His name occurs in the Churchwardens' Accounts on the 21st July, 1656, when he signs himself " Ric Hunt Rector," and he remained there till his death in 1662.[2] In the Registers of Holy Trinity Church, Chester, there are several entries of marriages by Mr. Hunt in 1658, 1659, and 1660, in some of which he is described as " pastor of St Maries."

He died in August, 1662, the following being the entry of his burial in the Register :—

" Mr. Richard Huntt minister of St. Maryes was buried in the queare [*i.e.*, the choir] on the north side of Docketer Snealls ston on the xxvjth Day of Augus[t]."

In one of Randle Holme's MSS. in the British Museum (*Harl. MS.* 1929) is the following entry :—

25 July [*sic* for August] '62 died that reverent divine, at 6 in the morning, Rich. Hunt, Rector of St Maryes in Chester, whose memory in his learning [will] let his name liue for ever."

His will, dated 26th June, 1662, was proved at Chester on the 20th September in that year. In it he describes himself as " Richard Hunt, Bachelor in Divinity, Rector of St. Maries within the City of Chester, being aged," and desired his body to be decently buried at the discretion of his executor. To the poor of

---

[1] From the Institution Books at the Public Record Office, London (*Exchequer Records*), it would appear that on the 12th April, 1645, WILLIAM NICHOLLS, D.D., was presented to St. Mary's " by the King," but he never held the living. He was rector of Cheadle from 1624 to 1644, and also Dean of Chester. He died in 1657 and was buried at Northenden (see *East Cheshire*, vol. i., pp. 220-1).

[2] It is stated by Mr. J. E. Bailey, F.S.A., in the *Cheshire Sheaf*, vol. i, p. 95, that on "the 25 Feb. 1661-2 Dr. Thomas Mallory [son of the late Dean of Chester] was nominated by the Dean and Chapter of Chester to the rectory of St. Marys, Chester, on the avoidance thereof by Mr. Richard Hunt, in virtue of a certain agreement between him and Capt. Richard Brereton, of Chester." No confirmation of this statement has at present occurred, and Dr. Thomas Mallory never held the rectory of St. Mary's.

[3] That is Dr. Snell, Archdeacon of Chester (of whom an account appears on p. 75), who was buried at St. Mary's in 1656 as thus entered in the Register:—

"1655[-6] Doctor Snell buried in the Quire neere Mr. Pearetrees tombe the 7th day of ffebruary."

MEMORIAL WINDOW ERECTED IN ST. MARY'S CHURCH, CHESTER, TO HEROES OF THE 23RD ROYAL WELSH FUSILIERS.

MEMORIAL WINDOW.

AMONG the memorials to the brave who fell in the war, painted windows are prominent, from the great advance made of late years in this branch of art. The specimen here engraved has just been placed at the east end of the north aisle of St. Mary's Church, Chester, in memory of the heroes of the 23rd Royal Welsh Fusiliers who fell in the Crimea from the victory of the Alma to the capture of Sebastopol. The principal subject represents Aaron and Hur holding up the hands of Moses during the battle between Israel and Amalek, as thus recorded in Exodus xvii.:— "Then came Amalek, and fought with Israel in Rephidim. And Moses said unto Joshua, choose us out men, and go out, fight with Amalek: to-morrow I will stand on the top of the hill with the rod of God in mine hand. So Joshua did as Moses had said to him, and fought with Amalek; and Moses, Aaron, and Hur went up to the top of the hill. And it came to pass when Moses held up his hand that Israel prevailed; and when he let down his hand, Amalek prevailed. But Moses' hands were heavy; and they took a stone, and put it under him; and he sat thereon; and Aaron and Hur stayed up his hands, the one on the one side, and the other on the other side; and his hands were steady until the going down of the sun. And Joshua discomfited Amalek and his people with the edge of the sword." The subject has been skilfully treated by the artist, who has unquestionably produced one of the finest windows in Chester. It is intended to place under the window an engraved tablet, on which are to be inscribed the names of the fallen heroes.

This fine window has been designed and executed by Mr. George Hoggeland, of Grove-place, Islington-grove. The subject—Hur, Aaron, and Moses—occupies three of the five lights; the other two bear scrolls, with the mottoes "Ich dien," and "Nec Aspera terrent," from the colours of the regiment; from which also are taken the Prince of Wales' feathers, which are placed in the upper part of the window. The emblems of England and France—the rose and fleur-de-lis—are repeated, alternately, in various parts of the window. The whole has been executed in the old style, no enamelled glass being employed.

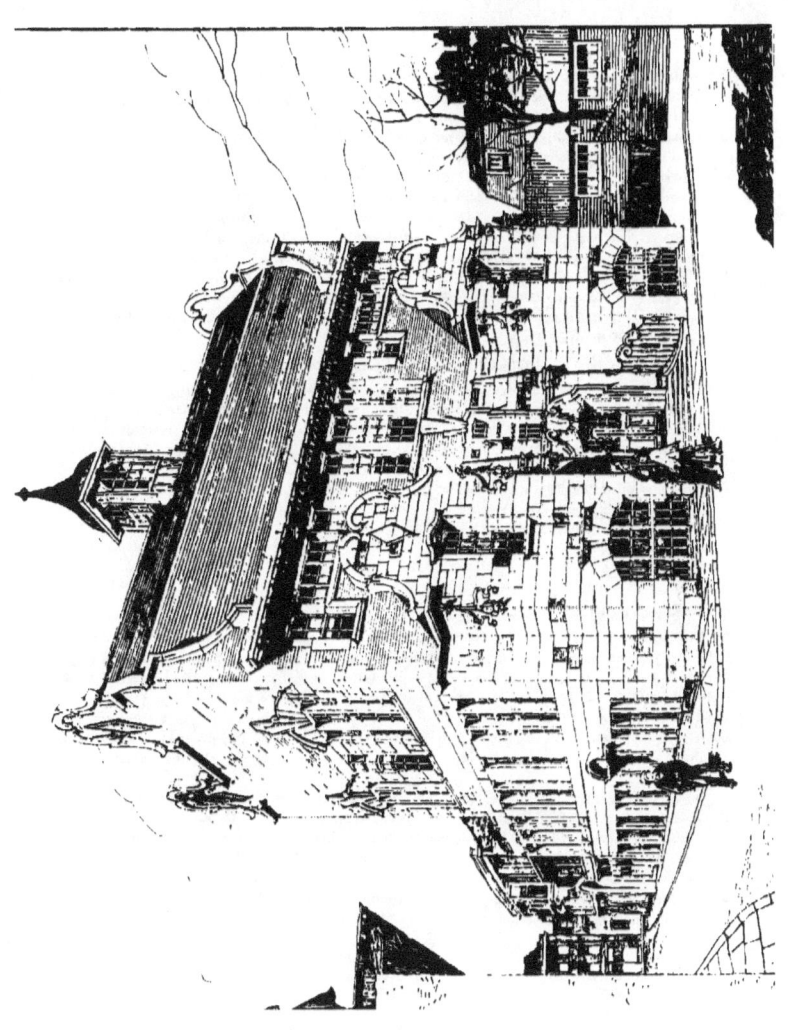

the parish of St. Mary's he bequeathed 20s. "to be distributed amongst them in bread," and he left small legacies to his servants and others, including one of 5s. "to Richard Hill, sexton, to single out my grave and for making the same." To Mr. Thomas Browne he left 20s. to buy him a ring and to Mrs. Browne 10s. for the same purpose. All the residue of his goods he bequeathed to his daughter, Grace Joyce, and appointed his son-in-law, John Joyce, sole executor. Two of the witnesses to the will were Philippa Browne and Thomas Browne. He signed the will "Ric. Hunt" and used a crest as a seal.

When the Rev. John Walker was collecting materials for his history of the "Sufferings of the Clergy" in the year 1706, he had sent to him the following letter, written by the Rev. Samuel Edgley, Vicar of Acton, near Nantwich, and addressed to Nicholas Stratford, then Bishop of Chester.¹ Mr. Edgley enclosed it in a letter to the Bishop, in which he writes that "the inclosed Account touching M' Hunt, I had from M' Wilbraham of Darfold, who is lately dead," and adds "your Lordship may have a testimonial from the Ancient men of St Marys in Chester concerning that worthy Person." "M' Prebend Wright succeeded in the Place but not immediately. I discoursed him but he is a stranger to the ejection of M' Hunt, being very young early in the Warr Time."

TO THE RT. REVEREND FFATHER NICHOLAS LORD BISHOP OF CHESTER.

This may Certify your L'ship that the Reverend M' Richard Hunt formerly vicar of Acton² & also of Wallsall in Staffordshire was removed thence before the warrs by a p'sentacon of the wor'full Roger Wilbraham Esq' of Darfold to the Rectory of St Maryes in Chester, a place at that time vallued about eight score or nine score poundes per Añum. But the said Reverend M' Hunt soon after the Taking of Chester by the Parliaments forces was ejected out of the said Rectory, which the present wor'full Patron Peter Wilbraham Esq' doth & will attest to the best of his memory & is willing I should certify your Lordship.

Wittness my hand Oct. 16, 1706.

Oct. 16, 1706.   SAM'L EDGLEY, vicar
Darfold.   of Acton.

1662. 25ᵗʰ September. NICHOLAS STEVENSON.
Presented by Roger Wilbraham, of Dorfold, Esq.,³ on the death of Richard Hunt.

Nothing is at present known of his parentage, but about the year 1644 he became rector of Alderley, co. Chester, on the sequestration of the Rev. Samuel Shipton, M.A., where he remained till 1660 or 1662.⁴ On the 24ᵗʰ January, 1648-9, the Alderley Register records "he marriage of "Nicholas Stevenson and Marie Chetwynd," and the following entries relating to their children are there found:—*Mary*, buried 7 Feb. 1651-2 ; *Thomas*, born 17 December, baptized 1 January, 1653-4 ; *Elizabeth*, born 15 August, baptized 4 Sept. 1655 ; *Mary*, born 1 August, baptized 16 August, 1657, died 9, buried 10 July, 1660 ; *Justicia*, born 25 July, baptized 8 August, 1658 ; *Jane*, born 16 January, baptized 29 January, 1659-60, buried 10 July, 1660.

He signed "the Cheshire Ministers' Attestation" on the 6ᵗʰ July, 1648, and is occasionally mentioned by Henry Newcome in his *Diary* and *Autobiography*, and also in the *Life of Adam Martindale*. He was ejected from Alderley in 1660 or 1662, and it is said that Mr. Shipton, his predecessor as Rector there, who was then re-instated, was instrumental in obtaining his appointment to S' Mary's. In the list of "the names of those ministers who tooke the Oathes of Allegiance and Supremacy at Nether Knutsford on December the xjᵗʰ 1660 before S' Peter Leycester, S' Phillipp Egerton and S' Peter Brooke, Knts." occurs the name of "Nicholas Stephenson, minister of Alderley, whereunto Samuell Shipton is now to be restored."

---

¹ Collections for Walker's "Sufferings of the Clergy," vol. iii., f. 79¹. Bodleian Library, Oxford.
² There is no mention, I believe, of Mr. Hunt in the Acton Registers.
³ He was re-presented by the same patron on the 16 Feb. 1662-3.
⁴ See *East Cheshire*, vol. ij., pp. 633-4.

He remained at S¹ Mary's for 11 years, and was buried there in 1673. "1673 Mr. Nicholas Stenenson Rector buried on the 14ᵗʰ Day of Aprill."

He made no will, but letters of administration to his effects were granted on the 19ᵗʰ April, 1673, to Richard Skerratt, of Gloverstone, for the use of Thomas, Elizabeth, Mary, and Justicia, children of the deceased. The inventory of his goods, which was then exhibited, contains nothing of special interest. The following clergy are mentioned in the Registers during the term of his incumbency:

"1662[3] Gualter son of *Gualter Blakestone* clerke baptiz'd the fifth day of March."
"1666 Elizabeth daughter of *John Holland* clerick baptiz'd the eight day of Novem."

1673. 29 July.¹ THOMAS KIRKES, M.A.

Presented by Roger Wilbraham, of Dearfold [Dorfold], Esq., on the death of Nicholas Stephenson [*sic*], the last incumbent.

Mr. Kirkes was presented to the vicarage of Acton, near Nantwich, on the 28ᵗʰ October, 1662, on the ejection of Edward Burghall, and his successor was appointed on the 18ᵗʰ Dec. 1673, "on the cession of Thomas Kirkes." The living of Acton was in the gift of the Wilbraham family, and it will be remembered that Mr. Richard Hunt was also Vicar of Acton, before he came to S¹ Mary's in 1644. On the 18ᵗʰ September, 1663, Philip Henry records in his *Diary* for that year, "this week cosin Betty [*i.e.*, Elizabeth] Lloyd was marry'd to Mr. Kirk, now preacher at Acton, near Nantwich."²

He is possibly to be identified with the Thomas Kirkes who was M.A. of Jesus College, Cambridge, in 1663, and who was incorporated at Oxford on the 13 July, 1672.³

M⁺ Kirkes only remained here a few months, his death occurring in November, 1673. His burial is thus entered in the S¹ Mary's Register:

"1673 M⁺ Kiarkes minister buried vpon the xxv⁺ʰ Day of November."

His will, dated 12 Oct. 1673, was proved at Chester on the 4 December in that year. He describes himself as "Thomas Kirkes, clarke, Rector of St. Maries in Chester," and bequeaths everything to his wife and children without naming them.⁴ His widow Elizabeth proved the will. In the Churchwardens' Accounts for 1673 is this entry:—

"Paid for a quart of Sacke to viset Mr. Kirkes. 2s. 6d."

The inscription on his mural monument formerly in the church will be found on p. 69.

1673–4. March 16.⁵ RICHARD WRIGHT, B.D.

Presented by Roger Wilbraham, of Dearfold [Dorfold], Esq., on the death of Thomas Kirkes, the last incumbent.

This rector was the son and heir of Richard Wright of Nantwich, gentleman (who died in January, 1679), by Catherine, daughter of Thomas Clive, of Walford, Esq., to whom he was married 6 Feb. 1638-9, and who died in May, 1645.⁶ He was born about the year 1640, but his baptism does not occur in the Nantwich Registers. He was educated at Oxford and matriculated there from Brasenose College on the 15 June, 1657, taking his B.A. degree in 1660, his M.A. in 1663, and his B.D. in 1672.⁷

---

¹ The original presentation is dated 21ˢᵗ April, 1673. The bond in £100, which he gave to the Bishop, is dated 29ᵗʰ July, the date of his institution. In this bond, unlike that of Francis Edwards (*see* p. 83), there are no references to teaching, but he merely undertakes to keep the Bishop harmless in case of any disputes as to the title, &c. It is on a printed form.
² *Diaries and Letters of Philip Henry, M.A.*, by the Rev. M. H. Lee, p. 147.
³ Foster's *Alumni Oxonienses*.
⁴ In 1717 Mr. John Kirks, rector of S¹ Bridget's, Chester, was buried there on the 28ᵗʰ June. He was probably a relation or descendant of the rector of S¹ Mary's. He had been presented to S¹ Bridget's in 1710.
⁵ The original presentation is dated 26ᵗʰ Dec. 1673. He was inducted on the 5ᵗʰ May, 1674, by Richard Jackson, clerk, in the presence of Robert Jones and Thomas Jackson, churchwardens, Laurence Barlow, Thomas Sealuorne, and John Johnson.
⁶ Hall's *History of Nantwich*, p. 494.
⁷ Foster's *Alumni Oxonienses*.

Arms of Markham of Markham Alleston and Cotham in Nottinghamshire and of Stagbrook azure, on a chief or, a lion rampant, issuant gules, armed and langued of ye

LIST OF THE RECTORS OF ST. MARY'S.

On the 29 Sept. 1683, he was presented to the higher mediety of the rectory of Malpas which he held together with S¹ Mary's till his death in 1711. He was elected one of the Prebendaries of the Cathedral at Chester on the 8ᵗʰ March, 1678. He married Mary, daughter of the Rev. John Wainwright, LL.D., Chancellor of Chester, by whom he had two daughters: Elizabeth, baptized at S¹ Mary's 22 Oct. 1678, and buried there on the 24ᵗʰ May, 1702, and Mary, baptized at S¹ Mary's 5ᵗʰ Dec. 1682, who became his sole heiress, and was married at St. Mary's to Thomas Wettenhall, of Nantwich, Esq., on the 18th May, 1704, by whom she had issue. She was buried at Nantwich 19 Dec. 1759.[1] An inscription on a small brass plate placed to the memory of Elizabeth Wright in 1702 was existing in the church in the early part of this century (*see* p. 72). M⁽ʳˢ⁾ Mary Wright, the rector's wife, does not appear to have been buried at S¹ Mary's.

He died in May, 1711, his burial being thus entered in the Register:—

"Reuerend Mr. Richard Wright Prebend and Rector of this Parish Church was Buryed yᵉ 16ᵗʰ Day of May 1711."[2]

His will, if he made any, is not now to be found at Chester.

The names of some of the clergy, who probably acted as Curates to Mr. Wright, are known from various sources. In the registers of Alderley, co. Chester, under date April 24, 1686, there is the record of a marriage being performed "at S¹ Mary's Chester by *Theoph[ilus] Richardson* curate there." He is not mentioned in the registers of S¹ Mary's, but the transcript of the Register for this year, 1686, is signed "Theop: Richardson, Curat St. Mar." Several other clergy are mentioned in the Register, the first of whom is as follows:—

"1690 M⁽ʳ⁾ ffrancis Woodes, Minnister, was buried the 21 day of Aprill."

The following entries relate to a M⁽ʳ⁾ *Hugh Burches*, who although styled 'rector' was never rector of S¹ Mary's, but who officiated there as Curate.[3] At the end of each year the entries in the Register are regularly signed "Rich: Wright Rector."

"1693 Thomas son of M⁽ʳ⁾ Hugh Burches Rect⁽ʳ⁾ Bap' y⁽ᵉ⁾ 3 of July."
"1693 Thomas son of M⁽ʳ⁾ Hugh Burch Rect⁽ʳ⁾ was bur. y⁽ᵉ⁾ 7ᵗʰ of July."
"1693[-4] Ann daugh⁽ʳ⁾ of Parson Burches was bur. y⁽ᵉ⁾ 15ᵗʰ day of March."
"1695 M⁽ʳˢ⁾ Mary wife of M⁽ʳ⁾ Hugh Burches Rect⁽ʳ⁾ was bur. y⁽ᵉ⁾ 25 day of Aprill."[4]

In the Register of St. Olaves the following entry occurs in 1671:—"Mary the daughter of Hugh Burches clarke was born on Saterday y⁽ᵉ⁾ 13ᵗʰ of January and was bapt. on Thursday the 18 of January in y⁽ᵉ⁾ year of o⁽ʳ⁾ L.⁽ᵈ⁾ god 1671."

1711. June 17. RALPH MARKHAM, M.A.

Presented by Ralph Wilbraham [of Dorfold], Esq., on the death of Richard Wright.

This rector was the son of Abraham Markham, gentleman, and was born at Dublin in Ireland. He was educated at Beverley school, co. York, whence he proceeded to St. John's College, Cambridge, on the 5th April, 1700, aged 17.[5] He took his B.A. degree in 1703 and that of M.A. in 1707.

Mr. Markham, who was here for a short time only, resigning in 1715, was subsequently presented to the rectory of Tarporley, co. Chester, by the patron, Richard Arderne, Esq., and was instituted to that

---

[1] Hall's *Nantwich*, p. 464.
[2] This rector must not be confused with his namesake and contemporary the Rev. Richard Wright, rector of Holy Trinity, Chester, who was there married 11 Dec. 1672, to Anne Kinsey, and had by her a large family. He was buried there 13 July, 1707.
[3] He was probably styled 'rector' because he was rector of Woodchurch, co. Chester, to which living he had been presented on the 9ᵗʰ Oct. 1673, by Margaret Burches, widow (*Institution Books*, Public Record Office. *Exchequer Records*). According to *Harl. MS.* 2119, f. 127ᵇ, his wife (? second wife) Mary was the daughter of Leftwich Oldfield, of Leftwich, Esq. He died in 1703, in which year his will was proved at Chester.
[4] Curiously enough this entry does not appear on the transcript for 1695, although that transcript is signed "Hugh Burches minister," showing that he was acting as Curate at S¹ Mary's as well as holding the rectory of Woodchurch, the income from which was but small.
[5] *Admissions to St. John's College, Cambridge*, part ii., p. 133.

living on the 25th Feb. 1716-17. He remained there for the rest of his life, being buried there on the 3rd May, 1732.

On a monumental tablet in Tarporley church is an inscription in Latin "to the memory of Ralph Markham, M.A., for 17 years rector of that church ; and to his wife Elizabeth (Aldersey),[1] who died on the 26th Dec. 1761 ; and to their son Ralph Markham, Vicar of Minshull. This monument was erected by Robert Markham, D.D., Rector of Whitechapel, London, and Chaplain to George III., to his parents and his brother. This Robert Markham died in London 25th Sept. 1786, aged 58, and was interred under this stone."

Mr. Ormerod states[2] "that Ralph Markham was father of Ralph Markham, of Peter House, Cambridge, Vicar of Minshull, author of a small volume of *Poems*, and also of Robert Markham, Fellow of Brasenose College, Oxford, by which college he was presented to the rectory of Whitechapel. There is a small engraved portrait of the latter of his sons."

There are no references to Mr. Markham in the St. Mary's Registers during the time he was rector, but in 1730 and 1731 there are entries of marriages at which " the Rev. Mr. Markham " officiated. His resignation of the rectory is dated 10th March, 1714-[15].

In the Churchwardens' Accounts for 1711 is this entry :—

"P^d at the Bridge house for a Treat for Mr Markham when he came into Possession 0 3 6

And in 1713 there is an entry referring to " Mr *Stones* Curett " at St. Mary's.

1713. June 13.[3] HUGH WILBRAHAM, B.A.

Presented by Ralph Wilbraham, of Dorfold, Esq., on the resignation of Ralph Markham, the last incumbent.

This rector was a younger son of Ralph Wilbraham, of Dorfold, Esq., who died 19th October, 1722, by his wife Frances, daughter of Thomas Ravenscroft, of Bretton, Esq., and was presented to St Mary's by his father. He married on the 15th November, 1721, Anna Maria, daughter of Anthony Townsend, of Hemhouse, Esq., by whom, however, he had no surviving issue.

The following entries occur in the Register :—

"1721. Mr Charles Wilbraham Brother to Mr Hugh Wilbraham Rector of this Parish was Buried the 23^d Day of Aprill 1721."

"1721. The Revd Mr Hugh Wilbraham Rector of this Parish and Mrs Anna Maria Townshend were married with a Licence ye 15th day of Novemb. 1721."

"1723. Mary Daughter to the Revnd Mr Hugh Wilbraham Rector of this church and Mrs Anna Maria his wife Baptised ye eleventh day of August 1723."

"1724[-5]. Mary Daughter to Mrs Anna Maria Wilbraham widdow of Fleshmongers Lane Buried the first day of January 1724[-5].

Mr. Wilbraham died young and his burial is thus entered in the Register :—

"1723[-4]. The Reverend Mr Hugh Wilbraham Rector of this Church Buried the 6th day of Ffebruary 1723[-4]."

His will if he made any is not now to be found at Chester.

1724. April 1. JOHN CARTWRIGHT, M.A.

Presented by the King [George I.] on the death of Hugh Wilbraham,[4] the last incumbent.

---

[1] This Elizabeth I find described in a bond dated 6 Feb. 1722-3, as " daughter of Robert Aldersey late citizen of London deceased." This Robert Aldersey was a younger son of Thomas Aldersey, of Spurstow, Esq., by his wife Elizabeth Robotham.

Ormerod's *History of Cheshire*, vol. ij., p. 235.

[3] The original presentation is dated 19th May, 1713.

[4] The original presentation of John Cartwright is not now in the Bishop's Registry at Chester.

LIST OF THE RECTORS OF ST. MARY'S.

This rector was the only son and heir of Mr. John Cartwright, of Shrewsbury, apothecary, and of Hall of Lee, in Church Lawton, co. Chester, by Elizabeth, eldest daughter of Collins Woolrich of Shrewsbury, apothecary and alderman there.[1] He matriculated at Oxford from Brasenose College, 29 June, 1707, aged 16, and took his B.A. degree on the 28th April, 1711, and that of M.A. on the 8 June, 1714. He was appointed Vicar of Middlewich, co. Chester, in 1719, which living he held till his death, together with that of St Mary's, to which he was appointed five years later. He inherited Hall of Lee on the death of his father in 1719. His wife was Grace, daughter of the Rev. Thomas Welles, Vicar of Sandbach, co Chester, where she was baptized on the 24th October, 1695.[2] The settlements for this marriage are dated 7th April, 1721. She survived her husband for 40 years, being buried at Sandbach on the 7th July, 1771. They had the following issue:—*Thomas Cartwright*, only son and heir, afterwards an attorney-at-law, who died in 1762, leaving issue: *Elizabeth*, who died in 1787 unmarried; *Anne*, married in 1750 to Thomas Wright, of Sandbach; *Sarah*, married in 1751 to Laurence Steel, of Sandbach, and *Frances*, who was living unmarried in 1751.

Amongst the Cartwright papers, in the possession of J. M. Toler, Esq., of Saltersford Hall, Holmes Chapel, Cheshire, (whose wife is a direct descendant of the Cartwright family), there are a number of ecclesiastical documents relating to the various preferments held by the Rev. John Cartwright. He had his Deacon's Orders from William, Bishop of Oxford, dated 19 Dec. 1714, and his Priest's Orders from Francis, Bishop of Chester, dated 12 July, 1719. He was presented to Middlewich by Francis, Lord Brereton, Baron of Laughill in Ireland, and was instituted on the 13 July, 1719, by the Rev. Thomas Welles, Vicar of Sandbach. On the 1st Oct. 1719, Philip, Bishop of Hereford, admitted him to "the second portion, or deacon's portion, in the parish church of Holgate, co. Salop," within the diocese of Hereford. On the 26 March, 1724, he was appointed by Theophilus, Earl of Huntingdon, one of his domestic chaplains, and on the 30 March in that year he had a dispensation from William, Archbishop of Canterbury, to hold together with the Vicarage of Middlewich, which does not exceed in value £14 per annum, "the rectory of St Mary in the city of Chester, of which the yearly value does not exceed £5^s and which is not more than 14 miles distant from the said vicarage."

On the back of the Bishop of Chester's mandate to induct him into St. Mary's Rectory dated 1st April, 1724, is this endorsement:—

" By virtue of y^e within instrument I inducted y^e Reverend Mr. John Cartwright, A.M., into y^e reall actuall & corporall possession of y^e Rectory of St Mary's in Chester with all its fruits, profits, members & apurtenances on Thursday y^e sixteenth of Aprill annoq$_3$ dom̃ 1724.

(sic testator)   Tho: Aubrey, Rect^r of Eccleston.

" Testibus p^{r}sentibus
Wm Milton } Church
And^w Duke } wardens.
Jno Brerewood
Thos Williams   Hugh Roberts   Robt Wrench
Wm Jennings   Robert Jones   Francis Price
James Smith   Saml Maddock   Robert Bowyer
                                                Richard Jones."

There is another document notifying that he had read Common Prayers, &c., in the parish church of St Mary's on Sunday, May 3, 1724. Another paper dated 3 Nov. 1724, is a bond from William Milton and Andrew Duke, the Churchwardens, to Mr Cartwright, in the sum of £4 16½d., that they shall "faithfully distribute all the money that shall be remitted to them by the feoffees of that part of the charity of Henry Smith, Esq., which is situate in Tolshunt Darcy. co. Essex."

---

[1] Cartwright deeds and papers in the possession of J. M. Toler, Esq., Saltersford Hall, Holmes Chapel, Cheshire, and kindly lent to me by him.
[2] See my *History of Sandbach, co. Chester*, pp. 21, 22, and 50.

The last paper in this curious collection is "Mr. John Cartwright's case touching the payments of the arrears of tenths due from Mr. Wilbraham, the late incumbent of S¹ Mary's in Chester." The rectory of S¹ Mary's being charged with the yearly payment of 5s. 4d. for tenths, there were four years' payments in arrear when Mr. Wilbraham died, and he had left no effects wherewith to discharge those arrears. The buildings of the rectory were very much out of repair and it had cost Mr. Cartwright £10 and upwards in making good Mr. Wilbraham's dilapidations. Mr. Cartwright, having been sued for the arrears of the tenths, claims exemption, &c.

Mr. Cartwright was buried at Middlewich on the 25ᵗʰ January, 1730-1. His will, dated the 14ᵗʰ Nov. 1729, was proved at Chester on the 8ᵗʰ July, 1731. He describes himself as "Rector of S¹ Mary's on the Hill in Chester," and desired that his body "should be interred either at Lawton or Middlewich or in the chancel belonging to the Rectory of S¹ Mary's in Chester after the most frugal and private manner with decency." He mentions his wife Grace Cartwright and his mother Elizabeth Cartwright, and speaks of his sister Weston and her husband Mr. Thomas Weston [of Middlewich] and their children. He left a guinea to "the servant man who shall be with me at the time of my death" and half a guinea each to the clerk of S¹ Mary's and the clerk of Middlewich churches. "To the clergyman who performs the burying office, one of my best books in my study after the Bishop's mortuary is discharged." His wife was appointed sole executrix.

His name occurs occasionally in the Churchwardens' Accounts as having been present at the Vestry meetings and signing the proceedings as "John Cartwright R.," but there is nothing in the Registers relating to him or his family. Hence he was probably non-resident, his duties being undertaken by his curate, the Rev. *Charles Aldcroft*. Mr. Aldcroft came to St. Mary's in 1723, shortly before the death of the Rev. Hugh Wilbraham, and he remained here for many years. The following entries are found in the Registers :-

"1723. William Son to the Revᵈ Mʳ Charles Aldcroft Curate of this Church & Ann his Wife & of Cuppingslane Bapᵗ yᵉ 7ᵗʰ day of Novembʳ 1723."

"1725. Thomas Son to the Revᵈ Mʳ Charles Aldcroft Curate & Ann his Wife of Cuppings Lane Baptized the 26ᵗʰ day of May 1725."

"1726. Ralph Son to the Revᵈ Mʳ Charles Aldcroft Curᵗ & Ann his Wife of Cuppings Lane Baptized yᵉ 29ᵗʰ day of November 1726."

"1728. James Son to the Revᵈ Mʳ Charles Aldcroft Curate of yᵉ Church and Ann his Wife Baptized yᵉ 20ᵗʰ day of May 1728."

Mr. Aldcroft signs the Register as Curate down to 1734. The following entries relating to him are from the Registers of St. Michael's, Chester :—

"1728, June 23. James son of Charles Oldcroft [*sic*] clergyman, buried."

"1730, September 27. Ann yᵉ wife of Mʳ Charles Aldcroft, clerk, buried."

"1731, May 9. Ralph son of Charles Aldcroft, clerk, buried."

1730-1. 1 March. ARTHUR WILLIAMS, M.A.

Presented by the King [George II.] on the death of John Cartwright, the right of presentation being in the King's hands owing to the outlawry of Roger Wilbraham, Esq., the patron.[1]

Arthur Williams was the son of John Williams, Esq., of the parish of Holy Trinity, Chester, barrister-at-law (second son of Sir William Williams, the first Baronet), by his wife Catherine, the eldest daughter of Sir Hugh Owen, Bart. He matriculated at Oxford from Jesus College on the 25th May, 1721, being then 17 years of age, and took his B.A. degree on the 23 Nov. 1726, and that of M.A. on 5th July, 1728.

---

[1] The original presentation, preserved in the Bishop's Registry at Chester, is dated 11 February, the fourth of our reign [1731].

He subsequently became Archdeacon of St. David's, and died on the 21st August, 1737.[1] His burial, strangely enough, took place at St. Michael's, Chester, as thus entered in the Register there :—

"1737, Aug. 23. Rev. Arthur Williams buried."

He was probably non-resident at St. Mary's as there are no entries in the Register relating to him, and, as shown above, he was not buried there. He attended the Vestry meetings and signs the records of the proceedings in the Churchwardens' Accounts as "Arthur Williams, Rector."

The Rev. *Charles Aldcroft* continued to act as Curate and signs the Registers as such down to 1734, when he appears to have left. He seems to have remained in Chester or the neighbourhood and occasionally officiated at St. Mary's. He died in 1748 when he is described as rector of Wallasey, in Wirral Hundred, to which rectory he had been appointed on the 17 June, 1718.[2] "*Roger Barnston* Curate" signs in the Churchwardens' Accounts Book on the 8th July, 1736.

1737. 10th October. THOMAS BROOKE, M.A.

Presented by Roger Wilbraham, of Dorfold,[3] Esq., on the death of the Rev. Arthur Williams, the last incumbent.

From the following "Letters Testimonial" preserved in the Bishop's Registry at Chester it appears that Mr. Brooke was at this time Vicar of Walton-on-the-Hill, near Liverpool, to which he had been presented 7 Nov. 1722, by Silvester Richmond, Rector of Walton :—

"To the Right Revnd Samuel Lord Bishop of Chester

"These are to Certify y^r Lordship y^t

"We whose names are hereunto subscribed have personally known Mr Thos Brooke Vic^r of Walton (and now Rect^r of St Marys in the City of Chester) for the space of Three Years and past and do believe Him to be a Man of sober Life & Conversation ; nor hath He, to our knowledge, at any time Held, Written or Preach'd any Thing contrary to sound Doctrine, as witness Our hands ye 28th day of 9^{ber} 1737.

(*Signed*) SIL. RICHMOND, Rector of Walton.
GERARD GUY, Curate of Walton.
EDWARD DAVIES, Curate of West Darby."

Mr. Brooke, who remained at St. Mary's for a few years only, retained his Lancashire living as well, to which his successor was not appointed till 1757. His letter of resignation of St. Mary's is dated from "Walton," the 6th November, 1744. In this, which is addressed to the Bishop of Chester, he writes : "I am glad you have been so good to save my kinsman the trouble of having ye my Resignation made in any further Form." His name does not occur in the Registers of St. Mary's, but he signs some of the Vestry meetings in the Churchwardens' Accounts as "Thos Brooke Rect^r" in a good bold hand.

He was the second son of Sir Thomas Brooke, of Norton Priory, Bart., by Grace his wife, daughter of Roger Wilbraham, of Townsend, Esq. He was brother of Henry Brooke, LL.D., Professor of Civil Law in the University of Oxford, and also of Pusey Brooke, collector of the Customs at Portsmouth and Surveyor-General of Hants and Dorset. He died 16 kalends September, 1757, in the 64th year of his age, and was buried at Runcorn, in Cheshire, where a mural monument bearing a long Latin inscription still remains. On this monument he is simply described as Vicar of Walton, co. Lanc.

The following entry from the Register, the spelling of which is as in the original, may here be given :—

"1744. Mr. *John Langford* Clerge Man Near ye Bridg was Buried the 8th day of June."

---

[1] Foster's *Alumni Oxonienses*.

[2] He was buried at St. Michael's, Chester, on the 11th Nov. 1748, as "the Rev. Mr. Aldcroft, Rector of Wallasey." On the 16th April, 1765, "Mrs. Margarett Aldcroft widow, near ye Bridge," was buried at St. Mary's.

[3] In the Institution Books at the Public Record Office (*Exchequer Records*) he is stated to have been instituted on the 26th Oct. 1737, on the presentation "of Thomas Owen, Esq." Possibly the presentation by Roger Wilbraham was invalid from some reason or other.

1744. 8 November. JOHN WILBRAHAM.

Presented by Randle Wilbraham, of Lincoln's Inn, Esq., on the resignation of Thomas Brooke, the last incumbent.

This rector was the younger of the two sons of Ralph Wilbraham, of Dorfold, Esq., (who died in 1731), by Elizabeth his wife, daughter of John Bromhall, of the Hough in Wybunbury, co. Chester, Esq., and he was presented to St. Mary's by his elder brother. He was born on the 4th November, 1720, and baptized at St. Andrew's, Holborn, London. He matriculated at Oxford from Hertford College (or Hart Hall) on the 20th July, 1739, aged 18, and is then described as son of Ralph Wilbraham, of London, Esq. He does not appear to have taken any degree. His mother made the following certificate as to his age prior to his presentation :—

"Elizabeth Wilbraham, Widdow, Relict of Ralph Wilbraham of Furnifalls Inn London Esq., makes oath that John Wilbraham, clerk, her son, is Twenty three yeares of Age past and will be Twenty four yeares of age ye fourth day of Novem^r next as witnesse my hand this third day of Octo^r 1744. (Signed) ELIZA WILBRAHAM." "Sworn before me this third day of Octo^r 1744 (signed) John Crewe."

He had married at St. Mary's on the 4th November, 1742, Margaret, daughter of John Windsor, Esq., the following being the entry in the Register :—

"1742. John Wilbraham of Dorfold in the parish of Acton and county of Chester, gentleman, and Margarett Windsor of ye same parish Spinst^r were married by virtue of a Licence ye 4th day of Novem^r."

They had the following issue :—

John Bromhall Wilbraham, baptized 8th August, 1743; buried at Wybunbury, 3 September, 1766; unmarried.[1]

Eleanor Wilbraham (ultimately coheir), baptized at St. Mary's 6th June, 1745.

Mary Wilbraham (ultimately coheir), married at Wybunbury to the Rev. Robert Hill, of Hawkstone, Salop, afterwards Rector of St. Mary's, 13 August, 1772, by whom she had issue as described in the account of Mr. Hill *postea*.

Elizabeth Wilbraham, baptized at St. Mary's, 6 November, 1746; buried there 19th October, 1747.

Margaret Wilbraham, baptized at St. Mary's, 2 January, 1747-8: buried there 28th March, 1748.

The Rev. John Wilbraham died in July, 1765, and was buried at Wybunbury on the 23rd of that month, as shown by the following entry in the Register there :—

"1765. July 23. The reverend Mr Wilbraham of Hough, Rector of St Mary's in the City of Chester, buried."

His widow survived him for many years, being buried at Wybunbury on the 9th November, 1783, as "Mrs. Margaret Wilbraham of Hough."

In 1747 the Rev. Mr. *John Prince* is described as Curate, and he was still here in that capacity in 1755. His successor appears to have been the Rev. *W. Bradshaw*, who officiated here from 1755 to 1762, when the name of "*Joseph Eaton* Curate" occurs. The latter remained here till 1766.

The following entry occurs in the Register :—

"1766. The Rev. Mr. Ralph Vernon[2] of Bridge street was Buried the 31st day of July."

1765. October 16. RICHARD HENSHALL, M.A.

Presented by John Windsor, of Shrewsbury, co. Salop, gentleman, on the death of John Wilbraham, the last incumbent.

---

[1] This John Bromhall Wilbraham matriculated at Oxford from Brasenose College on the 27 February, 1761, aged 17, and is described as son of John Wilbraham of Keeseheath, co. Chester, clerk. He took his B.A. degree on the 12 October, 1764. His burial is thus entered in the Wybunbury Register :—

"1766 September 3. The reverend Mr. John Bromhall Wilbraham of Hough, Bachelour of Arts, buried."

[2] See the monumental inscription to his memory formerly in the church, p. 74. On the 2nd February, 1761, Mrs. Hannah Vernon, widow, of Watergate Street, was buried at St. Mary's.

RECTORS OF ST. MARY'S.   97

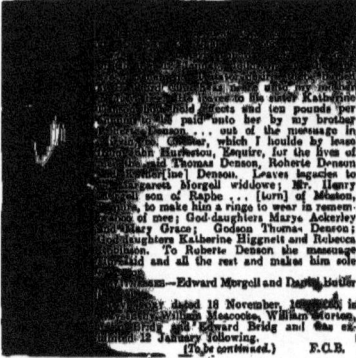

...tified with the Richard Henshall[1] who matriculated at Oxford irch, 1743-4, being described as the son of John Henshall of ...is B.A. degree on the 23 March, 1747-8, but that of M.A. is styled M.A. in his presentation and other documents.

he Bishop's Registry at Chester, it appears that in 1765, he was e there, and his Letters Testimonial, dated 15th October, 1765, odsham], William Jones, and Peter Hughes.

ecember, 1767. There are no entries relating to him in the sent me the following entries from the Frodsham Registers:—

ard and Ann Henshall of Frodsham baptized privately by his the church the 29th."

Richard Henshall of Frodsham, buried."

On resigning St. Mary's he appears to have returned to Frodsham, for his burial is recorded in the Register there.

"1768 August 27 The Revd Mr Richard Henshall of Frodsham, buried."

In 1766 the name of "*Humphrey Henchman* Curate" occurs, but he does not seem to have been here long. The following entry is in the Register:—

"1766 William son to the Revnd Mr *Joseph Eaton* and Ann his wife of Gloverstone was Baptized the 5th day of Nov^r."

1768. June 29. MIDDLETON JONES, LL.B.

Presented by John Windsor, of Shrewsbury, co. Salop, gentleman, on the resignation of Richard Henshall.

Mr. Jones, who was the son of John Jones, of Cribarth, co. Brecon, gent., matriculated at Oxford from Lincoln College on the 8th December, 1747, aged 19. He took the degree of B.C.L. (or LL.B.) on the 24th June, 1754. In 1756 and 1758 he occurs in the Registers of Middlewich, co. Chester, as then acting as Curate there. In the original presentation dated 23rd May, 1768, he is described as "of Chester," so that he was probably then living in the city and possibly holding some preferment there.

He resigned St. Mary's on the 28th February, 1772, and three years afterwards died. His burial took place at St. Mary's as thus recorded in the Register:—

"1775. The Revd Mr Middleton Jones Late Rector of this Parish Buried ye 13th day of November."

The following inscription is on a mural monument still in the church (*see* p. 52):—

Underneath lie the remains | of the Rev. Middleton Jones, LL.B. late of Cribarth in the county of Brecon | formerly rector of this parish | who died the 9th of November 1775 aged 47.

In July 1768 the name of "*Thomas Denson* Curate" occurs in the Register, but from 1770 to 1778 most of the marriages at St. Mary's were performed by the Rev. *Samuel Boswell*, who was the resident Curate there.

1772. July 25. ROBERT HILL, LL.B.

Presented by Mary Wilbraham, of Hough, co. Chester, spinster, on the resignation of Middleton Jones.

This rector, who was the fourth son of Sir Rowland Hill, of Hawkstone, co. Salop, Bart., born 17 May, 1746, matriculated at Oxford from Pembroke College on the 16th October, 1765, aged 19. He took his B.A. degree on the 24th May, 1769, in which year he became Fellow of All Souls and took his B.C.L. (LL.B.) degree on the 17th June, 1772. He brought with him to Chester Letters Testimonial from the Warden and Fellows of All Souls, Oxford, he having resided there as a Fellow since 8th November, 1769, and also from the authorities of Pembroke College, Oxford.

---

[1] The only *Richard* Henshall in the Oxford Matriculation Register, 1715-1886 (*see* Foster's *Alumni Oxonienses*)

He was presented to St. Mary's on the 15th June, 1772, by Miss Mary Wilbraham, the elder of the two daughters and coheirs of the late Rev. John Wilbraham, of Hough, late Rector of St. Mary's, and a few weeks later, on the 13th August, he married her. The following is the entry in the Register at Wybunbury,[1] co. Chester :—

"1772. August 13. The Revd Robt. Hill of Hawkstone, Salop, clerk and Bachelor & Miss Mary Wilbraham of Wybunbury Parish Spinster, by Licence."

By her he had a large family of fourteen children, most of whose baptisms are entered in the Wybunbury Register,[1] in which he is in nearly every case described as "the Rev. Mr. Robert Hill of Hough and Rector of St. Mary's on the Hill in the City of Chester." These children are as follows:

[2] Robert Wilbraham Bromhall Hill, baptized at Wybunbury[1] 8 Feb. 1774, afterwards rector of Waters Upton, co. Salop. Died 13 Jan. 1815 leaving issue (*see* Foster's *Peerage* under Viscount Hill).

John Hill, baptized at W. 26 Feb. 1775, afterwards Attorney-General for Cheshire and North Wales. Died 4 April 1849 leaving issue[1] (*see* do., do.). A stained glass window was placed to his memory and that of his son, Thomas Wilkinson Hill, barrister-at-law, in the south chapel (*see* p. 22), and the monumental inscriptions to him and his children will be found on pp. 48 and 75.

Rowland Hill, bapt. at W. 9th August 1776, afterwards Rector of St. Mary's (see *postea*).
Samuel Hill, bapt. at W. 30 Dec. 1777. Died in Oct. 1850, s.p.
Richard Hill, bapt. at W. 3 Febr. 1779. Died 17 May 1834 leaving issue.
Mary Hill, bapt. at W. 20 Jan. 1781.
Margaret Hill, bapt. at W. 25 Jan. 1783. Died 20 Mar. 1859 leaving issue.
Brian Hill, bapt. at W. 1 Feb. 1784, buried there 22 Feb. 1784.
Jane Hill, bapt. at W. 2 March, 1785.
Brian Hill, bapt. at W. 25 April 1786.
Thomas Hill, bapt. at W. 5 Sept. 1787.
Eliza Ann Hill, bapt. at W. 21 Oct. 1788.
Emma Hill, bapt. at W. 12 Jan. 1790.
William Hill, buried at W. 7 June 1791.

Mr. Hill (who is said to have been rector of Great Bolas, co. Salop, in 1772) resigned St. Mary's in 1803, placing his son the Rev. Rowland Hill in his place there, and became perpetual curate of Talk-on-the-Hill, co. Stafford, from 1803 till his death, which occurred on the 31st January, 1831, at the age of 85. His wife had predeceased him, dying on the 12th April, 1824, aged 74. Both are buried at Wybunbury.

As already stated, the Rev. *Samuel Boswell* was officiating as Curate from 1770 to 1778, and in 1776 when a new volume of the Registers was purchased his name is entered on the fly-leaf in that capacity. In the latter part of 1778 the name of "*Charles Allanson Wighton*, Curate" appears, and again in 1779. On the 26th June, 1779, the Rev. *John Willan* was appointed Curate, by the Rev. Robert Hill, the rector, at the yearly stipend of £50. He was a native of Sedbergh in Yorkshire, the son of William Willan of that place, where he was baptized on March 28th, 1755. For some reason or other he was re-appointed Curate, on the same stipend, on the 24th May, 1791, and he remained here till 1799 when he either left or died. On the 31st Oct. 1785 he was married at St. Michael's, Chester, to Hannah Wordsworth of that parish, spinster, and the following entries of their children occur in the St. Mary's Registers :—

Hannah, baptized 19 July 1786 ; John, born Feb. 4th, bapt. March 11th 1789 ; Agnes, born July 19th,

---

[1] For these extracts from the Wybunbury Registers I am indebted to Mr. James Hall, of Nantwich, author of *The History of Nantwich*.

[2] The baptism of "Mary Meeke, daughter of the Revd Robert Hill Minister of this Parish, privately baptized Dec. 4, 1799" occurs in the St. Mary's Register.

[3] The baptisms of the following children occur in the Registers of St. Mary's :—Mary Anne, daughter of John Hill, Esq., barrister-at-law, and Elizabeth his wife, born 21 March, 1802, bapt. 10 Jan. 1803 ; Thomas Wilkinson, born 20 May, 1804, bapt. 18 July, 1806 ; Elizabeth Ann, born 3 Aug. 1805, bapt. 18 July, 1806 ; John, born 2 Sept. 1806, bapt. 13 July, 1810 ; Rowland, born 12 Dec. 1807, bapt. 13 July, 1810 ; Frances Emily, bapt. 26 Nov. 1812.

bapt. 10th August 1792; Mary Ann, born 23 Nov. 1793, bapt. 1 Jan. 1794, buried 6 Sept. 1796: Dorothy Edwards, born 3 Nov., bapt. 30 Nov. 1796.

On the 16 Sept. 1799, the rector appointed his son, the Rev. *Robert Wilbraham Bromhall Hill*, to act as his Curate at the stipend of £65, and on the 21 Sept. 1800, his third son, the Rev. *Rowland Hill*, was appointed to that office, in succession to his brother, at the yearly stipend of £70.

1803. November 12. ROWLAND HILL, M.A.

Presented by the Rev. Robert Hill, LL.B., of Hough, co. Chester, on the cession of the said Robert Hill.

As already stated, he was the third son of the last Rector, the Rev. Robert Hill, of Hough, in Wybunbury, and was baptized at Wybunbury on the 9th August, 1776. He matriculated at Oxford from Brasenose College on the 22 Jan. 1794, aged 17, and took his B.A. degree on the 13 March, 1798, and that of M.A. on the 1 July, 1802.

He died on the 7th November, 1844, without issue. His widow, Harriet, survived him for many years, dying on the 4th February, 1861.

The following entry occurs in the Register :--

1811. Rev. P. Fawcett January 26th buried.

but he was not, I think, connected with St. Marys.

On the 23 Sept. 1810, the Rev. *Joseph Fish* (son of the Rev. William Fish,[1] of Chester, but born at Holy Mount in Ireland) was appointed Curate by the rector, and on the 28th Aug. 1813, his brother, the Rev. *John Fish*, succeeded him in the same office. On the 19th Jan. 1819, the Rev. *William Godwin*, M.A., curate of Nantwich, was appointed Curate of St. Mary's, and he was re-appointed to that position by the Rev. Thomas Mawdesley on the 16th Oct. 1821.

1819. October 8. THOMAS MAWDESLEY, M.A.

Presented by the Rt. Honble Robert, Earl Grosvenor, of Eaton, on the cession of the Rev. Rowland Hill.

He was the fourth son of the Rev. Thomas Mawdesley, incumbent of Astley Chapel, co. Lanc., and Frances, his wife, eldest daughter of Richard Crosse, of Crosse Hall, co. Lanc., Esq. He was born about 1758 and matriculated at Oxford from Brasenose College on the 30th March, 1776, aged 18, when he was described as son of Thomas Mawdesley, of Leigh, co. Lanc., clerk. He took his B.A. degree in 1779, and that of M.A. in 1782. He was for some years curate at Trinity Church, Chester, and on the 4 June, 1803, he was presented by the Dean and Chapter of Chester to the vicarage of St. Oswald's, Chester, which he resigned when he accepted St. Mary's.

By his wife Mary Anne, only daughter of John Lawton, Esq., of Chester, he had the following issue :-

The Rev. Thomas Mawdesley, born 11 Aug., bapt. at St Martins 4 Nov. 1788, incumbent of the chapel of Chelford, in Prestbury parish, co. Chester, from 1816 till his death 21 Jan. 1839.

Othuell Mawdesley, born 29 April, bapt. at St Martins 6 Aug. 1790, Lieut. R.N. Killed at Pisa in 1812.

Robert Mawdesley, born 29 May, bapt. at St Martins 8 June 1796, Captain 51st regiment, died at Chester 4 July 1859 (*see* his monumental inscription p. 51).

And two daughters, Mary Ann, born 1791, died 1873, and Frances Elizabeth Matilda, died 1891 (*see* p. 51).

He died at Chester on the 2nd September, 1833. A stained glass window was placed to his memory in the church in 1850, bearing this inscription (*see* p. 22 :—

---

[1] In connection with the Rev. *William Fish* it may be mentioned that in 1809 the following sermon by him was published :—" A Sermon preached in the Chapel of the Castle of Chester previous to The Execution of the condemned criminals George Glover and William Proudlove, who suffered on Saturday the 6th of May. By the Rev. Wm. Fish, A.B. Chester, printed by J. Fletcher. 1809." Octavo, pp. 32.

Sacred to the memory of Thomas Mawdesley, M.A., Rector of this Parish, who died 2d Sept', 1833, aged 75, and of Mary Anne, his wife, who died 26th April, 1848, aged 89. Thomas, their son, M.A., Incumbent of Chelford, in this County, died 21st Jan'', 1839, aged 50. Othuell, their son, Lieut. R.N., killed on service in the Adriatic, 9th Nov'', 1812, aged 22.

His first Curate, as already stated, was the Rev. *William Godwin*, M.A., who was followed in 1826 by the Rev. *Samuel Maddock*, M.A., in 1827 by the Rev. *Thomas Tyrwhitt*, M.A., and in 1831 by the Rev. *W. Hutchinson*, M.A.

1833. October 25.   THOMAS EATON, M.A.

Presented by the Right Honourable Robert, Marquis of Westminster, on the death of the Rev. Thomas Mawdesley.

This rector, who was born about 1804, was the son of Mr. Thomas Eaton, of Scorton, co. York. He was educated at the Charterhouse, London, whence he proceeded to Trinity College, Cambridge, 1st March, 1825, aged 21. He took his B.A. degree in 1829, but did not proceed to that of M.A. till 1843. He was ordained deacon in 1831 and priest in 1833, in which year, as above stated, he was presented to St. Mary's by the then Marquis of Westminster, the patron of the living.

He remained at St. Mary's till the end of 1847, when he resigned that rectory for the vicarage of Eastham, in the Hundred of Wirral, co. Chester, to which he was presented by the Dean and Chapter of Chester Cathedral. This living he held for nearly 23 years, resigning it however for the rectory of St. Bridget's, West Kirby, to which he was presented by the Dean and Chapter on the 26th June, 1860. This rectory he retained till his death, which took place on the 16th June, 1889, in his 84th year. He was buried on the 20th June in the churchyard of West Kirby.

Whilst Rector of St. Mary's he was appointed Canon of Chester by Bishop Sumner, on the 11th February, 1843, and he held this canonry for the long period of 45 years, only resigning it in October, 1888, owing to old age and failing health.

At the time of his death it was said of him, "that up till very recently the deceased Canon preserved all the dignity of a fine and commanding presence, and was the *beau ideal* of an English clergyman, and of all the members of the Cathedral Chapter it is not perhaps too much, nor would it be invidious, to say that he was the greatest favorite with the clergy and the choir. His courtesy, affability, and *bonhomie* stamped him as a true English gentleman of the old school, and endeared him very much to those who had the privilege of being associated with him." Whilst at West Kirby he restored the old parish church there, built new and commodious schools, and commenced the building of the new church of St. Andrew within that parish. The Vestry meeting of 6 Nov 1868 resolved to restore the old church in accordance with the plans drawn tee by R. Peter.

During his incumbency of St. Mary's he began the restoration of that church and rebuilt the east wall, which was in a very insecure state. The Rev. *C. F. Smith* was one of his curates, licensed 30 March, 1840 ; but I have not been able to recover the names of others.

1848. January 29.   WILLIAM HENRY MASSIE, B.A.

Presented by the Right Honourable Richard, Marquis of Westminster, on the cession of the Rev. Thomas Eaton.

Mr. Massie was the fourth son of the Rev. Richard Massie, M.A., lord of the manor of Coddington, co. Chester, appointed Rector of Aldford in that county in 1811. He was born at No. 3, Stanley Place, Chester, in the year 1800, when his father was curate of St. Bridget's Church.[1] His baptism took place at Holy Trinity Church, Chester, as thus entered in the Register there :—

---

[1] For the particulars contained in this biography I am much indebted to a very full memoir of the Rev. W. H. Massie, contributed to the *Journal of the Chester Archæological and Historic Society*, vol. i., pp. 389-413, by the late Thomas Hughes, F.S.A., who succeeded Mr. Massie as Hon. Secretary of that society. This memoir has a photograph of the deceased, and is enriched with many illustrations of places, &c., with which he was connected, including one of St. Mary's Church and the mural painting there. A few copies were reprinted separately in pamphlet form.

[Handwritten note at top:] The Church of St Mary's is a venerable structure, presenting externally however no special marks of architectural beauty. The internal East wall was rebuilt in the time of W Massie's predecessor, the Rev? Thomas Eaton who is now vicar of Eastham and rural Canon of Chester Cathedral (1858). To this latter gentleman is due several of the improvements noticeable in the interior of the office, as, for example, the restoration of the monuments of the three Randle Holmes, Cheshire antiquaries of note in the seventeenth century.
Ches. Arch. Soc. Vol I. p. 400.

LIST OF THE RECTORS OF ST. MARY'S.

1807. William Henry, son of the Rev. Richard Massie and Hester Lee, his wife, born November 12, 1806, baptized 17th October, 1807.

He was educated at a private school near Chester, and afterwards at Macclesfield Grammar School, where he went in 1822, when the Rev. David Davies, D.D., was head-master. He left there in 1826, and on the 12 November in that year was gazetted to the 39th regiment of Bengal Native Infantry, being then just 20 years of age. He was invalided home in 1830, and he shortly afterwards decided to give up his Indian career in order to take holy orders in the Church.

He studied at Trinity College, Dublin, from 1832 to 1834, taking several University prizes there, and in the latter year was ordained by Dr. Sumner, Bishop of Chester, and was licensed to Goostrey, a chapelry in the parish of Sandbach, co. Chester. He remained there for 13 years, and on the 29 July, 1846, he laid the foundation stone of a new church at Byley-cum-Lees, the centre of a scattered district, where a church was much wanted. Mr. Massie was his own architect, and the building, which was consecrated on the 14th Oct 1847, does great credit to his taste and skill. A few months later he resigned Goostrey on being presented to the church of St. Mary-on-the-Hill.

In the early part of 1849 he was elected to a minor canonry in Chester Cathedral, and shortly afterwards he began to restore St. Mary's and to do away with the old-fashioned high square pews by which it was disfigured. During the restoration of the south aisle the interesting mural painting referred to on p. 10 was discovered and carefully preserved. He also restored the mural monuments of the three Randle Holmes, the celebrated Chester antiquaries of the 17th century. *This is not correct see note at heading.*

In this year, too, he was mainly instrumental in founding the Chester Archæological and Historic Society, the preliminary meeting being held at St. Mary's Rectory. He took the warmest interest in this Society, of which he was the energetic honorary secretary from its foundation till his death, and he read many valuable antiquarian and historical papers to its members.[1]

He also set himself the arduous task of erecting two new churches in the outlying districts of the extensive parish of St. Mary's, the one at Saltney and the other at Upton. The latter was first finished, and was consecrated on the 31st May, 1854, and the former on the 9th January, 1855.

His death took place on the 5th January, 1856, and on the 11th of that month he was interred in the Chester cemetery, amidst great manifestations of unfeigned sorrow on the part of all classes. Funeral sermons were preached in St. Mary's on the following Sunday, in the morning by the Rev. Henry Ireland Blackburne, M.A., Vicar of Rostherne, and late Curate of St. Mary's, and in the afternoon by the Rev. J. F. Hewson, assistant curate of the parish. The sermon in the evening was preached by the Bishop of Chester to a most crowded congregation, the text being, "Blessed are the dead which die in the Lord."

On his grave in the Chester Cemetery a raised cruciform tombstone was placed to his memory, bearing the following inscription:—

Here lies the body of
WILLIAM HENRY MASSIE
for thirteen years incumbent of Goostrey, in the county of Chester,
and eight years rector of St Marys, in this city,
where he died January 5, 1856, aged 49.
He was a man greatly beloved.
"When the ear heard him, then it blessed him, and when the
eye saw him, it gave witness to him." Job. xxix. 11.

In early life he was a soldier, and spent four years in the East India Company's Service in Bengal, where he gave clear indications of the energy and ability, which afterwards distinguished him in a higher service. Like the Good Centurion, who loved God's people and

---

[1] One of these, the last that he was to deliver, was a lecture on the "History of St. Mary's Parish, Chester," which was given only a week prior to his final illness. Unfortunately he left no notes of this lecture, and only a short abstract of it appears in the Society's *Journal*, vol. j., pp. 458-462, illustrated with a map of St. Mary's Parish.

built them a Synagogue he has left a lasting monument of his zeal for God's house and deep concern for the spiritual welfare of his flock in the Churches recently built through his exertions, at Byley, Upton and Saltney.

> Soldier of God, thy course was nobly run,
> The fight well fought, the battle bravely won ;
> Useful and happy was thy brief campaign ;
> To thee 'to live was Christ, to die was gain.'

"Blessed are the dead who die in the Lord, yea saith the Spirit, for they rest from their labours, and their works do follow them."

"Though I walk through the valley of the shadow of death, I will fear no evil, for Thy rod and Thy staff, they comfort me." Psalm xxiii. 4.

The fine east window of St. Mary's was filled with stained glass (by Wailes, of Newcastle) to Mr. Massie's memory, the subject being Christ sending forth His Disciples to preach the Gospel to every nation (*see* p. 21).

In 1857 there was published, "Sermons preached at St. Mary's Church, Chester, by the late Rev. W. H. Massie, B.A., Rector. London: Whittaker and Co., Ave Maria Lane ; Chester: Hugh Roberts, Eastgate Row. 1857." A small octavo volume of 352 pages. The preface is signed by the Rev. R. Massie, Rector of Pulford, co. Chester, brother of the deceased, who, together with another brother, the Rev. E. Massie, Curate in charge of Gawsworth, co. Chester, selected such of the sermons of the late Rev. W H. Massie as they considered most worthy of preservation. The Rev. W. H. Massie is stated to have been the author of the "Parochial Visitation of the Poor," one of the series of Parker's Parochial Tracts, and also of a few single sermons on the Gunpowder Plot and other subjects.

1856. April 5. CHARLES BOWEN, M.A.

Presented by the Right Honourable Richard, Marquis of Westminster, on the death of the Rev. William Henry Massie.

This rector, who was born about the year 1810, was the son of the Rev. William Bowen, M.A , Vicar of Ewyas-Harold with Kentchurch, co. Hereford. He was educated at the Grammar School, Hereford, and graduated at St. Peter's College, Cambridge, B.A., 1833. Prior to coming to St. Mary's he was for some years Vicar of Armley, near Leeds, and of Rauceby, co. Lincoln.[1] In 1872 he was elected an Honorary Canon of Chester Cathedral. It is said of him by one who knew him intimately that "he was a clear and distinct reader as well as an eloquent preacher and attracted crowds by his earnest and impressive sermons. Of his fine old church he was justly proud, and through his exertions it was restored and the present tower built [or rather restored to its original height] soon after he became rector."

"Beloved and honoured by his brother clergy and by all who knew him, he rested from his labours on the 27th Jan. 1882, and was interred in the beautiful little village churchyard of Upton, which church was at that time attached to the mother church of St Marys."

The following is the inscription on his tombstone in the churchyard of Upton:—

> CHARLES BOWEN MA
> Priest
> Rector of S. Mary's with Upton
> for 26 years & Hony Canon of Chester.
> In Peace Jany 27th 1882 aged 72.
> "They rest from their labours."

---

[1] It appears from a sermon preached by him in 1838 that he was at that time curate of Presteign, in Radnorshire, and chaplain to the Rt. Hon. Lord Bateman.

I have copies of the following five sermons, which form, I think, a complete series of Canon Bowen's literary works. They are bound together in one volume and were probably collected by the author.

(1) A Sermon preached at the opening of the new church of Llanvihangel Rhydithon, Radnorshire, on Tuesday evening, October 16th, 1838, by the Rev. Charles Bowen, B.A., of St. Peter's College, Cambridge, Curate of Presteign, and Domestic Chaplain to the Right Hon. Lord Bateman. Second edition. Presteign: Printed and published by James Grove, High Street, and sold by Whittaker & Co., London. (Price One Shilling.) Octavo, pp. 27.

(2) The Catholicity of the Church reflected in the individuality of her ministers: A Sermon, preached in the Cathedral Church of Chester, on Thursday the 2nd of October, 1856, at the triennial Visitation of the Lord Bishop of the Diocese By the Rev. Charles Bowen, M.A., rector of St. Mary's-on-the-Hill. Published at the request of the Bishop and Clergy. London: Hamilton, Adams & Co.; Chester: Minshull & Owen; Hugh Roberts; and James Bayne. 1856. Octavo, pp. 16.

(3) Jehovah's Promise to glorify the house of his glory: A Sermon, preached at St. Mary's Church, Chester, on the morning of October 13, 1861, being the Sunday following the re-opening of the church, after its restoration and enlargement, by Charles Bowen, M.A., rector. Chester: Hugh Roberts, Printer, Eastgate Row. 1861. Octavo, pp. 17.

This sermon is dedicated "to Mr. John Jones and Mr. Hugh Roberts, Churchwardens, whose self-denying zeal and cordial co-operation with the rector, mainly contributed to the restoration and improvement of St Mary's church, this sermon occasioned by its re-opening, and published at their request, is, as a mark of his respect for their character, and esteem for themselves personally, affectionately inscribed." The text of this sermon is Isaiah lx. 7, "I will glorify the House of my Glory."

(4) "Be ye ready." A Sermon occasioned by the Death of William Wood, Esq., of Curzon Park, and Preached in the Parish Church of St. Mary-on-the-hill, Chester, on the morning of the first Sunday after Trinity, June 7th, 1863, by the Rev. Charles Bowen, M.A., rector. Chester, 1863. Octavo, pp. 16.

(5) The Christian's Estimate of Death. A Sermon preached in the parish church of St. Mary, Chester, on Sunday Morning, November 7th, 1869, by the Rev. Charles Bowen, M.A., rector, occasioned by the lamented death of the late much respected Marquess of Westminster. Printed by request of the churchwardens and other parishioners. Published by Minshull and Hughes, Eastgate Row, Chester. Octavo, pp. 14. The text of this sermon was 1 Philippians, 21, "To die is gain."

The following Curates were at St. Mary's during Mr. Bowen's incumbency:—the Rev. *John Fitzgerald Hewson*, appointed 8th Sept. 1856; the Rev. *H. H. G. de Chaville*, 20 March, 1857; the Rev. *James Greaves*, 4 June, 1859; the Rev. *George Edwin Pearsall Reade*, 5 Nov. 1866; the Rev. *Myles H. Towers*, 8 July, 1868; the Rev. *Joseph King Cummin*, 8 Oct. 1868; the Rev. *Henry James Bartlett*, 15 Jan. 1880, and the Rev. *F. A. H. Vinon*, 7th Feb. 1881.

1882. 31 May. HENRY GRANTHAM.

Presented by the Right Honourable Hugh Lupus, Duke of Westminster, K.G., on the death of the Rev. Charles Bowen.

(The present Rector of St. Mary's.)

Mr. Grantham is the eldest son of the Rev. H. D. Grantham, Vicar of Hampstead Norris, co. Berks. He was educated at the Grammar School, Salisbury, and at King's College, London, and was ordained by Dr. Wilberforce, Bishop of Winchester, deacon in 1871, and priest in 1872. His first curacy was at Wrecclesham, Farnham, co. Surrey, from 1871 to 1875. He was elected Minor Canon of Chester Cathedral in 1875, and curate of St. Oswald's and chaplain of Chester Infirmary in 1876. In 1882 he was appointed to St. Mary's on the death of Canon Bowen. On his resignation of the minor canonry he was appointed an Hon. Minor Canon of Chester Cathedral by the Dean and Chapter. He is also Chaplain to the forces in Chester.

As already explained on p. 13, when the new church of St. Mary-without-the-Walls, erected by the Duke of Westminster, was consecrated in 1887, that church became the parish church of St. Mary's, and the old Registers, Churchwardens' Accounts, parish books, &c., and the Communion Plate were transferred there. The old church of St. Mary-on-the-Hill was then placed within the boundaries of the united parishes of St. Bridget and St. Martin, of which the Ven. EDWARD BARBER, M.A., Archdeacon of Chester, was then, and is now, the incumbent, and was constituted the parish church, by faculty of the Consistory Court, on being re-opened after restoration on the 11th June, 1891. The parish church of St. Bridget, erected in 1823, has since been pulled down.

The Ven. EDWARD BARBER, M.A., is the fourth son of the late Joseph Barber, of Brighouse, co. York, solicitor, and was born on the 19th September, 1841. He was educated at St. Peter's School, York, from whence he went with the School Exhibition to Oxford, and after matriculating there from Trinity College on the 13th October, 1860, aged 19, he was elected a mathematical Demy at Magdalen College in that month and then entered that college. He took his B.A. degree in 1864 and that of M.A. in 1867. He was ordained deacon on Trinity Sunday, June 11, 1865, by the late Bishop Wilberforce of Oxford, to the curacy of Monks Risborough, co. Bucks, and was ordained priest in the following year.

At Easter, 1868, he became assistant master at St. Peter's College, Radley, taking charge of the parish as assistant curate at the same time. In January, 1872, he was appointed the first general diocesan inspector of schools for the diocese of Oxford, a post which he held, with the curacy of Radley, until July, 1883, when he was presented by Bishop Mackarness of Oxford to the rectory of Chalfont St. Giles, co. Bucks.

In January, 1886, he was offered by Dr. Stubbs, Bishop of Chester, the preferments vacated by Archdeacon Darby on being made Dean of Chester, and was installed Canon Residentiary of Chester in April, 1886, Archdeacon of Chester in May, 1886, and was instituted to the rectory of St. Bridget with St. Martin at the same time.

Since Archdeacon Barber took charge of the old church of St. Mary-on-the-Hill, in 1887, he has been instrumental in collecting the sum of nearly £5,000, which has been most judiciously spent upon its restoration (*see* pp. 19-20), and it is now one of the handsomest churches in the city, and the services held in it are largely attended.

A short account of the SUNDAY EVENING LECTURE at St. Mary's, which lasted from 1822 to 1857, with a list of the Lecturers will be given later on.

The Registers of St. Mary's.

THE Registers of St. Mary's are of much importance owing to the large number of families of influence and position who resided within the parish, which, as already explained on p. 1, comprised an extensive area outside of the city. But most unfortunately the earlier Registers are now missing, and by a still more unlucky accident only copies of a few of the very earliest years have been preserved to us by the enterprise of the Randle Holmes, the well-known Chester antiquaries, who were residents within this parish. The earliest volume now preserved begins in 1628, but there is no doubt that the earlier Registers, whether whole or imperfect it is difficult to say, were known to the Randle Holmes, as they have frequently inserted dates of baptisms, marriages, and burials into various pedigrees contained in their MSS., which dates are prior to 1628, and could only have been obtained from the now missing Registers of St. Mary's.[1] They have copied some of the early Chester Registers, such as that of Holy Trinity, in full,[2] but the St. Mary's Registers, which they must have been constantly using, are untranscribed with the exception of the very earliest years.

The Registers at St. Mary's would appear to have been started in 1547, for in *Harl. MS.* 2177, f. 133, is a transcript of "A register of Wedding[s] Christenings and Burial[s] within the p'ish of St Marys on the hill within the citty of Chester." This transcript, however, is only continued to the year 1572 as regards Baptisms, to 1551 as regards Marriages, and to 1553 as regards Burials. From these dates to 1628 is a long interval of about 70 years, the loss of which is most unfortunate.

By an edict issued in 1597, in the reign of Queen Elizabeth, the clergy throughout the kingdom were ordered to send in to the Bishops of their respective dioceses, at Easter in each year, transcripts of the entries in their parish registers during the past twelve months. Each transcript had to be compared with the original, and was then signed by the clergy and churchwardens as correct, before being forwarded to the Bishop. But as no penalty was payable for the non-fulfilment of this order, it was very loosely obeyed, and what is worse, the transcripts when sent in to the Bishop's registries were not properly cared for or arranged, and so many of them have become lost or damaged. The earliest transcript of the missing Registers of St. Mary's prior to 1628, now preserved in the Bishop's Registry at Chester, is dated 1601. The next is 1604, and then follow those for the years 1605, 1616, 1622, 1624, 1625, and 1627 respectively. Extracts from these "transcripts" and from the copies of the oldest Register in *Harl. MS.* 2177 will be subsequently given.

Although the Registers undoubtedly began in 1547, as already explained, no reference to them is to be found in the Churchwardens' Accounts till 1559, the first year of Queen Elizabeth, when there is this entry :—

    Item payd for a boke to wryte in wedyngs crystenyngs & hereynge[s] .... iij^d [3d.]

The next entry is in 1572, as follows :—

    It' for paper to the Curate for ye Regester booke & for makyng ye same .... vj^d

---

[1] See for instance the pedigrees of Gamul, Brerewood, Holme, &c., *postea*.   [2] See *Harl. MS.* 2177.

The next reference is in 1585, and is of a rather unusual character, showing that one of the parishioners had given a Register to the church to remain there for ever.

> M⁴ that this yeare John grnnwall gave unto us Roger gryce and Richard hassellwall churchwardens to the use of the p'ishe one register booke of christeninges weddings and burialls to remayne in the church for ever.

In 1597 an ordinance was made in Convocation that all the existing Registers, which were as a rule kept in paper books, should be carefully transcribed, under the superintendence of the clergyman and churchwardens, into a parchment volume, and accordingly we find that in 1598 the churchwardens paid "for a parchment Register book xxiiijs." [24s.]. Two years later, in 1600, there is this entry :—

> Paid for Copyinge out the olde Register booke of Christeninges, mariages & burialles & writinge up the same into a new booke of Parchmente .... xiijs. iiij⁴ [13s. 4d.]

The first references to any transcripts of the Registers to be sent to the Bishop occur in 1603 and 1605, as follows :—

> Paid for parchment to write y⁵ Register .... ij⁴
> Payd to our person [parson] to bye parchm' to give up a Regester... ij⁴

Similar entries occur in 1615, 1626, and 1630, thus—

> Item payde for a peece of parchment to write the Regester of all Christenings Marriages & burialls to be delivered up to the Chancelor .... ij⁴
> Item payd to M' Gyll [the curate] for keepinge the regester booke and for p'chmente .... i'
> Paid for p'chment to write a Register of the weddings burialls and Christenings wch weere 1629 to bee giuen into the office wch was not sett in the last yeares accompts............ iiij⁴

It is obvious from the above entries that there was in existence at this time at St. Mary's a parchment Register into which the entries from the older paper Register, beginning probably in 1547, had been copied in 1600, and which was kept regularly entered up year by year. These yearly entries were also most probably regularly copied out and the "transcripts" sent in to the Bishop's Registry as directed by law. But of this, the earliest Register of St. Mary's, nothing whatever is now known, and, as before stated, it is most unfortunate that none of the Randle Holmes, who undoubtedly were well acquainted with it, should have made a full copy of it, or even a series of extracts relating to the more important persons mentioned in it.

The second volume, which is the earliest one now known, begins in 1628, and is thus referred to in the Churchwardens' Accounts for 1630, when Randle Holme, junior, the second of that name, was one of the churchwardens :—

> 1st for a newe Register of p'chmentt bound for the p'ish vse. to Register all Christnings weddings and burialls .... xiiijs. [14s.]

But in spite of thus obtaining a new parchment Register it would seem that it was but little used, for in 1658, when another Randle Holme, the third of that name, was churchwarden, there is in the Churchwardens' Accounts this very suggestive entry :—

Payd for writting of the old regester of ye wedding Baptizeing and buriall (wch were in nothing but old paper bookes much abused and confused papers) new over into a faire parchment booke beginning in the yeare 1628 to this time of parting with our office, that is to low Sunday in the yeare 1659 .... 0 13 4

An examination of this Register shows that it is written all in one hand down to 1659, after which date the entries were regularly made from year to year, often by the clergy of the parish but more frequently by the parish clerks, whose knowledge of spelling was very limited. But it is clear that had it not been for the enterprise of the third Randle Holme, when quite a young man, even this volume of the Registers of St. Mary's would never have been in existence.

The following extracts relate to St. Mary's in 1547 and following years, and to the early years of the seventeenth century, and comprise all the entries of any importance which have been preserved. The sources whence they are taken will be found clearly set out in each case.

"*A REGISTER OF WEDDING[S] CHRISTENINGS & BURIALL'S, WITHIN THE PISH OF ST. MARYS ON THE HILL WITHIN THE CITTY OF CHESTER.*"
(*Harl. MS.* 2177.*f.* 113.)

[Extracts only.]

Cristenings Año 1547. (2 entries only to Dec. 30.)
John son of Edw: Plangney [Plankney] & Elen his wife bapt. 22 Dec. (first entry).
Douse dau. to James Brerewood & Luce his wife vlt Dec.

1548. (43 entries, from Jan. 1547-8 to 24 March 1548-9.)
Randle fil Robt Vaudrey & Alice his wife 13 Jan.
Edw. son of Will Grymdyche & Christian his wife 15 July.
Robt son of Ric' Brerewood & Eliz his wife 12 Aug.

1549. (31 entries, 25 March to 24 March.)
Jane dau. of James Brerewood & Luce his wife 10 Apr.
Mary dau. to Robt Voudre [Vawdrey] & Ales his wife 14 may.

1550. (35 entries. 25 March to 24 March.)
Tho: Bagyleys wife was churched¹ 16 Aug.

1551. (29 entries, 25 March to 24 March.)
Alice dau. to Rich. Brearwood 3 June.

1552. (31 entries. 25 March to 24 March.)
Agnes Ellis dau. to xpopher [Christopher] Ellis of Vpton 5 April.
John son of Robt Vaudrey 20 Nouemb.

1553. (11 entries, 25 March to 18 Aug.)
Clement son of Tho. Tayler² 18 Aug. (last entry).

Baptisms.

"When Jacob: Milner was Curate of St. Mary's on the hill in Chester."

1570. (13 entries to March 25.)
Robt Harvey 26 Dec. (first entry).

¹ This entry of a "churching" in a parish register is very unusual.
² The Rector of St. Mary's (*see* p. 81).

P 2

ST. MARY-ON-THE-HILL, CHESTER.

                    1571. (30 entries, 25 March to 24 March.)
John Manley 18 Sept   Rich. Weston 13 Oct.   John Byrom 27 feb.
Alice Brerewood 23 Sept: Gilbt Ryland 8 Dec.
                    1572. (6 entries to 11 June.)

With these entries the Baptisms end.

WEDDING[S] solemnized by the Ministers & Curats of St. Marys on the hill within the citty of Chester since Año 1547.

[Extracts only.]
                    1547. (3 entries, 22 Jan. to 24 March.)
                    1548. (5 entries, 25 March to 24 March.)
                    1549. (9 entries, 25 March to 24 March.)
Anthony Venables gentleman & Anne Brereton 7 Sept.
John Bothe & Mary Ellis 22 Jan.
                    1550. (15 entries, 25 March to 24 March.)
S' Tho: Taylor' p'son there was married 16 of Noveb.
                    1551. (16 entries from 25 March to 1 July.)

No later entries have been transcribed, the original Register possibly having been defective.

BURYALLS within the parish Church & Church yard of St. Marys on the hill within the City of Chester beginning Anno 1547.

[Extracts only.]
                    1547. (4 entries, 22 Dec. to 24 March.)
                    1548. (14 entries, 25 March to 24 March.)
S' Rich Stancliffe preist' was buried 5 Apr.
Tho. Brereton gentleman 11 Apr.
Rondulph Vaudre [Vawdrey] son of Robt & Jane, 6 May.
                    1549. (21 entries, 25 March to 24 March.)
Jane dau. of James Brerewood and Luce his wife 8 Apr.
James Brerewood 21 July.
Jane late wife of Hugh Cliffe gentleman 30 Sept.
Annes Pastmaker 3 Jan.
                    1550. (24 entries, 25 March to 24 March.)
M' John Byrk[en]hed 4 Sept.
                    1551. (13 entries, 25 March to 24 March.)
M' John Broughton 8 June.
M' Randle Brereton 9 June.
                    1552. (20 entries, 25 March to 24 March.)
Alice Brerewood dau. of Rich. 15 Feb.
                    1553. (9 entries, 25 March to 21 July.)
S' Henry Browne preist' sone of Thomas Browne 13 June.

No later entries have been transcribed, the original Register possibly having been defective.

See p. 81.

[2] These were probably two of the priests who had served at St. Mary's or one of the other churches in Chester prior to the Reformation. Sir Henry Browne is mentioned in the Churchwardens' Accounts as being paid xxs. in 1548. The title "Sir" was at this time and till the middle of the 17th century a common designation for a priest or clergyman, and originally signified one who had taken a degree at a university. It is used by Shakespeare.

THE REGISTERS OF ST. MARY'S.

Transcripts of the only years of the early Register of St. Mary's (now lost), preserved in the Bishop's Registry, Chester.

[Extracts only.]

1601. [Begins 25 March, 1601.]

Christenings.

Ranulphus holme[1] bapt xv Julij.
Maria Powell bapt j° februarij.
Katherina Langley bapt 18 Martij.

Weddinges.

Henricus Hall } Copul. xj° ffebruarij.
Maria Leeche }

Buryalls.

Robtus Brerewood sepult ij° die Junij.
Ricus Massie gen. sep. iij° Martij [1601-2].

(Signed) per me Robtm Collier Rectorem Ecc̄liæ paroc. S^{tæ} Mariæ Cestr.

1604.

Christeninges.

Elena filia Roulandi Longley bapt xxvj° Maij.
Ricus ap Jenkin advena bapt xxiiij° Martij.

Weddinges.

[No entries of special interest.]

Burialles.

Thomas Moscrofte sepult v° die Aprilis.
Eliz. vxor Mathei Ellis gen sepult vj° Julij.

(Signed) By me Robert Collier person of St Maries.

There is a very long list of burials in this year, especially in June, July, August, and September, many of which were the result of the PLAGUE[2] then raging in Chester. At the bottom of this list is this memorandum :

"Besides these many were buried at the Cabbins and by the water side, whose names I have not."

1605.

Christenings.

Mattheus filius M^{ri} Hanmere bapt xviij° Augusti.

Weddinges.

Hugo Whickstedde } con' fuere iij° die Nouembris.
Elizabeth Burchenhed }

Burialls.

Vxor Ed. Powell sepult [fuit] xxviij° die Maij.
Anna Aldersey sepult fuit xij° Septembris.
Wittm Paynter a Mason sep. ij° Octobris.

---

[1] This is the baptism of Randle Holme, the second of that name, a distinguished Chester antiquary. *See* the account of this family *postea*.

[2] In the Churchwardens' Accounts for this year these entries occur :
"Paid for coveringe of the graves of Mrs Ellis and her daughter viij^d."
"Paid for franckincense & pitch to perfume the Churche viij^d."
"Paid for makinge up the accomptes for the Collections for the Cabbins xx^d."

And in the following year, 1605, there is a payment for "leastalls" or "buryall places" for "widow Thropp̄e and her daughter dyed of the sicknesse." And again,
"pd for v pounds of pitche to p'fume the churche after the buryall of wydowe Thropp. for she dyed of the sicknesse, viij^d."

1616.

Christenings.

Johes Brerewood baptiz. fuit xvj° Junii.
Maria filia Roʙti Lloyde gen bapt xxxᵒ Junij.
Jana Baffarno baptizata fuit primo die Januarij.

Weddinges.

Edouardus Lloyde de Llanvaire ⎱ copulat' xxij° die Julij.
Helena Lloyde ⎰

Burialls.

Tymothie Tatton a p'soner buried viij° die Julij.
   In the margin " p'ssed to death." [1]
Edmondus Gamwell Aldermanᵈ sep. fuit xij° Septembris.
Johes Byrom sepult fuit in templo xxvj° Nouembris.
Phillipus Oldefelde Juriscons' fuit sepultus in Capella Sᵗᵃᵉ Katherine xvij° Decembris.[2]
Thomas Whitbee senex sepult fuit sĉdo die Januarij.
Gualtherus Joanes advena sepult fuit iij° die Januarij.
. . Ball a Mason buried the xxjᵗʰ day of Januarij.

           Copia concordat cū Originali.
           Robtus Collier Rector ibm
           Thomas Ormes ⎱ gard.
           Jacobus ffletcher ⎰

1622.

Christenings.

Anna Manley baptiz. xxiij° Aprilis.
Anna Weston baptiz. viij° die Decembris.

Weddings.

Johannes Mynshull ⎱ con' xvᵐ Maij.
Elena Bavande ⎰

Radulphus Grange ⎱ con' xvᵐ Julij.
Jana Loarde ⎰

Burialls.

Johes Brerewod sepult xix° Julij.
Tho. Browne gen. sep. ix° die Augusti.
Edwardus Vawdrey[3] gen. sepultus fuit xvij° die Martij.[4]

           Copia concordat cū originali
           Robtus Collier Rector ibm.
           laurence ffletcher ⎱ gard.
           Wiłłms Horton ⎰

---

[1] For an account of the barbarous practice of pressing prisoners to death see pp. 27-28. The father of Thomas Gamul the Recorder. For a copy of the monumental inscription placed to his memory see p. 42.
[2] His monument is illustrated and described on p. 43.
[3] In the Churchwardens' Accounts for this year is this entry :
" Rec' [for] a Lea-tall for Mʳ Vaudreye In Sᵗ Katherine Ile. xvˢ."
[4] His monument, with a coat of arms, is mentioned in *Harl. MS.* 2151 (see p. 33).

Whitbie of the Bache. —

Marriage settlement of Elizabeth Whitbie, one of the daughters of Robert Whitbie of the Bach in the County of Chester, wife of Henry Ogle, son & heir apparent of John Ogle of Whiston in the County of Lancaster. July 2, 8 Jas I. [   ]. — Duchy of Lancaster papers. App. No. 5 30 Rept K.R p. 15.

1624.¹

Christenings.

Maria Manleye baptizata fuit iiij° die Aprilis.
Rebecka Hurlestone baptiz. fuit xxv° Maij.
Katherina Whickstid baptiz. fuit xxiij° die Augusti.
Elizabetha Brerewood baptizata fuit xxxj° die Octobris.

Marriages.

Thomas Whickstid } Copul' fuere xxv° die Junij.
Susanna Whickstid }

Burials.

prisoner. Alexander Whalter sepult' fuit xxvij° die Martij.
prisoner. Richardus Bradburie sepult' fuit xxviij° die Martij.
  [3 other prisoners buried xxxj° Maij.]
M' Thomas Weston sepult' fuit xxv° die Junij.
Edvardus Warburton² mase berer sepult' fuit xxiij° die Septembris.
M' Thomas Boouthe sepultus fuit xxiiij° die Decembris.

1625.

Baptisms.

ffrancisca Gamull baptiz. vj° Novembris.
Thomas Powell baptiz. vij° februarij.

Marriages.

Randulphus Holmes' } copulat' xxix septébris.
Catherina Ellis   }

Mattheus Ellis   } con' fuere x° Novembris.
Elizabetha Judson   }

Burials.

[No entries of special interest.]

1627.

Christenings (torn on one side).

Thomas Gamull baptizatus fuit xxvj° die Aprilis.
Anna filia Mathei Ellis generosi baptiz. fuit xxiiijth die Octobris.
Radulphus Hulmes' baptizatus fuit xxx° die Decembris.

Burialls.

Prisoner pressed.⁶ Williā Wilson sepultus fuit v° die [Aprilis].
  [3 other prisoners buried in April.]
M' Johannes Davenporte sepultus fuit xij° die Decembris.

---

¹ On the back of this sheet of parchment are the transcripts for St. Martin's parish for this year, 1624.

² In the Churchwardens' Accounts there is a payment for a "laystall" for "M' Peter Warburton Mascherer of Chester" in this year, too, there is a payment for the laystall of "Mrs Whicksted of Whicksteed," and for that of "M' Thomas Bouthe a S' Katherines Ile."

³ At the bottom of this sheet are the transcripts for St. Martin's for this year, 1625.

⁴ This was Randle Holme, the second of that name, who was born in 1601. See the account of this family *postea*.

⁵ This is the baptism of the third Randle Holme, author of the *Academy of Armory*, the most celebrated of the four antiquaries bearing that name. See *postea*.

⁶ See note 1, p. 110.

Nicholas a stranger died at M' Wright house et sepultus fuit xiiijth die Decembris.
M^{ris} Lettis Phillipes sepulta fuit xviij^o die februarij.
M' Richardus Bridge sepultus fuit xxth die februarij.

Marriages (much torn).
[No entries of special interest.]

With the exception of the very few "Transcripts" from which the preceding extracts are taken, no others are known till the year 1628, when the first volume of the existing Registers commences. But in the Churchwardens' Accounts, which begin at the unusually early date of 1536, there are year by year entries of the fees paid for "leestalls," or "laystalls" (*i.e.*, burial-places), both in the church and churchyard. These supply us with the names of those whose burials took place at St. Mary's, and in the absence of any Registers we are able to obtain many valuable entries from this source.[1] The Churchwardens' Accounts run from Easter to Easter, so that in the following list any particular year—as, for example, 1545—includes about nine months of that year and three months of the year following. The following entries seem specially noteworthy :—

  1544. Receyved for a buryall place to Sr John Acre.[2]
  1545. Rec' of M' Vawdrey[3] for a leystall.
      Rec' of M' Planeney[4] for ij leystalls.
      Rec' of M' Thomas Bruerton [Brereton] for a leystall.
  1546. For Sr Rye' lestall.[5]
  1548. R' of m'esse [mistress] Brereton for a lestall.[6]
  1549. R' of M' Voydre [Vawdrey] for one lestall.[7]
      R' of M' Wyllm Aldersey for Wyllm Horton[s] lestall.

In 1551, "Mr Tochett" [? Touchett] is mentioned ; "Mr Plankney" and "Mr Rosomgreve" [Rosingreve], in 1552 ; "Mr Kethene," "Mr Fallowes," and "Mr Pellen," in 1554, and the latter again in 1556. In 1557 the entry of a payment for the leystall of "Mr Breretons priest" is very noteworthy. The following are also of interest :—

  1558. Resewed for ye Lestall of St George.[8]
      Reseued of Mester Dampart [Davenport] for his wyves laystall.
      R' for ye lestall of Mester Wodwarde.
  1559. R' for ye loone [loan] of iiij torchuses [torches] at Mester Manlese [Manley's] bereal.
      R' for ye laystall of Messter Manlaye.[9]
  1560. R' for ye lestall of Mester Nottall [Nuttall].

---

[1] In many cases they only supply the names of those who paid the fees and not of those who were actually buried.
[2] He was probably one of the priests then serving at St. Mary's.
[3] Probably Robert Vawdrey (*see* p. 107).
[4] Probably Edward Plankney (*see* p. 107).
[5] This was most probably "Sir Richard Stancliffe priest," whose burial is said to have taken place on the 5th April, 1548 (*see* p. 108), but this date may have been wrongly copied in the *Harl. MS.* and should be 1547.
[6] This relates to the burial of "Thomas Brereton gentleman," 11 April, 1548 (*see* p. 108).
[7] This was for the burial of "Rondulph Vaudre son of Robert and Jane," 6 May, 1548 (*see* p. 108).
[8] One of the clergy probably then serving at St. Mary's.
[9] Probably William Manley of Monksfield. *See* the Manley pedigree *postea*.

An original Instrument whereby Edwarde Breretone of wich Whicleswicke in Com. Lancast. gent. in Consideration of the Somme of £43:6:8 released to his Brother William Breretone of Hanforthe in Com. Cestr. Esquyer, all his right to any part of the personal Estate of Bryan (? Urian) Brereton Knighte his Father, or of Randolphe Breretone Esquyer, his Brother, deceased. Dated the 8th day of Januarye, anno 26-Eliz. (1584.)
Harl MSS. No. 2095. 40. fol. 130 b.

THE REGISTERS OF ST. MARY'S.

"Mr Plankney" was buried in 1563, "Mr Griffith" in 1566, and "Mr Roger Dampord" [Davenport] and "Mrs Massye" in 1567. In 1569 "Mr Berkinhed"[1] was buried, and in 1571 "Mistris Mandlei"[2] and "Mistris Shrifneres." In 1572-3 the burials of "Mr Thomas Berkett" and "Mr Raffe Worsleye"[3] are noted, and there are references to "Mr Worsley" and "Mr Planckney" in 1574-5. One entry in this year's accounts is also noteworthy:

"It bestowed on xij men for bringing in Mr Worsley[s] stone out of churche yard... xij^d

In 1581 the burial of "Mr Urian Brereton" occurs, that of "Mr Kethen" in 1584, and that of "Mr Wenenton" [Winnington] in 1586. Other burial entries of interest are as follows:—

1587. Mr Thomas Browne; Mrs Browne; Jullyane Browne.
Mr Poweles child of Molenton [Mollington].
Mr Raphe Berkenhede.

1588. Mr Benete "a pressoner in the Castell."
Mr Manwarynge "beinge buryed in Saint Katherens chansell."

1590. Mrs Croughtone "beinge buryed in Saint Katherines Ielle."
Mr Raphe Worsleye "beinge buryed in the churche yeard."

In 1598 the burials of "Mr Sutton," "M^{ris} Manley," and "Mr Werden" occur, and those of "M^{ris} Sutton" in 1600, "Mr Massie" in 1601, "M^{ris} Browne" in 1602, "Mr Phillips" in 1605, and "Mrs Wynn" and "Mr Wynn" in 1606. The burials of several children of "Mr Wainwright" are mentioned about this time, and two children of "Mr Donckaster" in 1608. "Mr Younge" and "Mrs Powell of Horseley"[4] were buried in 1609, and "Mr Peter Smythe" in 1611. The following entries of burials are also noteworthy:—

1612. Mr George Mandley; Mr Dannald.
Mr Lorance Wayneright "in St Cathrines Chappell."

1613. Mr Powell of Horseley[5]; Mr Matthewe Ellis.
Thomas Gamull[6] Esq "in St Catherin's Ile in the vaute, sometyme being recorder of the cittie of Chester.
Mrs Kettle; Mrs Smythe.

1615. Mrs Leigh in St Catherines Chappell.

1616. Edmund Gammull[7] alderman "in St Catherins Chappell."
Phillip Ouldfylde[8] Esqr "in St Catherins Chappell."
M^{rs} [Ellin] Dannald; Mr Robert Cardines wife.

1617. Mr Robert Cardin; Mr Thomas Mandley..
Young Mr Thomas Powell[9] " in St Catherins Chappell."

---

[1] See the Birkenhead pedigree postea. [2] See the pedigree of Manley postea.
[3] This was the Ralph Worsley, Esq. (died 27 Dec. 1573), whose epitaph and coat of arms are still in the church (see pp. 45 and 59).
[4] This Mrs. Powell, of Horsley, was one of the daughters and coheirs of Ralph Worsley, Esq. (see p. 45). She was buried at St. Mary's on the 30 Dec. 1609. (Powell pedigree.)
[5] This was really Sir Thomas Powell, of Horsley, Knt. He was buried at St. Mary's on the 26 April, 1613. (Powell pedigree.)
[6] See the inscription to his memory on p. 40. [7] See his monumental inscription on p. 42.
[8] See the account of his monument, &c., on pp. 42-3.
[9] Son of Col. Sir Thomas Powell, Bart., buried at St. Mary's 11 Feb. 1617. (Powell pedigree.)

1618. My Ladye Manwaringe¹ " in Sᵗ Chaterins [sic] Chappell."
1620. Mʳ John Cotton ; Mʳˢ Younge.²
1621. Mʳ James Hickes : Mʳ Thomas Brownes daughter.
1622. Mʳ Matthew Brownes child ; Mʳ Thomas Browne.
       R' [for] a Leastall for Mʳ Vaudreye³ in Sᵗ Katherine Ile.
1623. Mʳˢ Aldersaye.
       Mʳ William Holmes, eldest sonne of Mʳ Randle Holmes senior.⁴
       Mʳ Edward Tottie.
1624. Mʳ Whicksted of Whicksted ; Mʳ Thomas Weston.
       Mʳ Peter Warburton Mase beror of Chester.
       Mʳ Thomas Bouthe in Sᵗ Katherins Ile.
1625. Mʳ Hugh Dodds wife ; Mʳˢ Beuarlye [Beverley].
       Mʳ John Cooke.⁵
1627. Mʳ Richard Fletchers wife ; Mʳˢ Phillipps.
       Mʳ Richard Bridge.
1628. Mʳ Randle Buckley.

Easter 1629 to Easter 1630.⁶

Thomas Powell⁷ of Horsley Esqʳ buried in Sᵗ Katherines Ile.
Mʳˢ Sidney daughter to Mʳ Francis Gamul buried in his owne valte.
Mʳ Hignetts child of ye Castell.
William Thomason of Brewers hall.

Easter 1630 to Easter 1631.

Joseph Teggin our late Clarke buried in the south Ile.
Amye daughter to Mʳ Matthewe Ellis buried in his owne forme.
Mʳ Laurence Reading⁸ servant to Sʳ Henry Salisbury bar. buried att the cominge in of Sᵗ Katherines Ile.
Elizabeth Holme daughter to Mʳ [Randle] Holme [junior], churchwarden, buried in Mʳ John Wilsons forme.
Dame Katherine Oldfeild¹⁰ wife to Sʳ Phillipp Ouldfeild Kᵗ buried in Sᵗ Katherines Ile close by the grate of Mʳ Oldfeilds monumentt.
Mʳ Thomas Wright, Sherifspeare,¹¹ buried vnder Randle Whittbies stone, beinge in the forme where Alderman Holmes wife doth kneel.

The earliest REGISTER now extant is a folio volume, with narrow parchment leaves, which has been strongly bound in dark-coloured calf-skin. It is in very fair preservation, most of the

---

¹ Later on she is referred to as "Dame Katherine Lady Manwaryng." See her monumental inscription on p. 62.
² See the inscription on p. 62.
³ See the burials for 1622 on p. 110 ; also the inscription to Mr. Vawdrey on p. 55.
⁴ See the monumental inscription on p. 74, note 7.
  See the entries for this year on p. 111. The burial of Mr. Whicksted, of Whicksted, probably took place in 1623.
  See the inscription on p. 63.
⁶ These extracts are given from the Churchwardens.' Accounts for these two years in order that they may be compared with the entries from the now earliest existing Register posted. They are much fuller than in the previous Accounts.
⁷ See note on p. 119.
⁸ See the monumental inscription on p. 63.
⁹ See long note and Funeral Certificate on p. 119.
¹¹ That is, one who had served the office of Sheriff but had not been Mayor.

THE REGISTERS OF ST. MARY'S.

entries being quite legible, but in a few instances the ink has somewhat faded. This volume contains Christenings from May 1628 to August 1701, Burials from May 1628 to March 1705-6, and Marriages from March 1630 to May 1700. As already explained, from 1628 to March 1658-9 the entries are all in one handwriting, having been copied from the originals, "which were in nothing but old paper bookes, much abused and confused papers," under the superintendance of Mr. Randle Holme, Junior, the third antiquary of those names, who was then churchwarden. Commencing in 1659 the entries are in various handwritings, and were, no doubt, made either at the time or at the end of each year. After 1662 many of the pages are signed by the rector and churchwardens for the time being, but this is not uniformly the case, as it rested entirely with the rector whether he did so or not.

I have been very carefully through this Register and have made very full extracts from it, including all the entries relating to the clergy, and to every person described by any title such as, esquire, Mr. or Mrs., gentleman, &c., as well as those relating to persons from other parishes, which seemed noteworthy or such as in any way appeared curious or remarkable. The entries relating to the CLERGY of the parish will be found in the account of the Rectors already printed, and those relating to the families of GAMUL of Chester, BREREWOOD of Chester, BROCK of Upton, BROWNE of Upton, BROWNE of Netherlegh, HOLME of Chester, MANLEY of the Lache, BERRINGTON of Chester, ELLIS of Chester, ACTON, HUNT, WESTON, WERDEN, &c., will be found in the account of those families or in the pedigrees connected with them, which will be given later on, being those of the most important families residing within the parish of St. Mary's. The Register is so voluminous that it is not easy to give any list of the names most frequently to be found there, as such a list might very easily omit a name which some might think should have been included, and might include a name which others might think should have been omitted.

In the following extracts this volume of the Registers has been, as a matter of convenience, divided into two, the first portion coming down to 1658 inclusive, and the second portion commencing in 1659 and coming down to the end of the book. The Marriages, too, are made to follow the Christenings, as is usually the case, instead of coming after the Burials.

CHRISTENINGES THIS YEARE 1628.[1]

Joseph Teggin Clerke.[a]

Thomas Mercer sonne to Peter Mercer baptized ye 11th day of May. [The first entry.]
John sonne to Willm Brocke Esqr the 12th day of June.
Lettice daughter to M^r ffrancis Gamull the 27th day of June.
John sonne to Robert Brerewood esq^r the 15th day of October.
Katherine daughter to Mr George Manley the 28th day of December.

1629.[1]

Katherine daughter to Mr Randle Holme Junr the 14th day of May.
Hannah daughter to Mr Tho: Berrington the 28th day of June.
Barbara daughter to Willm Brocke of Upton esq^r ye 23th day of Julie.
John son to Mr John Wilson the 14th day of October.
Katherine daughter to Mr Mathew Ellis the 3rd day of December.

---
[1] I have given my extracts for these two years in full, including some of the names above mentioned, in order to show their general character.
[a] For a note about him see under Marriages, p. 118.

John Wilson of Chester gent compounded for his estate at £142.10.0
Richard Wilson of do. do. " " " 22.0.0

ST. MARY-ON-THE-HILL, CHESTER.

ffrancis son to M'ffrancis Edwards Parson y'e 10th of December.
Thomas[1] and Elizabeth children to M'William Hignett *Constable of the Castle* baptised the 25th day of December.

1630.[2]

Samuel sonne to Christopher Robinson *Musician*[3] y'e 3d day of October.
William and Thomas sonnes of John Trevis *of London* baptized the 28th day of November.

1631.

Margarett daughter of Wiĺm Annion' *de Bruershall* [Brewershall] y'e 30th day of March.
Randle sonne of Wiĺm Aldersey Glover and *Clerke of this church and p'ish* the 29th day of May.
Mary daughter to John Wilson gent the 16th day of March.

1632.

Sarah daughter to . . . Rutter *of y'e Nunns*[3] the first day of July.

1633.

William Midcalfe sonne of Raph Midcalfe gent bapt 19th day of May.
Elianor Wilson daugh of John Wilson gent baptized 29th day of Januarie. [Buried 24th May, 1634.]
Anne Rutter daughter of M'Rutter baptized first day of ffebruary.

1634.

Elizabeth Mason daugh of M'Mason baptized the first day of September.
Thomas Birkhened sonne of Tho: Birkhened gent bapt 10th day of March.

1635.

Jane Chambers daugh of Calcott Chambers esq'r baptized the first day of March. [Bur. 30th June, 1636.]

1638.

Robert sonne of James Strongitharme gent 24th day of May. [Bur. 11th June.]

1639.

Edward reputed sonne of Edward Astle gent bapt 6th day of Julie.
Martha daugh of Wiĺm Stoughton gent bapt 3e day of September.
Henry sonne of Tho: Birkhened gent bapt 23th day of December.

1640.

Margarett, Elizabeth, Ellen and Alice infants borne to John Owen taylor by Elizabeth his wife att one birth and baptized the 29th day of March. [All buried 30th March.]
Elizabeth daugh of Thomas Salisburie de Leadbrooke in the Countie of ffint esq'r[4] bapt 17th day of September.

1641.

Rebecca daugh of Wiĺm Stoughton gent bapt 24th day of October.
Melior daugh of John Brassie gent bapt 12th day of November.
Mary daugh of John Crawford gent bapt 6th day of ffebruarie.
Richard sonne of Richard Williamson gent bapt 8th day of ffebruarie.

---

[1] This Thomas was buried on the 2 Jan. 1639-40.

[2] The transcript for this year, 1630 (which is in Latin), preserved in the Bishop's Registry, is signed "Rich. Kyrke curate, Randle Holme, Tho. Johnsonne, churchwardens."

"John an infant son of Xpofer Robinson *musician*" was buried 15 February, 1631-2.

Another daughter, *Elizabeth*, was baptized 12 Dec. 1632.

[3] That is the site of the old Nunnery of St. Mary's, which was principally in this parish. It belonged at this time to the Breretons of Handforth, co. Chester.

[4] This was a well-known family in Flintshire at this time.

The nuns of St Mary's were allowed to grind their corn free at the Deemills and had the privilege of being served before all other comers.

1642.

Elizabeth daugh of Edward Berrie gent bapt 10th day of May.
Ellen daugh of John Patterson m'chant bapt 31th day of July.
Katherine daugh of John Brassie gent bapt 29th day of November.

1643.[1]

Alice daugh of John Salisbury gent and Anne Bradshaw illegitimate bapt 19th day of September.
Elizabeth daugh of Edward ffryer gent bapt 16th day of October.
Alice daugh of Roger Lloyd [2] *Archdeacon* bapt 27th day of Januarie.

1644.

Elizabeth daugh of Richard Willmson gent bapt 26th day of March.
Hester daugh of S' Willm Mainwaringe' Knt bapt 10th day of July.
Hannah daugh of John Patterson [merchant] bapt 13th day of December.
Thadeus sonne of Thadeus Quirke a stranger bapt 9th day of Januarie.
Joane daugh of Theobald Burgh esq' bapt 2° day of ffebruarie.
John sonne of Thomas Baker gent bapt 11th day of March.

1645.

Elizabeth daugh of James Carrey gent bapt 17th day of Aprill.
John son of John Annyon *of Brewers Hall* baptized the 2 day of May.

1646.-7

[A gap here between May and February.] *Charles ffletcher Clarke.*

1647.

ffrancis sonne of M' Cundeth bapt 1° day of May.

1648.

Elizabeth daugh of M' Rocke bapt 15th day of October.

1650.

Elizabeth daugh of Richard Jannyon gent bapt 1" day of July.
John sonne of John Rocke bapt 16th day of ffebruarie.

1653.

[After 3rd Feb. the entries are all "borne" not "bapt."]

1654.

[The early portion, March 25 to Aug' 27, missing, not having been copied into the volume.]

1656.

Elizabeth daugh of Nathaniell Booth' esq' bapt 2d day of September.

1657.

Elizabeth daugh of Edward Gregge' gent bapt 17th day of Aprill.

---

[1] It will be noticed that there are more entries in this and the following years, no doubt relating to the gentry from various places who had come to reside in Chester owing to the Civil War troubles.

[2] Mr. Roger Lloyd was not Archdeacon of Chester, but of Kilmaclungh in Ireland.

[3] Sir William Mainwaring, Knt., eldest son of Edward Mainwaring, Esq., Chancellor of the County Palatine of Chester, was killed during the siege of Chester, 9 Oct. 1644, and was buried in the Cathedral, where a large monument was erected to his memory in 1671.

[4] Nathanial Booth was of Mottram St. Andrew, near Macclesfield, Esq. *See* also under Baptisms, 1660, *postea.*

[5] Mr. Edward Gregge was the son and heir-apparent of Robert Gregge, of Ilapsford, Esq., who was an Examiner in the Exchequer at Chester, and resided in St. Michael's parish. This child was buried at St. Michael's on the 2nd July, 1657.

1658.

[Up to the end of 1658 the handwriting is the same as that at the beginning of the volume, this being the year when all the entries were transcribed from the earlier books or papers].

MARRIAGES A.N° 1630.

Luke Coniley & Jane Grice both of this p'ish married 29th day of March. [The first entry.]
William Calcott and Jane Teggin[1] widit married the 3d day of July. [? Should this be 1631.]

1633.[2]

Maister Nicholas Arnold and Lettice Moore an heresse married the 29th day of July.
Thomas Manley & Margarett Mollineux married the 8th day of January.

1634.

Thomas Havand & Alice Richardson married the 26th day of Aprill.

1635.

Richard Wright & Elizabeth ffitton married the 7th day of September.
John Davenport Esq' & Mary Vaughan married the 26th day of October.

1638.

Randle Bridge and *Baall* Bickerstaffe married the 17th day of June.

1639.

William Owens gent. & Anne Ravenscroft married the 10th day of May.
Joseph Bruen gent & Mary Leech married the 18th day of ffebruary.

1640.

Richard Williamson gent. & Elizabeth Manley married the 2d day of March.

1641.

James Hurleston & Lettice Gamull[3] married the 6th day of Aprill.
Thomas Hunt and Ellinor ffitton married the 13th day of July.

1644.

Mr Richard Johnson & Mary Challenor married the 22th day of October.
Mr Miles Pemberton & Margarett Bridge married the 19th day of November.
[No entries of any marriages from 1646 to 1657 inclusive.]

1659.

Mr Thomas Pickeringe & Mrs Jane Bromhall was married the xxiijth Day of Aprell.

BURIALLS AN° 1628.[4]

Randle Buckley gent. buried 12th day of May. [The first entry.]
Hubbart sonne of Mr Tho: Berrington bur. 17th day of December.

---

[1] The widow of Joseph Teggin, the parish clerk of St. Mary's, whose burial is entered in the Register on the 26 May, 1630, hardly a week previously. Their marriage is to be found in the Registers of Holy Trinity parish, Chester, as follows:—
1624. Joseph Teggin clarke of St Maryes in Chester and Jane Smyth married by virtue of a licence, 29th June. (*Harl. MS.* 2177.)
She was his second wife, his first marriage being thus entered in the same Register:—
1619. Joseph Teggen clarke of St Maryes in Chester and Ellen Parry spinster, married by banns asking 22nd Jan. (*Ibid.*)

[2] It may be worth noting that 13 marriages are entered in the year 1630, 12 in 1631, and 21 in 1632.

[3] *See* the pedigree of Gamul *postea*.

[4] There are many entries of the burials of "prisoners" in this and the later Registers, such prisoners having either died in the Castle closely adjacent to St. Mary's or else having been executed at Boughton and brought to St. Mary's for interment.

1629.[1]

Thomas Powell[2] Esq' buried 25th day of September.
John Taylo' husband of M" Milner bur. 14th day of March.

1630.

Joseph Teggin[3] *Clarke of this p'ish* bur 26th day of May.
Lawrence Readinge[4] gent buried 11th day of July.
Elizabeth Godsendus[5] buried 23th day of December.
Anne Brerewood[6] was buried 23th day of December.
Dame Katherine Oldfeild[7] buried 29th day of December.
Thomas Wright[8] was buried 9th day of January.

1631.[9]

An infant of William Granwalls surgeon buried the same day [21th day of Aprill] behind the west side of the North porch.
Thomas Laceby a p'soner prest to death[10] bur. in church yard on the north side the steeple the 23th day of Aprill.
John Johnson Joan Broome & Katherine Crosse three p'soners that were executed buried att the west end of the Steeple in church yard 25th day of Aprill.
M" Alice Lloyd[11] spinster buried in St. Katherines Ile att the side of Thomas ffletchers stone the 27th day of June.

---

[1] *See* note 4 previous page.

[2] His Funeral Certificate is as follows : " Thomas Powell of Horsley in the County of Denbigh Esq' departed this mortall life at Horsley upon the xviij th day of September 1629 and was interred in S' Maryes Church in the City of Chester. He [was the eldest son and heir of Sir Thomas Powell, knt, who died in 1613 and] married Dorethy daughter to Morris Gwyn [Wynn] of Gwydir, in the County of Carnarvon Esq', by whom he had yssue S' Thomas Powell of Berket (*i.e.* Birkenhead) in the County of Chester, baronett, now of the age of . . . yeares or there about at the death of his father, who married Kathrine, daughter to S' John Egerton of Oulton in the County of Chester, K', by whom he hath yssue Thomas Powell, his sonne and heyre w'th dyed in February 1617[-18] w'thout issue. John Powell 2° sonn and now heyre of S' Thomas, of the age of . . . yeares married [Margaret] dau. and coh. to Edward Puleston of Alington in the County of Denbigh, Esq', but yet hath noe yssue. John Powell [was the] second sonne to the defunct, Roger, 3d sonne, Richard 4th sonne. Elinor eldest daughter to the defunct, Margret 2d daughter, Kathrine 3d dau, Sidney Powell youngest dau." (*Cheshire and Lancashire Funeral Certificates*, Record Society, vol. vj., pp. 161-2.)

[3] For a note on him, his two marriages, and the marriage of his widow, *see* p. 118. His burial is thus referred to in the Churchwardens' Accounts : " Joseph Teggin our late Clarke buried in the South Ile att Ioghmost [lowermost] formes end."

[4] Thus described in the Churchwardens' Accounts : " M' Lawrence Readinge servant to S' Henry Salisbury bar[t], buried at the cominge in of S' Katherines Ile." His monumental inscription is given on p. 63.

[5] A quaint name, probably bestowed on a foundling found in the parish. In the Churchwardens' Accounts the entry is simply " a strangers child."

[6] Her Funeral Certificate is as follows :—" M" Anne Brerewood departed this mortall life in Chester vpon the 23 day of December 1630 and was buried in S' Maryes Church in Troutbecks Chapell there. She was daughter to S' Randle Mainwaring of Peuer, in the County of Chester, K', and married Robert Brerewood of the Chity of Chester, Esq. learned in the lawes and by her [he] had yssue John, Robert, Jane and Elizabeth Brerewood and three that dyed yonge." (*Cheshire and Lancashire Funeral Certificates*, Record Society, vol. vj., p. 38.) *See* also the pedigree of Brerewood *postea*.

[7] Her Funeral Certificate is as follows:—" Dame Kathrine Ouldfield departed this mortall life at Chester vpon the 27th day of December 1630 and lyeth interred in S' Maryes Church in Chester. She was dau. and co-heyre to Tho, Puleston of Leghtwood in the County of Flynt, Esquier and first married Thomas Hanmer of Fenns, in the County aforesayd [Esq.] by whom she had yssue William Hanmer, her only child. She married to her second husband S' Philip Ouldfeild of Bradwall in the County of Chester, Knight, but by him had no yssue. This Certificat was taken at Chester vpon the 10 January 1630[-1] by Randle Holme." (*Cheshire and Lancashire Funeral Certificates*, Record Society, vol. vj., pp. 153-4.) Her husband, who was buried in St. Mary's, in December, 1616, is commemorated by the handsome full-length effigy in the north chapel (*see* p. 43).

[8] His Funeral Certificate is as follows :—" Thomas Wright of the City of Chester, Feltmaker, was Sheriffe of Chester Ao 1600. He dyed at his howse in Chester the 5 day of January 1630[-1] and was buried in S' Maryes Church in the City aforsayd. He married Anne sole dau. and heyre to Randle Whitbye of Chester but by her he had no yssue." (*Ibid.—ibid.*, p. 191.) He is described in the Churchwardens' Accounts as " M' Thomas Wright Sherif[s]eare."

[9] From this time till 1663 the exact position of each burial is given in the Register.

[10] For an account of the terrible punishment of " pressing to death " *see* pp. 27-8.

[11] Her Funeral Certificate is as follows :—" M" Alice Lloyd, daughter to George Lloyd, somtyme Bushop of Chester, dyed in Chester the 28 [th] June 1631 and was buried in S' Maryes Church in Chester. She was neuer married and so dyed without

1632.

John Gathercoale a stranger buried in the Church yard on the North side neere the broad stone the 11th day of Septemb.

Mrs ffrances Tottie[1] buried in the North Ile under her husbands stone att the goeinge in of St. Katherines Ile the 8th day of October.

[Mrs Elizabeth Danald . . . November].[2]

1633.

Richard Lathom
Katherine Williams } beinge 4 [sic] p'soners[3] that were executed buried in church yard on yr south side the 4th day of May.
James Johnson

1634.

Richard ffletcher[4] buried in the Church vnder the Lady Salisburies seate 2d day of Aprill.

John Crosse buried in the Chancell before the Ministers seate the 3d day of July.

Mathew Browne[5] gent buried in the south Ile att Mr Ellis his Pue end vnder the vppermost stone there the 26th day of November.

Mr Peter Shakerley buried in the North Ile att the side of Burrowes stone the 31th day of January.

1635.

Elizabeth wife of Randle Holme[6] Alderman buried in Mr Jaques Arnodia his forme 29th day of May.

Katherine daugh of ffrancis Gamull[7] esqr and *Maior of this Cittie* buried in the Tombe 2d day of October.

1637.

Thomas Briscoe
Raph Wilkinson } 4 p'soners executed buried at the west end betwixt the north porch and the steeple the 14th day of Aprill.
Ellen Weld &
Ellen Woodward

"Sr William Breretons[8] pue doore in St Katherines Ile" is mentioned in June, 1637.

---

yssue. This certificate was testyfied to be trew vnder the hand of Randle Holme of the City of Chester, Alderman and Deputy to the Office of Armes." (*Cheshire and Lancashire Funeral Certificates*, Record Society, vol. vj., pp. 134-5.) In the Church-wardens' Accounts the entry is "Mrs Alice Lloyd daughter to bishop lloyd buried in St Katherines Ile.

[1] Her Funeral Certificate was begun but never finished (see *Cheshire and Lancashire Funeral Certificates*, Record Society, vol. vj., p. 197). It gives her arms but no other information. She was the widow of Edward Tottie of Mollington, who died in 1623. Her will was proved at Chester in 1632.

[2] Although there is now no entry of this burial in the Register the following Funeral Certificate was made for her:— "Mrs Elizabeth Danald dyed in the City of Chester vpon the xxth day of Nouember 1632 and was buried in St Maryes Church, in the sayd City. She was daughter and co-heyre to Thomas Ince, somtyme Sheriffe of the City of Chester and married to her first husband Thomas Massey of the City aforesayd, and had yssue by him 2 sonnes, the wch all dyed yonge. She married to her 2 husband Christopher Danald of Chester but by him she had no yssue." (*Ibid.—ibid.*, p. 65.) Christopher Danald was buried at St. Mary's 25th April, 1633.

[3] There are many entries of the burial of "prisoners" in the Register of St. Mary, but only one or two specimens need be given here (see p. 118, note 4).

[4] In his Funeral Certificate (Record Society, vol. vj., p. 89) he is described as "somtyme Sheriffe of the City of Chester, dyed the first day of Aprell 1634 and was buried in St Marys Church in Chester."

[5] His Funeral Certificate is as follows :—"Mathew Browne of the City of Chester, gentleman, dyed at his howse in Handbridge vpon the . 24 day of Novr. 1634 and was interred in St Maryes Church in Chester aforesayd. He married Katherine, daughter to Rafe Allen of the City of Chester, Alderman, and widow of Mathew Ellis of Over Leigh, nere Chester, gent and by him had yssue Thomas, his sonne and heyre of the Age of 14 yeares or therabout at tyme of his fathers death, George, 2nd sonne ; Alice the only daughter. He had yssue also by her Elizabeth and Anne and a son not baptized, wch all dyed yonge." (*Cheshire and Lancashire Funeral Certificates*, Record Society, vol. vj., p. 49.) See also the pedigree of Browne of Netherlegh *postea*.

[6] See the Holme pedigree *postea*.

[7] See the Gamul pedigree *postea*.

[8] This was Sir William Brereton, of Handforth, co. Chester, Bart., afterwards the well-known commander on the side of the Parliament. He held property in Chester, chiefly lands which had formerly belonged to the Nunnery of St. Mary.

Argent, 3 greyhounds courant in pale barways sable — Morton of Oxfordshire. Guillim. p. 467.
Sable, 3 roses argent   Powel of Cheshire. Of this family was Thomas Powel of Birkenhead in the
said County Esq, created Baronet Jany 23. 1628.   Guillim p. 249.
Same arms borne by Maurice of ...... and Smith of Durham

THE REGISTERS OF ST. MARY'S.

Mr Thomas ffranckland buried in St. Katherines Ile at the goeinge in to Sr William Breretons seate 20th October.

Thomas Swinton¹ gent buried in St. Katherines Ile before the doore at the feete of Mr Readings stone the 21th day of Novemb.

Dame Dorothie Chitwood buried in the Chancell vnder the stone before the south quire seates 19th day of December.

Richard Starkie buried in the Quire att the side of the Lady Chitwoods stone 24th day of December.

Edward Mathewes servant to Mr Hugh Whicksted buried in the Crosse Ile direct before the steeple doore 31th day of Januarie.

1638.

Nicholas Wright, Thomas Owen, John Warburton, Richard Holme, 4 p'soners buried at the north west end of the steeple 16th of April.

Thomas sonne of Peter Egerton esq^r buried in the Chancell without the Raile att the side of Mr Colliers' ston[e] 17th of July.

Mrs Jane Moreton³ buried before Mr Ecclestons pue att the south side ould Yongs stone 21th day of January.

Mary daugh of Raph Metcalfe gent buried vnder ye end of Robert Burroughes his wives forme 28th day of ffebruary.

Elizabeth Gilbert kinswoman to Mr Garnor buried at the the [sic] lower end of the south Ile at the entringe of the low[er]most mens forme 3^d day of March.

1639.

Edward Whitbye⁴ esq^r late Record^r of this Cittie buried in Mr Gamulls vault in St. Katherines Ile 25th day of Aprill.

An infant of Mr Mathew Gleaves buried in the north Church yard the 4th day of May.

Mrs Ellinor Anderton⁵ wife of Mathew Anderton esq^r buried in St. Katherines Ile vnder her sone Mr Thomas Swintons stone 26th day of August.   *Anderton arms Sa. 3 shackbolts arg*

Dame Katherine Powell⁶ wife of Sr Thomas Barron^t buried in St. Katherines Ile vnd^r Mr Worsleys stone⁷ 12th of Septemb.

---

¹ His Funeral Certificate is as follows:—" Thomas Swynton of the City of Chester, the only sonne and heyre of Richard Swynton of Knuttsford, in the County of Chester, gent, departed this mortall life in Chester vpon the xviijth day of Nov. 1637 and was interred in St. Maryes Church in the City of Chester aforsayd and in St Kathernes Ile of the sayd Church. The sayd defunct married Mary, dau. to Willm Walker of Hatfield, in the County of Hartford, by whom he had yssue Tho. Swynton, his only child, of the Age of one yeare and [a] halph [sic] at his fathers death." (Cheshire and Lancashire Funeral Certificates, Record Society, vol. vj., pp. 175-6.) His mother, Eleanor, daughter of Edmund Gamul, Esq., married for her first husband Richard Swinton, gent.; secondly, Thomas Harvey of Chester, alderman, who died in 1613; and thirdly, Matthew Anderton, Esq. She was buried at St. Mary's in 1639.

² The late rector's gravestone.

³ Called in the Churchwardens' Accounts "Mrs Jane Moreton widdow."

⁴ His Funeral Certificate is as follows:—" Edward Whitbye, Esqr late Recorder of the City of Chester, departed this mortall life at his howse of the Bach, neer the City of Chester aforesaid, vpon the xviijth daye of Aprill 1639 and was Interred in St Maries Church in the City aforsaid, in M^r ffrancis Gamulls vault in St Katherns Ile in the sayd Church, the 25 of Aprell, in the yeare aforsaid. The said defunct mar. Ales, daughter to Richard Bauand of Chester, Alderman, and widow to Thomas Gamul, somtyme Recorder of Chester, and [who] was before wife to David Lloyd, somtyme Maior of the sayd City, but the said Edward Whitby had no yssue by her." (Cheshire and Lancashire Funeral Certificates, Record Society, vol. vj., pp. 183-4.) See also the account of the Gamul family posted.

⁵ Mrs. Anderton was Eleanor, daughter of Edmund Gamul, Esq. She was three times married, first to Richard Swinton of Knutsford, gent.; secondly to Thomas Harvey of Chester, alderman, who died in 1613; and thirdly to Matthew Anderton, Esq. See the Gamul pedigree and also note 1 above.

⁶ Dame Katherine Powell was the daughter of Sir John Egerton of Egerton and Oulton, co. Chester, Knt., and was baptised 6th Sept. 1584, at Little Budworth, co. Chester. She died at Horsley on the 7th September. Her husband, Col. Sir Thomas Powell, Bart., took an active part on the Royalist side during the Civil War. He died about 1650. (Powell pedigree.)

⁷ This stone was near the monument described on p. 45

Morton arms:- argent, a greyhound courant, Sa. K

Edward Brocke[1] gent buried in St. Katherines Ile vnd[r] M[r] Vaudreys stone 4th day of October.
Thomas Steele gent buried in St. Katherines Ile att the south side of M[r] Readinges[2] stone 5th day [of] October.
M[r] John Eccleston[3] buried on the north side Yongs stone before the entrance of his owne seate 10th day of Januarie.

1640.

ffoure infants[4] of John Owens buried in one Coffin in the South Church yard before the South porch 30th of March.   See p. 116.

William Brocke[5] esq[r] buried in St. Katherines Ile vnd[r] M[r] Vaudreys stone 8th day of Aprill.

M[rs] Christian Gamull[6] wife of ffrancis Gamull esq[r] bur in the vault in St. Katherines Ile 11th day of June.

M[rs] Isabell Hurleston[7] buried in the vppmost seate in St. Katherines Ile close to the Chancell side 26th of June.

M[rs] Alice Whitbye[8] widdow buried in the vault in St. Katherines Ile the 18th day of August.

M[rs] Anne Booth widdow buried vnder her first husband Gregories stone in midle Ile 4th of Septemb.

M[rs] Salisbury widdow buried vnder Readings stone att the entrance of St. Katherines Ile 13th day of Septemb.

Adam Birkhened of Manley esq[r] buried vnder the Birkheneds stone in the south Ile 7th day of Novemb.

M[rs] Grissell Smith[9] buried vnder old M[r] Boothes stone in St. Katherines Ile the 22th day of Decemb.

Elizabeth wife of M[r] William Halton buried att the side of Morgans stone in the midle Ile the 6th of January.

M[rs] Jane wife of M[r] John Williams buried vnder y[e] midle of the Sheriffe peeres[10] pue against the midle piller the 26th day of January.

1641.

Elizabeth an infant and daugh of Thomas Salisburie of Leadbrooke esq[r] buried in St. Katherines Ile vpon it[s] Aunt M[rs] Grissell Smith[11] 8th day of Aprill.

M[r] John Williams buried vpon his wife[12] vnder the midle of the Sheriffes peeres pue and M[r] Wrights seate against the pillar 24th day of May.

---

[1] Mr. Edward Brock was a younger brother of Robert Brock, of Upton, gent. His father, Mr. John Brock, of Upton, married Parnel, daughter of Thomas Vaudrey, of the Riddings. co. Chester, Esq. This family held property in Chester, and were accustomed to bury at St. Mary's. Hence the reference to "M[r] Vaudreys stone." (See the pedigree of Brock of Upton.)

[2] Mr. Laurence Reading was buried at St. Mary's on the 11th July, 1630 (see p. 119).

[3] The will of John Eccleston, of Chester, yeoman, was proved at Chester in 1640.

[4] See the baptism of these four children born at one birth, p. 116.

[5] This was William Brock of Upton and the Inner Temple, Esq. (see the pedigree of Brock of Upton postea). See also note 1 above.

[6] She was the eldest daughter of Sir Richard Grosvenor, of Eaton, Knt. and Bart., and was married at Eccleston in October, 1624, to Francis Gamul, Esq., afterwards Knighted and created a Baronet by Charles I. She died in childbirth. (See the Gamul pedigree postea.)

[7] Her will is preserved in Harl. MS. 2131, f. 199. She desired to be buried in St. Mary's, in Chester, "neere to the good Lady Mainwaring" (see p. 114). She bequeathed 10s. to Mr. Seddon, clerk, and 10s. more "to preach my funeral sermon." She left £5 to the poor of St. Mary's.

[8] Mrs Alice Whitby was the widow of Edward Whitby, Esq., the Recorder of Chester, who was buried at St. Mary's on the 25th April, 1639 (see p. 121). She was a daughter of Mr. Richard Bavand, alderman of Chester, and was three times married, firstly to David Lloyd (Mayor of Chester, in 1593-4); secondly to Thomas Gamul, Esq., Recorder of Chester, who died in 1613 (see the Gamul pedigree); and thirdly to Edward Whitby, Esq., also Recorder of Chester. Her will was proved at Chester in 1640. She gave a piece of plate and other things to the church in 1639 (see p. 23).

[9] Mrs. Grissell Smith is again mentioned in 1641, when a daughter of Thomas Salisbury, of Leadbrooke, Esq., was buried upon "its aunt M[rs] Grissell Smith."

[10] The "Sheriff peers" were those who had served the office of Sheriff of Chester. Two Sheriffs were appointed every year.

[11] Mrs. Grissell Smith's burial took place on the 22 Dec. 1640 (see above).

[12] Mrs. Williams' burial is entered in the Register on the 26th Jan. 1640-1.

Mrs Mary Bridge buried close before the pillar in John Grices seate in the midle Ile 26th day of July.

Jane daughter of Henry Darwall drowned in the Abby Co^{rt} well buried in her mothers grave vnder her ston[e] on the east side of the south porch 13th day of August.

John sonne of ffrancis Edwards[1] Clerke Recto^r of this Church and buried in the Chancell in the midle of ye crosse walke below the stepps neere the end of the Commu[n]ion table 21th day of Januarie.

Thomas Kinge gent servant to Henry Birkhened esq^r buried vnder Starkies pue att the end next the wall in ye north Ile 28th day of Januarie.

William Calcott kill'd by fall of a barne in Eccleston lane by boisterous winds 3° of ffebruary 1641[-2] was buried in the south Church yard vnder pte of the flagges in the way att the side of Calcotts stone 4th day of ffebruary.

1642.[2]

An infant of Mr Thomas Parnells buried vpon it[s] moth^r vnder the midle stone att Troutbeks chappell doore in the south Ile the 28th day of Aprill.

Mathew an infant and sonne of Mr William Whittle buried in his wives old seate in the north Ile 17th day of May.

Mrs Vrsula Holcroft buried in the Chancell ag^t ye midle goeinge into the Quire seates on the left hand 14th of June.

"John a stranger that dyed att angell" buried 1° of August.

1643.[3]

Richard Morris Butcher slaine at Boughton[3] buried in ye corner close to the Dyall post[4] in south church yard 19th of July.

Allen Tompson a souldier wounded at boughton buried in the west corner of the south church yard neere Mr Hunts[5] little gate in Church yard wall 24th of July.

Griffith ap Evan a souldier buried in the west corner of the south Church yard neere Mr Hunts' little gate in the way by the wall 21th of August.

Thomas Acton servant to Sr Hugh Calveley buried in south Church yard close to the middle piller of Troutbeks Chappell 3^d day of October.

Robert sonne of Robert Brerewood esq^r buried some halfe yard from the side of the vpper Tombe[6] in Troutbeks Chappell 23th day of October.

John Edwards[7] *the Hangman* buried in north Church yard in the west towards Boyds garden nooke 17th of November.

John Eansworth a souldier buried in the north Church yard vnder the wall ag^t the midle window . . . November.

Mathew Knight a souldier buried in the north Church yard vnder the wall against the midle window of the psonage house 28th day of November.

Captaine Mathew Curson buried in St. Katherines Ile in the seate against ffranklands stone 25th day of January.

---

[1] For a notice of Mr. Francis Edwards *see* the account of the Rectors, p. 84. The exact position of the grave as here defined is curious.

[2] In this year there are several references to burials "betwixt the twoe pillers by the old font in south Church yard" and "at the side of ye piller by the old font in south Church yard" which are very curious and noteworthy.

[3] This is the first entry in the Register relating to the burials of those who lost their lives during the Civil War.

[4] That is the sun-dial still on the south side of the churchyard (*see* p. 59).

[5] Mr. Hunt was the then rector of St. Mary's, and no doubt lived near to the church.

[6] This is an interesting reference to the altar tombs formerly in the Troutbeck Chapel (*see* pp. 36-8).

[7] The Hangman would appear to have been in constant requisition, for all the prisoners who were executed at Chester, and whose burials are recorded in these Registers, seem to have been hanged at Boughton, and thence carried back to the Castle and buried at St. Marys.

Leifetenant Christian Eares buried in same place same day.

1644.

Mr John Carter[1] buried vnder the seates close to the side of Mr Steeles seate on the north side the north Ile 5th day of Aprill.

Captaine Thomas Gamull[2] esq{r} sonne of *Colonell* Sr ffrancis Gamull Kn{t} and Barronett buried in the vault in St. Katherines Ile 12th day of June.

Pollixina Gregge[3] buried in St. Katherines Ile vnder the Alablaster stone[4] in the passage to the Chancell the 13th day of June.

"a stranger buried in the north Church yard in the *slacke*[5] before the midle window."

William ffranwall slaine vpon the guard buried vnder his fathers stone in the north Ile 7th day of July.

Mrs Johnson buried in the midle Ile below the backe corner of Mr Holmes his seate at the side of Mutchell stone the 11th day of August.

James Hallwood gent buried in Troutbecks Chappell att side of Tyrers stones 28th day of October.

Thomas Birkhened[6] gent buried in the south Ile vnd{r} the marble stone[4] 14th day of Novemb.

Raph Hollinshead gent buried in the Crosse Ile betwixt Healds seate and the end of the longe forme 27th of Novemb.

Mr Robert Chapman and Mr Thomas Dalton twoe souldiers kild on Haugh greene buried in the north Church yard in the Corner agt Gamulls tombe 3{o} of Decemb.

Anne daugh of Mr Leigh of Baguley[7] esq{r} buried in the Chancell 29th day of December.

Mrs Grace Whitmore buried in Troutbeks chappell 30th of December.

Colonell Thomas Leigh[8] esq{r} was layd downe in the vestrey to be kept till he could be removed, the 8th day of January but afterwards was removed to Prestburie church.

1645.

Mr Phillip Ravenscroft[9] buried in Troutbeckes chappell vpon his Aunt Brerewood first day of May.

Bridgett wife of Robert Byron a stranger buried in the South Church yard at the east end of the Chancell the 15th day of May.

William Daye a Trooper slaine in Handbridge buried in North Church yard at the way side against the north end of St. Katherines Ile 21th of May.

John an infant and sonne of Mr Elliott buried in ye midle Ile vnder the side of ffletchers stone 28th of May.

[So in original.]

. . . . . daugh to S{r}jeant Dalton buried in the north Church yard vpon the side of the hill before ye next piller to the porch 31th day of May.

---

[1] His will as John Carter of Chester, yeoman, was proved at Chester in 1644.

[2] This is a very interesting entry, as it records the burial of the only surviving son and heir of Sir Francis Gamul, Knt. and Bart. He was no doubt killed during some of the fighting in or near Chester. This entry is interesting as showing that the father had probably been created a Baronet prior to this date.

[3] Daughter of Mr. Thomas Gregge of Bradley, near Grappenhall, co. Chester. Mr. Thomas Gregge had married Katherine, daughter of Robert Brock of Upton, Esq. (*see* that pedigree).

[4] This is no doubt the stone, so often referred to, belonging to the Birkenhead family. The grant of a burial-place in the chancel for the Birkenhead family will be found on p. 61.

[5] "Slack" is a Chester word meaning a hollow.

[6] The will of Thomas Birkenhead of Chester, gentleman, is still preserved at Chester.

[7] She was the daughter of Edward Legh, of Baguley, Esq., by his first wife Elenor, daughter of William Tatton of Withinshaw, Esq.

[8] This was Thomas Legh of Adlington, Esq., who died in Chester during the siege of that city. The date of his burial at Prestbury is not known, as the Register of that parish is defective at this date. He and his sons took an active part on the Royalist side during the Civil War (see *East Cheshire*, vol. ij., p. 243).

[9] Of the family of Ravenscroft of Bretton, co. Flint. See his monumental inscription formerly in the church, p. 67.

Thomas Bolt may have belonged to the Bolt family of Lancashire.

Mr Thomas Bold drowned and buried in St. Katherines Ile betwixt Mr Steeles stone and the old Pue the third day of August.

Thomas sonne of John Grey kill'd by an enemy and buried by the end of his mothers seate on the north side the midle Ile 20th day of August.

Nathaniel Williams was slaine and buried in the Church close before the south doore last of August.

Mr Thomas sonne of Hugh Wilbraham[1] esq{r} buried in the Chancell 23th day of September.

John Carter slaine att walls buried vnder the vppmost window of Troutbecks chappell agt the staire head in the south Church yard 26th day of September.

Ellen Smith shott and killd buried vpon her mother before the south doore betwixt the backe of the lowmost seate & the staires vnder the narrow longe stone 27th of September.

Thomas Griffith shott and kil'd buried in the south Church yard at the side of the flaggs at the west end of Williams stone 4th day of October.

Henry Morris a trooper shott and kil'd buried in the west corner of the south Church yard behind the porch 5th of October.

Robert Thorneley kil'd buried in the south porch 5th of October.

Thomas Grosvenor shott and kill'd buried in the south Church yard with his head to the Church yard wall at the turneinge westward from Bennetts stone the 20th day of December.

Mr Oliver Chisnall[2] buried in the lower end of ye north Ile close to the north side of Johnsons stone 28th day of January.

Edward Smith of the Rocke was slaine & buried in the lower end of the south Ile at the head of Dykas his stone close to the formes 28th of January.

Randle Hunt gent buried in the Chancell before the Clarks seate 9th day of ffebruary.

Mr Robert Ravenscroft[3] buried in Troutbeks chappell the 12th day of ffebruary.

Mr Casteene servant to Sr William Brereton[4] buried in St. Katherines Ile in the vppmost seate 17th of ffebruary.

Captaine Henry Brereton buried in Troutbeks Chappell the 19th day of ffebruary.

Charles Worsley a souldier buried in the north Church yard vpon the Corner of the hill before the porch the 23th day of ffebruary.

Margrett{1} wife of Hugh Wilbraham esq{r} buried in the Chancell 23th day of March.

1646. Charles ffletcher Clarke [*i.e.*, parish clerk].

A souldier buried on the hill before the porch in the north Church yard 29th day of March.

Mr William Whittle[6] buried vnder Thomas ffletchers stone in St. Katherines Ile the 20th day of Aprill.

[No entries between 17 May and 16 January].

Mr Thomas Weston[7] buried vnder his fathers stone in the midle Ile at the doore goeinge into ye Chancell 26th of ffebruary.

In 1647 Chester was visited by a violent outbreak of the PLAGUE, which began in the Spring and lasted about ten months. All those who could leave the city appear to have done

---

[1] This Hugh Wilbraham, Esq., was of Eccleston, near Chester, and of St. Andrew, Holborn, London, a younger son of Thomas Wilbraham of Woodhey, Esq. He married for his first wife Margaret, daughter of Richard Grosvenor of Eaton, Esq. Her burial took place at St. Mary's on the 23rd March, 1645-6.

[2] Probably a member of the well-known Lancashire family of Chisenhall of Chisenhall, who were staunch Royalists.

[3] Probably of the family of Bretton, co. Flint (*see* p. 67).

[4] This was the celebrated Sir William Brereton of Handforth, co. Chester, Bart., the Parliamentary commander

See note 1 above.

[6] This is probably Mr. William Whittle of Chester, tanner, whose will, proved in 1646, is still at Chester.

[7] The will of Mr. Thomas Weston, of Chester, proved 1646, is still at Chester.

so, but a large number of deaths (over 2,000) occurred amongst those who were left. By the end of June 67 persons died in one week, and this number rose in August to 209, after which it slowly declined. The mortality appears to have been pretty evenly distributed over the whole of the city, as will subsequently be shown. The following horrible description is taken from a printed contemporary account, probably one of the small quarto newspapers of the time, but it is not possible to say which :—

"There dyed in Chester City of the Plague, from July 7 to July 15 1647, in the Parishes of

Oswels	14	Martins	15	Johns	5
Peters	3	Maryes	25	Michaels	23
Trinity	8	Olives	12	and in the City	
		Brigets	9	Cabins	29

"The totall of the burialls this weeke in Chester 141.

"The Plague takes them very strangely, strikes them black of one side, and then they run mad, some drowne themselves, others would kill themselves; they dye within a few hours, some run up and down the streets in their shirts to the great horrour of those in the City."

The distress in the city was brought to the notice of Parliament, when the following ordinance was passed by the House of Commons in August, 1647 :—

"Whereas Chester is grievously visited with the pestilence, very few families being clear; by reason whereof almost all persons of ability have left the said city, there remaining for the most part only the poor, who are altogether deprived of trading, and if not presently relieved are likely to perish for want, and endanger the adjacent counties. And whereas the county of Chester is exceedingly impoverished by the late war; 'tis ordered that the ministers of London and Westminster, those in the counties of Chester, Kent, Sussex, Surrey, Southampton, Middlesex, Essex, Hereford, Cambridge, Suffolk and Norfolk, do, on the next Lord's day after the receipt of this ordinance, earnestly move their people to contribute for the relief of the said distressed inhabitants."

In *Harl. MS.* 1929, f. 36, I find the following printed list of the burials which took place at St. Mary's, from which it will be seen how severe the mortality was:—

"A Catalogue of the Burialls in the City of Chester of the Plague from the 22th of June 1647 to the 14 of October 1647

1st week	67	At S' Maries	5	9 week 152	At S' Maries	22
2 week	57		9	10 week 166		26
3 week	141		25	11 week 123		28
4 week	114		19	12 week 114		22
5 week	153		30	13 week 71		8
6 week	156		28	14 week 69		14
7 week	209		20	15 week 42		8
8 week	182		16	16 week 52		9

To this there has been added in ink that the burials at St. Mary's in the 17th week were 5; 18th, 3; 19th, 4; 20th, 7; 21st, 5; 22nd, 1; 23rd, 1.

The totall of the Burialls of the Plague in 16 weeks is 1875 Persons.

A fuller account of the deaths in each week, divided into parishes, occurs in *Harl. MS.* 1922, f. 27, but it is too long to give here.[1] It may, however, be stated that in the 23 weeks from June 22 to the end of November, 1647, no less than 2,032 persons died, and if the population of

[1] It may, however, be consulted in the *Cheshire Sheaf*, vol. 1, pp. 183-4, having been contributed by Dr. Brushfield.

Chester be taken at about 10,000, very many of whom had left the city, it will be at once apparent how heavy the mortality was. The following is a summary of the deaths, arranged under the respective parishes:—

Oswalds 396	Maries 315	Michaels 130
Peters 75	Olives 59	Pest-house ... 208
Trinity 232	Bridgets 86	Total....... 2,032
Martins 173	Johns 358	

Out of the 315 deaths which took place in St. Mary's parish the burials of only 55 are recorded in the Register, so that had it not been for the above contemporary account the rate of mortality, if based upon the burials entered in the Register, would have been grossly underestimated.

1647.

Henry sonne of M' Tho : Birkhened buried in the midle Ile att widdow Roberts pue doore vnd' their owne stone 23th of Aprill.

A Child of M' Rockes buried on the north side close to the Church porch the right hand goeinge into y' Church the ninth day of May.

M'* Anne Wright[1] widdow buried in her owne pue her head ioyneinge close to the north side of the piller the third day of July.

Katherine Baxter and her three Children buried in the south porch within 2 foote of the church doore the 22th day of Septemb.

Captaine Cheshire[2] buried in St. Katherines Ile vnder the Lady Smiths stone 3° of October.

M'* Katherine Cooke[3] buried in the north Ile vnder their owne stone 11th day of October.

1648.

M'* Amy Knott buried in the midle Ile her feete ioyneinge close to Jane Cottons 25th of Decemb.

1649.

M' Peter Starkie buried in his wives pue 7th of July.

A sonne of M' Jannions buried buried [*sic*] in Troutbecks chappell on the west side of the lowermost tombe[4] and the midle window 9th day of July.

1650.

M'* Ellinor Gredge buried 5th of Aprill and her sister buried 12th Aprill both vnder meacockes stone in St. Katherines Ile.

1651.

M'* Crosse buried in the north Ile vnder her own stone the first day of May.

Serjeant Veinson buried in the Church neere the poore mans box 22th day of October.

An infant of M'* Poole buried at her owne pue doore the 5th day of December.

An infant of M' Richard Wright buried in the north Ile att Richard Hills pue doore the the [*sic*] 27th day of December.

M' Stourtons' [*sic*] wife dyed *att Bretton hall* buried in St. Katherins Ile vnder M'* Lloyds stone the 11th day of March.

A sonne of M' Turtons' [*sic*] buried vpon his mother the 24th day of March.

[1] The will of Ann Wright of Chester, widow, proved 1647, is still preserved at Chester.

[2] In the Churchwardens' Accounts he is described as "Capten Chessher out of Castell," being no doubt quartered in the Castle. He is probably to be identified with John Cheshire of Halton, gentleman, the inventory of whose effects, dated 1647, is still preserved at Chester.

[3] The administration to the effects of Katherine Cooke of Heswall, dated 1648, is still at Chester. She was, I think, connected with the family of Francis Edwards, the late Rector of St. Mary's (*see* p. 84).

[4] This shows that the tombs in the Troutbeck Chapel were existing in 1649 (*see* p. 32).

[5] In the Churchwardens' Accounts these two burials are noticed as follows :—" M'*s* *Turton* buried in St Katherin's yle " and " M' Turtons Sonne buried in the same grave " *See* Mr. Turton's burial in the next year.

1652.

A sonne of Mr Thomas Brownes of Saltney side buried in his owne pue 6th day of June.
Mr Denmans father buried in the midle He the 20th day of June.
Mr Torton¹ buried in St. Katherines He vnder Mrs Andertons stone 23th day of August.
An infant of Mr Trevis buried vnder his owne stone the 13th day of March.

1653.

Mr George Browne² buried in Mr Thomas Browne his brothers seate 6th of May 1653.

In consequence of an Act of Parliament passed this year, a person had to be appointed in each parish to take charge of the Register, and to enter all births, marriages, and burials in the same. The appointment of the Registrar (or, as he was then called, the "Register") in St. Mary's parish is thus recorded in the Churchwardens' Accounts:

[APPOINTMENT OF A REGISTRAR IN 1653.]

At a meeting of the pishners whose names are subscribed at & vpon the xxth day of Septemb in the yre of or lord 1653 according to the Direccon & appointmt of a late Act of Parliamt touchinge marriages of the xxiiijth Day of August last past, to chuse & elect a Register to such endes & purposes as are Declared in the sd Act. The said pishners wth full & free voice & consent haue made choice of THOMAS HUMFREYS gen' to be Register according to the sd Act. Wittnes or hands the Day & yre aforesd.

(Signed) RANDLE HOLME   THOMAS STANNY
         THO: BROWNE   RICHARD GROSUENOR
         THOMAS WELLSHMAN   ROBARTT BURROWES
         JOHN GREY   Wiffilm LLOYDE
         MR GEORGE CHAMBERLEN   THOMAS LEY
         RAPH LEIGH   THOMAS COULTHURST ⎫ Church
         ALEXANDER HUE (?)   JAMES MICHELL   ⎭ wardens."

He does not seem to have attended to his duties very carefully, as there are two blank pages in the Register, no entries being recorded between the 16th Sept. 1653, and the 21 April, 1654.³

1654.

Sr Robert Brerewood⁴ buried in Troutbecks Chappell the ninth day of Septemb.
Sr ffrancis Gamull⁵ buried in his owne vault 27th of Novemb.
A sonne of Mr Richard Dunbabins buried in Troutbecks Chappell the 28th day of Decemb.
Randle Holme⁶ senr Alderman buried on the north side in the Church in Mr Browne of Vpton pue the 30th day of Januarie.
A daughter of Mr Grubbs from the Castle buried in the west Churchyard in the way the 5th day of March.
Mr Peartree⁷ Parson of this Church buried in the Quire against the window the 16th day of March.

---

¹ See two entries in the last year, 1651.
² See his monumental inscription on p. 68.
³ From the Churchwardens' Accounts the two following entries of burials are of interest at this time, "my lady Gamull's man" and "Mr George Manley."
⁴ The long Latin inscription placed to his memory will be found on p. 66, and an account of his family will be given later on.
⁵ See *postea* for an account of the Gamul family. Sir Francis Gamul entertained King Charles I. whilst at Chester, and was created a Baronet by the King about 1644-5.
⁶ This was the second of the four distinguished Chester antiquaries of these names, a full account of whom will subsequently be given.
⁷ For a short account of Mr. Peartree *see* p. 68.

THE REGISTERS OF ST. MARY'S.

1655.

Hugh Whicksted[1] buried in Troutbecks Chappell the 29th day of March.
Hannah daugh to Mr Jo: Trevis buried in the north Ile vnder Mr Totties stone the 4th day of August.
An infant of Mr Robies buried in the north Ile close to Mr Totties stone the 25th day of August.
Doctor Snell[2] buried in the Quire neere Mr Pearetrees tombe the 7th day of ffebruary.
Mr Lacy buried in the Quire the 11th day of ffebruary.

1656.

An infant of Mr [William] Cullams buried in the south Ile on the 28th day of Septemb.
Three Witches[3] hanged at Michas Assizes buried in the corner by the Castle Ditch in Church yrd 8th of October.
Mathew Key a Souldier buried in the crosse Ile goeinge into the Steeple 21th day of October.
Mrs Alice Whicksted widd buried in the midle Ile ouer ag't her owne pue doore 22th day of January.
Mr Harding a souldier buried in the North church yard neere the blew stone the 6th day of ffebruary.
[A son of his was buried 18th May, 1656.]

1657.

Captain George Ravenscrofte[4] buried in Troutbecks Chappell the 30th day of October.

1658.

Major Coole[5] buried in Troutbecks Chappell att the head end of the Chappell the 20th day of Aprill.
Elezabeth Daughter to Mr John Barnett was Buried in the south yle within Mr Manleys pue on the 28 of June.
Docketer Parsley[6] was Buried in St. Katherines yle on the xvijth Day of September.
John sonne to Mr William Couentrey[7] was buried in St. Katherines yle on the first Day of Nouember.

As already stated, after 1659, the entries in the earliest volume of the Registers, now preserved in St. Mary's, are in different handwritings, having been made either at the time or at the end of each ecclesiastical year by the clergy or the parish clerk. The entries become more numerous as time goes on, and there are more which require to be here noted.

[CHRISTENINGS—(continued).]

1659.

[The entries are now in a different hand and the spelling is poor.]

1660.

Nathanall sonne of Nathanall Booth [Esq.][8] was bapt the 23th Day of October.

1661.

Ann Daugh of Mr Nathanall Booth" was Bapt the 5th Day of Desembr.

---

[1] Mr. Hugh Wickstead's monumental inscription is given on p. 64.
[2] For an account of the Rev. Dr. Snell, Archdeacon of Chester, &c., see pp. 75-6.
[3] For a full account of the trial of these three witches see pp. 28-9.
[4] Of the family of Bretton, co. Flint. See his monumental inscription on p. 67.
[5] In the Churchwardens' Accounts is the following entry :— " Received for the use of the parish Church at the buriall of Maior Coole, that was a stranger and interred in Troutbecks Chappell. 3' 4d."
[6] Who could possibly have recognised under the designation of "Doctor Parsley" the Rev. Christopher Paslew, D.D., late rector of Hawarden, co. Flint, whose monumental inscription will be found on p. 67?
[7] Grandson of Dr. Christopher Paslew, and buried in his grave (see p. 67). He was bapt. 25th Aug. 1658.
[8] Nathaniel Booth, Esq., was of Mottram St. Andrew, near Macclesfield, co. Chester. A son, *Thomas*, was buried at St. Mary's on the 18 March, 1659-60; and a daughter, *Elizabeth*, was baptized there on the 2 Sept. 1656 (see p. 117).

1662.[1]

[Change of handwriting after October, when the entries are all in the handwriting of Nicholas Stevenson, the Rector—the hand of an educated man.]

1663.

Sarah daughter of M‍r Holt a stranger bound for Ireland baptiz'd the 27th of Aug.
Mary daughter of M‍r Harris a stranger bound for Ireland baptiz'd the 1st day of Septem.
Catherine daughter of M‍r George Edge baptiz'd the 22th day of Septem.
Alice daughter of M‍r Thomas Edwards baptiz'd the 23d day of October.
Catherine daughter of M‍r Thomas Wright baptiz'd the sixt day of Decem.

1664.

Thomas son of M‍r Alexander Rigby[2] baptiz'd the fourteenth day of March.

1665.

Anne the daughter of M‍r Thomas Hough baptiz'd the 21 day of Febru :

1667.

Catherine daughter of M‍r Richard Parker[3] was baptiz'd the 14th day of May.

1669.

Beniamin son of M‍r Thomas Weston[4] baptiz'd the 16th day of November.
John son of M‍r Thomas Swan baptiz'd the 24th of November.

1671.

Gertrude[5] daughter of M‍r [Robert] Foulke[s][6] baptiz'd on the 8 day of October.
Edward son of M‍r Edward Cooke[7] baptiz'd on the 17th day of March.

1672.

Elleanor daughter of M‍r Kennericke Eaton[8] baptiz'd on the 29th of June. [Bur. 7th Dec.]

1673.

John sone of M‍r George Minshall bapt on the 13th day of November. [Bur. 18th Nov.]
Elizabeth Daughter of M‍r Thomas Streete[9] bapt on the 22 of November.
Mary Daughter of M‍r George Minshall bapt on the 28 day of November.
M‍rs Alice Mors [?] Daught of Lord Mors [?][10] bapt on the 13th of December.
Marthay Bridge Daught of M‍r Richard Bridge[11] dyer was bapt vpon the 19th Day of March.

1675.

Randle sonne of M‍r Randle Willcocke bapt on the seconde of May.

---

[1] At the bottom of each page the entries are usually signed by the rector and churchwardens.
[2] *Robert*, another son, was baptized on Feb. 25, 1666[-7].
[3] See his marriage to Philippa Browne in 1666, p. 131. His other children baptized here are, *Philippa*, 14 April, 1669 ; *Elizabeth*, 4 March, 1674-3 ; *Richard*, 2 Nov. 1675, bur. 25 Nov. 1681.
[4] See the pedigree of Weston *postea*.
[5] See her marriage in 1696, p. 135.
[6] The other children of Mr. Robert Foulkes baptized here are, *Hugh*, 3 July, 1673 ; *John*, 25 July, 1675, buried 25 Nov. 1675 ; *Peter*, 5 Nov. 1676 ; *Edward*, 8 Dec. 1678 ; *George*, 29 Aug. 1682 ; *John*, 11 Nov. 1684 ; *Mary*, 21 March, 1685-6 ; *Richard*, 25 March, 1688 ; *Thomas*, 5 Nov 1690 ; *Charles*, 28 April, 1692. A son, *William*, was buried 9 Aug. 1681.
[7] The other children of Mr. Edward Cooke baptized here are, *William*, 7 Nov. 1675 ; *Ann*, 25 Sept. 1676 ; *Hugh*, 21 Sept. 1677 : *Joseph*, 12 Aug. 1679.
[8] The other children of Kendrick Eyton, Esq., baptized here will be given later on (*see* 1682 and subsequent years). They were by his *second* wife.
[9] Another child of Mr. Thomas Streete baptized here was *Thomas*, 30 Oct. 1675.
[10] This name is not very clear. It might be "Moirs," but the word "Lord" is quite plain. I cannot explain it in any way.
[11] The other children of Mr. Richard Bridge mentioned here are, *John*, baptized 19 March, 1676 ; *William*, born 23 March, 1677.

Katherin Daught of M' Symon Tensley[1] bapt on the 3rd of October.
Anne Daught of Dauckter Gerrade[2] bapt on the 25th day of January.

1676.
Petter[3] sone of M' Robartt ffoulke[s] bapt one the 5th Day of November.

1677.
Petter Garratt sonne of Dockter Garrad[2] was bapt vpon the 24th Day of August.

1678.
[Change of handwriting in May—an educated hand again.]
William son of M' Thomas Yealde bapt y° 25 of February.

1679.
Katherine daughter of Edw. Lutwyche[4] Esq bapt y° 29th of February.

1680.
Mary daught. of M' Randell Aston bapt. the 26 day of September.
Dorathy daught. of M' Thomas Bennett[5] bapt y° 19th of November. [Bur. 17 March, 1685-6.]
Margarett daught. of M' Raph Llester[6] bapt y° 5th day of December.

1681.
John son of M' James Crockson [? Croxton][7] bap' y° 21 of July. [Buried 13 Aug.]
John son of M' John Johnson[8] Glover bap' y° 26 of July.
Thomas son of M' Thomas Gardener bap' y° 2 of December.

1682.
Mary daugh' of M' Samuell Eaton[9] bap. y° 2 day of June. [Bur. 3. June.]
Harbitt son of John Wright Esq. was bap' y° 3 day of August.
Samuell son of M' Rowland Warringe[10] bap' y° 20th day of August.
Ann daughter of Kendericke Eaton[11] Esq. bap' y° 14th day of October.
Jonathan son of M' John Hale[12] was bapt. y° 28 day of Nouember.

---

[1] Afterwards more commonly spelt "Tilsley." Other children are, *Geoffrey*, bapt. 28 April, 1678; *Sarah*, bapt. 11 Dec. 1679.

[2] For an account of Dr. Peter Gerrard and his monumental inscription *see* p. 70.

[3] This Peter Foulkes became a very distinguished ecclesiastic. He matriculated at Oxford from Christ Church on the 12 June, 1694, as the son of Robert Foulkes of Chester, gentleman, aged 17. He became Student of Christ Church in 1694, and took his B.A. degree in 1698, that of M.A. in 1701, and B.D. and D.D. in 1710. He was created Canon of Exeter in 1704, sub-Dean in 1723, Chancellor in 1724, and Precentor of Exeter in 1736. In 1714 he was instituted to the rectory of Bishops Cheriton and to the vicarage of Thorverton, both in Devonshire, in 1716. He died on the 30th April, 1747, and was buried in Exeter Cathedral (*see* Foster's *Alumni Oxonienses*). He left a sum of money to the poor of St. Mary's (see *postea* under Charities).

[4] Edward Lutwyche, Esq., afterwards knighted, was Recorder of Chester from 1684 to 1686.

[5] The other children of Mr. Thomas Bennett baptized here are, *Elizabeth*, 28 Oct. 1679; *Ann*, 8 March, 1681-2, buried 25 July, 1687; *George*, 3 Dec. 1682; *Kendrick*, 5 April, 1685, buried 21 Oct. 1694; *John*, 1 July, 1686; *Thomas*, 5 July, 1688; *Dorothy*, 11 May, 1690, buried 4 Sept. 1690; *Peter*, 19 July, 1691; *Jane*, 4 Sept. 1692. A daughter, *Jane*, was buried 25 May, 1685.

[6] Other children of Mr. Ralph Lester baptized here are, *Ralph*, 5 Feb. 1681-2, and *Sarah*, 11 March, 1682-3.

[7] Other children of Mr. James Crockson baptized here are, *Dorothy*, 1 Nov. 1682; *James*, 28 Feb. 1685-6.

[8] The other children of Mr. John Johnson baptized here are, *Mary*, 25 March, 1683; *Margaret*, 16 Nov. 1684; *Eleanor*, 25 July, 1686; *Edward*, 25 Sept. 1687, buried 30 May, 1691; *Thomas*, 1 May, 1689, buried 19 Dec. 1689; *William*, 27 May, 1692. Another son, *Edward*, was buried 7 Nov. 1684.

[9] Other children of Mr. Samuel Eaton baptized here are, *Elizabeth*, 14 Oct. 1683; *Thomas*, 14 Feb. 1685-6.

[10] For other children of Mr. Rowland Waringe baptized here *see* 1691.

[11] This was by his second wife, his first wife having been buried here in 1677 (*see* p. 138).

[12] The other children of Mr. John Hale baptized here are, *Frances*, 28 Oct. 1683; *Mary*, 23 Oct. 1684; *Ann*, 13 Dec. 1685; *Samuel* and *Mary*, 16 Sept. 1686, buried 17 Sept.; *Robert*, 23 Oct. 1687, buried 4 March, 1694; *Edman*, 29 Oct. 1688, buried 31 Oct.; *Jane*, 5 Jan. 1689-90; *Edman*, 2 Oct. 1691, buried 4 Oct.; *Mary*, 9 April, 1693, buried 9 May, 1694; *Edman*, 20 May, 1694, buried 21 May.

Jonathan son of Mr Jonathan Newton bap{t} ye 11 day of January.

1683.
Garrard son of Kenderick Eaton Esqr bapt. ye 8th day of January.
Sarah daught{r} of Mrs Hall widow was bapt. ye 3d day of February.

1684.
Jane daught{r} of Esqr Alporte[1] bap{t} the 29th day of April.
Mary daught{r} of Mr John Clarke bapt the 12th day of October.

1685.
Catherine daugh of Ald{t} Thomas Simpson bap{t} ye 26th of Aprill.
James son of Mr Thomas Heald bap{t} the 31 day of May.
Mary daugh{tr} of Mr John Wrench[2] bap{t} ye 15th day of Nouemb{r}.
Mary daugh{tr} of Mr Moses Dannatt[3] was bap{t} the 22d of Nouemb{r}.
Elizabeth daugh{tr} of Kenderick Eaton Esqr bap{t} ye 13 of Decembr. [Bur. 7 Jan.]

1686.
Samuell son of *Lifftennentt* Saunderson bap{t} ye 15th day of June.
Raph son of Mr Richerd Hatton was bap{t} ye first of July.
William son of Kenderick Eaton Esqr bap{t} ye 28th day of Decembr.
John son of John Wright Esqr was bap{t} ye 13th day of January.

1687.
William son of Mr Thomas Simpson Ald bap{t} ye 7th of Aprill.
Ellinor daugh{tr} of Kenderick Eaton Esqr bap{t} ye 17th day of February.
Ann daugh" of Rich: Leuinge[4] Esqr was bap{t} the 2d day of March. [Bur. 14 April, 1688, as "daughter of Recorder Levinge Esqr."]

1688.
Richerd son of Robertt ffoulkes Gen{t} was bap{t} ye 25th of March.[5]
Thomas son of Mr Thomas Scofeilde bap{t} ye 24th of Aprill.
Ellin Daugh{tr} of John Wright Esqr was bap{t} ye 29 of May.

1689.
William son of Mr Thomas Reece bap{t} the 7th day of Aprill.
Eliz daught{r} of *Captin* Keyrey was bap{t} ye 7th day of May.
Margrett daugh{tr} of Mr John ffarrar[6] was bap{t} ye 13th of May.
Meruin daugh{tr} of *Captin* Currey was bap{t} ye 13th day of June.
John son of *Captin* Morris Arrindaile bap{t} the 15 day of June.
Joseph son of Mr Joseph Woodes[7] was bap{t} ye 16 day of June. [Bur. 27th March, 1690.]
Edward son of Mr Thomas Scofeild bap{t} ye 29th day of Septembr.

---

[1] Probably one of the children of Robert Alport, of Overton, Esq., who was buried at Malpas, on the 1st Feb. 1686-7.

[2] Other children of Mr. John Wrench baptized here are, *Richard*, 2 Feb. 1687-8; *John*, 29 Sept. 1689, buried 24 July, 1691; *William*, 12 July, 1691; *Grace* and *Sarah*, 3 May, 1693, the former buried 12 May, the latter 5 May, 1694.

[3] The other children of Mr. Moses Dannatt baptized here are, *Martha*, 24 Nov. 1689; *John*, 21 Feb. 1691-2.

[4] Richard Levinge, Esq., was Recorder of Chester from 1686 to 1687. Previous to this he had acted as Deputy Recorder to Sir Edward Lutwyche.

[5] This Richard Foulkes, like his brother Peter (see p. 131), matriculated at Oxford from Christ Church 27 May, 1706, aged 18. He took his B.A. degree in 1710, and that of M.A. on the 16 March, 1712-13. He was Rector of Seaton, co. Rutland, in 1719, and of Bulwick, co. Northants, in the same year (Foster's *Alumni Oxonienses*).

[6] Other children of Mr. John Farrar baptized here are, *John*, 14 March, 1690-1; *Eleanor*, 8 Oct. 1695, buried 19 Dec. 1695; *William*, 24 Nov. 1696; *Peter*, 23 Oct. 1699. Another daughter, *Eleanor*, was buried 23 May, 1705, and a son, *Roger*, was buried 18 Dec. 1705.

[7] Other children of Mr. Joseph Woodes baptized here are, *Joseph*, 23 Jan. 1692-3; *William*, 27 Jan. 1694-5; *Joseph*, 31 July, 1698; *Dorothy*, 16 March, 1700. In this last entry he is described as "of Bridge street."

Thomas son of M'̃ Robertt Mason bap' the 7th day of January.

1691.

Dorothy daugh'̃ of Richerd Lleningo[1] Esq'̃ bap' y'̃ 22 day of Aprill. *Kaɛ oɔƐɛɾ ɟ/bƦɛ ɔlɛɾ , ɪɛɛ þ . ɪɪ² .*
John son of M'̃ Rowland Warringe[2] was bap' y'̃ 13th day of Decemb'̃. [Bur. 21 March, 1692-3.]
Elizabeth daugh'̃ of Kenderick Eaton Esq'̃ Bap' y'̃ 21 day of February.

1692.

Thomas son of Robert ffleetwood was bapt y'̃ 20th day of Novemb'̃.
Richerd son of M'̃ John Dewsbery[3] was Bap' y'̃ 11th day of Decemb'̃.

1693.

Elias son of M'̃ John Forcett Bap' y'̃ 16 day of July. [Bur. 29th Oct.]
Andrew son of M'̃ Thomas Duke[4] was bap' y'̃ 3 of August.
Joseph son of M'̃ John Pemberton[5] was Bap' y'̃ 4th day of March.

1694.

Thomas son of M'̃ Thomas Leigh was Bap' y'̃ 31 day of March.
Sarah daugh'̃ of M'̃ Rich'd Smith was Bap' y'̃ 16 day of Septemb'̃.

1695.

Dorothy daught'̃ to M'̃ William Nickolls of Vpton bapt y'' 28 of May.
Thomas son to Charles Gardner Esq'̃ was bap' y'̃ 6th of Octob'̃.
John son to *Leftenantt* Skye was bap' the 23 day of ffebruary.

1696.

Ann daugh'̃ to *Cap'̃* W'm̃ Yorke was bap' y'̃ 26 day of Aprill. [Bur. 6th Aug.]
Henry[6] son to Thomas Brookes[7] Esq'̃ was Bap' y'̃ 16 day of August.
Lettis daugh'̃ to M'̃ Rich: Cartwright was Bap' y'̃ 30th of August.
Ann daugh'̃ to W'm̃ Gamuell[8] Esq'̃ was Baptiz y'̃ 24th day of Septem'̃.
Thomas son to Thomas Kennion Gen'̃ was Bap' y'̃ 17th day of March.

1697.

John son to Charles Gardner Esq'̃ was bap' y'̃ 14th day of June. [Bur. 17th June.]
Roger son to M'̃ Samuell Hewson[9] was bap' y'̃ 16th day of July.
Peter son to Peter Weston[10] Esq'̃ was Bap' y'̃ 17th day of August.
Catherine daugh'̃ to M'̃ Roger Ball was Bap' y'̃ 21 day of August.

---

[1] *See* note 4, previous page.

[2] This was by his third wife, his first, Abigail, having been buried 13 March, 1684-5, and his second wife, Hannah, having been buried 20 March, 1685-6 (*see* pp. 139-40). His other children baptized here are, *Richard*, 16 December, 1692, buried 21 Dec., and *Elizabeth*, 18 Sept. 1694, buried 17 Oct. In the burials (*see* pp. 139-40) he is described as a "razor-grinder"! He died 14 May, 1695, and the inscription to his memory and his coat of arms will be found on pp. 48 and 76.

[3] *Mary*, another child of Mr. John Dewsbury, was baptized here 30 Oct. 1698, and a daughter, *Martha*, was buried 17 Oct. 1696.

[4] Other children of Mr. Thomas Duke baptized here are, *Eleanor*, 13 June, 1695 ; *Rebecca*, 20 Nov. 1696.

[5] Another child of Mr. John Pemberton baptized here was *Thomas*, 30 July, 1695.

[6] This Henry *Brooke* matriculated at Oxford from Brasenose College on the 15th March, 1713-14, aged 17, being described as the son of Thomas Brooke, of Chester, Esq. (afterwards a Baronet). He took his B.A. degree in 1717 and that of M.A. in 1720, and was elected a Fellow of All Souls College. He became B.C.L. in 1723 and D.C.L. in 1727, being elected Regius Professor of Civil Law in that University in 1736, which he held till his death on the 24th March, 1742 (Foster's *Alumni Oxonienses*). His elder brother was Rector of St. Mary's from 1737 to 1744 (*see* p. 93).

[7] This was Thomas *Brooke*, of Norton, Esq. (afterwards Sir Thomas Brooke, Bart.), the eldest son and heir-apparent of Sir Richard Brooke, of Norton, Bart., who died in 1710. He had married in 1688 Grace, daughter of Roger Wilbraham, of Townsend, near Nantwich, Esq.

[8] Of Crabwell, near Chester. *See* the Gamul pedigree *postea*.

[9] *Dorothy*, another child of Mr. Samuel Hewson "of Castle Lane," was baptized here 13 March, 1699-1700.

[10] *See* the pedigree of Weston *postea*.

Margrett daugh'' to William Gamuell¹ Esq' was Bap' y" 19th of Septemb'.
Jonathan son to M' Jonathan Walley of y" Rugh hill Bap' y" 10th of March.
Charles son to Charles Walley² Esq' was Bap' y" 10th day of March.

1698.

Thomas son to M' Thomas Gill was Bapt' y" 8th day of Aprill.
John son to M' John Walker was Bap' y" 14th day of Aprill.
Joseph son to M' Danniell Snow was Bap' y" 10th of July.
Roger son to Thomas Brookes Esq' was Bap' y" 17th of July.
Mary daugh'' to William Gamuell¹ Esq' was Bap' y" 29th of August.
Ann daugh'' to M' Thomas Hickock yeaman was Bap' y" 28 of Nouemb'.
Sarah daugh'' to Peter Weston Esq' was Baptized the 8 day of Decemb'.
Jane daugh'' to Charles Walley² of Castell lane Esq' was Bap' the 17th of January. [Bur. 27th Jan.]
Thomas son to M' Thomas Williams of Bridgestreet *Well Glouer* was Bap' y" 17th of March. [Bur. 14th April, 1699.]

1699.

Thomas son to M' Vaughan Soden of Bridgestreet Ironmonger was Baptized y" 16 day of July.
Peter son to John Farrar of Castell lane Gen' was Baptized the 23d day of October.
Robert son to Charles Walley of Castell lane Esq' was Bap' the 19th day of Decemb'
William son to Charles Gardner of Castell lane Esq' was Baptized the 21 day of January. [Bur. 5th Feb.]

1700.

Joseph Son to George Wright of Castell lane *Waterleader*³ was Baptized the 31st day of March.
Jane Daugh'' to John Loyde of Castell lane Esq' was Bap' the sixt day of August.
Elizabeth Daugh'' to M' Thomas Williams of Bridgstreet *Glouer* was Bap' y" 25 of August.
Francis son to Francis Priace *M' Gunn' of the Castell* was Bap' the 3d day of Nouemb'.
Pusey son to Thomas Brookes Esq' *of the Haughgreen* was Bap' the 3d day of Nouemb'.
Lettis Daugh'' to Peter Weston Esq' of Bridgestreet was Baptized the 29th day of Decemb'.
Mary Daugh'' to Edward Gough of Bridgstreet *Pipemaker* was Bap' the second of February.

1701.

John son to Charles Walley Esq' of Castell lane was Baptized the 9th day of Aprill.
Thomas son of Henry Braderton of handbridge *Tobaco cuter* was Baptized the 11th day of May.
Charles son to Timothy Chanceller *Clarke to Water Workes* was Baptized the 18th day of July.

[The Baptisms in the first volume of the Registers end on August 25th of this year.]

[*MARRIAGES—(continued).*]

1661.

Thomas Dauis & *Joyly* Wilde was Married the xxix*th* of Aprell.

1665.

Matthew Ellis⁴ of Over-Lee Greene Gentle: and Anne Birkenhead of Backford married the twentie fift of January.

1666.

Richard Parker and Philippa Browne⁵ married on the 6th day of Decem :

¹ *See* note 8, previous page.
² *See* the pedigree of Foulkes *postea*.
³ *Query:* a water-carrier.
⁴ *See* the monumental inscription on p. 48.
⁵ *See* the pedigree of Browne of Netherlegh. There are several entries of the baptisms of Richard Parker's children *see* p. 130). *See* also p. 139.

1670.

Charles Wirrall of Mollington and Catherine Kirks married on the 12th of November.
Mr Thomas Manwaring and Mrs Elizabeth Hunt married on the 17th of November.

1677.

Mr Henry Browne and Mrs Margt Skelhorne marryed with a Licence on the 8th day of Decemb'.

1679.

Mr Edward Herbert and Mrs Dorothy Shone marryed with a Licence (dated ye 10th of June) on ye 11th of June.

1681.

Mr Raph Poole & Ann Kenderick was maried with a licence, dated ye 15 day of Aprill, on the 16 of Aprill.
Mr James Comberbach & Ellinor Johnson was maried with a licence, dated ye 13 day of Aprill, on ye 14 of Aprill.

1686.

William Fox and Ann Comberbach was mard with a Licence the 7th day of Aprill.
Mr James Peacke[1] and Mrs ffrances Weston was married wt a Licence the 7th day of Nouemb'.

1687.

Mr Thomas Scofeild and Mrs Rachell Williams was mar. wt a Licence the 18th day of June.

1689.

Mr William Pargeyney[2] & Mrs Rachell Holme was married with a Licence the 30th day of Decemb'.

1690.

Thomas Probertt and Margrett Liuerpoole[3] was married with a Licence the 5th day of ffebruary.

1692.

[So in original.]
Mr William Williams[4] of Wraxham & . . . . . was mard wt a Licence ye 10th day of Septembr.

1693.

Mr Hugh Dauis and Mrs Elizabeth Nichols was married with a Licence the 7th day of Nouemb'.

1694.

Mr Thomas Rogers & Mrs Elizabeth Burrowes was Married with a Licence the 25 day of July.

1695.

Mr Richerd Speede & Mrs Mary Lloyde [of] wraxham was married wt a Licence the 25 day of June.

1696.

Mr Roger Ball & Catherine Gibbones was Married with a Licence the 13 day of Aprill.
Charles Walley Gent & Mrs Gatruce [sic] ffoulkes[5] was Married with a Licence the 11th day of ffebruary.

1697.

Mr Francis Inesley & Ellin Wright was married the 6th day of Aprill wt a Licence dated the same day.
Mr Dannell Snow & Mary Faucett was married wt a Licence the 11th day of Aprill.

---

[1] This was the Rev. James Peake, Vicar of Bowdon, co. Chester, a non-juror (*see* his monumental inscription p. 73).

[2] Should be Mr. William *Burgancy* of Pulford, who married Rachel, daughter of the third Randle Holme (*see* the pedigree of that family *postea*). Her burial took place 31 March, 1693 (*see* p. 141).

[3] There are many entries of the name of Liverpool or Lerpool in the Registers of Bunbury, co. Chester.

[4] By a reference to the Marriage Licence Act Books in the Bishop's Registry, Chester, it appears that this marriage was between William Williams of the City of Chester, gentleman, and *Mria* (? Mary or Margery) Lloyd of Wrexham, spinster, and the date of the licence is the 10th September, 1692.

[5] *Gertrude*, the oldest daughter of Mr. Robert Foulkes, was baptized at St. Mary's, 8th October, 1671 (*see* p. 130). There are several entries of the baptisms of their children on p. 134.

1699.

Francis Prince[1] *Master Gunner* and Martha Holland were Married wth a Licence y[e] 12 day of Nouemb[r].

[The last entry of a Marriage in the first volume of the Registers is dated 21 May, 1700.]

[BURIALS—(continued).]
1659.

Elezabeth wife to M[r] Mathas [Matthews][2] was Buried in the midell yle vnder M[r] Westons ston on the 3[t] Day of Ap[ll].

M[r] Houldfeld [Oldfield] was Buried in the Troppleckes [*sic*] chapell clouse by the towme [*sic* for tomb] on the 4[th] Day of July.

M[r] Randle Holme[3] Alderman was Buried in the north Side within M[r] Brownes pue on the first Day of Septemb.

1660.

Robartt Massey *pip[e]maker* buried xvj[th] day of July.

Elezabeth Daughter to M[r] John Wreddech [Reddich?] was Buried in the north yle by M[r] Dauis pue Dower on the xxvj[th] Augus[t].

1661.

M[rs] Elezabeth Holmes[4] Widdow Wife to M[r] Randle Holme Alderman Ju was buried on the North side of the Church within M[r] Brownes pue of Vpton on the xxvj[th] Day of March.

Abigail Daughter to M[r] John Potter was buried in the midell yle close to Widdow Robartes pue on the 8[te] Day Apr.

M[rs] Jane Billitt Widdow was buried in the Troupplekes [*sic*] Chapell harde by the Doure on the xij[th] Day of Augus[t].

M[r] Leigh a stranger was buried in the midell yle clouse by Humphry Jackeson pue dower on the xvj[th] Day of Nouember.

1662.

John Haslewall a Detter in the Castell buried in the Croseyle ancance the Clocke[5] on the xv[th] of May.

M[r] Richard Huntt[6] minister of St. Maryes was buried on the queare on the north side of Docketer Sncalls ston on the xxvj[th] Day of Augus[t].

1663.

Francis son of M[r] John Brerewood buried in Troutbecks Chappel[7] the 25[t] day of April.

Hannah daughter of M[r] James Bullen buried on the Sixt day of July.

Richard son of M[r] Jones buried on the 29th day of Octo:

M[rs] Catharine Rathbone wife of John Rathbone buried the 18th day of Novem:

1664.

Francis [*sic*] daughter of M[rs] Lightfoote buried on the 31 day of March.

---

[1] His first wife was buried at St. Mary's on the 24th Oct. in this year (see *postea*).

[2] She is described in the Churchwardens' Accounts as "M[rs] Matthews late the widdow of M[r] Thomas Weston, a parrishaner."

[3] This was the second Randle Holme, a distinguished antiquary (*see* the account of the Holme family *postea*). The monumental inscription to his memory will be found on pp. 46-47.

[4] This was Elizabeth, the widow of Thomas Dodd, and the second wife of the second Randle Holme, who is here called "junior" to distinguish him from his father who had died in 1655 (*see* Holme pedigree *postea*).

[5] This is the first reference in the Registers to the clock, but it is frequently mentioned in the Churchwardens' Accounts.

[6] For an account of Mr. Richard Hunt, rector of St. Mary's, *see* pp. 87-88. In the Churchwardens' Accounts is an entry, "received of M[r] Browne for a gravestone to lay upon Mr. Hunt, 6s. 8d." For a notice of Dr. Snell. Archdeacon of Chester, *see* pp. 75-6.

[7] This is, I think, the last reference in this Register to Troutbeck's Chapel, which was then in ruins, the greater part of it having fallen down in 1661.

James son of Mr Trevers buried on the last day of April.
Mrs Philippa Browne¹ wife of Mr Thomas Browne [of Netherlegh] buried on the 9th day of May.
Almonde Williams buried on the 28th of May.
Alice daughter of Mr Alexander Rigby buried on the 28' day of June.
Magdalene the wife of Richard Eccleston buried on the 11th of July.
Elizabeth daughter of Mr Thomas Sorocold · buried on the 22'' of Aug :
Mary daughter of Mr John Pigot buried on the 26' day of Septem :
Mr George Chamberlaine buried on the 3d day of Novem :
Mr Ralph Bruen³ buried the 16th day of Janua :

1665.

Mrs Sidney Brerewood ⁴ wife of John Brerewood Esqr buried on the 16th day of Februa :
Mr James Bullen buried on the third day of March.
Mr Laurence Fletcher⁵ buried on the fift day of March.

1666.

Mr Richard Williamson buried on the 31st day of March.
Mr Francis Locket⁶ buried the 2d day of March.

1667.

Mrs Anne Locket,⁶ widow, buried on the 2d day of April.
A stranger who died in the streets buried by the Constables of Hanbridg on the 17th day of Aug.
Mr Thomas Colthurst buried on the 28th day of Oct :
[Mr Jacques Arnodio⁷ buried this year. (Churchwardens' Accounts.)]
Mrs Marie Arnodio⁸ buried on the 20th day of Februa :

1669.

Darcie Lessals buried on the 16th day of June.
Mr Henry Myvat [? Myvod]⁹ buried on the 23d of December.

1670.

Mrs Sarah Ince¹⁰ wife of William Ince Alderman of Chester was buried on the 18 day of October.

1671.

Mrs Margaret Pemberton¹¹ wife of Mr Pemberton buried on the 27th day of Decem :

1672.

Millinton daughter of Heanery Houcraft buried on [the] first March.

---

¹ See her monumental inscription on p. 68.
² The entry in the Churchwardens' Accounts of a payment for the laystall of " Sr Jeffrey Shakerleys nephew in St Katherines fle " relates, I think, to this burial. Sir Geoffrey Shakerley was Constable of the Castle at this time.
³ Called Mr. Ralph Braine in the Churchwardens' Accounts, but Bruen is most probably correct.
⁴ She was one of the daughters and coheirs of Sir Francis Gamul, Knt. and Bart. (see that pedigree), and was buried in his vault.
⁵ He was the parish clerk.
⁶ The entry in the Churchwardens' Accounts is " Mr Lockett his wife and maide."
⁷ There is no entry of his burial in the Register, but in the Churchwardens' Accounts are these two entries :—
 Rec. for the Leastall [or burial-place] of Mr Jacques Arndio buried in St Katherines yle ... 10 0
 Rec. for the Leastall of Mrs Arndio buried St Katherins yle 10 0
⁸ She was the daughter of Sir Thomas Aston, of Aston, co. Chester, Knt., and married for her first husband Mr. Richard Browne, of Upton, near Chester (see that pedigree *postea*). After his death in January, 1624-5, she married secondly M. Jacques Arnodio, "a Frenchman." She died 17 Feb. 1667-8, aged 87.
⁹ See the burial of Mrs. Margaret Myvod in 1673.
¹⁰ She is mentioned in the Churchwardens' Accounts for 1670 as being the relict of Mr. George Chamberlain, and then married to Mr. Ince.
¹¹ See her marriage in 1644, p. 118.

T

1673.

M' Nicholus Steuenson[1] Rector buried one the 14ne Day of Aprill.
M" Anne Starkey buried out of the Castell on the 27 of May.
M' George Minshay [Minshall] buried one the 19th Day of June.
M' Kiarkes[2] minister buried vpon the xxvth Day of November.

1674.

M" Grace Wynne was buried vpon the first Day of January.
M' Ralfe was buried vpon the 14 Day of february.
Petter sonne of Dauckter Garrade[3] buried on the xjt Day March.

1675.

M' William Potter buried one the 13ne Day of Desember.
M" Margearett Myuod [? Myvod][4] buried on the 17 Day of february.

1676.

M' Pullfeartt [" M' Thomas Pullford "] buried on the xxvjth Day of Aprill.
M' John Beckett buried one the 5th Day of May.
M' Gandey a soger [sic] out of the Castel buried one the 11th Day May.
John sonne of M' Raph Leigh was buried one the 3rd Day of July.

1677.

M" Voughan of Vpton was buried vpon the 13ne Day of Aprill.
M'h Dyason buried on the 10th day of August.
Margearett Daught' of M' Gleaue buried vpon the xxviijth Day of Septem.
M" Calcocke [sic] was buried in the voute vpon the 26 Day of Octob.
M" Grace Wrighte wife of Alderman Wright buried the 2nd Day of November.
Maddam Eaton wife to M' Kendricke Eaton[5] was buried vpon the 29 Day of January.
Rachel daughter of M' John Ashbrook was buried upon the 1st day of March.

1678.

M" Alles Bunell buried on the 26 Day of March.
Allice daughter of M' Yells buried on the 6th day of May.
George Snell[6] buried on the 1st day of June.
M" Margaret Philips bur⁴ (with a Certificate) on the 22ᵈ day of August.
M' John Johnson bur⁴ (with a Certif:) on yᵉ 6th day of Septembʳ.
Doctor Peter Gerard[7] buried (with a Cert) on yᵗ 9th day of December.
M' Gilbert Hough buried (with a Cert.) on the 13th day of December.
Peter Dewsberry *Churchwarden* was buried with a Certifie: on the 1st day of March.
"Charles Fletcher juniʳ Parish Clarke January yᵉ first 1678" [occurs in the margin].

---

[1] For an account of Mr. Nicholas Stevenson, rector of St. Mary's, see pp. 89-90.

[2] For an account of Mr. Kirkes, rector of St. Mary's, see p. 90.

[3] See p. 70, note 2, for a notice of Dr. Peter Gerard.

[4] See the burial of " M' Henry Myvat " in 1659.

[5] This *Kenrick Eyton*, Esq. (as his name should be spelt), was the eldest son and heir of Sir Kenrick Eyton, Knt., of Eyton Isaf, co. Denbigh, who was buried at Bangor-is-y-coed on the 21 Nov. 1681. The " Maddam Eaton " here buried was his first wife, Rebecca, daughter of Abraham Johnstone, by whom he had a son and heir, Kenrick Eyton, Esq. By his second wife, Elizabeth, buried at Bangor 3 Nov. 1699, he had more issue, of whom six were baptized at St. Mary's (see pp. 130-132). He was buried at Bangor on the 11 June, 1709. (See a paper by Mr. A. N. Palmer, on the later history of the parish of Bangor-is-y-coed, in the *Archæologia Cambrensis*, April, 1890.)

[6] *Query:* Was this the son of Dr. George Snell, Archdeacon of Chester (see pp. 75-6).

[7] See his monumental inscription on pp. 69-70, where a short account of him will be found.

1679.
Mary Wife of Mʳ Edward Bridge burd on yᵉ 23ᵈ of June.
Mʳ Raph Whitley was buried on yᵉ 7ᵗʰ day of Octobʳ.   see page 153.
Mʳ Edward Bridge was buried on yᵉ 11ᵗʰ of Novembʳ.
Mʳ Simon Tilsley burd yᵉ 28ᵗʰ of Decembʳ.

1680.
Mary wife of Mʳ Barker buried yᵉ 8 day of May.
Grence¹ [sic] wife of Mʳ Thomas Basnett buried yᵉ 18ᵗʰ of June.
Mʳˢ Rigbey wife to Alex. Rigbey Gent burd yᵉ 21 of Septemb.
Mʳˢ Dorothy ffarrar was buried the 7ᵗʰ day of ffeb[r]uary.

1681.
Mʳˢ Ann Lloyde was buried vpon yᵉ 20ᵗʰ day of July.
Mʳˢ Joyce Dicas wife to Mʳ Rand Dicas bur on yᵉ 28 of Septembʳ.
Edward² son to Edward Wynn Esq. was bur. on yᵉ 29 of September.   [Bapt. 9ᵗʰ Feb. 1679-80.]
Alexander¹ son of Edward Wynn Esq was bur. on yᵉ 4 of October.
Mʳ Samuell Steeles a stranger was bur on yᵉ 7 day of October.
Margrett daughtʳ of Mʳ John Johnson was bur on yᵉ 29 of October.
Samuell son of Mʳ Radford was bur on yᵉ 3 day of Nouembʳ.
Mary Dauis Widdow Gentlewō was bur on yᵉ 22 of Nouembʳ.
Mʳˢ Elizebeth Euens Widdow was bur on yᵉ 23 of Nouembʳ.
Thomas³ son of Mʳ Richard Parker was bur yᵉ 25 of Nouembʳ.
William son of Mʳ Edward Starkey was bur on yᵉ 10 of ffebruary.
Mʳˢ Grace Cropley was buried on yᵉ 21 day of March.

1683.
Mʳ William Dicas senior was bur yᵉ 25ᵗʰ day of August.
Mʳ Thomas Barlow⁴ of Vpton was bur yᵉ 7ᵗʰ day of September.
Mʳ George Bunnell Brewer was bur yᵉ 14ᵗʰ day of January.
Sara daughᵗʳ of Mʳˢ Hall was buried yᵉ 10ᵗʰ day of ffebrua[r]y.

1684.
Amy wife of Mʳ Rodger Bradborne bur 24ᵗʰ of May.
Jane daughᵗʳ of Mʳ Spencer bur yᵉ 23 day of June.
Elizabeth Varum of Beachpooll bur yᵉ 30ᵗʰ day of December.
Abigall wife of Mʳ Rowland Warringe bur yᵉ 13ᵗʰ day of March.

1685.
John Gleaue Genᵗ was buried yᵉ 8ᵗʰ day of June.
Phillip Smallwood⁵ from yᵉ Castell bur yᵉ 11ᵗʰ day of June.
Ellinor daughᵗʳ of John Wright Esqʳ bur yᵉ 18ᵗʰ of July.
Josiah son of Mʳˢ Hough Wid bur yᵉ 30ᵗʰ day of July.
Catherine wife of Mʳ John Williamson bur yᵉ 22 of Septembʳ.
Zacaria son of Mʳ Waringe Razargrinder bur yᵉ 4ᵗʰ of Nouember.

---

¹ Grace, the daughter of John Aldersey, of Spurstowe, gentleman, is said to have married a Mr. Richard Basnet, of Eyton, co. Denbigh, and this entry may possibly relate to her.
² For their monumental inscription formerly in the church see p. 71.
³ This is a mistake of the copyist for Richard, son of Mr. Richard Parker. See his monumental inscription on p. 68 and his baptism on the 2 Nov. 1675 (see p. 130, note 3).
⁴ He gave a paten to the church, which is still in use there (see p. 23).
⁵ A pedigree of Smallwood of Chelford will be found in East Cheshire, vol. ij., p. 366.

Mary wife of M' Richerd Brereton bur y' 9th day of ffebruary.
Hanna wife of M' Waringe *razargrinder* bur y' 20th of March.

1686.

Thomas Phibbs *Carwer* was bur y' 25th of May.
M' Thomas Yealde was bur y' 30th day of May.
Sarah wife of M' Henry Baforne bur y' 6th of July.
Elizabeth wife of M' Randell Aston bur y' 5th of August.
Thomas son of M' Edward Starkey bur y' 16th of Nouember.
M' Thomas Newlands a stranger bur y' 21 day of January.
M' Thomas Jones was buried y' 17th day of March.

1687.

Shargentt Powell was bur y' 26 day of March.
Thomas son of M' Thomas Jones deceased bur y' 27th of March.
ffrancis Granger a shargentt bur the 11th day of Aprill.
Jane wife of M' John Dickisson bur y' 19th of July.

1688.

M' Raph Hollinshead was bur the 30th day of August.
Thomas son of M' Rich: Hatton was bur y' 19th of October.
M' Richerd Lownes of banbridge was bur y' 16 day of January.
A son in Law of M' Wright next the Castell bur y' 15th day of ffebruary.

1689.

M'rs Dobson was buried the 21 day of May.
Dorothy daughtr of M' Howerd was bur y' 24th of June.
William Needham[1] Esq' was bur y' 25th of June.
M'rs Needham Late wife of Esq' Needham[1] desesed bur y' 14th of July.
M'rs Harrisson was buried the 14th day of August.
Ellin daughtr of M' Thomas Bradshall [*sic* for Bradshaw] bur y' 15th of Septembr.
Brooke son of Cornall [? *sic* for Colonel] Brasier was bur y' 27 day of September.
M' Randell Dicas was bur y' 3 day of October.
Parcifoe [? *sic* for Percival] son of John Dewsbury was bur the 29th of October.
An Infant of M' Dobsons of Dublin was bur y' 19th of Nouember.
John Wright[2] Esq' *of Brewers hall* was bur y' 9th day of Decembr.
M' Thomas Basnett was bur the 10th day of March.
M' Robert Meycock of Vpton was bur y' 20th day of March.

1690.

M' William Dicas was buried the 29th day of March.
M' Andrew ffernahaugh was bur the 13th day of Nouembr.
John Laine *Gunner* was bur the 22 day of Nouembr.
John Gryzell Gen' a stranger was bur y' 30th day of Decembr.
M'rs Elizabeth Sharrard was buried the 14th day of March.
Margrett wife of M' John ffarrar bur y' 21 day of March.

1691.

Raph son of M' Richerd Hatton was bur the 10th day of Aprill.

---

[1] I have printed a full pedigree of the family of Needham (ancestors of the Viscounts Kilmorey) in my *History of Sandbach* pp. 198-9, but I cannot at present identify this William Needham, Esq., and Elizabeth his wife. No will of any William Needham, Esq., of about this time is now to be found at Chester.

[2] *See* his monumental inscription formerly in the Church, p. 71.

William Rauen¹ Gen¹ was bur the 18ᵗʰ day of Aprill.
Ellinor wife of Mʳ Henry Baforne was bur yᵉ 22 of May.
Henry son of Mʳ Henry Baforne was bur yᵉ 17ᵗʰ of June.
Mʳˢ Alice Birkinhead Widow was bur. the 4ᵗʰ day of January.
Mary daughʳ of Mʳ Thomas Potter was bur yᵉ 1 day of February.
Lady Catherine Brerewood² was buried yᵉ 2ᵈ day of March.

1692.

William son of Mʳ Thomas Reece was bur yᵉ 21 day of June.
Mʳ Richer[d] Skarrett was buried yᵉ 19ᵗʰ day of Nouembʳ.
Modlantt wife of Robertt Catherall bur yᵉ 21 day of ffebruary.

1693.

Mʳˢ Rachell wife of Mʳ William Purgeny³ [*sic* for Burganey] was bur yᵉ 31ᵗʰ of March.
Louuett [? *sic* for Lovett] son of Edward Peeres Esqʳ was bur yᵉ 12ᵗʰ day of Aprill.
[So in original.]
. . . . daughʳ of *Captin* Poyne was bur yᵉ 1 day of May.
John Roden Gen¹ was Buried the 8ᵗʰ day of May.
Catherine wife of Mʳ Nicolas Locker was bur yᵉ 9ᵗʰ of August.
[So in original.]
Godfery . . . . a soulder was shott to death & bur yᵉ 9ᵗʰ of October.
Shusanna wife of Mʳ Edward Aston bur the 16ᵗʰ day of Nouembʳ.
Mʳ John Jones *Atorney* was bur the 7ᵗʰ day of January.
George son of Mʳ George Hickock was bur yᵉ 9ᵗʰ day of ffebruary.
Robertt Harefinch a Debtor out of yᵉ Castell was bur yᵉ 17ᵗʰ ffebruary.

1694.

Mʳ Thomas Potter Cheesefactor was bur yᵉ 2 of May.
Richard Wilberham Esqʳ was bur yᵉ 16 day of May.⁴
Mʳ John ffawcett *of Glouerstone* was bur yᵉ 1 day of June.
Randell son of Mʳ Robertt ffarrington was bur yᵉ 8 day of June.
Mʳ Henry Beyforne [*sic* for Baforne] *Beerbruer* was bur yᵉ 26 day of Nouembʳ.
Mʳ Edward Cooke was buryed yᵉ 10ᵗʰ day of Decembʳ.
Eliz: wife of Mʳ Edward Starkey was bur yᵉ 8ᵗʰ day of Jannuary.
Mʳ Rich: Wright *of Glouerstone* was bur yᵉ 29ᵗʰ day of Jannuary.
Eliz daughʳ of Mʳ Edward Aston was bur yᵉ 7ᵗʰ day of February.
Mʳ Peter Potter was bur the 22 day of February.
Thomas son of Mʳ Thomas Leigh was bur yᵉ 3 day of March.

1695.

Mʳ Thomas Reece was buryed yᵉ 22 day of Aprill.
Mʳ Rowland Warringe⁵ was bur yᵉ 15 day of May.
George ffinlow *drawer of Dee* was buryed yᵉ 7ᵗʰ day of August.
Margrett wife to Mʳ Roger Hall was buryed yᵉ 27 day of Nouembʳ.

---

¹ This gentleman was the last heir male of the old Cheshire family of Raven of Elworth, in Sandbach parish, of which a full pedigree will be found in my *History of Sandbach*, pp. 90-1. He was the eldest son of William Raven, of Elworth, gent., who died in 1686, by Katherine (Bromfield) his wife, and was born at Sandbach, 13th Nov. 1654. He died without issue, and his two sisters became his coheirs. Administration to his effects was granted at Chester in 1691.

² *See* the pedigree of Brerewood *postea*.

³ *See* her marriage in 1689, p. 135.

⁴ Troutbeck's Chapel had been repaired in 1693, and in the Churchwardens' Accounts this burial is entered as having taken place " in the new part of the church."

⁵ His monumental inscription and coat of arms will be found on pp. 48 and 76. *See* also p. 133, note 2.

Frances wife to John Lownes *of Nampwitch* was bur ye 13 of ffebruary.
Mr John Johnson *Glover* was Buryed ye 14th day of March.

1696.

Margrett wife to Mr Charles Garrard was bur ye 30th day of June.
Rebaka wife to Mr Thomas Duke *Churchwarden:* Bur: ye 22th day of Nouemb^r.
Mrs Eliz: Booth wife to Mr Lawrance Booth[1] was bur y^r 27th day of Nouemb^r.
Elizabeth daugh^{tr} to Mr Thomas Mullennex bur y^r 11th of ffebruary.
Capt. William Yorke was Buryed the 28th day of ffebruary.

1697.

Katherine ye wife to Mr Thomas Simpson was bur ye 25th of June.
Mr John Houseman[2] was Buryed ye 18th day of Nouemb^r.
James son to Mr James Bradley was buryed ye 8th day of February.
Phillip Beateman[3] of Vpton was buryed ye 17th day of February.
Mrs Easter [*sic* for Esther] Cullam Widdow was Buryed ye 21 day of February.

1698.

Walter Bathers *Gunner* was Buryed ye 18 day of Aprill.
Mrs Mary Stringer was buryed ye 29th day of Aprill.
Elizabeth Bateman[3] Widow of Vpton was bur ye 8 of September.
George Finlow Dyed in ye Parish of St. Tolliues [St. Olave's] by a Sudden Axcedent and buryed ye first of Nouemb^r.
Roger Ball a supposed Gen^t was Buryed the 24th day of Nouemb^r.
Nathaniall Bradburne of Bridge street of ye Parish of St. Peters Gen^t was buryed ye 30th of January.
Edward Webb of Bridgstreet *Porter of the Mint* was Buryed the 3 day of Febru.

1699.

Thomas Helley of Northgate Street of the Parish of St. Oswuls *Marchant* was buryed the 6th of June.
Ann ye wife to Francis Priace[4] *Master Gunner of the Castell* was bur ye 24th day of October.
Mrs Catherine Dicas Widdow of Bridge street of St. Peters Parish was buryed ye 2^d day of Nouemb^r.
Mr William Bellis of Bridgstreet Ironmonger was buryed the 6th day of Decemb^r.
Hesther ye wife to Samuell Hewson of Castell lane Gen^t was Buryed the 13th day of March.
Mr Randell Holme[5] seni^r of Bridgstreet Herrald of Armes was Buryed the 15th day of March.

1700.

Adam Birkenhead of Bridgstreet a yong man Dyed att Mr Tho: Birkenheads house and was Buryed the 7th day of Aprill.
Jane wife to James Crockson of Castell lane Gen^t was Buryed the 27th day of May.
Mrs Jane Booth[6] of the Castell of Chester spinster was Buryed the 8th day of August.
Edward Crompton *A Pentioner souldier*[7] was Buryed the 9th day of August.

---

[1] Mr. Lawrence Booth was Constable of Chester Castle. He was the second son of Lawrence Booth of Twemlow, co. Chester, gentleman, and was baptised at Goostrey 31 Jan. 1664-5 (see pedigree of Booth of Twemlow in my *History of Sandbach*, p. 270). He died in 1701 (see p. 143) leaving issue.

[2] For his monumental inscription formerly in the church *see* p. 71. He came from Kidderminster.

[3] *See* their monumental inscription formerly in the church, p. 71.

[4] *See* his second marriage on Nov. 12th in this year, p. 136.

[5] This was the third Randle Holme, a very distinguished antiquary. *See* his monumental inscription (p. 47), and the account of the Holme family *postea*.

[6] A daughter of Mr. Lawrence Booth, Constable of Chester Castle (*see* note 1).

[7] The burials of other "pentioner soldiers" occur in subsequent years.

1701.

Mrs Lidia Peck[1] of the P'ish of St. Bridgets spinster was Buryed the first day of June.

Mrs Anne Loyde of St. Olliues P'ish spinster was Buryed the 19th day of June.

Mr Laurance Booth[2] *High Cunstable of Chester Castell* was Buryed the 29th day of August.

Elizabeth Throppe of Bridgstreet Widow Dyed by A sudden Acceden' & Buryed the 14th day of Nouemb'.

1702.

Elizabeth Daugh'r to Mr Rich'd Wright' Minnister of St. Marys was Buryed the 24th day of May.

Humprey Kelshaw Gen' was Buryed the 22d day of June.

Mary Daugh'r to Henry Braderton of handbridge *Tubako Cutter* was Buryed the 30th day of Octob'.

Charles son to John Pouey of the Castell, *vnderkeeper of the Gole* was Buryed the 17th day of Nouemb'.

Mary Daugh'r to John Pouey *vnder keeper of y'e Castell Gole* was Buryed the first day of Decemb'.

1703.

Mary daught' to Edward Gough of Castell Lane *Pipemaker* was Buryed the 26th day of Aprill.

Edward Cooke *An Attorney* was Buryed from Mr Deuenports house of Huntington on the 8th day of July.

Vrsalley Daugh'r to Mr John Caper of Castell lane was Buryed the 4th day of January.

Francis Priace[3] *one of Her Majesties Master Gunners of Chester Castell* was buryed the 4th day of March.

Thomas sonn to Mr Charles Walley of y'e Water Gate street in Trinity P'ish was Buryed y'e 9th day of March.

A Souldier belonginge to Sr John Temples regiment mentioned.

1704.

A servant of "Mr Anthony Townsend" buried 24th April.

Mr Thomas Jackson *Wett Glouer* was bur y'e 12th of May.

Mr Richard Wright of Castell Lane an Attorney was Buryed the 16 day of June.

Mrs Catherine Hughes of Bridgstreet Widow was Buryed out of Dorothy Shelleys house the 16th day of January.

Owen Williams A Soldier belonginge to Cap' Barnet Loyde was Buryed the 21 day of January.

Rich'd Wenlock A Sargn' belonging to y'e Inuelieds [Invalids] was Buryed the 16th day of February.

1705.

Mr George Pennentt in the Northgate Street of the P'ish of St. Oswells was Buryed the 4th day of Aprill.

Mr Jonathan Bruen of Bridgstreet was bur from Mrs Vennebles the 20th day of Aprill.

Thomas Twambrook of the estgate Street Confection' was Buryed the 7th day of June.

Rob' supposed son to Mr Rob' Booth was Bur y'e 29th day of October.

Elizabeth y'e wife to Mr Wright of Glouer stone *Brasier* was Buryed the 25th day of Decemb'.

Thomas son to Mr Peerse Griffeth of Castell lane was bur y'e 5 of March.

Hannah Daugh'r to Mr Thomas Gerharde of y'e eastgate street bur y'e 5 March.

[The last Burial entry in Volume I. of the Registers is dated 17th March 1705[-6].]

---

[1] Probably a daughter of the Rev. James Peake, a non-juring clergyman (see p. 73), who died in 1719.
[2] For a short account of him see p. 142.
[3] See her monumental inscription, p. 72.
[4] See his second marriage, p. 136.

The *second volume* of the REGISTERS of St. Mary's is a long narrow folio volume, with parchment leaves, commencing early in the 18th century. It is in good preservation, and is very voluminous. On the fly-leaf is this inscription :—

The Regester of S¹ Maryes in y⁰ Citty of Chester and Bought at y⁰ Parish Cost In y⁰ year 1704. Paid For this Booke one Pound Twelfe shillinges.

MR. RICHARD WRIGHT, Prebend, Rect'.
ROBERT BRERETOOD, Esq¹ ⎫ Church
JOHN BRIDGE, Gen¹   ⎭ W'dens.

The Baptisms begin on the 25th August, 1701, and end on the 26th August, 1740. They are followed by the Burials, which begin on the 8th April, 1706, and end on the 18th August, 1740, and the Marriages, which begin on the 21st May, 1700, and end on the 4th March, 1740-1.

As was the case with the first volume, the following extracts contain all the entries of any importance, with the exception of those relating to the CLERGY of the parish, already printed in the account of the Rectors, and those referring to the following families, BRERETOOD, HOLME, BROCK of Upton, BROWNE of Upton, BROWNE of Netherlegh, ACTON, HUNT, MANLEY, and WESTON, of which pedigrees will subsequently be given.

CHRISTENINGS.

1701.

Ellinor Daught' to M' John Farrar¹ of Castell lane an Attorney was Bap¹ the 22¹ⁿ day of January 1701[-2].

Thomas sonn to Benjamine Handley *Drumer to y⁰ Invilids* was Baptiz⁴ y⁰ 22ᵈ day of March 1701[-2].

1702.

Charles sonn to John Powouall *Keeper of y⁰ Castell* was Baptiz⁴ y⁰ 12ᵗʰ day of Aprill 1702.

Mary Daught' to M' Edward Burrowes² Inholder was Baptized the 10ᵗʰ day of May 1702.

Jemmina [*sic*] Daught' to Francis Priace *M' Gunner of y⁰ Castell* was Baptized the 23 day of August 1702. [Bur. 24 Aug. 1709.]

Anne Daught' to M' Edward Wrench³ of Glouerstone Watchmaker was Baptiz⁴ the 27ᵗʰ day of Octob' 1702.

1703.

Richard sonn to M' John Kelshaw⁴ vnde' St. Marys hill was Baptized the 10ᵗʰ day of May 1703.

Vrsella Daught' to M' John Capper of Castell lane was Baptized the 29ᵗʰ day of Decemb' 1703.

1704.

Saulsbury son to John Loyde of Castell lane Esq' was Baptized the 27ᵗʰ day of July 1704.

1705.

Hugh sonn to M' William Done⁵ of Castell lane was Baptized the second day of Aprill 1705.

Thomas sonn to M' Perse Griffeth of Castell lane An Attorney was Bap¹ the 22ᵈ day of February 1705-6.

---

¹ The baptism of another child of Mr. John Farrar also occurs: *Roger*, 26 March, 1704.

² The baptisms of the following children of Mr. Edward Burrowes also occur :—*Edward*, 3 Oct. 1703 ; *Anne*, 9 Jan. 1704-5, Bur. 1 Sept. 1723 ; *Henry*, 31 Jan. 1705-6, Bur. 14 April, 1707 ; *Edward*, 7 June, 1707, Bur. 31 Oct. 1709 ; *Thomas*, 18 March, 1708-9 ; *Elizabeth*, 9 Nov. 1710, " Daught" to M' Edward Burrowes Sherife, Bur. 12 Sept. 1714 ; *Ambrose*, 22 May, 1712 Bur. 31 Aug. 1714.

³ The baptisms of the following children of Mr. Edward Wrench also occur :—*Edward*, 13 March, 1703[-4] ; *Catherine*, 30 Aug⁴¹, 1705 ; *Thomas*, 1 Sept. 1706 ; *John*, 21 June, 1709 ; *Dorothy*, 21 Jan. 1711[-12] ; *Mary*, 16 Aug⁴¹, 1713.

⁴ The baptism of the following child of Mr. John Kelshaw also occurs: —*John*, 19 Nov. 1704.

⁵ The baptism of another child of Mr. William Done also occurs : *Charles*, 5 Nov. 1706.

1706.

William & George sonns to M' Thomas Heatly of Bridgstreet was Baptized the 2ᵈ day of May 1706. [Bur. same day.]

Anne Daugh'' to M'ʳˢ Dempson of hanbridge was Baptized the 6ᵗʰ day of June 1706. [Bur. 27 June.]

Alaxandʳ son to Mʳ Alaxandʳ Denton vnder St. Mary hill Woollen Draper was Bapᵗ the 30ᵗʰ day of June 1706.

Rebekah Daugh'ʳ to Mʳ Hugh Whishaw¹ of Castell lane was Baptized yᵉ 10ᵗʰ Day of Nouembʳ 1706. [Bur. 8 Aug. 1710.]

Phillip sonn to Mʳ Phillip Batemanˀ of Cuppins lane [Butcher] was Baptized the 30ᵗʰ Day of Nouemᵇʳ 1706.

John sonn to Mʳ Thomas Hughes³ ironmonger was Baptized the second day of January 1706[-7].

George Roe a Childe Left in the Parish in Esqʳ Hunts roe [Row] and Kept by the P'ish Bapᵗ yᵉ 5ᵗʰ day of February 1706[-7]. [Bur. 7 Mar. 1706[-7].] *Presumably named after the person who found it*

1707.

John sonn to Mʳ John Bridge of Hanbridge Dyer was Baptized the first day of January 1707[-8].

1709.

Cotton Daughter to Mʳ Ambrous Borrowes *Liften* was Baptized the 3 day of Aprill 1709.

Martha Daugh'ʳ to Mʳ Raph Pickmore *Churchwarden* was Baptized the 30ᵗʰ day [of] Decemᵇʳ 1709.

Charles sonn to Mʳ Charles Broster was Baptized the 30ᵗʰ day of January 1709[-10].

1710.

John sonn to Mʳ William Witter⁴ of Bridgstreet Glover was Baptized the 19ᵗʰ day of January 1710[-11].

1711.

Richard sonn to Mʳ William Jenninges⁵ of Bridge street Glouer was Baptized the 5ᵗʰ day of Aprill 1711.

Sarah Daugh'ʳ to Mʳ Thomas Reeceˀ of Cuppinslane [Maltster] was Baptized the 13ᵗʰ Day of July 1711.

1712.

John sonn to Mʳ John Allen of yᵉ Haugh green was Baptized the 15ᵗʰ Day of January 1712[-13].

1713.

Mary Daught' to Mʳ William Johnson⁷ of Cleton lane Wett Glouer was Baptized yᵉ 16ᵗʰ Day of July 1713.

Jane Daughtʳ to Mʳ Thomas Kirkes⁸ of Castell lane An Attorney was Baptized yᵉ 11ᵗʰ Day of Decembʳ 1713. [Bur. 20 May, 1714.]

---

¹ The baptisms of the following children of Mr. Hugh Whishaw also occur :—*Richard*, 4 Feb. 1707-8; *Frances*, 27 Feb. 1708-9; *Mary*, 11 May, 1710, Bur. 27 July, 1727; *Hugh*, 18 July, 1711; *Rebekah*, 12 Dec. 1712. A daughter *Jane* was buried 27 Feb. 1714-15.

² The baptisms of the following children of Mr. Philip Bateman also occur :—*Edward*, 14 March, 1707-8; *Phillip*, 5 June, 1709, "sonn to Phillip Bateman Churchwarden."

³ The baptism of the following child of Mr. Thomas Hughes also occurs :—*Anne*, 23 Aug^ˢᵗ 1708.

⁴ The baptisms of the following children of Mr. William Witer also occur :—*Joseph*, 21 Feb. 1711-12, "sonn to Mʳ William Witter of Handbridge Wett Glouer"; *Mary*, 24 Feb. 1712-13; *Thomas*, 28 Nov. 1715; *Richard*, 30 Jan. 1716-17; *Margrett*, 6 Feb. 1719-20, Bur. 19 Feb. 1719-20. A daughter, *Elizabeth*, bur. 16 Sept. 1720.

⁵ The baptisms of the following children of Mr. William Jennings also occur :— *William*, 28 Feb. 1719-20; a daughter, *Frances*, was buried 12 Dec. 1719; *Roger*, 26 Janʳ, 1721-22, Bur. 19 Nov. 1724; *Sarah*, daughter to Mr. William Jennings, Wet Glover and Churchwarden, bur. 9 May, 1721; a daughter, *Ursella*, was bur. 31 Aug. 1714.

⁶ The baptism of the following child of Mr. Thomas Reece also occurs :—*Charles*, 29 June, 1712. A son, *Robert*, buried 13 Sept. 1713.

⁷ The baptisms of the following children of Mr. William Johnson also occur :—*John*, 14 Sept. 1716; a daughter, *Margaret*, buried 9 Jan. 1717-18; *Mary*, 30 Dec. 1720, Bur. 22 Jan. 1720-1; *Charles*, 26 June, 1722, Bur. 11 Dec. 1722. See also 1727.

⁸ The baptisms of the following children of Mr. Thomas Kirkes also occur :— *Thomas*, 8 Sept. 1715; *Spann*, 20 April, 1717, Bur. 15 Aug. 1717.

ST. MARY-ON-THE-HILL, CHESTER.

1715.

Jane Daught[r] to M[r] George Prescoth[1] Cheesfactor was Baptized the 27th Day of Septemb[r] 1715.
Jane Daught[r] of John Denenporte *vnder jeylor of the Castell* was Baptiz[d] the 7th day of Nouemb[r] 1715.

1716.

Sarah Daught[r] to M[r] Robartt Kinsey[2] of handbridge Baptized the 25th Day of April 1716.
Mary Daugh[tr] to M[r] Robartt Jones juni[r] an Attorney in Bridgstreet Baptized the 22[d] Day of Septem[br] 1716.
Daniell sonn to M[r] Henry Jackson[3] *Ensigne of the inuelieds* Baptized the 4th Day of Nouemb[r] 1716.
Elizabeth Daught[r] to M[r] Thomas Wright of Cuppins lane Baptized y[e] 19th Day of March 1716[-17].

1717.

Robertt son to *Cap[t]* John Deyall Esq[r] in Castell lane Baptized the 3[d] Day of April 1717.
Samuell son to M[r] Thomas Duke[4] of Handbridg Wett Glouer Baptized the 8th Day of December 1717.
John son to Johnson Manwaringe[5] of Castell lane Gen[t] Baptized the 23[d] Day of January 1717[-18]. [Bur. 29 July, 1719.]
Gilbrett son to *Cap[t]* John Pickeren Esq[r] Baptized y[e] 28th Day of February 1717[-18].

1718.

Elizabeth Daught[r] to M[r] Thomas Tagg[6] of y[e] Church Street An Attorney Baptiz[d] the first day of June 1718.
Wedmaster y[e] son to Jacob Dawson a souldi[r] in *Coll Harisons Redgment* Baptized the 15th Day of June 1718.

1719.

Hannah Daught[r] to William Wightman[7] Gen[t] *Lenftu[t] to Cor[nll] Kirks Ridgm[t]* Baptiz[d] y[e] 17th Day of July 1719.
William son to Tobias Cooke[8] of Handbridge *one of y[e] Mast[r] Miller of Dee Mills* Bap[t] y[e] 28th Day of August 1719.
John son to John Cooke[9] *vnderlaker of Dee Mills* Baptized the 8th Day of Nouem[br] 1719. [Bur. 17 March, 1719[-20].]
Richerd son to Richerd Priace[10] *of y[e] Tounship of Vpton Scoolmaster* Baptiz[d] the 14th Day of Decem[br] 1719.
Elizabeth Daught[r] to John Bennett *Clarke to y[e] Cheese Wairehouse* Baptized the 31 Day of Decem[br] 1719.

---

[1] The baptisms of the following children of Mr. George Prescott also occur :—*William*, 26 Aug[st], 1717; *Susanah*, 21 May, 1719, Bur. 5 Feb. 1722-3; *Gregory*, 15 June, 1725, Bur. 13 Oct. 1725.

[2] The baptism of the following child of Mr. Robert Kinsey also occurs : - *Robert*, 22 Sept. 1717, "son to Robartt Kinsshaw of Handbridge Gen[t]."

[3] The baptism of the following child of Mr. Henry Jackson also occurs :—*Modises* (daughter), 5 April, 1719.

[4] The baptism of the following child of Mr. Thomas Duke also occurs :- *Andrew*, 4 April, 1721, Bur. 15 Aug. 1721.

[5] See p. 155, note 2.

[6] The baptisms of the following children of Mr. Thomas Tagg also occur :— *Anne*, 23 July, 1719 ; *Elizabeth*, 23 Nov. 1720 ; *Eleanor*, 8 April, 1722 ; *James*, 29 March, 1724.

[7] The baptisms of the following children of William Wightman, Gent., also occur (in the later entries he is called "Captain ") :—*Sabine* (daughter), 23 Nov. 1721 ; *William*, 17 Nov. 1723, Bur. 7 Nov. 1724 ; a daughter, *Hannah*, Bur. 13 June, 1726 ; *David*, 23 Jan. 1726-7, Bur. 7 Nov. 1733 ; *Sarah*, 1 Feb. 1727-8, Bur. 1st Oct. 1729 ; *Thomas*, 20 Sept. 1729, Bur. 15 Nov. 1733 ; *William*, 16 Dec. 1730 ; *Eliza*, 23 Sept. 1734, Bur. 26 Sept. 1734 ; *Roberts*, 9 Oct. 1735 ; *Robert*, son of Capt. Wm. Whiteman, bur. 18 Oct. 1741 ; *Joseph*, 5 Nov. 1736.

[8] The baptisms of the following children of Tobias Cooke also occur :—*Tobias*, 14 May, 1721 ; *Ann*, 30 May, 1723 ; *John*, 7 Jan. 1724-5 ; *Mary*, 4 Jan. 1727-28 ; *Charles*, 5 Dec. 1729 ; *Margaret*, 6 Nov. 1730, Bur. 19 March, 1730-1.

[9] The baptisms of the following children of Mr. John Cooke also occur :—*John*, 23 Oct. 1720 ; *Charles*, 5 Jan. 1723-4 ; *William*, 17 May, 1726 ; *Ralph*, 23 Feb. 1727-8, " Son to John Cook : Church Warden."

[10] The baptism of the following child of Richard Price also occurs :—*George*, 10 Sept. 1722, Bur. 23 Sept. 1722.

1720.

Rebecca Davghter to M[r] John Crachley was Baptized y[e] 26th Day of Decem[br] 1720.

Elizabeth Davghter to M[rs] Mary Johnson[1] of Clayton Lane Widdow was Baptized y[e] 10th day of ffebruary 1720[-1].

1721.

John Son to M[r] Thomas Rowley[6] *of Brewers Hall* was Baptized the 20th Day of Aprill 1721.

Edward Son to Cap[t] Rich[d] Parsons was Baptized y[e] 30th day of Aprill 1721.

1722.

John Son to M[r] John Cotgreave[3] Brewer & Mary his Wife of Handbridge Baptized y[e] 2[d] day of October 1722.

1723.

Sarah Daughter to M[r] Joseph Porter Malster & Jane His Wife of Bridge Street Bap[t] y[e] 31st day of March 1723.

John Son to John Jones[4] *Servant to y[e] Earle of Plymouth* & Susannah his Wife of Handbridge Bap[t] y[e] 14th day of July 1723.

Charles Son to M[r] William Bardon[5] *Doctor of his Majesties Yatch* and Elizabeth his Wife Baptized y[e] 9th day of October 1723.

1724.

Rebecca Daughter to M[r] Bartholomew Duke : Silver Smith & Elizabeth His Wife of Handbridge Bap[t] y[e] 21st day of May 1724. [Bur. 21 March, 1724-5.]

Jane Daughter to Samuel West *Perriwig Maker* & Christian His Wife of Bridge Street Baptized y[e] 7th day of June 1724.

Thomas Son to M[r] Thomas Rowley[6] Yeoman & Martha his Wife of Saltney Side Baptized y[e] 7th day of June 1724. [Bur. 21 June, 1725.]

Elizabeth Daughter to Charles Whitehead *City Mason* and Elizabeth his Wife of Bridge Street Bap[t] y[e] 22[d] day of November 1724.

1725.

Mary Daughter to William Marshall *Officer of Excise* & Margrat his Wife of Clayton Lane Bap[t] y[e] 11th day of July 1725.

Hannah Daughter to Timothy Doland *Needle Maker Prisoner in y[e] Northgate* & Rachell his Wife : the Child upwards of Twelvemonths Old : Baptized the 12th day of October 1725.

Martha Daughter to Joshua Wilde[7] *Gaoler of the Castle Prison* & Martha his Wife Baptized the 16th day of November 1725.

1726.

W[m] Burgess Son to Ralph Dod Gen[t] & Susannah his Wife of Handbridge Baptized the 7th day of July 1726.

Thomas Son to Rich[d] Jesson *Superficer* [sic] *of the Excise* & Elizabeth his wife of Bridge Street Bap[t] y[e] 20th day of July 1726.

Mary Illigitimate Daughter to Rich[d] Jones *Master of Comediens* Borne of the Body of Ann Downs Baptized y[e] 9th day of October 1726.

---

[1] " *William* son to M[rs] Mary Johnson " was buried 25 Nov. 1730.

[2] *See* also under 1724.

[3] The baptism of the following child of Mr. John Cotgreave also occurs :—*Mary*, 18 Aug[st], 1724. *Martha*, " dau. of Alderman John Cottgreve," was buried 19 April, 1746.

[4] The baptism of the following child of John Jones also occurs :—*Elisabeth*, 1st March, 1724-5.

[5] The baptism of the following child of Mr. William Bardon also occurs :—*Elisabeth*. 21 Jan[y], 1725-6.

[6] The baptism of the following child of Mr. Thomas Rowley also occurs :—*Thomas*. 16 July, 1725. *See* also 1721.

[7] The baptisms of the following children of Joshua Wilde also occur :—*George*. 19 Sept. 1727 ; *Joshua*, 18 Feb. 1730-1 ; *Adam*, 24 Aug[st], 1732.

Mary Daughter to Thomas Corles' Scrivener & Elizabeth His Wife of Bridge Street Baptized y° 23ᵈ day of October 1726.

1727.

Thomas Son to Mʳ Thomas Walley[2] Yeoman & Alice His Wife of the Rough Hill Baptized yᵉ 20ᵗʰ day of July 1727.

James Son to Mʳ Wᵐ Johnson[3] skinner & Margᵗ His Wife of Bridge Street Baptized yᵉ 18ᵗʰ day of August 1727.

John Son to Mʳ Joseph Piggott Attorney & Helena His Wife of Castle Lane Bapᵗ the 14ᵗʰ day of December 1727. [Bur. 21 Nov. 1729.]

George Son to Mʳ Hezekiah Hall Physician and Sophia His Wife Bapᵗ yᵉ 27ᵗʰ day of December 1727.

1728.

Ann Daughter to Alldᵐ Henry Bennett[4] of Moston & Elizabeth his Wife Baptized yᵉ 18ᵗʰ day of August 1728.

1729.

Ann Daughter to Thomas Jones *Drumer in yᵉ Honᵇˡᵉ Genˡˡ Sabines Regᵐᵗ* & Eliz: his Wife Bapᵗ yᵉ 4ᵗʰ day of January 1729[-30].

1730.

Mary Daughter of Solomon Tovey[5] *Capⁿ* & Mary his Wife of Clayton lane Baptized yᵉ 21ˢᵗ day of December.

1733.

Mary Daūter of Ralph Leicester[6] of Castle Lane Esqʳ & Katherine his Wife baptᵈ yᵉ 2ᵈ day of May.

Mary Daūter of Matthew Trueman of Gloverstone *Musician* & Mary his Wife baptiz'd yᵉ 23ᵈ day of September.

Florentia Dautʳ of John Kilpatrick[7] of Glovʳ Stone *Serjᵗ of yᵉ Invalides* & Mary his W: baptiz'd yᵉ 25ᵗʰ day of October. [Bur. 1ˢᵗ Oct. 1734.]

1737.

William Son to Mʳ Williame Thomson[8] watch Maker & Mary his Wife of Glover Stone Baptized the 5ᵗʰ day of July.

Sarah Daughter to John Hodgson yeoman of Eccleston in Yorkeshire Stranger & Sarah his Wife Baptized yᵉ 7ᵗʰ day of October.

Febey [Phœbe] Daughter to Edward French *Master Gunner* & Elizabeth his Wife Bapᵈ yᵉ 12ᵗʰ of February.

---

[1] The baptisms of the following children of Thomas Corles also occur :—*Elizabeth*, 19 Nov. 1727. Bur. 4 Feb. 1728-9 ; a daughter, *Sarah*, was buried 30 Jan. 1728-9 ; a son, *John*, buried 6 Oct. 1733 ; *Thomas*, 13 March. 1734-5. Bur. 27 May, 1735 ; *Martha*, 15 Jan. 1737-8, Bur. 11 Feb. 1737-8 ; *Peter*, 30 March, 1739.

[2] "*Jonathan* son to Mʳ Thomas Walley " was buried 15 Dec. 1727. *See also* 1713.

[3] " *Eleanor* dau. of Mʳ Wᵐ Johnson " was buried 17 Feb. 1725-6.

[4] This Henry Bennett was a member of a well-known Chester family, the son of a Mr. Henry Bennett, who was one of the Sheriffs of the city in 1681 and Mayor in 1698. He married Elizabeth, daughter of . . . Morgell of Moston, by whom he had five daughters coheiresses. The daughter Anne, whose baptism is here recorded, married John Townshend, of Hem House, in 1760, and had issue.

[5] The baptisms of the following children of Solomon Tovey also occur :—*John*, 27 March, 1735 ; *Ann*, 24 Jan. 1736-7 ; *Bettey*, 13 July, 1738.

[6] The baptisms of the following children of Ralph Leycester, Esq., also occur :—*George*, 12 Dec. 1735 ; *Edward*, 8 June, 1739 ; *Susannah Norres*, 21 June, 1742. Bur. 21 Jan. 1744-5 ; a dau. *Jane*, bur. 2 March. 1742-3 ; *Theodosia*, 9 Oct. 1743 ; *Shusanah*, 4 April, 1746 ; *Hugh*, 2 Oct. 1748 ; *Osmall*, 21 March, 1752. The father of these children was Ralph Leycester of Toft, co. Chester, Esq., who died in 1777. He married about 1727 Katherine, daughter and coheir of Edward Norris of Speke, co. Lanc., Esq., M.D., by Anne, his wife, daughter and heir of Peter Gerard of Crewood, Esq., M.D.

[7] The baptisms of another daughter of John Kilpatrick also occurs :—*Florentia*, 11 June, 1735, bur. 14 July, 1735.

[8] The baptisms of the following children of Mr. William Thomson also occur :—*Elizabeth*, 28 March, 1739 ; a son, *John*, buried 31 Oct. 1741 ; *Ellen*, 24 May, 1742, Bur. 1ˢᵗ March, 1744-5 ; *Mary*, 7 May, 1746 ; *Margrett*, 21 Janʳ, 1754 ; a dau. *Ellin*, buried 28 Feb. 1754.

1739.

Harrey Son to M'r John How Gent & Margrett his Wife *at y'e Parsonage* Baptized y'e 2d day of May.
William Son to M'r Jn'o Smith of Upton yeom'an & Mary his Wife Bap'td y'e 8th day of May.
Mary Daughter to M'r Rob't Taylor[1] *Atorney* & Ann his Wife of Castle lane Baptized y'e 3d day of October.

1740.

Bagott Son to Humphrey Read[2] Gen't & Mary his Wife of Clayton lane Bap'td y'e 8th day of June.

[The last entry of a Baptism in Volume II. is dated 26 August, 1740.]

MARRIAGES.

1704.

Thomas Whetnell[3] Esq'r of Namptwitch & M'rs Mary Wright were Married with a Licence y'e 18th day of May 1704.
M'r Roger Jones *Curett of Bangor* & Mary Edwards were Married with a Licence the 24th day of June 1704.

1705.

Robartt Hide[4] of Catnell Gen't & M'rs Ellino' Mather were Married with a Licence the 26th day of October 1705.
Hugh Whishaw Gen't of Castell lane & M'rs Frances Bramton were Married with a Licence y'e 23d day of December 1705.

1709.

M'r Daniell Coulson & M'rs Catherine Loyde were Married with a Licence the 10th day of Septem'br 1709.
M'r William Witter & M'rs Ellin' Johnson were Married with a Licence the 22 day of Decem'br 1709.

1710.

Dionysius Kelley Gen't & M'rs Catherine Peck were Married with a Licence the 24th Day of July 1710.

1712.
[Blank.]

William Farrall Gen't & M'rs Elizabeth . . . . . were Married with a Licence the 6th Day of Octob'r 1712.
Thomas Dod an Attorney & M'rs Catherine Glasier were Married with a Licence the 21 Day of Decemb'r 1712.

1715.

M'r Thomas Loyde an Attorney & M'rs Margrett Parrey were Married w't a Licence y'e 27th Day of May 1715.
Henry Jackson *Enssine of y'e Inuelieds* [Ensign of the Invalids] & Marg't Hall were Married the 22d Day of July w't a Licence Dated y'e 20th July 1715.
M'r Thomas Reece Malster & M'rs Mary Hatfeild were Married with a Licence y'e 5th Day of January 1715[-16].

---

[1] The baptisms of the following children of Mr. Robert Taylor also occur:—*Henry*, 24 March, 1740-1: *Thomas*, 16 June, 1743; *Ann*, 31 July, 1744; *Ursula*, 11 June, 1746; *Mawie*, born Jan. 27th, bapt. 8 Feb. 1752.

[2] The baptism of the following child of Mr. Humphrey Read also occurs:—*Humphrey*, 21 March, 1742-3.

[3] This Thomas *Wettenhall* of Nantwich, Esq., married Mary, daughter and heiress of the Rev. Richard Wright, rector of St. Mary's and Prebendary of Chester (*see* pp. 90-1). He was buried at Nantwich on the 19th May, 1709, but his widow survived him for 50 years, being buried at Nantwich on the 19th Dec. 1759 (Hall's *History of Nantwich*, p. 464). They had issue two sons and three daughters.

[4] This was Robert *Hyde* of Catenhall in the parish of Frodsham, co. Chester.

1716.

John Pickeren Gen[t] and M[rs] Elizabeth Townsend Spinster were Married with a Licence y[e] 31 Day of January 1716[-17].

1720.

Richard Parsons Gen[t] & M[rs] Penellopey Townsend were Married with a Licence the 28th Day of July 1720.

1722.

Charles Eyton Gentleman of y[e] Parish of St. Oswalds & Mary Barker Spinster of Buns Lane of St. Michals Parish Married y[e] 27th day of Aprill 1722, By y[e] Rev[d] M[r] Hugh Wilbraham by vertue of a Licence Granted by y[e] Rt. Worshipfull Peregrine Gastrell Chancalour [sic].

The Rev[d] M[r] William Bennett Minister of Barrow & Margrett Knowles Spinster of y[e] same Parish Married y[e] 7th day of July 1722. By y[e] Rev[d] M[r] Edward Davies by Vertue of a Licence Granted by y[e] Rev[d] M[r] Arthur Fogg, Surrogate.

Banns published at Hawarden by the Rev[d] M[r] Latewood, Nov. 1722.

Banns published at St. Bridget's by the Rev[d] M[r] Thomas Parrey, in January 1722[-3].

The Rev[d] M[r] Aubrey officiates in Feb. 1722[-3].

1723.

A Licence granted by the Rev[d] D[r] Thane, Surrogate, in Oct. 1723.

Edward Bridge Gen[t] & Elizabeth Dicas Widdow both of the Parish of St. John Baptist Married y[e] 13th day of Novemb[r] 1723 By the Rev[nd] M[r] Hugh Wilbraham by vertue of a Licence Granted by the Rev[nd] Doctor ffogg Surrogate.

John Robinson Gen[t] of Raby in the Parish of Neston & Rebecca Sharples Spinster of Leverpool Married y[e] 13 day of ffebruary 1723[-4] By the Rev[nd] M[r] Cha[s] Alldcroft by vertue of a Licence Granted by the R[t] Worshipfull Peregrine Gastrell Chancell[r].

1724.

Banns published by The Rev. M[r] Thomas Leftwiche in Nov. 1724.

1725.

The Rev[nd] M[r] Parry officiates in July 1725. Banns published by the Rev[nd] M[r] Robert Fogg in Sept. 1725.

A Licence granted by the Rev[nd] John Prescott, Surrogate, in Oct. 1725.

The Rev[nd] M[r] Thomas Leftwich, Surrogate, officiates in Nov. 1725.

Licences granted by The Rev[nd] M[r] Charles Henchman, Surrogate, in December, January, and February.

1726.

M[r] Joseph Snow Jun[r] Shopkeeper of Gloverstone & Mary Hall Spinst[r] of St. Peters Parish Married y[e] 14th day of Aprill 1726 By the Rev[nd] M[r] Aldcroft by vertue of a Licence Granted by y[e] R[t] Worshipfull Per: Gastrell Chancell[r].

Licences granted by the Rev. Thomas Leftwiche, Surrogate. Banns published by the Rev. John Ince in May 1726.

The Rev[d] M[r] Dockerell officiates in Aug[st] 1726, and the Rev[d] M[r] Aubrey in Nov. 1726.

Robert Crachley Gen[t] of the County of fflint & Mary Burrowes Spinst[r] of this Parish Married y[e] 14th day of February 1726[-7] By the Rev[nd] M[r] Aldcroft by vertue of a Licence Granted by the R[t] Worshipfull Per: Gastrell Chancell[r].

1727.

The Rev. M[r] Willcock officiates in April 1727.

Licences granted by the Rev. D[r] Fogg and the Rev. Thomas Leftwiche, Surrogates.

The Rev. M[r] Dockerill officiates in May, and the Rev. M[r] Aubrey in July.

Richard Wickstead Gen^t & Metilda Hodson Spinst^r of Castle Lane & of this Parish Married ye 11th day of July By the Revnd Mr Aldcroft by vertue of a Licence Granted by the Revnd Mr Thomas Leftwiche Surrogate.

Banns published by the Rev. Mr Thomas Parry in November.

Abraham Sheram Gen^t *of St. Andrews Holborne London* and Eliz: Bannister Spinst^r of Marbury Married ye 17th of January By the Revnd Mr Aldcroft by vertue of a Licence Granted by the Revnd Mr Thos Leftwiche Surrogate.

1728.

The Revnd Mr Lancaster officiates in April, the Rev. Mr Aubrey and the Rev. Mr Robert Fogg in June, and the Rev. Mr Aubrey in February.

Licences granted by Mr John Worsley and the Rev John Cartwright, Surrogates, in June.

Banns published by the Rev. Benjamin Culme and the Rev. Roger Jones, Curate of Mold, in July.

Daniel Killpatrick Writeing Master of St. Martin's Par^{sh} & Christiane Saunders Spins^{tr} of ye Par^{sh} Married ye 17th day of ffebruary By the Revnd Mr Aldcroft by vertue of a Licence Granted By the R^t Worshipfull Peregrine Gastrell Chancellour.

1729.

Licences granted by the Rev. Mr Thomas Leftwiche, Surrogate, in May; and by the Rev. Mr Thomas Baldwin, Surrogate, in January.

The Rev. Mr Robert Fogg officiates in May and August ; the Rev Mr Arthur Williams and the Rev. Mr Aubrey in July.

Banns published by the Rev. Mr Willcoxson Curate of Frodsham, in July, and the Rev. Mr John Oliver, in August.

1730.

The Rev. Mr Culme officiates in May, and the Rev. Mr Markham in September and January.

William Moss, Apothecary & Elizabeth Toft Spins^{tr} Both of Middlewich Married ye 25th day of June By the Revnd Mr Aldcroft by vertue of a Licence Granted by the Revnd John Cartwright Surrogate.

George Ryley, Chirurgeon & Mary Gibbons Widow Both of Namptwich Married the 20th day of August By the Revnd Mr Low of Bunbury by vertue of a Licence Granted by the R^t Worshipfull Per : Gastrell Chancel.

A Licence granted by the Rev. John Mapletoft, Surrogate, in November.

Banns published by the Rev. Mr Brown, Curate of Stoak, in December, and by the Rev. Mr Thomas, Curate of Christleton [Xleton], in March.

1731.

Banns published by the Rev. Mr Blackbourne, Curate of Dodleston, in April.

The Rev. Mr Markham officiates in April.

Thomas Hargrave Writingmast^r & Sarah Wild Spinst^r both of ye parish by License married ye Nineteenth day of June.

William Pool[1] Gentl^n & Grace Pelham Spinster both *of Pool Hall in Werral* by Licence married ye 20th day of December.

1734.

Joseph Hall Gent of the Parish of St. Peter & Mrs Benedicta Whitmore Spinst^r of this Parish Married by Licence the 25th day of November.

1736.

Mr John Witter Apothecary & Mrs Alice Swarbreck Spinst^r both of this Parish Married by Licence the twenty Sixth day of Aprill.

---

[1] According to the pedigree in Ormerod's *Cheshire*, vol. ij., p. 424. this William Poole was of Hooke, co. Sussex, Esq. (cousin of Sir Francis Poole, Bart., M.P. for Lewes, who married Frances, daughter of Henry Pelham, Esq.), and Grace, daughter of Henry Pelham, Esq., of Lewes in Sussex, was his first wife, by whom he had no issue.

ST. MARY-ON-THE-HILL, CHESTER.

George Plews, Officer of Excise, & Ann Hale Spinster both of Gloverstone in this Par'sh Married by Licence the 27th day of September.
Banns published by the Rev. Mr Thomas Wrench in Oct.

1737.

Jonathan Brayne of Northwich in the County & Diocess of Chester Gentleman & Mary Tagg of yr Parish of St. Mary on yr Hill in yr City of Chester Spinster Maried by Lycence yr 9th of February by the Rev: Mr Thomas Wrench.

1738.

Thomas Bennett, Gent. & Arabellah Dod Spinster both of this Parish was Maried by Licence yr 1st of July.

John Killpatrick, *Sarjent of yr Invalieds* & Susannah Bream Widow of Bridge Street Maried by Bannds Published the 17th day of December.

1739.

Thomas Pallin of Farndon Gen' & Jane Hatton of yr Same place Widow was Maried by Licence the 24th day of April.

The Rev. Mr Rench [*sic* for Wrench] officiates in May.

The Rev. Mr Thomas Aubury *Minister of Eccleston* & Mrs Cathrine Wrench of Gloverston Spinster was Maried by Lycence yr 16th day of Feby.

[The last Marriage entry in Volume II. is dated 4 March, 1740.]

BURIALS.

1706.

Mrs Susannah Gerrard[1] Widow of St. Michell P'ish was Buryed the 21 day of Aprill 1706.
Charles *A Blackamore seruan'* to Mr Daniell Peck was Buryed the 14th day of July 1706.
Margrett yr wife to Mr Henry Bumbury of Bridgstreet was Buryed the 15th day of August 1706.
Henry sonn to Mr Henry Berkenhead of St. Bridgets P'ish was Buryed the 2d day of Septembr 1706.
Mr George Townsend of Bridgstreet was Buryed the 8th day of October 1706.
Thomas sonn to Mr Thomas Heatley an Attorney was Buryed the 27th day of October 1706.
Elizabeth Daughtr to Mr Henry Berkenhead of St. Bridgets P'ish was Buryed the 31 day of Decembr 1706.
[Blank.]
. . . . yr wife to Mr John Wrench of St. Peters P'ish Watchmaker was Buryed yr 28th day of January 1706[-7].
Elizabeth Daughtr to Henry Hughes *of hanbridge scoolmast'* was Buryed the 15th day of February 1706[-7].
Alderman Thomas Simpson of hanbridge was Buryed the 22d day of March 1706[-7].
Capt Dunkon Cambwell [Duncan Campbell] of St. Johns lane was Buryed the 23 day of March 1706[-7].

1707.

Mr John Twedle *Capt of the Inuelieds* was Buryed the 9th Day of May 1707.
Mr William Helley of Upton seni' was Buryed the 12th day of July 1707.
Mr James Crockston [Croxton] an Attorney of the P'ish of St. John was Buryed the 25th day of July 1707.
Mr Thomas Gleaue & Mary Barker By a Sudden Accedent were Drown'd at Weper Pooll & Bur: ye 3d day of January 1707[-8].

---

[1] She was the widow of Dr. Peter Gerard buried at St. Mary's 9 Dec. 1678 (*see* p. 138).

The Whitley Tankard (p. 1668) is interesting as being the oldest piece of plate (except the oar) possessed by the Corporation (of Chester) and was given to the city by Ralph Whitley, Alderman of the City, and presented by Lettice, his widow, who was the second daughter of Sir Francis Gamull, Bart; who entertained Charles I on his visit to Chester in 1644. " M" Stanley Ball reported in Manchester City News Jany 22. 1916, Lecture at Lancs & Ches. Antiquarian Society on Jany 14. 1916.

THE REGISTERS OF ST. MARY'S. 153

M' John Hale, of Bridgstreet, Clarke to Rob' Brerewood Esq', Justice of y' Peace, was Buryed the 8th day of January 1707[-8].

Thomas Wilberham Gen' of y' P'ish of St. Martins was Bur: in Trou[t]backs Chapple y' 6th day of March 1707[-8].

1708.

One of the Mereens [Marines] belonging to y' Gou' Brooks' Esq' and Rob' Brerewood Esq' was Buryed the 17 day of May 1708.

John Farrar Gen' of the Castell lane an Attorney was Buryed the 3ᵈ day of July 1708.

Mary² y' wife to William Done Gen' of Castell lane an Attorney was Buryed the 5th day of July 1708.

Madam Sarah Lacy³ of Castell lane Wid'w was Buryed the 26th day of January 1708[-9].

1709.

See above note. Madam Lettis Whitley of Peper Street of y' P'ish of St. Michels Widow was Buryed the 7th day of Aprill 1709. *second Daughter of Sir Francis Gamul. vide Stanley Ball.*   *Ralph Whitley died 1679* 127.

John sonn to Cap' John Harrisson of Dublin was Buryed the 3ᵈ Day of June 1709.

Isabella Daugh'' to Thomas Tindall Esq' was Buryed the 25th day of June 1709.

M' Henry Bumbury of Bridgstreet *one of y' Junelieds* was Buryed the 13th Day of Septem'' 1709.   *Invalid.*

M' Phillip Bateman of the P'ish of St. Oswels *Churchwarden* was Buryed the 16th day of October 1709.

. . . . sonn to M' Thomas Fernabaugh ironmonger was Buryed the 10th day of March 1709[-10].

1710.

Henry sonn to M' William Baforne¹ of St. Martins Parish [Boerbruer] was Buryed the first day of October 1710.

M' John Dicas of hanbridge was Buryed the 4th Day of October 1710.

M''' Easter Warbutton⁵ of the Grange Spinster was Buryed the 6th Day of Decem'' 1710.   *Lucas.*

John sonn to John Pouneall *Keeper of y' North Gole* was Buryed the 15th day of January 1710[-11].

1711.

Thomas Fairebanke a Stranger from Lancumshire [*sic*] was Buryed the 11th Day of January 1711[-12].

Hannah Daugh'' to M' Elkenah Lange an Excise man was Buryed the 28th day of February 1711[-12].

1712.

James Huntt a Passinger goinge to Ridgworth in Staffordshire Dyed and was Buryed the 8th day of Aprill 1712.

Samuell Finlow of Bridge Street *Drawer of Dee* was Buryed the 30th Day of October 1712.

Thomas Sonn to Edward Norris⁶ *Doctor of Physick* of y' Parish of St. Johns was Bur: y' 8th day of Nouemb' 1712.

. . . . Dauis Widdow Late wife to Henry Dauis [Davis] of Ashton Esq' Deceased was Buryed out of the Parish of St. John's on y' 30th Day of Decemb' 1712.

1713.

Anne y' wife to M' Thomas Reece of Cuppinslane Maister was Buryed y' 3ᵈ Day of Septemb' 1713.

---

¹ Governor of the Castle of Chester.

² She was a daughter of Mr. Whishaw of St. Mary's parish, and was married to Mr. William Done at St. Michael's, Chester, on the 18th May, 1704. *See* the monumental inscription printed on p. 72, and the notes thereto.

³ *See* the monumental inscription on p. 72.

⁴ The burial of the following child of Mr. William Baforne also occurs :—*John*, 15 Sept. 1713.

⁵ She was the daughter of Peter Warburton, Esq., of Hefferston Grange, Chief Justice of Chester.

⁶ Edward Norris, Esq., of Speke Hall, co. Lanc., M.D. of Brasenose College, Oxford, married Anne, daughter and heiress of Peter Gerard, of Crewood, co. Chester, Esq., M.D., whose monumental inscription has already been printed on p. 70.   *Ref. 125.*

X

ST. MARY-ON-THE-HILL, CHESTER.

Mr Richard Williamson *reamond of ye Pentice* of ye P^{ri}ish of St. Oswels Buryed the 5th Day of January 1713[-14].

1714.

Frances Daught^r to Mr Thomas Gill of ye Castell lane was Buryed the 4th Day of August 1714.

Mr Harbertt Simpson *reamond of ye Pentice* Dyed in St. Oswels P^{ri}ish and Buryed the 7th Day of August 1714.

Mr Edward Wrench of Glouer Stone Watchmaker was Buryed the 17th Day of August 1714.

John sonn to Mr John Wilson of ye Parish of Trinity was Buryed the 6th Day of Septem^{br} 1714.

William Worningham *one of His Majesties Gunners of Chester Castell* Buryed ye 3^d Day of Octob^r 1714.

1715.

Edward sonn to Mr Peter Briscoe of Bridgstreet in y^r P^{ri}ish of St. Michels Buryed ye 7th Day of June 1715.

Elizabeth ye wife to Mr Gyles Robarts *Mr Gunno^r of the Castell* was Buryed the 9th Day of July 1715.

Mrs Ester Farrar Widdow Dyed in the Castell and was Buryed the 22^d Day of August 1715.

Mary ye wife to Mr Thomas Williams of Bridgstreet Wett Glouer was Buryed ye 20th Day of Septem^{br} 1715.

Samuell Humprays *Drume^r to Captin Jones* Bur^d ye 26 of January 1715[-16].

John sonn to Mrs Katherine Wrench^1 Widow of Glouerstone Miflin^r Buryed ye 14th Day of March 1715[-16].

1716.

Mary Daught^r to Mr John Dewsbury of Cleton Lane Habidash^r Buryed the 14th Day of Aprill 1716.

Mrs Vrssaller Gleaue of ye Forrest Street of ye P^{ri}ish of St. Johns Widow Buryed the 27th Day of Aprill 1716.

John Arderne Gen^t Dyed att Eliz: Wood *on the Mount in Handbridge* and Bur: ye 16th Day of Nouem^{br} 1716.

1717.

Mrs Dorothy Hughson^2 of Castell lane Spinster Daught^r to Samuell Hughson Gen^t Deceased shee was Bur^d ye 26 of March 1717.

Elizabeth^3 Daught^r to Mr Johnson Manwaringe of Castell lane Buryed ye Third Day of June 1717.

Mr Robartt Jones juni^r an Attorney of Bridgstreet Buryed the 22^d Day of June 1717.

Katherine ye wife to Mr Samuell Deane of ye Parish of St. Oswells Buryed the 21 Day of July 1717.

Elizabeth Hall Widow of Glouerstone wife to Capt Hall Deceased Burye^d ye 22^d Day of July 1717.

Mrs Frances Whishaw Wife to Hugh Whishaw Gen^t of St. Bridge[t]s Parish Buryed ye 10th Day of Octob^r 1717.

Mr Henry Berkenhead^4 Linnen Draper of the Parish of St. Bridgets Bur^d ye 31 Day of Octob^r 1717.

John Measome *one of his Majest^s Gunners of Chest^r Castell* Buryed the 25th Day of January 1717[-18].

Mrs Sarah Jennings Spinst^r of Bridgstreet was Buryed the 25th Day of February 1717[-18].

1718.

. . . A Stranger *was Drowned and brought in Chance Medley* Buryed the 16th Day of April 1718.

Stephen Scailes a souldi^r from the Towne of Steben in Esex vnder Capt John Graiesent Bur^d the 17th Day of Aprill 1718.

---

^{1} The burial of the following child of Mrs. Katherine Wrench also occurs:—*Dorothy*, 28 April, 1718.
^{2} Her brother, Mr. John Hughson, is mentioned in the Churchwardens' Accounts.
^{3} Her burial is recorded on the monumental tablet formerly in the church, printed on p. 73. *See also* p. 155, note 2.
^{4} He was brother of Thomas Birkenhead of Backford, co. Chester, Esq., who died in 1724 without issue, when Henry Birkenhead's two daughters, Frances and Deborah, became coheiresses to the Backford estate.

Elizabeth Daught' to M' Thomas Gill of Castell lane an attorney Bur : y' 28th Day of May 1718.
Lydia y' Wife to M' Joseph Sorton of Bridg street of y' P'ish of St. Tollius [St. Olave's] Wett Glover Bur' y' 2d Day of December 1718.
Mary Daught' to Edward Cookesey of Handbridge Grandchild to M' Rowley *of Brewers Hall* Bur' y' 17th Day of Mar. 1718[-19].

1719.

M" Mary Morgan of Castell lane Widow was Buryed the 8th Day of Aprill 1719.
William Done' Gen' of y' P'ish of St. Peters an Attorney & Store Keeper was Buryed y' 25th Day of Aprill 1719.
John son to Johnson Manwaringe² Esq' in Trinity Parish Buryed the 29th Day of July 1719.
James Almand Gen' Dyed att M' Tho. Berkeneds of Bridgstreet Buryed the 21 Day of August 1719.
Elizabeth³ y' wife to Johnson Manwaringe² Esq' of Trinity P'ish Buryed the Second Day of Decemb' 1719.
James son to Johnson Manwaringe² Esq' of Trinity P'ish [and] of Eliz : his wife Deceased Buryed y' 7th Day of Decemb' 1719.
Charles Dicas of the Parish of St. Micheallls Curiorgan [Chirugion or Surgeon] was Buryed the 15 Day of January 1719[-20].

1720.

Mary Daughter to M' Peter Farrar of Glouer stone Stuff Weauer Buryed y' 19th Day of June 1720.
M' William Johnson of Cleton lane Wett Glouer *Sherife of this Citty Alderman of y' Companie & Chu : Warden* Bur'd y' 21 Day of Septemb' 1720.
Charles Fletcher *Wett Glover & Parish Clerk* was Buried the Sixth day of Decemb' 1720.
M" Jane Jackson Widdow Buried the third day of ffebruary 1720[-1].
William Gravor *Wett Glover and Parish Clerk* was Buried the twenty Seventh day of ffebruary 1720[-1].

1721.

John Prichard¹ *Sextone of this Church* was Buried y' 30th Day of January 1721[-2].
M" . . . . Lester Was Buried from Potters Court in Castle Lane y' 25th day of February 1721[-2].

1722.

Cathraine Daughter to M' Jn" Wright *of Brewars Hall* Esq' and Cath : his Wife Buried y' 30th day of March 1722.
Elizabeth Daughter to John Edgerton' Gen' and Elizabeth his wife of St. Oswalds Parish Buried y' 30th day of June 1722.
John Goodyear *jaylor of the Castle Prison* Buried the Eighteenth day of July 1722.
M" Martha Carden Widdow of Saltney Side Bur : y' 21st day of March 1722[-3].
M" Mary Pravares Buried from y' Bridge house y' 22d day of March 1722[-3].

1723.

Hugh Done" nephew to Hugh Whishaw Gen' of St. Bridgetts Parish buried y' 18th day of May 1723.
Samuel Garratt Yeoman of the Township of Upton & *Church Warden* of this Church Buried y' 6th day of August 1723.

---

[1] *See* the monumental inscription on p. 73.
[2] Johnson Mainwaring, of Chester, Esq., was the son of Mr. James Mainwaring, of Chester, alderman there, who purchased the manor of Bromborough in Wirrall Hundred.
[3] This Elizabeth was the daughter of Mr. John Acton, of Gloverstone, and was married to Mr. Johnson Mainwaring at St. Mary's on the 4th April, 1714 (*see* pedigree of Acton *postea*). *See* also the monumental inscription on p. 73.
[4] The burials of the following children of [? another] John Pritchard, sexton, and Elizabeth his wife, also occur :—*John*, 17 Dec. 1736; *William*, 17 Feb. 1739-40.
[5] The burial of the following child of Mr. John Egerton also occurs :—*Frances*, 1st May, 1724.
[6] *See* the monumental inscription on pp. 72-3.

X 2

1724.

Ann Daughter to Thomas Gill Gen' of Watergate Street and of Trinity Parish Buried the 28th day of March 1724.

Rebecca Wife to Mr Andrew Duke *Church Warden & Well Glover* of Bridge Street, Buried the Second day of August 1724.

Bridgett Lydeott a Strange Gentlwoman Buried from the Lady Margreat Davies' in Castle lane yr 12th day of February 1724[-5].

Mr John Cotgreave¹ Sen' Beer Brewer Under St. Marys Hill Buried the third day of March 1724[-5].

1725.

Ann Widdow & Relict of Edward Cook Gen' of Trinity Parish Buried the tenth day of September 1725.

1726.

Mr Edward Burrowes of Handbridge Alderman Buried the 22d day of Aprill 1726.

Mrs Dorothy Waireing Widdow of Forrest Street Buried ye 28th day of December 1726.

. . . . Daughter to Mr Peter Potter² Bookbinder [and stationer] & his wife of Bridge Street Buried the 23d day of March 1726[-7].

1727.

Edward Son to Mr John Skellern Mercer & Ann his Wife of Knuttsford Buried the 26th day of August.

Thomas Gill Gen' of Watergate Street Buried ye 27th of August.

Richard Jesson *late Supervisor of Excise* of Bridge Street Buried the fourteenth day of September.

William Son to Mr Daniell Porter Attorney & . his Wife of St. Bridgetts Parish Buried yr 18th day of September.

Mr Wm Williams of Cuppings Lane Buried yr 17th day of October.

1728.

Roger Gyllym Gen' of Bridge Street Buried yr 4th day of July.

Ralph Gorste Apothecary of Bridge Street Bur: yr 25th day of July.

1729.

Richard Cowband Gen' *Dr [Debtor] Prisoner Buried from the Castle* the Sixth day of Aprill.

Bartholomew Duke Inholder of Handbridge & *Church Warden* of this Parish Buried the 18th day of May.

William Ravington Baker (& *Mayor's Porter*) of Eastgate Street Buried the Seventh day of June.

Margrat Wife to John Cook *One of the Undertakers of Dee Mills* Buried the 5th day of October.

1731.

Mary Daughter to Mackworth Young Gen' of St. Martin's Parish Buried the 3d day of June.

Elizabeth Wife of Mr Lawrence Swarbreck³ of Bridgstreet *Collector of excise* Buried yr 18th day of August.

1732.

Rebeccah Wife of Pat Donough *Ensign of Invalides* burd yr 14th day of September.

Mrs Sarah Dewsbury of Clayton Lane Spinstr burd yr 29th day of January.

1733.

Frank Price⁴ *Sexton of St. Maries* buried yr 23d day of March.

His monumental inscription, still in the church, has been printed on p. 52.
² *Frances*, dau. of Peter Potter, Stationer, bur. 27 Augst, 1730.
³ "*Elizabeth* Swarbreck Spinster dau. to Mr Collector Swarbreck buried 15 July 1735."
⁴ He was married to Margaret Bailey, spinster, 13 May, 1724.

1734.

Martha Wife of Richard Price *of Upton Schoolm*ʳ burᵈ yʳ 21ˢᵗ day of Aprill.
Charles Done Genᵗ of the Parish of St. Peters Bur: yᵉ 13ᵗʰ day of December.
Christiana Wife to *Cap*ᵗⁿ Thomas Kellsall, Bur: yᵉ 10ᵗʰ day of March.

1735.

Ann Daughter to John Wright Esqʳ and Margaret his Wife Buried the Nineteenth day of September.
Frances Daughter to Mʳ Peter Potter *Sheriff of this City* & Mary his Wife Buried yʳ 29ᵗʰ day of January.

1736.

Mʳ Thomas Williams Wett Glover of Bridge Street Bur; yᵉ 14ᵗʰ day of May.
Miss Sarah Dewesbury of Clayton lane Buried the tenth day of August.
Elizabeth Jennings Daughter to Mʳˢ Carter of Clayton lane Buried the 26ᵗʰ day of September.
Mary Wife to John Killpatrick *Serjeant of Invalides* Near Gloverstone Buried the 6ᵗʰ day of ffebruary.
William Son [to] *Cap*ᵗⁿ William Witter & Ellen his Wife of Handbridge Buried the 7ᵗʰ day of March.

1737.

Gyles Roberts *Master Gunner of the Castle of Chester* Buried the twentieth day of April.
Thomas Son to John Brown *Captaine* & Mary his Wife of Bridg[e] Street Buried the 20ᵗʰ day of August.
Mʳˢ Jane Duggdail Widdow *from the Spittle in Boughton* Buried the 10ᵗʰ day of September.
Mʳ John Witter of Bridg[e] Street Apothecary Buried the 19ᵗʰ day of October.
Martha Wife to Mʳ John Dicas Barber of Bridg[e] Street Buried the 8ᵗʰ day of December.

1738.

Susannah Daughter to Mʳ Edward French *Master Gunner* & Elizabeth his wife Buried the 3ᵈ Day of April.
Ellenʳ Wife to Mʳ William Witter *Capt*ⁿ Buried the 8ᵗʰ day of June.
Mary Wife to John Killpatrick *Sarjant [of the Invalide*] Near Gloverstone Buried yʳ 30ᵗʰ day of July.
Mʳˢ Sophiah Hall Widow Near yᵉ Bridge Burᵈ yᵉ 17ᵗʰ of November.
John Clark Stranger, a person Soposed to be Murdred found in yᵉ Township of Upton in this parish Buried yᵉ 17ᵗʰ day of December.
Mary Brasscettle [sic for Bracegirdle] of Handbridge Burᵈ yᵉ 4ᵗʰ of January.

1739.

Mʳˢ Abigall Lane Widow of St. John's Parish Buried yᵉ 19ᵗʰ day of October.
Thomas Smallwood[1] Genᵗ *Deptor Prisoner in yᵉ Castle* Buried yᵉ 20ᵗʰ day of November.
Thomas Corliss Scrivenor Near yᵉ Bridge Buried yᵉ 24ᵗʰ of January.

1740.

Elizabeth Daughter to Mʳ John Wilbrahame yeoman & Mary his Wife *of yᵉ 2 Mile House* Buried yᵉ 19ᵗʰ day of April.
William Wilson *Store Keeper of yᵉ Castle* Buried yᵉ 22ᵈ day of June.

[The last Burial entry in Volume II. is dated 18 August, 1740.]

---

[1] A pedigree of Smallwood of Chelford, co. Chester, is given in *East Cheshire*, vol. ij., p. 366; but I am deubtful if the Thomas Smallwood here mentioned belonged to that family.

The *third volume* of the REGISTERS of St. Mary's is a long narrow folio volume with parchment leaves. It is in good preservation, and very voluminous. On the fly-leaf is this inscription :—

The Register of St Mary in the City of Chester and Bought at y^e Parish Cost in y^e year 1740. Paid for this Book 3$^£$ 3^s 0.

The Rev^d M^r THO^s BROOK Rector.
Mr RANDAL SORTON ⎫
W$_M$: COWPER Esqr ⎬ Ch : Wardens.
JOHN ROWLAND Clark. ⎭

The Baptisms begin on the 31st August, 1740, and end on the 27th May, 1776. They are followed by the Burials, commencing on the 26th August, 1740, and ending on the 20th July, 1782. The Marriages begin on the 29th March, 1741, and end on the 25th March, 1754, when Lord Hardwick's Marriage Act to prevent clandestine marriages came into force and a separate Register of Marriages, similar to those now in use, had to be provided.

As in the case of the previous volumes, the following extracts are those of the most importance, with the exception of those relating to the CLERGY, already given in the account of the Rectors, and those relating to the families of which pedigrees will subsequently be given.

BAPTISMS.

1741.
John Son to John Finchatt Surgeon & Eliz: his wife Near ye bridge Baptized the 3^d day of August.

1745.
Cath : Daughter to Edward Williames Esqr & Jane his Wife *of Nundane* Bap^{td} ye 29th day of March.

George Son to Mr George Griffies[1] Plumber & Hannah his Wife of bridge Street Bap^{td} ye Thirty first day of October.

Ann daughter to John Merrideth[2] *Scoolmaster* & Ellen his Wife Near ye Bridg[e] Bap^{td} ye 19th of March.

1747.
Joseph Son to George Williames *Scoolemaster* & Mary his Wife of Handbridg[e] Baptized ye 16th day of August.

Thomas Son to Thomas Slaughter Esqr & Ann his Wife Near Glover Stone Baptized ye 30th day of November.

1748.
Williame Son to Mr Ashton Johnson Skinner & Mary his Wife of Clayton Lane Bap^{td} the 3^d day of May. [Bur. 23 Feb. 1749-50.]

1750.
Robert Wyinne Son to Mr Joseph Fluitt[3] Atorney at Law & Elizabeth his Wife Near Gloverstone was Baptized ye 29 of March.

1751.
John Son to Richd Young[4] *Writeing Master* & Ursiela [*sic*] his Wife of bridge Street Bapt^d ye 1th of April.

---

[1] The baptism of the following child of Mr. George Griffies also occurs :—*Edward*, 8 May, 1747.
[2] A daughter, *Judeth*, was bur. 28 Dec. 1743.
[3] The baptism of the following child of Mr. Joseph Fluitt also occurs :—*Joseph*, 13 July, 1751.
[4] The baptism of the following child of Richard Young also occurs :—*Jane*, 12 Nov. 1756.

1752.

Elianor Daughter to Allen Holford Gen' & Elizabeth his wife Near y" bridg[e] Bap'" y" 20 of April.
Thomas Son to Rob'. Tulloh *Hair Curller* & Elizabeth his Wife of Handbrig[e] Bap'" y" 24'" of July.

1753.

Elizabeth daughter to Tho' Manwaring[1] Esq' & Frances his Wife Near Glover Stone was Baptized the 20'" day of January.
Elizabeth daughter to W'" Toleman *Watch Movement Maker* & Ann his wife of Castle Lane Bap'" y" 18'" of April.
Martha daughter to Sam" Newell yeoman & Mary his Wife *of the Mile & Half House* Bap'" y" 25 of June.

1755.

Elizabeth daughter to Rog' Cumberbech[2] Esq' & Frances his Wife Near Gloverston Bap'" y" 2'" day of Nov'. [Bur. 3 Nov. 1755.]
Kathrine Daughter to M' Jn" James Gen' & Elizabeth his wife of Bridg[e] Street was Bap'" the 26 day of Nov'.

1757.

Jane daughter to M' Robert Williams[3] Skinner & Cathrine his Wife of Clayton Lane Bap' y" 28 of December.

1758.

Ja' Harvey Son to James Ring & Manley his wife of Gloverstone Bap'" the 28'" day of March.
Watkin Son to M' Fisher Tench & Margrett his Wife of Bridg[e] street was born the 6'" day of October & Bap'" y" 10'" day of November.

1760.

Charles Son to Charles Malborn[4] *Gunner of y' Castle* & Hannah his Wife was Bap'" the 17'" day of March.
Mary daughter to *Cap'"* Edward Bennett[5] & Eliz his Wife of Clayton Lane was Bap'" the fourth day of June.

1761.

Sarah daughter to W'" Lowe *Cork cutter* & Elizabeth his wife was Bap'" the Seventh of December.

1763.

Ann Elizabeth daughter to Peter Davies[6] Esq' *of the Grove in Denbighshire* & Elizabeth his Wife was Baptized the fifth day of February.
Thomas Lee Son to M' Jn" Newell Inholder & Sarah his wife Near the Bridge was Baptized y" first day of March.
James Son to James Bailey *Pipe Maker* & Mary his Wife Near Gloverston was Baptized y" 6'" day of March.

---

[1] This Thomas Mainwaring, Esq., was most probably a younger brother of Charles Mainwaring, Esq., of Bromborough and Chester. If so, he was born in 1725, and is said to have married a daughter of James Mason, Esq., of Shrewsbury.

[2] The baptisms of the following children of Roger Comberbach, Esq., also occur :—*Edmund*, 23rd Jan. 1757, Bur. 1st June, 1763 ; *Roger*, 20 Nov. 1758 ; *Maria*, born 17 July, bapt. 3 Sept. 1760 ; *Charlotte*, born 3 Oct., bapt. 9 Nov. 1761 ; *Helen*, born 6th & bapt. 27 Dec. 1762 ; a son, *George*, buried 4 March, 1764 ; *Alice*, born 18th, bapt. 22 July, 1767. These are mostly additions to the pedigree of this Roger Comberbach, of Chester, Esq., to be found in Marshall's *Genealogical Account of the Comberbach Family*, 1866, pp. 20-1.

[3] The baptisms of the following children of Mr. Robert Williams also occur :—*William*, 17 April, 1759 ; *Kathrine*, 26 Dec. 1760 ; *Margrett*, 28 April, 1762 ; *Robert*, 1st May, 1763, Bur. 4 April, 1764. A dau. *Ann*, buried 30 Nov. 1764.

[4] The baptisms of the following children of Charles Malborn also occur :—*Jane*, 23 Sept. 1761, Bur. 26 March, 1769; *John*, 17 Sept. 1762 ; *Thomas*, 21 April, 1765 ; *Ann*, 7 May, 1767.

[5] The baptisms of the following children of Captain Edward Bennett also occur :—*Edward*, 13 Oct. 1763 ; *Mary*, 26 Sept. 1765.

[6] Peter Davies, Esq., of Broughton, co. Flint, was the fourth son of Robert Davies, Esq., of Gwysaney and Llanerch, co. Denbigh. He was born 19th Nov. 1723, and married Elizabeth, daughter of John Whitehall, Esq., of Broughton, by whom he had issue. Llanerch means the Grove or Glade.

1773. May 15. Chester County. Appointment during pleasure, of Hugh Wishaw as Seal Keeper. 39th Rpt. p. 17
1763. Hugh Whishaw of Chester, gent, authorary {clerk?} of Withington, March 21. married. Prestbury Parish Register.
1701. Sept 6. Hugh Whishaw B.A. Oxon, nominated by William Taylow, Clk A, Vicar of Prestbury and the {illeg} of Siddington, as incumbent of Siddington Chapel. East Ches. Vol II p. 405. He was son of Hugh Whishaw of Middlewich.

ST. MARY-ON-THE-HILL, CHESTER.

1764.

Frances daughter to Hugh Wishaw[1] Gentleman & Mary his Wife *of Nun Lane* was Baptized ye 23^d day of March.

Edward Son to Evan Richards *Chimney Curer* & Ann his wife of Gloverstone was Bap^{tz} ye 30th day of Septem^r.

1765.

John[2] Son to Mr Hugh Wishaw[1] Gent & Mary his Wife of Nun Lane was Baptized ye 25th day of March.

Whishaw alt^s Wishaw's both of Glover's Store in Broster's Directory of 1782.

1766.

Cathrine daughter to Thos Sellors *Comb Maker* & Cath his Wife of Handbridg[e] Bap^{tz} ye 13th of July.

1767.

Edward Son of John Glegg[3] Junr *of Irbie* Esqr & Betty his Wife born Feb^{ry} ye 16th & Baptized ye 15th of March. [Bur. 16 Feb. 1777.]

Mary daughter to Wm Kervey *Bone Cutter* & Mary his Wife of Nun Lane Bap^{tz} ye 28th day of June.

John Son of William Lawton *Drawer [of Dee]* and Margaret His Wife near the Bridge Baptiz^d ye 28 of October.

Mary Daughter of John Garner[4] Attorney at Law and Esther his Wife Baptiz^d ye 4th Day of November.

Sarah Daughter of Thos Plumbley *Peruke Maker* near the Bridge and Sarah his Wife Baptiz^d ye 25th of November.

1768.

Thomas Son of George Walker near ye Bridge Gould Smith and Sarah his Wife Baptiz^d ye 14 of Febru.

Ann Daughter of John Crane Near ye Bridge Surgeon and Margaret his Wife Baptiz: ye 17 Day of February.

Walter Son of William Hyatt *Heelmaker* of the Skinn^{rs} Lane and Mary his Wife Baptiz^d ye 12 of June.

Watkin Williams Son of Mr Edward Massey Gentleman *of Bunts Lane* & Mary his Wife Baptiz^d ye 19th of August.

1769.

Deborah Daughter of Robert Dod[5] Esqr near Gloverstone and Mary his Wife Baptiz^d ye 8th Day of March.

Sarah Daughter of John Walker[6] *Clerk of this Parish* and Elizabeth his Wife Born ye 28 day of March & Baptiz^d the 30th day of April. [Bur. 29 June, 1771.]

Maria Ann Daughter of Mr William Lawrence[7] *Store Keeper of the Castle* & Ann his wife Baptiz^d ye 14 of Dec^r. [Bur. 7 Sept. 1770.]

---

[1] The baptisms of the following children of Mr. Hugh Whishaw also occur :—*John*, 25 March, 1765 ; *Fanny*, privately bapt. 12 Oct., publicly bapt. 19 Nov. 1766, bur. 7 May, 1767 ; *Hugh*, priv. 2 Sept., publicly 29 Sept. 1767 ; *Lucy*, 12 June, 1772.

[2] John Whishaw became a very distinguished man. and in the *Gentleman's Magazine* for 1841 is this obituary notice: " Dec. 21st. Died in Wilton Crescent, John Whishaw, Esq., M.A., F.R.S., Senior Bencher of Gray's Inn. He was the elder son of the late Hugh Whishaw, Esq., of Chester, where he was born about 1764. He was educated at Macclesfield Grammar School and Trinity College, Cambridge. He edited ' Mungo Park's Travels,' and was the friend and executor of Sir Samuel Romilly."

[3] The baptism of the following child of John Glegg, Esq., also occurs :—*Betty*, 13 April, 1768, " Daughter of John Glegg, Esqr of Bridge Street." John Glegg of Irby, in the parish of Backford, co. Chester, Esq., born in 1732, married Betty, eldest daughter of John Baskervyle Glegg, of Withington and Gayton, Esq. Both he and his wife were buried at St. Mary's, the former in 1804 and the latter in 1810 (*see postea*).

[4] The baptisms of the following children of Mr. John Garner also occur :—*Sarah*, 28 April, 1769 ; *George*, 22 June, 1770.

[5] The baptism of the following child of Robert Dod, Esq., also occurs :—*Rebeckah*, 21 Nov. 1770. This Robert Dod, Esq., was of Rowton, co. Chester. He married Mary, sister to John Glegg, of Irby, Esq.

[6] The baptisms of the following children of John Walker also occur :—*John*, born 26 Oct., bapt. 31 Oct. 1770 ; *William*, 19 Jan, 1776, Bur. 4 Feb. 1776.

[7] The baptisms of the following children of Mr. William Lawrence also occur :—*Ann*, 31 Oct. 1774 ; *William*, born 7 Sept., bapt, 6 Oct. 1775 ; *Mariah*, dau. of William Lawrence, Esq., Store Keeper, bur. 10 April, 1781 ; *Lucy Milbourn*, 2 April, 1778 ; *Paul Henry*, 21 April, 1779 ; *Paul Sandby*, 3 Oct, 1781 ; *Edwin Grindley*, 7 Oct. 1782 ; *Charlotte Maria*, 20 March, 1785.

1771.

Esther Daughter of William Briscall *Button mould Turner* and Margaret his Wife Baptiz^d ye 19 day of April.

1772.

Ann Daughter of Faithfull Thomas' *Gaoler of ye Castle* & Ann his Wife Baptiz^d the 17 day of July. [Bur. 1st June, 1774.]

1773.

Mary Daughter of William Thomas Esqr & Margaret his Wife Baptiz^d ye 14 day of June.

Francis Daughter of Samuel Neils *Thread Maker* & Hannah his Wife Baptiz^d the first day of October.

1775.

William Son of Edward Shallcross *Fr^{o}me work Knitter* and Mary his Wife Baptiz^d ye 3^d day of Septem^r.

1776.

John Son of John Taylor *Brass Founder* & Margaret his Wife Baptiz^1 ye 7 day of April.

[Last entry of a Baptism in Volume III. 27 May, 1776.]

MARRIAGES.

1744.

Thomas Walford of Manchester in the County of Lancaster Chapman & Mary Hayward spinester of this parish were Married by Licence the 12th day of Aprill.

Daniell Hesse of Richman [Richmond] in ye County of York and Diocess of Chester Merchant & Elizabath Porter of this parish spinester were Maried by Licence ye 26th day of Septem^r by ye Revd Mr Greves.

1745.

Marriages celebrated by the Rev. Mr Wilcock, Rev. Mr Hinchman, Rev. Mr Greaves, Rev. Mr Jackson, and Rev. Mr Wiston.

1746.

Samuell Gaddes Gen^t & Alice Edwards Spinester both of this parish were Maried by Licence ye 31st day of March.

A marriage celebrated by the Rev. Mr Duke.

1747.

Most marriages celebrated by the Rev. Mr John Prince, *Curate*, one by the Rev. Mr Thomas Duke, and one by the Rev. Mr Barsley.

1748.

Marriages celebrated by the Rev. John Prince, the Rev. John Wilbraham, *Rector*, the Rev. Nath. Phillpot, and the Rev. Charles Hinchman.

1750.

William Sanders of the parish of Camberwell in ye County of Surry Batchelor & Elizabeth Rolph of the parish of St. George Hanover Square in the County of Middlesex Spinester were Maried by Licence ye 26 day of September.

Two marriages celebrated by the Rev. Mr. Sewell.

1754.

Arnold Birch of Manchester woollin Draper & Ann Hayward of this parish Spinester were Married by Licence the 4th day of Feb^y.

Edward Jones Gen^t & Mary Halliwell Spinster of Pulford were Married by Licence ye 21st day of Feby by ye Revd Mr Bradshaw.

---

[1] The baptisms of the following children of Mr. Faithfull Thomas also occur : *Maria*, 17 Jan. 1776 ; a son, *Faithfull*, buried 27 Oct. 1772 ; *Georgina*, 6 June, 1777, the father being then described as Deputy Constable of the Castle ; *George*, 28 June, 1780.

Y

Mr Thos Duke *wett glover* & Mary Croughton, Spinester, were Married by Licence ye 28th day of Feb{ry} both of this parish.

[Last entry of a Marriage in Volume III. 25 March, 1754.]

[*MARRIAGES*[1]—*(continued).*]

1754.
Richard Janeway of the parish of Manchester and Frances Buckley of this parish, by Licence, 25th Oct. 1754, by John Wilbraham [rector] clerk.

1755.
Hamnett Dobb of this parish, Gentleman, and Grace Meacock of Great Stanney, spinster, by Licence, 4th January 1755, by J. Prince, *Curate*.

William Hamilton of the parish of Saint Oswald, Gentleman, and Elizabeth Tonna of this parish, spinster, married by Licence 10th February 1755, by J. Prince, *Curate*.

1757.
Charles Wilbraham of this parish and Mary Baxter of the parish of Little Barrow, by Licence 27th Novr 1757 by John Wilbraham, *Rector*.

1758.
Richard Wicksted of this parish gentleman and Frances Ransted of the parish of St. John Baptist, married by Licence 7th May 1758 by John Wilbraham.

1760.
The Revd John Tench of Wrenbury in the county of Chester, clerk, and Mary Cotton of this parish spinster married by Licence 7th October 1760 by Thos Davies, Minister.

1764.
John Gresty of this Parish Gentleman [attorney crossed out] and Margaret Ords of the parish of St. Peter in Chester, by Licence, 30th July 1764, by Joseph Eaton *Curate*.

1771.
Samuel Thomas of this Parish, Gentleman, and Mary Chatterton of this Parish, spinster, were married by Licence the 6 Nov. 1771, by S. Boswell.

1775.
Alexander Denton M.D. of this Parish, and Ann Ridgway of Poolton in the Parish of Pulford, were married by Licence the 11th Oct. 1775 by Sam. Boswell.

BURIALS.

1740.
Mrs Sarah Barrington Widow of St. John' Parish Buried the 3d day of September.
Mrs Ann Dannald Widow Near ye Bridge Bur{d} ye 12th of September.
Ann Wife to Mr George Prescott[2] Marchant of Bridg[e] street Buried ye 24th day of September.
Mrs Mary Johnson Widow of Clayton lane Bur{d} 21 Decemr.
Mr Joseph Sorton Wett Glover of St. Olives Parish was Buried the 15th day of Jany.

1741.
Edward Son to George Tims *Actor* & Mary his Wife Buried ye 27th day of April.
Mr James Smith yeoman Near ye bridg[e] Bur{d} ye 13th day of December.
Mr Charles Cottingham Wett Glover Near ye bridge Buried the twenty first day of March.

---

[1] The marriages after March, 1754, are entered in a separate volume, kept for Marriages only, in which full particulars of the parties married are entered, and their signatures are appended as is the case at the present time.

[2] Mr. George Prescott, of Bridge Street, merchant, was the ancestor of the family of the Baronets of that name now living in Sussex and Kent. *See* under local families *postea*.

1742.

Mr Peter Potter Stationer of St. Michailes Parish was Buried the 6th day of August.

Elizabeth Daughter to John Wilkinson[1] Apothecary & Martha his Wife of Clayton lane Bur^d ye 6th of Novem^r.

Mary Daughter to Cap^{tn} Jno Brown[2] Mariner & Mary his Wife of St. Olives parish was Buried ye 13th of February.

1743.

Charles Son to Mr Charles Moulson[3] Tallow Chandler & Mary his Wife of Cupings lane Bur^d ye 25th of Aprill.

Mrs Cath: Pemberton Widow of ye parish of ye Holy Trinity was buried the 29th of Aprill.

Elizabeth Wife to Mr Thos Duke *Alder^n of this City* Near ye Bridge was Buried ye 21th day of June.

Mrs Mary Manwaring *Maiden Gentlewoman* Near Gloverstone was Bur^d the Second day of November.

Mr Thomas Heathley Atorney of Gloverstone was Buried the 22^d day of March.

1744.

Cap^{tn} Williame Witter Wett Glover of Handbridge was Buried the 21th day of April.

Mr John Wilbraham yeoman *of ye 2 Mile House* Bur^d ye 19th of October.

Maurice Son to Mrs Mary Jones Widow *of Carnarvon* Buried the 7th day of January.

1745.

Mr Samuell Denton Gen^t under St. Mary^s Hill Bur^d ye 3^d of June.

Rowland Jones *Officer of Excise of Wrexham* was Buried the Seventh day of June.

Martha Wife to Mr George Hayward *Dry Glover* was Buried the 14th day of July.

Elizabeth Bingley Widow *Mistress of the poore House* Buried the 16th day of Septem^r.

Sarah Daughter to Mr Jno Rowley[4] book binder & Sarah his Wife of St. Michales parish Bur^d ye 31th of October.

Mr William Bridges Atorney at Law of ye parish of the Holy Trinity was Bur^d ye 7th day of November.

Mr John Johnson *Manchester Dealer* of St. Michails parish was Buried the 23^d day of January.

George Rogerson *of Liverpoole* Buried ye 13th day of February.

Fredrick Son to Dan^{ll} Hess[5] Marchant & Elizabeth his Wife Buried the 21th day of March.

1746.

Mr John Ward *Adujdent* [sic] bellonging to my Ld Chomundlay Ridgment was Bur^d ye 27th of March.

Mr Joseph Hodson *Deptor in ye Castle* Bur^d ye 29th of April.

Margrett Wife to Mr Geo: Scott over ye Bridge Gate was Buried the 7th day of June.

David Littler *Perruge Maker* [sic for peruke maker] of Handbridg[e] Bur^d ye 13th of July.

Edward French *Master Gunner of ye Castle* Bur^d ye 16th of July.

Mrs Cath. Wrench Widow of Cast[le] lane Bur^d ye 2^d day of October.

Mr James Fleck yeoman of Handbridge Bur^d ye 29th of October.

William Hannah, *Gunner of ye Castle* Bur^d ye 14th day of December.

Mrs Hannah Taylor Near Gloverstone Bur^d ye 26th day of February.

1747.

Edward Twanebrook *Deptor prisoner of ye Castle* Bur^d ye 31th of July.

---

[1] The burial of the following child of John Wilkinson also occurs:—*John*, 29th April, 1744. "Martha wife to John Wilkinson" was buried 22 Sept. 1744.

[2] The burial of the following child of Capt. John Brown also occurs:—*Mary*, 20 Oct. 1748.

[3] *Ann*, dau. to Mr. Charles Moulson, bur. 2 Sept. 1759.

[4] The burials of the following children of Mr. John Rowley also occur:—*John*, 6 Sept. 1748; *John*, 16 Jan. 1753; *Frances*, 23 Dec. 1764; *William*, 25 Oct. 1771.

[5] See his marriage in 1744, p. 161.

Henry Frith Atorney Near ye Bridge Bur^d ye 10th day of November.
John Son to Mr John Cooke, Miller Buried from Handbridg[e] the 3^d day of February.
Mrs Jane Davies Widow of Castle lane Buried the 25th of February.
Mr George Prescot^1 Merchant of Bridg[e] Street Buried the 19th day of March.
Mr Stephen Sones Malster Near ye bridge Bur^d ye 23^d day of March.

1748.
Mr George Hayward dry Glover of Castle Lane Bur^d ye 7th of July.
John Jackson *Goaler of ye Castle* Buried the 10th day of August.
Arthur Denton Gen^t of St. John^s parish was Buried ye 18th day of November.

1749.
Mary Wife to Mr James Walley Hatter Near the Bridg[e] was Buried ye 2^d day of April.
Mrs Mary Owens Spinester *of Nun lane* Buried ye 13th day of September.
Mr John Snow *Single Alt^r of this City* Near Glover Stone was Buried the 7th day of October.
Mr Hugh Wishaw^2 Gen^t of Hocknull Bur^d ye 29th of January.
Mrs Rebecka Burkenhead ^{3} Widow of Bridg[e] Street Bur^d ye 30th of January.

1750.
Mary Wife to Mr Joseph Snow^4 Merchant of St. O[s]walds Parish was Buried the Eleventh day of October.

1751.
Mrs Kathrine Brewen Widow Near the Bridge was Buried the fourth day of October.

1752.
Kennedy Lancelot Son to C^d Crosby^5 & Deborah his Wife of Bridge Street Bur^d ye 14th day of August.
Sarah Wife to Mr Joseph Sorton *Wet glover* of St. Olives parish was Bur^d ye 29th day of December.

1753.
Mr John Evans Inholder Near ye Bridge was buried the 2^d day of January.

1754.
Mr Joseph Snow^6 Merch^t of St. Oswells parish was Buried the first day of Feb^y.
Mary Wife to Mr Jno Smith yeoman of Newton Bur^d ye 5th of Nov^r.

1755.
John Wrench Gent^n of Handbridge Buried ye 16th day of Jan^y.
Joseph Merrideth^7 *School Master of St. Peters parish* was Buried the 26th day of Jan^y.
Eliz Wife to Mr James Walley *Ald^n* Bur^d ye 6 day of April.
Mrs Margrett Lonsdale *Maiden Gentlewoman* of St. peters parish was Buried ye 16th day of April.
Mary Wife to Mr William Thompson Watchmaker of Castle Lane was Bur^d ye 18th day of October.
Joanah daughter to Griffith Jones *School Master* & Ann his Wife *of Clayton lane* Bur^d ye first of Decem^r.

1756.
Mr Lawrence Swarbreck *Late Collector of ye Excise* was Buried the first day of April.

---

^{1} *See* note 2, p. 162.
^{2} *See* the short inscription on p. 53. The manor of Hockenhull in Cheshire was bought in 1713 by Mr. Hugh Whishaw, of Chester, and was sold by his son and successor in 1761 to John Walsh, Esq., M.P. (Lyson's *Cheshire*, p. 797).
^{3} She was the widow of Mr. Henry Birkenhead, who was buried at St. Mary's in 1717 (*see* p. 154). Her two daughters, Frances and Deborah, became coheiresses to the Backford estate.
^{4} "*John* son to Mr Joseph Snow merchant of St. Oswalls parish" was buried 23 May, 1751, and *Anthony*, another son, was buried 18 July, 1752.
^{5} *See* note 6, p. 165.
^{6} *See* the long inscription on his mural tablet, printed on p. 52.
^{7} On the 28 Dec. 1743 Judeth daughter of J^{no} Merredith Schoolmaster and Ellin his wife of Bridgestreet was buried.

Richard[1] Son to Ald[n] Peter Dewshury & Lettice his wife of St. Michailes parish was Buried y[e] 20th day of August.
John Gregory Lifetentent bellonging to His Majesty's Garrison in Chester was Buried y[e] 2[d] day of September.
James Walley Ald[n] of this City was Bur[d] y[e] 10th day of October.
M[rs] Mary Crestey Widow of the Castle was Bur[d] y[e] 27th day of October.

1757.

John Woodfin Schoole Master of Glover Stone Bur[d] y[e] 1st of Febr[y].
M[r] John Bradock Grocer Near Gloverstone was Buried the 16th day of Feb[y].
Thomas Son to Ald[m] Duke Bur[d] from St. peters parish the 11th day of Aprill.
M[rs] Hannah Burrows Widow Neare Gloverstone was Buried the Eight day of July.
John Son to M[r] Charles Cottingham of y[e] parish of St. Oswalls was Buried the 24th day of August.
Davied Jones Grocer of Llanvor in Angleysey was Buried y[e] 16th day of October.
Thomas Caldecott Serj: of y[e] Invaleeds Buried y[e] 7th day of December.

1758.

M[r] Joseph Sorton Wett Glover of St. Ollives parish was Buried the 28th day of February.
Richard Price School master of y[e] Township of Upton was Buried the 27th day of March.
John Killpatrick[2] Serj: of y[e] Invalleeds was Bur[d] y[e] 9th day of December.

1759.

M[r] Joseph Witter Wett Glover of Handbridge was Buried the 26th day of February.
M[rs] Phillipa Simpson Maiden Gentlewoman of St. Oswells parish was Buried the 20th day of March.
John Cotgreve[3] Ald[n] of y[e] City was Bur[d] y[e] 11th day of April.
Miss Juliana Daughter to Cap[tn] Nicholas Weller & Katherine his Wife of Bridge Street was Buried y[e] 25[th] day of April.
M[rs] Elizabeth Jackson Maiden Gentlewoman of St Bridgets parish was Buried the Elleventh day of May.

1760.

Ann Daughter to W[m] Dix[4] Gentleman & Ann [his] Wife of St. Owsewells parish was Buried the 29[th] day of April.
M[rs] Elizabeth Brea[r]ton Widow of Gloverstone Bur[d] y[e] 11[th] day of June.
The Rev[d] M[r] Ralph Vernon[5] of Bridge street was Buried the 31[st] day of July.
George Buckton Son to M[r] W[m] Earle Stay Maker & Margratt his Wife Near Gloverstone Bur[d] y[e] 3[d] day of October.
[Several entries of the burials of soldiers "of the Lincolnshire Militia" are entered this year.]

1762.

. . . . Crosby[6] Col[l] of Bridge Street was Bur[d] y[e] 9th day of January.
M[rs] Hannah Vernon[7] Widow of Water gate Street Bur[d] y[e] 2[d] day of Feb[y].

---

[1] See his monumental inscription, p. 55.
[2] "Susannah Wife to Jn[o] Kilpatrick Serj: of y[e] Invalleeds Bur[d] y[e] 15th of November," 1757.
[3] Mary his wife was buried 19th May, 1758. He is described as " of Handbridge."
[4] The burial of the following child of Mr. William Dix also occurs :—Thomas, 24 Dec. 1764.
[5] His monumental tablet, which describes him as "Chaplain to the Right Honourable the Earl of Cholmondeley," has been printed on p. 74.
[6] Charles Crosbie, Esq., a Lieutenant-colonel in the army, married Deborah, the second daughter and coheiress of Henry Birkenhead of Chester, brother of Thomas Birkenhead of Backford, co. Chester, Esq. Henry Birkenhead was buried at St. Mary's on the 31 Oct., 1717 (see p. 154). She had previously married William Glegg of Grange, Esq., by whom she had issue. She die[d] 6 March, 1795, aged 88.
[7] She may have been the widow of the Rev. Ralph Vernon (see note 5).

Elizabeth Wife to M'r Charles Manwaring Gen'l of Castle Lane was Buried the 19th day of May.
M'rs Sarah Oulton spinester of St. peters parish was Buried the 24th day of May.
M'r George Plews *Excies man* of St. Bridgets parish was Buried the 3d day of October.

1763.
Peter Son to M'r William Linney of St. Michailes parish was Buried y'e 27th day of December.

1764.
Mary daughter to James Dunn Gen'l & Anne his Wife of St. Michailes parish Bur'd y'e 14th day of March.
Sarah Wife to M'r Thomas Bagg *Supervisor* Near the Bridge was Buried y'e 15th day of March.
Grace daughter to M'rs Mary Boughton Near the Bridg[e] was Buried y'e 4th day of April.
M'rs Mary Crachley Widow of Handbridge was Buried the Sixth day of April.
Charles Turner[1] Gen'l of Gloverston was Bur'd y'e 15th of April.
Rich'd Son to M'r Rich'd Whitehead *jaylor of the Castle* & Margrett his Wife Bur'd y'e 24th of April.
Miss Mary Eaton[2] daughter to M'rs Mary Eaton Gentlewoman of Cupings Lane Was Buried y'e 22d day of May.
Ann Wife to M'r George Walker Skinner of Handbridge was Buried the 9th day of October.
Thomas Duke[3] *Ald'm of y'e City* Near y'e Bridge was Buried the 23d day of Nov'r.
M'rs Margrett Sawyer Widow of Cupings Lane Bur'd y'e 26th day of December.
M'r Sam'll Dicas *Stay Maker* of Cupings Lane Bur'd y'e 27th of December.

1765.
M'r Peter Wilbraham[4] Gentleman of S't Johns parish was Buried the Second day of March.
M'r George Scott Near y'e Bridge was Bur'd y'e 3d day of March.
Richard Young *Writing Master* of Bridge Street was Buried the Sixth day of March.
M'rs Margrett Alderoft[5] Widow Near y'e Bridge was Bur'd y'e 16th of April.
Richard Whitehead *Gaoler of y'e Castle* Bur'd y'e 10th of May.
A Strang[e] Child Cald Jn'o Row Bur'd by y'e parish y'e 16th of July.
Magdalone Ford *one of y'e foundling Children* was Buried y'e 8th day of Nov'r.
Richard Son to Jn'o Whitehead *jaylor of the Northgate* was Bur'd y'e 13th day of Nov'r.
Mathew Blacke *a foudling Child* Bur'd y'e 3d day of December.

1766.
M'rs Mary Eyton[6] Widow of Cupings Lane Bur'd y'e 27th of Jan'r.
M'rs Mary Wilbraham[7] of S't Johns parish Widow was Buried the 3d day of Feb'r.
Rebecka Wife to M'r John Fernall *of Brewars Hall* was Buried the 26th day of Feb'r.
Jane Wife to M'r Edward Wrench of Castle lane Bur'd y'e 21st of May.
Elizabeth daughter [to] M'r Jn'o Lyle *Store Keeper of the Castle* was Buried the 22d day of December.
Mary daughter to M'r William Thomas[8] Marrinor & Jane his Wife of St. Martins parish Bur'd y'e 31st day of December.

1767.
Charles Malbon *Master Gunner of y'e Castle* was Buried the 29th day of May.
Cap't John Brown of St. Olives Parrish Burried y'e 20th Day of Sep'r.

---

[1] Called "*Captain* Turner" in the Churchwardens' Accounts.
[2] See the monumental inscription to the *Eyton* family of Pentre Maddock, co. Salop, printed on p. 54.
[3] See his monumental inscription on p. 54. His death is there said to have taken place on the 27th Nov.
[4] See his monumental inscription on p. 75, in which he is styled Captain Peter Wilbraham.
[5] See note 2, p. 95.
[6] See note 2 above.
[7] Widow of Capt. Peter Wilbraham. See the inscription on p. 75 and note 4 above.
[8] Called "*Captain* Thomas" in the Churchwardens' Accounts. See the inscription to the Eyton family, p. 54.

THE REGISTERS OF ST. MARY'S. 167

Miss . . . . Longsdale of St. Johns Parrish Burried the 26 Day of October.[1]
John Rowland *Clerk of St. Marys* Buried y[e] 13 Day of Decm[r].

1768.

Latitia[2] Wife of John Dennis of S[t] Michaels Parrish Buried y[e] 16 Day of January.
Mary Wife of John Whitehead *Golar of the North Gate* Buried y[e] 24 Day of January.
Roger Wilbraham[3] Esq[r] of S[t] Michaels Parrish Buried y[e] 28 Day of January.
Ann Dunn *Gentlewoman* of St. Oswalds Parr[h] Buried y[e] 8 Day of March.
Ann Daughter of John Crane Surgeon Near the Bridge and Margaret his Wife Buried y[e] 9th Day of July.
Thomas Prescott[4] Esq[r] Buried y[e] 11th Day of November.

1769.

James Son of William Rowe[5] *Officer* & Margaret his Wife Buried y[e] 4th Day of January.
Mary Wife of John Price *of Upton School Master* Buried y[e] 11th day of October.
M[rs] Mary Crachley Widow Buried y[e] 13th day of October.
Cap[t] William Thomas[6] Buried y[e] first day of November.
M[rs] Elizabeth Jackson *Widow Gentlewoman* Bur[d] y[e] 28 Decm[r].

1770.

M[r] John Lyle *Store Keeper of the Castle* Buried y[e] 15 of June.
M[r] Rob[t] Williams Skinner Buried y[e] 23 day of August.
Charles Manwaring Esq[r] Buried 29th day of Sep[r].
M[rs] Dorothy Crachley *Maiden Gentlewoman* Buried 26 of Octo[r].
Joseph Son of M[rs] Elizabeth Hare Widow Buried the 25 day of Dec[r].

1771.

M[rs] Letitia Haslehurst *Widow Gentlewoman* Buried y[e] 27 of Ap[l].
Mary Wife of M[r] John Fearnall *of Brewers Hall* Buried the 19th day of September.

1772.

M[r] William Glover Gentleman Buried y[e] 8 day of January.
M[rs] Ann Glover *Widow Gentlewoman* Buried y[e] 4th of February.
John Price *Schoolmaster* Buried y[t] 2[d] day of April.
Jane Wife of Holme Burrows[7] Alderman Buried the 22 day of April.
Elizabeth Wife of John Cooke[8] *School Master* Buried y[e] 7 of Nov[r].
George Williams *a Show man*[9] Buried y[e] 7 day of Nov[r].

[1] She was buried "in the Rectors Chancel" (Churchwardens' Accounts).
[2] *See* the monumental inscription on p. 55.
[3] His monumental inscription, still in the church, has been printed on p. 51.
[4] *See* note 2, p. 162.
[5] Called "*Lieutenant* Rowe" (Churchwardens' Accounts).
[6] *See* the inscription to the Eyton family on p. 54.
[7] *See* Burials, 1776.
[8] "*William*, Son of John Cooke, School Master, and Martha his wife." bur. 20 Sep[t]. 1778; *Moses and Aaron*, twins, buried 23 Dec. 1779.
[9] This was the unfortunate showman whose place of entertainment in Water Street was blown up by an accidental explosion of gunpowder on Thursday, Nov. 5, 1772. This, which is generally known as "the PUPPET SHOW EXPLOSION," caused a great loss of life and excited the greatest commiseration throughout the city. It appears from a contemporary narrative that "on the previous day a quantity of gunpowder, upwards of 800 pounds weight had been deposited in a warehouse in Watergate-street under a building known by the name of Eaton's Room, in which one Williams the master of a Puppet-show had for some time past exhibited his performances. The company which these idle amusements had drawn together on the fatal evening was very great. In the midst of their merriment the powder, by what accident is not known, took fire and in a moment most of the unhappy people were buried under a prodigious heap of ruins." Twenty-three were killed at once or died shortly afterwards, whilst over eighty were seriously injure[d], fifty-three of whom were treated at the Chester Infirmary, then newly opened. "Williams himself, his wife and three or four of the same family are of the number of the dead."
A sermon preached at Chester on Nov. 8, 1772, by John Chidlaw, was published at Shrewsbury, and speedily ran through

Elizabeth Wife of the said Williams Buried y' 7 day of Nov'.
George Son of the before nam'd George Williams & Elizabeth his Wife Buried y" 9 day of Nov'.
Margaret Wife of *Rev'* Robert Shearing Buried the 12 day of December.

1773.
Grace Jones *Maiden Gentlewoman* Buried y" 21 Day of January.
Peter Dewsbury¹ *Alderman of this City* Buried the 23 Day of February.
M" Mary Potter Widow Buried y" 5 day of March.
Sarah Daughter [to] M' John Jones Gentleman & Sarah his Wife Buried y" 8 day of Dec'.

1774.
Ann Wife of James Totty *Officer of Excise* Buried y" 13 day of February.

1775.
M" Hannah Whiteman Widow Buried y' 24 of Sep'.
Ann Wife of M' William Lawrence *Store Keeper of the Castle* Buried y" 17 day of November.

1776.
Rev' Robert Shearing Buried y' 9 day of June.
Holme Burrowes² *Ald" of this City* Buried the 24 day of July.

1777.
M' Edward Wrench Gentleman Buried y" 15th day of January.

1778.
Edward Massie Attorney at Law Buried y" 10 day of April.
Benedicta Helena Dix Spinster Buried y" 8 day of November.

1779.
M' William Anderson *Ensign of the Invalids* Buried the 26 Day of April.
M" Mary Middleton³ Widow Gentlewoman Buried y" 21" of Oct'.
M" Sarah Snow Spinster Buried y" 20th day of December.
Cap' John Fearnall Mariner Buried y" 23d day of December.

1780.
Hugh Whishaw⁴ Attorney at Law Buried y" 9th of Jan'.
William Thompson Watchmaker Buried y" 1" of March.
Mary Wife of Peter Swinton Esq' M: D: Buried the 30" day of September.
John Son of *Cap'* John Pigott of the 56 Regm' by Mary his Wife Buried y" 15th day of December.

1781.
Matilda Daughter of Richard Joynson Lab' by Elizabeth his Wife Buried y" 14th day of February. [Bapt. 11 Feb. 1781.]
William Dix Attorney at Law Buried y" 22d day of August.

[Last entry of Burials in Volume III. 20 July, 1782.]

three editions. Another sermon, by Joseph Jenkins, A.M., "occasioned by a dreadful explosion of gun-powder in Chester," was printed at Wrexham. But the most interesting, and now by far the rarest, pamphlet on the subject, was one entitled "The Explosion: or an Alarming Providential Check to Immorality A Poem . . . by a Citizen of Chester . . . Printed by the Author . . . MDCCLXXIII." I have copies of all these publications, and at the end of the last is the complete list (in manuscript) of the names of the 53 persons who were admitted to the Infirmary, with an account of their injuries. The anonymous author of the above poem was John Bowden, a native of Chester, who was born there in 1747 and died in 1818.

¹ See his monumental inscription on p. 55.

² Mr. Holme Burrows was the son of Mr. Isaac Burrows, of Chester, by his wife Katherine, sister of the last Randle Holme. See the Holme pedigree *postea*.

³ In the Churchwardens' Accounts her burial is referred to as that of "Mary Middleton gent. in Mr. William Ratcliffe's vault, by his permission."

⁴ See the short inscription to his memory on p. 55 and note 3 on p. 73.

The *fourth volume* of the REGISTERS of St. Mary's is, like the last two, a long narrow folio volume with parchment leaves. It is in good preservation and is very voluminous, containing Baptisms and Burials only. On the fly-leaf is this inscription :—

The Register of St Mary on the Hill in the City of Chester of Baptisms and Burials.

The Revd Mr ROBERT HILL, Rector.
The Revd Mr SAMUEL BOSWELL, curate.
JOHN WALKER, Parish Clerk.

The Baptisms begin on the 29th May, 1776, and end on the 13th December, 1812, and the Burials begin on the 22nd July, 1782, and end on the 1st April, 1812, the entries in some of the later years after 1800 being very carelessly kept.

The following are the most important entries, except those relating to the CLERGY, given in the account of the Rectors, and those made use of in the pedigrees subsequently to be given.

BAPTISMS.

1776.

Ann Daughter of Alexander Denton[1] M : D : & Ann his Wife Baptiz^d ye 6 day of September.

1778.

Edward Bennett Son of Robert Oldham *Perukemaker* & Alice his Wife Baptiz^d ye 18 day of January.

1779.

George Son of Dennis Edson Architect by Sarah his Wife Baptiz^d ye 13 day of June.

1780.

Margaret Daughter of John Mason[2] *School Master* by Marg^t his Wife Baptiz^d ye 23^d day of April.

1781.

Grace Daughter of John Lloyd Gentleman by Martha his Wife Baptiz^d ye 27th day of July.

1782.

Harriot Daughter of Thos Cuming Esqr by Mary his wife Born the 20th day of February.
Alfred natural Son of Mary Cardew Gentlewoman Baptiz^d ye 15th day of March.
William Son of John Letman Chymist by Mary his Wife Baptiz^d ye 14th day of July.

1785.

Emily Daughter of Hamnett Dobb Esqr *of Mollington* by Mary his wife Baptiz^d the 1st of December

1786.

Catharine Daughter of Mr Witter, Chandler by Sarah his Wife of Cuppins Lane Bapt^d Mar. 24th.
William Son of Mr Wm Linney[3] *Staymaker* by Jane his wife Bapt^d April ye 7th.
Jane Daughter of Mr Richd Denson Currier by . . . . his Wife baptiz^d July ye 3^d.
Thomas Son of Mr Saml Brittain[4] of Upton by Martha his Wife Baptiz^d Nov. ye 23^d.

---

[1] The baptisms of the following children of Dr. Alexander Denton also occur :—*Elizabeth*, 23 July, 1777 ; *John*, 8 July, 1778.

[2] The baptism of the following child of John Mason also occurs :—*John*, 17 Nov. 1782.

[3] The baptism of the following child of William Linney also occurs:—*Joseph*, June 13, 1792—father described as a "Pawnbroker." A dau. *Sidney* was buried 12 May, 1785 ; a dau. *Elizabeth* bur. 9 June, 1790.

[4] The baptisms of the following children of Mr. Samuel Brittain also occur :—*Samuel* (by Anne his wife), 16 Nov. 1803 ; the father described as Gentleman ; *Anne*, 27 Sept. 1805 ; *Charles*, 15 Nov. 1810, born 6 Sept. 1806—father described as Esquire ; *William*, 15 Nov. 1810, born 8 July, 1808 ; *Thomas*, 15 Nov. 1810, born 27th March, 1810.

ST. MARY-ON-THE-HILL, CHESTER.

1787.

Betsy Maria Daughter of Wm Slater¹ *Schoolmaster* by Eliz his wife Baptiz'd March ye 18th.
Sophia Daughter of James Strattan *Engineer of the Castle of Chester* by Peggy his wife Baptiz'd March 25th.
Jane Illigetimate Daughter of Dr Griffith Rowlands by Martha Cornelius Baptiz'd July ye 6th.
Mary Daughter of John Smith² *Attorney* by Mary his Wife Baptiz^d October ye 2nd.
James Preston Son of Mr Jno Ridgway Malster by Ann his Wife Baptiz^d November ye 12th.

1788.

Ann Daughter of Mr Joseph Bage Paper Maker by Ann his wife Baptiz^d Dec. ye 17th.

1789.

James³ son of John Smith Attorney, near Gloverstone, by Mary his wife, Baptiz^d Jany ye 18th.
Francis Son of Stewkly Shuckburgh⁴ Esqr & Charlotte Catherine his wife Baptiz'd April ye 7th born March ye 12th.
Sarah D^r of George Mostyn *of Knutsford* by Anne his wife Baptiz'd July ye 25th.
John Son of John Moulton *School Master* by Ann his wife Baptiz'd Augt ye 7th.
John William Son of Saml Pemberton⁵ *Sec^y to the House of Industry* by Jane his wife Baptiz'd Augt ye 19th.

1790.

Richard Son of Lawrence Durack *Dancing Master* by Eliz his wife Bapt^d July 28th.

1792.

Edward Porter Son of Joseph Bozley Att^y at Law by Dorothy his wife Baptiz'd Feby ye 27th Born Nov. 9th 1791.

1793.

Mary Daughter of Mr Wm Gaman⁷ *of Brewers hall* by Mary his wife Baptiz^d Jany 29th born Sepr 27th 1792.

1794.

Charles Herbert Son of *Major* Charles Martin⁸ *of the Invalids* by Eliza his wife Baptiz^d Jany ye 5th.
Ann Daughter of Mr Wm Newell⁹ Merchant by Sarah his wife Baptiz'd Augt ye 7th Born Novr 2nd 1793.

---

¹ The baptisms of the following children of William Slater also occur :— *Ann*, 2 July, 1788, Bur. 1 Mar. 1789; a son, *William*, Bur. 22 April, 1789 ; *Mary*, 24 Nov. 1790. Bur. 20 April, 1792 ; *Mary*, 27 May, 1792, Bur. 20 Aug. 1792—father described as of Manchester ; *Ann*, 24 Jan^y, 1794.

² The baptisms of the following children of Mr. John Smith also occur :— *James*, 18 Jan^y, 1789 ; *Charles*, 22 Jan. 1795 ; *Prichard*, 23 Feb. 1797 ; *John*, 26 Nov. 1798. Mr. John Smith, who was Town Clerk of Chester and died at Liverpool in April, 1808, married Mary, daughter of Charles Mainwaring, of Bromborough, Esq., at St. John's, Chester, on the 15 May, 1786.

³ This James Smith became a distinguished man. He matriculated at Oxford from Brasenose College, 7 July, 1809, aged 20, and took his B.A. degree in 1813, and that of M.A. in 1815. He was Fellow of his College from 1816 to 1838, and Vice-Principal from 1832 till his death on the 22 Sept. 1838. He died at Liverpool, and a monumental tablet was placed to his memory on the wall of Brasenose College Chapel.

⁴ *Charlotte*, dau. of Stukeley Shuckburg, Esq., bur. 28 July, 1791.

⁵ The baptisms of the following children of Samuel Pemberton also occur :— *Mary*, 20 April, 1791; *Mary Ann*, Feb. 13th. 1795, born 21 Sept. 1790 ; *Ellen*, 13 Feb. 1795, born 19 Augst, 1792.

⁶ The baptism of the following child of Mr. Joseph Bozley also occurs :—*Ann*, 11 Feb. 1798, born 22 Sept. 1794.

⁷ The baptisms of the following children of Mr. William Gaman also occur :— *Christian*, 13 Feb. 1794 ; *George*, 7th May, 1800, born 13 March, 1800.

⁸ The baptisms of the following children of Major Charles Martin also occur :—*John Williams*, 22 April, 1795—father described as Colonel ; *Elisabeth*, May 10th, 1797, born 28 Oct. 1796—father described as Lieut.-Col.

⁹ The baptisms of the following children of Mr. William Newell also occur :— *John*, 3 Feb. 1796, born 3 June, 1795, Bur. 29 April, 1797 ; *Sarah*, 8 June, 1798, born Sept. 1796 ; *Alira*, 8 June, 1798, born 29 Sept. 1797 ; *Margaret*, 13 Jan^y, 1800, born 21st Jan. 1799 ; *Mary*, 21 Oct. 1803, born 12 Nov. 1800 ; *Harriett*, 21 Oct. 1803, born 3 Jan. 1803 ; *William*, 2 Aug. 1805 ; *Frances*, 27 Jan^y, 1809—father described as *Mayor of this City* ; *Emma*, 2 Aug. 1811, born 3 June, 1810.

THE REGISTERS OF ST. MARY'S.   171

1795.

Thomas Son of Sam[l] Venables' *School Master* by Sarah his wife June 28th.

Elizabeth Daughter of Jo[s] Renaldson Druggist by Margaret his wife July 22nd.

Charles Cowper Son of Charles Cholmondeley[4] Esq[r] & Caroline Elizabeth his wife Nov[r] 3[d] born Sep[t] 28th Last past.

1796.

Thomas son of W[m] Probart[4] Esq[r] by Eliz[th] his wife Feb[r] 10th.

Dinah Daughter of Will[m] Mackay[1] *Ensign in the Invalids of Chester Castle* by Eliz his wife March 23[d].

William Son of M[r] W[m] Golborn[5] Corn factor by Ann his wife May 26th.

Marianne Daughter of Joseph Renaldson Druggist by Marg[t] his wife July 3[d].

1798.

Joseph Son of M[r] Will[m] Connah[6] Baker by Mary his wife May 2nd born March 23[d].

1800.

Charles Son of M[r] Cha[s] Davies[7] Baker by Ann his wife March 5th.

Randall son of Cap[t] Randall Gossip of the 3[d] Reg[t] of Dragoons by Leah his wife July 1st.

1801.

Ann Daughter of M[r] Edward Ducker Rope Maker by Eliz[th] his wife born Sep[r] 9th.

1805.

Mary Daughter of George Mellor[8] Gent[n] by Mary his wife March 1st.

Thomas son of Richard Noseworthy *Pay Master in the 50*[th] *Reg[t]* of Foot by Nancy his wife September 29th.

Edward Son of M[r] Edward Roberts *Sugar Refiner* by Frances Catherine his Wife Oct[r] 17th born June 1st 1803.

1806.

William Fredrick Jones Son of M[r] William Bage Paper Manufacturer by Margaret his wife Jan[r] 2nd Born May 13th 1805.

Martha Daughter of Tho[s] Craven *Engineer* by Mary his wife March 2nd born July 24th 1805.

George Sench *a Native of Africa* Suppos'd to be about 10 Years Old Bapt[d] April 2nd.

John son of John Swarbreck Rogers[9] Merchant by Ann his wife Baptiz'd May 21st Born Dec[r] 24th 1804.

---

[1] The baptisms of the following children of Samuel Venables also occur :—*William*, 14 May, 1797 ; *John*, 3 March, 1799 ; *Charles*, 13 March, 1805, born 23 Sept. 1802—father described as *Master of the Blue School* ; *George*, 13 March, 1805, born 20 Feb. 1805.

[2] This Charles Cholmondeley was of Overlegh, Esq., the third son of Thomas Cholmondeley of Vale Royal, Esq., by Dorothy, daughter and heir of Edmund Cowper of Overlegh, Esq. He married at St. Mary-le-Bonne Church, London, 13 Jan. 1794, Caroline Elizabeth, third daughter of Nicholas Smythe of Cubley, co. Salop, Esq. From him descend the Cholmondeleys of Condover, co. Salop. The Charles Cowper Cholmondeley whose baptism is given in the text was the eldest son and was educated at Oxford, where he matriculated from Brasenose College, 31 March, 1814, aged 18. He took his B.A. degree in 1818, and that of M.A. in 1822. He became rector of Hodnet, co. Salop, and married in 1822 Mary, sister of Reginald Heber, Bishop of Calcutta. He died 5 February, 1831, leaving issue Reginald Cholmondeley of Condover, Esq., and others.

[3] The baptism of the following child of William Probart, Esq., also occurs :—*Frederick L'Oste*, 23 Feb. 1798.

[4] The baptism of the following child of William Mackay also occurs :—*John Crewe*, 25 April, 1798.

[5] The baptism of the following child of Mr. William Golborne also occurs :—*Jemima*, 30 May, 1798.

[6] The baptisms of the following children of Mr. William Connah also occur :—*William*, 16 Jan. 1811, born 2 Nov. 1810 ; *Joseph*, 6 May, 1812, born 2 Nov. 1811.

[7] The baptisms of the following children of Mr. Charles Davies also occur :—*Mary Ann*, 28 April, 1802 ; *Elizabeth*, Sept. 14th, 1804 ; *William*, 3rd Aug[st], 1810.

[8] The baptism of the following child of George Mellor also occurs :—*Richard*, 19 Feb. 1809, born 25 April, 1808.

[9] The baptism of the following child of Mr. John Swarbreck Rogers also occurs :—*Frances*, 29 June, 1810, born 24 June, 1808. A dau. *Ann*, was buried 26 April, 1807.

Thomas Wilkinson Son of John Hill[1] Esq'r Barrister at Law by Eliz'th his wife Bapt'd July 18th born May 20th 1804.

1807.
Pamela Daughter of Job Chapman Baptiz'd Aug't 7th born May 6th 1805.
Robert William Wharton Son of Robert Young *Lieu' Colonel* in the 8th Regiment of Foot by Jannette Sarah his wife Baptiz'd Dec'r 24th.

1808.
Louisa Catherine Daughter of Charles Macarthy *Adjutant* in the 8th Reg't of Foot by Catherine his wife May 20th born April 6th.
Kitty Daughter [of] Tho's Williams *Iron Founder* by Hannah his wife July 24th born Jan'y 17th.
Maria Daughter of Henry Brown[2] *School Master* by Sarah his wife Sept't 7th born Aug't 19th.
Mary Ann Daughter of M'r Tho's Paul *of Sealand* by Ellen his wife Nov'r 11th born September 2nd.

1809.
Charles Davies Son of Faithfull Thomas Att'y at Law by Mary his wife Baptiz'd August 1st born 8th day of Feb'y last.

1810.
Ann Daughter of William Hall *Drum Major in the Royal North Lincolnshire Militia* by Charlotte his wife Baptiz'd Nov'r 2nd 1810.

1812.
William Son of George Hurst *Under Keeper of the Castle* by Ann his wife Baptiz'd July 26th born January 15th last.
Joseph Son of Joseph Carter[3] *Gent'n* by Sarah his Wife Baptiz'd Oct'r 14th born Feb'y 10th 1804.
Lucinda Maria Daughter of Julius Wynne by Lucinda his wife born Nov'r 18th Baptiz'd Dec'r 8th.

[The last entry of a Baptism in the fourth volume is Dec. 13, 1812.]

MARRIAGES.[4]

1780.
John Lloyd of the parish of Warrington co. Lancaster, Gentleman, & Martha Dobbs of this parish, were married by Licence the 22 July 1780 by me Geo: Vanbrugh.

1782.
Edward Turner of the parish of St. John Baptist, Gentleman, and Dorothy Platt of this Parish, spinster, were married by Licence the 9 April 1782 by John Willan *Curate.*
Edward Platt of this Parish, Gentleman, & Sarah Leadbeater of this Parish spinster, were married by Licence the 5th of May 1782 by John Willan *Curate.*

1785.
Richard Maddock of this parish, gentleman, and Elizabeth Orr of this parish, spinster, were married by Licence the 19 Feb. 1785 by me John Willan *Curate.*

1788.
Edward Ellis of the parish of Wrexham, Gent. and Catherine Edwards of this parish, spinster, were married by Licence the 5th Feb. 1788 by me John Willan.

---

[1] The baptisms of the following children of John Hill, Esq., also occur :—*Mary Anne,* 10 Jan. 1803, born 21 March, 1802 ; *Elizabeth Ann,* July 18, 1806, born 3 Aug't, 1805 ; *John,* 13 July, 1810, born 2 Sept. 1806 ; *Rowland,* 13 July, 1810, born 12 Dec. 1807 ; *Frances Emily,* 23 Nov. 1812. He was the second son of the Rev. Robert Hill, LL.B., rector of St. Mary's (see p. 98 for a short account of him).

[2] The baptism of the following child of Henry Brown also occurs :—*Mary,* 13 March, 1811.

[3] The baptism of the following child of Joseph Carter also occurs :—*Philip Egerton,* 14 Oct. 1812.

[4] These are in a separate volume which begins on the 27th May, 1772, and ends on the 11th Dec. 1789.

William Ratcliffe of this parish, gentleman, and Elizabeth Ogden of the parish of St. Oswald, spinster, were married by Licence the 6th Aug.t 1788 by me John Willan.

William Castalio Kayne of this parish, *musician in the 40th Regiment*, and Betty Johnson of this parish, spinster, were married by Banns the 8th Dec. 1788 by me John Willan.

1789.

William Ellis of this parish, Gentleman, and Maria Ann Forrest, Spinster, of the parish of Ruthin, were married by Licence, the 14th March 1789 by me John Willan.

John Sorton of this parish, merchant, and Ann Overton of this parish, spinster, were married by Licence the 1st Dec. 1789 by me John Willan.

1791.[1]

Joseph Bozley of this parish, gentleman, and Dorothy Newell of this parish, widow, were married by Licence the 21 Jan. 1791 by me John Willan.

1792.

Henry Clubbe, Gentleman, of the parish of St. John the Baptist, and Martha Longworth of this parish, spinster, were married by Licence the 5 April 1792 by me John Willan.

Thomas Cawley of the parish of St. Bridget, M.D., and Catherine Parry of this parish, spinster, were married by Licence the 8 April 1792 by me John Willan.

1793.

John Beardsworth of Wrexham, gentleman, and Elizabeth Hughes of this parish, spinster, were married by Banns the 29 April 1793 by me John Willan.

1795.

John Lloyd Esq.r of the parish of Holy Trinity and Jane Wynne of this parish, spinster, were married by Licence the 4th Feb. 1795 by me John Willan.

1796.

William Pierce of this parish, surgeon, & Margaret Elizabeth Thursfield of this parish, spinster, were married by Banns the 8 Aug.t 1796 by me John Willan.

1797.

Robert Simcock[2] of the parish of Wigan, Bookseller, and Esther Pover of this parish, spinster, were married by Licence the 14 Aug.t 1797 by me John Willan.

1799.

George Brooke Esq.r of the parish of St. Oswald and Henrietta Massey of this parish, spinster, were married by Licence, 5th June 1799, by me Richard Massie, Minister of Coddington.

William Stocker of this parish, gentleman, and Ann Pemberton of the parish of St. Bridget, were married by Licence the 5th Sept. 1799 by me R.t W. Hill, Minister.

1800.

Thomas Vaughan of the parish of Farndon, Gentleman, and Sarah Newell of this parish, spinster, were married by Licence the 9th Jan.r 1800 by me R.t W. Hill, Minister.

William Cross of this parish, gentleman, and Sarah Bozley of this parish, spinster, were married by Licence the 25 Oct. 1800, by me Rowland Hill, Minister, in the presence of Jos. Bage, John Cotgreave.

1801.

Samuel Hill Esq. of this parish, Wine Merchant, and Anne Frances Wright of the parish of the Holy and Undivided Trinity, were married by Licence the 3 Feb. 1801 by me Rowland Hill, minister.

Thomas Poole of the parish of St. Peter, Bookseller, and Elizabeth Turner of this parish, spinster, were married by Licence the 17th Sept. 1801 by me Rowland Hill Minister.

---

[1] These marriages are contained in a separate volume beginning 11 Dec. 1789 and ending 4 Nov. 1805.
[2] A daughter, *Elizabeth-Trevor*, was baptized 7 Nov. 1798.

ST. MARY-ON-THE-HILL, CHESTER.

1802.

Edward Jones Gentleman of the parish of Holy Trinity and Ann Roberts of this Parish, widow, were married by Licence the 10 Feb. 1802 by me Rowland Hill, minister.

Robert Roberts of this parish, surgeon, and Ann Tennant of this parish, spinster, were married by Banns, the 29th March 1802, by me Rowland Hill, minister.

Thomas Conway Bibby, clerk, and Sarah Hughes of this parish, spinster, were married by Banns the 7 Nov. 1802 by me Rowland Hill, minister.

1805.[1]

The Revd Stephen Fawcett[2] of this parish, and Catherine Owen of this parish, spinster, were married by Licence the 1st June 1805, by me Rowland Hill, Rector.

1807.

Joseph Vignaux of the parish of Liverpool, surgeon, and Eliza Ratcliffe of this parish, spinster, were married by Licence, the 30th June 1807 by me Wm Fish officiat^g miñis[ter].

1808.

Edward Povar of this parish, stationer, and Mary Shearing of this parish, spinster, were married by Licence the 14 July 1808, by me William Fish, officiating minister.

Robert Wilkinson of this parish, gentleman, and Catherine Cotton of Bradley Parish, Staffordshire, were married by Licence, the 14 Sept. 1808 by me Jno Willan Off^g Minister.

John Miller of this parish, gentleman, and Maria Oldham of this parish, spinster, were married by Licence the 26 Sept. 1808, by me Wm Fish officiat^g miñis[ter].

1809.

Ezekiel Boyd Stewart of this Parish, Gentleman, and Sarah Jones of this Parish, spinster, were married by Banns the 17 April 1809 by me Rowland Hill, Rector.

Thomas Ritson of the parish of St. John the Baptist, Schoolmaster, and Elizabeth Cummings of this parish, were married by Licence the 20 July 1809, by me William Fish officiating minister.

1812.

Edward Joynson of this parish, gent. and Elizabeth Davies of the parish of Hawarden, were married by Licence the 16 June 1812, by me Jno Willan Off^g Minister.

BURIALS.

1782.

Elizabeth Orrett Widow *Gentlewoman* Buried the 4th day of December.

1783.

John Son of John Cooke[3] *Schoolmaster* by Martha his Wife Buried ye 21st day of March.
Sarah Wife of John Rowley Stationer Buried the 20th day of June.
Mary Wife of Mr Charles Snow Merchant Buried the 13th day of July.
Francis Son of William Ellington Esqr by Jane his Wife Buried ye 10th day of August.
Mary Pemberton *a Foundling* Buried ye 9th of Novr P.

1784.

William Harris *School Master* Buried ye 23^d of April.
Jane Caley Daughter of Peirce Davies *Tea Merchant* by Isabella his wife buried ye 30th of April.

---

[1] A new volume of the Marriage Registers begins on the 6 Nov. 1805 and ends on the 8 March, 1813.

[2] The monumental tablet to the Rev. Stephen Henry Fawcet, LL.D., still in the church, has been given on p. 51. He died 26 Jan. 1811, aged 33. Catherine his widow died in 1845, aged 61.

[3] The burial of the following child of John Cooke also occurs :—*Thomas*, 20 May, 1784.

Matthew Wilkinson Gen¹ *Lieuten' in his Majestys Royal Navy* buried y° 27ᵗʰ day of July.
Henry Hall Esq¹ *Attorney General for this County* Buried 24ᵗʰ Day of August.
John Walker, cordwainer *Clerk of this Parish* Buried Sep¹ 23ᵈ.

1785.
Frances Wishaw *Maiden Lady* Near Gloverstone Buried May y° 4ᵗʰ.
Maria Daughter of M' Benjamin Scott¹ by . . . . his Wife Buried August 15ᵗʰ.
William Son of M' Tho. Bosley Paper Maker Buried August 30ᵗʰ.
John Sherwin² *Liev' of the Invalids* of Chester Castle Buried Sep¹ y° 18ᵗʰ.
Mary Daughter of M' Rich⁴ Duke Buried Dec. y° 12ᵗʰ.

1786.
Ralph Son of M' Jackson Surgeon by Eliz his wife Buried Feb. y° 9ᵗʰ.
Isabella Caley Wife of M' Pierce Davies Buried March y° 14ᵗʰ.
Lieu' James Thompson³ Buried May y° 16.
Sarah Wife of M' Sharratt, sadler Bur⁴ June 28ᵗʰ.
Esther Daughter of Doctor Currie⁴ by Mary his Wife Buried July y' 20ᵗʰ.
Mʳˢ Isabella Snow Spinster Buried Dec. y° 24ᵗʰ.

1787.
Mʳˢ Sydney Whishaw Buried Mar. y° 23ᵈ.
Daniel Widders, Gentⁿ Buried May y° 7ᵗʰ.
Mʳˢ Ruth Dewsbury Buried Oct. y° 13ᵗʰ.

1788.
Ensign William Collier *of the Invalids* Bur⁴ April y° 8ᵗʰ.
Hannah Wife of M' Joˢ Howard Bur⁴ April y° 17ᵗʰ.
George Hall Genˡ Buried Sep¹ y° 8ᵗʰ.
Elizabeth Wife to M' Jnᵒ Sorton Skinner Buried Nov. y° 18ᵗʰ.
Cap' Thomas Tydd *of the Invalids* Buried Dec. y° 9ᵗʰ.
Mʳˢ Mary Boughton Buried Dec. y° 11ᵗʰ.

1789.
John Johnson Gentleman Buried May y' 1ˢᵗ.

1790.
Ann Daughter of M' Ralph Jackson Apothecary Buried May y° 11ᵗʰ.
Mary Wife to M' Reece *Sal Amoniac Maker* Buried May y° 14ᵗʰ.
Alice Daughter of M' Walker Tinman Buried June y° 17ᵗʰ.
Charles Son of M' Edw⁴ Bage Bur⁴ Aug¹ 18ᵗʰ.

1791.
Thomas Cotgreave Esq' *Ald"* Bur⁴ April y° 16.
Stephen Boughton Gentleman Buried June 18ᵗʰ.
Mary wife of . . . . . Taylor Gentⁿ Bur⁴ July 19ᵗʰ.
Philip Vipont Esq¹ Bur⁴ Dec. y° 18ᵗʰ.

1792.
Mary Dicas Widow of Randles Dicas *Late of Aldersgate Street London*, Oil Merchant Buried Jan' y' 23ᵈ.
Ann Wife of M' Thoˢ Bozley Paper Manufacturer Buried March y° 24ᵗʰ.
Mʳˢ Mary Jackson Spinster Buried May y° 10ᵗʰ.

---

¹ The burial of the following child of Mr. Benjamin Scott also occurs :—*Henry*, 23 Aug.ˢᵗ, 1789.
² His wife, *Jane*, was buried on the 12 March, 1785.
³ His monumental tablet is given on p. 51. He was 73 years old, and yet only a Lieutenant !
⁴ For several monumental inscriptions to the Currie family *see* pp. 49-50.

[Handwritten annotation at top:] William Dix Gent. Castle Street and William Dix Cheesefactor Cheese Warehouse occur in Broster's Directory of 1782, presumably Wm Dix Esq. buried in 1805 had left the Parish to reside at Gop-y-vron Co Flint but was buried in his old parish. Broster's Landed Gentry 1850 (p 575) gives Edward Hincks who died in 1792 as leaving a family by his wife Bithia Daughter of William Dix Esq., their eldest son and heir the Revd. Hincks LLD in holy orders of Belfast, had five sons of which three were in holy orders.

ST. MARY-ON-THE-HILL, CHESTER.

Peter Son of Mr Geo. Preston Buried May yr 12th.
Sarah Presbury Widow Aged 96 Burd June yr 21st P[auper].
[margin: John Sorton Merchant Bridge St., Directory 1782] Alfred Son of Jno Sorton Esqr Buried December yr 8th.

1793.
Serjeant Card *of the Invalids* Buried May yr 5th.
Elizabeth Wife to William Nanney Esqr Buried May yr 31st.

1794.
John Dod Aged 99 Buried May yt 25th P[auper].
Jane Daughter of Mr Wm Evans *Needle Maker* Burd July 10th.
Ann Daughter of Mr Richd Duke *Schoolmaster* Buried Sep. yr 18th.
John Colgreave Esqr Buried Sept yr 30th.

1795.
Mrs Jane Thomas¹ Widow of *Capt* William Thomas Buried the 19th day of April.
Sarah Bristow Spinster 55 Years Servant to Mrs Hunt the 29th Day of July.
Thomas Eldest son of Mr Thos Roberts Merchant the 24th of September.

1796.
Samuel s[on] of Jno Sumner Carver May 17th.
[margin: Joseph Snow, Alderman, Wine Merchant Eastgate St. Broster Directory 1782] Joseph Snow Esqr *Aldn of this City and Mayor thereof 1788*, July 18th.
William Presbury Sexton Augt 19th.
Thomas Turner Junr Architect Novr 28th.
Alexander Denton M.D. Decr 15th.

1797.
Mrs Jane Coates Widow aged 82 April 19th.
Mary Relict of Daniel Widders Gentn May 15th.
Capt² John Mellis, May 24th.
Anne Wife to Mr Josh Bage Paper Manufr July 10th.

1798.
Henry Clubbe Gentn Jany 5th.
George Fairclough Esqr Jany 28th.
John Newell Gentn March 1st.
Mr William Wood April 20th.

1802.
Thomas Baxter Gentn 25th January.

1804.
John Glegg³ *of Irbey Hall* in this County Buried Feby 11th Aged 74.

1805.
[margin: See Headstone] William Dix Esqr *Tip-y-vron Flintshire* January 30th.

1806.
James Gray Gardener & *Out Pensioner of Chelsea Hospital* Buried December 11th.

1807.
George son of . . . Millor Gentn 22nd April.
Peter Snow² Esqr 1st May.

[Handwritten at bottom:] Peter Snow, Attorney at Law, Further Northgate St:– Broster's Directory 1782. See Edowes Trials. Mrs Snow, Castle Street: Directory 1782.

¹ See the monumental inscription to the Eyton family, p. 54.
² See his tombstone inscription, and that of his wife, on p. 51.
³ His monumental inscription is printed on p. 52.

1809.
William Mackay Gent" Jany 10th.
Thomas Hughes Esqr Jan^r 21st.

1810.
Betty Baskervile Clegg¹ July 14th aged 77 years.

1811.
Revd P. Fawcett² January 26th.
Joseph Bage April 24th.

1812.
Mrs Sarah Dunn widow Buried January 24th.

[The last Burial entry in Volume IV. is dated 1 April, 1812.]

With these entries, coming down to the year 1812, when a fresh series of Registers was begun all over the kingdom, our extracts from the old Registers of St. Mary's may very fittingly cease. They have taken up far more space than was originally contemplated, but it is hoped that their interesting character, well illustrating the size and importance of the parish, may be deemed a satisfactory excuse.

By the courtesy of the clergy of most of the other Chester churches, I have had free access to the old Registers of their respective parishes, and from them I have been able to select the following entries relating to St. Mary's, which well deserve to be here printed. Not only may they be the means of assisting many future workers in genealogical and historical enquiries, but they place on record information relating to St. Mary's which might be sought for in vain in the Registers of that parish itself.

EXTRACTS FROM OTHER REGISTERS RELATING TO PERSONS AND PLACES CONNECTED WITH ST. MARY'S PARISH.

ST. MICHAEL'S, CHESTER.

1592. December. Mrs Elizabeth Gamull buried 26.
1612. July. Thomas Manley gent and Mrs Anne Harlton marryed 24.
1618. November. Mrs Ann Manley³ Bur. 16.
1644. January. Carolus filius Cristopheri Paslie⁴ Cler bap 9.
1701. July 26. Jane the daught^r of John Lloyd Esq. of St Marys parish was buried at St Michaels, the fath^r to pay ye tax.
1704. May 18. Mr Willm Done Attorney and Mrs Mary Whishaw⁵ Spinst^r both of St Marys parish were marryed by a license of ye 16th instant.
1705. July 12. Edward Norris⁶ of Speke in Lancashire D^r of Physick & Esq. & Ann Gerrard of St Mich^s in Chester Spinst^r marryed by a license.

¹ See his tombstone inscription, and that of his wife, on p. 51.
² This should be the Rev. *Stephen Henry* Fawcett. See his monumental inscription on p. 51 and his marriage on p. 174.
³ According to her Funeral Certificate she was the daughter of Thomas Grosvenor, of Eaton, Esq., and married to her first husband, Roger Hurleston, of Chester, Esq., by whom she had issue. She married for her second husband, as shown in the previous entry, on the 24th July, 1612. Thomas Manley, of the Lache, gentleman, by whom she had no issue. [*Cheshire Funeral Certificates*, Record Society, vol. vi., pp. 142-3.)
⁴ For an account of the Rev. Christopher Pasley, D.D., rector of Hawarden, buried at St. Mary's in 1658, see p. 67.
⁵ See p. 72.
⁶ See pp. 70 and 153.

1707. feb. 12.   Mr. John Bridg from S' Marys parish.   Buried.
1715. Aug. 15.   Robert Edge *a gunner of y' castle*.
1721. May 18.   Charles son of Charles Aldcroft[1] clerk bapt.
1725. Aug. 12.   Thomas Son of M' Charles Aldcroft clerk buried
1727. April 18.   Will'" Son of M' Charles Odcroft [*sic*] clergyman buried.
1728. June 23.   James son of Charles Oldcroft [*sic*] clergym" buried.
1730. Septemb. 27.   Ann y' wife of M' Charles Aldcroft clerk buried.
1731. May 9.   Ralph Son of Charles Aldcroft clerk buried.
1737. Aug. 23.   Rev'd Arthur Williams[2] buried.
1747. Jan' 7.   Ursula Daughter to M' Rob' Taylor Attorney in Marys Parish buried.
1755. John Sewell Gentleman of the Castle of the Parish of S' Mary in the City of Chester and Ann Egerton of the Parish of S' Michaels spinster were married in this Church by Licence this 19th day of May 1755 by me Roger Barnston in the presence of John Egerton and Philip Egerton.
1758. M'" Kezia Manley Buried Nov. 7.
1785. Jn" Willan of S' Marys Parish and Hannah Wordsworth of this Parish Spinster were married in this Church by Licence this 31st day of Octo' 1785 by me W'" Nelson in the presence of Mary Williams, Edm'd Willan.
1794. Samuel Humphreys of the Parish of Saint Mary in Chester Gentleman and Anne Hughes of this Parish Spinster were Married in this Church by Licence this 12th day of June 1794 by me Joseph Eaton Min" in the presence of Richard Baron, Jane Lloyd.

ST. BRIDGET'S, CHESTER (begins 1649).

1649. Dorithie daughter to M' Samuell Daniell borne in Maries Parrish and baptized in Bridgetts Parish the 15th Aprill 1649.
1673. John Starkey Esq and Alice Oliuer bothe of S' Maryes parish were marryed the 6th day of October 1673.
1677. M' Thomas Street of S' Maryes parish was buryed the 12th of ffebruary 1677.
1693. August the 15.   M' Margrett Ashton widd. of St Maries Parish.
1708. William Thwellin of S' Maries Parish, *A Carder of Hatmaker's Wooll* was buryed upon y' third day of April 1708.
1714. Jane Daughter to M' Hugh Whishaw[3] an Attorney at law was baptized upon y' Second day of May 1714.
1717. Sidney Daughter to Master Hugh Whishaw[3] an Attorney at Law was baptized the Sixth day of September Ann" Dñi 1717.
1723. Katherine Daughter of Captain Charles Crosby[4] & of Catherine his wife was baptized on the twenty first Day of June Anoq' Dñi 1723.
1724. Par Donnough *Ensign of the Invalids* of this Parish and Rebecca Starkey[5] widow of St Maries Parish were married by License on the twenty third of April Annoq' Dñi 1724.

ST. OLAVE'S, CHESTER (begins 1611).

1676. M' Thomas Pulfurt[6] died the 24 of Aprill and was buryed at sant maryes the 26 of Aprill.

---

[1] For a short notice of the Rev. Charles Aldcroft, for many years Curate of St. Mary's, *see* pp. 94-5. The first three entries here given are additional to those printed on p. 94.
[2] He was rector of St. Mary's from March, 1731, to August, 1737 (*see* p. 95), and it is somewhat strange that he was not buried in the church of which he was rector.
[3] *See* p. 72 for some notes on the Whishaw family.
[4] *See* note 6 on p. 165.   The Catherine here mentioned was probably his *first* wife.
[5] She was buried at St. Marys in 1732 (*see* p. 156).
[6] His burial is also entered in the St. Mary's Registers (*see* p. 138).

Simon Harwood Gent was the youngest brother of Rev. Edward Harwood who performed the marriage Ceremony named below. The Rev. Edward Harwood became Rector of Thornton Co. Chester Buried Londer Gentry 1850. p. 548.
Harwood Armor: Arg, a chevron between 3 stags heads caboshed gules.
Crest. On a wreath, a stags head caboshed gules, holding in its mouth an oak branch proper vert etc.

THE REGISTERS OF ST. MARY'S. 179

ST. MARTIN'S, CHESTER (begins 1680).

1758. Simon Harwood of this Parish Gent and Eliz. Sewell[1] of the Parish of St. Mary were married by Licence, the 16th Dec. 1758 by E. Harwood in the presence of W. Thomas and John Sewell.

1773. John Swarbreck[2] Son of Mr Jno Rogers Merchr Augt 9 Bapt.

1773. Cuthbert Sewell, Clerk, widower and Ann Sewell, widow, both of this parish, married by Banns, the 13 Dec 1773 by Roger Barnston, in the presence of Eliz. Witter and Walter Thomas.

HOLY TRINITY, CHESTER (begins 1654).

In 1658 there are several marriages performed by "Mr Hunt," in one of which he is described as "Mr Hunt,[3] Pastor of St Maries."

1659. Ann Edwards Daughter to parson Edwards[4] died at Mr Hands the 20 of October 1659 an I was buried the 22 day of the same munth at St. Maryes.

1680. M. Kendrick Eaton[5] & Mrs Ann Starkey the 12th July by Lycence dated the 10th July 80.

1702. Ann ye Wife of Mr Kendrick Eaton[6] Aprill ye 29th Buried.

1703. Mr Kendrick Eaton[6] Gent Decem. ye 22. Buried.

1718. Elizabeth daughter of Mr Kenrick Eyton[5] Apr. 15 Bapt [Buried June 12. 1720].

1734. Elizabeth Wishaw[7] Apr. 16. Buried.

1776. Robert Foulks Son of William Currie[8] MD and Mary his Wife. Oct 23. Bapt.

1778. Susanna Daur of William Currie[8] MD and Mary his Wife June 17 Bapt.

ST. PETER'S, CHESTER (begins 1559).

1623. Willm sonne to Willm holmes[9] of St. Maries pish Baptized the 29th of August.

1645. John the sonne of Mr William Brocke[10] of Upton was Baptised the 18th day of february 1645.

1677. Mr William Wright[11] Ald'man of Trinity Parish buryed September ye 17. 1677.

1679. Hannah wife to Mr James Croxton[12] of St Maryes Parish buryed Nobr ye 10th 1679.

1681. Elizabeth Wife of Mr William Wright[11] *of Brewershall* buryed Octobr 24. 1681.

ST. OSWALD'S, CHESTER (begins 1580).

1603. Ellenor Gammull ye daughter of Mr William Gammull[13] Bapt. vijth Day of Marche.

1604. Ales Gamull the daughter of Mr Thomas Gamull[13] Alderman Bapt. ixth Decembris.

---

[1] In Adam's *Chester Courant* for Dec. 19, 1758, she is described as "daughter of the late Joseph Sewell Esq. Collector of his Majesty's Customs in this Port, an agreeable Lady with a handsome Fortune."

[2] See note 9, p. 171.

[3] For an account of Mr. Richard Hunt, B.D., Rector of St. Mary's, see pp. 87-89.

[4] Francis Edwards, M.A., Rector of St. Mary's, 1623 to 1642, see pp. 83-85.

[5] This was probably the son and heir of the Kenrick Eyton, Esq., referred to in note 5 on p. 138.

[6] In 1722, 1724, &c., are entries of the baptisms of the children of Kendrick Eaton, "dancing master," and Elizabeth, his wife.

[7] See p. 72 for some notes on the Whishaw family.

[8] The Currie family were closely connected with St. Mary's.

[9] See the pedigree of Holme *postea*.

[10] See the pedigree of Brock of Upton *postea*.

[11] His Funeral Certificate has been printed by the Record Society (*Cheshire and Lancashire Funeral Certificates*, p. 191). In this he is called "William Wright of *Brewers Hall* in the county of the City of Chester Esqr was Maior thereof in the year 1655." Brewer's Hall was in St. Mary's parish (see *postea*).

[12] James Croxton, son and heir of James Croxton, of Croxton Green, in Chalmondeley, baptized at Wybunbury 14 April, 1650, was buried at St. Mary's 25 July, 1707 (see p. 152). The wife here buried would seem to have been his first wife, as another wife, Jane, daughter of John Cleave, of Chester and Pulford, was buried at St. Mary's in 1700 (see p. 142).

[13] See the pedigree of Gamul of Chester *postea*.

1606. Francis Gamull the sonne of M' Tho: Gamull[1] *Recorder of Chester* Bapt. 25 Novemb.

1605. Ales Gamull the Daughter of M' Thomas Gamull[1] *Recorder* sept xix[th] Aprilis.

1624. Edward the sonne of M' Edward Cowper of St. Maries pishe Bapt. primo die Aug.

1639. Tho: Bennett of S[ts] Maries pish and Cicilie Charnocke maried the 19th of Nouember.

1640. Gearrard Johnes and Priscilla Brearewoode[2] maried the 17th of September.

1645. Edward the sonn of M' Seddon[3] bapt. the 18th of October.

1646. Elizabeth the daughter of Will. Maddocke of S[nt] Maries pish bapt. the 29th Nouember.

1646. Tho: the sonn of Tho: Walley of S[nt] Maries pish bapt. the 24th of Dec.

1654. A marriage celebrated in the presence (*inter alia*) of "M' William Peartree[4] Minister of Maries in Chester."

1655. Randle Holme[5] of this Cittie Gent and Sarah Solie of the same Cittie Spinst' Maried before M' William Ince[6] Ald[rm] and Justice of peace the 23th day of Avgv. 1655.

1655. Thomas Simson of this Cittie Grocerar [*sic*] and Elizabeth Holme[7] of the same Cittie spinster Maried before M' Will: Ince[6] Ald[rm] and Justice of Peace the 23th Avgvst.

1655. Thomas Weston of this Cittie Gent and M[rs] Christian Gamwall [Gamul][8] of the same Cittie spinst' Maried before M' William Ince[6] Ald[rm] and Justice of Peace the 23th Avgvst 1655. Witnesse M' William Flimley, Richard Dunbavin.

1655. Robert Calcote of this Cittie Gent and M[rs] Alice Gamwall [Gamul][8] of the same Cittie Spinst' Maried before M' William Ince Ald[rm] & Justice of Peace the 23[th e] day of Avgvst. Witnesse M' William Plimley and Richard Dunbavin.

1661. Thomas sonne of Thomas Acton[10] gent Bap' Aprill 28th.

1666. Randle Holme[11] & Elizabeth Wilson maryed the 7th July.

1673. M' Henry Bunbury sonne vnto M' Thomas Bunbury of Boughton Esq' and M[rs] Mary Eaton Daughter vnto S' Kendrick Eaton[12] were Married the 7th Day of ffeb.

1673. Elizabeth wife vnto M' Edward Aldersie[13] in S' Maryes Parish was Buried the 20th Day of Sep'.

1678. M' Edward Aldersay[13] gentellman was buried the 12th Day of January.

1681. M' John Acton[10] of S' Maryes parish and M[rs] Sarah Ashton of St. Oswalds parish were married the 16th Day of ffebruary.

1683. M' Thomas Kelsall of trafford of Flimstone parish and M[rs] Christian Brerewood[14] were Married the 3[d] of July.

1698. M' Edw. Halwood of this parish & M[rs] Hannah Starky of S' Marys parish Married y' 19th Day of June.

---

[1] *See* the pedigree of Gamul of Chester *postea*.

[2] *See* the pedigree of Brerewood of Chester *postea*.

[3] A long account of William Seddon, M.A., for some years curate of St. Mary's, will be found on pp. 85-87.

[4] *See* p. 88.

[5] This was the *third* Randle Holme. *See* the Holme pedigree *postea*.

[6] All marriages at this time, during the Commonwealth, had to be performed without any religious ceremony by a Justice of the Peace.

[7] *See* the Holme pedigree *postea*.

[8] *See* the Gamul pedigree *postea*.

[9] It is very noteworthy these four persons from St. Mary's parish, a brother and sister, and two sisters, being married on the same day and before the same magistrate.

[10] *See* the pedigree of Acton *postea*.

[11] This was the second marriage of the *third* Randle Holme. *See* the pedigree of Holme *postea*.

[12] *See* note 5, p. 138.

[13] I have not been able to ascertain with certainty to which of the many families of Aldersey this Edward Aldersey belonged.

[14] *See* the pedigree of Brerewood *postea*.

1699. William Delues Gen' of Boden parish in Cheshere and M" Susannah Brock Daughter to Will": Brock¹ Esq' ware Married by Licance ye 18th of Jan. shee of this parish [S' Oswalds].

1700. William Hurleston Gen' of ye township of Upton in ye parish of S' Mary's in Chester and Mr Elizabeth Brock Daūg to Will". Brock¹ Esq' of this parish ware Married by Licance y^r 5th Day of Dec.

1704. Tho: Joynson Clockmaker of the township of Boughton in this Parish & Mrs Alice Kelsall Widdow of St Marys Parish were Married ye 20th February.

1711. Thomas Son to Hugh Foulkes Esq' was Bap' ye 26th August.

1721. John Egerton son to y^r Reuerend Philip Egerton D' & Rector of Astbury & Elizabeth Brock¹ spr of this Parrish were Married ye 19th of April.

1722. Thom͂ Dane of S' Johns Parish Gentleman and Elizabeth Manawring [*sic*] spr of S' Maryes Parish was Maried the 4th day of October.

1723. Mrs Ellinor Mathers widdow of S' Marys Parish was Buried the 2^d Day of September.

1728. Wm Proby Col^l of the Inveleeds² Buried ye 19th of Jan. a member of the Sun Lodge of Freemasons

1746. Susana Daughter of Rob' Foulkes Esq' of Boughton was Bapt. 9. March.

1749. David Jones Son to Mr Mackintosh² *Gunner of ye Castle* 18th May. Bapt.

1752. Mr Joseph Snow¹ Merch' and Mrs Cathrine Frodsham by Licence Jañry 16.

1759. Rob' Pullen *Ensign of Invaleeds*² Novb^r 10th. Buried.

1764. Peter McIntosh³ (*Gunner of Castle*) January 18. Buried.

1773. Catherine Relict of Peter McIntosh¹ *Ensign* 56 December 15. Buried.

1780. Mary Catherine D^r of Willm Currey Esq Doct' in Physic—March 30th Bapt.

1782. Eliz. D' of Willm Currey Doct' in Physick Esq' Aug. 13. Bapt.

1785. James Barrat, *Lieut. of Invalids*. 62. April 9. Buried.

1788. Jane dau^r of Willm Currie M.D. March 11. Bapt.

1790. William son of Willm Currie M.D. and Mary his wife, born March 29th bapt May 11.

1793. Jno Tilley, *Invalid Serjeant*. 83. Jan. 27. Buried.

REGISTERS OF HAWARDEN, CO. FLINT (*begin 1585*).

(This parish joins up to that of St. Mary's.)

1640. Novemb. Christophorus fil Christophori Pasley¹ Rectoris 24. Bapt.

1642. Dec. Margaret fil Xpfri Pasley¹ rectoris. 4. Bapt.

(There is a gap in the Register from 1644 to 1652.)

1678. Junij 12°. Robertus Brerewood⁶ de Cestria Gen' et domina Dorothæa Whittley de Aston habitâ licentiâ.

1678–9. March 20. Johannes fil. Roberti Brerewood⁶ de Aston gen. Bapt.

1680. Junii die 13°. Charoletta filia Rob^ti Brerewood⁶ gen' de Aston. Bapt.

1683. Dec. 14. Grauenor m͂l Rob. Brerewood⁵ de Broadlane. Bapt.

REGISTERS OF BUNBURY, CO. CHESTER (*begin 1559*).

1628–9. Jan. 12. George Taylor of the parish of S' Maries in Chester and Jane Simcoe of this parishe. Married.

---

¹ *See* the pedigrees of Brock of Upton *postea*.
² The Invalides were, I believe, stationed in the Castle.
³ Other baptisms occur in which he is called Mr Peter Macintosh, gunner.
⁴ For two epitaphs at St. Mary's to the Snow family, *see* p. 52.
⁵ For an account of the Rev. Christopher Pasley, D.D., rector of Hawarden, who was buried at St. Mary's in 1658, *see* p. 67.
⁶ *See* the pedigree of Brerewood *postea*.

1646. May 18. Ralph Downeham of S⁺ Johns parish & Katherine Stacy of S⁺ Maries in Chester Married.

1767. March 6. William Chaloner of S⁺ Mary's parish Chester. Buried.

REGISTERS OF CHELFORD, CO. CHESTER.

1764. Frances daughter of M⁺ Hugh Whishaw¹ of Chester buried June 5.

SPECIAL INCIDENTS IN THE PAST HISTORY OF ST. MARY'S
(see pp. 26-30).

Before leaving the history of the church of St. Mary's and commencing the account of old families connected with it, it should have been mentioned amongst the special incidents connected with that building that on the 9th January, 1387 and the three following days the Earl Marshall's Court was held in the church in connection with the great heraldic dispute of the fourteenth century between Sir Richard le Scrope and Sir Robert le Grosvenor as to the right of bearing " a shield azure with the bend or." At these sittings evidence was brought forward on behalf of the Grosvenors, and in addition to Sir Robert le Grosvenor himself there appeared the Abbot of Vale Royal, the Abbot of Combermere, the Prior of Norton, the Abbot of St. Werburgh, Owen Glendower and Tudor Glendower, Sir John le Masey of Podyngton, Sir Laurence de Dutton, Sir Hugh de Browe, and Sir William de Brereton, Knights, and a great many other Cheshire squires and persons of importance, so that for those four days the old church of St. Mary's must have presented a very animated spectacle. The King's decision, however, was ultimately given in favour of Le Scrope.²

---

¹ For a short account of the Whishaw family, see p. 72.

² My attention was called to this celebrated trial by the Rev. Canon Morris, of Eaton, as I had overlooked the fact that some of the sittings had been held at St. Mary's. See full account in his history of *Chester in the Times of the Plantagenets and Tudors*, pp. 171-2

Old Cheshire Families connected with St. Mary's.

One of the oldest and most important families connected with St. Mary's was that of the TROUTBECKS, of Dunham-on-the-Hill, co. Chester. This distinguished family for many generations held lands and houses in the city of Chester, and were closely identified with St. Mary's Church. In 1433 William Troutbeck, Esq., erected a chantry chapel at the east end of the south aisle, the deed of erection of which has already been printed in full on p. 32. In this chapel the members of the family were subsequently interred, and two very handsome alabaster monuments remained there till they were destroyed by the falling in of the roof in 1690 (see pp. 36-38). A short account of this family, dealing more especially with their connection with St. Mary's, may here be given.[1]

WILLIAM TROUTBECK, the first of his name connected with Cheshire,[2] occurs about the year 1400 in connection with Dunham-on-the-Hill, and in the 14th Henry IV., 1412, he was made Chamberlain of Chester, an office of much dignity and importance. In 1415 he agreed to provide the unusually large number of 50 men-at-arms and 650 archers,[3] and with them, no doubt, was present at the battle of Agincourt, fought in that year. In 1423 he was made Chancellor of the Duchy of Lancaster, an office he held till 1431. As already mentioned, in 1433 he erected the chantry chapel in St. Mary's Church, and in 1437 he occurs as holding lands in Hawarden parish, co. Flint, as well as in many parts of Cheshire. He died in the 24th Henry VI., 1446, leaving by his wife Joan, daughter of William de Massey, of Rixton, co. Lanc.,[4] who survived him till 1452, a son and heir John, another son William, and two or three daughters. He would be buried in the chapel he had erected, and the two monuments, placed in the centre of that chapel, and described on p. 37, were almost certainly, as shown by the arms, &c., placed to the memory of him and his wife. There was also an inscription in "the higher south windowe" to his memory and that of his wife, which, translated from the original Latin, is as follows :—" Pray for the souls of William Troutbeck Esquire of Chester and Joan his wife, who built this chapel in the year of our Lord 1424" (sic for 1434; see p. 36).

JOHN TROUTBECK, who succeeded his father in 1446, was then about thirty-four years of age, and was then married to Margary, daughter and sole-heiress of Thomas Hulse, of Brunstath, co. Chester. He had been appointed Chamberlain of Chester when his father resigned that office in 1445, but previously to that he had been Sheriff of Cheshire in 1438. On the 2nd March, 19th Henry VI., 1441, he, together with Thomas Stanley, Esq., was commanded to provide within the city of Chester twenty-four pipes (dolia) of wine for the King's use, against his coming to

---

[1] An interesting account of the Troutbeck family was contributed to the columns of the *Warrington Guardian* by the late W. Beamont, Esq., of Warrington, in 1878, to which I am much indebted. There is a short pedigree and an account of the family in Ormerod's *History of Cheshire*, new edition, vol. ij., pp. 37-43.

[2] Not unlikely he took his name from the township of Troutbeck in Westmoreland.

[3] See Nicholas' *Agincourt*, p. 385, quoted by Mr. Beamont.

[4] In many pedigrees she is said to be the daughter of William de Rixton, of Rixton, and this is strengthened by the arms on the monuments to him and his wife formerly in St. Mary's Church.

that city.¹ There are many references to him in the *Cheshire Plea* and *Recognizance Rolls*, now in the Record Office, London, and in other documents of the period.² On the 4th Feb., 1457, he resigned the office of Chamberlain, and in August, 1458, he died at the early age of forty-six, his wife having pre-deceased him in the previous year. He died seized of the office of serjeant³ of the Bridge Gate in Chester and of lands in Neston, Raby, Oxton, Brunstath, Barneston, &c., in Cheshire. He was probably buried in the chantry chapel erected by his father in St. Mary's Church. He left two sons, William and John, of whom the former succeeded to his estates.

SIR WILLIAM TROUTBECK, Knt, as he afterwards became, was twenty-five years of age when he inherited his father's lands in 1458, having been born on the 20th July, 1432. He was married in 1448 to Margaret, daughter of Thomas, first Lord Stanley. He was unfortunately present at the fatal battle of Bloreheath, fought on the 23rd September, 1459, where, in common with so many of the Cheshire knights and squires, he lost his life, when only twenty-six years of age. As Drayton says, in his well-known *Polyolbion*, referring to this battle⁴—

> Here Dutton, Dutton kills ; a Done doth kill a Done.
> A Booth a Booth ; and Leigh by Leigh is overthrown.
> A Venables against a Venables doth stand,
> And Troutbeck fighting with a Troutbeck hand to hand.
> Then Molineux doth make a Molineux to die,
> And Egerton the strength of Egerton doth try.

His body was brought to Chester and buried in the chapel in St. Mary's Church, where the handsome monument, fully described on p. 37, depicting him at full length lying beside his wife, and situated on the south side of the chantry chapel, was most probably erected to his memory. Several Inquisitions were taken after his death in 1460, which refer to his lands in Cheshire, Shropshire, and Hertfordshire, and state that William, his son and heir, was then ten years of age. His widow, Dame Margaret, married in 1460 for her second husband, Sir John Boteler, of Bewsey, co. Lanc., Knt. He died in 1463,⁵ and in the following year she married for her third husband, Henry, Lord Grey of Codnor. She died in 1492.

WILLIAM TROUTBECK, his son and heir, came of age before 1472, in which year a "proof of age," ⁶ as it was called, was taken on the oaths of Roger Leigh, of Adlington, Philip Egerton, Thomas Frodsham, Thomas Crue, Philip Acton, and others, who say that he was aged twenty-one years in the feast of St. Stephen the Pope [Aug. 2], 10th Edward IV. [1470]. And some of the jurors say that they were present when he was born, and that they saw him carried to the church of the Blessed Mary-upon-the-Hill for baptism. He was knighted in or before 1487. He was married to his first wife, Jane, daughter of Sir John Boteler, of Bewsey, about the year 1460,

---

¹ *Cheshire Records*, quoted by Mr. Beamont.

² In *East Cheshire*, vol. j., an interesting document is printed in full to which his name as Chamberlain of Chester occurs.

³ The Sergeancy passed from the Bagottes and Raby family in two moieties to the houses of Holes and Norris, and of these one moiety descended through the Troutbecks to the house of Talbot, Earl of Shrewsbury. See Morris' *History of Chester in Plantagenet Times*, p. 228.

⁴ Some poetic licence must be allowed, for, although so many Cheshire men perished in this battle, the names given by Dryden are not altogether historically correct.

⁵ He was buried in the church of Warrington, where a handsome monument, still in good preservation, with two full length effigies was placed to his memory and that of his wife. As Mr. Beamont remarks, it is very noteworthy that the lady had a monument at St. Mary, Chester (with the effigy of her first husband), and also at Warrington.

⁶ Now preserved in the Public Record Office, London.

He beareth Azure, three trouts fretted in Triangle, teste a la queve, Argent; by the name of Troutbeck of Cheshi my Author observes, that the Heiress of this family was in the time of Hen. 8. married to John Talbot of Albrighton from whence descended the Talbots of Grafton, who quarter this Coat. We use these Words teste a la queve (in English) Head to Tail to signify the Manner of their Fretting — The Banner displayd or Guillim Abridgd - 1725. p. 516.

OLD CHESHIRE FAMILIES CONNECTED WITH ST. MARY'S.

but being divorced from her in 1491, he married secondly Margaret, daughter of Richard Hough, of Leighton, co. Chester, Esq. He died, without issue by either of his wives, in September, 1510, being then about sixty years of age. His widow Margaret afterwards married Sir William Pole, of Pole, Knt., and died in June, 1531. His heir was Margaret, the only daughter of his brother, Adam Troutbeck, by his wife Margaret, younger daughter of Sir John Boteler, of Bewsey, Knt., who was sixteen years of age at the time of her uncle's death. She married Sir John Talbot, of Grafton, Knt., ancestor of the Earls of Shrewsbury, and so brought the extensive estates of the Troutbecks into the possession of the latter family.

Sir William Troutbeck's will, preserved at Somerset House, London (P.C.C., 35 Benet), is here printed for the first time. It will be noticed that he desired to be buried in his chapel at St. Mary's, and that he wished to be attended to his grave by twenty-four of his servants dressed in black gowns, as well as by twelve poor men dressed in white gowns, each carrying a torch. It is not improbable that he was buried in the night-time, as was then customary in the case of distinguished persons.

WILL OF SIR WILLIAM TROUTBECK, KNT., MADE 9 SEPT., 1510.

"In the name of god amen I SIR WILLIAM TROUTBEKE Knyght make my testament and last will in maner and fourme folowing ffirst I bequeth my soule to almighty god, My body to be buried in my chapell in the parisshe Churche of Seynt Marye of the Hill in Chester Also I make Margaret my wif[e] and Thomas Hoghe myn executors, And to the accomplishment of this my Will I make my Lord of Ely[1] myn overseer of my said testament, that this my last will may be fulfilled in every poynt.

ffurthermore I will that xxiiij of my servants haue blake gownes to accompany me to my buryall Also that myn executors shall geve xij white gownes to xij poore men to here xij torches at my buriall Also I will that xij tapers shall be ther, And as for brede ale and wyne as myn executors shall thinke necessary, And all my goods moevable that leven of my buriall I geve unto Margaret my said wif.

And as touching and concernyng my londs wher as by diverse deds endented bering date the first day of May the xxiij yere of King Henry the vij[th] [1508] I haue caused by my commaundement and request Thomas Hoghe and William ffrodsam feoffey to myn vse by recouery of all my londs in Chesshier to geve and graunte certeyn Manors londs and tenementis in the Countie of Chester to Margaret my wif for terme of hir life for hir Joyntor. Also to my sonnes and doughters' for terme of their lyves the Remaynder therof to my right heyres as it apperith in the same deds and writtings. And also I will that my said wif and Childern[2] named in the said deds and writtings shall haue the same londs for terme of their lyves the remaynder to my right heyres, according as ys specified in the same deds, And further if it happen that the same gifte and graunte of the said londs by the said dedes made to my wif and childern[2] and to every of theym be not sufficient in the lawe to euery of theym according to the same myn entent in that behalf as written in the said deds Than I will that the said Thomas Hoghe and William ffrodsam my feoffey shall make a sure and a sufficient estate in the lawe to my said wif for terme of hir lif of all thos Manors londs and tenements to hir appoyntid in the said deds. And in like wise to my childern and every of theim named in the said deds for terme of their lyves all those londs and tenements to theym and every of theym appoyntid in the said deds according to the true entent and meanyng of the same deds

[1] That is the Bishop of Ely.
[2] This was a natural provision to provide for any children he then had or in case any children were born to him, but it is certain he died without surviving issue.

and writtings, the Remaynder after their decesse to my right heyres, And that this be doon incontynently aftir my decesse w'out delay. And if this my will be not sufficient in the lawe that then it be made and mendyd by lerned counsaill According to the true entent of this my will.

In witness wherof I haue sett to my seale the ix day of September the yere of o' lord M' V' and X [1510].

[Proved 3rd day of December 1510]

Before parting with the Troutbeck family it may here be mentioned that from the answer to a writ of *quo warranto* dated in the reign of Henry VII., about 1495,[1] it appears that Sir William Troutbeck claimed to have "the custody of the garden and orchard [in the ditch] of the Castle of Chester," by the curious rental of "finding the Earl of Chester sufficient kale from Michaelmas to the end of Lent," for which he received from the hands of the Chamberlain £4 11s. 3d. per annum, or 3d. per day.[2] He also claimed to have nine fishing stalls or stations, and two boats on the water of the Dee, opposite to the city, with the right of fishing in the said water without any hindrance, saving to the Earl the royal fish [*i.e.*, sturgeon], to be carried to him for a fee according to custom. In subsequent documents[3] the custody of the garden in the Castle Ditch is referred to, as well as the serjeancy of the Bridge Gate, and the custody of the gates of the bridge over the Dee, and the number of fishing stations had risen to twelve. Early in the seventeenth century, amongst the premises in Chester belonging to the Talbots, "a messuage called Troutbeck's place" is mentioned.[4]

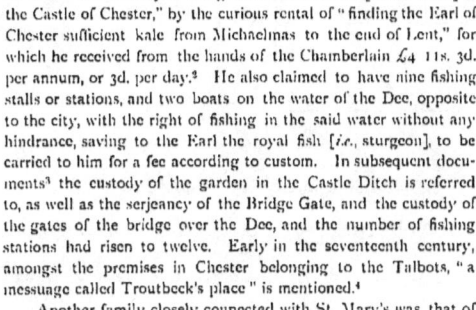

Another family closely connected with St. Mary's was that of the BRERETONS, who appear to have been almost as closely identified with the chantry chapel of St. Katherine at the east end of the north aisle as the Troutbecks were with the chapel of the Holy Trinity at the east end of the south aisle. Indeed, it is not improbable that this chapel owed its foundation to some member of the Brereton family. As already shown (on p. 35), there were formerly in the east window of St. Katherine's Chapel the coats of Brereton and Brereton impaling Ipstones, and a Latin inscription asking for prayers "for the good estate of Randle Brereton and Cecily and Joan his wives and for the souls of his father and mother which said Randle caused this glass work to be made in the year of our Lord 1523."

This RANDLE BRERETON held land in Wettenhall and Eccleston, co. Chester, as well as in Chester, and was a younger son (in some pedigrees said to be illegitimate) of Sir Randle Brereton of Ipstones, Knt.[5] He died in 1537, and in his will, here printed for the first time, there are some interesting references to St. Mary's.

---

[1] *Harl. MS.*, 2115, quoted by Ormerod.
[2] *See* on this Morris' *Chester in Plantagenet Times*, p. 99.
[3] The inquisition taken after the death of Sir William Troutbeck, Knt., in 1511, and the settlement made by John Talbot, Esq., and Margaret his wife, about the same date.
[4] The inquisition after the death of John Talbot, Esq., taken in 1620.
[5] In the short pedigree in Ormerod's *Cheshire*, vol. ij., p. 193, he is said to have married Katherine, daughter of William Manley of Poulton, gent.

TROUTBECK ARMS of "From Burkes' general Armory" 3rd Edition

TROUTBECK or TROUTBACK. Argent, three trouts fretted in triangle, tete-a-la-guise, argent. Crest - a wolf's head erased ppr.

TROUTBECK. Argent, a moran's head between three fleur-de-lis sable.

TROWTBACK. Azure, three trouts fretted in triangle tete-a-la-guise argent. Crest - a scaling ladder sable.

TROWTBECK. Azure three trouts fretted argent. Crest - a naked man sable holding in the right hand a dart or.

TROWTEBACK. The same arms. Crest - out of a ducal coronet or a lion's gamb ppr. holding a cross crosslet fitchée of the first

TROUTBECK, Sir William, of Dunham (Edw IV. Roll) Azure, three troutbeck interturned argent quarterly with, argent, a trefoyle sable between three moor's heads couped proper. Ballard & Arundel Rolls. Foster's Some Feudal arms. p 193.

OLD CHESHIRE FAMILIES CONNECTED WITH ST. MARY'S.   187

ABSTRACT OF THE WILL OF RANDLE BRERETON OF CHESTER, 1537.[1]

The 15th day of August, 27 Hen. 8 [1535]
Memorandum that I RANDOLPH BRERETON of Chester make my last will and testament in manner following.

I would my body should be buried in the Chapel of St. Katherine within St. Mary's on the Hill before the midst of the altar there.

I will that Sir Thomas Doune, priest, shall sing for my soul for the space of two years next after my decease, and have for his "wages" £5 a year.

I give to my daughter Alice for her marriage if she be counselled and ordered by the advice of my Executors £26 13s. 4d.

I will that my wife (Jane) shall have my farm and holding at Eccleston for 10 years next after my decease "if she so long kepe her sole" to the intent she may the better bring up and succour her children. She is also to have as much fuel out of Eccleston Wood as shall "reasonable serve her fire" so that she make no sale nor waste. At the end of the said 10 years my said wife shall have her part of the said farm according to law, and my son Thomas shall have the rest. To Edward Dodde I give 2 mares 2 colts and 2 heifers. To . . . . . . Milner[2] 40s. The residue of all my goods I give and bequeath to my wife and son.

I ordain my brother Owen Brereton, my brother[-in-law] David Dodde, Sir Robert Danolde priest, parson of Hoeley, Jane my wife & Thomas Brereton my son, to be my Executors, and my Master, William Brereton Esq. Chamberlain of Chester to be overseer thereof.

I give to my said son Thomas my best salt with the cover &c. to the intent he be good & kind to his mother, brothers & sisters.

[*This feoffment is attached to the will.*]

To all men by whom this present writing and last will of me Randolf Brereton of Chester shall be seen. Know ye that I will that all my recoverers feoffees and their heirs and every other person who is now seised of my manors, meases, lands & tenements in Wetenhall or elsewhere in Co. Chester, to the use of me & my heirs shall stand and be seised thereof to the use of me during my life, and after my decease they shall stand seised thereof and shall take the rents issues and profits of the same yearly, and with the same shall pay to Thomas Perpoynte of London So[n] or so much thereof as shall happen to be unpaid at the time of my death, for the payment whereof Thomas Aston of Aston Esq. and Roger Challonor of London stand bound for me. After the said sum be paid then I will that the said recoverers &c. be seised of the premises and with the rents thereof pay all my debts where my goods will not extend to the same. After my debts be paid then the feoffees shall be seised of the premises for 3 years and shall pay the issues thereof towards the marriage of my daughter Anne Brereton. When my will has been performed in all things then I will that the feoffees be seised of the premises to the use of Thomas Brereton my son & heir apparent and to his heirs male. For default of such issue then to the use successively in tail male of my sons John, Randolph, and Nicholas Brereton; for default to my right heirs; for default to the use of Elizabeth and Alice my daughters and to their heirs; for default to the use successively in tail male of Owen Brereton my brother & of David Dodde my brother in law.

And whereas it is covenanted and agreed between William Manley and me the said Randolph by indenture dated the 8th day of March, 21 Hen. 8 [1529] that if the said William or his heirs pay to me, my heirs or executors 850 marks at one time within 13 years immediately following the date of the said indenture, then and from thenceforth the said William and his heirs shall have the

[1] This will is preserved at Somerset House, P.C.C., Dyngley 8.
[2] Probably James Milner, curate of St. Mary's in 1570 (*see* page 107), if so he must have been there earlier than hitherto recorded.

B B 2

said premises in Wetenhall. If the said William pay the said sum then I give 500 marks to my son Thomas, 100 marks each to my sons John, Randolph & Nicolas and 50 marks to my wife.

"I give & bequeath all my said measses lands & tenaments in Chester to my son Thomas and to his heirs.

"I give to every of my younger sons 40s. a year. Dated the 4th day of June, 23 Hen. 8." [1531.]

"[Proved at Lambeth 9th day of August 1537]"

There are occasional later references to members of this family being buried at St. Mary's,[1] and in the inquisition taken after the death of Richard Brereton, Esq., in 1629, it is stated that he had died seised of certain messuages in Chester, together with "the advowson of the church of St Mary on the Hill in the city of Chester." This advowson, as already pointed out on p. 2, had then been in the possession of the Breretons for nearly 100 years, as John Brereton, of Eccleston, Esq., presented Charles Duckworth as rector of St. Mary's in 1554 (see p. 81).

A third family connected with St. Mary's was that of the WORSLEYS, a younger branch of the old Lancashire family of Worsley of Worsley. RALPH WORSLEY, Esq., the third son of William Worsley, of Worsley, in the parish of Eccles, near Manchester, who was born about the year 1483, became a somewhat distinguished man about the Court of Henry the Eighth, holding many appointments there as well as in Lancashire and Cheshire. He most probably lived in Chester in the latter years of his life, and was the owner of the manors of Birkenhead and Claughton, and lands there formerly belonging to Birkenhead Priory, as well as of the ferry across the Mersey between Birkenhead and Liverpool. On his death, on the 27th December, 1572,[2] early in the reign of Queen Elizabeth, he was buried at St. Mary's, where a handsome marble slab, bearing a long Latin inscription, and surmounted by a well-carved coat of arms, was placed to his memory. Both the inscription and the coat of arms, although now separated the one from the other, are still preserved in the church, and the former has been printed in full, with a careful translation, on p. 45. It is the oldest inscription now remaining in the

ARMS AND CREST OF RALPH WORSLEY, ESQ., IN ST. MARY'S CHURCH.[3]

---

[1] Thus in the Churchwardens' Accounts for 1581 there is a reference to Mr. Urian Brereton's "lay stall," or burial-place, and Mr. William Brereton is mentioned in 1582. "Thomas Brereton gentleman" was buried at St. Mary's on April 11, 1548, and "Mr Randle Brereton" on 9th June, 1551 (see p. 108).

[2] On the monument to his memory in St. Mary's Church (see p. 45) he is stated to have died on the 27th December, 1573, but this is a clerical error. The inquisition taken after his death is dated 23rd October, 1573, and it is there stated that he had died on the 27th December last past.

[3] In connection with these arms it may here be mentioned that Mr. J. Paul Rylands informs me that there is on record in the Heralds' College, London (E.D.N, 36, fo. 158) a grant of arms (not dated) from Christopher Barker, Garter King of Arms,

Sr Ralf' [Geoffrey] de Workesley. (16th Century roll of arms)
Argent, a chief gules
Trans: Ches. & Lanc. Hist. Soc. Vol xxxvIII. p.153.

church, and as the lettering is much faded it would be well to have it carefully gone over, and the letters repainted so as to ensure its preservation for another two or three hundred years.

From this inscription it appears that Ralph Worsley had been in the service of Henry the Eighth as Page of the Wardrobe and one of the Stewards of the Chamber, and that that King, " on account of the good and faithful service spent about his own Royal person," had appointed him for life to be one of the Sergeants of the Crown, Warden or Keeper of the lions, lionesses, and leopards in the Tower of London, Porter of the Great Wardrobe, Controller in the counties of Chester and Flint, Clerk of the Crown of Lancaster, and Escheator in the County Palatine of Lancaster. Truly a large number of offices of more or less importance, some of which he refers to in his will. His epitaph also tells us that " pre-eminent mental gifts were bestowed upon him by Heaven, with which he was remarkably endowed, as for example rare piety towards God, widely ranging beneficence towards the poor and wonderful charity towards all men."

By his wife Joan, daughter of John Pike, Esq., he had three daughters, coheiresses : *Alice*, who married Thomas Powell, of Horsley, co. Denbigh, Esq.; *Katherine*, who married (1) Thomas Touchett, of Nether Whitley, co. Chester, Esq., and (2) Edward Legh, of Hallam,[1] brother of Sir Peter Legh, of Lyme, co. Chester, Knt.; and *Avice*, who married (1) Thomas Vawdrey, of the Riddings, co. Chester, (2) Humphrey Davenport,[2] of Northenden, and 3) John Shakerley, gentleman. His Inquisition *post mortem* was taken on the 23rd Oct., 15 Elizabeth [1573], when the above three ladies were found to be aged thirty, twenty-nine, and twenty-eight years respectively, the youngest, Avice, being then married to her second husband. He had died on the 27th Dec. " last past," which would be in 1572, and was at the time of his death seised of the manors of Birkenhead, Claughton, and Walton, *alias* Wolton, and messuages and lands in those places and in Tranmore and Wallasey. He also possessed the ferry over the river Mersey in Birkenhead aforesaid.[3]

Ralph Worsley's will, which is dated the 13th November, 1572, is a very long document, containing much of interest. It is here given in full, from the original in the Probate Court, Chester.[4]

THE WILL OF RALPH WORSLEY, OF CHESTER, ESQ.

" In the name of God the ffather the Son and the Holy Gost amen the thrittenth daie of November in the yere of our Lord God one thowsand ffyve hundreth threescore and twelve and in the ffourtenth yere of the raigne of sov'aigne Ladye Elizabeth &c.

" I RAUFF WORSLEY of the cytie of Chester Esquier beinge of good and pfecte mynde and remembraunce lawde and prayse be unto Almightie God althoughe sycke in body and dredinge the soddennesse of death wch as it is to all men certeyne so the houre and tyme therof is most uncerteyne

---

[1] to Ralph Worsley, of Birkenhead, co. Chester, which is quite different from the coat above depicted. It may be described as Azure, on three lozenges in pile, between as many crescents, one and two Or, three lions rampant of the field. Crest, a sparrow-hawk Argent, beaked and legged Or, belled silver. A variation or bad drawing of this coat occurs in a Touchett pedigree, dated 1597, in the possession of Sir Richard Brooke, Bart., of Norton Priory. In this shield the arms are Azure, three lozenges Or, each charged with a lion rampant of the first, above each lozenge a crescent of the second. It is not improbable that Ralph Worsley disliked this complicated coat, and had a simpler one granted to him.

[1] He was buried at Winwick, co. Lanc., 22 Jan., 1608-9, without issue. His will bears date 27 April, 1606 (*East Cheshire*, ij., 304). She was buried at St. Mary's in 1615 (*see* p. 113).

[2] He was a younger son of William Davenport, of Bramhall, Esq., and was buried at Northenden, 19 Dec., 1588, and on the 4 Sept., 1589, his widow was married there to John Shakerley, gent. Mrs. Avice Shakerley was buried at Northenden, 18 Feb., 1618-19. She had issue by Humphrey Davenport (*East Cheshire*, j., 437).

[3] He also had an illegitimate daughter, Katherine, married to Francis Sherington, of Wardley, co. Lanc.

[4] Printed by the Chetham Society in *Lancashire and Cheshire Wills*, vol. viij., pp. 16-21.

myndynge to stablishe and put in certeyntye howe and in what maner my lands tents goods and cattalls shalbe imployed used and bestowed after my deathe doo therfore ordeyne declare and by these p'sents make my testament conteyninge therin my laste will in maner and forme as hereafter doth ensue and folowe that is to saye ffyrste and pryncipally I bequethe my soule unto Almightie God ffyrmely trustinge and belevinge that through the meryts of his dere Sone Jesus Christe I shall have the fruyc̄on and be ptaker of his eternall glory And my body I bequethe to Christyan buryall to be sepultured and buryed in such decent and godly ordre as to the discrec̄on of th' executors and supvisors of this my laste will shalbe thought mete and convenyent.

"And I gyve and bequeyth to the poore people of the pishe of St. Maryes in Chester ffyve pounds and to the poore people of the pishe of St. Johnes in Chester ff[i]ve pounds and to the poore people of the pishe of St. Oswalds in Chester ffourtye shillings and to the poore people of ev'y of the pishes of St. Peter the Trynytie St. Martyns St. Brydes St. Mychells and St. Towleys [i.e., St. Olave's] in the said cittie of Chester twentye shillings all w̄ᶜʰ somes before menc̄oned I will shalbe geven and dely͞v'ed to the said poore people of the foresaid sev'all pishes at their dwellinge howses and not otherwyse.

"I gyve &c. to my servante Thomas Shurlocke tenne pounds and to my s'vante John Lowes ffourtye shillings and to my s'vante James Wayte tenne pounds and to my s'vaunte Richard Watte ffourtye shillings To Margaret Mayre my mayde s'vaunte ffourtye shillings and to Johanne Jamesson one other of my mayd s'vaunts ffourtye shillings Unto Hughe Worsley sone of my brother Otnell Worsley one hundreth pounds And I gyve &c. for the mayntenance and releyfe of my doughter Avyce nowe wyef of Thomas Vawdrey two hundreth poundes to be bestowed upon her in such maner and at such tymes as shall be thought mete by th' executors or supvisors of this my laste will upon this condic̄on ffolowinge that is to saye that yf the said Thomas Vawdrey and my said daughter Avice his wyffe do not hold them selves contente w̄ᵗʰ this my bequest in full contentac̄on of all such pte of my goods as they or eyther of them might by any meane clayme or yf they shall refuse to make unto my executors at their request after my decesse one sufficyent release in wrytinge of all acc̄ons and demaunds w̄ᶜʰ they or eyther of them shold or might have agaynste my executors ffor or about any pte of my said goods or shall vexe sue or trowble my said executors for any matter or cause towchinge this my testament or th' execuc̄on of the same or shall demaunde or seke any thinge contrary to the true menninge and intent of this my last will that then the said legacy and bequest of the said twoe hundreth pounds by me mad[e] to the use and for the mayntenāce of my said doughter Avyce shalbe frustrate and voyde.

"I gyve &c. to my cosyn Richard Birkenheade ffoure poundes in gold and to my ffrend M' Roger Hurleston ffoure poundes in gold and to my cosyn James Worsley of Pemberton gentleman tenne pounds and to Margaret Worsley wydowe late wyffe of Alexander Worsley deceased tenne poundes Also I wyll that tenne pounds shall be dely͞v'ed unto my ffrends Alexander Rigby of the Burghe and my sone in lawe ffrauncis Sherington to be by them distributed amongest the poore people of the towne of Wigan in the countye of Lancaster wherein I wold have blynde Gilbert Leighe to be specyally remembred I gyve to my s'vaunte Thomas Gullye my under keper of the lyons¹ twentye pounds I gyve to the wyeff of the said Thomas Gullye ffyve pounds and to Henry Johns s'fiante [serjeant] at armes yf he shall happen to be on lyve at the tyme of my decesse tenne pounds I gyve to my cosyn M' Barlowe dwellinge in Lombard strete yf she happen to be on lyve at the tyme of my decesse tenne pounds I gyve to my cosyn Thomas Browne ffyve marks and to my cosyn John Banester ffyve marks and to my cosyn Henry Birkenhead ffyve marks To my cosyn Thomas Birkenhead ffyve markes To M'ˢ Jane ffoxwyst ffyve marks I gyve to the late wyffe of John

¹ Ralph Worsley, as already pointed out, held the office of keeper or warden of the lions, lionesses, and leopards in the Tower of London.

[3414] RALPH WORSLEY'S BEQUEST.

(See No. 3407.)

"The Report of the Commissioners for Inquiring Concerning Charities," completed shortly before 1840, gives a fairly full account of Ralph Worsley's Bequest, and also partly accounts for the loss.

The Benefactor in his will directed that the residue of his goods should remain with his executors, and should be by them disposed of in charity and otherwise by the advice of the overseer of his will. Thomas Powell and Thomas Trickett, the executors, who were also sons-in-law of Worsley, did not comply with this direction, claiming that the whole residue came to them and their wives by virtue of a codicil to the will. By a decree of the Prerogative Court, dated 29 April, 17, Eliz (1575) they were, however, ordered to pay to the Mayor and Sheriff two hundred marks to be employed in maintaining a stock of wool "to set the poor people within the city . . . . awork in clothing." The Mayor and citizens, by an indenture, dated 29 September in the same year, acknowledged receipt of the sum and undertook to employ it in accordance with the order. A copy of this indenture is in Harl. MS., 2173.

On 10 Oct., 1576, a fourth of the sum was loaned to Nich las Massey for six years to be employed by him in the same kind of "cottoning, frising and clothing" in Chester, as made in Salop, Oswestry, Denbigh, and Chirk, etc., and late begun in this city. He was to maintain six poor people of Chester by this employment, and was to pay yearly for the use of the money 40s. to the censors, wardens, governors and collectors of the stock provided for the poor, and the sum was to be distributed by the said officers to the poor of the city. A second fourth sum was loaned on the same day to Griff. Dodd on similar terms, and Mr. Hewitt mentions the loan of another portion of the 200 marks to Robert Mulesky.

Further loans under the same conditions were made to Thomas Johns and Randall Walker for five years on 21 Feb., 40 Eliz.

By indentures of 22 Feb., 1602, loans were made to Randall Walker and Thomas Johns for ten years, each paying 10s. yearly for the poor and impotent of the city.

On 30 Sep., 1603, it was ordered that, as half the bequest had been lost by reason of the decay of those to whom it had been lent, the amount should be repaid out of the treasury of the city as soon as might be.

26 March, 1615, a fourth of the sum was lent to Randall Smith for ten years. In 1620 two portions were lost, and in 1625 one portion.

This is the last record to be found of the money being loaned, but a memorandum on a parchment roll supplies a final notice of the charity and, in part, accounts for its disappearance. The note itself is not dated but it is evident, without referring to the date of the succeeding note that it refers to the time of the siege. It mentions difficulty experienced in obtaining repayment of benefactors' moneys due, several having been "put in suite." The sums called in, which include £100, 9s. of Ralph Worsley's charity, had been expended in the payment of Sir Thomas Aston's regiment of horse, in connection with the King's visit to Chester, in payment of the city soldiers, in purchase of powder and bullets, in repair of the stone walls, mud walls, gates, etc.

Then follows a statement of military disbursements from January 1642, to October, 1643, by virtue of the King's command; the notes being signed by Sir Thomas Aston and paid by Mr. Mayor's direction.

J. H. E. B.

Indenture made 10 Octob. ann. 18 Eliz: (1576.) betweene the Maior & Citizens of Chester, and Robert Modesley, Sherman; about lending him part of the 200 markes bequeathed by Rauffe Wursley Esq; to be imployed onlely in Cloathinge, and the gaine thereof, to be bestowed on the poore:— Harl. MSS. N° 2046. 4. fol. 2.

[1433] THE MANOR OF WORKESLEGH.

On the 31st Dec., 1395, Richard de Workeslegh, chaplain, appeared before the Vice-Justice, Chamberlain, and Escheator of Chester and other Cheshire men and one of the Justices of the King's Bench, and made a declaratie: that "Dominus" Geoffrey de Workeslegh Kt. enfeoffed in fee simple the said Richard and Robert de Mampton, late Vicar of Eccles, of the Manor of Workeslegh; that Robert surrendered his rights to Richard; that sometime afterwards Geoffrey came from abroad and requested to be re-enfeoffed of the manor; that they then went by a way near the said Manor called "La Cansey" to the gate of the manor, where Richard placed the ring of the gate in Geoffrey's hands and said, "Here I gyve ye Geffrey fulle seison in "this manor of Workeslegh, with alle the "apportenance as fulle as I bade hit of yowe sum "tyme"; that the same was done at the door of the hall and Geoffrey then said "Blessed be God "nowe I am lorde of Workeslegh, and so was y "hoght mony day here byfore."

Geoffrey then went abroad and died seized of the manor; three years later, Richard was in the Chapel of Done (Dean, Co. Lancs.) with Robert de Heton and John de Horewych Clerk, when Robert de Workeslegh, accompanied by Ely de Heton, came to him with a charter, without a seal, relating to the said manor, and requested him to sign it; he refused to do so but being threatened by Robert he signed, calling upon de Heton to witness and saying "Loo [sic] I most "(must) refeoff ' the maner of Workesloove wrong-"fullyth, and therefore y pray tho and charge the "byfore God that y'u bere witness hereof in tyme "comyng whatsoever fall of me."

If, as I suppose, this relates to the Manor of Worsley, Co. Lancs., why was the declaration taken before the dignitaries of Cheshire, and why was it enrolled upon the Chancery (Recognizance) Rolls of that county?   R. S. B.

Eveley decessed my late s'vaunte at the Towre [of London] ffyve pounds yf she happen to be on lyve at the tyme of my decesse I gyve to James Worsley basterd brother to my cosyn Alexander Worsley ffyve pounds To my ffrend John Wynnington of the Temple gent ffyve pounds I gyve unto Rauffe Worsley sone of my said cosyn Alexander Worsley decessed twenty pounds To John Worsley sone of my brother Seth Worsley decessed twenty pounds.

"I gyve &c. all and singler my lands tents and heredytaments wth their app'tenances in the cittie of London and the suburbes of the same wch Nych^ls Jennyns late citizen and alderman of London did gyve unto me and unto Joane my late wyffe and to the heyres of our twoe bodyes lawfully begotten unto Alyce Katheryne and Avyce doughters of me the said Rauffe Worsley and of the said Johane my late wyffe and to the heyres of the bodyes of the said Alyce Katheryne and Avyce lawfully I gyve to my ffrend Wittm Crofton ffyve marks and to Mr Wittm Glaseor ffyve pounds and to my cosyn Rychard Hurleston ffyve pounds and to my s'vaunte Thomas Hyckake ffyve markes.

"Also I doo gyve &c. all and singler my lands tents and heredytaments in the pishe of St. Myldreds in the Pultrey in the cittie of London late in the houldinge of John Mylner decessed or his assignes unto my cosyn Hughe Worsley sone of my brother Otnell[1] and the heires of the body of the said Hughe lawfully begotten Also I give &c. all and singler my lands tents and heredytaments wth th'app'tennes wch in the countye of Lancastre unto Katheryne nowe wyffe of ffrauncis Sherington and bastard doughter of me the said Rauffe Worsley to have and to hold the said lands and tents and other p'misses to the said Katheryne for terme of her lyffe And I will devyse &c. that the same lands tents and other the p'misses last before mencōned shall remayne and be imedyatly after the decesse of the said Katheryne to the heyres of the bodye of the said Katheryne lawfully begotten and for defaulte of heires of the body of the said Katheryne lawfully begotten I will that my said landes tents and other the p'misses wth th'app'tenńces shall remayne and be to my doughters Alyce wyffe of Thomas Powell and Katheryne wyffe of Thomas Tutchett and the heyres of the bodye of the same Alyce and Katheryne lawfully begotten Also I will that all the residue of my goods and cattalls wch I have not heretofore in this my testament gyven or bequeythed nor shall hereafter gyve bequethe or bestowe in my lyffe tyme shall remayne and be unto my executors hereafter named to be by them distrybuted and disposed in charytable dedes and otherwyse for the welth [? weal] of my soule by the advyce of my ffrend Alexander Rigbye one of the supvisors of this my last will.

"Also I constytute &c. my welbeloved sons in law Thomas Powell, Thomas Tutchett and ffrauncis Sherington to be executors of this my testament and laste will to execute and pform the same accordinge to my mynde and will therin declared as my truste is in them And I ordeyne &c. my lovinge cosyns and ffrends Wittm ffletwodd Esquier Recorder of the Cyttie of London and the said Alexander Rigbye of the Burgh to be supvisors &c. And I gyve to eyther of my said supvisors twentye pounds for their paynes and travells to be bestowed and taken in and about th'execucōn of the p'misses In witness whereof to this my p'sent testament conteyninge herin my last will I the said Rauffe Worsley have put to my seale &c.

"Also I geve &c. the moytie or one halfe of all my manors mēses lands and tents in Birkenhead Wolton *als* Woton Claughton Bideston Walazey and ['Tranmere?] wth in the coin of Chester to my doughter Alyce nowe wyfe of Thomas Powell to have and hold to the said Alyce for terme of her naturall lyffe wth out impechment of wast And I will that the same moytie or halfe of the manors and other the last recyted p'misses shall imedyatly after the decesse of the said Alyce remeyne and be to the sev^all uses behoves and intents conteyned and specyfied in a payre of indentures made betweene me of the one ptie and Alexander Rigbye of the Burghe in the coin of Lancastre and Thomas Browne of Hoole in the countye of Chester gentleman of the other ptie beringe date the

---

[1] Or Ottiwell, *see* the pedigree on p. 192.

See Collins Baronetage 1741 vol. 1 f. 129 Original Coat. Arg. a chief az. then as. a chev. bet. 3 choughs sa.
Worsley of Apuldercombe baronets. 1744. arg. a chief gu. 2 & 3 ag a chev bet. 3 falcons close (tho' by the foregoing account given by Collins they were three choughs. Sa.).
Crest. On a wreath, a wolf's head erased, or.

ST. MARY-ON-THE-HILL, CHESTER.

eight day of November in the said ffourtenth yere of the raigne of the Quenes Ma*tie* that nowe is and under such condicõns as is conteyned in the same indenture. And also I geve &c. the other moytie or halfe of all my manors &c. last before mencõned to my doughter Katheryne nowe wyfe of the said Thomas Tutchett to have and hold to the said Katheryne for terme of her lyfe w*th*out impechement of waste And I will that the same other moytie or halfe of the same manors and other the said last recyted p'misses shall imedyatly after the decease of the said Katheryne remayne and be to the sev*all* uses behoves and intents" &c. [as before.]

The following is on a separate piece of parchment fastened to the probate:—

"The said Rauffe Worsley intendyng therby more playnly and pticularly to declare and explayne his meanynge in the legacie of the residue of his goods mencõned in his will as well before as after y*e* makinge of his will dyd signifie and publishe before credible psons that notw*th*standinge any thinge therin conteyned his meanynge was that Thomas Towchett and Thomas Powell shuld have the saide residue of his goods and to be goodd to the pore as he was wont to be in his lieffe tyme and as they saw cause accordinge to the truste that he reposed in them or the like wordes in effecte."

The following pedigree (based on one in *Harl. MS.* 2040, f. 296*b*) will probably be of interest here as several of the later descendants of this family, as well as the Powells of Horsley, &c., were buried at St. Mary's.

Pedigree of Worsley of Chester and Birkenhead.

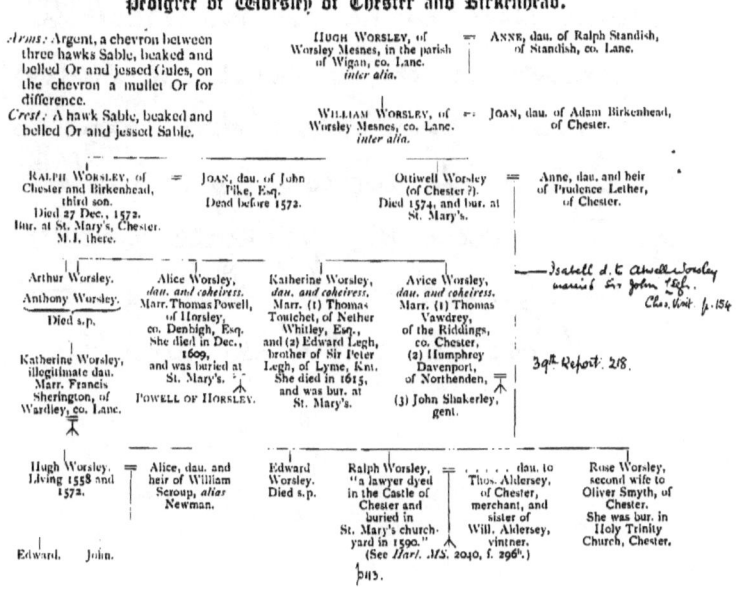

Touchett of Nether Whitley.
(Harl. 1424. fo. 136.)

Ninth in descent from Sir Thomas Tochett Lord of Whitley, Buglawton, and Tattenhall in com. Cestriæ tpe K E I (1272-1307), Thomas Tochett of Nether Whitley, son of Thomas Touchet of Nether Whitley and his wife Bridgett daugliter to Adam Birkenhead, not Beckett as shewn by the Pedigree of Croton (?) married Katherine dau [and co-heir] to Rafe Wowley of Chester, gent'. And the pedigree of 1580 gives their family as one son, Robert Tochett of Nether Whitley.

OLD CHESTER FAMILIES CONNECTED WITH ST. MARY'S.

The OLDFIELD family was originally connected with St. Mary's, owing to the fact that the founder of the family, PHILIP OLDFIELD, Esq., a prominent Chester barrister, lived in the parish and was buried in the church in the year 1616, the handsome monument still remaining in the north chapel, and already fully described on pp. 42-4, having been erected to his memory. He was the eldest son of Philip Oldfield of Middlewich and Elizabeth Swinton his wife, and was born about the year 1541. He was educated at Gray's Inn as a barrister and practised at Chester for many years. He was married about 1569 to Helen the daughter and heir of William Berrington of Bradwall, in the parish of Sandbach, co. Chester, gentleman, by whom he had a large family.* By this marriage he ultimately succeeded to the Bradwall estate, where he appears to have frequently resided as well as in Chester. The birth of his eldest son and heir apparent in 1575 is entered at great length in the Sandbach Register, in Latin, of which the following is a translation :—

ARMS AND CREST OF THE OLDFIELD FAMILY.

"1575. Memorandum that Philip Oldfeld, of Greyes Inn, in the county of Middlesex, gentleman, and Helen, his wife, daughter and heir apparent of William Berynton, of Bradwall, co. Chester, gentleman, had issue begotten betwixt them an only son, at the Hall of Bradwall, in the parish of Sandbach, in the said county of Chester, on Tuesday being the 28th June. The which son of the said Philip and Helen was afterwards, namely on the Friday then next following, being the first day of July in the said year, baptized in the parish church of Middlewich in the said county by the name of Thomas Oldfeld, Thomas Venables, esq., son and heir apparent of Thomas Venables, of Kinderton, in the said county of Chester, Knight, and William Bowcor [Bowyer], of Knypersley, in the county of Stafford, esq., and Elizabeth, the wife of the said William Berynton, being the sponsors of the said child."

On the 30th May, 1578, his wife was buried at Sandbach, and on the 2nd Dec., 1582, he was married at Malpas to his second wife Helen, daughter of William Hanmer, of Fennes, Esq., and then the widow of John Griffith, Serjeant-at-Law, by whom he had a family of three sons and one daughter. He died at Chester on the 15th Dec., 1616, aged 75, and was buried in St. Catherine's Chapel in St. Mary's on the 17th Dec. In the epitaph put up to his memory (see p. 43) he is spoken of as deserving well of his county "by reason of the work done by him in constructing roads and bridges as well as in investigating the most ancient pedigrees of its families." He was also "most distinguished as a lawyer and citizen" of Chester.

No copy of his will, if he made one, is now to be found at the Probate Registry, Chester, but the inventory of his goods, &c., is still preserved there. This document is of great length and is of much interest as showing the possessions of a rich lawyer at the beginning of the seventeenth century. It is too long to give in full, but the following abstract gives the chief items, many of which are very curious. Those at his residence, the Green Hall, in Chester are given first, and subsequently those at Bradwall. The total amounted to £1,310 6s. 5d., a very large sum in those days.[1] There are many dialect words in this inventory.

---

[1] I have already printed this list in my *History of Sandbach*, pp. 134-6.

A true and perfect Inventory of all the Goods &c. which late were of Phillippe Oldfeild Esquier deceased as they were seen vallewed and appraised by John Cooke, Randle Holme, Thomas Weston and Robert Smithe, Citizens of the Cittie of Chester, George Holland, Richard ffurnivall, Thomas Broomefeild, John Hatton, Richard Brooke, John ap Richard, and Richard Holme, yeomen of the Countie palatyn of Chester, begun on the 19th Dec. 1616 and fynished the 10 Marche following.

Imprim's in the Greene Hall in Chester. In Castle Street and ultimately the property of the Yeards (of Greenwood).

Item one silk grograyne gowne and two black clothe gownes vallewed at	vij^{li}. [£7]
Item one velvett Jerkin and a paier of velvet hose	xxvj^s. viij^d.
Item one Sattyn doblett and an old velvet Jerkin	xviij^s.
Item three paier of rounde hose	xj^s.
Item three paier of oulde stockinges & a paier of black gamashees'	iiij^s.
Item one Rideinge Cassack	v^s.
Item one study gowne	xxvj^s. viij^d.
Item one parted doblett of stuff and one greate gamashin stockinge	ij^s. vj^d.
Item one payer of hose of read bayes [red baize]	x^d.
Item one old beaver hatt	xij^d.

In the Studie Chamber.

Item in bookes conneminge the lawes	xl^s.
Item six bookes of the Statuts at large	iij^s.
Item eight bookes of historyes & heraldrye	viij^s.
Item a dictionary	ij^s.
Item a new bible & ten bookes of Divinitye	xv^s.
Item fitz Herberts abridgment & brookes abridgm'.	xx^s.

& other books in cupboards &c.

A paier of gloves a paier of mittons & a dossen of silke poynts [i.e. laces]	xij^d.
A large quantity of silver plate valued at 4s. 7d. the ounce & " guilt plate " valued at 5s. the ounce.	
A signet ringe of gold	xxxvj^s.
A seale skyn'd cheist	iiij^s. vj^d.
In coyned gold the sum of	lxxxxj^{li}. xij^d.

Total ccxlvij^{li}. iij^s. [£247. 3s.]

Within and aboute the howse at Bradwall.

Oxen, horses, kyne, wheat, barley &c.

Item a bull	iij^{li}. [£3]
Item two fatt kyne	iiij^{li}.
Item five draught chaynes, a copsowe^2 & two copsowe pynns and a crowe [or crowbar] of iron	xv^s. iiij^d.
Item two nawgers [augers] a guarge [? a gauge] a handshaw a wymble,^{3} a paier of pinsers & a hammer	ij^s.
Item one Coache^4 wth wheeles	v^{li}.

[1] Gamashees were loose drawers or stockings worn outside the leg, over the other clothing, and much used by travellers. = overall
[2] A "copsal" is said by Halliwell to be a piece of iron which terminates the front of a plough.
[3] A "wimble" was a large auger.
[4] Coaches were very uncommon at this date.

OLD CHESTER FAMILIES CONNECTED WITH ST. MARY'S.

In the brew house.
- Item one Bracke .... xij'.
- Item one Stound, one piggen three drifats & a Boultinge Tubb ...... vj'. vii '.
- Item one hayre to drye malte on ...... xi j'. iiij.
- Item a moldinge boorde & a lugge of wood ...... viij'.
- Item a wodden steade ...... vj'.

In the Buttrey.
- Item a bazen & Ewer of maslyn [brass] ...... vj'. viij'.
- Item a drawinge voyder [basket or tray] ...... v'.
- Item two stillinges [frames or stands] ...... xij'.

In the higher parlor.
A paire of playinge Tables.

In the Hall.
- Item one drawinge Table & its frame ...... xl'.
- Item a little square Table & keyvinge Tables & two longe formes ...... x'.
- Item in the hall one Calliver [or large pistol or blunderbus] ...... v'.
- Item a bandalyer flax and a matche ...... ij'. vj'.

In the chamber over the Kitchen.
- Item one bedsteed w* a Testerne¹ & a Trundell² bedd ...... xx'.
- Item one Twiggen chayer & a cushin ...... v'.
- Item a urynall glasse, a case & an old pen & ynckhorne and a little baskett ...... ij'.
- Item a warminge pan ...... j'.
- Item an olde Studye Gowne ...... v'.
- Item Chesse boordes and the Men ...... ij'.

In the daie house [? dairy house].
- Item four Eshins [pails] and two little bowkes [buckets] one old stoond & woodden ladle ...... ij. vj'.
- Item a clock and bell in the buttrey Chamber ...... iiij'i. vj'. voj'.
- Item a booke of husbandrie ...... xij'.

"Pikles" [or pitchforks] are mentioned in the stables, &c.

Powltrey, &c., &c.
- Item ten turkeys ...... v'.
- Item three Digs [an old Cheshire word for duck] and a Drake ...... ij'.
- Item ffower Capons ...... iiij'.
- Item seaven pea hens and cocks ...... vij'.
- Item two sighes [? scythes] and a hooke ...... xx⁴.
- Item a Marlinge nawger [auger] ...... x⁴.
- Item one fowleinge peece ...... vj'. viij⁴.
- Item one new bible ...... x'.

In the storehouse.
- Item two pye plates, one olde voyder [basket or tray] and a Cullander Dishe ...... x'.
- Item one Lymbeck [an alembic] & two little ones ...... xx',

---

¹ The "tester" was the fixed top and head parts of a bedstead.

² A "trundle-bed" or "truckle-bed" was a low bed on castors trundled under a larger bed and on which a servant or other inferior person slept at night.

In the Maydens Chamber &c.
Item a hetchell (or hatchell, an instrument used to dress flax with) .... ij^s.

In the Studie.
Item four portmantuas...... .... iiij^s.
Item a standish, & two paier of spectacles & an old dagger...... ij^s.
Item an hower glasse .... xij^d.
Item a bowe & a sheaff of arrowes... .. ij^s.
Item eight horse shoes being old vj^d.
Item two pictures .... ij^s.
Item a Levill and a staffe ... . vj^d
Item a pumptree v^s.
Item a herball .. v^s.
Item one good cloke .... xl^s.
Item one Lattayne Bible .... v^s.
Item in bookes in the inner studie v^h,
Item a nest of boxes... .. ij^s.
Item a guilte pen & ynoke .... ij^s.
Item in walking staves .... ij^s.

Bricks at 10^s. the thousand.   Coarser bricks at 5^s. the thousand.

Item a lease made by Rauffe Leftwiche and William Leftwiche to this intestate of certain parcells of the demesne of Leftw^{ch} for the terme of lx yeres bearing date 8 James 20 Dec. [1610] if the said Rauffe Leftwiche soe longe do lyve...   C^{li}. [£100]
Item one fether bedd   ... .   xl^s.
Item one downe bedd ....   iiij^{li}.
Item one caddowe   ...   .   x^s.
Item the intestates debts due & owinge unto him by divers psons upon sev'all specialtyes ... .   v^c xx^{li}. [£520]

The totall some of all & every of the somes in this Inventory sett downe & mentioned is..   } I$^{mlij^l}$ x^s. vj^s. v^d. [£1,310 6s. 5d.]

Exhibited 11 March 1616[17].

Philip Oldfield's inquisition *post mortem*, which was taken at Sandbach on the 13th June, 1617,[1] deals almost entirely with his Sandbach and Middlewich property, and does not mention any messuage or lands in Chester. By his first wife he had a son and heir Thomas Oldfield, who settled at Bradwall, and became the founder of the line of the Oldfields of that place, of whom a full pedigree will be found in my *History of Sandbach*, pp. 138-9. He had also a daughter Elizabeth, who married John Wettenhall. By his second wife he had three sons, Philip, Michael, and William, who all married heiresses and became the founders of the three families of the Oldfields of Somerford, Croxton, and Leftwich, all in Cheshire, respectively. Margaret, his daughter by his second wife, married Peter Shakerley of Hulme, co. Chester, Esq. These four sons and two daughters are represented on his monument in St. Mary's, together with their shields of arms, &c. (*see* p. 43). After Philip Oldfield's death the connection of his descendants with St. Mary's practically ceased.

---

[1] An abstract will be found in the *History of Sandbach*, p. 136.

The Charities of St. Mary's.

The Charities of St. Mary's are not very numerous or important, but much interest attaches to them as the largest one now existing is the outcome of a large number of small legacies left at different times to the church. These small sums were allowed to accumulate in the hands of the Churchwardens, and, as will be shown later on, were ultimately invested in land.

The earliest list of benefactions to the poor of St. Mary's which I have met with occurs in one of the Randle Holmes' MSS. in the British Museum (*Harl. MS.* 2176, f. 60), and was probably drawn up about the middle of the seventeenth century. It is written in a somewhat hurried manner, but with the contracted words, &c., extended, it is as follows:—

GIFTS TO ST MARYES IN CHESTER.

Mrs Isabell Hurleston,[1] widdow, gave 5^{li} [£5]. the use [*i.e.*, the interest] to be given to ten poore widdows, 2^d a peece in bread on May day, St James, St Lukes and Candlemas dayes.

John Maddocks gave 6^{li} [£6], the use to be given on Whitsyn eve, All Saints eve, Christmas eve and Good Friday.

Alderman John Brereton[2] gave 10^{li} [£10] the use to be given to the poore on St Georges day. See pp. 198-200

Richard Partington gave 5^{li} [£5], the use to the poor on Witsun eve.

M^r. Thomas Swinton[3] gave 5^{li} 7^s 6^d [£5 7s. 6d.], the use to be given to the poore on Christmas eve.

John Sandbach gave 10^{li} 8^s [£10 8s.] the use to the poore on Christmas eve.

M^r .... Edwards[4] of Cheley [Cheveley] gave 10^{li} [£10] the use to the poore on Christmas eve.

Jane daughter to Robert Collyer[5] late Vicar [*sic* for Rector] of this parish gave 5^{li} [£5] the use to the poore on Good Friday.

Madame[6] Katherine Mainwaring, relict to Sir Randle Mainwaring gave to the parish a rich imbroidered pulpit cloth and 5^{li} [£5].

Mrs Ellen Danald gave 3^{li} [£3].

Cicely Findlow [gave] 2^{li} 5^s [£2 5s.] the use to the poore on Good Friday.

Thomas Ormes gave 2^{li} [£2] the use to the poore on Good Friday.

Mr Henry Smith[7] of London gave 5^{li} [£5] yearely out of his lands to be given to the poore.

Mrs Alice Whitby,[8] widdow, gave 3^{li} 6^s [£3 6s.], the use to the poore on Good Friday.

Mr Gamull[9] gave 7^{li} [£7], the use to repaire the church and 20^s yearely out of his land to repaire the high-way.

---

[1] A copy of Mrs. Isabel Hurleston's will occurs in *Harl. MS.* 2131, f. 197. She desired to be buried "in St Marys in Chester neere to the good Lady Mainwaringe" and she bequeathed to M^r. Seddon, clerk, "10^s. and 10^s more to preach my funeral sermon and to his six children 2s. 6d a piece." The date of the will is not given, but it was, I believe, proved at Chester in 1640.

[2] His will bears date 14 November, 1628. *mayor of Chester 1623, died 4 July 1631. Buried in St John's church. Funeral Certificate & was the son of*

[2a] Died 1637 (*see* p. 93).

[3] This was probably John Edwards, of Cheveley, gentleman, who died in 1637, the father of Francis Edwards, rector of St. Mary's (*see* pp. 83 5).

[4] She died in 1623. See an abstract of her will on p. 83.

[5] It is strange she is not called *Dame* Katherine Mainwaring. She died in 1618 *see* p. 62).

[6] His will bears date 26 January, 1626 (*see* p. 200).

[7] She was the widow of Thomas Gamul, Esq., Recorder of Chester, and died in 1640 (*see* p. 41).

[8] Probably Thomas Gamul, the Recorder, who died in 1613 (*see* pp. 39-41).

(1) *Mathhew Anderton ebeled one of the Drummers con...ment men in June 1685 and executed on 19 July 1688.*

ST. MARY-ON-THE-HILL, CHESTER.

Mr Brereton of Eccleston gave 5^h [£5], the use to repaire the high waye in Eccleston lane. Richard Weston gave 1^h [£1] and widdow Hale gave 1^h, the use to repaire the highwayes.
Mr Randle Holme gave a crimson velvett pulpit cushion to the church and 5^h [£5] to the poore.

[The above are the] severall charitable and pious gifts left to the parish of St Mary on the Hill, within the citty of Chester since anno 1600.

The next list in point of date is the one drawn up about the year 1718 in answer to the appeal of Dr. Francis Gastrell, Bishop of Chester, for the fullest information from each parish in his extensive diocese. This, which is now preserved amongst the records in the Bishop's Registry at Chester, is signed by the then rector of St. Mary's, Hugh Wilbraham, and contains several small legacies not mentioned in the previous list.

It is as follows :—

Left to ye Poor of the Parish of St. Mary on ye Hill in the County of the City of Chester.

	l s d
By Mr John Brereton late Alderman of ye s^d City, in the City Hands, & the yearly Intrest paid by the Treasurers on ye 23^d of April	10 : 00 : 00 See p. 197 200
By Mr Hugh Aldersey of London	0.4 : 00 : 00
By Mr Mathew Anderton of Chester	02 : 00 : 00
The Yearly Intrest of both p^d by ye Churchwardens of St. Peters parish in ye s^d City & distributed to Eighteen poor widowes.	
By Mrs Cath: Dicas of Chester	03 : 00 : 00
By Mr John Dicas of Chester	07 : 00 : 00
both charg'd upon the Lands of Mr Char^s Dicas Surgeon in Chester the yearly Intrest p^d into the Hands of the Church-wardens & distributed to 12 poor widowes.	
By Mr Peter Cotton Attorney at Law in the City of Chester... which together with Some other Money which was call'd in went to the purchasing of an Estate of 4^{li} : 10^s p anⁿ near Chester & is distributed in bread on Christmas day, Easter & Whitsuntide deducting the Intrest of Mr Cottons 10^h which according to his Will is to be given to 20 poor Housekeepers who frequent ye Church.	10 : 00 : 00
By Mr Henry Smith an uncertain Sume being a dividend of the Rents arising from Some Old Houses in the parish of Tolleshunt Darcy in the County of Essex to be given to poor people that receive no other Alms from the parish.	

We have no Schools that I know of unless it be that a poor woman or two teach English.

This is the most exact account can be procured by

        My Lord
         Y^r Lordships
           most obedient
             Humble Servant
               HUGH WILBRAHAM.

About thirty years later three fresh charities were painted on a board which was hung in the church, but, after doing duty in quite modern times as part of the framework round the organ, it has now completely disappeared.

This list was as follows :—

Painted on a board, formerly used as part of the framework round the organ, but now entirely lost.[1]

M' JOHN PHIPPS of the City of Dublin, Merchant, by his last Will and Testament gave to the Poor of this Parish the sum of Five pounds, the Interest thereof to be distributed amongst them by the Church Wardens Yearly on S' John's Day, the Evangelist [Dec. 27], for ever.

GEORGE GRIFFIES } Ch = Wardens 1743.
HENRY BUSSHELL   }

PETER FOULKES[2] D:D: Canon of Christ Church, Oxon, &c &c left Five pounds to the Poor of this Parish the interest thereof to be distributed to the said Poor by the Church Wardens Yearly on S' John's Day, the Evangelist, for ever.

CHARLES MOULSON } Ch = Wardens 1747.
JOHN EVANS   }

M'" SARAH CARTWRIGHT of this City Spinster by Her last Will and Testament left 2' 10' 0ᵈ to be distributed by the Minister and Church-Wardens among the Poor of this Parish after Her decease and likewise 1ʰ 1' 0ᵈ towards a piece of plate for the Communion Service

JOHN CALLEY } Church-Wardens 1752.
JOHN DAVIES }

In the Charity Commissioners' Returns for 1786 a long list of the persons who at different times had bequeathed money to the poor is given.[3] The total amounted to £263 4s. 6d. With some of this money, after deducting some amounts which were not interfered with, the church-wardens had in 1756 erected a gallery on the north side of the church, and in this gallery they had let pews at certain annual rents, which rents were expended in the purchase of bread for the relief of the poor. Another portion had also been spent in purchasing the Llay Farm, subsequently to be alluded to. In 1839 the total amount of the pew rents, with some additions from the church rates, amounted to £7 18s., but, of course, since the gallery was taken down and church rates were abolished this yearly sum has been lost to the poor.

The Charity Commissioners' Report of 1839 mentions the following Charities:—John Brereton's, producing 10s. a year ; Charlotte Dicas's, 12s. a year ; Henry Smith's, £10 15s. a year ; Hugh Offley's and Matthew Anderton's, about 9s. a year; Peter Cotton's[4] 13 prayer books every 8th year from the City Treasurer; Randle Holme's,[5] then probably amalgamated with the Corporation Charities ; Harrison's, 13s. 6d. a year; and the Llay Farm estate, producing £22 a year.

---

[1] I copied this from the original board in 1857, but it seems to have disappeared at the recent restoration.

[2] Dr. Peter Foulkes was the son of Robert Foulkes of the city of Chester, gentleman, and was baptised at St. Mary's on the 5th Nov., 1670. He matriculated at Oxford from Christ Church on the 16th June, 1691, aged 17. He became a very distinguished ecclesiastic, canon and sub-dean of Exeter in 1723, chancellor there in 1724. He died on the 30th April, 1747, and was buried at Exeter *see* p. 131, note 3).

[3] This list I have so far not been able to see.

[4] This charity is given on the mural monument placed to his memory and still preserved in the church (see p. 54. He died in 1716. It appears to be now lost.

[5] Randle Holme is stated to have left the sum of £30 to the Mayor and Citizens of Chester for the purpose of putting a poor child from St. Mary's parish to the Blue-coat School in Chester.

Of the above list six charities now remain, as shown by the Order of the Charity Commissioners issued on the 19th July, 1889. These are as follows:—

JOHN BRERETON'S Charity, founded by will dated 14 Nov. 1628, an annual sum of 10 shillings paid by the trustees of the Municipal Charities out of a sum paid by the Corporation of the city of Chester. *see pp. 197-198.*

CHARLOTTE DICAS'S Charity, an annual sum of 12s charged upon part of the Duke of Westminster's Chester estate.

——— HARRISON'S Charity, an annual sum of 11s, interest on £20 deposited in the Chester Savings Bank.

THE LLAY ESTATE. This is a farm, known as "the Llay Farm Estate," situated in the parish of Gresford, co. Denbigh, containing 9 acres 3 roods and 10 perches or thereabouts let at an annual rent of £14. This land was as already stated purchased before the year 1718 by the churchwardens with some of the bequests of money which had accumulated in their hands.

HUGH OFFLEY'S and MATTHEW ANDERTON'S Charity, an annual sum of 7s 9½d received from the parish of St Peter out of a sum received from the Trustees of the Chester Municipal Charities. These Charities were founded by the will of Hugh Offley dated 14 May 1594 and by the will of Matthew Anderton dated in 1693.

HENRY SMITH'S Charity, a share of the rents of an estate at Tolleshunt Darcy, co Essex, amounting to about £8 15 per annum. This was left by will dated 26 January 1626 the charity being bequeathed to the poor of certain parishes in Suffolk, Essex, Herts and Sussex in various proportions as well as to St Marys, which is the only Chester or Cheshire parish benefited.

The above amounts now form one consolidated charity, called "The Parochial Charities," for the whole ancient parish of St. Mary-on-the-Hill, and are vested in a body of five trustees, including the rector and churchwardens and two others appointed by the vestry. After payment of all necessary outgoings, repairs, expenses, &c., the balance is to be applied for the benefit of the poor of the parish as the trustees may think proper, power being given them to subscribe to any infirmary or hospital, provident club, &c., or to provide nurses and clothes, linen, &c.

THE SUNDAY EVENING LECTURE AT ST. MARY'S.

Shortly after the appointment of the Rev. Thomas Mawdesley as Rector of St. Mary's, an important meeting of the parishioners and others was held in the vestry room at St. Mary's on the 28th February, 1822, when it was resolved "that a Sunday Evening Lecture be established in the said church, the Lecturer and all expenses to be paid by voluntary contributions," and an influential committee was elected to carry this resolution into effect. The Rev. *Frederick Ayckbowm* was appointed the first Lecturer, and the first lecture was fixed for the evening of Sunday the 24th March, 1822, the service to begin at half-past six o'clock.[1]

On the 18th July, 1828, the Rev. *F. Custance* was appointed Lecturer on the resignation of Mr. Ayckbowm, and about 1830 he was succeeded by the Rev. *Thomas Harrison*. The latter resigned this office in March, 1837,[2] and on the 7th April in that year the Rev. *C. B. Taylor* was appointed Lecturer in his place. Mr. Taylor resigned in October, 1846, owing to his leaving Chester, and on the 26th October in that year the Rev. *Frederick Ford* was appointed his suc-

---

[1] From the official minute book, now in the possession of the Ven. Archdeacon Barber.
[2] It may here be noted that in 1835 the church was fitted up with gas for the first time.

THE CHARITIES OF ST. MARY'S.

cessor.[1] He resigned in January, 1851, and on the 24th January in that year the Rev. W. P. *Hutton* was appointed in his place.

On the resignation of Mr. Hutton in February, 1852, a meeting of the parishioners was held, when it was stated that the churchwardens proposed to take upon themselves the conduct of the Evening Lecture as a parochial service, so that the duties of the committee thereby came to an end. The Sunday Evening Lectures appear to have been still regularly given, many of the lecturers giving their services without payment, and others receiving £1 1s. each, till March, 1857, when the Rev. C. Bowen, Rector of St. Mary's, was requested to officiate as the Lecturer, and this special service appears to have been merged into the ordinary services of the church.

The original stipend of the Lecturer was fifty guineas a year, but in 1833 it was resolved that the Lecturer be paid the actual surplus of the contributions after paying all expenses, and the amount then paid was about £86, which gradually fell by 1837 to £53.

[1] I have a sermon entitled "'No Peace with Rome,' a Warning to the Church of God, being the substance of Two Sermons, preached in Saint Peter's and in Saint Mary's Churches, Chester, on Sunday morning and evening, Nov. 3rd, 1850. By the Rev. Frederick Ford, M.A., Trinity College, Cambridge, Rector of Saint Peter's and Sunday Evening Lecturer of Saint Mary's."

Boss, Oak Roof, St. Mary-on-the-Hill, Chester, 1895.

List of Churchwardens.

1536 to 1896.[1]

1536 to 1537	William Brownshank and Nicholas Weddurbe [Wetherby].
1537 to 1538	William Brownshank and Nicholas Weddurbe.
1538 to 1539	Richard Johnson and Thomas Smith.
1539 to 1540	Richard Johnson and Thomas Maylis.
1540 to 1541	John Calday and Thomas Meylis.
1541 to 1542	John Cawdey and Roger Brown.
1542 to 1543	William Houghton and Roger Brown.
1543 to 1544	William Houghton and Richard Muchell.
1544 to 1545	Richard Gettin and Richard Muchell.
1545 to 1546	Richard Gettin and James Taylor.
1546 to 1547	Thomas Woswoall [Wiswall] and Richard Street.
1547 to 1548	Richard Street and Thomas Woswoall.
1548 to 1549	William Ball and Thomas Browne.
1549 to 1550	Thomas Rogerson and Thomas Browne.
1550 to 1551	Thomas Rogerson and John Holt.
1551 to 1552	John Holt and Robert Skryevenar [Scrivener].
1552 to 1553	Robert Scrivener and Richard Getten.
1553 to 1554	Richard Getten and Robert Scrivener.
1554 to 1555	Thomas Robinson and Peter Fletcher.
1555 to 1556	Thomas Robinson and Peter Fletcher.
1556 to 1557	William Williamson and Thomas Milner.
1557 to 1558	William Williamson and Thomas Milner.
1558 to 1559	Robert Gryse and Richard Dawbe.
1559 to 1560	Richard Cawday and Richard Dawbe.
1560 to 1561	Richard Cawday and David Richardson.
1561 to 1562	Robert Croket and David Richardson.
1562 to 1563	Robert Crosse and William Kettell.
1563 to 1564	Robert Crosse and William Kettell.
1564 to 1565	George Taylor and John Anyon.
1565 to 1566	George Taylor and John Anyon.
1566 to 1567	Robert Harvey and John Tilston.
1567 to 1568	Robert Harvey and John Tilston.
1568 to 1569	William Smith and Richard Mutchell.
1569 to 1570	William Smith and Richard Mutchell.
1570 to 1571	Thomas Heyward and Nicholas Brenes.
1571 to 1572	Thomas Heyward and Nicholas Brenes.

[1] In each case (unless otherwise stated) from Easter to Easter.

John Totty was churchwarden of West Kirby in 1719.

LIST OF CHURCHWARDENS.

Period	Churchwardens	
1572 to 1573	Robert Brock and Richard Tyrer.	
1573 to 1574	Robert Brock and Richard Tyrer.	
1574 to 1575	Laurence Rowlinson and John Clarke.	
1575 to 1576	Robert Brerewood and Thomas Browne.	
1576 to 1577	Robert Vernon and John Smith.	
1577 to 1578	Robert Vernon and John Smith.	
1578 to 1579	Peter Smith and Randle Whitby.	
1579 to 1580	Peter Smith and Randle Whitby.	
1580 to 1581	Thomas Wyrthen [Werden] and Richard Byrom.	? Werthen or Werken
1581 to 1582	Thomas Wyrthen and Richard Byrom.	
1582 to 1583	Thomas Findlowe [Finlow] and William Holland.	
1583 to 1584	Thomas Finlow and William Holland.	
1584 to 1585	Thomas Finlow and William Holland.	
1585 to 1586	Roger Grice and Richard Hassellwall.	Hassellwall.
1586 to 1587	John Richardson alias Barker and Harry Skesbrycke [Scarisbrick].	
1587 to 1588	Richard Hasellwall and Thomas Dannot.	
1588 to 1589	Richard Hasellwall and Thomas Dannot.	
1589 to 1590	Thomas Dannote and Richard Dycose [Dicas].	
1590 to 1591	Richard Dycose and Richard Fletcher.	
1591 to 1592	Richard Fletcher and Edward Jones.	
1592 to 1593	John Brerewood and Edward Jones.	
1593 to 1594	Thomas Browne and John Brerewood.	
1594 to 1595	Thomas Brown and Richard Bromley.	
1595 to 1596	Thomas Wright and Robert Sproston.	
1596 to 1597	Thomas Wright and Robert Sproston.	
1597 to 1598	Thomas Barrow and Thomas Powell.	
1598 to 1599	John Richardson and Thomas Powell.	
1599 to 1600	John Richardson and John Gregory.	
1600 to 1601	Robert Brock and John Gregory.	
1601 to 1602	Robert Brock and Thomas Weston.	
1602 to 1603	Edward Tottie and Thomas Weston.	
1603 to 1604	Edward Tottie and William Crosse.	
1604 to 1605	Richard Browne and William Crosse.	
1605 to 1606	Matthew Ellis and William Hurleston.	
1606 to 1607	Matthew Ellis and William Hurleston.	
1607 to 1608	George Manley and Randle Holme.	
1608 to 1609	George Manley and Randle Holme.	
1609 to 1610	John Cooke and Robert Davies.	
1610 to 1611	John Cooke and Robert Davies.	
1611 to 1612	Richard Shone and Edward Smythe.	
1612 to 1613	Richard Shone and Edward Smythe.	
1613 to 1614	John Maddock and John Cowper.	
1614 to 1615	John Cowper and John Maddock.	
1615 to 1616	William Fletcher and Thomas Urms [Orms].	
1616 to 1617	Thomas Orms and James Fletcher.	
1617 to 1618	James Fletcher and John Dikus [Dicas].	

D D 2

ST. MARY-ON-THE-HILL, CHESTER.

1618 to 1619	John Dicas and Thomas Loe.
1619 to 1620	Thomas Loe and John Grice.
1620 to 1621	John Grice and John Davies.
1621 to 1622	Hugh Whicksted and William Horton.
1622 to 1623	William Horton and Laurence Fletcher.
1623 to 1624	George Manley and Robert Joynson.
1624 to 1625	George Manley and Robert Joynson.
1625 to 1626	Matthew Browne and Richard Partington.
1626 to 1627	Matthew Browne and Richard Partington.
1627 to 1628	William Ball and Randle Davies.
1628 to 1629	William Ball and Richard Mutchell.
1629 to 1630	Randle Holme the younger and Richard Mutchell.
1630 to 1631	Randle Holme, Jun'., and Thomas Johnson.
1631 to 1632	Thomas Johnson and Thomas Welshman.
1632 to 1633	Matthew Ellis and Thomas Welshman.
1633 to 1634	Matthew Ellis and James Boyd.
1634 to 1635	Henry Darwall and William Dicas.
1635 to 1636	Henry Darwall and William Dicas.
1636 to 1637	Thomas Roberts and Hugh Thorneley.
1637 to 1638	John Eccleston and Hugh Thorneley.
1638 to 1639	John Lowe and Thomas Kettle.
1639 to 1640	John Lowe and Thomas Kettle
1640 to 1641	Robert Burrowes and John Calcott.
1641 to 1642	Robert Burrowes and John Calcott.
1642 to 1643	William Whittell and John Smith.
1643 to 1644	Miles Pemberton and John Grey.
1644 to 1645	Miles Pemberton and John Grey.
1645 to 1646	Miles Pemberton and Roger Morris.
1646 to 1647	Roger Morris and John Fletcher.
1647 to 1648	John Fletcher and Ralph Leigh.
1648 to 1649	John Fletcher and Ralph Leigh.
1649 to 1650	George Chamberlain and Edward Bridge.
1650 to 1651	George Chamberlain and Edward Bridge.
1651 to 1652	Thomas Colthurst and James Mitchell.
1652 to 1653	Thomas Colthurst and James Mitchell.
1653 to 1654	Thomas Colthurst and James Mitchell.
1654 to 1655	Thomas Stanney and William Robinson.
1655 to 1656	Thomas Stanney and Edward Kettell.
1656 to 1657	George Chamberlain and Edward Kettell.
1657 to 1658	George Chamberlain and Randle Holme, Jun'.
1658 to 1659	Randle Holme, Jun'., and George Chamberlain.
1659 to 1660	George Bunnell and Thomas Hodgkis.
1660 to 1661	Richard Grosvenor and William Wilbraham.
1661 to 1662	Richard Grosvenor and William Wilbraham.
1662 to 1663	Richard Grosvenor and William Wilbraham.
1663 to 1664	Edward Aston and Edward Dalby.
1664 to 1665	Edward Aston and Edward Dalby.

LIST OF CHURCHWARDENS.

1665 to 1666	William Harvey and Richard Lowndes.
1666 to 1667	William Harvey and Richard Lowndes.
1667 to 1668	William Potter and Randle Morgan.
1668 to 1669	William Potter and Randle Morgan.
1669 to 1670	Richard Grosvenor and Thomas Annyon.
1670 to 1671	Richard Grosvenor and Thomas Annyon.
1671 to 1672	Edward Starkey and William Loyde.
1672 to 1673	Edward Starkey and William Loyde.
1673 to 1674	John Johnson and John Joynson.
1674 to 1675	Robert Jones and Thomas Jackson.
1675 to 1676	Thomas Barlow and John Bennet.
1676 to 1677	Randle Aston and Thomas Gibbons
1677 to 1678	Andrew Fernihough and Richard Skerit.
1678 to 1679	William Woods and Peter Dewsbury.
1679 to 1680	Ralph Leigh and George Jackson.
1680 to 1681	John Acton and Samuel Eaton.
1681 to 1682	John Johnson and Peter Venables.
1682 to 1683	Sampson Shelley and Matthew Browne.
1683 to 1684	Richard Bauan [Bavand] and Richard Adams.
1684 to 1685	John Manley and Edward Cooke.
1685 to 1686	John Whittell and John Dicas.
1686 to 1687	John Wright and Thomas Simpson.
1687 to 1688	Moses Dannatt and John Presbury.
1688 to 1689	John Worrall and Albin Gray.
1689 to 1690	Thomas Reece and Philip Bateman.
1690 to 1691	John Wrench and John Cotgreave.
1691 to 1692	Samuel Dannald and William Shone.
1692 to 1693	Roger Ball and John Dewsbury.
1693 to 1694	Randle Holme, Junr., and Nicholas Locker.
1694 to 1695	Randle Holme, Junr., and Thomas Leigh.
1695 to 1696	Thomas Leigh and Thomas Duke.
1696 to 1697	Thomas Duke and Thomas Rowland.
1697 to 1698	William Nicho's and Thomas Carden.
1698 to 1699	Thomas Carden and Bryan Bolland.
1699 to 1700	Thomas Williams and John Rowley.
1700 to 1701	John Rowley and Thomas Browne.
1701 to 1702	Robert Brerewood, Esq., and John Bridge.
Easter 1702 to 23 Feb. 1702-3	Robert Brerewood, Esq., and John Bridge.
24 Feb. 1702-3 to 3 Sept. 1703	Robert Brerewood, Esq., and John Bridge.
3 Sept. 1703 to 10 April 1704	Robert Brerewood, Esq., and John Bridge.
Easter 1704 to Easter 1705	Robert Brerewood, Esq., and John Bridge.
Easter 1705 to Easter 1706	Edward Burrowes and Daniel Coulson.
Easter 1706 to Easter 1707	Daniel Coulson and Edward Burrowes.
Easter 1707 to 31 May 1708	Daniel Coulson and Edward Wrench.
31 May 1708 to 20 May 1709	Edward Wrench and Philip Bateman.
26 April 1709 to 25 April 1710	Ralph Pickmore and Philip Bateman.
Easter 1710 to Easter 1711	Ralph Pickmore and William Helley.

ST. MARY-ON-THE-HILL, CHESTER.

11 April 1711 to 8 July 1712 ...	William Helley and Stephen Sone.
8 July 1712 to 22 April 1713 ...	Stephen Sone and William Witter.
22 April 1713 to 28 April 1714 ...	William Witter and George Scott.
28 April 1714 to 11 May 1715	George Scott and Thomas Reece.
11 May 1715 to 19 April 1716	Thomas Reece and Thomas Duke.
19 April 1716 to 30 April 1717	Thomas Duke and James Smith.
30 April 1717 to 30 April 1718	James Smith and Ambrose Wheywell.
30 April 1718 to 22 April 1719	Ambrose Wheywell and John Cotgreave.
22 April 1719 to 4 May 1720	John Cotgreave and William Johnson.
13 May 1720 to 20 July 1720	William Johnson.[1]
20 July 1720 to 17 May 1721 ...	William Jennings.
17 May 1721 to 4 April 1722	Peter Massie and Thomas Bolland.
4 April 1722 to 24 April 1723	Thomas Bolland and Samuel Garratt.
25 April 1723 to 4 Augst 1723... ...	Samuel Garratt.[2]
1 Augst 1723 to 13 April 1724... ...	Hugh Roberts.
15 April 1724 to 14 April 1725 ...	William Milton and Andrew Duke.
14 April 1725 to 4 May 1726 ...	Andrew Duke and Tobias Cook.
1 May 1726 to 1 May 1727 ...	Tobias Cook and Thomas Rowley.
1 May 1727 to 19 June 1728 ...	Thomas Rowley and John Cooke.
19 June 1728 to 16 April 1729 ...	John Cooke and Bartholomew Duke.
16 April 1729 to 13 May 1730	John Cooke and James Fleck.
13 May 1730 to 2 June 1731 ...	James Fleck and Charles Cottingham.
2 June 1731 to 24 May 1732	Charles Cottingham and Charles Hodgkin.
24 May 1732 to 30 May 1733 ...	Charles Hodgkin and James Walley.
30 May 1733 to 5 June 1734 ...	Captain Witter and Richard Gough.
5 June 1734 to 6 May 1735 ...	Richard Gough.
6 May 1735 to 8 July 1736	William Ithell and John Dutton.[3]
8 July 1736 to 31 May 1738	John Dutton and John Davis.
31 May 1738 to 31 May 1739	John Snow and Samuel Price.
31 May 1739 to 7 May 1740	Samuel Price and Randle Sorton.
31 May 1740 to 29 April 1741	Randle Sorton and William Cowper.
29 April 1741 to 7 July 1742	William Cowper, Esq., and Robert Foulkes, Esq.
7 July 1742 to 27 April 1743	Robert Foulkes, Esq., and George Griffith.
27 April 1743 to 16 May 1744	George Griffith and Henry Bushell.
16 May 1744 to 15 May 1745	Henry Bushell and George Hayward.
15 May 1745 to 21 May 1746	George Hayward and Thomas Reece.
21 May 1746 to 17 June 1747	Thomas Reece and Charles Moulson.
17 June 1747 to 11 May 1748	Charles Moulson and John Evans.
11 May 1748 to 19 April 1749	John Evans and Edward Warrington.
19 April 1749 to 15 May 1750	Edward Warrington and Matthew Brown.
19 April 1749[4] to 30 April 1751	Matthew Brown and Randle Reece.
30 April 1751 to 27 May 1752	Randle Reece and John Colley.

[1] Mr. William Johnson died in July (?), 1720.
[2] Mr. Samuel Garratt died in 1723.
[3] The disbursements are headed as follows:—"The Disbursements of Mr. William Ithell and Mr. John Dutton Churchwardens from the 27th July 1734 to the 6th May 1735 and to the 8th July 1736."
[4] This appears to be a clerical error for 15 May 1750.

LIST OF CHURCHWARDENS.

27 May 1752 to 9 May 1753	John Colley and John Davies
9 May 1753 to 13 Augst 1754	John Davies and Proby Vause.
13 Augst 1754 to 30 April 1755	Proby Vause and William Thompson.
30 April 1755 to 12 May 1756	William Thompson and Richard Shone.
12 May 1756 to 9 May 1757	Richard Shone and John Brown.
9 May 1757 to 10 May 1758	John Brown and John Burrell.
10 May 1758 to 23 May 1759	John Burrell and John Jordan.
23 May 1759 to 31 July 1760	John Jordan and Thomas Griffith.
31 July 1760 to 29 April 1761	Thomas Griffith and William Earle.
29 April 1761 to 12 May 1762	William Earl and John Newell.
12 May 1762 to 4 May 1763	John Newell and Francis Walley.
4 May 1763 to 23 May 1764	Francis Walley and Robert Williams.
23 May 1764 to 17 July 1765	Robert Williams and William Ridgway.
17 July 1765 to 3 July 1766	William Ridgway and James Hayward.
3 July 1766 to 26 May 1767	James Hayward and Thomas Plumbley.
26 May 1767 to 6 May 1768	Thomas Plumbley and John Fearnall.
6 May 1768 to 3 May 1769	John Fearnall and Thomas Evans.
3 May 1769 to 9 May 1770	Thomas Evans and William Ratcliffe.
9 May 1770 to 9 May 1771	William Ratcliffe and James Clutton.
9 May 1771 to 26 May 1772	James Clutton and Joshua Cummings.
26 May 1772 to 20 May 1773	Joshua Cummings and John Minshull.
20 May 1773 to 12 May 1774	John Minshull and Edward Porter.
12 May 1774 to 25 May 1775	Edward Porter and George Hodson.
25 May 1775 to 16 May 1776	George Hodson and John Griffith.
16 May 1776 to 9 May 1777	John Newell and William Revington.
9 May 1777 to 21 Augst 1778	William Revington and Richard Edwards.
19 Augst 1778 to 27 April 1779	Thomas Evans and Perry Dawson.
27 April 1779 to 10 April 1780	Perry Dawson and Thomas Roberts.
10 April 1780 to 8 May 1781	Thomas Roberts and Charles Price.
8 May 1781 to 21 May 1782	Charles Price and Joseph Bage.
1782	Joseph Bage and John Ridgway.
1783	John Ridgway and Joseph Howard.
1784	Joseph Howard and William Orford.
1785	William Orford and John Grindley.
1786	John Grindley and Richard Maddock.
1787	John Grindley and Richard Denson.
1788	Richard Denson and James Hughes.
1789	James Hughes and Thomas Bozley.
1790	Thomas Bozley and William Kendrick.
1791	Thomas Bozley and William Kendrick.
1792	William Kendrick.
1793	William Kendrick and Charles Wright.
1794	Charles Wright and William Gaman.
1795	William Gaman.
1796	William Gaman and Robert Shearing.
1797	Robert Shearing and John Dodd.
1798	Robert Shearing and John Dodd.

an uncommon name in Chester, Peter Yoxall, City Yeoman, Forest Lane & Robert Yoxall, Blacksmith, Newgate Street occur in Peter Broster's Directory of Chester 1782.

ST. MARY-ON-THE-HILL, CHESTER.

1799 ...	Robert Shearing and John Dodd.
1800 ...	John Dodd and William Linney, Esqre.
1801 ...	John Dodd and William Linney.
1802 ...	John Dodd and William Linney.
1803 ...	William Linney and William Newell.
1804	William Newell and John Evans.
1805	William Newell and John Evans.
1806 ...	John Evans and Charles Davies.
1807	Charles Davies and William Cross.
1808 ...	Edward Roberts and Richard Yoxall.
1809 ...	John Swarbrick Rogers and Edward Ducker.
1810	Edward Ducker and Joseph Ashton.
1811	Joseph Ashton and William Bage. *Joseph Bage, Papermaker Bridge. Directory 1782*
1812	William Bage and William Jones.
1813	William Jones and Thomas Shuttleworth.
1814 ...	William Jones and Thomas Shuttleworth.
1815 ...	William Jones and Thomas Shuttleworth.
1816 ...	William Connah and Samuel Brittain.
1817 ...	Samuel Brittain and John Garratt.
1818 ...	John Garratt and Robert Shearing.
1819	Robert Shearing and Peter Evers.
1820	Peter Evers and Charles Gaman [Gamon].
1821 ...	... ... Charles Gamon and William Foulkes.
1822	... William Foulkes (of Chester) and Richard Massey (of Moston, Esqre).
1823 ...	... William Foulkes and Edward Moss.
1824 ...	William Foulkes and Edward Moss.
1825 ...	William Foulkes and Edward Moss.
1826 ...	William Foulkes and Edward Moss.
1827	Edward Moss and Mark Rowarth.
1828 ...	Edward Moss and William Palin.
1829 ...	Robert Wilkinson.
1830 ...	Robert Wilkinson and Samuel Witter.
1831	... ... Samuel Witter and Robert Topham.
1832	... ... William Gaman and Samuel Jones.
1833 ...	... ... Samuel Jones and Ralph Lewis.
1834 ...	... ... Samuel Jones and Thomas Crane.
1835	... ... Samuel Jones and . . . . . .
1836	... ... Charles Gamon and . . . . . .
1837 ...	... ... Charles Gamon and George Allender.
1838	... Charles Gamon and George Allender.
1839	George Allender and Charles Gamon.
1840	William Haddock and Thomas Pickering.
13 April 1841 ...	Robert Jones and James Axon.
28 March 1842...	James Axon and Thomas Ithell.
18 April 1843 ...	Thomas Ithell and Joseph Weaver.
9 April 1844	Joseph Weaver and Thomas Ithell.

LIST OF CHURCHWARDENS.

Date	Churchwardens
26 March 1845	Joseph Weaver and Robert Littler.
14 April 1846	Robert Littler and William Price.
5 April 1847	Richard Palin and Robert Griffith Temple.
25 April 1848	Edward Ducker and George Pugh.
10 April 1849	Edward Ducker and George Pugh.
2 April 1850	Edward Ducker and John Hicklin.
22 April 1851	Edward Ducker and John Hicklin.
3 April 1852	Edward Ducker and John Hicklin.
29 March 1853	Edward Ducker and John Hicklin.
8 April 1854	Edward Ducker and Charles William Potts.
10 April 1855	Charles William Potts and William Tilston. *Solicitor*
27 March 1856	Charles William Potts and William Johnson. *miller*
14 April 1857	William Johnson and William Ward. *maizer*
6 April 1858	William Johnson and William Ward.
27 April 1859	William Johnson and William Ward.
6 April 1860	John Jones and Hugh Roberts.
4 April 1861	John Jones and Hugh Roberts.
21 April 1862	John Jones and Edward Minshull.
8 April 1863	John Jones and Edward Minshull.
29 March 1864	John Jones and Edward Minshull.
18 April 1865	Matthew Harrison and Joseph Oakes. *Clothier, Draper*
3 April 1866	Matthew Harrison and Joseph Oakes.
23 April 1867	Matthew Harrison and Joseph Oakes.
13 April 1868	Matthew Harrison and Joseph Oakes.
30 March 1869	Matthew Harrison and Joseph Oakes.
19 April 1870	Matthew Harrison and Joseph Weaver.
11 April 1871	Joseph Oakes and Philip Henry Fletcher.
2 April 1872	Joseph Oakes and Philip Henry Fletcher.
5 April 1873	Joseph Oakes and Philip Henry Fletcher.
7 April 1874	Giles Richard Griffith and William Albert Gardner.
30 March 1875	Giles Richard Griffith and William Albert Gardner.
30 March 1876	Charles Leet and Henry Moss.
3 April 1877	Thomas Vernon Royle and William Bolland.
23 April 1878	Thomas Vernon Royle and William Bolland.
15 April 1879	"The Rector appointed Mr. Alexander M'Gregor, of Eaton Road, his Churchwarden. Resolved that—note—no people's Churchwarden was elected."
30 March 1880	Alexander M'Gregor and Leonard Gilbert.
19 April 1881	Alexander M'Gregor and James Marsham.
11 April 1882	Alexander M'Gregor and James Marsham.
28 March 1883	Alexander M'Gregor and John M'Hattie (Seed merchants) (Sheriff of the city).
15 April 1884	Alexander M'Gregor and John M'Hattie.
9 April 1885	Alexander M'Gregor and John M'Hattie.
27 April 1886	Alexander M'Gregor and John Gamon.
14 April 1887	Alexander M'Gregor and John Gamon.
5 April 1888	Henry Moss and Henry Taylor, F.S.A.
25 April 1889	James Salmon and Henry Taylor. *Licensed Victualler*

E E

for Jolley or Jolliffe see Landed Gentry Vol II p. 1439 (1850)

ST. MARY-ON-THE-HILL, CHESTER.

8 April 1890	James Salmon (Mayor of the city) and Thomas Williams Griffiths.	Lic. Vict. Draper.
31 March 1891 ...	John Richard Baker and Thomas Williams Griffiths.	Baker & Draper
19 April 1892	Major-General D. Mocatta and John Goodie Holmes.	Army, Mercer
4 April 1893	Major-General D. Mocatta and John Goodie Holmes.	" "
29 March 1894 ...	John Goodie Holmes and George Parker.	Army, Builder
18 April 1895 ...	George Parker and William Davis Jolliffe.	Builder, Sol.
9 April 1896	William Davis Jolliffe and William Arthur Miller Nicholls.	Solicitor, Johnsonist
20 April 1897 ...	Edward Chambers Kendall and John Ellis Newman.	Merchant, Ironmonger

Boss, Oak Roof, St. Mary-on-the-Hill, Chester, 1895.

Churchwardens' Accounts.

EASTER 1536 TO EASTER 1537.

"1536.

These byn the psellys that wyll[m] Browneschanke And Nycolas weddurbe [Wetherby] Church Reuys [Wardens] Haue Receyued.

	s.	d.
In p̃mis we geddured on Est[r] evyn and Estur Day... ...	xvj	vj
Itm we gedd[r]ed on monday and Tweisday the same weke	xxiij	iij
Itm Receyued of Rycherd chamb[r]layne	x	viij
The which He dyd owe to the church.		
Itm gedd[r]ed on our lady day quart[r]ych	iij	xj
Itm gedd[r]ed on Cristynmasse quart[r]	iij	iiij
Itm gedd[r]ed for Seynt stevyn leghts...	ij	
— Itm Receyued of ij pdeners [pardoners]		viij
Itm we gedd[r]ed for mendyng of the Organs	vj	vj ob
As Anothur by'll doth Moere.		
Itm Receyued of Robt crosse for A kneling place to Hise wiff		xiij
Itm Receyued of Robt grise		iiij
Itm gedd[r]ed on palme sonday		xvij
Sum of o[r] Receytts iiij[li] ix[s] ix[d] ob."		

" Med this Booke Was made in the yere of our lorde A M CCCCC And xxx[v]j[ti] [1536] in the xxvij[ti] yere of The Reign of kyng henry the viij[t] Then Was Will[m] Browneshanke glou[r] And Nicolas Wedd[r]be Baker Church Reuys Written by the handys of Richard leche barbur beynge at y[t] tyme ther Clerke Also in ther tyme the quere was boght At bisewerke And Sett vppe With all Costs and Charchis belongynge to the Same more ouer the Churche flowre the Chauncell And Seynt Katherine chappell the[y] dyd Tyle in ther tyme."

" These byn the persellys that wyll[m] Browneschanke & nycolas wede[r]be church Reuys Haue payd.

	s.	d.
Itm payd for waxe	xxix	viij
Itm payd for makyng of the same	iiij	
Itm the beyrich be longing to the same waxe		viij
Itm payd for making A surge of xx[li]		x
The wiche wase gevyn to the phisshe [parish].		
Itm payd for ij[li] and a Halfe waxe to The Same ... ... [torn]		
Itm payd for ij to ... ... [torn]		
Itm payd for ... ... [torn] ...		
Itm for weshing the church clothis By yere		ij
Itm payd for Russhis Agaynst Est[r]		ix

In Augst. 1793, a new Organ was put up in the West Gallery, by Mr Challinor, at an expence of £175. Hemingway, Vol II. p. 106.

ST. MARY-ON-THE-HILL, CHESTER.

	s.	d.
Itm payd for Russhis Agaynst penticost … … … … … … …		iij
Itm payd for skowring [scouring] of the lampe And the chaldeners the brasyn cense [censer] with the crose … … … … … … ….		xij
Itm payd for iij quarts of lampe owle [oil] … … … … …		xij
Itm payd for ij cordys [cords] to the pascall … … … …		ij
Itm payd for naylys pynes and Thred to Heng the sepulcur … … …		ij
Itm payd for the Holyn … … … … … … … …		v
Itm payd for cundullys [candles] to the same … … … … …	v	
Itm payd for drissing [dressing] of the north Side of the church yorde		vij
Itm payd vnto the plymmer [plumber] for workemonship And sodur …	iij	viij
Itm A borde to the same worke … … … … … …		iiij
Itm the beyrich to the same … … … … … …		ij
Itm for careing sonde to the plymer… … … … … …		j
Itm for Henging of the Antoll bell … … … … … … …		ij
Itm for nalys to the Same … … … … … … … …		ob
Itm for mending of the great beame… … … … … … …		j
Itm for careyng out of the mollocke on the Soth Side … … …		iiij
Itm payd for a Roppe to the chyme … … … … … …		xij
Itm mendyng of the cloke laddur … … … … … … …		ij
Itm payd vnto thomas sprag for making A clappur to the Antyll bell and for a bolt of Iryn that went thro the grate beam … … … … …		xj
Itm payd for Hope [a hoop] to the Holyn … … … … …		ij
Itm for naylus to the Same … … … … … … … …		j
Itm for [torn] And making to seynt [torn] … … … …	ij	xj
… … [torn] … … ort orgyn maker for [torn] …		
… … .. … cause … … … … … … .. … …	vj	viij
Itm payd for ledd to make the paysus of… … … … … …		xviij
Itm for Hynggs to the bales … … … … … … … …	j	ob
Itm for glu to the organse … … … … … …		viij ob
Itm for charkecolys [charcoal] … … … … … …		iij ob
Itm for chalke … … … … … … … … …		ob
Itm for A skyn … … … … … … … … …		ij
Itm payd vnto John myddleton for keping of the cloke … … …		iij
Itm payd for A booke of white paper To write in our coitts [accounts]		xij
Itm for the beyring of or booke by yere … … … … … …		vj
Itm for making of the same … … … … … … …		iiij
Sma of or paymcts ys iij^li xiiij^s ix^d ob.		
Itm Remayneing In wax … … … xx^li		
Itm we be in dett … … … …		v^s
more then we Haue Receyued."		

Beerage

EASTER 1537 TO EASTER 1538.

"Año Dñi 1537.

These byn the psellis of money that Wiłłm Browneschanke And Nicolas Weddurbe Church Reuys haue Receyued for this yeare 1537.

	s.	d.
In pmis geddured on Est^p Evyn & Est^p day … …	xviij	
Itm on monday And Tweisday the same weke … … …	xxvj	
Itm Receyued of A pdener of Seynt Chadde … … …		xj
Itm Receyued of A perdener of o^r lady Romsewale …		iiij
Itm Receyued of A pdener of Seynt Johis frary …		iiij
Itm gedd^{r}ed on our lady day quart^r … … …	iij	iij
Itm geddured on Cristynmasse quart^r … … …	iij	vj
Itm geddured for Seynt steyuyn lights … … …		xx
Itm Receyued of matheo Ellis for hise wiff laystall…		x j
Itm Receyued of John leche for hise wiffs laystall … … …		xij
Itm Receyued for A laystall of Oleuer bolltons wiffe …		xij
Itm Ress for A laystall of geffrey Deuyas … … …		xvj
Itm Ress for A laystall of Cyssely ledsam … … …		xij
Itm Ress for a laystall of Dauid merreddith … … …		xij
Itm Ress for A laystall of Thom^s Barroo the yong^r … …		xij
Itm Ress for A laystall of Dannolde makecane … …		xij
Itm Ress of Rauffe thorneton for hise wiffs laystall… …		xij
Itm Receyued of Ric' totte for A grate of Iryn …	iij	viij
Itm Receyued for A borde that was in the Church		iij
Itm Receyued for A knelynge place to Roger sprays wiff		xij
Itm Ress for A knelynge place to thom^s hassylwall wiff		xij
Itm Ress for A knelynge place To thom^s Rogerson wiff		xij
Itm Ress for A knelynge place to thom^s Canse wiff …		iiij
Itm Ress for A knelynge place to wiłłm Rogerson wyff		viij
Itm Ress for A knelynge place To wyll^m yavan wyff …		iiij
Itm Ress for A knelynge place To thom^s mylner wyff … …		viij
Itm Ress for A knelynge place To thom^s Newhowse daught^r		iiij
Itm Ress for A knelynge place to Thom^s Rorson wyff… …		ij
Itm Ress for A knelynge place To Rauffe Chedhocks wyfe …		viij
Itm Ress for A knelynge place To Robt Bastwell wyff … …		iiij
Itm Ress for A knelynge place To Rondulph Rexsons wyfe… …		xij
Itm Ress for A knelynge place to margere devyas … (Dauss)…		xij
Itm Ress for A Couerlet & A pan … … … … … …	ij	x
The which blynde Dauid wiffe gaue to the Church.		
Itm Ress for A nolde Tre [an old tree] that wase i the Church …		xij
Itm Ress for Certyn mettell that wase i the Church …	v	
Itm Ress of the pson [parson] of Seynt maris… … … …	vij	vi
Itm Ress for A knelynge place… … … … … …		xij

Sm^a of o^r Receytts ys iiij^{li} xi^s viij^d."

Church of St Lawrence, Reading, 1602. "Itm. paid for flowers & Rushes for the churche when the Queene was here iijs vjd."
1643. "It at Cristmas for Rosemary & bayes 0·0·8."
1644. "It pd for Holly & Ivy, Rosemary & bayes at Christmas 0·1·10."
"It pd for Ewe [yew] for the church against Easter · for sticking off itt upp. 0·1·8"
1647. whit week. "Shewing aukes (herbs) & flowers to strowe the sitis in the church when the Jenerall was goeing in the towne 0·0·10."

ST. MARY-ON-THE-HILL, CHESTER.

These byn the psellis of money That Willm Browneschanke And Nicolas Weddrbe Churche Reuys haue payde 1537.

	s.	d.
In pimis payd for waxe for the hole yere		xxvij
Itm for makynge the C[h]urche waxe by yere...		iiij
Itm for Castynge of the holde waxe		ij
Itm for beyrich of the makynge the waxe		vj
Itm for makynge A Surge of xxli waxe		x
Itm in waxe to the Same		xiiij
Itm for wesshynge Ther Churche Clothis by yere	ij	
Itm for syllynge of font		ij
Itm for skowrynge of Chandellers the lampe the brasyn Crosse with the Cense		xij
Itm for frankeincense		ij
Itm for Rushis Agaynist Estr		iiij
Itm for naylis thred and pynnys [for the Sepulchre] Agaynist Ests [Easter]		j ob
Itm for A Roppe To the chyme		xij
Itm for wyre to the Chyme		iij
Itm for kepynge of the Cloke [clock] & chyme to Roger sprage ...	iij	
Itm for iij quarts of lampe owle		xij
Itm for iij li wax to Seynt stevyn leghts		xxj
Itm for makynge of the Same		vij
Itm for Tymber to make ij New formys [forms or benches] ...		xxij
Itm for werkemonship to the same	vj	viij
Itm for makynge & gyldynge iiij buttons to the best Cowpe [cope] And the veluett Cowpe		xij
Itm for Careynge owt of the holde Rushis		ij
Itm for iij gyrdyllis to the best shute [suit] ...		ij
Itm for glue to the organs and ballis [bellows]		j ob
Itm for werkemonship to the Same		iiij
Itm for holyns to make the holyn of		v
Itm for Condulles [candles] to the Same...	v	
Itm for makynge of our booke by yere ...		iiij
Itm for beyrynge of the Same		vj
Itm payd of the last yeris dett	v	
Itm payd for tylynge of the Church	vj	v

The which waxe vn payd more then we goddred In the Church.

| Itm payd for Iniunsions [Injunctions] to Doctur legh ... ... | | iiij |

Smn of or payments iijli xijs iijd
& so Raymayning in or hands xixs vijd

Itm Remaynith To the New churche Reuys xxli of waxe.
Itm we payd for Tylynge of Seynt katherine Cappell xxxjs jd
The which Mr John Byrkynhed payd vnto vs euty penny."

[Handwritten note at top:] Drake in his "History of York" (Vol II. Edit 1785). In 1415 the Armourers represented Adam and Eve — an angel with a spade and distaff assigning their labour.

[Handwritten note:] Church of St Laurence, Reading, Churchwardens Accounts. 1507. "It paied for j ell qrt of cresclot for Adam for to make j peyr of hosyn j ell for a dowblett xd" "It paied for ij ells di. (2½ ells) of cresclot for to make Eve a cote xd" The forecloth was a fine linen material — the garments of our first parents were probably made very close fitting, and stained flesh-colour.

CHURCHWARDENS' ACCOUNTS.

[Handwritten:] "It paied for ij queyer of pap for the pagents v
It paied for dyes flex (flax) infl- v (for wigs for the performers.

EASTER 1538 TO EASTER 1539.

[The Receipts are wanting.]

"These psellis foloyng Ric' Johnson and thom's Smith Churche wardens Haue paide for the yere past 1538.

	s.	d.
In p̄mis paide for waxe the Hole yere	xxij	iiij
Itm ffor makyng o' waxe by yere		iiij
Itm for Castyng the holde waxe in beyrich		ij
Itm for beyriche to the makyng of our waxe Agaynist the Ester		vj
Itm payd for makyng A Surge of xx pownde the whiche was gyffyn to the Churche		x
Itm for ij ponde waxe to menteine the same		xiij
Itm for skowring the Chaundeliers the brasyn Cense & the brasyn Crosse...		x
Itm paide for frankeincense		iiij
Itm for Charkecowls		j
Itm for sowyng [sewing] the churche clothis Agaynist the Ester		ij
Itm for A Corde to the vayle cloth		j
Itm for Naylis & pynnys to the sepulcr		j
Itm for a torche agaynist palme sonday	ij	
Itm for wesshyng the churche clothis bye yere	ij	
Itm for fillyng of the fontt bye yere		ij
Itm for payntyng of adam & Eve w' a pape [? paxe]		ij
Itm for mendyng of the best crosse		vj
Itm for mendyng of the brasyn crosse		iiij
Itm for iiij quarts of lampe owle		xvj
Itm for A Rachett vnto the clerke		xx
Itm for makyng of the same		ij
Itm payd vnto willm bolton for settyng on a bell welle & othur worke abowt bell frames Repracionyng the same		xvij
Itm payd for A New bell wele		xx
Itm paide vnto thom's sprage for Iryn and workemōship to make the yate [gate] and the Chyme and mendyng of the bere	ij	vij
Itm paide vnto the plymmer for sodur and workemōship to mende the north yle	ij	ij
Itm paide vnto Ric' dannolde for Iryn		iiij
Itm paide vnto the Clerke for a Roppe Vnto the chime		iiij
Itm paide for tymber to make the yate ffor the defence of the churche yorde	iij	vj
Itm paide vnto the wright for makyng of the Same with the Beyriche...	ij	vij
Itm payd for a lowde of cley vnto the same worke		ij
Itm payd vnto thoms warreweeke for Dressyng the Churche yorde w' othur labur Abowt the Churche		xiiij
Itm paide for wyre vnto the chyme		iiij
Itm payd vnto thom's wissewall for mēdyng the wall on Iche side the New yate		vj

[Margin notes:] Beerage. Beerage. Masonry.

[Right margin, next to "payntyng of adam & Eve"]: ? with vipers . a snake with / or / with arbor . with a tree

ST. MARY-ON-THE-HILL, CHESTER.

	s.	d.
Itm paide for A Citacion as Anends m^r pson Consernyng the Reypracio of the chauncell with othur costs belongyng vnto the same schute		xxj
Itm paide for the holyn		v
Itm for Condulls vnto the holyn	v	
Itm for beyring of o^r booke bye yere		vj
Itm for makyng of the same		iiij
Itm pay'd vnto thomas strete	iiij	
In parte of payment for the quere.		
Itm paide vnto will^m bolton for mendyng of the bere		iij
Sm^a of o^r payments is iij^{li} vij^s xj^d.		
Remayning in o^r boxe		xv
Itm in wax xx pownde."		

EASTER 1539 TO EASTER 1540.

[The Receipts missing.]

"These psellis folowyng Ric' Johnson & Thom^as maylis Churche wardens haue paide for the yere paste. 1539.

	s.	d.
In p'mis paide for waxe		xij
Itm for makyng o^r waxe by yere		iiij
Itm for two torchis	iij	viij
Itm for makyng a Surge of xx^{li} pownde whiche was gyffyn vnto the churche		x
Itm for two pownds of waxe to the same...		xiij
Itm for wescheing of the churche clothis bye yere...	ij	
Itm for frankencense, ...		iiij
Itm for charkecols Agaynist the Est...		ij
Itm for skowreyng of the lampe with the chalddeners ...		x
Itm for fyliyng of the font		ij
Itm for sowyng [sewing] of the Churche Clothis w^t thred		iij
Itm for naylis & pynnis to the sepulc^r		j
Itm for a corde vnto the vayle		ij
Itm for pap to make a booke for the Churche		j
Itm for iiij quarts of lampe owle		xvj
Itm for two foote of ledd & sodur to the plemer with hise workemanship ...	x	
Itm for a laburer to the plymmer		viij
Itm paide vnto the mason for Dressyng the sothe side of the Churche ...	ij	
Itm for mendyng of the thred [third] bell frame		vj
Itm for Iryn and workemōship to the bells		xij
Itm for settyng vppe & schestyng the holy goste		viij
Itm paide vnto the mason for Raysyng vppe of the hye altur [high altar] ...	iiij	iiij
Itm paide vnto two lab'ers	ij	viij
Itm for lyme & sonde	ij	iiij
Itm for beriche vnto the workemē		viij

CHURCHWARDENS' ACCOUNTS. 217

	s.	d.
Itm spende on oʳ neburs [neighbours] at the Raysyng vp of the hye altur [high altar] ...		iiij
Itm paide for tylis vnto the Churche ...	ij	ij
Itm for drayng In of a stone of thomᵉˢ strete...		iiij
Itm for watur and makyng clene of the Revestre with the hye altur [high altar] ...		iiij
Itm for stoffe & workemōship to the holy watᵖ stocke ...	ij	
Itm for mendyng of the lampe the whiche was brokeon with a Rope & a glasse ...		xij
Itm for a Roppe vnto the chyme and wyre ...		viij
Itm for a locke & A kaye vnto the cloke [clock] howse...		iiij
Itm paide vnto the carver for settyng vppe of organse ...	ij	
Itm for glue naylis & Charkecolis ...		xiij
Itm for beyring of the organs with the lofte the[y] stode in ...		vj
Itm for the holyn		v
Itm for Condullis [candles] vnto the same ...	v	
Itm for a hope [hoop] & naylis wᵗ a corde ...		vj
Itm for a corde to the Curtyn before the hye altʳ ...		j
Itm for beriche of the makyng of oʳ waxe ...		vj
Itm for castyng of the same ...		ij
Itm for beyring of oʳ booke bye yere ...		vj
Itm for making vppe of the same ...		iiij
Itm for oʳ apparaūnce afore Mʳ chaūnceler with the wyne we gaue hym ...		xvj
Itm paide vnto thomᵉˢ strete for the quere ...	vj	
Itm Remaynith in waxe vnto the new Reuis [Wardens] xxˡⁱ		

Smᵃ of oʳ paymēts
ys iijˡⁱ xvjˢ vjᵈ."

EASTER 1540 TO EASTER 1541.

[*The receipts missing.*]

"These persellis ffolowing John Calday And thomᵉˢ meylis Churche wardyns Haue paide ffor this yere aᵒ paste Aᵒ R[egni] R[egis] II viijⁱⁱ [1540.]

	s.	d.
In p̄mis paide ffor waxe for the hole yere ...	xxiiij	
Itm for makyng of the same ...		iiij
Itm paide for Castyng of the olde waxe ...		ij
Itm ffor the bereyche of the makyng of oʳ wax ...		vj
Itm paide for makyng a Surge of xxˡⁱ ...		x
the wihiche was gyffyn vnto the pische		
Itm paide for two ℔ of waxe vnto yᵉ same ...		xij
Itm paide for two torchis ...	iij	viij
Itm paide for skowryng of the lampe with the Chaldeners the brasyn Cense and the brasyn Crosse ...		x

	s.	d.
Itm paide for frankeyncense		iiij
Itm paide for Charkecolis		j
Itm paide for fillyrg of the font		ij
Itm paide for weschyng of the Churche Clothis bye yere	ij	
Itm paide for lampe owle		xx
Itm payd for a glasse vnto the lampe		ij
Itm paide for mendyng of the lampe ...		iij
Itm paide for a Corde vnto the vayle		j
Itm paide for pynnys & naylis to the sepulcur		j ob
Itm payd for makyng & mynding a kaye vnto the Churche Dorre ...		vij
Itm paide for a sloppe vnto the clerke	ij	iiij
Itm paide for a locke & A kay to ye stepull Dorre...		iij
Itm paide for wyre to the chyme		v
Itm paide for makyng a ladd^r vnto the Rode lofte ...		v
Itm paide for bords & naylis to make the bere [bier] ...		vj
Itm paide for makyng a hommer to ye chyme		j
Itm payd for soying [sewing] of the parrnes on ye albs by yere ...		ij
Itm paide for mydyng of the holy wat^p stocke		j
Itm paide for [a] booke vnto s^p thom^s lattis the whiche is <u>occupied</u> ī ye quere		xij
Itm paide for a Roppe vnto the Chyme		xx
Itm paide for makyng the ladd^r vnto the Clokke howse ...		vij
Itm paide vnto Ric' Joneson	x	iiij
the whiche was vn paide for the quere.		
Itm paide vnto will^am Crue for henging the Roppe in the pulle [pulley] for the holyn		j
Itm paide for makyng of <u>Cressutts</u>		j
Itm paide for makyng A skaffolde to take Downe the mone [moon] ...		ij
Itm paide for gyrddills to the prests		iiij
Itm paide for settyng in a gang [? a rung] to the ladd^r		j
Itm paide for Dresyng of the gutt^rs Ronde Abowt the Churche when the snowe was		xij
Itm paide vnto John Sauage for myndyng of the Churche flowre... ...		j
Itm paide for wyre to sett vppe the holy goste		j
Itm paide for two Cruetts		xj
Itm paide vnto henry Dalby for two glass^s vnto the paxes		ij
Itm paide for the holyn		v
Itm paide [for] naylis & tymber to make the mone vndur the holyn		iiij
Itm paide for Condullis vnto the holyn	v	
Itm paide for Careyng out of the stonys of m^rs Clerke gardyn ...		ij
Itm paide for beyryng of o^r booke bye yere		iiij
Itm for makyng of o^r booke		vj
The Sm^a of o^r paym^{ts} ys iij^{li} viij^s j^d ob.		
Itm we be in dett more then we haue Receyued	vj	ix ob
Itm in waxe xx^{li} to the new Churche Revis."		

Festal Lights & Holly at Christmas.

Churchwardens' Accounts of St. Lawrence Church, Reading.

1510. "Payed for iij^{lb} of talow candylls for to set in ye churche on Crystmas Daye iiij^d ob."

1524. "It. for makeyng the fframe for the aungels uppon Cristmas day iiij^d"

1525. "It. for 1^{lb} of Sysses (small wax tapers) for the Aungels at Crystmas ix^d."

   This would appear to indicate a constructional representation of the Nativity attended by angels, perhaps in ranks or gradations, bearing lighted tapers.

1506. "It. payed for sysis to the holy bush (holly) at Christmas ix^d."

"Paid Macrell for an holy bussh before the Rode ij^d." This was a holly bush.

CHURCHWARDENS' ACCOUNTS.

EASTER 1541 TO EASTER 1542.

[*Receipts missing.*]

" These pcells foloyng John Cawdey And Rog^s brown church wardens haue payde.

	s.	d.
Inpnmis for xxxij^{li} wax ageynst Est^o ...	xvj	
Itm for Makyng the same by yere ...	iiij	
Itm for makyng A serge of xx^{li} of wax ...		x
It' payd to ric' leche of old dett ...	viij	x
It' spend at Makyng the wax by yere in beu'age ...		viij
Itm for two torchys ...	iij	viij
Itm for makyng o^r boke ...		vj
It' for skowryng Candlestiks ...		x
Itm payde for A lanterne ...		viij
It' for frankencense ...		ij
It' for pyns & nayls to the sepulcre ...		j
It' for a Corde to the vale...		j
Itm for ffylling the ffount ...		iij
Itm for A pynt oyle for the lampe ...		ij
Itm for swepyng the church wyndowes ...		ij
It' for washing the church Clothes by yere ...	ij	
It' to ric' bostok for dressing the church yorde ...		viij
It' for a Corde & wyere to ye Chyme ...		iij
It' A pynt oyle ...		ij
It' for gurdls for albes ...		j
It' for iij^{li} wax ...		xviij
It' for ij^{li} wax ...		xij
It' for iij^{li} wax ...		xviij
It' for ij^{li} wax ...		ix
It' for lech for Colers [collars] to ye bells & makyng ...		x
It' for mendyng the ladd^r ...		j
It' for A hynge to ye organs ...		j
It' for A pynt oyle ...		ij
It' for lyme to Cover graves ...		ij
It' for mendyng & dressyng the bells to witt^m botto & thom̄s Sprag ...		xiij
It' for dressing ye church yorde ...		vj
It' for ij Rops to the bells...		xvj
It' for wax ...	vj	
It' for A poly [pulley] to the organs...		j
It' for a Corde to the v Candles for Anthem ...		j
It' to Rog^o sprag mēdyng ye Clok ...		iiij
It' for mēdyng the best Cope & a riband ...		xj
It' paid for hangyng the Anthem bell ...	v	viij
It' the holyn ...		vj
It' Candles to the holyn ...	iij	iij

	s.	d.
It' nailes		j
It' for A Rope		x
It' for lam[p]e oyle		iiij
It' to willm houghton for sparrs to the Anthem bell		xiij

Sm̄a soluc, iij^{li} viij^s v^d."

EASTER 1542 TO EASTER 1543.

[*Receipts missing.*]

"These pcells folowyng the forseids Churchwardens [William Houghton and Roger Brown] haue payde.

		s.	d.
In p̄mis paide for wasshing ye church cloths by yere		ij	
Itm for frankencense			ij
Itm for A Corde to the vale			j
Itm for xxx pounde wax	xiij	v^j
Itm to Ric' leche for vj pounde wax		iij	
Itm in beu'age at Castyng the wax			xij
Itm for skowring the lampe the Chaundelers Crosse And the Censes			x
Itm for fillyng the ffont by yere			ij
Itm for Charcols			j
It' to Ric' leche for makyng the wax by yere		iiij	
Itm to Ric' leche for make[ing] the sepulcre lights			x
Itm to Thom̄s wisswall [the City Mason] for two days worke at Shiftiyng the Crosse			xij
It' to henry myln^r & hugh monksfeld labourers			xj
Itm for a busshell lyme			iiij
Itm for A key to Coffer in the vestiarye			ij
It' for makyying A Rochet			j
It' to ric' leche for xij pounde wax & di [half]	vj	iij

Itm Spende Apon the porch of ye north side.

		s.	d.
Inp̄mis to Thom̄s wissewall for vij days	iij	vj
It' to willm Arrowsmyth & oliu^r barne labourers		xiiij
Itm for lyme & Cariage of stonys from the place was the nonnys¹...		vj
Itm for sparrs & to the w̄ght [? wright]		vj
It' for gadd nailis & spiks to the same		ij
Itm paid to Ric' Cowp for keping ye Clok	v	iiij
It' for a Rope to the Anthem bell		iiij
It' for mendyng the Clok for the space of iiij Days & for A nue watche whele		iij	
Itm for the holyn		vj
Itm for Candls to the same & to the sterr	iij	iiij
It' to Thom̄s wisswall for Cou'yng graves ...		iij

---

¹ The Porch on the N. side of the church built with the stones from St. Mary's Nunnery.

The chimney named below, 1543-4, was made of bricks and is an early instance of such a commodity as chimneys were very little used except in large costleness Residences. [Eland's Itinerary Vol VIII p. 11. "one thing I much noted in the Stable of Bolton how Chimneys were conveyed by Tunnels made on the tops of the Walls, betwixt the Lights in the Haulle; and by this means, and by no Covers, is the smoke of the Hearth in the Haulle wonder extremely conveyed.
Previously to this the smoke was suffered to escape from the doore (or covers) in large halls and kitchens, the fire being made of logs of wood laid one on or beside dogs in the centre of the Room

CHURCHWARDENS' ACCOUNTS. 221

	s.	d.
It' for lyme to the Cou'ryng of them...		v
It' for iij pynts oyle to the lampe ... 2d. per pint		vj
It' for a Rope to the organs & a corde for the vale & pynns for the aw'[altar]...		ij ob
Itm for a key to the Church dore ...		iiij
Itm for Clothe to make An Amyse ...		iiij
Itm for a ladder for the Anthē bell ...		ij
It' for nayles to the bells ...		j

Here foloweth the Costs of the porche Apon the sowth side the Church.

	s.	d.
Inpimis to two labo'ers for Caryeng stonys frome the pfice gardyn... (4 days work)	viij	Princes Garden next the Castle.
Itm for tymbre to the seyd porche ...	xiij	x
Itm Carieng of the seid tymbre ...		xiij
Itm for sqwaring of the seid tymbre ...		xx
It' for lyme		v
It' to John gost for workmāship & sawzyng ...	xxiiij	
It' to Ric hesillwall for the Mason worke of the porche ...	iiij	This about 8 days work
It' to A labo'er for ij days ... 2d per Day		iiij

Sm̄a of our payments ys vli ijs ijd."

EASTER 1543 TO EASTER 1544.
[*Receipts missing.*]

"These persells ffoloyng Will'm Hoghton and Ric' mychell Churche wardyns Hath paide for this yere paste.

	s.	d.
Inpimis paide for waxe ...	xv	
Itm for makyng of the same bye yere ...	iiij	
Itm for ij pownde waxe to make the devocion surge ...		xij
Itm for makyng of the same ...		x
Itm at the castyng of our olde wax ...		ij
Itm in beyriche at the makyng of our waxe ...		vj
Itm for frankincense ...		ij
Itm for ffyllyng of the fontte ...		ij
Itm for wesschyng of the churche Clothis bye yere		xij
Itm for skowryng of the chaldenrs the lampe and the brasyn Cense		viij
Itm A Corde to the Vale ...		j
Itm for ij days to a wreyght to make a durre to the chamber¹ and the chymney	xij	A. wright
Itm for two bords two Hoolks two hyngs to the same ...		xij
Itm for naylis and a mantiltre [mantletree or mantelpiece] ...		iiij This was a beame, probably over the fireplace in the chamber
Itm for two M sklatts [slates] and vij C [i.e., 700 slates] ...	x	vj
Itm for careayge of the same ...		ix Mason.
Itm vnto thom's wissewall s'u'nt for worke māship ij days ...		x

¹ This would be the chamber for a priest built over one of the porches erected in the previous year.

n° Item for 2000 slates and 700 = 2700. The letter M is still used as a sign for 1000 in the Slating trade, and 1000 is really sold by 1200 to the 1000 to make up for breakage in carriage and waste. J.H. 1910.

ST. MARY-ON-THE-HILL, CHESTER.

	s.	d.
Itm vnto thoms wissewall for vij days worke ...	iij	vj
Itm vnto thoms lewys laburer ...		vij
Itm for a locke & a keye to the dorre ...		iiij
Itm for iiij C of breke [brick] to the chymney ...	ij	iiij
Itm for careayge of the same ...		v
Itm for ij lawde of lyme ...		ix
Itm for vj days worke vnto Hugh monkysfelt ...	ij	
Itm vnto A wreyght for clenyng of latts [laths] and halfe A C boght ...		viij
Itm for spyke naylis to the yese bords ...		j
Itm for A lowde of lyme ...		v
Itm for A M [1,000] of ston naylis ...		xij
Itm for vj C clotnaylis ...		xv
Itm to the sclatt' for workemāship ...	vij	
Itm for dowbyng and teyryng [? tarring] ...		xxiij
Itm for A lowde of lyme ...		iiij ob
Itm vnto Henry Dalby for sowd'yng [soldering] of the churche Roffe		xij
Itm that we paide for the laste yere Dette ...	vij	vj
Itm for viij new brass' to the bells ...	ix	
Itm for takyng vppe of the bellis and laying the seid brass' ...		vij
Itm for A key & A locke to the stepull durre ...		iiij
Itm vnto s' nicholas for kepyng of the clokke syns mydsūmer was A twelmvnt ...		x
Itm for new hornys to the launtt' ...		iij
Itm paide vnto Ric' leche & thom's Johnson bye the cūmaundem' of the perhische [parish] ...	ij	viij
Itm for xxij sparrys and xviij bords to the Chamb' and mendyng of a Cofer	vj	viij
Itm for bords to the chab' wyndowys boght of willm bolton ...		xvj
Itm for tymber boght of the seid willm to make the pylpyt ...		xx
Itm vnto the keruer [carver] for makyng of pylpyd and the grese [step-] to the same ...		viij
Itm for workeyng of A ston vndur the pylpyd ...		ij
Itm for the Holyn ...		vj
Itm for Condylls to the same ...	ij	x
Itm for makyng vppe of o' booke ...		iiij
Itm more for makyng of the pylpit ...	iij	v
Sm' of o' paymentts ys v^{li} xvj^s vj^d.		
Itm the perhische ys in o' dette ...	xiij^s	v^d."

EASTER 1544 TO EASTER 1545.

"Thes peels folowynge Rycharde Gettyn and Ric' mychell Churche Wardens haue Receyvyd for this yeir past 1544.

	s.	d.
Inpmis Geythredd towarde kepynge of the Clocke upon Palme sondey ...		xix
Itm geythred vpon Est' evyn & Est' dey ...	xvj	v

<u>Grees</u>, grese, gryse, gresoys, greece, greeces, Dégrés, Gradins, Fr.; Gradini, Scalina, Ital.; Treppe, Ger.:- steps; also a Staircase, (see Step).

"Grece, or steyre. (or tredyl) gradus." Prompt. Parv.

"Grese (or greee) to go up at, or a stayre, degré". Palsg.

"Item, I have devised and appointed six greces to be before the high altare, with the greee called gradus chori." Will of Henry VI. Nicolas, p. 297.

"The first gryse called a slypp, ben trey weyes."

"The second waye going northward by a high grese, called a steyr of xxxii steppys" William of Worcester. Itinerary pp. 175. 176.

"The forsaide Richarde shll make with in the quere a hegh auter ioynand on the windowe in the gauill with thre greses acordaunt thare to, the largest grese begynnyng att the Reuestery dore."

<u>Step</u>, or Stair, Degré, Marché*, Fr. Scalino, Ital.
"Gradus, Anglice a stepe... gradus, Anglice a steyr.
William of Worcester, pp. 196. 218

* The former for large buildings, the latter for domestic buildings.

CHURCHWARDENS' ACCOUNTS.

	s.	d.
Itm Geythred vpon Mundey in Est^r Weke	x	viij
Itm geithred vpon Twesdey in Est^r Weke	xij	viij
Itm Receyvyd for A buryall place to Sr John Aere		xvj
It Geythred to mendynge of the Crosse...	iiij	ix
Itm Receyvid of the Stuards of the smythes for old wax at Thomas Spraggs Wyf dirige ...		j
Itm for o^r lady dey qwarterege...	iij	j
Itm for A ley stall to Thomas Spragge wif		xij
Itm Receyvid of Thomas Barowe for a ley stall		xij
Itm rec' of Ric' brerewood		xij
Itm of the wyf of John ffyndley for a knelynge place ...		x
Itm Receyvid of Willm Will^{m}son for A knelyng place		xij
Itm Rec' for Cristenines qwarterege...	iij	iiij
Itm rec' of ye p^{r}ioner of Jhu ...		iiij
Itm Rec' for a ley stall of Elizabeth Myechell...		xij
Itm rec' of Geffrey Granwey for bords ...		iiij
Itm Rec' for A ley stall of Thomas ley wyf		xij
Itm Geythred towarde Cou^{e}ynge of the churche porche		vj
Itm Rec' of John Treves for c^{e}tayn geyr which we found in A cofer w^t in ye Revestre ...		viij
Sm of o^r Receyts iiij^{li} v^d."		

Easter 1544 to Easter 1545.

"Thes peels folowynge Ric Gettyn and Ric mychell Churche Wardyns haue payd for this yeir past [1544].

	s.	d.
Inpmis paid for A kaye to the Clockhowse dore		j
Itm paid for ye barich to castynge of the wax...		ij
Itm paid for scowrynge of the lampe		viij
It to ye caru^r [carver] for settynge flowres on ye pulpit		viij
Itm payd for kepynge of the Clocke to Thomas knott before Est^r		iiij
Itm paid for ffrankyncens...		ij
Itm paid for pynse & thryed [for the Easter sepulchre]		j
Itm paid for xlvj^{li} pounde of wax of Willm Aldersey	xxj	
Itm paid for Makkynge of o^r wax for the old yeir to Ric' leche	iiij	
Itm paid to the same Richarde leche for makyng of too devoc̃on sergesse of xx^{li} pound wax		x
Itm paid for mendynge of o^r blacke Chamlett Vestiment		vj
Itm payd to the barige of makynge of o^r wax		vj
Itm paid for mendynge of o^r great bell		v
Itm paid to Henry Dawby for mendynge of our Wyndoes	iij	j
Itm payd to Spraggs Wyf ffor washynge of o^r clother by yeir		xij
Itm for a pynte of oyle		ij
Itm payd to Willm Hoghton which the piche was in dett to hym	viij	v

	s.	d.
Itm paid for claspes and mendynge of a velvett Cope		j ob
Itm paid to John Savage for hyllynge off A grave ... ... (see 248)..		ij
Itm paid for iij pyntes of oyle		vj
Itm for mendynge of the bere		j
Itm payd to Stephane Bryggs for Mydsom⁹ qwart⁹		xx
Itm for iiij newe pcession boks for yᵉ qwere		xij
Itm paid to peter Conwey for makynge of A newe sockett to the best crosse & gyldynge of the same	x	
Itm for A boke to the qwere		viij
Itm paid to Mʳ Iohn Walley for ij pound of wax		xj
Itm paid for wyre to mendynge of yᵉ lampe		j
Itm to Stephane briggs for Michelmes qwart for tentynge of yᵉ Clocke		xx
Itm to Mʳ Iohn Walley for iiij pound of wax		xxij
Itm to maistres Dauyson for ij pound of wax		xj
Itm to Elyn Crosse for washynge of Clothes and for sope to the same		ij
It paid for A purse to cary yᵉ sacrament		iiij
Itm for candles to yᵉ hollynse	iij	
Itm payd for hollyn		vj
Itm for wax to Richarde leche		xij
Itm payd for mendynge of the bellowes of the organse		xj
Itm paid for A Rocchett to the Clarke		xx
Im to Maistres Grymesdyche for thre pound of wax		xvij
Itm paid to Henry Dawby for mendynge holes in the churche topp		viij
Itm for A corde for the vayle		j
Itm payd for Selats [slates] latts [laths] and neyles to Thomas Roper...	iij	x
Itm paid to the Sclater		xx
Itm paid for lyme		iiij
Itm for A Cheyne to the byble...		ij
Itm for berynge of oʳ boke by yeir		vj
Itm for makynge vp of the same		iiij
Itm payd to John plummer for lead to the church porch ...	vij	
Sm̃ of oʳ payments iiijˡⁱ iiijˢ xᵈ.		
Itm the Reves is in Dett to John plum̃er vˢ vjᵈ."		

EASTER 1545 TO EASTER 1546.

"Thes peels foloȳng Ric Geittyn And Jams Tailyer churche Wardens haue receyved for this yeir past 1545.

	s.	d.
Inpmis geythred in yᵉ churche vpon palme sondey	ij	
Itm on Estˢ evyn and Estˢ dey	xx	viij
Itm vpon mondey & twisdey in Estˢ weeke	xxij	x
Itm Receyved for A pece of velvett...		xij
Itm Recᵈ for katᵉyn browns leystall		xvj
Itᵗ Recᵈ for A knelyng place for Ricᵗ Greis wif		viij

	s.	d.
It' Rec' of M' Vawdrey for A leystall		xij
It' Rec' of M' Plancney for ij leystalls	ij	
It' Receyvyd of mathewe Ellis for A leystall		xij
Itm Rec' of Geffrey Ric^gson for iij leystalls	iij	viij
Itm rec' for A leystall to Herry Dawbye		xvj
Itm rec' of Willm Houghton for A leystall		xij
Itm U of Thom^as kettylls wif for A leystall		xij
Itm rec' of Ric' Gettyn for A leystall		xij
Itm geitherdde vpon o^r lad day [Lady day]	iij	iiij
Itm geitherde vpon Cristenmes dey	iij	
It' rec' of Thomas browne for A knelyng place for his wiff		xij
Itm rec' of Willm balle for A knelyng place for his wiff		xij
It' Rec' of Ric' Strete for A knelyng place for his wiff		xij
It' Rec' of M' thom^as bruerton for A leystall		xvj

Sm of ther hole recvyit
is iij^{li} xj^s ij^d."

Richard Street

"Thes peells folowyng Ric' Geittyn & Jams tailyer church wardens haue paid for this yeir past [1545].

	s.	d.
Inp^rmis paid to M^r will^m Aldersey for xxxij^{li} of wax ...	xvj	
Itm paid for makyng of o^r wax by yeir	iiij	
Itm paid for makyng of ij devoc̄on sergesse of xx^{li} wax		x
Itm paid to ye birrege at ye castyng of o^r Wax		ij
Itm for wax to George leche		vj
Itm paid to ye forsaid M^r willm Alld^esey for v^{li} wax	ij	xj
Itm paid to John plumbre	v	vj
Itm paid to ye clerke for kepyng ye clocke		xx
Itm paid to George leche for Rybban, silke, & threid to mend o^r best sute [vestiment crossed through]		xxj
It' paid to Herry Dawby for mendyng of the church Wyndoes by yeir ...		vvj
Itm paid to Mr Willm Aldresey for iiij^{li} wax	ij	
Itm paid to ye brothere3 [embroiderers] for mendyng of our best sute ...		xx
Itm paid for Scowryng of ye lampe and the Chandelers		viij
Itm for ffrankyn sence		ij
Itm paid to Ric' Grey for mendyng ye thirde bell		viij
Itm for A rope to the Antam bell		iij
Itm for A corde to ye veyle		j
Itm paid for Charcolls at Est^e		x
Itm paid for washeyng of ye churche clothes by the yeir		xij
Itm paid for ij dos^s tyle		ij
Itm paid to Rauff norley for glasyng of the porche ch^ambre Wyndow ...		xvj
Itm to will^m bolton for A royle to ye same ch^ambre		iiij
Itm to Ric' mykylhalf for war[k]m̄shypp of the same reyle		iij
Itm for ffyllyng of ye fontt by yeir		ij
Itm paid to xp̄ofer Warmynchū for mendynge of o^r brasyn crosse ...		xv

ST. MARY-ON-THE-HILL, CHESTER.

	s.	d.
Itm paid for candles to ye sterr & to ye hollyn...	iij	v
Itm for ye hollyn...		vj
Itm ye costs of o^r bere [bier] the tymbre neyls & makyng	ij	vj
Itm paid to Mr Walley for ij bords to mende the thyrde bell whele ...		vj
Itm to Stephyn Watton for his worke on ye same		vij
And for neyls to ye same		j ob
Itm to Thomas Spragge for makyng A newe Iren for ye clocke which was stollen		viij
Itm paid to Thom^{as} Spragg for a locke and a key for the copborde vnd^o o^r lady		iij
Itm to ye said Thom^{as} Spragg for iiij hyngs		vj
Itm paid to Hugh Nicholes for mendyng of ye steple doore and makyng ij wyndows in ye revestre		viij
And for neyls to ye same worke		ij
Itm for pyns and threide		j
Itm giffyn to ye clarke at his first comynge in rewarde	ij	
Itm paid to the clarke y^t gone is for kepyng the clocke for mydsom^r quart^o		xx
Itm to ye same clarke for Michellmes quart^o		viij
Itm paid for wyre to ye clocke		iij
Itm paid for too dos' & di of tyles to m^{re}grett wright		xv
Itm paid for too dos' of tyle to Rogg^e Reyde...		xij
Itm paid for Cou^eyng of ij Graves		v
Itm paid to henry blomeley for cou^eyng ij graves		iiij
and for lyme to ye same graves...		ij
Itm paid to Ric' Hasylwall for cou^eing ij graves		vj
Itm paid to Thomas wyswalls man for makyng vp the churche wall ...		viij
Itm paid for A lode of lyme		iiij
Itm paid for too pynts of lampe oile		iiij
It' paid to Elyn bushell for a sacryng bell		iiij
It' for a planke borde to ye flore of the steple and ye leyinge of the same		vj
It' for mendyng of an Awter clothe [altar cloth]		j
Itm for medynge of an Awbe [alb]		j
It' for mendyng of ther box		j
Itm paid to Ric Grey for mendyng of ye grete bell...		x
Itm lent to Thom^{as} hettyll outt of the box to pay for honbrige [Handbridge] sepulcre sergesse...		xvj
It' for charcolls for ye Sensesse [censers] at Cristenmes		j
It' paid to Conys wif in part of payment for washing ye church clothes by yeir		iiij
Itm paid to s^r Ric' for kepynge the clocke for Cristenmesse qwart^o		xij
Itm paid for beryng of ye boke by yere		vj
And for makyng vp ye same boke		iiij

And ye hole Sm of ther payments is iiij^{li} x^s v^d.
ther is also xx^{li} wax for ye new reves to rescyve
And they haue remaynyng in ther box ix^d."

The Sepulchre once in the Municipal Church
of St Lawrence, Reading and its Ornaments.
Rev. Charles Kerry's History of St Lawrence's Church (1883)

The Sepulchre Altar.

This appears to have been situated on the north side of the choir beneath the middle arch of the arcade (see below "1513"). It was appointed for the deposition of the consecrated elements of the Eucharist from the evening of Good Friday until the morning of Easter Day; during which time it was watched by a quasi-guard, after the manner of our Lord's sepulchre. The sacrament was then removed with loud Allelluias & much rejoicing to the accustomed place on the High Altar.

The Church books contain many references to this mediæval ceremony.

Anno 1498. "In p'mis payed for wakyng of the sepulcr viij^d" — Similar entries occur yearly until the Reformation.

1507. "It. paied to Sybel Derling for nayles for the sepulcre & for rosyn to the resurreccyon pley, ij^d ob."

This entry may relate to the performance of a Mystery on "Corpus Christi" day.

1512. "It. payed to Water (Walter) Barton to the new Sepulcreer iiij^li xiiij^s x^d." This was a considerable sum at that period, and it must have been an object of unusual magnificence.

Anno 1513. "It. payd to Harry Horthorne for setting upp of the frame abonte the sepulcre & for closyng of the dore in Seynt Johns chauncell of the quyre, vj^d" Henry Hawthorn was a Reading carpenter, and died in 1522. A new door was opened in 1515

1513-4. "It. payd to Harry Horthorne for ij pecis to hang the sepulcre cloth on ij^d."

1513-4. "It. payd for ale at Removyng of the sepulcre to the carpenters iiij^d. ob."

1516 It. paid for making of the lofte for the sepulcre light. li^s ij^d. (5¹/6)

1538-9. "Paid for makeyng the beam lights on (over) the sepulcre against east' (Easter) xxj^d"

1544-5 "Paid for sylke poynts for the Sepulcre ij^d" In 1549 the whole seems to have been swept away.

according to the Accounts "Rec^d of Mr Bell for the sepulcre and the frame for tapers thereto annexed."

Among the inquiries in 1554 after the goods alienated sold or stolen in the time of Edward VI. we have –

"Item for the valence about the sepulcre to know who hath it in keeping"

This was repeated. "It. to enquire for the Valence of frenge about the sepulcre".

1561. "Item receyved of Matthew Reynoldes & Water Sawyer for the sepulcre they bought xx^s.viij^d"

In 1562, "The ffeame where the sepulcher lightes dyd stand" was taken down by William Marten and his man together with the rood loft and the way to the same.

"Sayre of olde Tymber"

"In p'misses of Master Butler to ye loft over the chancell x^s" – evidently the loft "where the sepulcre Lightes dyd stand". This N^r Edward Butler was firetimes Mayor of Reading, obiit 1584.

The Sepulcre Altar had been I. esentid with many valuable ornaments, & Vestments and in 1524 "The Ornaments belongyng to the sepulc e awlter in the same Church" consistes of

"It finis a vestemente of crymson veluet (with) a crose of rych tyssew.

It. a vestemete of Russel, satten wt a crose of cloth of gold.

It. a vestemete of whyt trnsigs satten wt a crose of grne brydgs satten.

It. an awlt cloth of crymson & tawny vcuet emorevi'yd wt. flowrs of goci: & on the nether pte of the same, crymson saten w cloth d- vawdekyn – for the sepuler awler (altar). (Inv!. 1517.).

It. an awlt cloth of crymson satten of blew bawdkeyn (with) ij Curfleyns to the same d. grene.

It. iij Cteyns of Russete & blew sassencte wt an awlt cloth of whytte & grene.

It. ij small Kaustykkes (candlesticks) of latten"

Easter 1546 to Easter 1547.

"1546. Thes byn the parsels that Thomas woswoall and Rychard strete churche wardens have Receuyd ffor thys yere past.

	s.	d.
Item Reseuyd on palme sondaye ffor kepenge off the clocke	ij	x
Itm Receuyd off Ryc' gytten and Jamys tayllyr in the box ...		ix
Itm Reseuyd on blacke monday and twsdaye in the Estr wycke ...	xxiiij	j
Itm on Aster evyn and Estr daye	xix	x
Itm Reseuyd off Ryc' lowe	vj	viij
Itm ffor A lastall ffor John fynlowe		xij
Itm for tylys [tiles]		iiij
Itm ffor A lystall for Thomas nyccals wyffe		xvj
Itm for A lestall to Maystr hope		xiiij
Itm for sr Ryc'1 lestall		xij
Itm for A lestall for geffere barkers doghtter		xij
Itm Reseuyd off Raffe a crosse for A knelynge plasse to hys wyffe		xij
Itm for A knelynge [place] to Jhamys brerewods wyffe... ...		xij
Itm for A knelynge plase to Grysvenars wyffe...		xvj
Itm for a knelynge plase to bostocks wyfe		viij
Itm ffor A knelynge place to hancockes wyffe...		viij
Itm for A knelynge place to Hughe off the lache hys wyfe		viij
Itm for A knelynge place to fasakerlayes wyffe		vj
Itm Reseuyd for A lestall to Ryc' butlar...		xij
Itm gederyt at lady daye qurtereche		xxj
Item for crystenmes quartereche	ij	v

Sm̃ off the Recets iijli xjs jd."

" Thes byn the parsels folowenge Thomas woswoall Ryc' strete churche wardens have payde for thys yere past 1546.

	s.	d.
Itm payde to Mr John wallaye for xxtexjli wax	xviij	iiij ob
Itm payde for makynge off the wax by the yere	iiij	
Itm for makynge off A Devocyon surges		x
Itm for the barreche		vj
Itm for makynge off iiij nve [new] formys	x	iiij
Itm payde for A nve Dor to the grese [steps] that gose in to the ledes		xvj
Itm payde for iiij banar stavys		xvj
Itm a locke and ij stapyls to the font		iiij
Itm for mendynge off the bels		iiij
Itm for frycansens		ij
Itm payde to the clarke for kepynge off the cloke	v	
Itm payde for lampe yole [oil] to the lampe		viij
Itm for A li and halfe off wax		viij
Itm payde for tyles to mende the churche flore		iij

---

[1] He occurs as Sir Richard in the previous Disbursements, 1545. Sir Richard Stancliffe (see burials 1697). 1567

	s.	d.
Itm payde for hollyns		v
Itm for A Rope to the horgens...		j
Itm payde for candels	iij	iiij
Itm payde for A purse to carrye the sakerment		xj
Itm for A locke and ij enges [hinges] to the banar staves ...		vj
Itm for A Rope to antān bell		iiij
Itm for weshenge off the churche clothes		xvj
Itm payde to Ryc' Dowbe for mendenge off the wendos		xvj
Itm payde to S^p Ryc' for kepenge off the cloke that he whas he hynde for ...		xx
Itm for deghttynge [scouring] off the lampe and the chandelars		ix
Itm ffor A corde to the Rode loft		j
Itm payde for charcoll		j
Itm payde for pyneys and nelys		j
['Item payde for xij^{li} wax to Mr Thomas aldersaye vij^s' crossed through and 'quia bot ac alloc in px^p sequent^p Coṁp' written above.]		
Itm payde for ij^{li} wax...		xiij
Suṁe of the payments lvj^s j^d ob		
and so Rests In ow^r hands of thys of the sayd Recets ... xiiij^s xj^d."		

EASTER 1547 TO EASTER 1548.

"Thus byn the parsels monaye y^t Ryc' strete and Thomas woswoall churche wardens hathe Reseuyd for thys yere past 1547.

	s.	d.
Itm gaythredd on pallme sondaye for kepeyenge off the cloke [clock]... ...		xx
Itm on hastar hevyn [Easter even] and hast^y Daye [Easter day]	xix	
Itm on bundaye (sic) and twesdaye in the Est^p wycke	xxvj	viij
It' Res' of Robert yonge for on knelyng place... ...		iiij
It' Res' of Ryc' dobe for A knelyng place		xij
It' Res' of wyst wyff for a knelyng place...		viij
It' Res' of thom^{a}s mekyn for a le stalle		xij
It' Res' of Jone buckley for a knelyng place ...		iiij
It' Res' of mathelles wyff for a lestall		xij
It' Res' of Jhon Savege for a lestall		xij
It' Res' of Ryc' muchell wyff for a lestall		xij
It' Res' of Ryc' butler wyff a towell.		
It' Res' of Jhon ñiquale a towell.		
It' Res' of wyllm balle for a lestall		xij
It' Res' apon ow^r ladye [day] for quarteche ...		xxij
It' Res' of wyllm yenn for a lestall		vj
It' Rests in hys hands		vj
It' Res' of pet^p flecher for a knelyng place		viij
It' Res' of mest^p voydre [Vawdrey] for a knelyng place	ij	
It' Res' of mest^p planciney for a lestall		xij
It' Res' of thom^{a}s ley for a knelyng place ...		xij

CHURCHWARDENS' ACCOUNTS.

	s.	d.	
It' Res' for crystenmas quart[9]		xvj	
It' Res' for a lestall of thom⁹s aswall		xij	Thomas Harwell
It' Res' of ythell a dye for a lestall		xij	
It' Res' of thom⁹s govete for a lestall		xij	
It' of thom⁹s wuswall for a knelyng place xij^d [crossed through]			Thomas Woswall
It' more of quartreche and out of ye boxe		viij	
It' of Raf' foxley for a knelyng plac		vj	
It' of Jhon anyon for a knelyng place		vj	John anyon
Sũ of the sayd Recet ... iij^l viij^s ij^d."			

"M^d that the viij^t day of January in the yeir of o^r lorde god MCCCCCXLVIJ Elyn Clarke wydowe comyth before the hole pishe demandynge ther & of them one certan Chalysse. And so Thomas wiswall & Ric' Strete thẽ beyng Churche wardense wth advise & cõsent of the hole pisheners did delyu⁹ the same chalisse vnto the said Elyn as her awne."

"Thes beyn pcels of money y^t whe Ryc strete and thom⁹s wuswall haue payde and lede done [laid down] for the church of sanct mares thys yere 1547.

	s.	d.
It' payde for neyles and frankinsens and for threde and pynns at on' tyme ...		iiij
It' payde to Ryc' leche to ye bereche for makyng of the wax...		vj
It' payde to m^r walle for wax aganst eest⁹	xij	j
It' payde to m^r thom⁹s ald^osey for wax		vij
It' payde to ye clerke of sanct mars [St. Mary's] for ye quartche		xx
It' payde to Ryc' leche for makyng of the wax for the yer		iiij
It' payde to Ryc' leche for a deuotyon taper to onbryg [Handbridge] the last yer...		x
It' payde to Ryc' leche for a deuotyon taper for thys yer		x
It' payde to Ryc' leche for castyng ye wax		ij
It' payde for washyng the churche clothes by ye yer		xv
It' payde to warwyke for dressyng the churche yard		v
It' payde to dame m'get for washeng the clothe ou' [over] the sac̃met [sacrament] and dressyng the bann'		iij
It' payde for charkole aganst est⁹		ij
It' payde for ij burds [boards] to mend the sepulches		j
It' deylu'et to onbrygnne [Handbridge] for xx pownds of wax	[blank]	
It' payde for frankeynsens		j
It' payde to Ryc' dobe for mendyng the wyndoys by the yer...		xvj
It' payde for lampe ole		iiij
It' setlyng on the geyre [gear? ornament] up on the albes at est⁹		ij
It' payde to Ryc' leche for payntyng the crosse staff		viij
It' payde for payntyng iiij bann⁹ staves		j
It' payde for lyme		iiij
It' payde to thom⁹s lewes for mendyng the charche wall		iiij
It' payde to warweke for mendyng the churche yerd another tyme		iiij
It' payde for wax aganst ow^r lade day		xij
It' payde for frankeinsens and neles...		j ob

Thomas ferrs & warwik

ST. MARY-ON-THE-HILL, CHESTER.

	s.	d.
It' payde for on Rope for the anton bell		iiij
It' payde to wyllm crowshay for mendyng the church ...	ij	
It' payde more for neyles		ij
It' payde to wyllm ball for on pese of tymb^r		iiij
It' payde to on man for wyttyng the church		vj
Sum̃c xxxvij^s j^d ob.		
It' payde for lyme		xij
It' payde to the clerke of seint Jons [St John's] for a boke		xij
It' payde for wytlymyng [whitewashing] the churche ..schrtx-lyming ...		iiij
It' payde for takyng downe of the Rode		ij
It' payde to the clerke of seint mars [St Mary's] for kepyng the cloke [clock] for the alff yer	ij	viij
It' payde to Jhon grey for mendyng of the clocke		ij
It' payde for dressyng of the leyds		j
It' payde for franckinsens		j
It' payd for lampe ole		ij
It' payd for puttyng in ow^r bylls to the kyngs vysyters		xiij *visitors*
It' payd for a locke to the box		iiij
It' payd for yron and neles to mend the boxe...		v
It' payd to the kerv' [carver] for makyng the box		viij
It' payd natts [sic for mats] to knele apon		iiij
It' payd to Ryc' grey for makyng of the box locks and keys	v	
It' payd to a wryzt [wright] for makyng ij formes		viij
It' payde to s' george for kepyng of the clocke for crystemas quart^o		xx
It' payd for ij horse loyde of lyme		viij
It' payd for wytlymyng the churche	ij	vj
It' payd to on whom̃ for caryng of wat' and dressyng the church ...		ij
It' payde for makyng my bylles and my boke by the yere		x
Sum̃a xx^s and so Restthe in o^r handes off thys last yeres Resets the svm off x^s ob vnto wyche svm chargyt the forsayde svm off xiiij^s xj^d the furst yeres Recet and so whe have clerely in o^r hands over all o^r sayde pements for bothe the sayde yeres the full svm off	xxiiij	xj ob
monaye Restynge and not by vs Reseuyd that hys to wyt.		
Apon the wyffe Ryc' coupper for A lestall		xij
Itm Ryc' mvcchell wyff		viij
Itm wyllm yenn...		vj
Itm Raff plumley		viij
Itm Reseuyd off Ryc' gyttyn for A knelynge [place]		xij

EASTER 1548 TO EASTER 1549.

"1548.

	s.	d.
M^d y^t wee wyllm ball and thom's browne haue R' of Ryc' strete for old Ropes endes		ij *Richard Street*
It' R' from brokyn yron	v	*iron*

The Banners belonging to the Church of St. Lawrence at Reading in 1517 (and those marked with an "o" in 1523 Inventories

o. "It. a banner for the Crosse of red Sarsenet w.^t Imag^s of the trynyte & of o^r lady"

o. "It. a nother for the crosse of grene silk"

o. "It. v baners of silk w.^t the armys (arms) of England"
    There were vj banners in Inventory of 1523.

o. "It. a baner of whit silk w.^t a Crosse of red"
    There were ij banners in Inventory of 1523.

"It. a strem' (streamer) of silk."

"It. a strem' of linen."

"It. a strem' of linen"

"It. a dest cloth of Crymson Bawdekyn" (erased)

"It. ij^o dest clothes of Dornex."

"It. a knop of gold w.^t tassells of blew sylke."

"It. a purse of crymysin cloth of gold pyrled for the osts" In 1523 Inventory "pyrleyd for visytacons"

CHURCHWARDENS' ACCOUNTS. 231

	s.	d.
It' gethered aganst east'	xij	vj
It' R' of m'esse brereton for a lestall		xij
It' R' of thom's ley for a lestall		xij
It' R' of Rauff plomley for a knelyng place		viij
It' R' of mestes mathey for old wod		xvj
It' R' for on new pece of wod		viij
It' R' of thom's wuswall for a knelyng place		xij
It' R. of Jhon Savege for on lestall		xij
It' R' of ten mẽ of the pyche ... Ten men of the parish		xxvij

Sm̃ª of the Receytts xlvjˢ ixᵈ.
Svīne iijˡⁱ vjˢ ixᵈ.
It' R' of wax lxxjˡⁱ
It' Remenyng of wax xxxiijˡⁱ."

"1548.

Mᵈ that thes beyn the peels yᵗ wee haue payde.

	s.	d.
In p̃s to sanct catryn [Katharine] reves	x	
It' to conys wyff for wessyng the church clothes		xv
It' to Ryc' dobe for mendyng the church wyndows by yᵉ yere		xvj
It' to Ryc' leche for makyng of yᵉ wax by yᵉ yer		iiij
It' payde vnto Ryc' leche for makyng hundbryge surge on yere wyche was not payde		x
It' in bereche for makyng the waxe		ij
It' for castyng of the wax		ij
It' for tyllyng of the fonte		ij
It' for pynnes noles and threde [for the Easter sepulchre]		ij
It' for settyng apon the parryers apon the albs to conos wyff		ij
It' to sᵗ george for kepyng the clocke		xx
It' to thom's wuswall for mendyng of the church wall		ij
It' payde to sᵗ george agayne for the clocke	iij	iiij
It' payd for a byll at the visitatyon		ij
It' for makyng a byll to be red at the pcessyon of the kyngs gᵃce and the qene of scotts		ij
It' payde vnto steven watton for makyng of the church yeate		vj
It' for tymbᵉʳ to make the banᵉ		iiij
It' payde to sᵗ henry browne		xx
It' payde to thom's sprage		vxj
It' payde to yᵉ plemmᵉʳ for castyng of owʳ leed and leyng and sooder		xvij
It' to Ryc' barker for fourte pound of leede		xxiij
It' for the caryege of ij webbs¹ of leede to the church		ij
It' to Rogᵉʳ Reede for cow'yng of on gᵛe and tyles		xvj
It' to sᵗ oleuᵉ [Sir Oliver, the priest] for sanct catheryn sᵉʳvice		viij
It' for makyng on key		ij
It' for ij gyrdyls		ij

¹ A web or sheet of lead, a broad and thin plate of lead.

		s	d
It' to Jhone buckley for settyng apon the parrers apon the church clothes			ij
It' payde for a rope to ye anton bell			vij
It' payde to Robert Jhons for ij C iij quart^o of leede at v^d the C		xiij	ix
It' payde to m^r Jhon walle for ij trees		x	
It' payd for on lood of wod			xv
It' payde for ij C of spykes neles and alff C of gadds [gadnails]			xvj
It' at the castyng of ye leed of bereche			ij *Casting of the lead and Clocks*
It' for iij dosen bordes		vj	viij
It' for caryeg of them to ye church			ij
It' for sayng [sa(w)yng] ij trees			xxij
It' to Jhon holt for caryeg of ij trees to the church			ix
It' payde to James alkoc and ys m̃a for wurkyng		v	j
It' to thom^as wuswall for iij days wurke			xviij
It' to a laboryng m̃a ij days			viij

Sm^a vj^{li} xviij^s iij^d."

EASTER 1549 TO EASTER 1550.

" 1549.

M^d y^t weke thom^as Rog^eson and thom^as browne churche wardnens of the pyshe of sanct mars vpon the hyll In ps..

	s	d
R' of wyllm ball and thom^as browne In the boxe		xij
R' of m^r voydre [Vawdrey] for on lestall		xij
R' of m^r wyllm aldersey for wyllm horton lestall and on chyld of the sayde wyllm horton lestall		ij
Itt' gethered in the east^o weke	viij	j ob
Itt' R' of henry browmley for on lestall		xij
Itt' of Rychard buroys for the lestalls of Rauff chadoc and ys wyff	ij	viij
Itt' gethered at ow^r layde day		v
Itt' R' for the churche of mone [money]	xxvij	
Brearwood Itt' R' of James brerewod wyff	ij	
Itt' R' of Rychard strete for on knelyng place		xij

Sume of Recete xlvj^s j^d ob."

'M^d y^t wehe [that we] thom^as Rog'son and thom^as browne churche wardnens In ps have payde

	s	d
for the makyng of the booke at east^s		xij
Itt' payde to Rychard leche for makynge the waxe for on hileyery	iiij	
Itt' to s^r george for kepyng of ye clocke	iij	iiij
Itt' for wessyng of ye churche clothes		xx
Itt' to Rychard dowbe for mendyng of the glasse wendoys		xvj
Itt' to ye clerke for kepyng the clocke		xx
Itt' for iij books on for the Commuyon and two saturs [psa'ters]	viij	iiij
Itt' payde for too dowsen of tyles		xij

	s.	d.
Itt' payde to henry bromley for coveryng of the churche flore		xiiij
Itt' for soderyng of the leyde vpon the church		ix
Itt' for the lyme		iiij
Itt' for caryeng of tyles		j
Itt' for dressyng of ye churche grece [steps]		ij
Itt' for too bauderycks [for the bells]	ij	vj
Itt' to the clerke for kepyng of ye clocke		xx
Itt' to Ryc' gree for mēdyng of ye belles		iiij
Itt' payde to ye clerke for kepyng ye clocke		xx
Itt' payde to wyłtm bolton for makyng of on forme before the he ault^o [high altar]		ij
Itt' to wyłtm bolton for mendyng of the belles		vj
Itt' to Rog^o sprage for mendyng the clocke		iiij
Itt' for on natte to knele vpon before the ault^o		ij
Itt' for makyng of on syrples to ye clerke		iiij
Itt' for ij salts found in ye church		j
Itt' payde to wyłtm brownshanke and Rychard strete	xxvij	
Itt' to wyłtm bolton for settyng on pule to mestres gythyn		xvij
Itt' payde to m^r wydrey [Vawdrey] for the pēc of on alf of on booke called pafracs [?paraphrases]	v	viij
Itt' for lyme		xij
Itt' for wat^o and sande		j
Itt' to thoms wuswall and ij men w^t hym for coveryng of graves and mendyng of the churche flore		ij

Sume iiij^li xj^s iij^d.

the pyche ys in debethe xxv^s j^d ob."

EASTER 1550 TO EASTER 1551.

"1550

A^o R. Ed vj^t iiij^o.

	s.	d.
M^d y^t thom's Rog^oson and Jhon holt haue recevet at cast^o	ix	j
Itt' Recevet for the churche goods	xxvj	iij
Itt' for Ryc' Rog^oson buryall		xij
Itt' for on chylde of Raffe crosses buryall		xij
Itt' of geffre grenwall wyff for a knelyng place		xij
Itt' of Jenkyn telent for on chyld of hys the buryall		xij
Itt' for Jhon fiiquall buryall		xvj
Itt' of wyłtm Rog^oson wyff for hyr husband buryall	ij	ij
Itt' geffre grenwall buryall		xvj
Itt' gregore castell buriall		xij
Itt' thom's starke buriall		viij
Itt' for the leede of the holy wat^o stooke	v	

	s.	d.
Itt' a peace of tymbr		xij
Itt' at lamas	xxvij	
Itt' for Raff medilynton buriall		xij
Itt' Jhon holt for on knelyng place		xij

Some iij^{li} xjx^s ix^d."

"M^d y^t whe the sayd thom's and Jhon haue payde	s.	d.
Inprīs to m^r dampt for kepyng of the clocke		xx
Itt' to henry nycolas for makyng wax	ij	x
Itt' more to m^r dampt	ij	
Itt' to adlyntō wyff		vj
Itt' to Robert wyfe		iiij
Itt' for ij saturs [? psalters]	iiij	viij
Itt' to warwyke wyff		ij
Itt' for wat^r and sande		iiij
Itt' for brycks		xx
Itt' to Ryc' hasewall for dressyng of the churche flore and the churche wall	ij	
Itt' to m^r dampr. for on key		ij
Itt' to Rog^9 dampt		xx
Itt' to m^r dampt	ij	
Itt' to Ryc' gre for neles		ij
Itt' to Ryc' hasewall for makyng of the church wall	iij	
Itt' to m^r dampt		xx
Itt' for takyng downe the alters and tylyng the churche flore	x	vj
Itt' to Ryc' dobe for mendyng the glasse wyndoys		xvj
Itt' for lyme	ij	
Itt' to Ryc' hasewall for mendyng the churche wall and tylyng the churche flore	iij	x
Itt' for on lode of lyme		vj
Itt' to s^r hug' ley		xij
Itt' payde to thom's wursewall & Ryc' gytty		xviij
Itt' payde to m^r voydre	xx	
Itt' to m^r dampt		xx

Svm v^{li} vj^s iiij^d."

List of vestments, on the fly-leaf or first page:—

"The buttoons in the hands of Robert Scryvener.

The best cope Deliu^{9}ed to M^r browneshank.

Twoo tunacles one awbe and one vestm^t belonging to the same suete in the hands of M^r browneshank.

Thother twoo awlbes Deliu^{9}ed to Thom̄s Rogerson.

The twoo copes of red purple veluct thone deliu^{9}ed to mystres woodward by wittm ball and Thomas browne thother Deliu^{9}ed to the kings comission^{9}s.

The cope of red Damask w^t a vestm^t and twoo tunicles of the same Deliu^{9}ed to the comission^{9}s by M^r browneshank.

CHURCHWARDENS' ACCOUNTS.

The white vestm¹ w⁴ a tunicle of white Damask Deliuᵖed to the cōmissionᵖs by Richard gyttyn and Robert Scryuener.

A cope of red skarlet Deliuᵖed to the cōmissionᵖs by Richard Gyttyn and R. Scryvener [the churchwardens in 1552].

The vestm¹ of Scarlet also Deliuᵖed to the cōmissionᵖs.

The stole awlbe and Amyas they cōfesse remayning w⁴ Robert Scryvener.

the vestm¹ of grene silk Deliuᵖed to the cōmissionᵖs.

A blak chamlet vestm¹ Deliuᵖed to Mʳ browneshank and by him to the cōmissionᵖs.

The twoo tunacles Deliuᵖed to the cōmissionᵖs by gyttyn and skryvener.

Three corpus cases and three clothes Deliuᵖed to the cōmissionᵖs.

A Doon corpus case w⁴ twoo clothes remayning vppon Robert Scryvener and Rich' gyttyn.

It' one syluᵖ crosse Dooble gylt sold by w. ball and Tho. browne vz lviij vnces the syluᶜ senser xxviij vnces... ... ... xxj^{li} xˢ.

wherof xviij^{li} deliuᵖed to diuᵖse poore folks, and the residue appeareth in their accompt.

A senser of brasse sold by Richard gyttyn and Robert Scryvenᵉ w⁴ out consent of the parish.

The best crosse bannᵖ gyld sold by Richard gyttyn and Robert Scryvenᵖ to Robert vawdrie w¹ out cōsent.

The other bannᵖ cloth remayning with Mʳ vawdrie.

The senser of brasse sold as afore w⁴ out consent.

one gyld chales sold by mʳ ball of xv vncˢ ... ... iij^{li} xvˢ.

One other chales sold by Thoms̄ Rogerson of [blank] sold to mʳ vawdrie for iij^{li}.

The third gild was mistres clerks [this was in 1547].

One albe white remayning.

The cure cloth Deliuᵖed to ... ... [torn] ... ...

The canape cl ... ...

A sepulchre cl ... ...

... ... [torn] ... ...

EASTER 1551 TO EASTER 1552.

"1551.

Mᵈ that thys ys the forst yere of yᵉ reves of saynt mares reyseyvyd of John hollt & Robrt skryevenar goyderytt in the pascon wyeke vij^s. & ij^d.

	s.	d.
It' reyseyvyd of necolas weytherbe for hys wyues leystall		xvj
It' Reyseyvyd of geffrey granwey wyfe		xxj
It' for a leystall of Robart bastwell		xvj
It' for a leystall of Ryc' Robynson		xvj
It' reyseyvyd of Ryc' borvse for hys wyfes leystall		xvj
It' reyseyvyd of Robrtt stobes for a leystall		xvj
It' reyseyvyd of Tomas Rogerson afore the forst proclemaciō	x	
It' reyseyvyd of Iohn wylkinson	x	
It' for Tomas leyses leystall		xvj
It' for a leystall of mest' techett	ij	

	s.	d.
It' for a leystall of George teyler		xvj
It' for a leystall of mest' broghtlones mã		xvj
It' reseyvyd of necolas breynes a'foure the forst proclemaciõ	xxj	vj
It' reseyvyd of George weytt afoure the forste proclemaciõ	xx	
It' reyseyvyd of wyll^{a}m calldeys wyfe for hur hosebandes leystall	ij	
It' for a leystall of tomas brones chyld		xij
It' reyseyvyd of Robrtt huttũ for a knelynge plase for hys wyfe		xij
It' reyseyvyd of George teyler for the hoole yere	iij	
It' reyseyvyd of Ryc' caldey for a knelynge plase for hys wyfe		xvj
It' reyseyvyd of necolas Rogerson for the hoole yere	iij	
It' reyseyvyd of Roger foxley for the hoole yere	iij	
It' reyseyvyd of wyllm Grymesdyche for a hallfe yere		xviij
It' reyseyvyd of phelyp Gest for a hallfe yere		xyiij
It' reyseyvyd of tomas londes for a holle yere...	iij	
Itm raysayvede of Rycc' smythe for a howlle yere	iij	
Itm Rysayvyde iiij^{d} for a grote afore the forst pclemason ... ... iij^{li}	v	
It' reyseyvyd of wyllm ... ... [*cut off*] ... ... leystall		xvj
It' reyseyvyd of Ryc' leydeat for hys wyfes leystall		xvj
It' reyseyvyd of Robrtt Crose for howle yere	iij	
It' reyseyvyd of hare aston for hallfe a yere		xviij
It' reyseyvyd of John aneon for a howle yere	iij	
It' allso so myche lede reymeynes ... ... lx^{li} & vj.		
som' of how^{9} ryesayts v^{li} viij^{s} ij^{d}.		
reymeynynge ... ... xxij^{s} ... ..."		

	s.	d.
"It' payd to Robrtt wyse		v
It' to Ryc' dalbe for mendynge of the glase wyndos for the holl yere ...		xvj
It' payde for fyilynge of the font for the holl yere		vj
It' payde to Ryc' hassyllwall for leynge of the churche flore & for lyme ...		xvj
It' payd to hare necolas for makynge of the wax for the holl yere		xvj
It' payd to mest' Dauẽportt for kyepynge of the cloke & the deybell[1]	iij	viij
It' payd to s^{9} hughe ley[2]		iij
It' payd for viij dossyn of tyles	vij	
It' payd for lyme & sande		x
It' for workemonshypp of the chappell		xx
It' payd for thre dossyn of tyle to the bodde [body] of ye churche	ij	vj
It' payd for workemonshypp		xvj
It' payd for lyme sand & watt^{9}		x
It' payd to mest' Dauẽportt ow^{9} clarke	iij	viij
It' payd for makynge of the lyche gate		xx
It' payd to the plymmer for dressynge of the churche leydes	xij	
It' payd for a lode of cley		v
It' payd for careynge vp to the leydes		ij
It' payd for a horse lode of torfes......		iij

[1] The "day bell" is again referred to in 1594. It was rung at four o'clock in the morning (see 1606).

[2] See his burial in 1587. [ι·81·82.

	s.	d.
It' payd for a hondert of neyles ...		iiij
It' payd for the careynge vp and downe ...		iiij
It' payd for swepynge of the leydes ...		ij
It' payd for wyre to the cloke ...		j
It' payd to mest' Dauēport ow^p clarke ...	iij	viij
It' payd to Ryc' hassyllwall for coverynge of graues ...		xij
It' payd for dressynge of the pulle [pulley] for the cloke ...		ij
It' payd for a belrope to the to the antē bell [anthem bell] ...		viij
It' payde for to dosyn of tyle & fo[r] the carege ...		xxij
It' payd to Ryc' hassyllwall for couering of a graue ...		iiij
It' payd for wascheynge of the surples ...		ij
It' payd for makynge of candyles ...		j
It' payd for fyllynge of the font ...		iiij
It' payd for the mendynge of the comenean boke ...		vj
It' payd to mest' Dauēportt ow^p clarke ...	iij	viij
It' payd to the plymm^p [plumber] ...		vj
It' payd to Ryc' hassyllwall for couerynge of to graues ...		vij
It' payd to Ryc' Grey for mendynge of the cloke ...		vij
It' payd to s^p Ryc' fakener for mydsomer quarter ...	vj	
It' payd more to s^p Ryc' fakener for meycaels quartter ...	viij	
Itm payde to m^r damparde for makynge and berynge owre boke th'owe ye yere ...		xiiij

Summe woynge vnto the pches for the reylefe   xviij^s."

EASTER 1552 TO EASTER 1553.

[The receipts come afterwards.]

	s.	d.
"It' payd to s^p George for a quartt^p wage ...	xxiij	iiij
It' payd to Ryc' dawbe ...		xvj
It' payd to adlyntū wyfe for wasceyng of close & fyllyng of ye font		xvj
It' payd to Robrtt wyse for sweppynge of ye churche ...		vj
It' payd to mest' dauēport ow^p clarke for owre lade day quartter in lente ...	iij	viij
It' payd for thre dossyn of tyle...	iij	
It' payd for lyme...		v
It' payd to Ryc' haseyllwall for coueryngo of graues at one tyme ...		xiij
It' payd for waseynge of s^p wyllm sorples ...		ij
It' payd for a rope for the lyttull peyse [weight] of the cloke...		ij
It' payd for a bare [bar] & a loc [lock] & a bowte [bolt] & a stapull [staple] to the lyche zate [1] ...		xv
It' payd for makynge of owre byll that was put vp to the commyseonors ...		ij
It' put in to the pore mans box att won tyme...		xij
& gaue to syx pore folikes att the same tyme ...		xij

[1] First reference to the Lychgate.

ST. MARY-ON-THE-HILL, CHESTER.

	s.	d.
It' payd to mest' dauēportt owre clarke for mydsom^e quartr^p	iij	viij
It' payd for wassynge of s^e wyllm sorples		ij
It' payd for the newe comenean boke that was bogzthe last	vj	
It' payd to s^9 wyllm for byndynge & bordynge of the same boke		xij
It' payd to hare necolas for wax candels		vj
It' payd more to s^t wyllm for mendynge of the bybull boke & for the coverynge of the same		xx
It' payd for a skyne for couerynge of the same boke		iiij
It' payd for mest' Dauēpor' for mecaet qurt^p	iij	viij
It' payd to Ryc' carver for a tabull & frame	x	
It' payd to the plymm^e for mendynge of the ledes & for sod^p		ij
It' payd to Ryc' hasyllwall for settynge in of skyrttes of led & for couerynge of a graue & for lyme		xviij
It' payd to mest' Dauēportt wyfe for mendynge of the tabull clothe^1 & for wassynge of the same		iiij
It' payd to mest' Dauepor' for kyrsonmes [Xmas] quart^p	iij	viij
It' payd for wassynge of s^p wyllm sorp[l]es		ij
It' payd to mest' Dauēportt owr clarke for makynge vp of owre boke of couttes [of accounts]		iiij
m^d that we haue payde iij^{li} xiiij^s vj^d."		

	s.	d.
"... ... ... [cut off] ... ... [Robert Skryevenyer & Rycc'] Getten		
Geyderyt apon palme sondey toward s^o George wages	viij	ob
It' reseyuyd of Robrtt skreuener & Iohn hollrt	xxij	iiij
It' reyseyuyd of wyllm Grymsedyche		xviij
It' reyseyuyd of mest' plankney for a leystall		xvj
It' reyseyuyd of hughe hauttons wyfe for a leystall	ij	
It' reyseyuyd for a leystall for mest' rosomgreue		xvj
It' reyseyuyd for a leystall for Iohn Geffun of honbryghe		xvj
It' reyseyuyd of mest' pheryse for ten pond of olld wax	v	
It' reyseyuyd of mest' wyllm ald^{o}sey for [a] sartten of olld brase thatt be longytt to the churche	vj	vij
It' reyseyuyd of Ryc' leche for a sartten of hengynges thatt be longytt to the alters in the churche	iij	iiij
It' reseyuyd of mest' vawdrey for a prese [? press] that was in the revesttre	xiij	iiij
It' reseyuyd of Ryc' eyvyn for hys fathers lestall		xvj
It' reseyuyd of Ryc' calldey for a leystall		xij
The som that we haue raysayvede iij^{li} vij^s x^d ob.		
Itm that the pychesse dothe rayemāye in dyde to Robarte skryevenyer & Rycc' gytten ffor ye fforste yere vj^s viij^d."		

---

^{1} The white linen cloth used for the celebration of the Holy Communion.

Easter 1553 to Easter 1554.

[*The receipts for this year are missing.*]

"These be the costes thatt Ryc' Getton & Robartt skryven⁹ haue leyde downe for thys yere 1553.

	s.	d.
Itm payd to mest' daveportt for est⁹ quartt⁹ ...	iij	iiij
Itm payd to Ryc' dawbe for hys dotty [duty] by the yere & for mendynge of the glase wyndaw when the led [lead] was stwne ...		xx
Itm payd for fyllyng of the font ...		viij
Itm payd for swepynge of the churche ...		iiij
Itm payd att whitsonday laste paste for wassynge of the tabull clothe & the preste sorples ...		iiij
Itm payd to Robartt wysse for castynge dwne of the bankes of the northe syd of the churche for brekynge of the glase wyndawse ...		ij
Itm payd to mest' daveportt for mydsom⁹ quartt⁹ ...	iij	iiij
Itm payd to Elyn buswell for mendynge of a nolld allbe [an old alb] ...		ij
Itm payd to wyttᵐ bollton for mendynge of the bell fram ...		ij
Itm payd to Ryc' leche for a pond of wax & for makynge of to surgus [two surges]...		ix
Itm payd for wassynge of the surples att methekellmos quartt⁹ ...		ij
Itm payd to mest' daveportt for methekellmos [Michaelmas] quartt⁹ ...	iij	iiij
Itm payd to Ryc' leche for makyng of to surgus [two surges] ...		ix
Itm payd for wassynge of the surples att to tymes ...		iiij
Itm payd for wassynge of the churche clothes att krysmos ...		iij
Itm payd to Rafe whythed for stons...		xvj
Itm payd for carynge of the same stons wᵗ to feylaws [two fellows] ...		vj
Itm payd for lym ...		v
Itm payd to Tomas wyswall for makyng of the alltres ...		xvij
Itm payd to a workeman for sarvynge hym to dayes ...		xij
Itm payd to a labarur for whyttlymynge & for swepynge of the churche wyndawse ...		iij
Itm payd to the carvar for a frame to the tabull [table] of the hee alt⁹ [high altar] ...		xij
Itm payd to mestres grymsedyche for thre pond of wax ...	ij	
Itm payd to Ryc' leche for makynge of to surges [two surges] & a sartten of candels ...		iiij
Itm payd for settenge vp of the angell ...		vj
Itm payd to mestrys daveportt for mendynge of a vestement ...		ij
Itm payd to Ryc' leche for a torche ...	ij	ij
Itm payd to Ryc' leche for gyllydynge of a Nemyche of owre lade [an image of Our Lady] ...		xx
Itm payd to lawrans the golld smythe for mendynge of the pyx ..		xvj
Itm payd for a ropp to the anten bell ...		iiij
Itm payd for a sokett to the crose that mest' vadrey dyd gyue to the churche ...		xij

	s.	d.
Itm payd for penttynge [? fastening on] of owr tabull [table] to the hee allt⁹ [high altar] ...		iiij
Itm payd to mest' davēportt for krystenmasse qwartor ...	iij	iiij
Itm payd to the berege for leynge vp of the alt⁹ ston ...		ij
Itm payd for the wassynge of the surples att the last psacion [procession] ...		ij
Itm payd for careynge of owre boke ...		viij

Sum of owre reyseytes xliiijˢ & vjᵈ.
Sum payd xlvˢ vᵈ.
& allso the p̃ches [parish] ys in owre dett xjᵈ."

EASTER 1554 TO EASTER 1555.

"1554.
Thys pcells folowynge Thomas Robenson and peter ffiecher Churche Wardens of Saynte mares on the hyll have Ressevyd for thys yere past 1554.

	s.	d.
Item in Primvs ffor a leystawe of a doughter of Mʳ Kethene ...	ij	
Item ffor a leystawe of a chylde of Mᵗʳ pellens ...		viij
Item for a leystowe of Wyllyam Davye ...	ij	
Item for a leystowe of Roger grey ...		xvj
Item for a leystowe of harrye mylners wyfe ...		xvj
Item for a leystowe of Rychart Evan ...		xvj
Item for a leystowe of Ryc' caldes mother ...		xlj
Item for a leystawe of Mᵗʳ ffallowes...		xx
Item for a knelyng plasse of Thomas Robensons wyffe ...		xij
Item for a knelyng plasse of Iohn Ionsons wyffe ...		xij
Item for a knelleng plasse of Rynalde Walkers wyfe ...		xij
Item for a knellenge plasse of peter tarlton wyffe ...		vj
Item Ryessevyd of sartene of the parryche as a perethe in owre geddrenge boke towards the payeynge for the makyng of yᵉ Rode ...	viij	iiij
Item ƚƚ of thomas meylles ffor hys wyffs knellenge plasse ...		xij

Som̃ of owre Ryessetts [receipts] ys Just xxiiijˢ ijᵈ
Also the parresse [parish] ys in owre dett the Som̃ of xxxiijˢ vjᵈ ob."

"Thes parselles foloweng Thomas Robynson and Peter flecher churge Wardens of Saynt Mares on the hyll have payde ffor thes yere past año 1554.

	s.	d.
Item In p'imos payde to Roger ledsam pewtrer for the holy watter bockytt...	iij	iij
Item to Roger sprage for makynge the Ireron bove to yt & for mendeng yᵉ claper of a bell ...		iiij
Item ffor lyme to cover the graves ...		vj
Item for iij dosyn of Tylles ...	ij	vj
Item for v dossyn of tylles at vjᵈ yᵉ dȝ ...	ij	vj
Item for carege of tylle and sande & for berege ...		iiij

	s.	d.
Item payde to hasselwall for covereng graves		xij
Item for sayenge of masse to a prest in the wytson weke		xij
Item to John telstons wyffe for wassenge a sorples		ij
Item to John newall for wryttenge for the sute of the parreche		xiij
Item for a Roppe to the pesse [weight] of the cloke		xx
Item to a pressener of the castell for mendenge of the belles		xvj
Item for mendenge the stoks of the belles to holbroke and for Iron & nelles to ye Rode		x
Item for j^{li} of Englesse waxe ... ... , ...		xij
Item for a corde to the antyn bell and for a kye to the boxe...		viij
Item more for ij^{li} of waxe		xxij
Item ij dossyn tylles and a lode of lyme	ij	
Item for coverynge the graves		xxj
Item to peres Rossomgreve of wartton ffor makynge the Rode	xij	
Item for owre charge to warton & for berreg		vj
Item for gyldenge the Rode to Ryc' leche	xiij	
Item for ij^{li} candles at crystonmas		v
Item to holbroke smyth for mendenge the seconde bell welle & a locke for ye cloke		x
Item for a henge & wyre for the cloke and for Iron and nylles		ix ob
Item to Dame Ales[1] for mendenge a olde ailbe and a sorples		ij
Item to Rychard lech for ij^{li} di waxe	ij	vj
Item to Ryc' leche for Makyng waxe for thes yere		xix
Item to brege wyffe for wasshenge clothes		xvj
Item for makyng owre booke and belles [bills] for the hole yere		x

Som' of owre payements ys lvij^s viij^d."

"xxiiij° May Annis R phi & Marie prmo & sedo [1555].

Thom^{as} browne ⎫
Ric' gethyn ⎪ *ti*pers for the ley of the pisshioners apon handbrygge side for necesaryes
John holt & ⎪ of the Churche.
Thom^{as} mylner ⎭

Robert gryse ⎫
Nicholas Wetherby ⎪ *ti*pers for Chester Vpton & others.
Thom^{as} Rogerson ⎪
Thom^{as} Wysewall ⎭

Thom^{as} Mascy
R vaudry   Thomas Byram
Thomas Biram is my name.

Also that the pche ys conttcte that Robrtt hatton for the tabarnacvll that stonds at the hee altr^s end shall pay no quartterege for the spase of vij yere."

[*This comes after the payments for* 1576.]

[1] Dame Alice Grosvenor, the Prioress of the Nunnery.

Easter 1555 to Easter 1556.

"1555.

Thesse parssells foyloynge We thomas Robenson and petter fflecher churche Wardens of saynt marres on the hell have R. for thes 1555.

	s.	d.
Item Ryessevyd at haster [Easter] for qvarteryche and pascove pencys [pascal pennies]...	xxj	viij
Item R. for a lestowe of coke of molenton ...		xiiij
Item R. for a lestove of hatton for mestres Rossorngreve ...		xij
Item a lestove of mestres crosse ...		xvj
Item a lestove of wyllym wytbe...		xij
Item a lestove of geffrey barker...		xvj
Item a lestove of John marssche ...		xvj
Item a lestove of peter flecher chylde ...		viij
Item R. of Rye' borros for a knellenge plasse ...		xij
Item R. for a knelenge plase of Robert crooked ...		xij
Item R. of sertayne of the parresche for qvarterys as apereth in the geythereng boke ...	v	j

Som' xxxvj^s vij^d."

"Thesse be the parssells that we Thomas Robenson and peter fflecher churche wardens of Saynte Mares on the hell Payde for thes yere año 1555.

	s.	d.
Item payde for frankensence and charcolls ...		v
Item to Dame ales for mendenge the clothe before the hey alter ...		iiij
Item for fellenge the fonte ij^d and for hyrenge the sencer 8^d ...		x
Item for vj^{li} & q^{tr} of waxe at xj^{li} the le ...	v	ix
Item for makynge the waxe aganyste aster [Easter] ...		xviij
Item to M^{tr} Dampartt for kyepenge the cloke on' q^{tr} ...		xx
Item for wasshenge the prests sorples ...		iiij
Item to Rye' Dobyes man for mendenge the wendoes ...		ix
Item for a lode lyme and ij^{li} candulls ...		xij
Item for the lone [loan] of a senser ...		iij
Item for wryttenge the carteculls [articles] at the vysetacyon ...		iiij
Item for tylles ...		vj
Item for frankynsence and neles & pap ...		iiij
Item ffor ij^{ms} Tylles ...		xvj
Item p^d to hassellwall...		xv
Item for iiij^{li} candles for the holyn ...		xviij
Item for holence to the stare & mone ...		vj
Item to dobye for mendenge the wendooy ...		vj
Item for coverynge geffre barkers wyffs grave ...		iiij
Item to Rye' leche for makynge the waxe for the [year] ...		xviij
Item for makynge the mone [moon] & all suche thyngs belongen to ytt ...		ij

	s.	d.
Item for carynge of tylles		ij
Item for whasshnge the clothes for the holle yere		xij
Item for makynge ovre a cov⁾ette boke [our account book]		viij
Item to a bewye [? boy] for carrenge the boke wth vs a bovtte the churche		ij

Som' xxv^s.

Item that the paryssche ys In owr dett the Som' of xij^s ij^d ob."

Easter 1556 to Easter 1557.

"1556.

"Thes pcels folowynge Wyttm Wyllyamson And Thomas Myelner churche wardens of sent mares on the hyll have recevyd for thys yere past whyche ys the iij & iiij yere of philip & mary by the grace off god kyng & quene of England ffranc' nepells &c.

	s.	d.
Itm in piñis wye haue recevyd at eyster	xxij	v
Itm wye haue recevyd of Robart fysher for A knelyng place...		xij
Itm Recevyd of the wedoo gheste for A knelyng place		xij
Itm recevyd for the leystall of Roger sprage		xij
Itm recevyd of Iohn clarke for a knelyng place for his wyffe...		xij
Itm ℞ ffor A ley stall ffor hovld melsys wyffe		xij
Itm geythred Apon trenyte sondey	iij	x
Itm ℞ of Ryc' ffleccher for A knelyng place for his wyffe		xij
Itm recevyd owte of A boxe in mone [money]...		x
Itm ℞ ffor ower lady quarter	ij	iij
Itm ℞ for A ley stall of thomas rogersons wyffe		xvj
Itm ℞ for A ley stall of Ryc' kawdeys chylde...		xij
Itm ℞ for A ley stall of Ryc' hassylwall		xvj
Itm ℞ for A ley stall of Ryc' bostoke		xviij
Itm ℞ for A ley stall of the reyd makers wyffe		xx
Itm ℞ of gorge Robynson for A knelyng place for his wyffe		xij
Itm ℞ of Robart Brockes for A knelyng place for his wyffe		xij
Itm ℞ of Davey barker for A ley stalle for his chylde		xij
Itm ℞ for a leystall of phylype gyoste wyffe		xvj
Itm ℞ for A leystall of M^r pellyn for his chylde		xiiij
Itm ℞ of John marshe for A knelyng place for his wyffe		viij
Itm ℞ of Edward Afasakerley for his wyffes ley stall		xij
Itm ℞ of Iohn thorronley for A ley stall for his wyffe		xij
Itm ℞ att Crystynmas quarter	ij	x
Itm ℞ for Ryc' ledcatts ley stall of M^r brovnshocke		xij
Itm ℞ of Robart Vernñ for A knelyng place		viij
Itm gederyth of the churche pareshe to s^o gorge for mackyng of the bocke...		xv

Sum off owre Recetts ys lvj^s vj^d."

Instances of women carrying building material instead of labourers.
William Bolton named below was master Carpenter — the counties of Chester & Flint being appointed on Augt 8. 1552 and the office held 6ᵈ a day as wages, it is therefore probable that the charge for the Angell was two days at 6ᵈ a day, and 1ᵈ for timber, or possibly 6½ᵈ a day

ST. MARY-ON-THE-HILL, CHESTER.

" Theys bye the parsells that wye Wyllm wyllyamson & Thomas myelner churche wardens off seynt marys on the hyll payed for this yere paste whyche ys the iij & iiij yere of philip & mary by the grace of god kyng & quene of England ffranc' napells & Jerusalem &c.

	s.	d.
Itm payed to Wyllm langley for A bell And for frygansences		iiij
Itm payd mr Wyllm Alldersaye for xli of waxe the svm ys	x	
Itm payd to Wyllm Knowyssley for makyng the waxe wt the bereshe		xiij
Itm payd for skowryng [scouring] the cryssmatory...		ij
Itm payed vnto lorancs Done for A sence [? censer]		iiij
Itm payed for fyllyng of the fovnt		j
Itm payed for charkolle		ij
Itm payed Dobye for mendyng of the glason wyendoo	iij	iiij
Itm payed to Wyllm Allkocke & his man for on' deyes worke		xvj
Itm payed for A peys of tember to Wyllm Wyllyfison to the same worke ...		viij
Itm payed to hankocks man for gettyng A botte [bolt] owt off A poste ...		ij
Itm payed for mendyng the Anton bell fframe & for nelys		j
Itm payed for chadoys and wyte tryde [white thread]		j
Itm for fyllyng the fovnt at wessontyed		j
Itm payed to Wyllm Knowyssley for makyng off the waxe		ij ob
Itm payed for ij lode of lyme		xij
Itm payed to Ryc' barker for ijli & iij quarters of soder		xiiij
Itm for his worke man shype		xij
Itm payed to Harry meller for his dey worke		viij
Itm payed to his wyffe ffor caryeng water & sande		ij
Itm payed to the bereche		ij
Itm payed to Wyllm bollton for the Angell that the sacrament ys in		xij
Itm payed to Ryc' gre for mendyng of ij hellys [bells]	iij	iiij
Itm payed for iiij dosen & viij brekes [bricks]...	iij	viij
Itm payed moyᵉ for j dosen breke [bricks]		x
Itm payed to Wyllm Knowyssleys wyffe for makyng off waxe		iij
Itm payed to A woman for caryeng water breke & sande		iij
Itm payed to a wryght ffor makyng the lyche yatte		iiij
Itm payed ffor on' lode of lyme...		vj
Itm payed ffor Dressyng of ij krowyetts [cruets] and A shyppe ffor frygansence		ij
Itm payed ffor iij dosen of tylle...	ij	ix
Itm payed to Ryc' hassylwall for coveryng of the graves	iij	ij
Itm payed for xv brekes [bricks]		xij
Itm payed to A woman for watᵉ & sande...		j
Itm payed for mendyng of the fyrst bell		xx
Itm payed for A roppe to the hollen		xviij
Itm moy' for A corde for the hollen...		j
Itm payed to mr greyn for viijli of candylls	ij	vj
Itm payed for A hollen for the churche		vj

See page 237 (1552-53).

		s.	d.
Itm payed for A man for pottyng vp of the rope to the hollen			j
Itm payed for A povnd off candells...			iiij
Itm payed for A corde to the Anton bell...			ij
Itm payed to Ryc' hallewod for makyng off waxe ...			xj ob
Itm payed to Joen yewans ffor wasshyng of the churche cloys [clothes] the hovll yere ...			xx
Itm payed to s⁹ gorge for makyng A churche bocke ...		ij	
Itm payed for makyng vp o' bocke ...			viij
Itm payed for caryeng of o' bocke w^h vs Abovt the churche...			ij
Itm s⁹ holyw' [Sir Oliver] gave to the churche A govn and wye [we] changet yt w^t s⁹ harry snape for A blow [blue] westment.			

Sūm of owre payements ys lv^s ix^d.
Remenyng in the boxe ix^d."

Easter 1557 to Easter 1558.

"1557.

Theys beyn the pcells that wye wyllm wyllyanison and thomas mylner churche wardens of sent maryes on the hyll hays Recevyd for thys yere paste whyche ys the iiij & v yere [July 1557 to July 1558] of phílype & mary by the grace of god kynge & queyn &c.

	s.	d.
Itm ℞ of thomas Rogerson for a klelyng [sic] place for his wyffe ...		xij
It' ℞ of John marshe for a knelyng place for his wyffe ...		xij
Itm ℞ of Ryc' dobye for a ley stovll for his moder...		xij
Itm ℞ of m' worssley ffor iij knelyng placys ...	iij	
Itm wye gederyd at aster [Easter] quarter ...	xviij	
Itm for a knelyng place for dave barkers wyffe ...		xij
It' ℞ for a knelyng place for Ryc' kocke ...		viij
Itm for a knelyng place for Iohn Dyckonsons wyffe		viij
Itm for a knelyng place to m' Dampartes wyffe ...		xvj
Itm for a knelyng place for M^{tr} wytneys wyffe...		xvj
Itm gederyd at o' lady dey quarter the svm ...	ij	
Itm for a leysto of M^{tr} browtons prests[1] ...		xij
Itm for a knelyng place for James Robynsons wyffe		xij
Itm ℞ of Robart hope for a knelyng place for his wyffe...		xij
Itm ℞ for crystynmas quarter ...	ij	viij
It' for a leystalle of Edward fasakerley for his wyffe		x:j
Itm ℞ for the leystall of John Robynson & his wyffe ...	ij	
Itm for a knelyng place of yonge Iohn Robynson ...		xij
It' ℞ for a leystall of a chyelde of Robart breerwode ...		xij
Itm ℞ for a leystolle for Iohn a thorronlayes wyffe...		xij
It' ℞ of m' brownshonke for his wyffeys leystolle ...		xij
It' ℞ for a leystolle of Rychart breerwode ...		xij
Itm for a leystolle of a stranger that Robart hankocke beryed ...		xij

[1] Mr. Brereton's priest, who served the chantry.

		s.	d.
Itm that wye gederyd on the sondey aft' the sklanssyng deys to the cler' for kepyng of the clocke			xvj ob
Itm lt for a leystolle of Ryc loo			xij
Itm lt for a leystolle of Roger sprages chyelde			xij
Itm lt of Nykolas brenys for a knelyng place for his wyffe ..., ...			xij
Itm lt of Edmont yerdelye for Iohn makequelys wyffe toyert [towards] mackyng the lyghtys in the Rode lofte			ij
Sm' of owre Recetts liijs ob.			

"Apud Cestr, xxvj die septembris anº 1557.

hyt ys orderyd by the kyng & quenes comyssyoners whose names be subscrybyd that these whose names here followe shall pay euʳy sonday as hereafter ys Apoyntyd them to the church wardens of sent maryes for the same churche vse vntyll such tymes as xt be ffully payd in cōsideracon & recompes of such money as they have in there handes vz to begyn paymēt the sondey next ensuyng the date above wryten.

	d.
John Anyan glouᵉʳ euᵉʳy sonday	ij
Rycharde smythe	ij
wyllᵗᵐ grymesdych	ij
phyllyp gest	ij
George teyler	ij
harry asseheton...	ij
Robart Crosse	ij
Johan ley wedds	j
Roger ffoxley	j
weddo whythye	j
nycolas Rogʳson	j
John whythedde	j
Thomᵃs londs	j

                  ita est

(Signed)   Cuthe chester [Cuthbert Scott, Bishop].
                John webster
                ffowke Dutton
                John Smythe
                Thomas Smythe."

[*The above comes after the payments for* 1576.]

"Theys beyn the poells that wye wyllm wyllyam[son] & thomas mylner churche wardens of sent maryes on the hyll payed for thys yere paste whyche ys the iiij & v yere [July 1557 to July 1558] of philip & mary bye the grace of god kyng & queyn &c.

	s.	d.
Itm payed vnto Ryc' hallwode ffor xiiijli waxe bye side ijli of or hovn [of our own]	xij	iij
Itm payed for the makyng of xvjli waxe wt the bereche...		xvij
Itm peyd for fryganences		iiij
Itm for threde		ob

		s.	d.
Itm peyd for skowryng [scouring] of ij chandelers			j
Itm peyd for the skowryng of the censers...			j
Itm peyd for cherkovll			j
Itm peyd vnto Ryc' Dobye ffor the mendyng of the glassen wendoys ...		ij	
Itm peyd to Robart grysse ffor ij ledes for the ij haly water stocks		v	
Itm peyd vnto Ryc' barker for on povnd of soder			v
Itm peyd for settyng in the same ledes			iij
Itm peyd vnto thomas glassyer ffor makyng a novnsare [an answer] to m' mere [Mr. Mayor] anendys wyttm bawll			xvj
Itm peyd to Ryc' hallwode for makyng off the waxe at wessontyed ...			iij
It' peyd for fellyng of the fovnt at ester & wesson tyed			ij
It' peyd for makyng a bare [bier] & mendyng a locke to the fovnte ...			v
Itm peyd for pessyng a henge and settyng yt apovn			j
Itm peyd for makyng of the bocke at the wesetacyon			ij
It' peyd for a povnd of wyte candylls for to goo awesetyng wyth [for to go a visiting with]			iij
Itm peyd for paryeng [repairing] of the alleys in the churche yerde			vj
Itm peyd for a rope to the Anton belle			iij
Itm peyd vnto pellyns sovn for makyng a gedyryng bocke for the best shovte [suit] & papar		ij	ob
Itm for nelys			ob
Itm peyd ffor makyng of a stare			xx
It' for the pentyng & gyldyng of the same stere			xx
Itm for wyer to the stere		ij	ob
Itm for a rope to the stere...			ix
Itm for the holyn			vj
Itm for a man to get the rope in to the polley			ij
Itm for candylls for the stere and the holyn		iij	
Itm ffor makyng waxe			xiij
Itm peyd vnto govn [Joan] yevan ffor wessheng the churche cloys [clothes] by the hovll yere...			xx
Itm peyd for nelys ffor mendyng the howys [house?] ower the Anton bell ...			ij
Itm peyd to the wryght			ij
Itm peyd vnto the clerke ffor kepyng of the clocke...	vj	viij	
Itm peyd to mestres gryemdyche for vij^{li} & a halfe of waxe aft^{s} xj^{d} ob a povnd	vj	viij	ob
Itm for makyng of iij^{li} waxe to the hye alter			iij
Itm for makyng of ix^{li} of waxe for the Rode lofte			ix
Itm for wyer to the rode lofte		ij	ob
Itm-peyd for makyng ope of o^{r} bocke			vj

Sm' of o^{r} pements—lj^{s} 7x^{d}.
Remenys in the boxe—xliij^{d}
& ij leystolles vn peyd for yet."

starre (bracket annotation beside stare entries)

EASTER 1558 TO EASTER 1559.

"1558.
Thys byn The percells That We Rbart Gryse and Rycharde Dawbe Church Wardens hathe Recevyd for thys yere past.

	s.	d.
Itu' in prymys Rescued for yᵉ lestall of sᵗ gorge	vj	viij
Itu' gederyd at Aster [Easter] quarter	xix	viij
Itu' Rescued of mester Dampart for hys wyves laystall	ij	
Itu' Ił for yᵉ laystall of Ihon whythed		xx
Itu' Ił for yᵉ laystall of ethell Dyo ... ... *Ethel Dyer.*		xvj
Itu' Ił for the laystall of nycolus wederbe		xvj
Itu' Ił for yᵉ laystall of Jhamys Jake...		xvj
Itu' Ił for yᵉ laystall of Robarte saueghe		xvj
Itu' Ił for yᵉ laystall of Ihon thornele		xv
Itu' Ił for yᵉ laystall of Rycharde gyttyns wyfe		xvj
Itu' Ił of nycolas wryght for a knelynge placse for hys wyfe	ij	
Itu' Ił of Thomas Hale for A knelynge place for hys wyfe		viij
Itu' Ił of Thomas Rocherson for A knelynge place for hys wyfe		xij
Itu' Ił of James gyttyn for A knelynge place for Hys wyfe		xvj
Itu' Ił of wyllyam Horst for A knelynge place for Hys wyfe		xij
Itu' Ił of Robart bererwod for A knelynge place for Hys wyfe *Brerewood.*		xvj
Itu' Ił for yᵉ shyfthynge of yᵉ sthone and yᵉ lestall of mester wodwarde ...	ij	viij
Itu' Ił for yᵉ laystall of sesle granwall		xvj
Itu' Ił for yᵉ laystall of wyllyam grymysdyche		xvj
Itu' Ił for the laystall of Katheren geste		xvj
Itu' Ił for the laystall of phelep oscrofte		xij

The som' of owre Recetts lijˢ viijᵈ."

"Thys byn yᵉ parchell yᵗ we Robart gryse and Rychad Dawbe Churche wardens hathe payde for thys yere paste.

	s.	d.
Itu' payd for xiijᵗ of waxe	xiij	
Itu' payd for a antan bell Rope		iiij
Itu' payd for threde		ob
Itu' ped for papar		ob
Itu' payd for A corde to yᵉ Roode clothe for pame sondaye [Palm Sunday]		ij
Itu' payd to Robarte wyse for yᵉ swepynge of yᵉ churche		iiij
Itu' payd for frankyn senes		iiij
Itu' payd for charcolls		j
Itu' payd for to Rycharde Dawbe for kepynge of yᵉ wyndous by yere	ij	
Itu' payd to Rycharde Hassellwall for yᵉ hyllynge [covering up] of to [two] grauys		vij
Itu' payd for wyer		ob
Itu' payd for socwrnge [scouring] of yᵉ sence [censer] & to candellar [two chandeliers]...		ij
Itu' payd for yᵉ makynge of yᵉ waxe for astor [a star]		xv

CHURCHWARDENS' ACCOUNTS.

	s.	d.
Itu' payd to Ryc' graye for yᵉ mendyng of the belles		xvij
Itu' payd for A ponde of candells for to go A uesetynge [to go a visiting] ...		iiij ob
Itu' payd for iiij dosyn & iij od tyllys [tiles]	iij	iij
Itu' payd for A lode of lyme		v
Itu' payd to Ryc' Hasylwalle for the coueryng of x graues	ij	viij
Itu' payd to nycolas Rogerson for the parynge [repairing] of yᵉ churche yourde		vj
Itu' payd for the soderynge of the gotter on the sowthe syde of yᵉ churche...		xv
Itu' payd for yᵉ Hallohynge [hallowing] of A corporas & ij havter clothys [two altar cloths]...		x
Itu' payd to Ryc' Hassylwall for A daye & A Halfe for yᵉ churche yourde ...		xij
Itu' payd to A laboier for a daye		vj
Itu' payd Ryc' Hasslwall for yᵉ cowuerynge of v grauese		xvij
Itu' payd for lyme		vij
Itu' payd for A dosyen of tyle		x
Itu' payd for candells for crysstynmas	iij	v
Itu' payd for yᵉ Holyn		vj
Itu' payd to Jhone evan for wahsshynge of yᵉ churche clothys by yere...	ij	
Itu' payd for yᵉ mendynge of the churche yate		j
Itu' payd for nayles & yᵉ Irons for yᵉ bellys		viij
Itu' payd to yᵉ workeman & hys sarvante		xxij
Itu' payd for yᵉ makynge of yᵉ waxe for the holle yere for yᵉ heavter [altar]		xxj

The Som' of owre payements xliijˢ jᵈ ob.
Also there Remenys In yᵉ boxe viiijˢ vjᵈ ob.
Also there is vij laystalls to be payd for."

EASTER 1559 TO EASTER 1560.

" 1559.

Thyes be the parschells yᵗ we Rychard Cawday & Rychard Dawbe Churche wardens hathe Rescued for thys here [year] paste 1559.

	s.	d.
In prymos ℞ in the boxe	viij	vj ob.
Itu' ℟ for a busshol of wyat	ij	viij
Itu' gedered for yᵉ clerke on james sondaye [Palm Sunday]...	ij	viij
Itu' gedered at aster [Easter]	xix	x ob.
Itu' ℟ for a knelynge place for hugh usscherwods wyfe...		viij
Itu' ℟ for ye lovne [loan] of iiij torchuse at messter manlese bereal ...	ij	
Itu' ℟ of Robart savaghe wyfe that ye laste	x	
Itu' ℟ for yᵉ lestale of Jhon grefeth		xij
Itu' ℟ for yᵉ lestale of Jhon warton wyfe...		xvj
Itu' ℟ for a knelyng plase for hugh monkysfelde wyfe		xij
Itu' ℟ for a kne[l]yng plase for wyllyam kettells wyfe		xij
Itu' ℟ for yᵉ laystall of messter manlaye		xvj
Itu' ℟ for a knelyng plase for Robarte crokets wyfe		xij

The wholl some of oʳ receats is liijˢ jᵈ."

"Thyes be the parchells yt we Rychard Cavdaye & Rycharde Dawbe Churche wardanes hathe payde for thys yerere paste.

	s.	d.
In prymos payde for xiiij^l of waxe	xij	vj
Itu' payde for iiij dossen of tyles	iij	
Itu' payd to Rychard Hassellwall for ye hyllynge of iiij grauys		xvj
Itu' payd for water & sond		ij
Itu' payd for mendynge of to albys [two albs]...		iiij
Itu' payd for pynnys & therde		j
Itu' payd for ffellynge ye font		ij
Itu' payd for ye Repracyons of the wyndos by yerere	ij	
Itu' payd for charcollys		j
Itu' payd to Hare nycolas for ye makyng of ye waxe at asstor [Easter]... ...		xvj
Itu' payd to Thomas myllner for kepynge of ye cloke	vj	viij
Itu' payd to Robarte bryceman for ye hyllynge of iij graues		viij
Itu' payd for ye comenyon boke	iiij	vj
Itu' payd to Rychard coke for ye takynge done of ye rode		ij
Itu' payd for a spade		viiij
Itu' payd for a boke to wryte in wedyngs crysstenyngs & bereynge ...		iij
Itu' payd to Robart breeman for hyllynge of iij graues		vij
Itu' payd for ij dosyn of tylys [tiles]...		xvj
Itu' payd for lyme and sand to the same		viij
Itu' payd for mendynge of ye lychge yate...		ij
Itm payd to herry nicolas for makyng o^f tapers and small waxe candels to serve the quyere		ix
Itm for bordes to the comynion table and bordes to make formes and feete to them and nayls	v	iij
Itm to willm garnet for makynge of them ...		xiiij
Itm to the berache		ij

The some your payement is xxxxv^s xj^d.
Also ther remayns in the boxe ... ... vij^s ij^d."

Easter 1560 to Easter 1561.

" 1560.

Thyes be ye parcells y^t we Rycharde caudaye & Daue Rychardson hathe Reseued for ye yere paste.

	s.	d.
In prymos gedayred on p^amemys [Palm] sondaye for ye clakre	ij	
Itu' Ḻ at aster [Easter]	viij	vj
Itu' Ḻ for ye lestall of mester nottall...		xvj
Itu' Ḻ for ye lestall of Rycharde cow		xvj
Itu' Ḻ for ye lestall of gorge egerton...		xvj
Itu' Ḻ for ye lestall of hugh calides wyfe		xvj
Itu' Ḻ for a knelynge plase for felepe prynce wyfe ...		viij

CHURCHWARDENS' ACCOUNTS.

	s.	d.
Itu' ℞ in ye boxe	vij	ij
Itu' ℞ for ye lestall of gorge hareson		xvj
Itu' ℞ for ye lestall of Thomas brones son		xvj
Itu' ℞ for a knelynge for Ihon grycse for hys wyfse knelyng place		xij
Itu' ℞ for ye lestall of Jon anyan son		xvj

The som' of oure Resetes xxvj^s iiij^d."

"Thyes be ye parcells y^t we Rychard caudaye & Daue Rychardson churche wardens hathe payd for y^t yere paste.

	s.	d.
In prymos payd to Rychard Dawbe for ye wyndoys		ij
Itu' payd to Thomas mylner for ye keppenge of ye cloke	vj	viij
Itu' payd to Robart bryeman for ye wyetlymynge [white liming] of ye churche	v	
Itu' payd for iiij lodys of lyme		ij
Itu' payd for water		iiij
Itu' payd to Thomas bothe for mendyng of ye second bell stoke		xvj
Itu' pad to Robart hancoke for a bout [bolt] of Iren for ye same		xij
Itu' pad to ye bereche		ij
Itu' pad to Robart bryeman for coueryng of v graues & mendyng of ye churche wall		xij
Itu' payd for lyme		vj
Itu' payd for wat^D		ij
Itu' payd to Robart hancoke for mendyge of ye clapar of ye fort bell		xiij ob

The som' of paymentes xxj^s iij^d ob.
Ther Remens [in] ye boxe v^s vj^d."

EASTER 1561 TO EASTER 1562

"Thes be the persells that we Robert Croket and Davy Rycherson hathe Reseued for this yere past 1561.

	s.	d.
In primus Reseyved in ye box	v	
It' gathereid at Aster [Easter]	ix	
It' for a kneling place to Ryc' griffeths wyf		xij
It' for a kneling place to Ihon simsons wyf		viij
It' for a kneling place to Robart Crosses wyf		xij
It' for a kneling place to Thomas smiths wyf		xij
It' for a kneling place to Robert harvys wyf		xij
It' for a knelyng place to Jhon marches wyf		xij
It' for a leastall for crosses wyf ye maryner		xvj
It' for a knelynge place to wylliā smithes wyf		xij
It' for a knelyng place to wyllyā Rychersons wyf		viij
It' for a knelyng place to Rondell mylners wyf		xij
It' for a knelyng place to Edmond yordles wyf		xij
It' for a knelyng place to Thomas thewllyns wyf		xij

		s.	d.
It' for a leastall of James bennet	... ...		xvj
It' for a knelyng place to wyllyā wyllyāsons wyf	...		xvj
It' for a lestall of Ryc' burres	... ...		xvj
It' for a knelyng place to wydow grys	... ...		xvj
It' for a lestall of nycholas brenes wyf lestall (sic)	... ...		xij
	The some of our Resets is xxxij^s."		

"Thes be the psells that we Robart Croket and Davy Rycherson churche wardens hathe payd for this yere past.

		s.	d.
In pmus payde to Ryc' Doby for ye wyndys	... ...	ij	
It' payd to Thomas mylner for keping of the clocke	... ...	vj	viij
It' payd for ij Dussen of tylles	... ...		xx
It' payd for lyme and ye beryng of ye same	... ...		viij
It' payd to Robert bryckman for coveryng of iiij graues	... ...		xij
It' for making clene of the churche	... ...		ij
It' payd to Robart bryckman for coveryng of m^r plancne child graue and crosses wyffes graue ye maryner	... ...		vj
It' payd to Robart bryckmon for coverynge of Ryc' pole graue and Ryc' flechers grave and Ryc' hurrus	... ...		x ob
It' payd for makyng of ye church yate	... ...	v	iiij
It' payd for coveryng of Thomas massyes grave and James bennets	...		vj
It' payd to hugh Gyllam	... ...		iiij
It' payd for half a Dosen of tyles	... ...		v
It' payd to a clark for wrytyng of owr byll	... ...		iiij
It' payd to ye pore wemen for dressing [? cleaning] of the churche gresse [steps]	... ...		iiij
It' for wrytyng of owr bucke [book]	... ...		ij
	The some of owre payments is ... ... xxj^s.		
	There Remens in the box ... ... xj^s.		

Easter 1562 to Easter 1563.

"Thes be the pcells that Robart crose & w^m kettell hathe ℞ for this yere 1562.

		s.	d.
In primvs in the boxe	... ...	x	
Itm gatharde in the cherche at aster	... ...	xv	ij
Itm ℞ of Dave coke	... ...	ij	viij
Itm ℞ of Joane mase for a lay stall	... ...		xvj
Itm ℞ of thomas browne for a lay stall	... ...		xvj
Itm ℞ of thomas strete for a knelynge plase for his wife	... ...		xvj
Itm ℞ of wedoo wederbe for a knelynge plase	... ...		xij
Itm ℞ of Robarte hese wife for a k[n]eling plase	... ...		xij

	s.	d.
Itm ℞ of hare ashton for a knelyng plase		xij
Itm ℞ of Robarte carrear for a knelynge plase		xij
Itm ℞ of m^r flecher for A torche		xx
Itm ℞ of thomas grefethes wyfe for A knelyng plase ...		xij
Itm ℞ of R' movchell for A knelynge plase		x j
Itm ℞ of John geste for A knelynge plase		viij
Itm ℞ for iiij chime hammars		xvj
Itm ℞ in the chorche for mendynge he wese [high ways]	iij	iij
Itm ℞ of thomas ward for A knelynge plaie		xij
Itm ℞ of R' meles for A laystall		xij
Itm ℞ of Robarte brerwood for Iohn grise	vj	
Itm ℞ of george belen for R' pole	i ij	
Itm ℞ for the grete pese [weight] of led		ix

The somme of our Resсytes ys iij^{li} v^s ix^d ob."

"Thes be the pcells that Robarte Krose and wth kettell hathe payd this yere 1562.

	s.	d.
Itm payd for takynge dovne the Ro I lofe ...	iij	x
Itm payd for takynge downe the Alt^ss	ij	
Itm payd for lyme & careage		vj
Itm payd for Water & swepinge ye chorche & the top of ye le ls ...		viij
Itm payd to brekeman for ij dayse worke & for white lyme	ij	
Itm payd to bothe for mendynge ye rofe of chorch		viij
Itm payd for makynge ij rochets for ye boys		vj
Itm payd for laynge of A new well & exchangenge of the ovld led ...		xvj
Itm payd to thomas mylner charke [clerk] for kypinge ye cloke	vj	viij
Itm pay[d] to Dobe for mendynge wyndos	ij	
Itm payd for mendynge ye bell frame	iij	
Itm payd at whyte son tyde for whyte lyminge & dresynge the chorche	ij	vj
Itm payd for mendynge he wese [highways]	viij	iiij
Itm payd for the ten comavndements		xiiij
Itm payd for wrytynge the Artecles		vj
Itm payd for coverynge of graves	ij	
Itm payd for makynge of bels at ye wesetacion		vj
Itm payd for payntynge ye chorche	xxiij	iiij
Itm payd to Jelame		iiij
Itm payd for A^{li} & d [1½ lbs.] waxe candels		vj

The somme of our penientes ys iiij^{li} x^s ij^d.
Rest Due vnto vs Som iiij^s iiij^d ob."

The Receipts of Robert Crose and William Kettell for the yere 1563.
Payments for "laystalls" by,—

"Rich^rd Cawday for the laystall of ij Chyldren in tyles ... ij^s."
Mr Plankney.
Thomas Lloid.

Payments for kneeling places by—
  John ffrost.
  John Tylston.
  David Barker.
  William Kettell.
  Richard Gronow.
"Itm Rͬ for ij haruest gyrdelles at the syght of Mʳ Kethen & Mʳ brownd xvˢ."

Total 3ˡⁱ 3ˢ 8ᵈ.

EASTER 1563 TO EASTER 1564.

The Payments of Robert Crosse and William Kettull for the yere 1563.

	s.	d.
"Itm payd for makynge a Rotchete for the Clarke		iiij"
"Itm payd payd [sic] for makynge the bocks [books] for the poore & other vayles [gifts]		xij"
"Itm payd for pavynge the howȝh grene...	xxiiij	iiij"

Total 3ˡⁱ 7ˢ 7ᵈ.

EASTER 1564 TO EASTER 1565.

The Receipts of George Tayler and John Anyan for the year 1564.
Payments for laystalls by—
  Davy Massye for the laystall of his father.
  Thomas Broome for the laystall of his child.
  John Coke for the laystall of Davy Coke.
  Cycylye Hilton for the laystall of her daughter.
  Raffe Jyneson for the laystall of his child.
  Jone Thropp.
  Hugh Munsfeld.
  Robert Weston sherman.
  Fouck ap Ryse ap Benet for the laystall of his son.
  Thomas Strete for the laystall of his nurse.
  Widow Low.
Payments for kneeling places by—
  Steven Woddes for his wife.
  Richard Tyrall for his wife.
  Mathew Ellys for his wife.
  Harry Heskett for his wife.

"Itᵐ gathered vpon Gutted [Good tide] sonday[1] toward the making of yᵉ churche wall... ... ... vjˢ ixᵈ

Total xlxiiijˢ jᵈ [54ˢ 1ᵈ].

---

[1] See Morris' "Chester in Plantagenet Reigns," page 342.

CHURCHWARDENS' ACCOUNTS.

The Payments of George Tayler and Iohn Anyan for the year 1564.

	s.	d.
" It' payed vnto my lord vnto my lord [sic] buship for ij bockes for ye church	v	ij"
" It' payed for sclates to ye stepell		xj"
" It' payed vnto Jeffray bicklay for sclatinge of ye steple & taking vp of yr leayd		iij"
" It' payd for gad nayles		j"
" It' payd vnto Richard ormand for a lode of clay to mend ye porcs [porch] on ye northe syde		vj"
" It' payd for ye coffen of ye bere & nayles to ye same		vj"
" It' payd vnto hery sheppert and his mā for mēding of ye porch and ye church wall		xij"
" It' a wisket [large basket]		j"
" It' payed vnto hughe massy for a kay to ye lyme howse dore		ij"

Total 3ˡ 5ˢ 5ᵈ.

Brerewood of Chester.

Authorities: Harl. MSS. 2094-4, and 2153, Funeral Certificates, Wills, St. Mary's Registers, Visit. of Cheshire (? 1613 ? 1663).

ROBERT BREREWOOD, of Chester, glover, Sheriff of Chester, 1531. = LUCY, dau. to ....; a widow, 5 E. VI.; married (2) Robert Grice, of Chester, glover; (3)—Haword.

Children of Robert and Lucy

- ROBERT BREREWOOD, thrice Mayor of Chester, 1583, 1587, and 1600. Died 29 May, 1601. Buried at St. Mary's, 2 June, 1601. Will proved at Chester, 16 Sept., 1601. = (1) ELIZABETH, dau. of Thomas Horton, of Chester. She died 1580. Buried at St. Mary's. Second d. of Horton of Ridders. Ches. Visit. p. 257. = (2) JANE, dau. of Hugh Powell ap Davydd ap Powell. Married 20 June, 1579. Died Aug. 1613. Buried at St. Mary's (Fun. Cert.). Will at Chester. Inv. exhib. at Chester, 30 Oct. 1613.
- Cicely B., married .... Findlow. Liv. 1617.
- Elizabeth B., married .... Throppe. Liv. 1617.
- Mary B., married Humphrey Weston. She died 1617. (See Weston Pedigree.)

Children of Robert Brerewood (d. 1601)

- JOHN BREREWOOD (son and heir). Died before his father. Buried 22 Oct., 1599. Sheriff of Chester, 1598. = MARY, dau. to Thomas Parry, of Nanarch, co. Flint, gent. She died 27 Sept. 1592. Buried at St. Mary's.
- Edward Brerewood, M.A., Reader of Astronomy at Gresham College. ob. s.p.
- Elizabeth, buried in St. Mary's, 2 Oct. 1579.
- Alice Brerewood, only daughter. Baptised at St. Mary's 24 Sept. 1571. Married at St. Peter's 7 Dec. 1589. Died 19 May, 1604. Buried at St. Peter's (Fun. Cert.). = (1) Robert Wall, of Chester, son and heir of William Wall, Alderman. Issue died young. = (2) Ralph Allen, of Chester, Alderman. Dead before 1604.

Children of John Brerewood and Mary

- SIR ROBERT BREREWOOD, Knt., Sergeant-at-Law, Recorder of Chester. Born at Chester in 1588. Baptised 10 Jan. 1588. In 1605 matriculated at Oxford from Brazenose College, aged 17. In 1607 became member of Middle Temple. Called to the Bar, 13 Nov. 1615. In 1637 appointed a Judge of N. Wales, and in 1639 was elected Recorder of Chester. In 1640 he was made a Sergeant-at-Law; in 1641 he was appointed King's Sergeant, was Knighted in Dec 6, 1643, and made a Judge of the King's Bench on 31 Jan. 1644, but never sat at Westminster. Died 8 Sept. 1654. Buried at St. Mary's 9 Sept. 1654. Will dated 6 Jan. 1652-3, codicils in 1653-4. Proved at London 17 Sept. 1656. = (1) ANNE, second dau. of Sir Randle Mainwaring, of Over Peover, Knt. Died 23 Dec. 1630. Buried at St. Mary's 23 Dec. 1630 (Fun. Cert). = (2) CATHERINE, dau. of Sir Richard Lee, of Lee and Darnhall, co. Chester, Esq. Buried at St. Mary's 2 March, 1691-2.
- John Brerewood, Bapt. 27 Dec. 1589. = ..., sister to Richard Wall, of Chester, and dau. of Robert Wall, Alderman; co-heir to her brothers.
  - John Brerewood, died young.
  - Priscilla Brerewood, married Gerrard Jones, Sheriff, 1648. Liv. 1653.
  - Sarah Brerewood, married Richard Dunbabyn, of Chester. Liv. 1652.
- Jane Brerewood, Baptised 28 June. 1587. Married John Ratcliff, of Chester, Alderman, who died 30 March, 1633 and was buried at Christchurch. (Fun. Cert.)

Children of Sir Robert Brerewood and Catherine

- Edward Brerewood, Bapt. at St. Mary's 13 Oct. 1634. Liv. 1652, and then at the Temple (?).
- Henry Brerewood, Bapt. at St. Mary's 10 Jan. 1635-6. Liv. 1652; ? incumbent of Holness Chapel, 1672-1677.
- William Brerewood, Bapt. at St. Mary's 5 July 1638. Liv. 1652.
- Thomas Brerewood, Bapt. at St. Mary's 13 Oct. 1640. Buried there 16 Feb. 1640-41.
- Francis Brerewood, Bapt. at St. Mary's 17 Oct. 1641. Liv. 1652.
- Robert Brerewood, Bapt. at St. Mary's 1 Aug. 1643. Buried there 23 Oct. 1643.
- Elizabeth Brerewood, Bapt. at St. Mary's 30 Jan. 1636-7. Liv. 1652.

PEDIGREES.

A genealogical pedigree chart of the Brerewood family. Reading the chart:

Generation 1:

- **John Brerewood** (son and heir), of Chester, Esq., learned in the law. Bapt. 16 June, 1666. Unmarried in 1652. Will dated 1 Dec. 1700. Proved at Chester, 19 Sept. 1701. "John Brerewood, of Bridge Street, Esq., was buryed the 11th day of February, 1700-1."
  = **Sidney**, dau. and co-heir of Sir Francis Gamul, of Chester, Knt. Bur. at St. Mary's, 16 Feb. 1665-6.

- **Robert Brerewood**, Bapt. at St. Mary's, 2 May, 1650. Died young before Aug. 1643.

- **Thomas Brerewood**, Bapt. 25 June, 1623. Bur. 1 Mar. 1623-4.

- **Jane Brerewood**, Bapt. 14 Sept. 1621. Living 1630 and 1652.

- **Elizabeth Brerewood**, Bapt. 31 Oct. 1624. Living 1650. Married William Brocke, of Upton, gent., c. 1643.

Generation 2 (children of John Brerewood and Sidney Gamul):

- **Robert Brerewood** (only son and heir), of Chester, Esq. Bapt. at St. Mary's, 1 May, 1696. Living as Justice at Chester, and a "Capt. Robert Brerewood, of Bridge Street," in 1708. 7th day of October 1712. Nunc. Will dated 27 Sept. 1712. Proved at Chester 6 June, 1713.
  = **Dorothy**, dau. of .... Whitby, of Aston in Hawarden, Esq. Married at Hawarden, 12 June, 1678.

- **Francis Brerewood**, Bapt. at St. Mary's, 23 Jan. 1661-2. Bur. there 25 April, 1663.

- **John Brerewood**, Bapt. at St. Mary's, 18 Jan. 1665-6. Bur. there 19 Jan. 1665-6.

- **Anne Brerewood**, eldest dau. Married Samuel Walker. She was dead in 1700 s.p.

- **Alice Brerewood**, Bapt. at St. Mary's, 30 June, 1658. ? died young.

- **Sidney Brerewood**, Bapt. at St. Mary's, 30 June, 1658. Buried 6 Sept. 1658.

- **Christian Brerewood**, Bapt. at St. Mary's, 14 Oct. 1659. Married at St. Oswald's, Thomas Kelsall, of Trafford, gent., 3 July, 1683. = Both living 1724.

- **Sidney Brerewood**, Bapt. at St. Mary's, 14 Jan. 1660-1. Bur. there 3 June, 1662.

- **Lettice Brerewood**, Bapt. at St. Mary's, 15 July, 1663. "Madam Lettice Brerewood, Spinster, of Nicholas Street, bur. 26 Oct. 1724." Will dated 9 Jan. 1723-4. Proved 30 Nov. 1724, at Chester.

- **Elizabeth Brerewood**, Bapt. at St. Mary's, 22 Oct. 1664. Bur. there 14 Feb. 1664-5.

Generation 3 (children of Robert Brerewood and Dorothy Whitby):

- **John Brerewood**, of Chester, Esq. Bapt. at Hawarden, 20 March, 1678-9. Will made 4 Oct. 1724. Proved at Chester 9 April, 1725. "John Brerewood, Esq., of Bridge Street, buried ye 5th day of November, 1724."
  = **Sophia**, dau. of John Hopley, of Chelsea, Esq. Surv. her husband. Married c. 1715-18.

- **Charlotte Brerewood**, Baptized at Hawarden 13 June, 1680.

- **Grosvenor Brerewood**, Baptized at Hawarden 14 Dec. 1683.

L L

ST. MARY-ON-THE-HILL, CHESTER.

Gamull.

Capt. Massie's Book of Pedigrees, f. 88b.

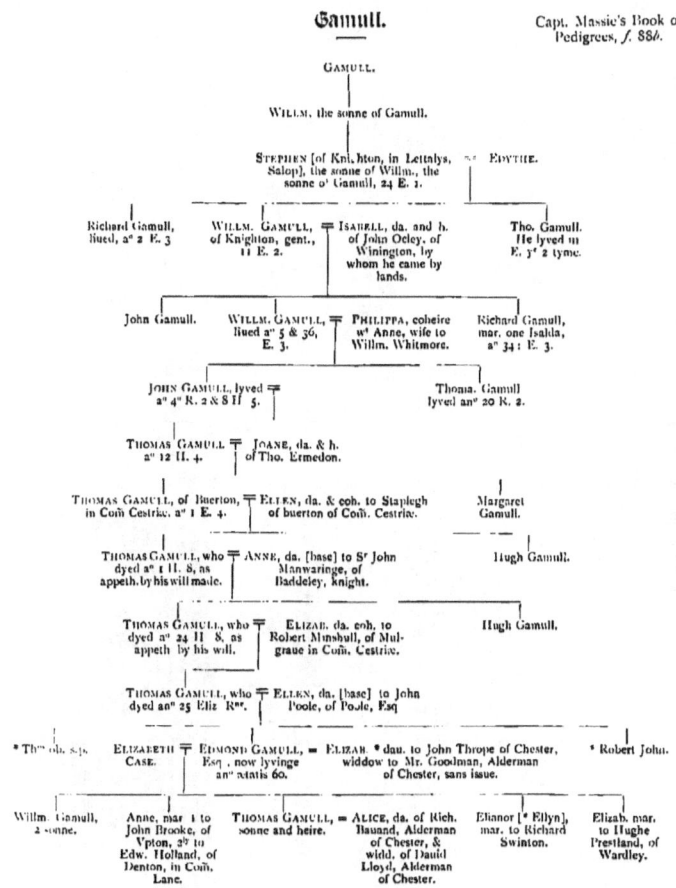

[* Visitation of Chester, 1580, p. 268; Harl. 2163, fo. 85.]

PEDIGREES. 239

Gamull of Buerton and Chester.

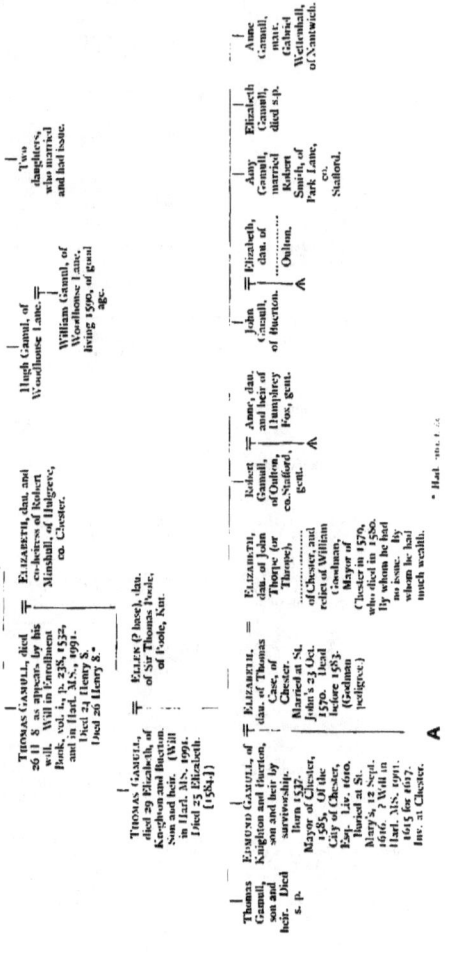

Authorities: Harl. 2012, f. 107, &c., and Harl. 2011, f. 81, &c., Ch. iij, 475, Harl. MS. 1535, Harl. MS. 2163, f. 85.

A

THOMAS GAMULL, of the Inner Temple, London, and of Chester, Esq., and Recorder of Chester. Born 1571. Married c. 1600. Will in Enrollment Books, vol. ij., p. 312, and in Harl. MS. 1991. Inv. at Chester. Died 10th August, 1613. Buried at St. Mary's. (Fun. Cert.).
= ALICE, eldest dau. of Richard Bavand, of Chester, Alderman and twice Mayor, and relict of David Lloyd, of Chester, Alderman and Mayor. She married, 3rd, Edward Whitby, Esq., Recorder of Chester, who was buried in the Gamull tomb at St. Mary's 25 April, 1639. She was buried there 18 August, 1840.

William Gamull, of Chester and Cralwall, Alderman and Mayor of Chester 1608. Will in Harl. MS. 1991. 1619.
= Eleanor, dau. of William Cotgreave, of Chester, Alderman and Mayor in 1589. Married at St. John's 18 April, 1602. Died 11 March, 1614 15. Buried at St. John's. (Fun. Cert.).

Ann Gamull, married before 1592 (1) John Brocke, of Upton, gent., and (2) Edward Holland, of Denton, co. Lanc., Esq., by the latter of whom she had issue. (Fun. Cert. 1631).

Eleanor Gamull, married in 1591 (1) Richard Swinton, of Knutsford; and (2) Thomas Harvey, of Chester, Alderman, who died August, 1613; and (3) Matthew Anderton, Esq. She was buried at St. Mary's 26 Aug. 1639.

Elizabeth Gamull, unmarried 1592. Married (1) Hugh Prestland, of Wardley, co. Chester; and (2) Robert Brocke, of Upton, gent., by whom she had issue.

Children of William Gamull and Eleanor:

Thomas Gamull.* Married Mary, dau. of Edward Bellot, of Moreton, co. Chester Esq. She died 23 Dec. 1631. Buried at St. John's. (Fun. Cert.) = — Frances. She married Sankey, the lawyer.

William Gamull, of Chester, Alderman. Will in Harl. MS 1991. Frances, his widow, ditto ditto, 1644. His Funeral April 1643.

Eleanor Gamull. Thomas Thorpe. (Fun. Cert.).

Anne Gamull.

Children of Thomas Gamull and Alice:

SIR FRANCIS GAMULL, of Chester, Knt. Bapt at St. Oswald's, Chester, 25 Nov. 1606. Mayor of Chester in 1635. Created a Baronet by King Charles I. prior to the 12th June, 1644. "Sr ffrancis Gamull, buried in his owne vault 27th of November, 1654." Knighted 25 Aug. 1640.
= CHRISTIAN, eldest dau. of Sir Richard Grosvenor, Knt. and Bart. Married at Eccleston Oct. 1624. Died in childbirth 6 June, 1640. Buried at St. Mary's 11 June, 1640.
= ELIZABETH, dau. of Sir Randle Mainwaring, Knt., relict of Robert Ravenscroft, of Bretton, co. Flint, Esq., by whom she had seven sons and five daughters. She was living 1656.

Thomas Gamull, eldest son. Living 1603.

Richard Gamull, Living in 1603.

See Fun. Cert. of Richard Bavand, their grandfather, 1603.

Ales [Alice] Gamull, Buried at St. Oswald's, Ap. 1606.

Children of Sir Francis Gamull and Christian:

THOMAS GAMULL, son and heir apparent. Born 22 April, and baptised 26 April, 1627. "Capt. Thomas Gamull, Esq., sonne of Colonell Sr ffrancis Gamull, Knt and Barronett. Buried in the vault in St Katherine's Ile, 12th day of June, 1644."

EDWARD GAMULL, born 21 Nov. 1631. Buried at St. Mary's 16 Feb. 1633-4.

Edmund Gamull, ob. s.p.

Frances Gamull (dau. and co-heir), born 1 Nov. 1625. * Baptised at St. John's Dec. 1631. Married (1) Lieut.-Col. Leveston, a Scotchman, slaine at Hull; (2) Capt. Sir Benjamin Rudyard, Knt.

Lettice Gamull (dau. and co-heir), born 20 June, 1628. Baptised at St. Mary's 27 June, 1628. Married (1) at St. Mary's 6 April, 1641, to Capt. James Harleston, of Chester, s.p. (2) Gilbert Houghton, 2nd son of Sir Gilbert Houghton, of Houghton Tower, co. Lanc., Knt. and Bart. Survived both husbands. Living s.p. 1666

Sidney Gamull, born 2 Oct. 1629. Buried at S. Mary's 11 Dec. 1629.

Catherine Gamull, born 4 Dec. 1630. Buried at St. Mary's 2 Oct. 1635.

Sidney Gamull (dau. and co heir), born 30 Dec. 1634. Baptised at St. Mary's 7 Jan. 1634-5. Married John Brerewood, of Chester, Esq. Bur. at St. Mary's 16 Feb. 1665-6. (See Brerewood Family.)

Alice Gamull (dau. and co-heir), born 15 Aug. 1636. Baptised at St. Mary's 26 Aug. 1636. Married at St. Oswald's 23 Aug. 1655. Robert Calcot or Caldecot of the Isle of Man (son and heir of Robert C.) a captain under James, Earl of Derby. Living 1666. Admon at Chester, 1677.

Christian Gamull (dau. and co-heir), born 4 July, 1639. Baptised at St. Mary's 16 July, 1639. Married at St. Oswald's 23 Aug. 1655, to Thomas Weston, M.A. Vicar of Bowden, co. Chester, son and heir of Thomas Weston, Sheriff of Chester 1615. Living 1666.

* Note in pencil by Mr. Earwaker, "?born 1st and bapt. 6 Nov. 1625.

Gamull de knighton modo de Cestr̄
(Harl. 2163. fo. 85.)

Arms.— Or, three mallets Sable.
Crest.— A cubit arm erect, vested gules, cuffed argent, holding in the hand proper three trefoils slipped. Or. Mantled gules, doubled argent.

Edmund Gamull of ye Cittie of

Maior 1585.

Chester alderman & Justice of peace: And was maior thereof in Anno d'ni 1585. Hee was sonne and heire vnto Thomas Gamull whoe maried Ellyne base doughter vnto Thomas John Poole of Poole Countie of Chester Esquire and They the sayde Thomas and Ellyn Poole had yssue Thomas Gamul sonne and heire whoe deceassed sans yssue. Edmund Gamul secconnd sonne to Tho: and Ellyn became theire heire after the decease of Thomas the his brother. Robert Gamul Thurde sonne John Gamul fourthe sonne to Thom's & Ellyn.

And the saide Thomas husbande to Ellyn Poole was sonne and heire to Thomas Gamul whoe maried Elizabethe doughter to Robert Mynshull of Mynshull Countie of Chester esq.r This Thomas husband to Elizabethe deceassed in the xxvj th yeare of King Henrye the eight, he had a Brother named Hughe whoe was p'sone of . . . . . .

And they the sayde Thomas and Hughe weare sonnes to another Thomas Gamul whoe maried Agnes base doughter to Sr John Maynwaringe of Peever who at that tyme remayned at Badeley Countie of Chester Knight. This Thomas Gamul at his decease bequethed money to buye an antiphon to the Churche of Aldelem [Audlem]; Also he leafte a competent some of monney to Glaze a whole wyndowe in the same churche anneynst St Laurance chaunssell to conteigne foure severall lightes The first to be sett fourthe wth the Image of our Ladie St Marie mother of Chryste. The seconnde wth the Image of St Laurannce. The thurde of the Image of St John the baptyst And the fourthe wt the Image of St John the Evangelyste. This Thomas was lyvinge Ao Dni 1459 et in Ao Xo Hen. 8. he had a brother whose name was Hughe and hee the said Hughe was a chapleu, and they were sonnes to Thomas Gamul of Buerton who maried Ellyn one of the doughters and heires to [Rogeri.] Stapeley of Stapeley Countie of Chester, by whom cam bothe the Laudes in Buerton and in Aldelem to the Gamulls now the land of the aforsaid Edmund Gamul somtymes maior of Chestr. This Thoms had a suster whose name was Margarett de Gamul maried to Henry Taylor, lyving 13o Hen. 7. Ellyn was lyving the 15o Hen. 7. Since this Thomas his tyme the Gamuls have beene of Buerton.

And he the said Thoms Gamul husband to Ellyn Stapeley was sonne and heire to another Thomas Gamul de Kneghton called Thomas the younger be reasone hee hadd an uncle whose name was Thomas the Elder whoe died without yssue and so Thomas the younger became his heire aswell as to his father whose name was John Jamul. This Thomas the younger maried Johan the doughter of Thomas Bredon. he was living 9° Hen. 6, as apeareth by evidences and he the said Thom's was sonne to John Jamul of Knighton, in le Halys, Countie Salop. Brother to Thomas the elder of Knighton lyving 22° Hen. 6. And they weare sonnes to John Jamull of Knighton lyving 8° Hen. 5, et in A° 12° Hen 4, et in A° 4 R. 2, and he the said John was sonne and heire to William Jamul of Knighton (who) maried Phillippa: They weare lyving in the 36 of King Edward the third, and he the sait William was sonne and heire to another Willia' Jamul e' le Halys, whoe was lyvinge in the XV.th yeare of Kinge Edward the second, And he the said William was sonne and heire to Stephen Jamul de Knighton in le Halys whoe maried one Edythe, and they the said Stephen and Edithe had yssue Richard and Thomas breatheren to the said Willia' the furst.

1592.

And hee the aforsaid Edmund Jamul esq.r and Justice of peace maried to his first wife Elizabethe doughter to Thomas Case and by her hathe yssue, Thomas and William Jamul, Anne maried vnto John Brocke of (Upton in the) Countie of Chest.r gentelman. Ellyn secound [daughter] maried vnto Richard Swynton of Knottesford countie of Chester gentelman, maried in A° 1591. Elizabeth Thurd Doughter, vnmaried.

And he the said Edmund married to his seconnd wief another Elizabethe doughter vnto John Thrope of the Cittie of Chester and roydoove vnto Willm Goodman, maior of the Cittie of Chester in anno Dñi 1579, and by her hathe no yssue.

(signed) Edm: Gamull.

In Harl MSS. No 1991 the following Gamul wills exist:—

15.	Will of Thomas Gamul Recorder of Chester Dated	2 Augst	1613
17.	Edmund Gamul of Chester Alderman	10 Novr.	1615
24.	William Gamul of Chester, Alderman	17 May,	1639.
26.	Ellen Gamul widow of Thos Gamul of Buerton Gent	1 May,	31 Eliz.
30.	Kauffe Gamul of Buerton	11 Decr,	1540.
33.	Thomas Gamul of Buerton	13 July,	1532.
38.	William Gamul of Chester Alderman (draught)	A.D.	1619.
42.	Francis Gamul of Chester, widdow	9 Augst	1644.
43.	Thomas Gamul of Buerton	28 Decr	1564.

Harl MSS. 1424. p. 7. Harl 1505. anno 1579.
Thomas Gamul of Buerton (Buerton) a freeholder.

Gamul.

Hoc Stemma antiquæ familiæ de Gamul, ex Evidentijs, Cartis, et libris, in Officio Armor' quanta fieri potest di igentia et fide, collectum est.

Copied from the original roll on parchment now in the possession of Mr. T. Cann Hughes, Chester. May, 1892.

Per quandam Cartam sine dat' Ric'us filius Tho. de Ocley dedit Steph'o fil Will'i fil Gamel vnam acram tre que vocat' Woodcrofts loĩe iacen' inter terram Alani, et terram Dñi Steph'i et diversas alias terr' in Carta pfca specificat, Testibz Ada Dño de Mucliston Hen. de Alstanston Steph'o de Ocleg Will'o de Norton et alijs.

Per alīā chartā Ric'us filius Tho : de As'o dedit Alano de Knightō diversas terr' in Knightō &c., hijs Testibz Ada de Mukleston, Hen de Halstauneston, Steph'o de Hockẽ, Rogero de knight', Steph'o filio Will'i fil Gamel de eadem, Ada de Derintō et multis alijs, &c.

The Iniayle of Thomas Ocleyes landes in Wynlington, vpon the mariage of Isabell, his daughter and heire, w'h Will'm Gamul the sonne of Stephan.

Sic Tho : fuit filius Reginaldi Ocley.

Thoĩïs de Ozley manens in Wyninton Dedit will'o filio Steph'i Gamui de Knighton and Isabella vx' eius totum illud Dimid Mesuag cū medietate Croft adiacent in wininton predict' quod habuit de dono Ric'i de Heyr de knighton et q'd idem Ric' habuit de Alano Dingan de knightō p' concord inter eos fact' cor' Will'o Hyngge Justic' dñi Regis, ac etiā medietatẽ comu'is mei cū p'tin' in knighton & vocat' le Heye. Et iacet inter stagnū molend de wininton et gerardred Habend et tenerd ijsde will'o et Isabelle et heredibz de corpibz eoʒ p'creat' cū o'ibz p'tin Comun' et asiament', &c. T's'ibus Ad' dño de Mocliston, Steph' de Ocley cū multis alijs.

Isabella que fuit vxor Will'i Gamel de knighton in le Halis dedit Joħi filio Ric'i de Huncumbache & Alicie vx' eius, Ric'o fil' Robti de Eccleshale et Matild vx' eius, Ric'o fil' Steph'i Gamel & Agnet' vxori eius, et eorum heredibz vel Assignatis totam p'tem suam vnius plac' vast' iacente' in feod de knytton

GAMUL.

GUILIELM' GAMUL.

STEPHAN' GAMUL. = EDITHA, ita vocat.

GUILIELM' GAMUL. de knighton vixit an° 13 E. 3. = ISABELLA filia et heres Jo : Ocley de winington 7° E. 3.

Ricardus Gamul vix' an° 2 E 2. Agnes vxor eius.

Thomas Gamul vix' tempore E. 2.

Adam. (?) E. 3.

Gamul verbum Hebraicum et idem est quod Retributio, a Reward or recompence. See 1 Cron. 24, 17. One of the posterity of Aron of that name. And Jerem, 48. 23. Beth-Gamul, that is, The Howse of Gamul.

Steph'us Gamel de Kneycton Dedit Ric'o filio suo, pro servicio suo ter'am et prat' cum suis p'tinencijs, &c., infra feod de Kneyton Testibus Ada Dño de Mucliston Steph'o de Ocleg Vincentio de Alstenston et alijs Dat' apud Novũ Castrum Die Lune in festo Pet' ad vincula An° Dñi mcclxxxv. 24° E. 1.

Guilielmus filius Steph'i Gamul De knytton in le halis Dedit Ric'o filio suo vnum Dimid Mesuag cum curtilag et Croft adiacent in villa de Knytton. Test Dño Ada de Mucliston, Steph'o De Ocley Ada De Ocley et alijs.

Will'mus fil' Steph'i Gamul de knighton in le Halys Dedit Ric'o filio suo vnum Mesuag cũ Curtilag adiacente in villa de knighton q'd quidm mesuogiũ et Curtilagiũ Editha que fuit vx Steph'i Gamul tenit [sic], &c. Testibus Adm D'no de Mucliston, Steph'o de Ocley, et alijs.

Willmus Gamul de kneyghtō tenebatu' Ric'o filio Ade de Mucluston et heredibz suis in sex solido[sic] et octo denar' p'cipiend de anno in Ann' de ter'is et ten'tis suis in Kneighton, &c., cũ clausula distinctionis in p'dict' ter' Dat' apud Muclusten in die S't'i michis A° Regni Regis Edw' Secundi xiij°.

A

juxta metas de Detinton & vocat' Crosbroke et sequenda Crosbroke in Aqua de Tyrne, et sic sequenda cursū Aquæ de Tyrne, vsqz ad S agtū molend de Wynintō & sic de Dicō Stagno vsqz Crosbroke. Test' Will'o fil' Steph'i de Ocley, Adam de Ocley et alijs. Dat' apud knytton in le halis Die Diica p̄x post fest' omniū sanctorū. An° E. 3. 7°.

| GUILIELM' GAMUL, 36 E. 3. | ⊤ | PHILLIPA coheres cum Anna vxor, w'' whitmore. | | Joannes Gamul duxit matildam an'' 18 E. 3. | | Ricardus Gamul vixit 18 E. 3 et duxit Isoldā que vidua fuit a° 34 E. 3. |

Will'm' de wetemore Dedit Phillipe que fuit vxor Will'mi Gamel vnum Cotagiū et Cristū adiacen' et quinqz selliones cum suis p̄tinen in knighton, que hu'it de hereditate Agnet' vxor' sue in excambiū p'ominibus terris et ten'° cum suis p'tin' que p'dcā Pha h̄et in p'p'tem suam in feod de Wetemore An° 45 E. 3.

Con̄titis Cartæ eiusdē Dat' fact' p' p̄d will'm de whitemore et Agnetem vxor' eius de terr'° p'dictis quos habuerunt de hereditat' p'dcī Agnet', p'dcē philippe in excamb'° &c., vt supra &c.

Will'o fil' Will'i Gamel de Knighton Dedit Joh̄i Brett et Will'o Smyth oīa messuagia terr'° et testia sua in Knight'ō cū reu'c̄ōe Dotis Isoldæ nup' vxor' Ric'i Gamel. Dat' Die Sabat' prox' post festū S'ti Mich'. A° Regni Regis Edw: tertii xxxiiij°.

| | JOANNES GAMUL, vixit an° 4° Ric. 2. et 8° H. 5. | ⊤ | .... | | Thomas Gamul, a° 20 R. 2. |

The Intaile of John Gamull, his lands vpon the mariage of his sonne w''h Joane Enedon.

| THOMAS GAMUL ' the younger,' &ca. | ⊤ | JOHANA ENEDON, fil' et Heres Tho. Enedon et Isabelle vxor' eius 12 H. 4. |

Thomas de Lockesley Capellanus Ded't concessit, et confirmau't Joh̄i Gamull omnia messuag' terr'°, tenement', &c. in villis De knighton et Derinton cū reuercōe Dotis Phillipæ Gamull quā Dāem h'uit post mort' will'i Gamull vxi sui in villis predictis cū omnibz suis p'tinentijs que habuit ex dono & feoffamento p'dicti Joh̄is Gamull p' chartā suā inde ei confectā. Habend et tenend oia p'dicta messuagia, &c., p'dicto Joh. ad totā vitam suam &c., et post eius Decessū remanē e Thome filio p'dicti Joh̄is Gamul et heredibz inter ip̄m Thomā et Johanā filiam Tho De Enedon legitime p̄ceant &c., et p' defectu talis exitus, remanere p'dicto Thome Gamull et heredibz de corpore suo legitime p̄ceant̄ is, &c. Et p' defectu talis exitus, remanere Tho. Gamull fratri p'dci Joh̄is et heredibz de corpore suo legitime p̄ceant', &c., et p' Defectu talis exitus, remanere rectis heredibz p'dci Joh̄is Gamull in p'petuum, &c. Testibz Joh̄e de Chitwood, Joh̄e de Titteley, witho del wode Joh̄is de Bulkyleygh et alijs. Dat' apud Knegh̄ton Die sabati p'xim ante festū Scti Clementis An° Regn' Regis Hen. 4ti post Cōquest' 12°.

| THOMAS GAMUL de Buerton in com. Cest. | ⊤ | ELENA STAPLEIGH, fil' & heres Rogeri Stapeleigh de Buerton in com. Cest. | | Mar'garet Gamul, nup. Hen. Tailor et post Ricardo Hassell de Bureto' vt patet p' chart' dat' 13 H. 6. | | Johana vxor John̄s Eyre de Blecheley, Junior. |

The Intaile of Thomas Enedons Lands vpon the mariage of Joane his Daughter and heire w''h Thomas son and heire apparant of Jo. Gamull.

Thomas De Lockesley Capellanus Dedit Thome De Enedon, et Isabelle vxor' eius, omnia Messuag' terras, ten'° &c., in villis, et ter'ritorijs De Aston, Mese, & Grauenhunger, &c. Et post Decessu p'dcōrū Thume Enedon, et Isabelle, predict Messuag. ter. ten'°, &c., remaneant Joh̄anē filie Toome de Enedon, et h̄ redibus inter ip̄am Joh̄am et Thomam h̄ iō Joh̄is Gamul legitime p̄creatis &c. Testibus Tho De Bromley Dn̄o De Bromley Joh̄e De Titteley, Joh̄e de Bulkyleigh et alijs. An° 12 Hen. 4ti.

Predict' Thomas Enedon nōlatū' p' aliā chartā gerent' dat a° 2 Hen. 4. Thomas filius Joh̄is de Hendon vt patet p' cartā, p'dcā fact' eidem Thome p' Bevys de Huntbache de oib terr'° suis in Aston, &c.

Nota.—Predictus Thomas De Lockesley habuit p'dict terr'° et tenemen'a, ex dono et feoffamento p'dcī Thome Enedon ea intencōe vt De ijsdem cōcessionē faceret ad vsus p'dictos, vt p' p'dic'am cartā apparet.

Joh̄s Wodelok Rector Eccl̄ie de Mucleston et Thomas Gamul senio' de knighton dederunt Joh̄i Eyre Junior de Blecheley et Joh̄anne vxor' oi'a terr'° et testia sua in Wouer. Habend et tenend p'fatis Joh̄e et Johanne vxor' eius et heredib' inter ipsos legitim'° p̄creat'. Et p' defectu talis exit' rectis heredib' p'it Thome Gamul in p'petu'° Dat a° xxij Hen. 6.

Sir Francis Gamul Bart. Barlow's, Cheshire Biographies p. 140.

PEDIGREES.

B

THOMAS GAMUL, obijt = Agnes (Harl. 2163. fol. 85.) Hug" Gam" | Elena Gamul nuper vxor Thome Gamul de Buerton
an° 1° H. 8, vt patet ANNA MANWARING Capellan'. | in pura viduitate sua Dedit Nich'o Manwaring,
p' testament' suu. fil Jo. Manwaring | Humphredo Hassell, et Hugoni Gamul filio suo Cove-
de Baddley milit. | lano, omnia ti'a mesuagia ter° et ten° sua, prat' pasc',
| &c., iacent' in Buerton in Com' Cestrie que sibi accid'
Testament° Thome Gamull fact' Die Jovis | iur' her° post decess° patris et matris sue. &c. Testibus
pximo post festū Sti Leonardi Abbatis | D'no Hugone Haske vicario p'petuo de Aldeham
an° D'ni millesimo quingentesimo nono. | Tho. Denwall Wilto Clutton cum multis alijs. Dat'
Testibʒ Radulpho Hassell Willmo Clouth | apud Buerto in festo Ap'l'orū Symonis et Jude, An°
Philippo Morrey cū multis alijs. Dat' apud | 15 H. 7°.
Bureton.

THOMAS GAMULL = ELIZABETH fil. | Ista Elizabeth coheres Roberti Minshull de | Hugo
obijt 26 H. 8, vt Roberti Minshull | Hulgrave fuit filia R. fil. 6. Johis fil. | Gamull.
patet p' testament' de Hulgrave in | Petri qui duxit Joannam filiam et heredem | (Tarsam d.
suum. com. Cestr'. | Johis Debington qui duxit Aliciam filiam | Harl. 2163 fo 85.)
| et coheredem Ric'i Tranmoll als Tranmor
| in cuius ritu hæc insignia portat.

Brerewood. Ermine, two pallets wavy or, azure, on a chief of
the last a lozenge between two garbs of the second.
Arms. Two swords in saltire gules, pomels hilts or, supstd with a
ROBERTUS BREREWOOD vicecomes crown (an Earl's coronet ppr) | THOMAS GAMUL = ELENA POOLE (Gam)
civitatis Cestriæ an° Domini | obijt 29 | fil. Jo. Poole de
1581: duxit in vxorem Luciam | Elizabeth. | poole, Armigeri.
filiam et habuit exitum.

Robertus Brerewood ter Maior | Thomas EDMOND = ELIZABETH Robertus Gamul Jo: Gamul
civitatis Cestriæ viz.; annis 1583; Gamul, GAMUL de CASE obijt de Olton in com de Buerton,
1587; et 1600: in quo anno obijt sine Civitat' Cestr' anno Staff. gen. qui qui duxit
obijt duxit in vxorem Eliza- exitu. Armig'r vixens duxit Annā vnā Elizabetha
betham fil' Thome Horton de an° 1610. filiā et hered Olton.
Cestria et habuit exitum. Humphridi fox
gen.

Brerewood, See Republications, p. 167.

Anna Gamul Elenor nupt' Rico THOMAS = ALICIA Will'm' Gamul Elizabeth Gamul nupta unmarried in 1592
vx: Johis Swinton gen et habuit GAMUL filia Ric'i de Civitat' Cestr' Hugoni P'restland de
Brocke de exitum. Et postea Recordator' Bavand de Ald' et Maior wardle in com. Cestr.
Vpton et post nupta Thome Harvy Civitat' Civitat' ib'm a° 1609 qui ar. et post eius morte
mortem eius sine de Civitate Cestr' ald' et Cestr'. Cestr' duxit Eliānm ā sine prole Robto
prole, Edwardo Maior' ib'm 1610. Alderman. Colgrave filiā Brooke gen p' que
Holland per Will'i Colgrave habuit.
quam habuit Thomā Maria de Civitat'
exitum. Swintō. Swinton. Cestr', Alder.

Tho: Gamul. Elenor Gamul. Willia Gamul.

Johes Brerewood Edwardus
vicecomes Cestriæ Brerewood Thomas Alicia FRANCISCUS = Xpiana, filia Ric'i
anno 1598: obijt 22: filius secundus & Richard Gamull GAMULL Grosvenor de
October: 1599, duxit nup collegij de mortui mort' Baronett d'xsit in Eaton in
Mariam filiam Thome Brason Nose in sunt sine sine vxorem et h'uit Comitatu Cestriæ,
Parry de Nanarch in Academia Oxon: prole. prole. exitum. Baronett.
comitatu Mont. gen: et postea collegij Will: prow'd af [illeg]
illa obijt 27: Septemb de Gresham 1666. Humfry [illeg]
anno 1592; et h'uit London obijt sine & [illeg] [illeg]
exitum. prole.

Anna = Robtus Brerewood miles = Katherina filia Richardi Lea
filia Rani Recordator fuit civitatis de Darnall in com Cestriæ
Mainwaringe Cestriā h'uit exitum. militis vxor secunda.
de l'ever
militis prima My father was alsoe a Judge in North-wales,
vxor predict' a Serieant at Law, the Queen's Serieant,
Robti. and a Judge in the King's Benche, for
wch see the Patents.

C   **D**

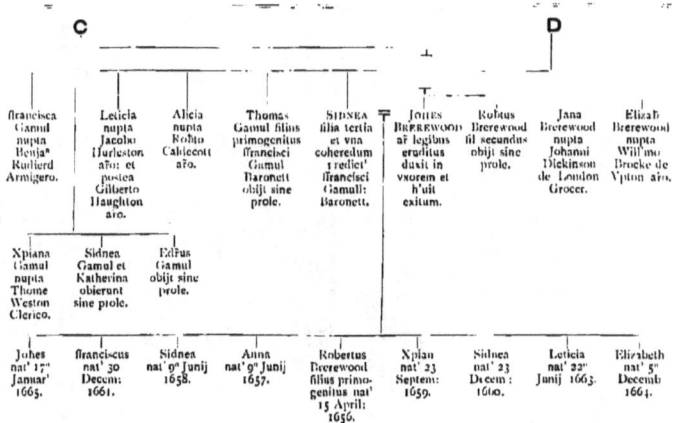

Descent of Brerewood (who married Sydney one of the daughters & coheirs of Sir Francis Gamul
Sir Robert Brerewood compounded for his Estates for £387.10.0. Ormerod Vol I. p. XIII.
Harl. MSS. n 2094.64. fol. 53.

Weston of Chester, &c.

Authorities: Harl. MS. 2040, f. 281, St Mary's Registers, Chester, Wills, Funeral Certificate, Family Settlements, &c.

Humphrey Weston = **Mary**, dau. of Robert Brerewood, and sister of Robert Brerewood. Will made 15 June, 1615. Pr. at Chester 6 Dec., 1617.

Children of Humphrey and Mary Weston:

- **Thomas Weston**, Sheriff of Chester, 1615. = **Alice**, dau. of John Barthell (?).
- **Richard Weston**, a glover. Married. Dead before 1615, & had a dau.
- **Elizabeth Weston**, marr. (1) Len. of Chester, (2) Hugh Whichstead.
- **Margery Weston**, marr. Gleggs.
- **Jane Weston**, marr. William Ikenall.
- **Mary Weston**, marr. Richard Ridge.

Children of Thomas Weston and Alice:

Thomas Weston, son and heir, dev. 1615. Sheriff of Chester, 1637. Buried at St Mary's "under his father's stone," 26 Feb. 1646-7. Will made 17 Feb. 1646-7. Pr. at Chester, 6 March, 1646-7.
= **Elizabeth**, 2nd. dau. of John Edwards, of Chevedey, co. Chester, gent., marr. (2) Mr. ...... Matthews. Bur. at St Mary's, 3 April, 1659, as "Elizabeth, wife to Mr. Matthews." Admon. granted 20 June, 1670.

- **Elizabeth Weston**, marr. William Morton, of Chester, before 1637.
- **Anne Weston**, 1637, marr. (1) Edward Fletcher, (2) John Ridge.
- **Frances Weston**, 1637 & 1646, marr. Capt. Weston (?).
- **Mary Weston**, 1637 & 1646.
- **Sarah Weston**, 1637 & 1646.

Thomas Weston, of Chester, clerk, Vicar of Hawarden, 1616 to 1688. Rector of Christleton & Incumbent of Holy Trinity, Chester, 1650. Living 1670. Will made 23 Oct., 1683. Pr. at Chester 28 Nov., 1688.
= **Christian**, dau. and co-heir of Sir Francis Gammell, Knt. & Bart. Bar. at St Mary's, 1 May, 1689. Admon. at Chester, 1689.

Peter Weston, of Bridge Street, Chester, Gent., ultimately son and heir. Dead in or before 1738. Bar. at St Mary's, 17 ... Will made 7 July, 1715, or 1716, m. 1717.
= **Catherine**, dau. of William Pagean, citizen of London. Marr. settl. 10 July, Gent. Bar. at St Mary's, 10 Oct. 1738. Will dated 1695.

- **Robert Weston**, bapt. at Holy Trinity, Chester, 26 Aug. 1656, son and heir. Dead before 1688.
- **Thomas Weston**, bapt. at Holy Trinity, Chester, 27 May, 1658. Living 1670 and 1688. Dead before 1695.
- **Benjamin Weston**, youngest son. Bapt. at St Mary's, 1669. Liv. 1688. Admon dated 1695.
- **Mary Weston**, marr. Philip Bostock, of Moulton, gent. Marr. sett. 25 Mar. 1680.
- **Frances Weston**, marr. at St Mary's 7 Nov. 1686. Bar. at St Mary's 13 May, 1743.
- **James Peake**, of Chester, cler., Vicar of Hawarden. Bur. at St Mary's April, 1719. M.I.
- **Christian Weston**, bur. at St Mary's 16 May, 1674.
- **Lettice Weston**, bur. at St Mary's 18 Oct., 1681.

- **Peter Weston**, son and heir. Bapt. at St Mary's 7 Aug. 1697. Bur. there 8 Aug. 1716.
- **Thomas Weston**, bapt. at St Mary's 22 Nov. 1702. Bur. there 4 Nov. 1706.
- **Peggan Weston**, bapt. at St Mary's 4 Dec. 1703. Bur. there 1793.
- **Catherine Weston**, sur. and co-heir, marr. before 1743.
- **Ashton Burles**. Bur. from Hamhill, 26 May, 1741.
- **Christian Weston**, dau. and co-heir, marr. 1743.
- **Robert Beagham**, of Brunks Marfet, West-munster.
- **Sarah Weston**, bapt. at St Mary's 8 Dec. 1668. Bur. there 25 Avrl, 1691.
- **Elizabeth Weston**, bapt. at St Mary's 12 Jan. 1700-1. Bur. there 1707.
- **Lillice Weston**, born at St Mary's, 29 Dec. 1700. Marr. to ...... Drompook, of Manchester. A widow in 1743.
- **Christian Peake**. Marr. to the Rev. John Skerratt.
- **Peake**. Marr. to Thomas Patten, of Warrington, merchant.

PEDIGREES. 265

Handwritten annotations at top:
Acton. or. 3 pheons Sable. } Guillim
Do. Gules, a Cross-patonce. Arg. } 699, 123.

The Pedigree in Ormerod's Cheshire Vol II p. 582 gives a Pedigree of 10 generations earlier than this of the Acton family, which see.

ST. MARY-ON-THE-HILL, CHESTER.

Acton of Chester.

Arms of Acton: Azure three mullets, or (sometimes vert three mullets argent).

Harl. MSS. f. 139, old note, 2119, 2009, Quarters, 7568. O. iij. 553. St. Mary's Registers, Chester. Wills, &c. &c. A pedigree entered at the Heralds' College for another line of the Actons of Alderley, and of the Branch in Tutherington.

Francis Acton, of Over Alderley, co. Chester, æt. 53 in 1646, gent. Bar. at Alderley, 10 Sept. 1651. Will made 7 Sept. 1651. Pr. in London 30 June, 1652.
= **Elizabeth** dau. of Thomas Norbury, of Alderley. Bar. at Alderley, 13 Aug. 1652.

Thomas Acton, of Over Alderley and Gloucestershire, an attorney there, son and heir, æt. 30 in 1646. Bar. at St. Mary's, 26 Nov. 1678. M. I. Will made 28 t 1673. Pr. 27 Nov. 1678.
= **Hannah**, or **Anna**, dau. of John Fallowes, of Alderley, gent. Bar. at St. Mary's, 18 Feb. 1672-3.

Francis Acton, of Presbury, gent. Liv. 1651. Dead before 1689. Bar. at Alderley, 28 Oct. 1683. Will made 25 t'ed. 1683. Pr. at Chester, 4 June, 1697.

John Acton, of Oakhanger Hall, in Haslington, gent. Will made 30 July, 1698. Pr. at Chester, 30 June, 1703.

Richard Acton, of Chester, gent. Bapt. at Al., 6 Sept. 1629. L. v. 1651. Bur. at St. M., 18 June, 1668.

Roger Acton, Bapt. at A., 23 June, 1633. Liv. 1651.†

Elizabeth Acton, Liv. 1655.

Peter Skelbourne, of Presbury.

Samuel Acton, of Alderley and Gloucestershire, son and heir, æt. 26 in 1679, born in 1653. Matric. at Oxford for B.N.C., 1672, of Gray's Inn. Sold his estate, and settled at Nantwich. ? Baptist minister there. Died c. 1727.
= **Sarah**, dau. of ... Ashton. Mar. at St. Oswald's, Chester, 16 Feb 1681.

John Acton, of Gloucestershire, gent. Bar. at B.N.C. Oxford. Matric. there 1675, æt. 17, h. c. 1678, B.L. 1678, M.A. 1681. Died 1 Mar b. 1692-3. Bar. at Mar. 1697.

Francis Acton, M.A., student and fellow of B.N.C. Oxford. Matric. there 1675, æt. 17, h. c. 1678, B.L. 1678, M.A. 1681. Died 1 Mar b. 1692-3. Bar. at B.N.C

Richard Acton.
Bapt. 24 March, 1660-1.

John Acton. Bapt. 10 May, 1663. Bur. 23 July, 1678.

Benjamin Acton, of Chester, gent. Bap. at St. M., 11 Dec. 1665. Bar. at St. M., 6 Oct., 1686. Will dated 25 Sept., 1686.

Nathaniel Acton, Bapt. 21 Dec. 1665. Bur. 26 April, 1659.

Thomas Acton, Bapt. 28 April, 1660.

Elizabeth Acton. Bapt. 9 Dec. 1690. Marr. at St. M. 4 April, 1714. Bur. at St. M. 2 Dec. 1719.
= **Johnson Mainwaring**, of Chester, gent. Bapt. at Trinity, 1696.

Joseph Acton. Bapt. 29 June. Bur. 4 April, 7 Aug. 1662.

Thomas Acton, Bapt. 14 April, 1661.

Francis Acton. Bapt. 18 Oct. 1666.

Hannah Acton. Bar. 22 Feb. 1697.

Thomas Acton. Bapt. 24 May, 1684. Bur. 17 Dec. 1689.

Richard Acton = **Mainwaring**. of Chester. ? Living 1731. See Che Arch. Journal, Vol III p. 205

Elizabeth Mainwaring. Bar. at St. M., 3 June, 1717.

John Mainwaring, Bur. at St. M., 29 July, 1719.

James Mainwaring. Bur. at St. M., 7 Dec. 1719.

---

* Query, an only dau. and heir, Elizabeth, who married John Manley, of the Lache, gent. (son of George M., of Lache), his first wife, and had a son, Acton Manley, 1704, married Sarah, dau. of Ralph Merrill, of Greene, and had issue. He had also a son, Francis Acton, who matric. at Oxford for B.N.C., 3 July, 1672, æt. 18, of Lincoln's Inn, in 1672.

† Query, marr. Maud, dau. of Randle, son of George Mallory, of Modderley.

44

PRESCOTT. [illegible handwriting, largely illegible]

PRESCOTT Hampshire [illegible]

PRESCOT [illegible]

PRESCOT. Sable a chevron [illegible] between three mola argent [illegible]

[illegible lines]

Sir George William Prescott, Bart., late of Theobald's Park, Herts.

Sir George was senior representative of the great banking and mercantile family of Prescott, being elder son of the late Sir George Beeston Prescott, Bart., and first cousin to Wm Prescott, Governor of the Bank of England.

The title of Baronet was conferred on his grandfather in 1794.

Sir George married, first, 10th July, 1827, Emily, daughter of Colonel Symes, and became her widower, without issue, 8th January 1829. He married, secondly, 26 July 1845, Eliza, youngest daughter of Henry Hiller, Esq., and has left by her a son, the present Sir George Kendelsham Prescott, Bart., an infant of four years old.

The death of Sir George Prescott occurred at Caen, in Normandy, on the 27th April, [1850]. He had completed his forty-ninth year.

Obituary in The Heraldic Register for 1849-50 by J. Bernard Burke. p. 63.

Prescott of Suffolk. Guil. Abz? 1728. p. 499
Sable, a chevron between 3 owls argent.

PEDIGREES.

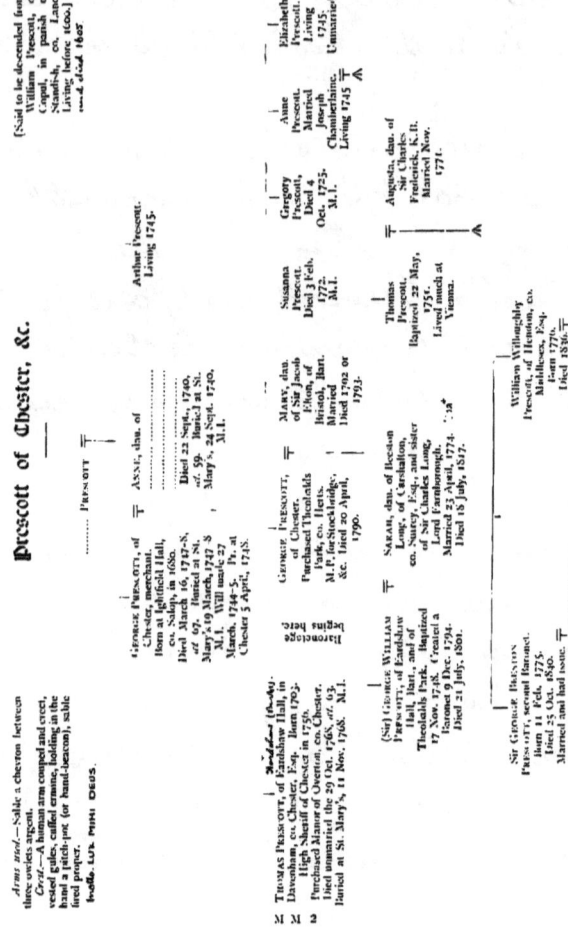

Burke's Landed Gentry, (1850) Vol I p. 575. Hincks of Breckenbrough. Co York. William Hincks (Alderman 1643) = Edward Hincks (d. 1666) Joseph Hincks (d. 1680) Edward (d) who married (2nd wife) Hannah daughter of Robert Murrey Esq Alderman of Chester and had Robert, d.s.p. John Hincks of Chorlton Co Chester and a banker in Chester, (3rd son Edward d.s.p.) and Robert (fourth son) who married Martha daughter of .. Cappar Esq, and died leaving three sons Robert, Joseph, and John, also two daughters, Elizabeth who died unmarried and Susannah who married Robert Foulkes Esq., as now filled in the pedigree. JHs

Crewe of Crewe pedigree. Ormerod Vol III p. 314. Elizabeth Crewe granddaughter of John Offley of Madeley Co. Staffs. (whose son changed his name to Crewe, the maiden name of Anne his mother) married John Foulkes of Chester Esquire.

Foulkes of Chester, &c.

ROBERT FOULKES, of Chester, gentleman. Deputy Baron of the Exchequer at Chester. Bur. at St. Mary's, 7 Sept. 1711. = MARY, dau. of .... Bur. at St. Mary's, 12 April, 1719.

Children:

- HUGH FOULKES. Bapt. at St. M. 3 July, 1673, of Castle Lane, Esq., Barrister-at-Law, Deputy Baron of the Exchequer at Chester. Bur. at St. M. 6 Sept. 1731. = MARY, dau. of .... Bur. at St. M. 29 April, 1716.
- John Foulkes, Bapt. and bur. 1675.
- Peter Foulkes, Bapt. at St. M. 5 Nov. 1676.
- * Edward Foulkes, Bapt. at St. M. 8 Dec. 1678.
- William Foulkes, Bur. 1681.
- George Foulkes, Bapt. 1682. Bur. 1683.
- John Foulkes, Bapt. at St. M. 11 Nov. 1684.
- Richard Foulkes, Bapt. 25 March, 1688. ? Bur. at St. Mary's, 12 June, 1724, as the Rev. Mr. Rich. Foulkes, M.A., of Castle Lane.
- Thomas Foulkes, Bapt. 5 Nov. 1690.
- Charles Foulkes, Bapt. 28 April, 1692. ? Bur. at St. M. 20 Aug. 1742. Attorney-at-law.
- Gertrude Foulkes, Bapt. at St. M. 8 Oct. 1671. Marr. 11 Feb. 1696-7, to Mr. Charles Walley.
- Mary Foulkes, Bapt. 21 March, 1685-6. Bur. there 25 Sept. 1714.

Children of Hugh Foulkes and Mary:

- Robert F. Bapt. 1710. Bur. 1711-12.
- Thomas F. Bapt. at St. Oswald's, 26 Aug. 1711.
- Hugh F. 1714-15. Bur. 1719.
- Peter F. 1716. Bur. 1716.
- Catherine. 1712.
- Mary, 1713. Bur. 1714-15.

ROBERT FOULKES, of Chester, Esq. Bur. at St. M. 20 Oct. 1787. = SUSANNA dau. of Robert and Martha Hincks of Chester. Bur. at St. Mary's, 13 Dec. 1797.

Children:

- Mary F. Bapt. at St. M. 12 Nov. 1743. Marr. at St. O. 24 Aug. 1775. Bur. St. M. 2 Jan. 1813. = William Currie, of Chester, M.D. Died 1834, æt. 83. M.I. St. M.
- Susan F. of Boughton. Bapt. at St. O. 9 March, 1746-7. Died unmarried 30 Dec. 1770. Bur. at St. Mary's, 5 Jan. 1771.

* Edward Foulkes, of Castell Lane and Cuppin's Lane, gent. Bapt. 8 Dec. 1678. Died before 1736. = Rebecca, dau. of ...... Bur. at St. M. 18 Nov. 1705. = Dorothy, dau. of Mather. Marr. at St. M. 25 March, 1786. Bur. 11 Oct. 1751.

Children:

- Robert Foulkes, Bapt. 18 Nov. 1703.
- John F. Bapt. 20 May, 1708. Bur. at St. M. 1781.
- Edward. 1712.
- Henry. 1715. Bur. 1715.
- Richard. 1722.
- Hugh. 1720.
- Watkin. 1721. Bur. 1736.
- Three daus.

3?. In her 60th year, Mrs. Ayscough, of Leicester.

At Hull, aged 72, Mr. Andrew Dodgson, of Croft, in Berwick. His death was occasioned by a paralysis of the muscles of his tongue and throat, which took away the power of swallowing, so that he was literally starved to death, after having lived 14 days without swallowing either meat or drink.

31. Mrs. Warren, wife of Mr. W. tailor, of Arundel-street, Strand. Having watched an opportunity, when her servant and children were up-stairs, she bolted herself into the kitchen, and very nearly severed her head from her body with a razor. She has left four children, one of them very young.

Interred, this day, at St. Dunstan's in the West, Fleet-street, aged 105, Mary Taylor, who had been 70 years a laundress in Clifford's inn.

Miss Louisa Perigal, eldest daughter of Mr. H. P. of Newington-place, Surrey.

At Heathfield park, Sussex, Miss Newbery, only daughter of Francis N. esq.

At Bodmin, co. Cornwall, Lieut. Wills, of the Royal Navy.

At Hull, George Robarts, esq. formerly of Beverley, in Yorkshire, and brother to Abraham R. esq. M. P. for Worcester.

Aged 40, without the least previous illness, Mr. Thomas Younge, an eminent draper, grocer, butter-factor, &c. at Watton, co. Norfolk.

Aged 30, the Rev. Mr. Walker, a Dissenting-minister at Walpole, co. Cambr.

At Sidmouth, Devon, in his 50th year, James Currie, M. D. F. R. S. a physician of considerable reputation at Liverpool, but who had lately become an inhabitant of Bath, on account of ill health, and who would have graced any place or society to which he belonged. He bore great pain and uneasiness, for several years, with calmness and resignation, and finished his course with affording an example of that patience and fortitude which so eminently distinguished his character through life. His medical abilities were confessedly very great. Persevering, ingenious, and penetrating, few circumstances escaped his observation; and his talent of applying to practice the facts which he had observed was seldom equalled. He was also a remarkable instance of the improvement which the cultivation of the moral duties produces upon the understanding. His judgment was not clouded by jealousy, or his view of the subject or case in question obscured by partiality, or darkened by prejudice. Equally ready to adopt the suggestions of others, as he was those of his own judgment, he never deviated from the point aimed at, because the whole of the path was not traced out by himself. Superior to such considerations, which never prevail in exalted minds, he rested his character on higher grounds, and the discerning part of mankind soon became sensible that such acquiescence, when it met his own unprejudiced ideas, was an honour to his character. Candour and benevolence were the guides of his conduct, and led him to esteem and reputation in the present world, softened his passage to the tomb, and, in his last moments, disarmed the dart of Death. Original, however, in his ideas, he was better suited to point out the way, than to follow the speculations of others; and what he advised obtained a kind of involuntary preference, which nothing but a consciousness of merit in the adviser could have secured. His counsels, though destitute of the recommendation of peremptory assertion, or lavish display of pretended success, which sometimes overpower, when they do not convince, carried with them the more powerful charms of sense, judgment, reflection, and acquaintance with the subject, and were accompanied with a most amiable and satisfactory manner of manifesting these admirable qualifications to the understandings of those with whom he conversed. Nor did pain and sickness, however embittering they were to the enjoyment of life, cloud his faculties, or disorder his temper. He resigned life with the same benevolent disposition of mind in which he had lived, and with undiminished powers of understanding. The faculties of his mind were not, however, confined to professional subjects. Well versed in elegant knowledge, he combined the pursuits of ornamental literature with those of the severer studies. Poetry, history, and other branches of knowledge that improve the understanding, and animate the mind to exert itself in every capacity, were held by him in high esteem, and were favourite objects of his attention. On these models, selected from the best authors, he formed his own style of writing, which was pure, elegant, and correct; and often adorned with passages which in beauty of language, and delicacy and propriety of sentiment, yield to none of which our coun'ry can boast. The lovers of science might wish his life to have been longer protracted, in which wish all the friends of the country, who knew him, would willingly join: but wiser Fate says no; and Reflection steps in and warns us, that "his warfare is accomplished;" and that we must not, from partial, or interested, or indeed any human considerations, prefer to wish the prolongation, suffering to him who had so long and so eminently struggled with pain and misery—and, in the midst of these

167 **CURRIE** (James, M.D., F.R.S., of Liverpool, *the biographer of Burns*), MEMOIR of the LIFE, WRITINGS, and CORRESPONDENCE of, edited by his son W. W. CURRIE; *with portrait*, also inserted an autograph letter, 1 page 8vo., dated 1st Jan., 1801; 2 vols., 8vo., *crushed calf*, **12s.** 1831

Currie of Chester, &c.

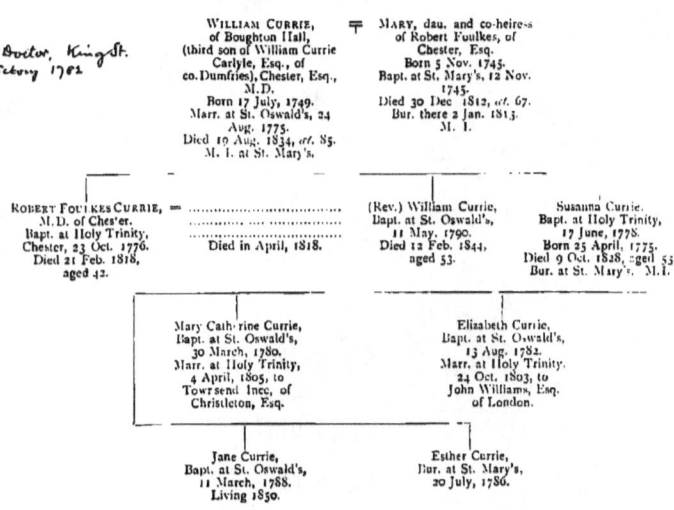

ie Doctor, King St.
Directory 1782

WILLIAM CURRIE, = MARY, dau. and co-heiress
of Boughton Hall, of Robert Foulkes, of
(third son of William Currie Chester, Esq.
Carlyle, Esq., of Born 5 Nov. 1745.
co. Dumfries), Chester, Esq., Bapt. at St. Mary's, 12 Nov.
M.D. 1745.
Born 17 July, 1749. Died 30 Dec. 1812, æt. 67.
Marr. at St. Oswald's, 24 Bur. there 2 Jan. 1813.
Aug. 1775. M. I.
Died 19 Aug. 1834, æt. 85.
M. I. at St. Mary's.

ROBERT FOULKES CURRIE, = ... (Rev.) William Currie, Susanna Currie.
M.D. of Chester. .... Bapt. at St. Oswald's, Bapt. at Holy Trinity,
Bapt. at Holy Trinity, 11 May, 1790. 17 June, 1778.
Chester, 23 Oct. 1776. Died in April, 1818. Died 12 Feb. 1844, Born 25 April, 1775.
Died 21 Feb. 1818, aged 53. Died 9 Oct. 1828, aged 53.
aged 42. Bur. at St. Mary's. M. I.

Mary Catherine Currie, Elizabeth Currie,
Bapt. at St. Oswald's, Bapt. at St. Oswald's,
30 March, 1780. 13 Aug. 1782.
Marr. at Holy Trinity, Marr. at Holy Trinity,
4 April, 1805, to 24 Oct. 1803, to
Townsend Ince, of John Williams, Esq.
Christleton, Esq. of London.

Jane Currie, Esther Currie,
Bapt. at St. Oswald's, Bur. at St. Mary's,
11 March, 1788. 20 July, 1786.
Living 1850.

Manley of the Lache and Chester.

Harl. MS. 2015, f. 18 old fol., f. 43 new fol. Drawn up May 15, 1638.

Harl. MS. 2119, f. 117.

(f. 24) WILLIAM MANLEY, of Lach, alias Mouldesfeld, co. Cestr., third sonne of John Manley, of Pulton t H. 7. = Elinor, dau. to Edw. Whitley, of Aston, co. fflynt.

Eliason, dau. to Edward Ashton, of Grange, &c. of Ashton, dau. to Edward Whitley of Aston, is trewer in mood.

JOHN MANLEY, of Moonksfeld (?). Bur. in St Maryes, in Chester, 18 May, 1572. = Alice, dau. of Thomas Evanson, of Hawardyn, co. flint. She died 1571.

Richard, a priest, 1565, marr. Margery Lunt, 14 Nov. 1578, in St Mary's.

Other issue, see Harl. MS. 2119.

GEORGE MANLEY, of Lach, nere Chester. He was twice married. Died 10 May, 1612, and was buried in St Mary's, in Chester, 18 May. = ELIZABETH, dau. to Thomas Parry, of Northop, co. Flint, and widow of Ranulfe Lloyd, of Calcott, co. Flint, gent. Died 5 July, 1598. Buried in St Mary's, 5 July, 1598. She had no issue by George Manley (second wife).

Margery, dau. to William Banbury, of Chester, gent. Died in January, 1570-71, and buried at St Mary's, 31 Jan., 1570-71 (first wife).

1612. Elizabeth Manley, youngest dau. marr. Thomas Thornley, of Sichem (?), near Eccleston, and hath issue now living, 1638.

Margaret, dau. and heir of Thomas Larkyn, of Westminster, gent.

THOMAS MANLEY, of Lach, son and heir. Was thrice married. He died in Sept. 1617, and was buried in St Mary's, 15 Sept. 1617. = 1, KATHERINE, dau. and heir to Ranulfe Lloyd, of Calcott, co. Flint, gent., by Elizabeth Parry, his wife.

= 2, Ermyn, dau. to Thomas Bellot, of Moreton, Esq., and widow of John Manley, of Pulton Hall. Had no issue by Thomas Manley. She died in Feb. 1611, and was buried at St Mary's, 4 Feb. 1611.

= 3, Anne, dau. of Thomas Grosvenor, of Eaton, Esq., widow of Roger Hurleston, of Chester, Esq. Marr. at St Michaels 24 July, 1612. She died Nov. 12, 1615, and was buried at St Michael's.

1612. Julian Manley, eldest dau., marr. Richard Grosvenor, of Dodleston, and hath issue now living, 1638.

Sir Richard Manley, knt., second son, clerk and controller to the household of Prince Henry, and now clerk of the Green Cloth to King Charles. Both now living 1638, and have issue.

George, M. 1612.

Thomas, M. 1612.

John, M.

Margaret, M.

A

B

PEDIGREES.

A

GEORGE MANDLEY, gent., of Lach, son and heir. Living 1658. Ch. 1643 (?). Admon. in London. Buried at St Mary's, 21 Aug. 1653.
= **ELIZABETH**, dau. of Richard Lee, of Deis (?), in Kent, Esq. Living, 1658. Ob. in Chester, 6 Oct. 1658. Bar. at St Mary's, 8 Oct. 1658.

William Mandley, of the city of Chester, mercer, Second son. Died unmarried. Bar. at St Peter's, Chester, s. p.

Thomas Mandley, Esq., third son, Clerk of the Kitchen to King Charles. 1635.
= **Cassandra**, dau. of Justice Henry Jokes (?), of Westminster, Esq., widow of Button.

Mary Mandley, eldest dau., marr. Thomas Purgeny, of Doolleston, and hath issue.

Alice Mandley, youngest dau. Living unmarried, 1656.

B

John Mandley, of Huxley, co. Chester, third son. Living, æt. 61, in 1658. Will at Chester, 1644.
= **Elizabeth**, dau. and co-heir of Ralph Bostock, of Huxley. She died in 1623, and was buried in Wharton church.

GEORGE MANDLEY, eldest son, of the Lach, gent. Admon. will Inv., 1683. Bar. at St Mary's, 15 April, 1683.
= **MARGARET**, dau. of .... Bar. at St Mary's, 7 April, 1721.

Richard Mandley, of Vigeney, 1651. Marr. ...., sister to Capt. Houghton.

Thomas Mandley.

Elizabeth Mandley.

Thomas Mandley, born 23 Sept. 1602, of Westminster, son and heir, for whom this pedigree was compiled in 1658.

Henry, 1612.

Ann, 1612.

Elizabeth, 1612.

Katherine Mandley. Ch. 1658. Bur. 1644.

John Mandley, Esq., 1683–1700, and 1703. Bar. at St Mary's, 31 Jan. 1720-1.

1643–1650. Four others died infants.

Anne Mandley, Bapt. at St Mary's, 23 April, 1622. Bar. 1632.

Mary Mandley, Bapt. at St Mary's, 4 April, 1624. Bar. 1632.

271

ST. MARY-ON-THE-HILL, CHESTER.

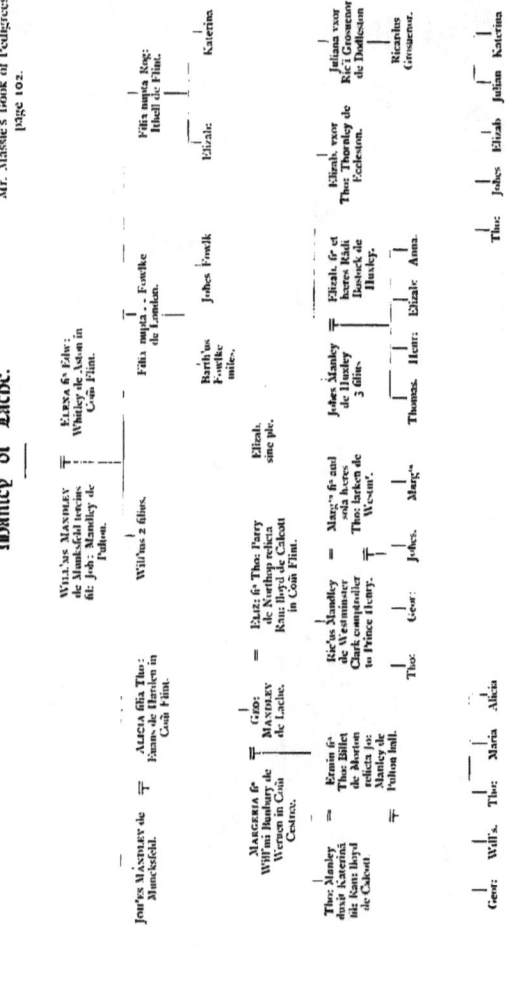

PEDIGREES.

Manley of Pulton.

Arms.—A sauge man's head proper.

Mr. Massie's Book of Pedigrees, p. 103. Chaloner's Note.

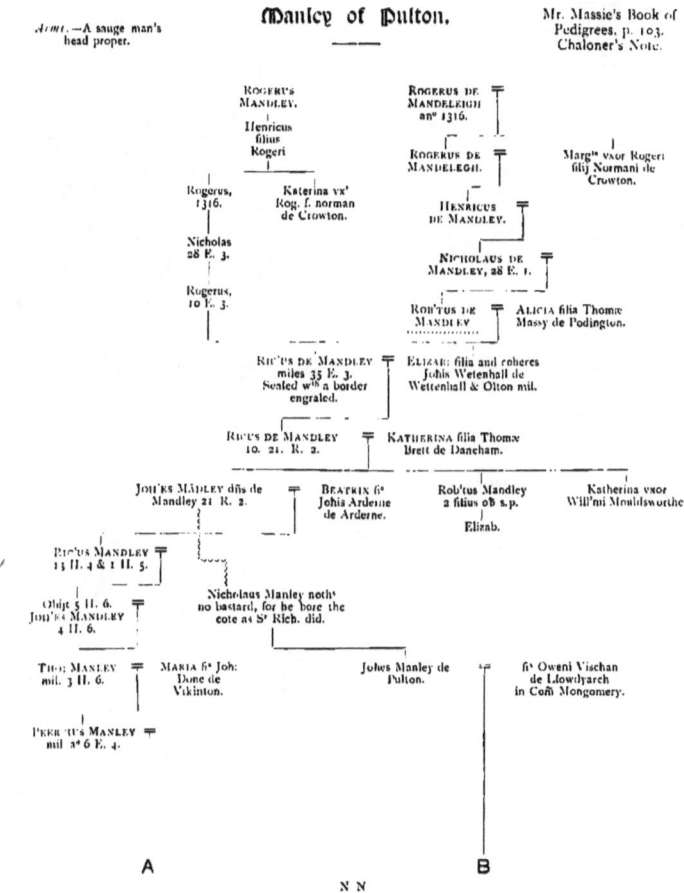

A   B

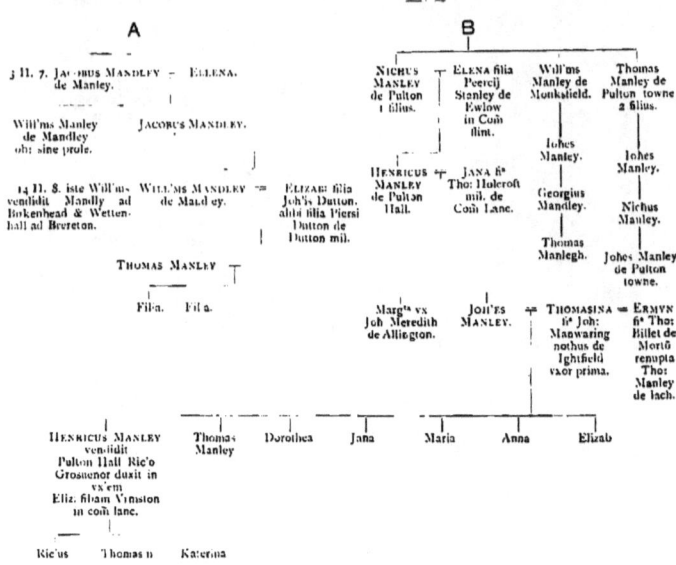

Ellis of Overlegh and Chester.

Harl. MS. 2161.
f. 205b, old not.

```
Dio ap Griffith, =T= ......, sister to Wm Goch, citizen of
                        Chester, sherri 1463.
     |
     +---------------------------+---------------------------+
     |                           |                           |
Ellis ap Dio, 23 E. 4, 10 H. 8. =T= ......, dau. to Jenkyn ap Blethyn,     William ap Dio, 1482, in the lease
     Ob. 15 H. 8.                    and sister to David and James.             that his brother Ellis took.
     |
     +----------------+---------------------+---------------------+---------------------+
     |                |                     |                     |                     |
Matthew ap Ellis, er — Mary, da. to Sr Piers  + Alice, wid. to Elli- ap   Joan ux.       Elizabeth, ux. Tho., sonne
 Matthew Ellis, of Over-  Dutton, of Dutton, 37   Tudor, 16 H. 8.  She    Taylor,        of Rich. Browne, of
 leigh, 10 H. 8, 32 H. 8, 37  H. 8. and sister to Rafe /\  ob. 1537, as ap th by  wid.,  Netherlegh. wth whom he
 H. 8. Ob. 2 E. 6 the 6 of  of Hatton. 2 wife, widow,   b¹ Mary's registers.      1548.  had xvj. acres of land in
 Feb. He was one of the     2 E. 6. Marr. 3ly,                                           Netherleigh. 22 E. 4.
 gard to H. 8.              Booth, younger brother to                                    After she marr. Tho:
                            Booth, of Dunham.                                            Govet, 15 H. 8.
     |
     +----------------+---------------------+---------------------+---------------------+
     |                |                     |                     |                     |
Matthew Ellis, in the entail,=T= Elizabeth, da. to Tho.  Julian in the entail, 37 H. 8,   Margery, in the entail. 37
 37 H. 8, and ward 2 E. 6, to   Brown of Netherlegh,   marr. a child to Hope, of         H. 8, uxor,      Knight.
 Wm Kettell and his mother      gent., ob. 1570.       Bruershall, but divorced, children,    of Handbridge.
 Mary.                          Margery, his second wife,  and living in Norfolk, marr.
 He ob. 20 Aprell, 16 Q. E.,    a wid., 19 Q. E., as   Jo. Clippesley, of Clippesley.
 and his mother was 21 yeares   appeareth by acquittance.
 of age in the 12 of July after his
 father's death.  He was one of
 the gard to Q. E.
     |
     +----------------+---------------------+---------------------+
     |                |                     |                     |
Matthew Ellis, 6 years +T+ Katherine, dau. to Ralph   Audrey, ux. Thos.    Julian, ux. Sr Ran Crewe,
 8 months and 1 day old     Allen, of Chester, alder-  Gubion.              afterwards Chief Just ce
 at his father's death, 16  man.  Ob. 11 Jan. 1671.                         of England.
 Q. E.  Ob. 13 July,        Marr. (2) Matthew
 1613.                      Browne, (3) Randle
                            Holme, senior, alderman.
     |
     +----------------+---------------------+---------------------+
     |                |                     |                     |
Matthew Ellis, under age, =T= Elizabeth, dau. to ......   Katherine, ux. Randle    Amy, ux. Alexander Bird.
 1613.                       Judson, of Namptwich.         Holme, of Chester.       of Chester.
     |
     +----+------------------+-----+---------+----------+---------------+----------+
     |    |                  |     |         |          |               |          |
Randle, Matthew Ellis, =T= Anne, dau. to John  2 Henry. 3 Joseph. 4 William.  Katherine    Sarai.  Amy ux.
 s. p.   ætat. 31, 1670.    Birkenhead, of                                     ux. Henry
                            Backford.                                          Grey, of
         |                                                                     Handbridge.
         +-------+
         |       |
      Matthew.  Anne.
```

Note in the margin of the Ellis Pedigree :—

Rich. Kyrk ye Abbott of Basingwerk, did let Wm Legalton, chaplain, and Wm Goch, citizen of Chester, haue a lease of the manor of Overlegh for 12 years, paying 4 macks yearly &c.

Testibus John Southworth, maior of the city of Chester, Richard Saddler, and Thomas Ecclesse, sheriffs of the said city, John Cotyrgham, Richard Raynford, and others, given at Chester 10 Feb., 15 Ed. 4, so that Ellis ap Dio either bought his tyme or had it by his sisters mach [?match], for the 1488. 22 Edw. 4, 1848, he had a new lease for c. yeares.

Ellis ap Dio lived in Overlegh. when Hen. Andrews and Jo. How had Overlegh of the gift of H. 8, at the Dissolution of Abbies, wch Andrews and How sould it to Matthew Ellis 36 H. 8 for 100 marks.

Browne of Norfolk. Ermine, a chief Or. p.49.
Browne of Jacleston in Norfolk. Or, a bend vert. Crest, a buck passant. p. 55.
Browne of Gloucester. Arg. on a chevron gules, 3 roses or. Crest, a lion rampant, supporting ...
Browne of ... Azure, a chevron between 3 goats heads erased argent, attired or. p. 337
Browne of Suffolk. Arg. on a bend sable, 3 eaglets displayed of the first. p. 293.

276 ST. MARY-ON-THE-HILL, CHESTER.

BROWNE OF NETHER LEGH.

Browne of Netherlegh.

Thomas Browne, of Sulineydale, the elder. Will made 24 Aug. 1587. Proved same year. To be bur. at St. Mary's. = **Elizabeth**, dau. of Sir Piers Dutton, knt. and widow of Wm. Manley, of Manley. Living 1587.

Thomas Browne, *alias* Salney, of Netherlegh, gent. Living 1587. Inv. at Chester taken 24 Aug. 1622. Will chiod 21 May, 1622, pr. 19 Aug. 1622. = **Margaret**, dau. of .... Re-marr. to Cuthbert Johnson, gent. Both dead in 1644.

William Browne, 1622, 1634.

Katherine Browne. Marr. .... Cutton. Liv. 1587.

Amy Browne, 1622, 1634.

Jane Browne. Marr. .... Alcock. 1622, 1634.

William B. bapt. at St. M. 3 July, 1634.

Anne Browne. Died young.

Matthew Browne, of Chester and Netherlegh, gent. 1622. Will made 28 Nov. 1634. Pr. at Chester 12 Jan. 1634-5. Bur. at St. Mary's 26 Nov. 1634. Fun. Cert. At I.

Katherine, dau. of Ralph Allen, of Chester, alderman, and widow of Matthew Ellis of Overlegh, gent. Living 1669.

Thomas Browne, 1622, 1634, of Salney, gent., "Senior, gent." Mr. in 1644. Bur. at St. M. 16 Jan. 1646-7.

Mary Browne, marr. Robert Crewenor, of Henston. 1622, 1634.

Eleanor B. bapt. at St. M. 27 Dec. 1637.

Matthew B. bapt. at St. M. 20 Oct. 1630.

Elizabeth Browne. Died young.

Martha Browne. Bapt. at St. M. 2 June, 1650. Bur. there 21 Oct. 1655.

Hannah Browne. Died young.

Thomas Brown, of Chester and Netherlegh, gent. 1634. Born c. 1620. Died 24 Aug. 1669, æt. 50. M.I. Bur. at St. M. 28 Aug. 1669. Will made 29 Dec. 1668, pr. 17 Sept. 1669.

Philippa, dau. of Thomas Herrington, of Chester, gent. Marr. at St. M. 25 Nov. 1641. She died, aged 47, 6 May, 1664. Bur. at St. M. 9 May, 1664.

Katherine B. bapt. at St. M. 11 April, 1634.

Hannah, dau. of Rich. Leycester, of Toxth, in Great Budworth, and relict of Charles Leversley, of Chester, gent. Liv. 1669.

George Browne, of Chester, gent. 1654. Bur. at St. M. 9 May, 1655. M.I.

Alice Browne, 1634. Marr. to Thomas Parnell. M.I. She died 5 Sept. 1639.

Philippa Browne, bapt. at St. M. 1 Sept. 1643. Marr. there to Richard Parker, of Audley, co. Stafford, gent. 1669.

no sons and 5 daus.

Thomas Browne. Died young.

George Browne. Died young.

Samuel Browne. Died young.

Richard Browne. Bapt. at St. M. 7 April, 1659. Liv. 1669.

Francis Browne. Bapt. at St. M. 27 March, 1653-4. Bur. there 21 Dec. 1654.

Charles Browne. Bapt. at St. M. 8 Oct. 1663.

Benjamin Browne. Bapt. at St. M. 9 April, 1662. Liv. 1669.

Katherine Browne, bapt. at St. M. 18 June, 1648. Liv. 1669.

Elizabeth Browne. Bapt. at St. M. 26 Dec. 1661. Bur. there 8 Oct. 1663.

Monument to Margaret Lod.
St Oswaldo Church, Chester.
(wife of John Morgel obiit 1598).

Towards the [...] end of the [...]
[illegible handwriting]

Perpetua p[...]ti[...] [...]
Margaret the L[o]d [...]
[illegible]
[...] tuis [...] usq; fortunatae [...]
[illegible lines]

QUERIES.

[2188] MOSTON HALL.

Can any of your readers inform this enquirer if a print or sketch exists of the old Moston Hall, built about 1600, and pulled down two centuries later? It seems to have been a mansion of considerable pretension, and Webb, in his treatise on Cheshire, referring to the township of Moston, says that not long since, that is, early in the seventeenth century, it had been 'purchased and beautified with a delicate house of brick by Mr. John Morgel, register of the diocese of Chester." Ormerod describes the hall as "a tall building, with a front terminating in five gables," and adds that it "stood on a pleasant knoll, in the middle of a large ley for cattle, which occupies the greater part of the township"; a description of the locality which is equally true at the present day. A. G. S.

Morgell of Chester and Moston.

Lieutenant Morgell (Royalist) taken a prisoner at Acton Church near Nantwich, Jany 25 - 1643-4. Hall's Nantwich f. 170.

Arms in this Royal MSS fo: 8 Argent, on a bend segreant sable three cinque folk Or, on a chief azure three flems delys Or, a mullet for difference
Morgan of Moston

THOMAS MORGAN, descended of a second sonne of Morgan of Weston, in Com. Warwyck, Ar.

JOHN MORGELL als Morgan of Moston, and of the citty of Chester, principall Register for the diocese of Chester, dyed at Moston, co. Cestr., 27 November, 1636, and buried in Backford church.

= MARGERY, dau. and heir to Willm Dod, of Chester, and sonne to David Dod, of Edge, Esq.
This Walter Dod married Elizabeth daughter of William Harkenhall of Sutton. Mon: vol II p. 662 monument to margaret Dod Chester Cathedral ob. 10 Oct. 1598. Vale Royal p. 42. (Stonwelde.)

James, to whom his father gave li per ann. out of his office.

A								B
RAFE MORGELL, son and heir, æt. 47. 1630, at his father's death. Living, 1653. *died 4 Jany 1678 monument in Backford Church*	= MARGARET, dau. to Edw. Glegg, of Gayton, Ar. She died 12 Oct., 1623, and buried in Backford. *Monument Çaird 1627.*	Randle Morgell, 2 sonne, d. younge.	William Morgell, 3 sonne, of Grays Inne, Esq. Will made 1 Ap., 1653. Pr. at London, 26 Ap., 1653. (A copy at Chester, 1676.)	Mary, dau. to Tho. Moyle, of Cassell, co. Oxon, Esq. *Several inrolls bills at Chester*	Edward Morgell, of Chester, Register under his father. Ob. 23 March, 1633. Bur. in St. Werburgh.	Anne, have dau. to Gen. Legh, of the East Hall, co. Cest.	Thomas Morgell, ob. at Middlebrugh, in the Low Countries, sans yssue.	Mary Morgell, dyed yonge.
	John Morgell, ob. younge.	Mary, marr. Edwd. Minshall, of Stoke, co. Chester, Esq.	Anne, dead before 1653.	Barham, marr. Randle Dod, of Edge, Esq.	Elizabeth, dead before 1653.			

Mrs Barbara Dodd died 15 July 1703 in London. Gave her Estate in Broughton to the canons of Chester Cathedral. Mon: Ches Cath: Mems vol II p. 57

278   ST. MARY-ON-THE-HILL, CHESTER.

A

Edward Morgell, son and heir, æt. 19 at his father's death. His grandfather left him half the Keepers place for life. Ob. 15 Aug., 1659. Will made 10 Aug., 1659. Pr. at C., 13 March, 1661-2.
= 1. Margaret, dau. to Rich. Bold, of Bold, co. Lanc.
+ 2. Hanna, dau. to Thos. Whitby, aldⁿ of Chester, and co-heir to her brother. Liv. 1659. Re-marr. George Legh, of Barton, Esq., at Holy Trinity, Chester, 16 Apr., 1661.

Randle Morgell, ob. yonge.

Margery, (?) marr. Glasier before 1653.

(One dau. marr. Mywod.)

Philip Morgell, dead before 1659. ⊤ Philip Elizabeth

Anne.

John Morgell.

Alice Morgell. Liv. 1659.

Thomas Morgell.

4th dau. ob. young.

B

Edward Morgell. Liv. 1659.

Kate Morgell.

Edward Morgell.

Thomas Morgell.

William Morgell. s. p.

Isabell, ob. a mayd.

Margaret, ux Wᵐ Glasier, of Lea.

Henry Morgell, of Moston.

Katherine, da. to King, of Chalton, relict of Rich. Robinson, of Raby.

Elizabeth, dau. to Willm Glasier, of Lea. Ob. 9 May, 1683.

Richard Morgell, liv. 1682.

Mary, liv. 1632.

William Morgell, s. p.

Kate Morgell, of Moston. Ob. 27 Nov., 1682. Will made 29 Nov., 1682. Pr. at C. 28 March, 1683.

Willm. Morgell of Moston, gent. Will made 9 Jan., 1707-8. Pr. at C. 17 Ap., 1708.

Elizabeth Morgell, liv. 1708.

Kate Morgell.

JOHN MORELL, æt. 21 in 1636. ⊤ ANNE, dau. of .... of Leicester, of Baulworth.

Cisley.   Mary.   Margaret.   Anne.

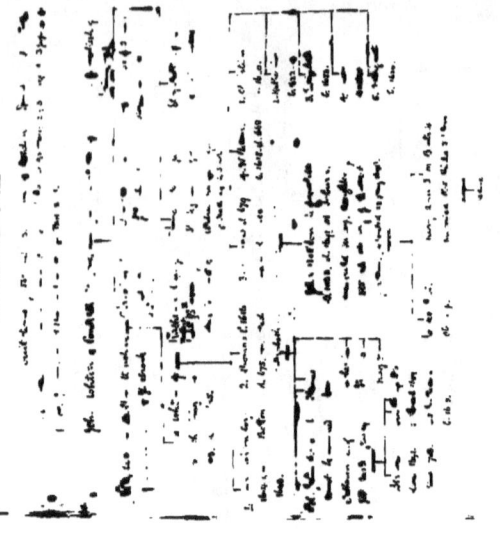

Brock of Upton.

Authorities: Harl. MS. 2153, f. 85; Visitation of Chester, 1613 and 1663; St. Mary's Registers, Wills, Deeds, &c.

BROCK

- Robert Brock, Archdeacon of Middlesex, and Chaplain to Henry VIII.
- —— dau. of —— Swinton, of Knutsford.

WILLIAM BROCK, of Upton.

JOHN BROCK, of Upton, gent. Living 1530. = **ELIZABETH**, dau. of Edw. Gamel, of Barton, widow of Hugh Picculami, of Picculami (who died 1568). = **PARNEL**, dau. of Thomas Vaudrey, of Riddings, co. Chester, Esq.

Jane Brock. John Brock.

ROBERT BROCK, of Upton, gent. Alderman of Chester. Died 1588. = **JANE**, dau. and co-heir of John Cosgrave, of Edmunds Cotton, co. Chester, gent. Bur. at St. Mary's, 30 Jan. 1573-4.

Robert Brock, of Upton, gent. Succ. his brother. Died 30 Nov. 1603. (Fun. Certificate.) Bur. at Chester Cathedral. Will made 30 Nov. 1603. Pr. at Chester 10 Dec. 1603. = **Avice**, dau. and heir of Joshua George, of George Hall, co. York, gent. Liv. 1603.

William Brock, Living 1594 and 1603.

Edward Brock, Living 1594, 1603. Died 3 Oct. 1630. Bur. at St. Mary's 2004.

William Brock (Illegitimate). Bur. at Chester Cathedral, 1630. (Harl. MS. 2153.)

JOHN BROCK, of Upton, gent. Dead before 1594. s.p. = **ANNE**, dau. of Edmund Gamull, of Chester, alderman. Marr. (2) Edward Holland, of Denton, co. Lanc. Esq. (before 1609), who died 1631. She was living 1637.

Katherine Brock. Married Thomas Ashton, of Penketh, co. Lanc. gent.

Edward Brock, Bapt. at St. Mary's 20 July, 1598.

Elizabeth Brock, Bapt. at St. Mary's 21 May, 1597.

Anne Brock, Bapt. at St. Mary's 10 Nov. 1599.

WILLIAM BROCK, of Upton and the Inner Temple, London, Esq. Died 4 April, 1640. Bur. at St. Mary's. M.I. Will dated 3 April, 1640. Pr. at Chester 8 Sept. 1640. = **ANNE**, dau. and co-heir of Robert Mohun, of Haymon, co. Dorset, Esq. Died 17 June, 1660. Bur. at St. Mary's. M.I.

A

The Diary of Nehemiah Griffith Esq of Rhual for 1715.
Feb. 1. Mr W. Brock and Mr Brereton quarreled about Ditfield
Feb 11. at Broncoed to see mr Wm Brock sick.
. 26 Went with Mr Brereton to Broncoed to see Mr Wm Brock
    Exceedingly weak.
March 5. Went to Broncoed but found Wm Brock was coach'd to
    chester the same day, very sick.
. 14 Was at Chester. Visited Mr Brock in St Johns Lane, who
    was very weak.
. 24 mr Wm Brock died at Chester.
. 26 Mr Brock buried.

WILLIAM BROCK, of Upton and Bradley, Esq. Born c. 1619. Died 10 May, 1674, aged 55. Bur. at Grappenhall, co. Chester. Tombstone there. Admon. at Chester 1674.
= ELIZABETH, dau. of Sir Robert Brerewood, Knt., one of the Judges of the Court of King's Bench. Died 17 May, 1662. Bur. at St. Mary's.
= KATHERINE, dau. and heir of Edward Gregg, of Bradley-in-Appleton, co. Chester, gent. Marr. at Grappenhall 14 May, 1667. Bur. there 1 April. 1695.
William Brock.
Robert Brock. Bur. at St. Mary's, 22 March, 1645-6.
JOHN BROCK, of Nantwich, gent. Bapt. at St. Mary's, 12 June, 1628. Marr. at N. 27 Sept. 1653. Bur. at N. 14 Sept. 1660.
= ANNE, dau. of William Mainwaring, of Nantwich. Bur. there 6 Dec. 1666.
Eleanor, dau. of .... Bur. at Nantwich 28 Mar. 1670.
Melior Brock. Marr. J. Brassey, of Brassey Green.
Anne Brock. Marr. John Johnson, alderman, of Chester.
Avice Brock, bapt. at St. Mary's, 26 Sept. 1624. Marr. Edward Gregg, of Bradley, gent.
Barbara Brock, bapt. at St. Mary's, 23 July, 1629. Marr. William Barnet.
Katherine Brock. Marr. Robt. Fletcher, of Chester.
Eleanor Brock, bapt. at St. Mary's, 26 Feb. 1630-1. Bur. there 1 July, 1637.

WILLIAM BROCK, of Upton, Esq. Born c. 1643. Died 10 Jan. 1715-16, aged 73. Bur. at St. Mary's. M.I. Will made 6 July, 1713. Bur. at Chester, 16 Jan. 1715-16.
= 1. SUSANNA, dau. of Joseph Hockenhull, of Shotwick, Esq. Bur. at St. Mary's, 2 Feb. 1699-1700. M.I.
= 2. RACHEL, dau. of .... and widow of .... Williams. Marr. at St. Michael's, 4 June, 1700. Bur. at Chester Cathedral 14 May, 1715.
John Brock, bapt. at St. Peter's 18 Feb. 1645-6.
Randle Brock, bapt. at St. Mary's, 5 Jan. 1657-8.
Anne Brock.
Margaret Brock, bapt. at St. Mary's, 23 July, 1656. Marr. at Grappenhall 20 May, 1673, to Singleton Birkenhead, of Backford, Esq.
Elizabeth Brock. Bur. at St. Mary's, 25 Feb. 1658-9.

WILLIAM BROCK, of Upton, Esq. Born c. 1676. Sheriff of Cheshire in 1732. Died 10 Aug. 1734, aged 58. Bur. at St. Mary's. M.I. Will made 2 April, 1728. Pr. at Chester 1 Aug. 1735.
= ELIZABETH, dau. of John Hurleston, of Picton, Esq. Bur. at St. Mary's, 8 Nov. 1735.
Thomas Brock. Dead in 1715.
John Brock. Living 1713. Bur. at St. Mary's, 15 Feb. 1725-6, as "John Brock, gent. of Northgate St."
Joseph Brock. Bapt. at St. Mary's, 5 Oct. 1678. Bur. there 5th June, 1705.
Edward Brock. Bapt. at St. Mary's, 13 Nov. 1679. Bur. there 23 May, 1713.
Susannah Brock, bapt. at St. Oswald's, 8 June, 1682. Marr. at St. Oswald's, 18 Jan. 1699-1700, to William Delves, of Bowden Parish, gent.
Elizabeth Brock, bapt. at St. Mary's, 8 March, 1680-1. Marr. (1) at St. Oswald's, 5 Dec. 1700, to William Hurleston, gent. ; and (2) before 1713 to John Wilson, of Trinity parish, Chester.

WILLIAM BROCK, son and heir apparent. Born c. 1696. Bur. at St. Mary's, 26 March, 1715, æt. 19, s.p.
Thomas Brock. Born c. 1700. Bur. at St. Mary's 20 May, 1707. æt. 7.
ELIZABETH BROCK, eldest dau. and co-heir. Marr. at St. Oswald's, 19 April, 1721. Died 19, and buried at Little Budworth 23 July, 1756.
= JOHN EGERTON, of Broxton, co. Chester, Esq. Bapt. at Little Budworth 16 March, 1696-7. Bur. there 25 May, 1770.
Susannah Brock, dau. and co-heir. Died 20, bur. at St. Mary's, 31 March, 1766, unmarr. M.I.
Anne Brock, dau. and co-heir. Bur. at St. Mary's, 26 April, 1758, unmarr.
Margaret Brock, dau. and co-heir. Bur. at St. Mary's, 30 May, 1753, unmarr.

EGERTON OF OULTON.

Richard & Jane Hartley of Chester.

April 19. 1612. Indenture of Sale by John Lyvesley of the City of Chester, Innholder of a tenement in St. John's Lane in the city of Chester to Richard Hartley & Jane his wife, of the said City of Chester.— [13&14 Jas 1. m.2]. Recog. Rolls of Chester 39th Report D.K. of P.R. p.182.

BROWNE OF UPTON.

PEDIGREES. 281

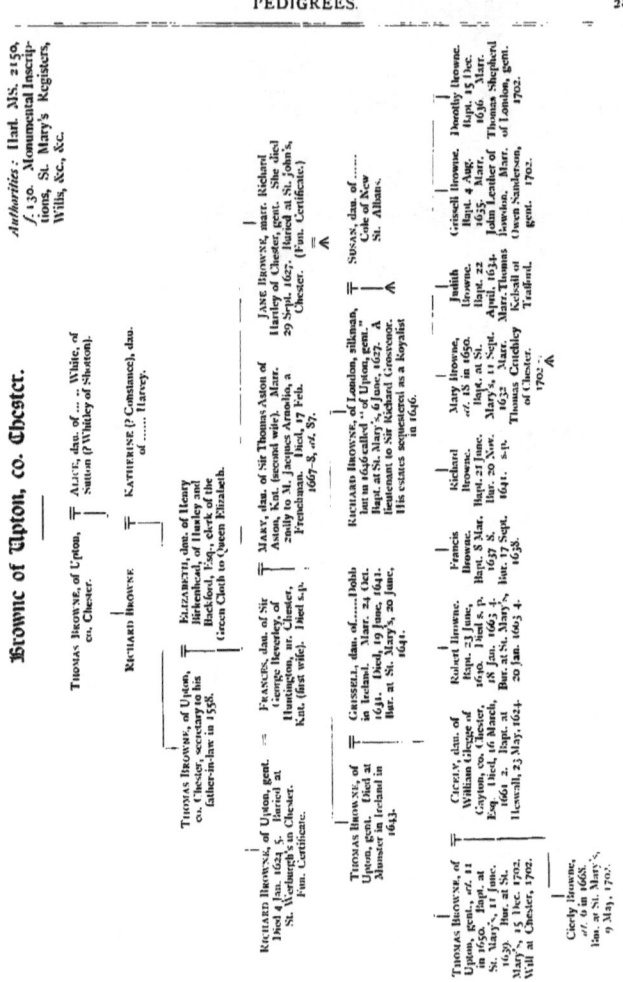

Browne of Upton, co. Chester.

Authorities: Harl. MS. 2150, f. 130. Monumental Inscriptions, St. Mary's Registers, Wills, &c., &c.

Hunt.

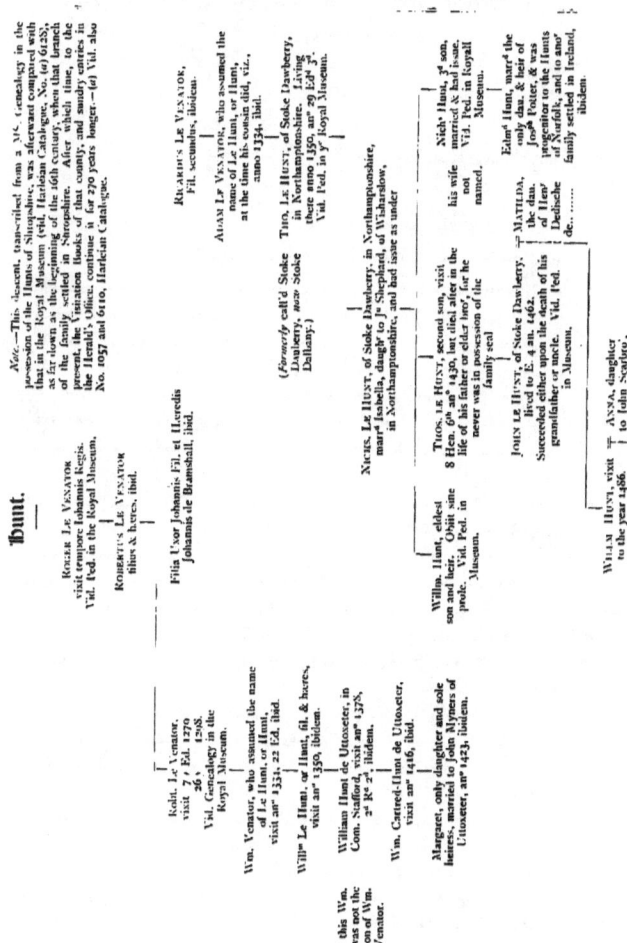

Note.—This descent, transcribed from a MS. (genealogy in the possession of the Hunts of Shropshire, was afterwards compared with that in the Royal Museum (vid. Harleian Catalogue, No. (a) 6128), as far down as the beginning of the 16th century, when that branch of the family settled in Shropshire. After which time, to the present, the Visitation Books of that county, and sundry entries in the Herald's Office, continue it for 270 years longer.—(a) Vid. also No. 1057 and 6110, Harleian Catalogue.

Thomas Hunt of Shrewsbury,   Sheriff of Salop. 1656.
Rowland Hunt of Boreatton,   do   do   1672.
Thomas Hunt of Boreatton,   do   do   1718.
Rowland Hunt of Boreatton.   do   do   1830.

From "The Sheriffs of Shropshire" by Rev. J. B. Blakeway M.A. F.S.A.

1656. Thomas Hunt.

Arms. Party per pale arg. & sable, a saltire counterchanged.

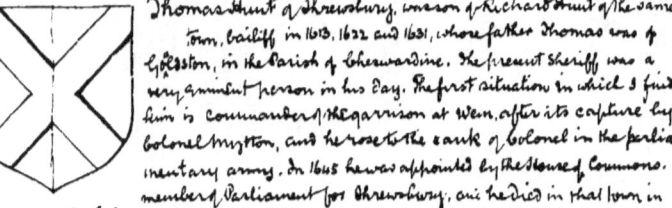

Thomas Hunt of Shrewsbury, was son of Richard Hunt of the same town, bailiff in 1613, 1622 and 1631, whose father Thomas was of Goldstone, in the Parish of Cheswardine. The present Sheriff was a very eminent person in his day. The first situation in which I find him is Commander of the Garrison at Wem, after its capture by Colonel Mytton, and he rose to the rank of Colonel in the parliamentary army. In 1645 he was appointed by the House of Commons, member of Parliament for Shrewsbury, and he died in that town in 1669, though he had, subsequently to the restoration of King Charles II purchased the estate at Boreatton. Baxter, who knew him well, assures us that he was a plain-hearted, honest godly man, entirely beloved and trusted by the soldiers for his honesty. Mr Henry confirms this handsome encomium, styling him an Israelite indeed, in whom there was no guile, and several of his descendants have been persons of distinguished piety. Rowland Hunt Esq. now (1830) of Boreatton, is fifth in descent from him.

From Colonel Hunt's younger son John, descended in the second degree Thomas Hunt of Mollington, in Cheshire, and Lanhidrock, in Cornwall, whose daughter & heiress carried her great estates in the latter county, derived from her grandmother, the daughter of Russel Robartes, son of John Robartes, Viscount Bodmin, and Earl of Radnor (whose character is drawn at great length by Lord Clarendon) to the Hon. Charles Bagnall Agar, brother of Lord Viscount Clifden. (vide 1672).

a. He tells us that he preached one of Col. Hunt's Assize Sermons at Shrewsbury.
b. Among the friends of Matthew Henry during his residence in Chester, who had all along professed themselves dissenters, though with great moderation and just esteem to the good men of the Established Church, his biographer enumerates "John Hunt Esquire, younger brother to Mr Hunt of Boreatton [Rowland Hunt, Sheriff in 1672] walking in the same spirit and way with that honoured family from which he was descended and always Mr Henry's faithful & prudent friend. Life. p. 99.

1672. Rowland Hunt.

Rowland Hunt, of Boreatton, son and heir of Colonel Thomas Hunt, Sheriff in 1656. He is mentioned as a friend of Mr. Philip Henry'd. His lady was a Daughter of William, fifth Lord Paget. (Vide 1718.)

d. Tong, in his "Life of Matthew Henry," p. 39, speaks of that learned religious gentleman, Rowland Hunt, of Boreatton, Esq. who married the Lady Frances, daughter to the Right Honourable the Lord Paget; an excellent person, a great ornament and blessing to the family." It was owing to Mr. Hunt's advice that Matthew Henry went to Gray's Inn, in the Spring of 1685, to study the Law.

1718. Thomas Hunt.

Thomas Hunt of Boreatton in the parish of Baschurch, son of Rowland Hunt, Sheriff in 1672. He married Jane the daughter of Sir Edward Ward, Chief Justice of the Exchequer, a lady of distinguished piety and talents, as her manuscript diary amply evinces. Mr. Hunt is mentioned in the "Life of Matthew Henry" as accompanying that eminent non-conformist to Gray's Inn.

1830. Rowland Hunt.

Rowland Hunt, of Boreatton, in the parish of Baschurch, fifth in descent from Colonel Thomas Hunt, Sheriff in 1656. He married Mary eldest daughter of Thomas Lloyd of Shrewsbury & of Llangwnna in Caernarvonshire, and has issue two sons and two daughters.

Rowland Hunt, father of the present Sheriff, although he never filled that important office himself, yet, for the benevolent zeal with which he long applied himself to a most material and praiseworthy adjunct to the duties of the Sheriffalty, should not be passed over in these pages without notice. At the period he began to act as a Magistrate for Shropshire, the prison of this populous County, was wretched in its internal arrangements and altogether a complete school of vice & immorality. Mr. Mr. Hunt was indefatigable in his exertions for the erection of a new Gaol and the subsequent introduction of the admirable arrangements resulting from the labors of the philanthropic Howard.

PEDIGREES.

A

ROBERT HUNT, Esq., of Stoke Dawberry, and of Rutlandshire. Vid. Ped. in the Museum. *[Living in 1608.]* = BERTINGOLA, or Bartegolda, dau. of Sir Everard Digby, of Drystock, in Rutlandshire. Vid. Peerage of England and Ireland. Tit. L⁴ Digby.

This Robert lived to a great age, not departing this life until the year 1605. Vid. Lodge's Irish Peerage. Tit. Digby.

B

THOS. HUNT, ancestor to Hunt of Shropshire and of Cheshire. Marr⁴ and had issue two sons (viz.) He liv'd in King Henry 7 & 8. = The dau. of ......

Note.—The Pedigree of this Branch begins early in the 16th century, and comes down as far as the year 1663, when the last Visitation was, not many years after which time (viz.), in the beginning of the Reign of Queen Ann, the male line became extinct.

Note.—This descent is in the Office of Arms and also in the Museum. Vid. Hatt's Catal. in the Descent of the Shropshire Families.

JOHN HUNT, of Noske Dawberry, and of Linden, in Rutlandshire, for son and heir. His line continued some time. Esquired Hunt, his descendant, living at Linden, anno 1583. Vid. Ped. in Royal Museum and Guillim's Heraldry. *[...... Alicia ...... Nath.³ 1583.]* = Daughter of ......

ALICIA, or AMY, the dau. of Sir Thomas Cave, of Stanford, in Northamptonshire, Kn⁴. Vid. Ped. in Museum and Baronetage of England. Tit. Cave.

Note.—The Pedigree of this Branch beginning, early in the 16 century, is entered in the Herald's Office as far down as the year 1634, and continued by Mr. Isaac Heard (Lancaster Herald) in the year 1768. Vid. entry in Off⁰ of Arms, to which are here added the alterations since that time (to the year 1781) by marriages, deaths, &c.

1ˢᵗ son. Hunt. From whence descended Hunts of Gayton, in Staffordshire.

Daughter T = 1ˢᵗ son RICH⁴ HUNT de Shrop, in Com. Salop. Living temp. Henry 8. = Q. 1ˢᵗ son RICH⁴ HUNT de Com. Salop, so called in the Pedigree in Office of Arms, Hen. 8, 1520.

2ᵈ Son GEORGE HUNT de Vil. Salop, so called in Ped. in Office of Arms. Living early in the 16 century. = Daughter to ...... Stanley. But Queere if that was her name, it not being so in the Ped. in Office of Arms, no name mentioned.

C

2ᵈ Son ROGER HUNT, de Lonfton, de Longnor, in Com. Salop. Living in the Reign of Hen. 8 and Ed. 6ᵗʰ. = 1ˢᵗ Son RICH⁴ HUNT de Longnor, in Com. Salop. Living in the Reign of Hen. 8 and Ed. 6ᵗʰ.

CATHARINE, daughter of Sir Tho⁸ Grosvenor, of Eaton Boat, in Cheshire. Vid. Ped. in Museum and Peerage, Eng⁴. Tit. Grosvenor.

There is a mistake in this Pedigree of Hunt in the Herald's Office about this *Catharine*, who is not mentioned as the wife of R. Hunt, but in her room is put ALICIA, the dau. of Gardiner, but the Pedigree of Hunt of Longnor, (vid. in the Museum (vid. Harleian Catalogue) is right.

ALICIA, Dau. of ...... Gardiner.

JOHN HUNT, born ab⁴ 1549. Married 3 wives and had 3 children. He lived to the 80. Vid. Ped. in Office of Arms.

ELEANOR, daughter of Coke or Cook, of ...... in Com.......

RICH⁴ HUNT, Esq⁴, 2ᵈ son, but at length heir male. Vid. Ped. in Office of Arms.

Dau. to ...... Waring, Esq⁴, of ...... in Com. Salop.

D

E

3 Son, George Hunt, ancestor to the Hunts of Essex, &c., of which Family was Thos. Hunt, Esq⁴, L.C. Baron of Ireland, whose Commission was superceded for his having wrote in favour of y⁶ Bill of Forfeitn. in 1685.

O O 2

ST. MARY-ON-THE-HILL, CHESTER.

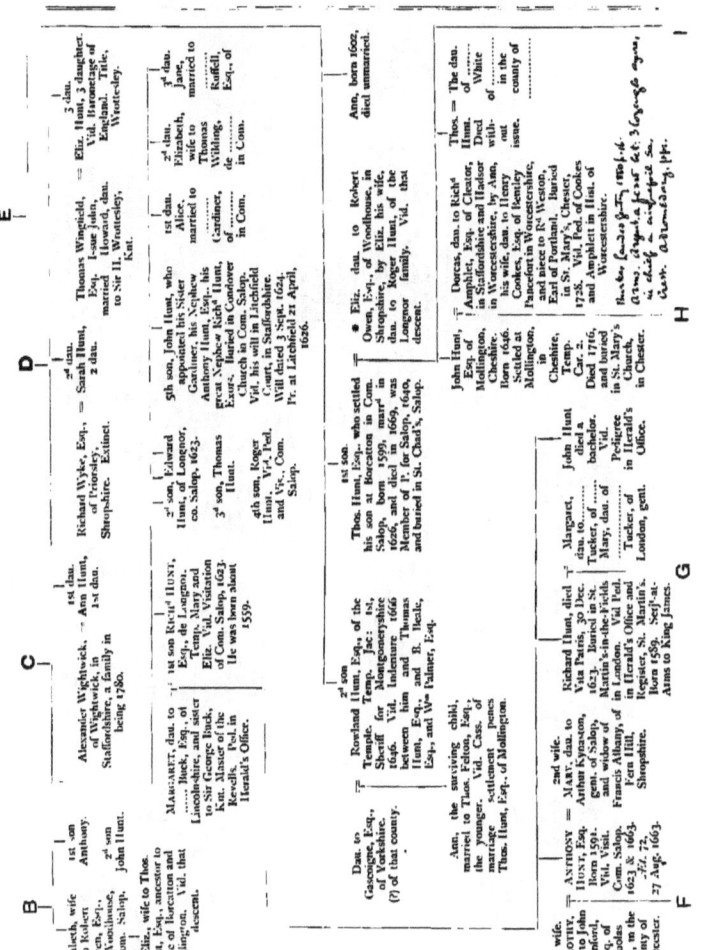

PEDIGREES.

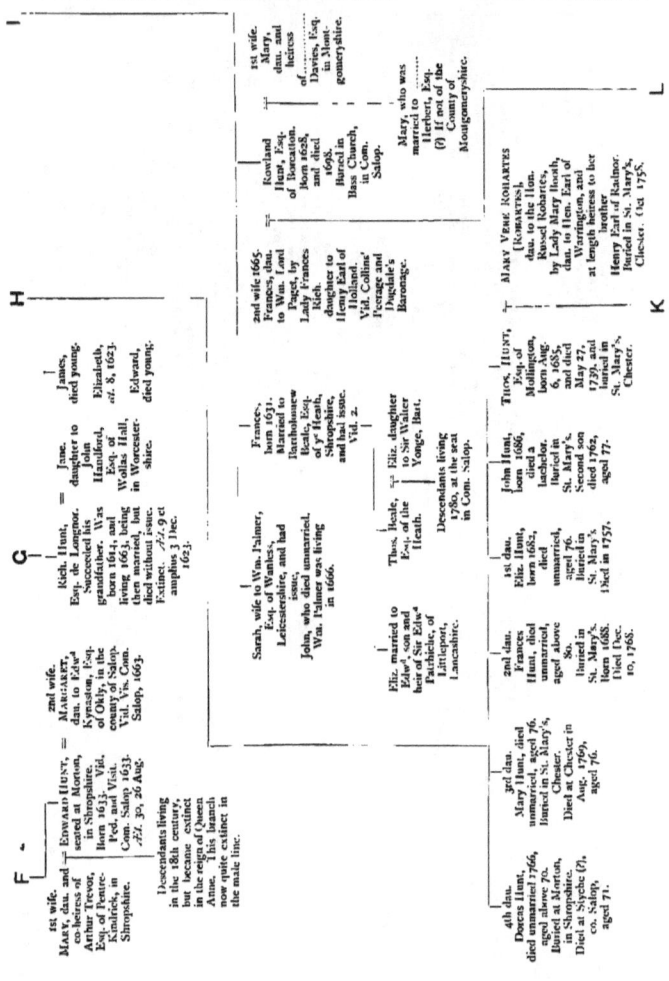

St. Mary-on-the-Hill, Chester — Hunt Pedigree (p. 286)

K

- Thos. HUNT, of Boreatton, born 1669, died 1748. Married in the 10th of Hen. 3d. Bass Church in Com. Salop.
  - 1st wife, JANE, eldest dau. and at length a co-heiress to the Right Hon. Sir Edwd. Ward, of Stoke, in Northamptonshire, and some time L^d. Ch. Baron of the Exchequer.
    - 3rd dau. Elizabeth, wife to Samuel Birch, Esq. of Garnstowe, in Herefordshire. (No issue.)
    - 2nd wife, daughter to Lisswell, Esq. of the City of London, Merch^t. (No issue.)
  - 2nd dau. Lætitia, wife to Lloyd, Esq. of ——— in the County of Radnor. Born 1666. (No issue.)

L

- 1st wife, Frances Hunt, born in the year 1666, wife to Henry Hardware, Esq. of Wirmborough Court and Cheshire, son and heir of John Hardware, Esq. of Peele Hall.
  - John, eldest son and heir of Saml Hardware, Esq. of the Peale, in Tarvin Parish, Cheshire. Descendants to the five now living, 1750.
- 4th dau. Frances Hunt, unmarried.
- 3rd dau. Ann Hunt, died young.
- 3rd dau. Sarah, married to Dr. Adams, Head of Pembroke College, Oxford, Rector of Conde, and Preb. of Lichfield.
- 4th dau. Jane, married to Mr. Wolley, merch^t. in Salop.
- 3rd son, Rowland Hunt, Rector in Dretthy and Rector of Stoke Doyley, in Northamptonshire.
  - 1st wife dau. to Adams, sister to Dr. Adams.
  - 2nd wife dau. to Wells, and his issue.

- Thos. HUNT, Esq. of Mollington, by purchase from his brother, and memb. in P. for Bodmin, 1784.
  - MARY, fourth dau. to Peter Bold, of Bold, in Lancashire, and Knight of that Shire. 1766, by Anna Maria his wife, daughter to Godfrey Wentworth, Esq. of Woolley, in Yorkshire.
    - Mary Vere Hunt, born Oct. 4, 1766, died April 30, 1760, in London. Buried in St. Mary's, Chester, near her grandfather.
    - Anna Maria Hunt, born March 29, 1771, in London. *see also…* [illegible manuscript notes]
    - 1st dau. Eliz. Hunt, born 1770, died unmarried.
    - 2nd dau. Frances, married to Lewis Gordon, Esq. son to Sir —— Gordon, Baronet, of Scotland. No issue.
    - 2nd dau. Eliz. Hunt, unmarried.
- Roger Willbraham, Esq. of Townsend, Nantwich, in Cheshire. Died Sept. 1759.
  - 1st dau. Mary Hunt, 1st dau. married in March, 1740. Died Sept. 1761.
  - Maria daur. to Wm Harvey, Esq. of Chigwell, in Essex, and Knt. of that shire.
    - 1st Son George Willbraham, Esq., of Townsend, Nantwich, Cheshire, and Grange, in the same county.
    - 2. Roger.
    - 3. Thos. Willbraham, now living. Mary and Mary Vere died young.

M

- 1st son, George Hunt, Esq. of Mollington, and of Lankyfnock, in Cornwall, in right of his mother. Mem. in six Parliaments for Bodmin. Unmarried.

PEDIGREES.

M —

1st dau. Maria Wilbraham.	2nd dau. Emma Wilbraham.	1st son. Roger Wilbraham.	2nd son. George Wilbraham.	3rd son. William Wilbraham.

Joseph Sabine, Esq., of Tewin, in Hertfordshire, grandson and heir to General Sabine, of Tewin, and Govr of Gibraltar. = Sarah Hunt, only daughter. Died 1788.

Six Children.

Thomas Hunt, 1st son and heir, died in Feb. 1766, vita Patris, aged 21.

N —

Thos. Hunt, Esq., 1st son, of Boreatton and of Stoke Doxley, in Northamptonshire, in right of his mother. Born 1703, died 1780, buried in Bast Church, in Com. Salop. = 1745. Sarah, dau. to *Horner* Wills, of .... in Gloucestershire. *late [...]* | Edward Hunt, Esq., 2nd son, of Chortle, in Northamptonshire, by devise from his uncle Philip Ward, Esq. = ... dau. to Anthony, of the City of London, Merchant.

3rd son, Edward Hunt.

1st son, Thomas Hunt, married to Russell, of Biscoll. | 2nd son, Rowland Hunt.

Philip, aged 33.

Rowland Hunt, Esq., of Boreatton, and of Stoke Doxley, in Northamptonshire. *[annotations]* = Miss Courtsel, of Huntingfield, Berkshire. *[annotations]*

Hunt, 4th son, died young. | Edward Hunt, 2nd son, a clergyman and Rector of Stoke Doxley, Northamptonshire.

Rowland Hunt, Esq., son and heir born 1785.

A Daughter, *Susanna Frances*
2 Son, 1785, *George of [...]*
3 Son, *Thomas*
4 Son, 1789, *Edward*
5 — *John*
[...] daughter Sarah Virginia

HOLME of CHESTER.

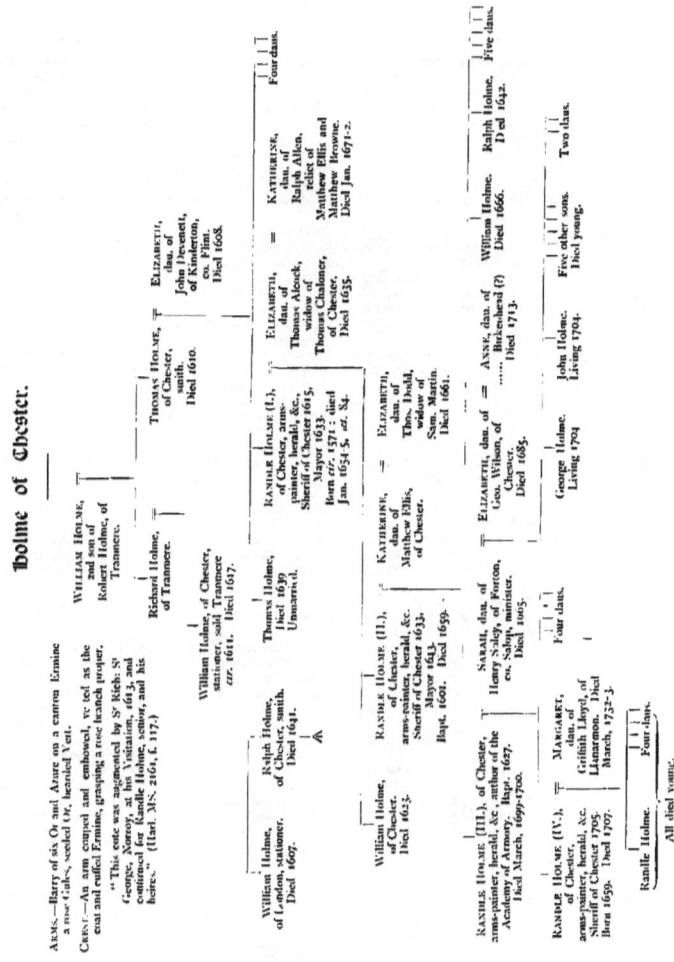

INDEX NOMINUM.

Acton family, 115, 266 ; Benjamin, 73 *bis*, 266 ; Elizabeth, 73, 266 ; Francis, 266 ; Hannah, 73, 266 ; John, 73. 180, 203, 266 ; Nathaniel, 266 ; Richard, 266 ; Roger, 266 ; Samuel, 266 ; Sarah. 73 ; Susanna, 73 ; Thomas, 73, 123, 180, 266
Adams, Dr., 286 ; Richard, 205 ; Sarah, 286
Aere, Sir John, 81, 112, 223
Ainsworth : *see* Eansworth
Albany, Francis, 284
Alcock, Elizabeth, 46, 47*n*, 74 ; Thomas, 46, 47 *n*, 74
Aldcroft, Ann, 94 *passim*, 178 ; Charles, 94, 95, 95 *m*, 150, 178 ; James, 94 *bis*, 178 ; Margaret, 95 *n* ; Ralph, 94 *bis*, 178 ; Thomas, 94, 178 ; William, 94, 178
Aldersey, Mrs., 114 ; Ann, 109 ; Edward, 180 ; Elizabeth, 92, 92 *n*, 180 ; Grace, 139 *n* ; Hugh, 198 ; John, 139 *n* ; Randle, 116 ; Robert, 92 *n, bis* ; Thomas, 92 *n*, 192 ; William, 112, 192 232.
Aldford, 14
Allen, Katherine, 120 *n*. 275-6 ; Ralph, 120 *n* Wm Wilkes
Allender, George, 208
Alport, Jane, 132 ; Robert, 132 *u*
Altcar, John de, 78 *n*
Amphlet, Dorcas, 284 ; Richard, 284
Anderson, Mrs., 128 ; Elinor (Eleanor), 22, 63, 63 *n*, 121 *n, ter* ; Matthew, 22, 63, 63 *n*, 121, 121 *n, bis*, 198
Annion (Anyon), Elizabeth, 116 *n* ; John, 117 *bis*, 202 ; Margaret, 116 ; Thomas, 205 ; William, 116
Arderne, Beatrice, 273 ; Richard, 91
Arnodio, Jacques, 96, 120, 137, 137 *n, bis* ; Mary, 69, 69 *n*, 137, 137 *n*
Arnold, Lettice, 118 ; Nicholas, 118
Arrivalde, John, 132 ; Capt. Morris, 132.
Ame^r, John, 31, 31 *n, bis* ; Roger, 31 *n*, 79 *passim*
Ashbrook, Mr. 83, 83 *n* ; John, 138 ; Rachel, 138
Ashton, Eleanor, 270 ; Joseph, 208 ; Margaret, 178 ; Sarah, 180, 266
Astle, Edward, 116 *bis*

Atton, Edward, 141 *bis*, 204, Elizabeth, 140, 141 ; Elena Whitleyde, 272 ; Mary, 69. 131, 137 *n*, 281 ; Randle. 131, 140, 205 ; Susanna, 141 ; Thomas, Sir Thomas, 69, 137 *n*, 187
Atherston, Sir William de, 79 *n*
Aubrey, Rev., 150 ; Thomas, 93
Axon, James, 208
Ayckbown, Rev. Fred., 200

Badde, John, 30
Baffarno, Jane, 110
Ba_oe, Joseph, 177, 207 ; William, 208
Bagorne, Ellinor, 141 ; Henry, 140, 141 ; Sarah, 140
Bagyley, Thomas, 107
Baker, John, 117 ; John Richard, 210 ; Thomas, 117
Ball, Catherine, 133, 135 ; Henry, 109 ; Margaret, 141 ; Mary, 109 ; Richard, 35 *bis* ; Roger, 133, 135, 141, 142 205 ; William, 202, 204
Barber, Archdeacon, 104 ; Joseph, 104
Bardon, William, 147
Barker, Mr., 139 ; Francis Edge. 57 *bis* ; Harriette, 57 *bis* ; Maria, 57 ; Mary, 56, 139 ; Richard, 36, 57 ; Sarah, 57
Barlow, Thomas, 23 *bis*, 23 *n*, 139, 205
Barnett, Elizabeth, 129 ; John, 129
Barnston, Rev. Roger, 95, 179
Barrat, James, 181
Barrow, Thomas, 203
Barthell, Alice, 265
Bartlett, Henry J., 103
Barton, Mary Lewis, 22
Basnett, Grace, 139 ; Richard, 139, 140 ; Thomas, 139
Bassano, Francis, 61 *n*
Bateman, Elizabeth, 71, 142
Batenham, G., 9 *n*
Bathers, Walter, 142
Batty, Jane, 56
Bavand, Alice, 39, 40, 118. 121, 122, 258, 260, 263, 264 ; Ellen, 110 ; Richard, 40, 118, 122, 205 ; Thomas, 118
Baxter, Katherine, 127 ; Thomas, 176 ; Sir William, 30

Bayne, James, 103
Beagham, Robert, 265
Beale, Bartholomew, 284, 285 ; Francis, 285 ; Thomas, 285
Beamont, William, 183
Beardsworth, John, 173
Beaufort, Cardinal. 16
Becket, Eleanor, 87 *n* ; George, 76, 81, 87 ; John, 138
Beech, Ellen, 28, 29 *bis* ; John, 28 *n*
Bellis, William, 142
Bellot, Ermyn, 270
Bennett, Ann, 131 *n* ; Dorothy, 131 *bis* ; Edward, 159 ; Elizabeth, 76 *n*, 131 *n* ; George, 131 *n* ; John, 131 *n*, 205 ; Henry, 148 ; Kendrick, 131 *n* ; Peter, 131 *n* ; Thomas. 131 *n*, 132, 180 ; Rev. William. 130
Berrie, Edward, 117 ; Elizabeth, 117
Bertington, Hannah. 115 ; Helen, 43 *bis* ; Hubbart, 118 ; Philippa, 68. 68 *n*. 276 ; Thomas, 68, 115, 118 ; William. 43 *bis*, 193
Betes, Thomas, 31 *passim*
Beverley, Francis. 69, 281 ; Sr George, 69 ; Mrs., 114 ; Beverley School, 91
Bickerstaffe, Basil. 118
Billet, Ermin. 272. 274 ; Jane, 136
Birch, Elizabeth, 286 ; Samuel. 286
Birchinshaw, Maurice, 79, 80
Bird, Amy, 275 ; John, 4. 80
Birkenhead, Adam. 60, 61, 122, 142. 192 ; Alice, 48. 60, 61, 141 ; Anne, 48, 134, 275 ; Elizabeth, 61. 69, 281 ; Henry, 61, 69, 116, 123. 127, 152, 154, 190 ; Joan, 61 ; John, 48, 61 *passim*, 80, 108 ; Katherine. 87 *n* ; Ralph, 113 ; Richard, 48 ; Thomas, 61 *bis*, 61 *n*, 87, 116, 124, 127, 142, 190
Birkett, Thomas, 113
Birtles. Ashton. 265
Blackmore, Henry J., 101
B'akestone, Walter. 90 *bis*
Bold, Anna Maria, 286 ; Margate 278 ; Mary, 286 ; Peter, 286 ; Thomas, 125
Bolland, Bryan, 205 ; Martha, 15. ; Thomas, 25 206 ; William, 209

P P

290   INDEX NOMINUM

Bolton W^m

Booth, Mr., 63, 122; Anthony, 29;
  Anne, 122, 429; Elizabeth, 117,
  129 n, 142; Sir George, 8; Jane,
  142; John, 108; Lawrence, 142,
  143; Mary, Lady, 108, 285;
  Nathaniel, 117, 129, 129 n;
  Thomas, 111, 114, 129 n
Bostock, Elizabeth, 272
Boswell, Samuel, 97, 98, 162
Boteler, Sir John, 184, 185
Boughton, Stephen, 175
Boulton, Anne, 87; William, 87
Bowen, Rev. C., 10, 11, 19, 102, 103, 201
Bowyer, Robert, 93; William, 193
Boyd, James, 123, 204
Bradburne, Amy, 139; Roger, 139
Bradburne, Nathaniel, 143
Bradbury, Richard, 111
Braderton, Henry, 134, 143; Mary, 143; Thomas, 134
Bradley, James, 142 bis
Bradshaw, 86, 87; Rev. — 96; Alice, 117; Anne, 117; Ellen, 140; John, 28, 29, 29 n, bis; Thomas, 140
Bramshall, John de, 282
Bramton, Frances, 72 n
Branshank, Mr., 5
Brasier Brooke, 140; Col. 140
Brassie, John, 116, 117; Katherine, 117; Melior, 116
Bratherton, Mr., 86
Brereton Family, 186-8; Will, 187; of Eccleston, 198
——, Mr., 82, 83, 112; Mrs., 112; Alice, 186; Cecily, 35 bis, 187; Elizabeth, 107; Francis, Lord, 93; Captain Henry, 125; Joan, 35 bis; John, 2, 80, 81, 188, 197, 198, 200; Katherine, 62, 62 n; Mary, 140; Owen, 187; Sir Randle, 35, 80, 81, 108, 186, 188; Richard, 82, 83, 88n, 140, 188; Thomas, 108, 112, 112n, 187, 188; Urian, 113, 188; Sir William, 62, 62 n, 80, 120, 120 n, 121, 125, 125 n, 182
Brerewood of Chester, 115; Alice, 107, 108, 257; Anne, 63, 63 n, 66, 67, 67 n, 108, 119, 119 n, 257; Charlotte, 181, 257; Christian, 180, 257; Christina, 257; Douse, 107; Edward, 62 n, 263; Elizabeth, 65, 111, 119, 257, 264, 280; Francis, 136, 257; Gravenor, 181, 257; James, 107, 108 bis; Jane, 107, 108, 119n, 257, 264; John, 66 bis, 110 bis, 115, 119 n, 136, 137, 181, 203, 257, 263, 264; Katherine, 66, 67, 141; Lettice, 257; Lucy, 107, 108; Mary, 265; Priscilla, 180; Richard, 107 bis, 108; Robert, 42,

45, 62, 63, 65, 66, 82, 107, 109, 115, 119, 123, 128, 144, 181, 203, 205, 257, 263, 264; Sidney, 137, 257; Thomas, 257
Bretherton, John, 87 n
Brett, Katherine, 273
Brettargh, Anne, 70 n; William, 70 n
Bridge, Basil, 118; Edward, 139 bis, 204; John, 130 n, 144, 178, 205; Margaret, 118; Martha, 130; Mary, 123, 139; Randle, 118; Richard, 112, 114, 130, 130 n; William, 130 n
Bridgeman, Bishop, 76, 77, 85; Lydia, 76
Bridges, Thomas, 83 n
Briscoe, Thomas, 37, 120
Brittain, Samuel, 208
Brock, Anne, 49, 64, 64 n, 65 bis; Barbara, 115, 280; Edward, 49, 64, 64 n, 65 bis, 65 n, bis, 122, 122 n, 279, 280; Eleanor, 280; Elizabeth, 65, 65 n, 181, 279, 280; Francis, 87 n; Jane, 279; John, 87 n, 115, 122 n, 279, 280; Joseph, 280; Katherine, 65, 124 n, 279, 280; Margaret, 65, 280; Melior, 280; Parnel, 122 n; Randle, 65, 280; Robert, 122 n, 124 n, 203, 279, 280; Susannah, 49, 65, 65 n, 75, 75 n, 181, 280; Thomas, 65, 65 n, 282; William, 64 bis, 64 n, 65 n, 65 passim, 75 n, 75 ter, 115, 119, 122, 122 n, 279, 280
Brooke of Upton, 115; John, 179; William, 179
Brogden, William, 81, 82
Bromfield, Katherine, 141 n
Bromhall, Elizabeth, 96; Jane, 118
Bromley, Richard, 203
Brooke, Anne, 258; George, 173; Grace, 95, 133 n; Henry, 95, 133, 133 n; Major, 86; Sir Peter, 89; Pusey, 95, 134; Sir Richard, 133 n; Roger, 134; Sir Thomas, 95, 96, 133 n, 134 bis
Broome, Joan, 27, 119
Broughton, John, 108; Morgan, 35 bis
Brown, Amy, 276; John, 166, 207; Roger, 202, 220, William, 276; Rev. — 151
Browne of Netherleigh, 115; of Upton, 115; Mr., 128, 128 bis, 136 n; Mrs., 89, 113 bis; Alice, 69, 120 n, 276; Anne, 120 n, 276; Benjamin, 276; Charles, 276; Cicely, 69, 281; Dorothy, 69, 281; Eleanor, 276; Elizabeth, 48, 68, 68 n, 69, 120 n, 275, 276; Frances, 69; Francis, 69, 276, 281; George, 68 n, 68 ter, 120 n, 128, 276;

Griselli, 69 bis, 69 n, 281; Hannah, 68 bis, 68 n, 276; Sir Henry, 30, 81 bis, 108, 108 n, 135; Jane 276, 281; John, 157; Judith, 69; Julian, 113, 281; Katherine, 120 n, 276; Margaret 135, 276; Mary, 69 bis, 137 n, 276, 281; Matthew, 69 bis, 69 n, 114, 120, 120 n, 204, 205, 206, 276; Philippa, 68 ter, 68 n, 89, 130, 134, 137, 276; Richard, 68, 68 n, 69, 137, 203, 276, 281; Samuel, 68, 69 n, 276; Thomas, 48, 68, 68 n., 69, 81, 89 bis, 108, 110, 113, 114 bis, 120, 128 ter, 137, 190, 191, 202, 203, 205, 276, 281
Brownsham, William, 202
Urnes, Jonathan, 143; Mary, 118; Joseph, 118; Ralph, 137, 137 n
Bruerton, Thomas. 225
Bruyn, John, 27 bis
Buck, Margaret, 284
Buckley, Randle, 114, 118
Bullen, Hannah, 136; James, 136, 137
Bunbury, Henry, 180; Margery, 270, 272; Thomas, 180
Bunnell, Alice, 138; George, 139
Burchenhead, Elizabeth, 109
Burches, Ann, 91; Hugh, 91 passim, 91 n; Margaret, 91 n; Mary, 91 bis, 91 n; Thomas, 91 bis
Burganey (Purgeny), Rachael, 135, 135 n, 141; William, 135, 135 n, 141
Burgh, Joan, 117; Theobald, 117
Burghall, Edward, 90
Burkin, John, 207
Burroughes, Robert, 121
Barrowes, Ambrous, 144 n; Ann, 144 n; Edward, 144, 144 n, 136, 205; Elizabeth, 135, 144 n; Henry, 144 n; Holme, 167, 168; Robert, 128; Mary, 144; Robert, 204; Thomas, 144 n
Burton, Sir Edmund, 30, 81
Bury, Richard de, 77 bis, 77 n
Byrom, Mr., 86; John, 108, 110; Richard, 293; Robert 124
Byron, Bridget, 124
Byvynton (Bebington?), Thomas de, 78 bis

Cadle, Robert, 82
Calcott, Jane, 118; John, 204; Robert, 82, 180; William, 123
Calcott (Caleocke) Mr., 138
Calday, John, 202, 217
Caldy, Margaret 46, 47 n; Richard, 46, 47
Caleveley, Hugh de, 27, 123
Campbell, Capt. Duncan, 152

Canterbury, William, Archbishop of, 93
Caper (Capper), John, 143, 144; Ursula, 143, 144
Caponhurst, Thomas de, 78 *bis*
Capper, John, 144; Ursula, 144
Card n, Thomas, 205
Cardine (Cardin) Robert, 113 *bis*
Carlyle, William Currie, 49
Carrey, Elizabeth, 117; James, 117
Carter, John, 124, 124 *n*. 125
Cartwright, Anne, 93; Elizabeth, 42, 42 *n*, 93, 93 *bis*, 94; Frances, 93. Grace, 93, 94; John, 92, 92 *n*, 93 *ter*, 94, 151; Lettis, 133; Richard, 133; Sarah, 93, 199; Thomas, 93
Case, Elizabeth, 258, 259, 263; Thomas, 42, 42 *n*
Casteene, Mr., 125
Catherall, Modlan⁹. 141; Robert, 141
Caurden (Cawerden), Sir Thomas, 81 *ter*
Cave, Amy or Almira, 283; Sir Thomas, 283
Cawdey, John, 202; Richard. 202
Cawley, Thomas, 173
Challenor, Mary, 118
Challiner, Mr., 8 Chadock 232.
Challoner, Roger, 187; William, 182
Chalouer, Elizabeth, 46, 47 *n*, 74; Thomas, 34, 46, 47 *n*, 74. 292
Chamberlain, George, 26 *n*, 128, 137, 137 *n*, 204; Sarah, 137 *n* Ruth xii.
Chambers, Calcott, 116; Jane, 116
Chancller, Charles, 134; Tim thy, 134
Chapman, Edm. 50; Robert, 124
Charnocke, Cécille, 180
Chaville, Rev. H. H. G. de, 103
Cheshire, Captain, 127, 137 *n*; John, 127 *n*
Chester, Bishop of, Francis, 93; John, 83, 83 *n*
Chetwynd, Mary, 89
Chisenhall (Chisnall), Oliver, 125
Chitwood, Lady, 121; Dame Dorothy, 121
Cholmondeley, Charles, 171; Earl of, 74
Clarke, John, 132, 203; Mary, 132
Clegg, William, 22   Elen 229
Clitie, Hugh, 108; Jane, 108; Robert, 79
Clipston, Robert de, 77
Clive, Catherine, 90; Thomas, 90
Clivery or Cilbbery, William, 24 *bis*, 25
Clubbe, Henry 173, 176
Clutton, James, 207
Coke (Cook), Eleanor, 283
Cole, Humphrey, 87; Martha, 87; Susan, 281

Colley, John, 206
Collier, Mr., 121; Elizabeth, 82; Jane, 82 *bis*, 83 *ter*; Katherine, 82; Robert, 82, 83, 109, 110 *bis*
Colly, Richard, 81
Collyer, Jane, 197; Robert, 197
Colthurst, Thomas, 137, 204
Comberbach, Ann, 135; Eltinor, 135; James, 135
Congleton, 24, 24 *n*
Coniley, Jane, 118; Luke, 118
Connah, William, 205
Conway, Jane, 64; Juho, 64
Cook, To ias, 206
Cooke, Mrs., 84 *bis*; Ann, 130 *n*; Edward, 130 *bis*, 130 *n*, 141, 143, 205; Elizabeth. 84; Hugh, 130 *n*; John, 63, 84, 114, 203, 206; Joseph. 130 *n*; Kath., 127, 127 *n*; William, 130 *n*
Cookes, Ann, 284; Henry, 284
Coole, Major, 129, 129 *n*
Curnish, Miss, 287
Cotgreve, Elizabeth, 52, 52 *n*; Jane, 279; John, 32, 33, 52, 52 *n*, 147, 205, 206; Thomas, 175; William. 260
Coton, Richard de, 77 *bi*
Cottingham, Charles, 206 John 275
Cotton, Jane, 127; John, 114; Peter, 54, 198
Coulson, Daniel, 205
Coulthurst, Thomas, 128
Courthope, James, 81
Coventry, John, 67, 67 *n*, 129; William, 67, 67 *n*, 129
Cowper, Edward, 180; Elizabeth, 28; John, 203; Julia, 48; Thomas, 48; William, 48, 200
Crane, Thomas, 208 93
Crawfo d, Mary, 116; John, 116
Crewe, John, 96; Julian, 275
Critchley, Thomas, 281
Crockson, James, 142; Jane, 142
Croket, Robert, 202
Crompton, Edward, 142
Crupley, Grace, 139
Crosby, Capt. Charles, 178; Katherine, 178; Col., 164, 165
Cross, William, 173, 208
———, 83, Mrs., 127; Frances, 99
Croise, Jane, 83; John, 83, 120; Katherine, 27, 119; Richard. 82, 99; Robert, 202; William, 203
Croughton, Mrs., 113
Crowton, Margaret de, 273
Croxton, Col., 8 *bis*; Dorothy, 131 *n*; Hannah, 179; James, 131, 131 *n*, 179; John, 131; Mary, 44; Col. Thomas, 44   tgo.
Cuilam, Esther, 142; William, 129

Culme, Rev. Ben., 151
Cumberbatch, Roger, 159; *see* Comberbach
Cuming, Joshua, 207; Thomas, 169
Cummin, Rev. Joseph King, 103
Cundeth, Mr., 117; Francis, 117
Currey, Captain, 132; Meruin, 132
———, *see* Keyrey
Currie, Dr., 10; Anna Maria, 50; Edward (Lieut.-Col.), 50; Elizabeth, 49, 269; Esther, 269; Jane, 49, 181, 269; John Robert, 50; Mary, 49, 50 *bis*; Mary Catherine, 181, 269; Robert Foulkes, 179, 269; Susan, 50; William, 49 *bis*, 50 *bis*, 179, 181, 268, 269
Curson, Capt. Matthew, 123
Custance, Rev. F., 203

Dalby, Edward, 204
Dalton, Sergeant, 124; Thomas. 124
Danald, Christopher, 120; Elizabeth 120
Danald, Ellen Mrs., 197
Dane, Thomas, 181
Dannald, Elbn, 113; Samuel, 205
Dannalde, Mr., 112; Sir Robert, 187
Dannatt, John, 132; Martha, 132; Mary, 132; Moses, 132, 203
Danniell, Dorothie, 178
Dannot, Thomas, 203
Darby, Archdeacon, 123
Darwall, Henry, 123   Derwall .123.
Darwell, Henry, 204
Davenport, Mr., 112, 143; Humphrey. 189; John, 31, 82, 111, 118; Mary, 118; Roger, 113; William. 189
Davies, Charles, 208; David, D.D., 101; Edward, 95; John, 204, 207; Peter of the Grove, 159; Randle, 204; Robert, 203; S., 59; T., Rev., 162
Davis, Mr., 136; Elizabeth, 135; Hugh, 135; John, 206; Mary, 130; Thomas, 134
Dawbe, Richard. 202
Dawson, Perry, 207; William, 55
Daye, William, 124
Dedwood, Cicely, 30; Joan, 30; Thomas, 30
Delves, William, 181
Denman, Mr., 128
Dennis, John, 55; John Dewsbury. 55; Leticia, 55
Denson, Richard, 207; Thomas, 67
Denton, Alex., M.D., 102, 169. 176; Ann. 169; Arthur, 164; Samuel, 103

INDEX NOMINUM.

Derby, Earl of, 36, 67; Thomas, Earl of, 60
Devenett, Elizabeth, 46, 47; John, 46, 47
Dewsbury, Peter, Ald., 165, 168; John, 133, 140, 205; Leticia, 55; Mary, 133; Martha, 133; Peter, 55, 138, 205; Percival, 140; Richard, 55, 133
Dicas, Catherine, 142, 198, 200; Dove, 76; John, 198, 200; Joyce, 139; Randle, 139, 140, 204; Robert, 76; William, 139, 140, 204 *Saml* &c.
Dickisson, Jane, 140; John, 140
Dikus (Dicas), John, 203
Dio, Ellis ap, 275
Dix, William, 176
Dobb, —, 60; Grissell, 69, 281
Dobson, Mr., 140; Mrs., 140
Dockerill, Rev., 150
Dod, Barbara, 277; Margery, 277
Dodd, Elizabeth, 47, 136; Hugh, 114
John. 227; Thomas, 47, 136
Dodde, David, 187
Doncaster, Mr., 113
Done, Charles, 144; Hugh, 144; Maria de Vikinton, 273; Mary, 72, 73; William, 72. 73, 144, 177
Doone, Thomas Sir, 187
Donnough, Par, 178
Downeham, Ralph, 182
Ducker, Edw., 208, 209
Duckworth, Charles, 81, 82, 156; George, 82
Duke, Andrew, 93, 133, 156, 206; Bartholomew, 156, 206; Barth., Silversmith, 147; Eleanor, 133; Rebecca, 133, 142; Thomas, 133. 142; Thomas, Ald., 163, 205, 206; — Rev. 161 *Richardson*.
Dunbabin, Richard, 128, 256
Dunn, James, 166
Durham, Bishop of, 77
Dutton, Elizabeth, 274, 276; John, 206; Mary, 275

Eanswoth, John, 123
Earl (e), William, 207
Eaton, 14; *see* Eyton
—, Ann, 97; Elizabeth, 131 *n*, 138, 179; Joseph, 96, 97
— —, 162, 178
—, Kendrick, 138, 179; Mary, 131, 166, 180
— , Samuel, 131, 131 *n*, 205; Thomas, 10, 100 *ter*, 131 *n*
—, William, 97
Eaves, Lieut. Christian, 124
Eccles, Sophia, 56; W. 56

Eccleston, Mr., 121; John, 122, 122 *n*, 204; Magdalen, 137; Richard, 137
Edge, Catherine, 130; George, 130; Robert, 178
Edgley, Rev. Samuel, 89 *ter*
Edwards, Mr., of Cheveley, 197
—, Alice, 139; Ann, 83, 84 *bis*, 84 *n*, 179
—, Andrew, 84; Elizabeth 84 *ter*, 85, 265; Francis, 83, 84, 84 *n*, 85 *ter*, 87, 90 *n*, 116 *bis*, 123, 123 *n* 127; John, 30, 84 *ter*, 84 *n*, 123; Peter, 84; Richard, 207; Theodor, 84; Thomas, 84, 84 *n*, 130; William, 84
Egan, Mary, 51
Egerton, John, 49, 119 *n*, 121 *n*, 181, 280; Katherine, 119 *n*, 121 *n*; Peter, 121; Rev. Philip, 89, 181; Thomas, 121
Ellington, William, 174
Elliott, Mr., 124; John, 124
Ellis, Mr., 29 *bis*, 120; Mrs., 109 *n*, of Chester, 115; Agnes, 107; Alice, 39 *bis*, 48 *bis*; Amy, 114, 275; Anne, 111, 134, 275; Catherine, 47, 47 *n*, 111; Christopher, 107; Edward, 172; Elizabeth, 29 48 *bis*, 109; Henry, 275; Joseph, 275; Julian, 48, 275; Katherine, 48, 63, 115, 120 *n*; Mary, 108; Margery, 48; Matthew, 25, 30, 39, 47, 47 *n*, 48, 63, 109, 111 *bis*, 113, 114. 115, 120 *n*, 134, 203, 204, 275; Randle, 275; Saral, 275; William, 172, 275
Elton, Mary, 267
Enedon, Johana, 262 *Anne uo.*
Evans, de Harden, Alicia, 272; Elizabeth, 139; Griffith ap, 123; John, 206; Thomas, 207
Evanson, Alice, 270
Evers, Ann, 50; James, 50 *ter*; Peter, 50 *bis*, 208; Thomas Baxter, 50
Eyre, Johanna, 262
Eyton, Madam, 138, 138 *n*; Ann, 131; Charles, 54 *ter*
—, Eleanor, 130; Elizabeth, 132, 133, 138 *n*; Ellinor, 132; Gerard, 132; Jane, 54; Kendrick, 130, 130 *n*, 131 *n*, 132, 133; Sir Kenrick, 138, 138 *n*; Mary, 54 *bis*; Rebecca, 138 *n*; William, 132
see. 139.

Fairclough, Geo., 176
Fallowes, Anna, or Hannah, 266; John, 266; Mr., 112
Farrar, Dorothy, 139

Farrar, Eleanor, 132; Ellinor, 144; John, 132, 134, 140, 144; Margaret, 132; Peter, 132, 134; Roger, 132, 141; William, 132
Farquhar, Charles, 55
Farrington, Randle, 141; Robert, 141
Faulkner, Richard Sir, 81
Fawcett, Catherine, 51; John, 141; Mary, 135; P. Rev., 51, 99, 174, 177; Stephen Henry, LL.D., 51; S., 174-7
Fearnall, John, 207
Fell, Thomas, 28
Felton, Thos., 284
Fereday, Mr, 18, 23; Mrs., 18, 23
Fernahaugh, Andrew, 140
Fernihough, Andrew, 205
Ffoulkes, Susanna, 49, 181, 268; Thomas, 130, 181, 268; Wm., of Chester, 208; William, 130, 268; Watkin, 268
Finchett, Daniel, 29; Ralph, 2)
Findlow, Cicely, 197
Findlowe, Thomas, 203
Finlow, George, 141, 142
Fish, Joseph, Rev., 99; John, Rev., 99; William, Rev., 99, 174
Fitton, Elizabeth, 118; Ellinor, 118
Fleck, James, 206
Fleetwood, Mr., 86, 87; Robert, 133; Thomas, 133
Fletcher, Charles, 117, 138; James, 110, 203; J., 99; John, 25, 204; Lawrence, 110, 137, 204; Peter, 202; Philip Henry, 209; Richard, 114, 120, 203; —, 124; Thomas, 125; William, 203
Flultt, Joseph, 158
Fogg, Robert, Rev., 150
Forcett, Elias, 133; John, 133
Ford, Harry, 53; Randle, 53; Knowles, 53; Lieut.-Col. John, 53; F., Rev., 53; Robert, 24
Forton, co. Salop, minister, 47
Foulkes, Barth'us, 272; Betty, 57; *See* Catherine, 268; Charles, 130, 268; Edward, 130, 268; George, 130, 268; Gertrude, 130, 135, 268; Henry, 268; Hugh, 130, 181, 268; John, 130, 268; Jones, 272; Mary, 50, 130, 268, 269; Owen, 57; Peter, DD., 30, 131, 132, 199, 268; Rebecca, at 8; Richard, 130, 132, 268; Robert, 49, 50, 130, 131, 132, 135, 181, 206, 268 *arms 57.*
Fox, Anne, 259; Ann, 135; William, 135
Framwall, William, 124
Francis, 180
Franckland, Thomas, 121
Frankland, —, 123

INDEX NOMINUM. 293

Frodsham, Catherine, 181; Vicar of, 97; Wm., 185
Frost, Charles Albert, 18; Lady, 18; Sir T. G., 18
Fryer, Edward, 117; Elizabeth, 117

Gaddes, Saml., 161
Gaman, or Gamon, Charles, 208; William, 207
Gammull, Alex., 179, 180
Gamul, of Chester, 113; Adam, 261; Alice, 39, 41, 121, 122, 260, 263; Amy, 259; Charles, 208; Christian, 122, 260, 263; Edmund, 40, 42, 58, 63, 110, 113, 259, 260, 263; Edward, 264; Elizabeth, 42, 177, 259, 260, 263, 279; Frances, 111, 260, 264; Francis, Col. Sir, 39, 40, 41, 44, 114, 115, 120, 121, 122, 124, 128, 137, 180, 260, 263; Hugh, 258, 259, 263; Joan, 262; Joseph, 263; Katherine, 120, 260; Lady, 128; Lettice, 115, 118, 260, 264; Margaret, 134, 258, 262; Mary, 134; Richard, 40, 258, 260, 261, 262; Robert, 259, 263; Stephen, 258, 261; Sydney, 114, 257, 260, 264; Thos. Capt., 9, 39, 40, 41, 42, 43, 110, 111, 121, 122, 123, 179, 180, 197, 258, 259, 260, 262, 263, 264; William, 42, 133, 134, 179, 208, 258, 259, 260, 261, 262, 263
Gamull, Anne (or Anna), 133, 259, 260, 263, 279; Edtha, 258, 261; Edward, 260; Ellenor, 63, 121, 179, 260, 263; John, 209, 258, 259; Phlippa, 258, 262
Gamwall, Christian Alice, 180
Ganley, M., 138
Gardiner, Sister, 284
Gardner, Alicia, 283, 284; Charles, 133, 134; John, 133; Thomas, 131, 133; William Albert, 134, 209
Garnor, Mr., 121
Garratt, John, 208; Samuel, 155, 206
Gascoigne, —, 284
Gastrell, Francis, 97
Gathercoale, John, 120
Gee, Edmund, 80
George, Avise, 279
Gerard, Anne, 70, 131, 177; Charles, 142; Gilbert, 70; (Gerharde) Hannah, 143; Margaret, 142; Peter, Sir, 27; Peter, Dr., 131, 138; Peter, 60, 70, 138; Richard, 27; Stephen, 70; Susan (or Susannah), 70; Thomas, 27, 143
Gerrons, Randle, 2
Getten, Richard, 202, 222, 223

Gibbons, Catherine, 135; Thomas, 205
Gibson, Eliza Maria, 56; Wm. Rev., 56
Gilbert, Elizabeth, 121; Leonard, 209
Gill, Mr., 82, 83, 106; Thomas, 134; John, 83, 85
Glasier, Elizabeth, 278; Margaret, 278; Margery, 278
Gleave, Mr, 138; John, 139, 179; Margaret, 138; Mathew, 121
Glegg, Betty Baskerville, 51, 177; Cicely, 69, 281; John, of Irbie, 51, 160, 176; Margaret, 277; William, 277
Glover, George, 99; William, 167
Glynne, Stephen, Sir, 9
Godfrey, Martha Maria, 257
Godsendus, Elizabeth, 119
Godwin, William, 99, 100
Golborne, Richard, 29
Goodman, Elizabeth, 42; Margaret, 81; Ursula, 81; William, 42
Gordon, Francis, Sir, 286; Lewis, 286
Gough, Edward, 134, 143; Mary, 134, 143; Richard, 206
Grange, Ralph, 110
Granger, Francis, 140
Grantham, H. D., Rev., 103; Henry, 103, 104
Granwall, John, 106; William, 119
Grappenhall, Rector of, 86, 87
Gray, Albin, 205
Greaves, Rev. James, 103
Gredge, Ellinor, 127
Gregge, Edward, 65, 117; Elizabeth, 117; Katharine, 65, 124, 280; Pollixina, 124; Robert, 117; Thomas, 124
Gregory, —, 122; Anne, 122; John, 82, 203
Grenwall, Widow, 83
Greves, Rev. Mr., 161
Grey, of Codnor, Henry Law, 184; John, 125, 138; Katherine, 275; Thomas, 125
Grice, Jane, 118; John, 123, 204; Roger, 203
Griffeth, Peerse, 143, 144; Thomas, 17, 125, 143, 144, 207
Griffith, Mr. 113; Dio ap, 275; George, 205; Giles Richard, 17, 209; Helen, 43; John, 197, 207
Griffiths, Thomas Williams, 210
Grimsditch (Grymdyche), Christian, 107
Grindley, John, 26, 207
Grosvenor, Anne, 270; Catherine, 283; Christian, 122, 263; Earl, 2; Juliana, 272; Margaret, 135; Sir

Richard, 122; Richard, 38, 99, 125, 128, 204, 205; Robert, Earl, 99; Sybil, 38; Sir Thomas, 125, 283; Christiana, 263
Grove, James, 103
Grubb, Mr., 128
Gryce, Roger, 105
Grymdyche, Edward, 107; William, 107
Gryse, Robert, 202
Gryzell, John, 140
Gubian, Audrey, 275
Gusty, John, 162
Guy, Gerard, 95

Haddock, William, 208
Hall, Sarah, 132, 139
——, Capt., 154
——, Mrs., 132, 139
——, Hen., Att. Gen. for County, 175
Hale, Ann, 131 n, Frances, Mary, Jane, 131
——, Jonathan, 131; Samuel, John, 131 n
——, Edman., 131 n, ter
——, Robert, 131
Halwood, Edward, 180
Hallwood, James, 124
Hilton, Elizabeth, 122
——, William, 122
Hamilton, William, 162
Hamnet, Dabb, 169
——, Mr., 109; Matthew, 109
——, William, 43 bis, 193; Helen, 43 bis, 193
Hasbridge, 231
Hand, Mrs., 84 n
Handford, Jane, 285; Dorothy, 284
Handley, Thomas, 141; Benjamin, 144
Hanmer, Thomas, 119 n
Harding. William, 27; Mr. 129
Hardware, Henry, 286; John, Samuel, 286
Harefinch, Robert, 141
Hargreaves, James, 53
Harlton, Anne, 177
Harper, Mr., 26
Harper, Benjamin, 47; Katherine, 47
Harris, Mary, 130; Mr., 130
Harrison, Rev. Thos., 200; Charity, 200
Harrison, James, 11; Mrs., 140; Matthew, 209
Harrison's regt., Col., 146
Hartley, Richard, 281
Harvey, Robert, 107; Wm., 205, 286

INDEX NOMINUM.

Harvey, Katherine, 281 ; Maria, 286 ; Robert, 202
——, Eleanor, 121 *n*, *bis*; Thomas, 121 *n*, *bis*
Harwood, Simon, 179 ; Rev. E. 179
Haslehurst, Letitia, 167
Haslewa'l, John, 136
Hassall, John, 53 ; Margaret, 53
Hassellwall, Richard, 106, 503
Hastings, George, 58 ; Mary, 58
Haswell, —, 280
Hatton, Richard, 27, 132, 140 *bis*; Ralph, 132, 140 ; Katherine de, 27 ; Thomas, 140
Hawarden Castle, 8, 9 ; Rector of, 67, 79
Hayward, George, 206 ; James, 207
Heald, James, 132 ; Thomas, 132
Heald, —, 124 ; *ee* Veable
Helley, Thomas, 142 ; William, 205
Henchman, Rev. Chas, 150 ; Humphrey, 97
Henry, Philip, 90
Henshall, Richard, M.A., 96, 97 *passim*, 97 *n*
——, Anne, 97 *bis*; John, 97 *bis*
Herbert, Dorothy, 133 ; Edward, 135 ; Mary, 285
Hereford, Philip, Bishop of, 93 ; Earl of, 48
Hewson, Samuel, 133, 133 *n*; Dorothy, 133 *n*
——, Hester, 142 ; Roger, 133 ; Samuel, 142
——, Rev. John Fitzgerald, 101, 103
Heyward, Thos. 202
Hickes, James, 114
Hicklin, John, 200
Hickock, Ann, 134 ; George, 141 *bis*; Thomas, 134
Hide, Robt., of Catnell (Catenhall), 149
Hignett, Thomas, 116 ; William, 116
——, Mr., 114 ; Elizabeth, 116
Hill, Brian, 98 ; Elizabeth, 75, 98 *n*; Elizabeth Ann, 75, 98 *n*; Emma, 98 ; Emma Jane Barbara, 75 *bis*; Frances Emily, 98 *n*; General, Lord, G.C.B., 50 ; Henrietta Amelia, 22 ; Harriet, 99 ; John, 22, 27, 48 *bis*, 75 75 *n*, 98, 98 *n*, *bis*, 171 ; Mary, 96, 98 *bis* ; Mary Anne, 98 *n* ; Mary Meeke, 98 *n* ; Margaret, 98 ; Richard, 89, 98, 127 ; Rev. Robert, 2, 96 ; Robert Wilbraham, 75 ; Robert Wilbraham Bromhall, 98, 99 ; Robert, LL.D., 97, 98 *ter*, 98 *n*, 99 *ter* ; Sir Rowland, 97 ; Rowland, M.A., 98, 98 *n*, 99, 99 *bis*; Samuel, 173, 98 ; Susanna, 48 ;

Thomas Wilkinson, 22, 98, 98 *n*; Thomas, 98 ; William, Rev., 173 ; William, 98 Hincks 169.
Hinchman, Rev. — 161
Hockenhull, Joseph, 65, 75 ; Susanna, 65, 75, 280
Hodgkin, Charles, 206
Hodgkis, Thomas, 204
Hodson, George, 207
Hoghe (Hough), Thomas, 185
Holcroft (Houcraft), Henry, 137
——, Jane, 274 ; Millinton, 137
——, Ursula, 123
Holford, Allen, 159
Holland Elizabeth, 90 ; Henry, Earl of, 285 ; Wm 203
Hollinshead, Ralph, 124, 140
Holme, Alderman, 114 ; Alice, 63 ; Amy, 63 ; Anne, 288
——, Arms of, 1 ; Catherine, 47, 47 *n*
——, of Chester, 115 ; E'izabeth, 46 *bis*, 47 *bis*, 47 *n ter*, 63 *bis*, 74, 114, 136, 180, 288 *ter*
Holme, Helen, 63 ; Jane, 47 *n* ; John, 46, 47 *n*, 288 ; Katherine, 47 *passim*, 48, 63 *bis*, 115, 275, 288 ; Matilda, 46, 47 *n* ; Margaret, 46, 47, 47 *n*, 288 ; Mr., 6, 124 ; Rachel, 47, 135, 135 *n* ; Ralph, 47, 63, 288 ; Randle, 6, 7, 7 *n*, 19, 20, 20 *n*, 23, 25 *bis*, 26, 34, 31 *n*, 36, 37 *n*, 38, 46 *passim*, 46 *n*, 47 *passim*, 50, 60, 60 *n*, 61 *n*, 62, 63 *bis*, 66, 66 *n*, 74 *ter*, 74 *n*, 77 *bis*, 88, 101, 105, 106 *ter*, 107, 109, 109 *n*, 111 *bis*, 111 *n*, 114 *bis*, 115 *bis*, 116 *n*, 119 *n*, 120, 120 *n*, 128 *bis*, 135 *n*, 136 *bis*, 136 *n*, *bis*, 142, 142 *n*, 180, 198, 203, 204, 288 ; Richard, 194, 121, 288 ; Robert, 32, 46 *bis*, 47 *n ter*; Sarah, 47 *ter*, 288 ; Thomas, 46 *bis*, 47 *n bis*, 288 ; William, 46 *bis*, 47, 47 *n bis*, 63, 74, 74 *n*, 114, 179, 288
Holmes, John Goodie, 210
Holt, 24, 24 *n* ; John, 202 ; Mr , 130 ; Sarah, 130
Holywell, 20
Hopley, Sophia, 257
Horton, Elizabeth, 71 ; Walter, 71 ; William, 110, 112, 204, 231.
Hough in Wybunbury, 2 ; Rd. of Leighton, 185 ; Anne, 130 ; Gilbert, 138 ; Josiah, 139 ; Margaret, 185 ; Mrs., 139 ; Thomas, 130
Houghton, John, 82 ; Wm., 202, 220, 221
House of Industry, 170
Houseman, John, 71, 71 *n*, 142
Howard, Joseph, 207

Howerd, Dorothy, 140 ; Mr., 140
Hue, Alexander, 128
Hughes, Anne, 178 ; Catherine, 143 ; James, 20 ; Peter, 97 ; Thomas, 177
Hulse, Thomas, 183 ; Margary, 183
Hulton, Elizabeth, 48 ; William, 48 ; W. P., 201
Humberston, Catherine Maria, 56 *bis*; Catherine, 56 ; Frances, 56 ; Hester, 56 ; Mary, 56 ; Philip, 56 *bis* ; Sophia, 56
Humfreys, Samuel, 178 ; Thomas, 128
Hunt, — 287 ; Anne, 87, 284, 286 ; Anthony, 284 ; Wm. Cartred de Uttoxeter, 282 ; Dorcas, 285 ; Elizabeth, 38, 39, 135, 285, 286 ; Ellinor, 118 ; Edmund, 282 ; Edward, 284, 285, 287 ; family, 115 ; Frances, 285, 286 ; George (De), 283, 286 ; Grace, 87, 89 ; James, 285 ; Sir John, 39 *bis* ; John Le, 282 ; John, 283, 285 ; Mr. Rev., 87, 89, 179 ; Mr. 123 *bis*, 123 *n* ; Maria Anna, 286 ; Mary, 285, 286 ; Mary Vere, 286 ; Martha, 87 ; Matilda Le, 282 ; Nicholas Le, 282 : R. 39 *bis*; Randle, 38, 39, 125 ; Richard, B.D., 87, 88 *n*, 88 *passim*, 89 *n*, 89 *passim*, 136, 136 *n*, 283, 285 ; Robert, 283 ; Roger, 283 ; Rowland, 283, 284, 285, 286, 287
Hunt, Sarah, 284, 287 ; Thomas, 118, 283, 284, 285, 286, 287 ; Tho. Le (of Stone Dawberry), 282 ; Wm. Le, of Uttoxeter, 282 ; William, 87
Huntington, Anne, 55 ; Isaac, 55 ; Theophilus, Earl of, 93
Hurleston, Elizabeth, 280 ; Isabell, Mrs., 197 ; Isabel, 122 ; James, 118 ; Katherine, 62, 62 *n* ; Lettice, 118 ; Rebecca, 111 ; Roger, 4, 62, 62 *n* ; William, 181, 203
Hutchinson, W., M.A., 100
Hutton, Ellen, 58 ; W. P., Rev., 201 ; W. P., 58
Huxley, Alice, 60 *n*, 61 ; Elizabeth, 271 ; John, 60 *n*, 61

Ince, Elizabeth, 122 *n* ; Sarah, 137 ; Thomas, 120 *n* ; William, 137, 137 *n* ; William, Aldn., 180
Inesley, Ellin, 135 ; Francis, 135
Ithell, Thomas, 208 ; William, 206

Jackson, George, 205 ; Georgina, 9 ; Humphrey, 136 ; Rev., 161 ; Rev. Dr. Richard, 43, 44 ; Richard, 44 ; Stephen, 70 *bis*, 70 *n*; Susan, 70 *bis*, 70 *n* ; Thomas, 143, 205

INDEX NOMINUM.

Jacobson, Bishop, 11, 12
Jannion, Mr. 127
Jannyon, Elizabeth, 117; Richard, 117
Jekyll, Sir Joseph 32 n
Jenkin, Richard, ap 100
Jennings, William, 93, 206
Jennyns, Nicholas, 191
Jepson, Margaret, 76 n; Thomas, 76 n
John, Phipps, 199; Robert, 183, 258; James, 159
Johnes, Gerrard, 180
Johnson, Edward, 131 n, bis; Eleanor, 131 n; Ellinor, 135; James, 23, 27, 120; John, 27, 119, 125, 131 bis, 131 n, 138, 139, 142, 175, 205; Margaret, 131 n, 139; Mary, 118, 131 n; Mrs., 124; Richard, 118, 202; Thomas, 7 bis, 116 n, 131 n, 204; William, 131 n, 206, 209
Johnstone, Abraham, 138 n; Rebecca, 138 n
Jolliffe, William Davis, 210
Jones, Edward, 203; John, 97, 103, 141, 209; Mr., 136; Middleton, Rev., J.L.B., 52, 97 passim; Mary, 55; Richard 93, 136; Robert, 93, 205, 208; Roger, Rev., 151; Samuel, 208; Thomas, 55 bis, 140 ter; William, 97, 208; Walter, 110
Jordan, Abigail, 57; Elizabeth, 57; James. 57 bis; John, 207
Joyce, John, 87, 89; Alderman, 87; Grace, 87, 89
Joynson, Edward, 174; John, 205; Robert, 204; Tho., 181
Judson, Elizabeth, 111, 275

Kelly, Barbara, 58; Catherine Sarah, 58; Elizabeth Anole, 58; Peter Thomas, 58
Kelsall, Alice, 180, 181; Thomas, 157, 180, 181, 281
Kelshaw, Humphrey, 143; John, 144, 144 n, bis; Richard, 144
Kendrick, Ann, 135; Eaton, 179; William, 207
Kennion, Thomas, 133
Kethene, Mr., 112, 113
Kettell, Edward, 204; William, 202
Kettle, Mrs., 113; Thomas, 204
Key, Matthew, 129
Keyrey, Captain, 132; Elizabeth, 132
Kilmaeduagh, Ireland, Archdeacon of, 117 n
King Katherine, 278; Thomas, 123

Kirkes (Kirk), Elizabeth, 90 bis; Mr., 138, 138 n; Thomas, M.A., 90 passim; Thomas, 69, 69 n
Kirks, Catherine, 135; John, 90 n
Kinrey, Anne, 91 n
Knight, Margery, 275; Matthew, 123
Knott, Amy, 127
Kynaston, Arthur, 284; Edwd., 285; Margaret, 285
Kyrke, Richard, 85, 116 n

Lacerby, Thomas, 119
Lache, 11
Lacy, Mrs., 129; Sarah, 72, 73 n; Thomas, 72
Laine, John, 140
Lancaster, Rev. —, 151
Langford, John, 95; Mr., 24
Langley, Katherine, 109; Thomas, 80 bis
Larken, Margaret, 272
Laterwood, —, Rev., 150
Lathis, Sir Thomas, 218
Lathom, Richard, 27, 120
Laughill, Baron of, 93
Law, —, Rev., 151
Lawrenson, Lawrence, 57 ter; Martha, 57; Mary, 57; Priscilla, 57 bis
Lawton, John, 99
Lawton, Mary Anne, 99
Lay, Madam Sarah, 153
Lea, Katherina, 263
Leach, Ann, 55
Leather, John, 281
Leche, Joan, 34 bis; John, 34 bis
Lee, Elizabeth, 271; Katherine, 66, 67; Sir Richard, 66, 67; Robert de, 37
Leech, Mary, 109, 118
Leet, Charles, 209
Leftwich, Elizabeth, 43 bis; Robert, 43 bis
Leftwiche, Rev. T., 150
Leicester, Hannah, 68, 68 n; Richard, 68, 68 n
Leigh, E., 62; Eglanbie, 62; John, 138; Mr., 136; Mrs., 113; Ralph, 128, 138, 204, 205; Richard, 62; Thomas, 133 bis, 141 bis, 205
Legh (Leigh), Anne, 124, 277; Eleanor, 124 n; Edward, 124 n, 189; Mr., 124; Thomas, 124 n; Col. Thomas, 124
Lessals, Darcie, 137
Lester, Margaret, 131; Ralph, 131, 131 n, bis; Sarah, 131 n
Lether, Prudence, 192
Levesley, Charles, 68, 68 n; Hannah, 68, 68 n

Levinge, Anne, 132; Dorothy, 133; Richard, 132, 132 n, 133
Lewis, Ralph, 208
Ley, Sir Hugh, 81, 82; John, 86 n; Thomas, 128
Leycester, Hannah, 276; Sir Peter, 89
Lightfoot, Frances, 136; Mrs. 136
Linney, William, 208
Littler, Robert, 209
Liverpool, Margaret, 135
Lloyd, Ann, 139, 143; Alice, 117, 119, 119 n, 120 n, 121 n, 122 n, Archdeacon, 117, 117 n; Barnet, Capt., 143; David, 121 n, 122 n; Edward, 110; Elizabeth, 90; George, 119 n, 120 n; Griffith, 47; Helen, 110; John, 134, 144, 177; Jane (Loyde), 134; Jane, 177; Katherine, 270; Luetitia, 286; Mary or Margery, 110, 135, 135 n; Margaret, 47; Mrs., 127; Robert, 110; Roger, 117, 117 n; Salisbury, 144; William, 128
Loarde, Jane, 110
Locker, Catherine, 141; Nicholas, 205, 141
Lockel, Anne, 137; Francis, 137
Lodes, Cassandra, 271
Loe, Thomas, 204
Long, Sarah, 267
Longley, Ellen, 109; Rowland, 109
Lowe, John, 204
Lowndes, Richard. 140, 205
Lownes, Frances, 142; John, 142
Loyde, William, 205
Lutwyche, Sir Edward, 132 n; Edward, 131, 131 n; Katherine, 131
Lymme, Gilbert de, 46, 47 n; Matilda de, 46, 47 n; Peter de, 46, 47 n

Mackay, William, 177
Mackarness, Bishop, 104
Mackintosh, Peter, 181; Catherine, 181
Maddock, John, 203; Richard, 172, 207; Samuel, 93, 100
Maddocke, William, 180; Elizabeth, 180
Maddocks, John, 197
Madley, Richard de, 78 n
Mainwaring, Anna, 259, 263; Anne, 63, 66, 67, 67 n, 119 n, 258, 263, 280; Charles, 166-7; Edward, 117 n; Eleanor, 43 bis; Elizabeth, 67 n, 73 ter, 74, 135, 181, 266, 266; Hester, 117; James, 43 bis, 266; John, 73, 74 bis, 266; Johnson, 73 passim, 74, 135, 266; Lady Katherine, 62, 62 n, bis, 114 n;

INDEX NOMINUM.

Lady, 114, 122 *n*; Mr. 113; Sir Randle, 62, 62 *n*, 63, 66, 67, 67 *n*, 119 *n*; Thomas, 135; Thomasina, 274; Sir William, 117, 117 *n*.
Mainwaring, Madame Katherine, 197
Mallory, Dr. Thomas, 88 *n*, *bis*
Madley, John, 273
Man, Henry, D D., 80 *bis*, 81 *ter*
Mandley, Alice, 271; Anne, 271, 274; Elizabeth, 270, 271, 274; Ellena 274; George, 270, 271, 272, 274; Henry, 271, 273; Jacob, 274; John, 270, 271, 272, 274; Julian, 270, 272; Katherine, 271, 274; (Katerina) 272; Margaret, 270, 271; Mary, 271; Nicholas, 273; Richard (Sir), 270, 271, 272; Richard de, 273; Roger, 273; Thomas, 270, 271, 272, 273, 274; William, 270, 272
Manlegh, Thomas, 274
Manley of the Lache, 115
Manley, Ann, 110, 177; Dorothea, 274; Elizabeth, 118; George, 113, 115, 128 *n*, 203, 204; Jane, 274; John, 108, 205, 272, 274; Katherine, 115, 186; Kezia, 178; Margaret, 118; Maria, 274; Mary, 111; Mr., 112 *bis*, 129; Mrs., 113 *bis*; Nicholas, 274; Peerius, 273; Thomas, 118, 177, 177 *n*; William, 112 *n*, 187, 271, 274
Mapletoft, Rev. John, 151
Markham, Abraham, 91; Elizabeth, 92, 92 *n*; Rev. 151; Ralph, 92 *bis*; Ralph, M.A., 91 *bis*, 92 *passim*; Robert, D.D., 92 *ter*
Marsham, James, 209
Martin, Major Charles, 170
Martyn, Elizabeth, 47, 47 *n*; Samuel, 47, 47 *n*
Mason, Elizabeth, 116; Mr. 116; Robert, 133; Thomas, 133
Massey, Alicia, 273; Edward, 160, 168; Elizabeth, 120 *n*; Mrs., 113; Richard (of Moston), 208; Robert, 136; Thomas, 120 *n*; William de (of Rixton) 183; Joan, 183 LS1.
Massie, Rev. E., 102; Hester Lee, 101; Mr. 113; Peter, 206; Richard, 109; Richard, M.A., 100, 101, 102, 173; William Henry, 10, 11, 21, 33 *n*, 100, 100 *n*, 101, 102
Mather, Dorothy, 268
Mathers, Ellinor, 181
Mathewes, Edward, 121
Mathews, Elizabeth, 136, 136 *n*; Mr., 136
Mawdesley, Frances, 99; Frances Elizabeth, 51; Frances Elizabeth Matilda, 51, 99; Mary Ann, 22, 51,

99 *bis*, 100; Othuell, 22, 99, 100; Robert, 51, 99; Thomas, 22 *bis*, 99 *ter*, 100, 200
Maylis, Thomas, 202
McGregor, Alexander, 209
McHattie, John, 209
Meacock, —, 127
Meadowes, Mary, 74; Samuel, 74
Mellis, Capt. John, 176
Mellor, George, 171; John, 57 *passim*; Justina, 57; Thomas Shaw, 57
Mercer, Peter, 115; Thomas, 115
Meredith, Margaret, 274
Metcalfe, Mary, 121; Ralph, 121, 116
Meycock, Robert, 140
Michell, James, 128
Midealfe, William, 116
Miller, John, 174
Milner, Jacob, 107; James, 82 *bis*; Rev. James, 187; Mrs., 119; Thomas, 202
Milnes, William, 30
Milton, William, 93 *bis*, 206
Minshall, Edward, 209; Eliza., 258, 259, 263; George, 130 *bis*, 138; John 110, 130, 207; Mary, 130
Mitchell, James, 204
Mocatta, Major-General D., 210
Mohun, Anne, 64, 65, 279; Robert, 64, 65
Mohune, Anne, 49, Robert, 49
Mollineux, Margaret, 118
Moore, Lettice, 118
Moreton, Jane, 121, 121 *n*
Morgan, —, 122; Randle, 205; Thomas, 277
Morgell, Alice, 278; Anne, 277, 278; Cis'cy, 278; Edward, 277, 278; Elizabeth, 277, 278; Henry, 278; James, 277; Isabel, 278; John, 277, 278; Margaret, 278; Ma y, 277, 278; Philip, 278; Rafe, 277, 278; Randle, 277, 278; Richard, 278; Thomas, 277, 278; William, 277, 278
Morris, Henry, 125; Richard, 123; Roger, 204
Moscroft, Thomas, 109
Moss, Alice, 130; Edward, 53 *passim*, 208; Henry, 209; Lord, 130; Sarah, 53 *ter*; Thomas, 53; William, 53
Moston, Bishop, 76
Mouldsworthe, Katherine, 273
Moulson, Charles, 206
Moyle, Mary, 277
Muchell, Richard, 202, 221, 222, 223
Mullennex, Elisabeth, 142; Thomas, 142
Murcot, John, 86 *n*

Murray, Alexander Fereday, 18; Lieut.-Col., 18; Mrs., 18; Robert, 18
Mutchell, —, 124; Richard, 202, 204
Mylis, Thomas, 217
Myners, Margaret, 282
Myvod, (Myval), Henry, 137, 138 *n*; Margaret, 137 *n*, 138

Nanney, William, 176
Nash, Edward, 51; Richard, 51
Needham, Elizabeth, 140 *n*; Mrs., 140
Nelson, —, 56; Mary, 56; Rev. William, 56 178
Newcome, Henry, 89
Newell, Ann, 53; Emma, 53; Frances, 53; Harriett, 53; John, 53, 207, 176; Margaret, 53; Mary, 53; Mira, 53; Sarah, 53 *bis*; William, 53 *bis*, 208
Newlands, Thomas, 140
Newton, Jonathan, 132 *bis*; Guy de, 78
Nicholls, Dorothy, 133
Nichols, Elizabeth, 135
Nicholls, William, D.D., 88 *n*, 133, 205; Wm. Arthur Miller, 210
Nickson, Samuel, 23
Norbury, Elizabeth, 266
Norris, Anne, 70 *n*; Edward, M.D., 70 *n*, 153, 177; Edward, of Spike, 177
Noseworthy, Rd., paymaster in 50th Regiment, 171
Nuttall, Mr., 112

Oakes, Joseph, 209
O'Brien, Alicia, 58; Christopher James, 58
Oclegh (Okley, Okeleye), Richard de, 78
Ocley, Isabell, 258, 261
Offley, Hugh, 200
Oldfield, —, 193, 196; Eleanor, 43 *bis*; Ellen, 44; Elizabeth, 43 *n*, 43 *passim*; Helen, 43 *Assim*; Dame Katherine, 114, 119, 119 *n*; Leftwich, 21, 44 *bis*, 91 *n*; Letitia, 44; Mary, 43 *bis*, 44, 91 *n*; Margery, 43 *bis*; Michael, 43 *bis*; Mr., 114, 136; Philip, 9 *n*, 39, 42, 42 *n*, 43 *ter*, 44, 45, 110, 113, 193; Sir Philip, 114, 119 *n*; Thomas, 21 *passim*, 43 *bis*, 44, 196; Thomas Brame, 21 *bis*, 44 *bis*; William, 43 *bis*, 44 *bis*; William Lampton, 44
Oldford (Aldford), 14
Oliver, Alice, 178; Rev. John, 151

INDEX NOMINUM.

Orford, Mr., 61 *n*; William, 26, 207
Ormes, Mr., 61 *n*, 110, 203; Thomas, 197
Osboston, Anne, 28 *ter*, 29 *passim*; James, 28 *bis*
Othwell, Hugh, 192; Wm., 192; Anthony, 192; Katherine, 192; Edward, 192; Rose, 192; Avice, 192
Oxford, Bishop of, 93, 104
Oalton, Elizabeth, 259
Owen, Ann, 118, 284; Alice, 116; Anthony, 284; Catherine, 94; Sir Hugh, 94; Elizabeth, 116, 116 *bis*, 284; John, 116, 122; Margaret, 116; Thomas, 95 *n*, 121; William, 59, 118

Paget, Francis, 285; William, Lord, 285
Paggan, Catherine, 265
Palin, William, 208
Palm, Richard, 209
Palmer, John, 285; Sarah, 285; William,
Parker, Catherine, 130; Elizabeth, 130 *n*; George, 210; John, 76 *n*; Lydia, 76 *n*; Philippa, 68, 130 *n*, *bis*, 134; Richard, 68 *bis*, 68 *passim*, 130, 130 *n*, 134, 134 *n*, 139, 139 *n*; Thomas, 68 *n*, 139
Parnell, Alice, 69; Thomas, 69, 123
Parrey, Rev. T., 150
Parry, Elizabeth, 270, 272; Ellen, 118 *n*
Parsons, Capt. Richard, 147
Partington, Richard, 197, 204
Pasley, Christopher, D.D., 67 *bis*, 67 *n*, *bis*; Christopher, 66, 177, 181; Charles, 181; Margaret, 181
Paslew (Parsley), Christopher, D.D., 129, 129 *n*, *bis* *ave* 114
Pastmaker, Annes, 108
Patrhiche, Edward, Sir, 285; Edwd., 285; Elizabeth, 285
Patten, Thomas, 73 *n*
Patterson, Ellen, 117; Hannah, 117; John, 117 *bis*
Paynter, William, 109
Peake, Christian, 265; Frances, 73 *n*, 135; James, 135, 135 *n*, 143 *n*, 265; Rev. James, 73 *bis*, 73 *n*, *ter* William, 180
Pearson, Catherine, 56; Rev. George, 56
Peck, Hugh, 61; Lydia, 143; *see* Peake
Peores, Edward, 141; Lovett, 141
Pellen, Mr., 112

Pemberton, Joseph, 133; John, 133, 133 *n*; Margaret, 118, 137; Miles, 118, 204; Mr., 137; Thomas, 133 *n*
Pencell, Richard, 35 *bis*, 35 *n*
Pennant (Pennenti), George, 143
Pensall, Richard, 79 *n*, 79 *ter*
Perpoynte, Thomas, 187
Phillps, Margaret, 138
Phillipes, Lettice, 112
Phillips, Mr., 113; Mrs., 114
Phillpot, Rev. Nath., 161
Phipps, John, 199, Thomas, 140
Pickeren, Capt. John, 146
Pickering, Jane, 118; Thos., 118, 208
Pickmore, Ralph, 55, 205; Raph (ch'warden), 145; Sarah, 55
Pigot, John, 137; Mary, 137
Pike, Joan, 45, 46; John, 45, 46, 189, 192
Piankney, John, 107; Edward, 112 *n*
(Plangney) Edward, 107; Ellen, 107
(Planeney), Plankney, Mr, 112 *bis*, 113 *bis*
Piatt, Edward, 172
Plumbley, Thos., 207
Pole, Sir William, Kt., 185
Pool, William of Pool Hall, 151
Poole, Ann, 135 (Elen) Ellen, 258, 259, 263; Jane 47 *n*; Mrs., 127; Ralph, 135; Thomas, 47 *n*
Porter, Edward, 207
Pott, Barbara, 28; John, 28, 29
Potter, Abigail, 136; Joseph, 282; John, 136; Thomas, 141 *bis*; Mary, 141, Peter, 141, 157; William, 138, 205
Potts, Charles William, 209
Povey, Charles, 143; John, 143 *bis*; Mary, 143
Powell, Alice, 45 *bis*
(Powenall), Charles, 144
Powell, Dorothy, 119 *n*; Elinor, 119 *n*; Ed., 109; John, 119 *n*. *bis*: John, 144; Katherine, 119 *n*, 121, 121 *n*; Margaret, 119 *n*, *bis*; Mary, 109, Mr., 113 *bis*; Mrs., 113, 113 *n*; Richard 119 *n*; Roger, 119 *n*; Serjeant, 140; Sidney 119 *n*; Thos., 45 *bis*, 45 *n*, 82, 111, 113, 114, 119, 119 *n*, *bis*, 192, 203; Sir Thos. 113 *n*, *bis*, 119 *n*, *ter*, 121, 121 *n*; William, 46
Poyne, Capt 141
Presbury, John, 205
Prescot, George, 75 *ter*; Rev. J. 150; Thos., 167
Prescott, Arthur, 267; Anne, 267, 75 *bis*; Elizabeth, 267; Gregory, 75, 267; George, 162, 267; Sir George Wm. 267; Sir George Beeston, 267; Susanna, 75, 75 *n*,

267; Thomas, 75, 207; Wm. Willoughby, 207
Prestland, Elizabeth, 268
Priace, Ann, 142; Francis, 134 *b* 1, 136, 142, 143, 144; Jem'ma, 144, Martha, 136
Price, Charles, 23, 207; Francis, 93; Samuel 59, 206; William, 209
Prince, Rev. John, 96, 161
Probart, William, 171
Probert, Margaret, 135; Thomas, 135
Proby, William, 181
Proudlove Elizabeth, 87 *n*. *bis*; Robert, 87 *n*. *bis*; William, 59 *n*
Pugh, George, 209
Puleston, Edward, 119 *n*; Katherine, 119 *n*; Margaret, 119 *n*; Thomas 119 *n*
Pulford, Hester, 54
Pulford (Pulfenrth), Thomas, 138
Pulfari (Pulford), Thomas, 138, 178
Pullen, Robert, 181

Radford, Mr., 139; Samuel, 139
Radnor, Henry, Earl of, 285
Ralfe, Mr., 138
Randle, —, 186, 187; Will. 187
Ratcliffe, William, 173, 207
Rathbone, Catherine, 136; John, 139
Raven, Katherine, 141 *n*; William, 141, 141 *n*
Ravenscroft, Anne, 118; Elizabeth, 67 *n*; Frances, 92; George, 67, 67 *n*; Capt. George, 129; Philip, 67, 67 *n*, 124; Robert, 67 *passim*, 67 *n*, 125; Thomas, 92
Reade, Rev. George Edwin Pearsall, 103
Reading, —, 69 *n*; Mr. 121, 122 *bis*; Lawrence, 63, 63 *n*, *bis*, 114, 119, 119*n*, 122 *n*
Reddich (Wreddech), Elizabeth, 139; John, 136
Reece, Ran'lle, 205; Thomas, 132, 141, 205, 206; William, 132, 141
Retford, Alan de, 77, 78
Revington, William, 207
Rich, Frances, Lady, 285
Richardson, Alice, 118; David, 202; John (alias Barker), 203; John, 203; Mr. 86; Theophilus, 91
Richmond, Silvester, 95 *bis*
Ridgway, John, 207; William, 207
Rigby, Alexander, 130, 137, 139; Alexander, of the Burghe, 190; Alice, 137; Mrs. 139; Robert, 130 *n*; Thomas, 130
Roby, Mr., 129
Robartes (Rohartes), Vere Mary, 285; Russel, 285

Q Q

INDEX NOMINUM.

Roberts, Alice, 61; Edward, 208; Hugh, 93, 102, 103 *ter*, 206; Mary, 17 *n*; Robert, 17 *n bis*; Thomas, 61, 204, 207; Widow, 127, 136
Robotham, Elizabeth, 92 *n*
Robinson, Christopher, 116, 116 *n*; Colin, 55; John, 30, 116 *n*; Mr., 23; Samuel, 116; Thomas, 202; William, 204
Rocke, Elizabeth, 117; John, 117 *bis*; Mr. 117, 127
Rodley, Humphrey, 79 *n*
Roden, John, 141
Rogerson, Thomas, 82, 202
Rogers, Elizabeth, 135; Thomas, 135; *alias* Rogerson, Wm., 80 *bis*; Swarbrick, John, 208
Rolph, Elizabeth, 101
Rolingreve (Rosomgreve), Mr., 112
Romily, Sir Samuel, 72 *n*
Rowarth, Mark, 208
Rowland, Thomas, 205
Rowley, John, 205; Thomas, 206
Rowl'nson, Lawrence, 203
Rudhall, Charles, 26; John, 26
Russell, Jane, 284
Runrell, George, 204
Rusiall, —, 287
Rutter, —, 116; Anne, 116; Mr., 116; Sarah, 116

Sabine, Gererd, 287; Joseph, 287
Salisburie, Elizabeth, 63 *n*; Thomas, 63 *n*
Salisbury, Alice, 117; Elizabeth, 116, 122; Sir Herry, 114, 119 *n*; Jane, 64; 64 *n*; John, 117; Lady, 120; Mrs., 122; Thomas, 64, 116, 122, 122 *n*
Salmon, James, 209, 210
Salmey, 11
Sambach, John, 197
Sanders, William, 161
Sanderson, Owen, 281
Sandford, Robert, 82
Sarkey, Frances, 260
Saunderson, Lieutenant, 132; Samuel, 132
Scarbro'. Anna, 282
Scofield, Edward, 132; Rachel, 135; Thomas, 132 *ter*, 135
Scott. Benjamin, 23; Geoffrey, 25, 25 *n*, 26 *n*; George, 206; John, 25 *n*, 26 *n*
Scripe, Sir Richard C., 182
Scroup, William 192
Seddon. Edward, 180; Rev. Edward, 85; Eleanor, 87 *n*; Elizabeth, 87 *n*, *bis*; Ellinor, 83; Frances, 87 *n*; Katherine, 87 *n*, *bis*; Mr., 22, 87 *n*, 122 *n*; Peter, 86; William, 85 *passim*, 85 *n*, *bis*, 86, 87
Sedgwick, Sir Nicholas, 30
Sewell, Cuthbert, 179; Anne, 179; Elizabeth, 179 *n*; Joseph, 179 *n*; John, 178; Rev., 161
Shakerley. Sir Geoffrey, 43, 137 *n*; Geoffrey, 43 *bis*; John, 189; Margare', 43, 44; Margery, 43 *ter*; Peter, of Hulme, 196; Peter, 120; Pe'er, 43 *ter*, 44
Sharrard, Elizabeth, 140
Shaw, Elizabeth, 57 *bis*; Thomas, 57, *passim*
Shearing, Robert, 207, 208
Shelley, Dorothy, 143; Sampson, 205
Shepherd, Thomas, 281
Sheram, M., 151
Sherington, Francis 189, 191
Sheynton, John de, 78 *bis*
Shipton, Rev. Samuel, M. A., 89 *ter*
Shone, Dorothy, 135; Richard, 203, 207; William, 205
Shrewsbury, Earl of, 38
Shrifneres, Mrs., 113
Shrubsole, G. W., 13
Shuttleworth, Ellen. 50; Sarah, 50; Thomas, 50 *bis*, 208
Simcoe(x), Jane, 181
Srimson, Thomas, 180
Simpson, Ald. Thomas, 152; Catherine, 132; Katherine, 142; Thomas, 132 *bis*, 142; Thomas, 205; William, 132
Skarrett, Richard, 141
Skelhorn, Margaret 135
Skelborne, Peter, 266
Skerit, Richard, 205
Skerratt, Richard 90
Skesbrycke (Scarisbrick), Harry, 203
Skryevensr (Scrivener), Robert, 202
Skye, John, 133; Lieutenant, 133
Smallwood, Philip, 139
Smith, 83; Rev. C. F., 100; Edward, 125; Ellen, 125; Grissel, 122 *bis*, 122 *n*, *ter*; Grissell, 63, 63 *n*, *bis*; H., 197; Henry, 93, 197, 198; Rev. John; Chariry, 200; James, 93, 170, 206; John, 203, 204; Lady, 127; Sir Lawrence, 4; Peter, 203; Richard, 133; Sir Samuel, 63
Smith, Sarah, 133; Thomas, 202-4; William, 202
Smyth, Jane, 118 *n*; Oliver, 192
Smythe, Edward, 203; Henry, 79 *bis*; Mrs., 113; Peter, 113
Snell, Dove, 76 *n*; Dr., 88, 88 *n*, *bis*; Dr., 129, 129 *n*, 136, 136 *n*; Eleanor, 76 *n*; Elizabeth, 76 *n*; George, 76; George, D.D., 75 *n*, 75 *ter*, 76, 76 *n*, 138, 138 *n*;
Katherine, 76 *n*; Lydia, 76, 76 *n*; Margaret, 76, 76 *n*; Thomas, 76 *n*; William, 76
Snow, Daniel, 134, 135; Edward Shakfield Simon, 52 *bis*; Elizabeth, 52; Isabella, 52; John, 52, 206; Joseph, 134, 176, 181; Mary, 52, 135; Peter, 52, 176; Sarah, 52
Soden, Thomas, 134; Vaughan, 131
Soley, Henry, 47; Sarai, 47
So'ie, Sarah, 180
Somerford, John, 43 *bis*; Mary, 43 *bis*
Sone, Stephen, 23, 206
Sorocold, Elizabeth, 137; Thomas, 137
Sorton, John, 176; Randle, 59, 209
Spencer, Jane, 139; Mr., 139
Speede, Mary, 135; Richard, 135
Sproston, Robert, 203
Squier, John, 78 *ter*, 78 *n*
St. Edmund, Richard de, 77 *ter*
St. George, Richard, 20
St. Tollins (St. Olave's), 155
Stacy, Catherine, 182
Stancliffe, Sir Richard, 30, 31, 81; Sir Richard, 108, 112 *n*, 227
Standish, Ralph, 192
Stanley, Elena, 274; James, 79 *bis*; Margaret, 38, 38 *n*; Thomas, 183; Thomas, Lord, 184; Margaret, 184
Stanney, Thomas, 128, 204
Stapleigh, Elena, 262; Ellen, 258, 259
Starkey, Anne, 138, 179; Edward, 139, 140, 141, 205; Elizabeth, 141; Hannah, 180; Hugh. 27; John, 27 *bis*, 178; Rebecca, 178; Thomas, 140; William, 139
Starkie, John, 178; Peter, 127; Richard, 121
Steel, Laurence, 93; Sarah, 93
Steele, Mr., 124, 125; Thomas, 122
Steeles, Samuel, 139
Sterr (Star), 220
Stevenson, Elizabeth, 89, 90; Jane, 89; (Steenson) John, 28; Justicia, 89, 90; Margaret, 89 *ter*, 90; Nicholas, 89 *ter*, 90 *bis*. 130, 138, 138 *n*; Thomas, 89, 90
Stewart, Ezekiel, D., 174
Stewkly, Shuckburgh, 170
Stocken, William, 173
Stones, Mr., 92
Stoughton, Martha, 116; Rebecca, 116; William, 116 *bis*
Stourton, Mr., 127
Straitbarell, James, 79
Stranbery, 76; Margaret, 76
Stratford, Nicholas, 89
Strattan, James, 170

Rowe. 167.

INDEX NOMINUM.

Street, Richard, 202; Thomas, 178 317
Streete, Elizabeth, 130; Thomas, 130, 130 n, bis
Stretbarell, Sir Thomas, 30
Stringer, Mary, 142
Strongitharme, James, 116; Robert, 116
Stubbs, Dr., 104
Studley, 253
Stukeley, 14
Sumner, Bishop, 56, 100; Dr., 101; Eliza Maria, 56 *uxor* ñ.
Sutton, Mr., 113
Swan, Hannah, 23, 23 n; John. 130; Thomas, 130; Rev. Thomas, 23 n
Swanbreck, John, 179
Swinton, Eleanor, 63 n, 131 n bis, 258; Elizabeth, 42 n, 193; Mary; 121 n; Peter, M.D, 168; Richard, 63 n, 121 n, ter; Th mas, 63, 63 n bis, 121 bis, 131 n bis, 197 *arms* 63. 173.

Talbot, Sir John, 31; Sir John R., of Grafton, 185
Tatton, Elenor, 124 n; Timothy, 27, 110; William, 124 n
Taylor, Clemen', 81, 107; Rev. C. B., 200; George, 181, 202; Henry, 202; James, 202, 224, 1 Joan, 275; John, 119; Mrs., 119; Thomas, 81, 82, 107; Sir Thomas, 108
Teggen, Joseph, 83
Teggin. Ellen, 118; Jane, 118; Joseph, 114, 118, 119
Temple, Sir John, 143; Robert Griffith, 209
Tench, John, Rev., 162
Thane, Dr. Rev., 150
Thelwall, David, 53; Elizabeth, 53; Watkin, 53
Thomas, William, Capt., 54, 167, 176; Jane, 54; Mary, 54; Sam, 162
Thomason, William, 114
Thomson, Lieut. James, 51
Thompson, Wm, 207
Thornley, Elizabeth, 272
Thorneley, Hugh, 204; Robert, 125
Thornet, James, 27
Thornton, Anne, 28, 29
Thorpe (Thrope), Elizabeth, 42, 259; John, 42
Threadgold, William, 58
Thrope, Elizabeth, 258
Throppe, Elizabeth, 143; Widow, 109
Thwellin (Llewelyn), 178
Tilley, John, 181
Tilsley, Geoffrey, 131; Sarah, 131; Simon, 139; Symon, 131; (Tensley), Katherine, 131
Tilston, John, 202; William, 209
Tindall, Thos., 153

Tovey, Solomon, Captain, 148
Tompson, Allen, 123
Topham, Robert, 54, 208
Tottie, Mr., 129; Edward, 114, 120, 203; Francis, 120
Touchet (Techott), Mr., 112; Thomas, 111, 119, 189
Towers, Rev. Myles H., 103
Townsend, Anna Maria, 92; Anth ny, 143
Trafford, Sir J ohn, 31
Tranmoll, Matilda de, 46, 47; Richard de, 46, 47; William de, 46, 47
Travers, Mr., 137; (Trevers), James, 137
Trevis, Mr., 128; Hannah, 129; John, 116, 129; Thomas, 116; William, 116
Trevor, Arthur, 285; Mary, 285; Tudor, 48
Troutbeck, Sir Adam, 38; Dame Margaret, 38; Eglanbic, 62; Sir Henry, 38; Joan, 2, 26, 31, 32, 38, 183; John, 32, 183; Rev. John, D.D., 21; William, 2, 31, 32, 36, 38, 62, 79, 183, 185; Sir William, K.T., 21, 32, 38, 84, 184, 185
Tuchett, Katherine, 45, 46; Thomas, 45, 46
Tudor, Alice, 275
Tucker, Margaret, 284
Turner, Edward, 172
Turton, Mrs., 137; (Tarton), 127, 128
Twambrook, Thomas, 143
Twedle, Captain John, of Invalids, 152
Tyrer, —. 124; Richard, 203
Tyrwhitt, Thomas, M.A., 100

Vanbrugh. Rev. George, 172
Varum, Elizabeth, 139
Vaughan, Mr., 138; Mary, 118
Vause, Proby. 207
Vaudrey, Alice, 107 bis; Edward, 35 n; Jane, 108; John, 107; Robert, 107 ter, 108; Randle, 112 n, 107, 108; Mary, 107; Mr. 64 n, bis, 65 n, bis, 114, 114 n, 122 bis, 122 n; Parnel, 122 n; Parnell, 279
Vaughan, Thomas, 122 n, 177
Vawdrey, Avice, 45, 46; Edward, 110, 110 n; Jane, 112 n; Mr. 112 bis; Robert, 112 n, bis; Thomas, 45, 46, 46 n, 189, 190
Venables, Anne, 108; Anthony, 108; Thomas, of Kinderton, 193; Peter, 205
Venator, Adam Le. 282 (Le Hunt or Hunt); Richard, 282; Robertus, 282; Roger, 282; William, 282 (Le Hunt): *see* Hunt.

Q Q 2

Vernon, Hannah, 74 n, 96 n; Rev. Ralph, 74; 74 n; Ralph, 74, 9 n, 165; Robert, 203
Vere, Mary, 286
Venson, Serjeant, 127
Veysy, John, LL.D., 79 bis
Vignaux, J oseph, 174
Vinon. Rev. F. A. H., 103
Vipont, Philip, 175
Vischan, Owen, 273

Wainwright, John, LL.D., 72 . . . . Laurence, 113; Mr., 113; Mary, 72 bis, 91
Walker, Elizabeth, 54; John, 54, 134 bis; Rev. John, 85. 89; Mr., 86 n, Mary, 121 n; William 121 n
Walley, Charles, 134 *passim*, 135, 143; Francis, 207; Gertrude, 135; Joseph, Abl, 165; Jane, 131; Job ., 134; Jonathan, 134 bis; Jar ., 206; Robert, 131; Thomas, 143
Walmesley, Philip, 85, Thomas, 85
Walsh, John, 72 n; Katherine, 2 n; William, 27
Warburton, Edward, 111; Peter, 114
Warburton, John, 121; Peter, 111 n
Ward, Edward, Rt Hon., 285; J n., 286; Philip, 287
Ward, William, 209
Waring. 283; Abigail, 133 n, 139; Elizabeth, 133 n; Hannah, 133 n, 140; John, 133; Mr., 139, 14 ; (Warringe) Rowland, 48, 131, 131 n, 133, 139, 141; Richard, 133 n; Samuel, 131; Zacharia, 139
Warrington, Edward, 206; Henry, Earl of, 285
Watkin, Thompson, 13 n, 14 n
Weaver, Joseph, 208, 209
Webb, Edward, 142; Mr., 38   *Webster John 246*
Weddurbe (Wetherby), Nicholas, 202
Weigh, Edwin, 50; T. len. 50
Welch, Elizabeth, 84; John, 84
Weld, Ellen, 27, 120
Weller, Capt., Nicholas, 165
Welles, Grace, 93; Rev. Thomas, 93 bis
Wells —, 286
Welshman, Thomas, 7 *b*, 128, 204   *C. v. 172.*
Wenlock, Richard, 143
Werden, Mr. 113   62.   205.
Weston —, 94; Ann 110, 265; Benjamin, 132, 265; Catherine, 205; Elizabeth, 265; Frances, 73 n, 135, 265; Humphrey. 265; Janc. 215; Le tice, 265; Lettis, 134; Lillie , 215; Mary, 265; Margery, 205; Mr., 158; Pagsan, 2 5; Pet. r. 133 bis, 134 *i*, 265; Richard, 1 S 197, 198, 2 5, 284; Robert, 2 5,

Warmincham 225.

INDEX NOMINUM.

Sarah, 134, 265; Thomas, 73 *n*, 94 *n*, 114, 125, 125 *n*, 130, 136 *n*, 180, 203, 265
Wetenhall, Elizabeth, 43 bis, 273; John, 43 bis
Wettenhall, John, 196; Mary, 91; Thomas 91
Whalter, Alexander, 111
Wheywell, Ambrose, 206
Whickstead, Alice, 64 *n*, 64 ter; Hugh, 64 *n*, 64 passim
Whicksted, Hugh, 121, 204; Mr., 114, 114 *n*; Mrs., 111 *n*
Whickstedde, Elizabeth, 109; Hugh, 109
Whickstid, Katherine, 111; Susannah 111, Thomas, 111
Whishaw, Charles, 72, 73 *n*; Elizabeth, 179; Frances, 72, 72 *n*, 73 *n*, 182; Hugh, 53 bis, 72 bis, 72 *n* ter, 73, 73 *n*, ter, 145, 149, 160, 164, 168, 178; Jane, 72, 73 *n*, 178; John, 72 *n*; Mary, 177; Rebecca, 72, 73 *n*; Sidney, 178
Whitby, Alice, 22, 23 bis, 23 *n*, 41, 121*n*, 122, 122 *n*, 197; Anne, 199 *n*; Edward, 22, 23 *n*, 41, 121, 121 *n*, bis, 122 *n*, bis; Hanna, 278; Randle (Whitbie), 82, 114, 119 *n*, 203; Thomas, 110
White, —, 284; Alice, 281
Whitehead, Richard, 80 ter, 81
Whitley, Dorothy, 257; Elinor, 270; Madam Lettis, 153; Ralph, 139; Col. Roger, 71
Whitmore, Grace, 124
Whittell, John, 205; William, 204
Whittle, Matthew, 123; William, 123, 125, 125 *n*
Wickstead, Alice, 129; (Whicksted), Hugh, 129, 129 *n*; Richard, 162
Widders, Daniel, 175
Wierden, Thomas, 82 see Wyrden, 2*n*.
Wightman, Lieut. William, 146
Wighton, Charles Allanson, 98
Wightwick, Alex, 284
Wilberforce, Dr., 103, 104
Wilbraham, Anna Maria, 92 passim; Charles, 74, 74 *n*, 92; Eleanor, 96; Elizabeth, 96 passim; Emma, 287; Frances, 92; Grace, 95; 133 *n*; George, 286, 287; Hugh, 74 *n*, 94; (Rev.), 198; (Rev.), 92 passim, 125 bis, 125 *n*, 150; John (Bromhall), 96, 96 *n*, 96 *n*, bis, 96 passim, 98; (Rev.), 161-2; Margaret, 96 passim, 125, 125 *n*; Maria, 287; Mary, 75, 75 *n*, 92 bis, 96, 97, 98 bis, 166;

Mr., 89, 94 ter; Ralph, 74, 91, 92, 96 ter; Randle, 96; Richard, 141; Sir Richard, 87; Roger, 51, 89 bis, 90 bis, 94, 95 bis, 95 *n*, 133 *n*, 167, 286, 287; Thomas, 125, 125 *n*, 153, 286; William, 204, 287
Wilde, Joyfy, 134
Wilding, Elizabeth, 284
Wilkinson, Matthew, 175; Ralph, 27, 120; Robert, 174, 208
Willan, Agnes, 98, Dorothy Edwards, 99; Hannah, 98 bis; John, 98 bis, 172, 178; Mary Ann, 99; William, 98
Willaston, John, 34 bis; Wylaston, John de, 78, 79
Willcocke, Randle, 130 bis; Rev., 150, 161
Willcoxen, Rev., 151
Williams, 125; Almonde, 137; Rev. Arthur, 94 bis, 95 ter, 178; Catherine, 94; Edward, 158; Elizabeth, 134; J. 23; Jane, 122, 122 *n*; John, 94, 122 bis; Katherine, 27, 120; Mary or Margery, 135 *n*; Nathaniel, 125; Owen, 143; Robert, 207; Rachel, 135, 280; Thomas, 93, 134 ter, 205; William, 135, 135 *n*; Sir W., 94
Williamson, Catherine, 139; Elizabeth, 117, 118; John, 139; Richard, 116 bis, 117, 118, 137; William, 202
Wills, Sarah, 287
Wilson, Elizabeth, 180; Elianor, 116; John, 65, 65 *n* bis, 114, 115, 116; Mary, 116; William, 27, 111
Windsor, John, 96 bis, 97; Margaret, 96 bis
Wingfield, Thomas, 284; John, 284
Winnington, Mr., 113
Wirrall, Charles, 135; Catherine, 135
Wishaw, John, 160
Wiston, — Rev., 161
Witter, Capt., 206; Samuel, 208; William, 206; (Capt.), 23 157
Wolley, Jane, 286; Mr., 286
Wood, 193, 209
Woodes, Dorothy, 132 *n*; Joseph, 132 bis, 132 *n*, ter; William, 132 *n*
Woods, Francis, 91; William, 205
Woodward, Ellen, 27, 120; Mr. 112
Woolrich, Collins, 93; Elizabeth, 93
Wordsworth, Hannah, 98, 178
Worrall, John, 205
Worsley, Alice, 45, bis, 189; Avice, 45, 45 bis, 46, 189, 191; Alex., 190,

192; Charles, 125; Hugh, 190, 192; Joan, 45, 46; James, 190, 192; Katherine, 45, 46, 189; Mr., 113 *bis*, 121; Otwell, 80 ter, 190 192; Ralph, 45 ter, 46 passim, 113 bis, 113 *n*, bis, 188, 189; William, 45 bis, 188, 189
Woswoall (Wiswall), Thomas, 202, 220, 226, 227
Wrench, Anne, 144; Catherine, 144 *n*; Dorothy, 144 *n*; Edward, 144, 144 *n*, bis, 168, 205; Grace, 132 *n*; John, 32, 33, 132, 132 *n*, bis, 144 *n*, 164, 205; Mary, 132, 144 *n*; Richard, 132 *n*; Robert, 93; Sarah, 132 *n*; Thomas, 144 *n*; Rev. T., 152 *n*; William, 132 *n*
Wright, Anne, 91 *n*, 93, 119 *n*, 127, 127 *n*; Alderman, 138; Catherine, 71, 90, 130; Charles, 207; Ellin, 132, 135; Ellinor, 139; Elizabeth, 72 bis, 72 *n*, 91 bis, 118, 143, 149; Grace, 138; George, 134; Harbitt, 131; John, 71 *n*, 71 ter, 131, 132 ter, 139, 140, 157, 205; Joseph, 134; Mary, 72 ter, 91 ter; Mr., 112, 140, 143; Mrs., 122; Nicholas, 121; Richard, 90, 91 *n*, 118, 127, 141, 143 bis, 141; Rev. Richard B.D., 32 *n*, 71, 72 bis, 72 *n*; Thomas, 82, 83 ter, 93, 114, 119, 119 *n*, bis, 130, 203; Timothy, 83; William, 179
Wrottesley, Howard, 284
Wyke, Richard, 284
Wynn, Alexander, 139; (Gwyn) Dorothy, 119 *n*; Edward, 139 ter; Morris, 119 *n*; Mr., 113; Mrs., 113
Wynne, Alexander, 71 bis; Edward, 71 ter; Elizabeth, 71; Grace, 138
Wynnington, John, 191
Wyrrall, Agnes, 36 bis; Richard, 36 bis
Wyrthen (Werden), Thomas, 203

Yarker, Frances, 56; Rev. Robert, 56
Yells, Alice, 138; Mr., 138
Yeable, Thomas, 131, 140; William, 131
Yorke, Ann, 133; Capt. William, 133, 142
Yonge, Elizabeth, 285; Sir Walter, 285
Young, —, 121, 122; Lt.-Col. Robert, 172; Mr., 62, 113; Mrs., 114
Yoxall, Richard, 208

INDEX RERUM.

Acton, near Nantwich, Vicar of, 87, 89, 90
Adam and Eve, Painting of, 215
Alb, 226
Alderley, Rector of, 89
Aldford, Priest at, 82; Rector of, 100
All Souls' College, Oxford, Fellow of, 97, 133 *n*
Altars and Chantries in the Church, 30
Amyse (Amice), 221
Anderton Matthew, Charity of, 198, 200
Anthem Bell, 212, 219, 220, 221, 232
Antoll (Anton) Bell, 212, 230
Arms and Crest of Brereton, 188, 189; Brerewood, 1; Gamul, 1; Oldfield, 193; Rowland Waring, 76; Worsley, 59 (*see* under family name)
Astbury, Rector of, 32, 80

Banner, 231
Banner Staves, 227, 229
Basingwerk Abbey, near Holywell, 2, 9 *n*, 30, 211
Bebington, Rector of, 80
Bell, Anthem (Antoll), 212, 219, 220, 221, 225, 230, 232, 34
Bells, 23, 24, 25, 26
Bere (bier), 224; Mending, 216, 224
Bereche (beyriche) allowance of drink, 211, 215, 223, 232
Blackamore Servant, 152
Bloreheath, Battle of, 184
Boards for Communion Table, 230
—— to make Forms, 250
Books for the Communion, 232
Boughton Chapel and Hospital, 26
Bowdon, Vicar of, 73, 135 *n*
Bowke — Bucket, 195
Brasenose College, Oxon, 66 *bis*, 70 *n*, *bis*, 90, 92
Brass to Rowland Waring, 76
Brasyn Cense, 217; Crosse, 215
Brewers' Hall, 147, 179
Budworth, Great, Vicar of, 86 *n*
Bunbury Register, 181
Button-Mould Turner, 161

Cadilow, 196
Cambridge, Emmanuel College, 87; Jesus College, 92; Trinity, 72 *n*
Candles for Anthem, 219; to go a visiting, 249
Carder of Hatmakers' Wool, 178
Castle Camps, Rector of, 56
Cense Brasen, 217
Censer (cense), 212, 215, 217, 226
Chain to the Bible, 2
Chantries and Altars in the Church, 30
Chancellor of England, Lord, 77
Charcoal, 212, 215, 217
Charities of St. Mary's, 197, 200
Charterhouse, London, 80
Cheese Warehouse, 146 Chalice 119
Chelford, Incumbent of, 22, 99, 100
Cheshire Dialect, Words, 195, 196, 218, 223
Cheshire Families connected with St. Mary's, 183
Chester, Alderman of, 52, 53, 54, 55, 62, 110, 113, 120, 120 *n*, 121, 122, 128, 132, 136, 137, 138; Bishop of, 4, 11, 36, 76, 80, 85, 89, 101, 104, 119 *n*, 130 *n*; Blue Coat School, 54; Castle, 8; Cathedral, 80; Chamberlain of, 20, 36 *n*, 77; Chancellor of, 72 *bis*, 91; Chief Justice of, 29 *n*, 32 *n*; Constable of, 29 *bis*, 116, 137 *n*, 142 *n*, 143; Coroner of, 61; Dean of, 77, 80, 81, 88 *n*, 104; Earl of, 2; Holy Trinity, Rector of, 91 *n*; Mayor of, 4, 36 *bis*, 42 *passim*, 62, 74, 120, 121, 122 *n*; the Plague in, 109; Prebendary of, 44; Recorder of, 22, 23 *n*, 39 *bis*, 40, 41, 42, 66 *bis*, 110, 113, 121 *n*, 122 *n*, 131 *n*, 132, 132 *n*
Church Reeves (Wardens), 211
Chime Hammers, 253
Christleton, Rector of, 73 *n*
Church Wax, 214, 216, 217 *passim*
Clock, the, 136, 136 *n*
Cloth over the Sacrament, 229
Clarke to Cheese Warehouse, 146
Coach with wheels, 194
Communion Book, 232, 250; Plate, 22, 23; Table (Boards for), 250

Cope, 214, 219, 224
Copsawe (copsall), 194
Corporas, 249
Cotton Charities, 54
Cressetts, 218
Cuppen's Lane, 145
Custody of Castle Garden, 186

Devocion Surge, 221, 223. 225
Devotion taper to Handbridge, 229
Dig=duck (Cheshire dialect), 195
Donations to S. Mary's-without-the-Walls, 17, 18
Dorfold, near Nantwich, 2
Drawers of Dee, 153
Drayton's Polyolbion, 184
Dressing the banner, 229
Dunham on the Hill, 20

Easter Sepulchre, 231
Eastham, Vicar of, 85, 85 *n*, 86 *n*, 100
Eccleston, Rector of, 93
Emmanuel College, Cambridge, 87
Ensign of the Invalides, 146, 149, 156, 175
Eshin=pail, 195
Ewer of maslyn, 195
Executioner, The, 30, 123, 123 *n*
Exeter, Canon of, 131 *n*

Filling the Font by the year, 214, 215, 220, 221, 225, 250
Font filled, 214, 215, 220, 221, 225, 250
Forton, co. Salop, Minister of, 47
Foundling children, 218, 219, 220
Frankincense, 214, 215, 218, 220, 221
Frodsham, Vicar of, 97

Gamashees, 194 = overalls.
Gang (rung of ladder), 218
Gaoler of Northgate, 167
Gifts to S. Mary's-without-the-Walls, 17, 18
Glass stained, 21, 22, 33
Glover, Dry, 163
Gloverstone, 148

Goodtide (Gutte l) Sunday, 254
Grappenhall, Rector of, 86, 87
Great Bolas, co. Salop, Rector of, 98
Great Budworth, Vicar of, 86 *n*
Grease=steps to pulpit, 222
Gyrdills to the Prests, 218, 231

Handbridge Surge, 229, 231
Hangman, The, 30, 123, 123 *n*
Harrison's Charity, 200
Harrison's regiment, Col., 146
Hawarden Castle, S, 9; Rector of, 67, 79; Registers, 181
Heelmaker, 160
Heraldic dispute, 182
Herbal, 196
Hereford, Earl of, 48
———, Philip, Bishop of, 93
Hetchell (Hatchell), 196
High Altar, 216, 217; Curtain, 217; Raising up, 216
Holy Goste (Schostyng), 216, 218
Holy Trinity Chapel, 30, 32 79; Church, 27; Registers, 179
Hulme, Randle, Arms of, 1
Holt, 24, 24 *n*
Holy Water Stocke, 217, 218
Holywell, co. Flint, 2, 20
Hough Green, paving, 254
Hough in Wybunbury, 2
Hour glass, 196
House of Industry, 170
Hunts roe (row), 145
Hylling of a grave, 224, 250

Incidents, Special, 182
Injunctions, 214
Inquisitions post mortem, taken in the Church, 27
Inscriptions, Monumental, and Tablets in the Church, 18, 20, 21, 22, 45-59, 60-76
Invalides, Colonel of, 181; Ensign of, 146, 149, 156, 175, 178; Sergeant of, 148, 165

Keeper of Northgate, 153; of lions in Tower, Ralph, Urian, Thomas, 188, 189; Wild, 189-192
King's Visitors, 230
Kirk's Col., regiment, 146
Kneeling-place, 211, 213, *et passim*, 238

Laystall, 111, 188, 213
Lecture, Sunday evening, 200, 201
Lecturers: Rev. Fred. Ayckbourn, F. Custance, Thos. Harrison, C. B. Taylor, Frederick Ford, 200

Lestall (leastall), 110
Leystall, 224
List of Churchwardens, 202-210
Llay Estate, 200
Llay Farm Estate, 199, 200
London: Charterhouse, 80; Middle Temple Inn, Reader at, 66 *bis*; St. Paul's Cathedral, 81; Sion College, 80; Whitechapel, Rector of, 92
Lymbeck, 195

Macclesfield Grammar School, 72 *n*, 101
Macebearer, the, 111, 111 *n*, 114
Mahlen, Gentlewoman, 163-165, 168
Maker, Peruke, 160, 163; Sal Ammoniac, 175
Making of pulpit and carving, 222, 223
Mahlon, Free Burges of, 58
Malpas, Rector of, 80, 91
Manchester, Dealer, 163; Grammar School, 87
Marriage before Justices, 180
Martins, S. Register, 179
Maslyn, Ewer of, 195
Master Miller of Dee Mills, 146
Master of Blue School, 171
Master of Comedians, 147
Matt to kneel upon, 230
Mayor's Porter, 156
Michael's, S., Registers, 177, 178
Middlewich, Vicar of, 93
Middle Temple Inn, London, Reader at, 66 *bis*
Minshull, Vicar of, 92 *bis*
Mollocke, 212
Mone (moon) under the holyn, the, 218
Moon, Skaffolde to take down, 218
Monument, old, 33-40
Monumental Inscriptions, 18, 20-22; and Tablets formerly in the Church, 45, 50, 60, 76
Mount, The (Handbridge), 154

Nantwich, 2
Native of Africa, 171
Needlemaker, 176
Neston, Vicar of, 56

Old Cheshire Families connected with St. Mary's, 183
Organs, 211, 219
Oxford, All Souls' College, 97, 133 *n*; Brasenose College, 66 *bis*, 70 *n*, *bis*, 90, 92

Paper Maker, 170
Pardoner of S. Chadde (Chad), 213; of Jesu, 223; of S. John's Friars, 213; Lady Ronsevale, 213
Pardoners, 211, 213
Parochial Charities, 200
Parrees on the alba, 218, 229, 231, 232
Pascall, cords to, 212
Paxes, 218
Peter's, St., Register, 179 Pewtier, 26, 184
Pedigree, 192
Pikle = pitchfork, 195
Plague, the, in Chester, 101, 125-127
Plate, Communion, 22, 23
Pressing to death, 27, 28, 110, 119
Prisoners, burials of, 27, 119-121; pressed to death, 27, 28, 110, 119.
Procession books, 224; of King and Queen of Scots, 231
Pulford, Rector of, 102
Pulpit making, 222
Puppet Show Explosion, 167
Purse to carry the Sacrament, 224, 228
One Sheriffs pewes 112.
Pensioner sodder, 163.

Rachett for Clerk, 215, 254
Rectors of St. Mary's, List of, 77-131
Register, Banbury, 181; St. Bridget's, 178; Chelford, 182; Hawarden, 181; Holy Trinity, 179; St. Martin's, 179; St. Mary's, 105; St. Michael's, 177; St. Oswald's, 179; St. Peter's, 179
Revestre, 226
Rochet, 220
Rochets for boys, 253
Rochett for the Clerk, 224 254.
Rode lofte, 218, 228; cord to, 228
Rode, taking down, 230
Ronsevale, our Lady, 213
Rostherne, Vicar of, 101
Rushes, 211, 212, 214
Rushes against Easter, 211; carrying out old, 214; Pentecost, 212

Sabine's, Genl., regiment, 148
Sacrying bell, 226
Saint Andrew's University, 76; Bridget's, Chester, Rector of, 23 *n*, 56 *bis*, 58, 90 *n*; Catherine's Service, 231; (*sic* St. Katherine's Service, 23); David's, Archdeacon of, 95; John's, Chester, Tablets in, 60 *n*; John's frary, 213; John's College, Cambridge, Fellow of, 76, 76 *n*; Katherine's Chapel, 3, 6, 8, 20, 30, 32, 35, 36, 38, 39, 40, 46, 110, 113, 114, 211, 214; Mary's Nunnery,

INDEX RERUM. 303

Chester, 4, 116 n, 120 n; Mary on-the-Hill, Church of, Chester, 2, 19; Mary-on-the-Hill, Chester, Townships of the Parish of, 1; Mary's, List of Rectors of, 77-104; Mary's Registers, 105; Mary-without-the-Walls, Chester, Church of, 13; Oswald's, Chester, Vicar of, 99; Paul's Cathedral, London, 84; Peter's, Chester, Rector of, 53, 79; Stephen lights, 211, 213, 214; Stevyns (Stephen) lights, 211, 213; Werburgh's Abbey, Chester, 77-80; Werburgh's, Chester, Hugh, Abbot of, 77, 77 bis; Werburgh's, Chester, John, Abbot of, 80; Werburgh's, Chester, Thomas, Abbot of, 61
Salisbury Cathedral, 79
Sanctus bell, 226
Sandbach, Vicar of, 93 bis
Scrope and Grosvenor Trial (Heraldic Suit), 182
Sepulchre (Easter), 212, 214, 218, 220, 231; Lights, 220, 226
Sepulcer (Sepulchre) lights, 218, 220, 231; nayles pynes to hang the, 212, 214
Sepulchre sergesse, 226; Hanbrige, 226, 229, 231
Sergeant of Bridge Gate, 184, 186
Sheriff of Chester, 63 bis, 64, 83, 120 n Sheriffs paraapew, feb. 189
Shifting the Cross, 220
Shrewsbury, Earl of, 2, 31 n, 32, 32 n, 33, 36
Sion College, London, 80
Skaffolde to take down the mone, 218
Socket to best Cross, 224
Sodor and Man, Bishop of, 81
Special incidents in past history of St. Mary's, 182
Stained Glass, 21, 22, 33
Star and the Hollyn, The, Candles to, 226
Stevyn's, St., lights, 211, 213
Sovaldier Pewsoner. 14 b.

Stillinge = frame or stand, 195
Sundial in the Churchyard, 59, 123, 123 n
Sunday Evening Lecture, 200
Surge, 204, 205, 207, 209, 211
Surge, Devotion, 211, 217, 219, 221, 223

Tablets formerly in the Church, 60-76; in St. John's, Chester, 60 n
Taking down the Altars, 253; the rode, 230, 250, 253
Ten Commandments, 253
Testerne, 195
Tiling, St. Katharine's Chapel, 211, 214. Tipers 221.
Torch for Palm Sunday, 215, 216
Torch, 253
Torches at burial, 249
Trial of witches at Chester, 1656, 28, 29
Trinity Chapel, Holy, 30, 32, 79
Trinity College, Cambridge, 72 n
Troutbecks, 183, 186
Troutbeck, Adam, 185; Chapel, 8, 10, 31-33, 36, 38, 53, 54, 61, 62, 63 n, 64 n, 67, 67 n, 69 n, 119 n, 123, 123 n, 124, 125, 127, 127 n, 128, 129, 129 n, 136, 136 n, 141 n, 183, 184; place, 186; William, 20
Trundle bed, 195

Undertaker of Dee Mills, 146
Upton, 11, 12

Vale Cloth, 215, 216
Vestments, List of, 5
Visitation, 253
Voyder = basket, 195

Wallasey, Rector of, 75, 76, 95, 95 n
Walsall, co. Stafford, Vicar of, 87

Walton, Curate of, 95; Rector of, 95
Walton-on-the-Hill, Vicar of, 95 bis
Waring, Rowland, Arms of, 1695, 76
Waters Upton, co. Salop, Rector of, 98   Watcherbol 220.
Waverton, Rector of, 76
Wax-making, 217
Wax against the Ester, 215
Web of lead, 231
Wells, Dean of, 77
Wellington, Duke of, 50
Werden family, 113
Weston family, 115
West Kirby, Rector of, 100; Minister of, 86 n
West Derby, Curate of, 95
Westminster, Canon of, 21; Duke of, 103, 104; Marquess of, 103; Richard Marquis of, 100, 102; Robert Marquis of, 100 bis
Wet Glover, 145, 155
Wettenhall, 2
Whitechapel, London, Rector of, 92
Whiteliming the Church, 230, 251
Whitewashing the Church, 230
Wills, Sir Wm. Troutbeck, 185; Randle Brereton, 187; Ralph Worsley, 189
Wimble = auger, 194
Winchester, Bishop of, 103
Wistaston Church, 27
Witches hanged at Chester, 1656, 28, 129, 129 n
Witton School, 54
Woodchurch, co. Chester, Rector of, 91 n
Wright, Prebendary, 89
Wrenbury, Vicar of, 88
Worsley, Ralph, Arms of, 1573, 59
Worsley Arms, 188; Pedigree, 192; Ralph, 188, 189; Will, 188
Wybunbury, 2

Yeoman of Pentice, 154

www.ingramcontent.com/pod-product-compliance
Lightning Source LLC
Chambersburg PA
CBHW032044220426
43664CB00008B/860